SMALL MAN, BIG HEART

Art Huinker's Baseball Days

Published, November 2012

Printed by Quad Graphics; Dubuque, Iowa

Cover illustration and other graphics by Stefani Wunderlich

Printers Press; Dubuque, Iowa

ISBN#: 978-1-4875-5195-3

If interested in additional copies of this book, write to: Huinker Books, P.O. Box 156, Peosta, IA 52068; or e-mail: Huinkana@aol.com. The cost of the book is $20.00 including sales tax. Shipping charges, if necessary, will be $2.50 per book. Check or money order accepted.

DEDICATION

This book is dedicated to our five older children who were part of my baseball playing days and to our two youngest sons who encouraged me to put together this "scrapbook" for them. Finally, it is dedicated to Ann who was always there.

SMALL MAN, BIG HEART

ABOUT THE TITLE: The title "Small Man, BIG Heart," comes from an editorial written By Waterloo Couri Sports Editor, Russ Smith, in the summer of 1967. The actual newspap copy, complete with water spots, is copied here.

ONCE UPON A TIME in the beautiful little hills of Northeastern Iowa in a tiny town named Festina there were three brothers.

These three brothers were teenagers in 1951 when they came out of the hills of Northeastern Iowa and the tiny town of Festina to throw a baseball and catch a baseball and hit a baseball.

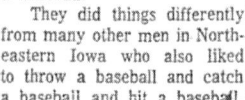

They did things differently from many other men in Northeastern Iowa who also liked to throw a baseball and catch a baseball and hit a baseball.

These three brothers from the hills of Northeastern Iowa and the tiny town of Festina threw the baseball and hit the baseball with their left hands and they caught the baseball with their right hands. And they did all three exceedingly well.

The oldest brother was named Linus. The middle brother's name was Kenneth. And the baby, a fuzzy-cheeked youth who had seen only 15 summers before the summer of 1951, was named Arthur.

Now the boy named Linus, who played, mainly, center field has returned to the hills and the tiny town to farm. The boy named Kenneth, likewise, except that he still ventures forth from those hills and that town occasionally on a summer afternoon to pick up the bat or the ball in his left hand and the glove in his right and do battle with the diamond foes of Fort Atkinson in the league named after that area of the state Iowa which is noted for its beautiful little hills.

So only one brother remains. That is the brother named Arthur. Today he is almost exactly twice as old as he was on that day in 1951 when they first ventured forth from those hills and that town to meet the best many other small towns in neighboring hills could provide in a tournament known as the Waterloo Daily Courier Northeast Iowa Tournament of Champions.

Brother Art 32 Now

THE BROTHER named Arthur is, as has been recorded, exactly twice as old in this year of 1967. And, physically, he may be only half as good as the lythe little man who appeared in Waterloo Stadium in 1951.

Hobbled by a painful knee, the man, Arthur, walks haltingly to the pitcher's mound. He takes ball in left hand, glove in right and he's just as good as ever was the fuzzy-cheeked boy named Arthur. And folks in, both his tiny town in the beautiful little hills of Northeastern Iowa as well as his adopted town with the twin-spired basilica named for St. Francis Xavier which stands just above the approaches to the valley of the Mississippi River, insist that, "There ain't none better."

At the age of 32, this brother named Arthur of the clan of Huinker faced 10 Waterloo Merchants in the final three and one-third innings of a 10-inning game in the state baseball tournament Tuesday night. With his still strong left arm he struck out eight of them. One, there was, hit the ball back into the glove on his right hand and was thrown out at first by his left hand.

Another stroked the ball into the glove of his right field playing teammate. And then it came time for this man to bat and he picked up the bat with his left hand and hobbled to the plate on his one good leg.

And another little lefthander from a much larger city with credentials ever as impressive and summers some 10 fewer threw two balls that were wide of the target. Then, and in these words spoke the brother named Arthur, "Tom got behind on me and he made the next pitch too good."

Double Despite Bad Leg

SMOTE FOR A TRIPLE it became a double. Remem this one bad leg. And today this leg is no better, but brother named Arthur, at the age of 32 has done something never has done before in his life.

Because a teammate followed his double with a single, because, on this one good and one bad leg, he slid h safely with the tie-breaking run in the 10th inning of state tournament game, he has defeated for the first tim all his 32 summers this left hander from Waterloo named ' Simpson.

And it was just over a month ago that the two met i tournament in another small town, located somewhere betw here and there — a town named Winthrop which has a tou ment for 16 teams from these Northeast Iowa hills. And e in those recent days the brother named Arthur had two g legs, not yet having slid into second base in such a man as to tear the cartilege in one knee. And this game was sc uled for seven innings as was that game which occurred in town of Dysart Tuesday night.

But this game went only eight innings because the h hander named Tom Simpson from the larger city named terloo smote one of the lefthanded pitches of the bro named Arthur over the fence in the town of Winthrop win that tournament semifinal game 2-1.

But that tournament was for the championship of the t of Winthrop. This tournament is for the championship of state of Iowa. And this lefthanded brother is more than pitcher for this team from Dyersville, he is its manager, athletic director and baseball coach of the high school nam Beckman, of that adopted town and he also is one fie competitor.

TABLE OF CONTENTS

FORWARD by Monsignor Francis P. Friedl
INTRODUCTION

FOREWORD

I had the rewarding experience of proof reading this amazing account of a baseball career. When I finished, the author suggested that I write a Foreword. I asked him what title he had chosen for the book. He smiled, shook his and said, "I still don't have one. I have tried a dozen titles, but none of them seemed to be just right." That was easy for me to understand. As I read chapter after chapter, I was amazed by the athletic achievements of a young man who grew up on a farm, polished his ability to pitch by throwing a ball against the house, and went on to become one of the most skilled players on the diamonds of northeast Iowa and beyond.

If I were Art, I would have in my files the record of every athletic victory of my life. But, not surprisingly, he has lost track of many of his successes. When I asked him the number of home runs he has hit, he could not answer. When I asked for his career batting average, again, he had no idea.

But some of his records are so remarkable that they are listed in the past issues of local newspapers. He played all four years of his college career for Loras College, with 19 wins and no losses. In his senior year, pitching against one of the best hitting teams of the circuit, he had 22 strikeouts in one game against Lewis College. He joined the St. Louis Cardinals, and his first three games were shutouts. All of these were shining moments, but Art sees as the peak of his career the 1956 Cascade Tournament when, playing for Dyersville, he pitched three games, two of which were no hitters, the other a one hitter. In another game during that tournament he did not pitch, but played in the outfield and drove in three runs. And so even a few of the outstanding achievements of Art's years in baseball are not available for this book, the players who worked with him, as well as his opponents, will enjoy reviewing the stories of many exciting games which they shared with pitcher Art Huinker.

Art graduated from Loras College in 1957 with a major in social studies and education. He returned to the College in 1970-71, to serve as Dean of Men. He continued playing baseball until 1968.

The athletic accomplishments of this young man mark a life of outstanding success. But that is only a part of the story. His family life was another home run. He married Ann, his high school sweetheart, in 1955, when he was a sophomore at Loras. He and Ann became the parents of seven children, three girls and four boys. All are living and in good health with the exception of a daughter Tammy, who died in 2002. Those who know Art are aware that he values his beloved family more than all the home runs, all the strikeouts, and all the championships won in his remarkable career.

Msgr. Francis P. Friedl

PREFACE

With every effort to write and produce a book, there is a purpose. For some, it is to sell millions of copies and make money. For others, it is to provide information on something, be it a project, a discovery, possibly a life. The latter, about a person's life, describes fairly well this production. But there have been many twists and turns to the life we are describing.

Initially, the purpose of this book was to organize a scrapbook of the baseball career that I have experienced. And that scrapbook specifically was geared to pulling the many different baseball accomplishments, some successful, some not successful, that covered the first 33 years of my life. The scrapbook was intended to provide information for our youngest daughter and the two youngest sons that my wife, Ann, and I have raised. By the time they came into this world, my baseball playing days had drawn to a close. The three of them talked often of their need for some kind of a memory book for them to keep for their family.

Their need for the story of my baseball career provided the beginning of what today is a "book." Having saved some write-ups and pictures from newspapers over the years, the task of organizing them began. Consequently, a search of old newspapers in libraries in the northeast Iowa area, as well as southern Minnesota and southwestern Wisconsin, led to frequent road trips to towns where I had played. Questions arose about the coverage that might be found in South Dakota or Michigan, or even Albany, Georgia where I had played professional baseball.

Just sitting around one evening at our home, doing nothing special, we started evaluating all the efforts to collect many missing materials desirable for the scrapbook, when Ann made the off-the-cuff remark, "All the effort you are putting forth, Art, why don't you just go a step further and put together a book about your baseball days?" There are times when she regrets having raised that possibility, but we decided to go the extra mile and put our experiences and thoughts connected to those experiences, into a book.

An opening chapter, or introduction was needed. That led to the question of why baseball was so important to the Huinker family in which I grew up. That piqued my interest but the more I wrote the more there were two key life-time goals that drove me throughout those early years and even beyond. The first goal, or maybe dream, evolved around the drive of playing professional baseball, and eventually the major leagues. The second goal centered on the pursuit of the love of my life, Ann, who eventually became my wife and mother of our children. That goal obviously began in my formative years when the opposite sex attracted my attention. Shortly, that goal became the specific beautiful and energetic young woman mentioned above. Those two goals basically directed my decision-making for almost everything. Sometimes they were in unison with each other. Sometimes they led to conflicts, major and minor. And decisions, based on the importance of the issues pertaining to the goals, are described and defined.

The two goals became the focus of the entire book and were necessarily addressed frequently throughout this writing. Based on those two driving forces and the original purpose of meeting the needs of our three youngest children, the content of this book began to take shape.

To accomplish the task before me, much time and effort were required. The effort proved an education in itself. Thanks has to go out to so many valuable sources who helped make this book possible. First, appreciation goes out to daughter Jennifer, who helped with the structure and the formation of the many revisions made throughout the entire writing of each chapter. And there were many major changes.

Thanks also to Monsignor Francis P. Friedl who graciously volunteered his time to proof every chapter as it was written. His corrections, revisions and suggestions were invaluable in reaching a successful ending to this effort. In addition, he was constantly sharing ideas from his many experiences as an author that added a more professional touch to the entire content of this book. Interestingly, classes I completed under Msgr. Friedl's tutelage some forty and fifty years ago, also had a vital influence on my outlook on the life I lead.

Thanks also to Jim Schneberger and Gene "Tiny" Potts who gave of their time to react to sections of the book and offered additional memories and other ideas from the time we spent together at Festina and Loras College respectively.

I wish to thank also the newspaper publishers who willingly allowed me to use write-ups of all the games that have been included in this book. It made it so much easier to let your write-ups cover my successes and failures over the eighteen years of playing the game best known as "America's favorite pastime." A special thank you to the Ossian Bee, the Dyersville Commercial, the Dubuque Telegraph Herald, the Loras College Lorian and the Waterloo Courier.

Finally, there is one person I will never be able to thank enough. That is Ann, that wonderful person who has shared her entire life with me. There were many days and evenings where Ann sat by herself while I buried myself in all the entities that have gone into putting this book together. Her love has never waned, and her dedication makes our love story complete. Simply, but with a depth of feeling impossible to describe, thank you, Ann.

BARN BALL

Most of us do not remember much of the first few years of our life. Our human brain is just not ready to build all those connections which help us form long-term memory of what is going on around us. It is no different for me. Being the youngest of three boys and two girls, the older siblings frequently enlightened me on what life was like back then, including how it related to why baseball was so important in the Huinker family. Coming into this life in 1935, during the middle of the "Great Depression," my older brothers and sisters describe the hardships they lived through, hardships not in my memory bank. The two older family members, Shirley and Linus, talked about going to school in horse and buggy. Also, they often boarded overnight at the sisters' convent (Franciscan nuns—four teachers and a housekeeper headquartered in La Crosse, Wisconsin) who directed our small 1-8 Catholic grade school in our little home town of Festina, Iowa. The boarding was utilized only during bad wintry nights.

The meaning of the concept, "subsistence farming" learned in one of the many college courses I experienced, best describes the life for the Huinker family on our small eighty acre farm, later increased to 120 acres sometime during those early depression years. Raising cattle (milk cows mostly), hogs and chickens (eggs and food), along with a huge garden plus a large apple orchard, provided most of the food we lived on. One car (a 1932 Ford) provided motorized transportation until 1946 together with horses to pull a two-seater buggy and to provide the strength to harvest corn, oats and hay (no tractor until 1941)

This paints a picture of the culture of our family in those early years. It is in this setting where baseball and our family's love of the game was planted and nourished.

Reflecting on some experiences I do remember, there is little doubt that the attachment to this "pitch the ball, catch the ball and hit the ball" game came from our daddy Leo (yes, that was the calling referring to our father). He himself was a catcher for many years for his hometown (and mine) of Festina. This is a small, precious village of about 100 people in the southern hills of Winneshiek County in northeast Iowa. Those of us from this little German community always say about a hundred, but then add to the count the dogs and cats in order to reach that century total. The entire community, including the circle of farm families, is centered around a Catholic Church and Catholic School. No other school or church is found there although in the 1930's to the 1950's there were three general stores that handled groceries, hardware, a bar and a limited food menu. One of the three was also the post office location. Interestingly enough, there was also a bank occupying a small building that was forced to close early in the depression.

Some additional mental images of our school. Built during the 1930's, it had six classrooms but no gym or multi-purpose room. The lower basement area served as a community center for church dinners and other related community functions. And there was a chapel on the second floor where Mass was offered

1

for the school and parish members during the winter months. No hot lunch program and above all, no inside restrooms. I will not share some images I have of that situation because they are not pretty. The school usually had an enrollment of about 80 to 100 students for grades 1-8. The number of students, the limited facilities, no coaching from school or community, and it helps paint a picture of why the only game in town was baseball.

The same system of schooling, grades 1-8, was true of my first ten years of education. In my grade there were eight boys and three girls. We started first grade with nine and four respectively. One nun taught both first and second grades. That system operated throughout all the grades. Most of the time class sizes numbered about 24-25 students per teacher. In talking with many people around Festina and also the Dubuque area, people speak about the number of times they witnessed, or "maybe even" experienced the famous ruler in a nun's hand slapping a student across the knuckles. Not so at St. Mary's in Festina. Our Franciscan nuns from La Crosse, Wisconsin must have completed a different teacher preparation program than other religious orders. Reflecting on that difference, could it possibly be that Festina students never required such harsh discipline? Just a thought.

We had good teachers, I think. Their weakest subject was mathematics. One particular instance recalled while in second grade prompted the nun to ask for a classmate and me to remove a couple of stars from our charts. Yes, there was a reason. When the two stars were brought to the desk, she stated that three stars were necessary. When this was questioned by the person whose name I will not divulge, four stars were removed from the chart. No further comment needed.

There is another facet of that Festina school experience that fits with the culture of this little farming community. Morning and afternoon recess as well as the extended lunch period gave us plenty of time to play. No gymnasium. What did we do during those times? You probably can answer that question. Yes, we played ball. Almost always, except for the winter time. The ball diamond for first and second grade was right next to the school. If you hit a ball down the right field line, a big window came into play. So, having an "astute understanding" of how a batted ball breaks windows quite easily, our nun asked that I bat right handed. Thus, the switch that made me a right hand batter, even though my brother Kenny played on that same space and probably hit the ball further than I did at that age (and always did). He batted left-handed, and did not recall breaking a window because of that. His first and second grade teacher must not have had that "astute understanding" that I referred to earlier.

Because I was the youngest in the family, I never had the privilege of seeing my father play baseball. He was a catcher and an early picture shows him with the gear on. Two other players on that picture were my uncles, Hubert Schneberger and Ted Einck. Hubert was the pitcher at that time. He later had six sons that played for the Festina team, two of whom were high school teammates

2

of mine. Ted Einck's two sons also played for Festina and Norb, the younger of the two, played at the same time my brothers and I were playing. Another player on the picture is Florian Buchheit, whose son Del is now our neighbor here in Peosta. Del's older brother "Sonny" played for Festina before he went into the service. Another player on that picture was a neighbor, Frank Elsbernd. His second youngest son, Romauld, played with the Festina team when I did. We have been unable to identify the other players on the picture. Most of the knowledge that I have of that team came from my older sister, Shirley, and I thank her so much for all the info she shared. Jim Schneberger, son of Hubert, was helpful in analyzing the picture.

That was to be one of the pictures that I planned to be included in the picture section of this book. I put the picture in a place where I was sure it would be safe for later use. Sadly, I cannot now remember that place of safe keeping, even after a thorough search of all possible hiding places in our home. This has proved to be very frustrating.

During my Daddy's playing days, the baseball diamond was located about a mile west of Festina. It was a farm pasture in a creek bottom where the outfield fence was the creek that flowed in a half circle beyond the outfield. Wonder what the ground rules were. And this creek bottom was a pasture for cattle throughout the week. For any readers from the Dubuque area, the diamond parameters were very similar to the baseball diamond in Placid in Dubuque County, except the creek was further from home plate. The Festina diamond had no fence around the outfield. Wonder if an outfielder could run through the creek to catch a long high fly ball. None of this knowledge was ever shared with me until my father's younger sister, Aunt Viola Tessmer, sat down with me and shared many fabulous stories. She herself married a baseball player from a neighboring small town of Waucoma. Ironically, my father became an umpire after his playing days and did many of the Sunday afternoon games that provided most of the entertainment in our home town area. Like father, like son.

Another note of interest in my baseball developing days relates to Daddy's interest in the major leagues. He listened to radio broadcasts of major league baseball, particularly the ones which involved his favorite team- - -the ST. LOUIS CARDINALS. Yes, he possibly indirectly influenced me into being a Cardinal fan all my life. Add to his loyalty the fact that when major league baseball was starting to be of interest for me, the Cardinals won four national league pennants and three World Series from 1942 to 1946. My idol was Stan, the Man, Musial. I finally had the privilege of talking with him, one on one, when I was about 65 years old. It was in his office at a business titled "Stan Musial, Inc." It has a huge collection of memorabilia with a special emphasis on Stan's professional career. After fifteen plus minutes of just interacting with each other (he asked me where I had played professional baseball in the Cardinal minor league system), he personally autographed a large Musial photo and presented it to me. You bet I still have that picture and vivid memories of the experience.

3

Upon my return to our son Dan's townhouse, and without delay sharing what had just taken place, he observed very quickly that I was behaving like a "kid that just had his first ice cream cone." Not far from being true.

Why baseball? Even though the town of Calmar, three miles from our farm, had a public high school with football, basketball and baseball, we did not attend any of their games. I think that was our family culture, or maybe the culture of the entire community impacting our decisions. The depression and World War II possibly impacted this culture also. For us it was all BASEBALL. Remember that we had no television until 1951 when I was a sophomore in high school. Some further explanation will come later. At the same time, Kenny and I did have a homemade wood backboard nailed against our corn crib. One-on-one games on dirt, packed snow, ice and/or wind pretty well described our basketball skill development. In fact, the first year the backboard was nailed to the corn crib, the only ball with air in it was a football. So that was what we used to play basketball. Try to bank that off the backboard.

With the existing culture of the Festina area and the love for the game exhibited by my father, is it any wonder that my two older brothers were baseball players as well? But for my first few years of recall, there was little baseball happening in Festina. There was a war going on. With the war ending in 1945 and men coming home from the war, the next year I remember Festina with a baseball team. A ball diamond had been built on the large school playground across the street from the church. That school and playground, including the baseball diamond, were developed in the 1930's, after my father had retired from the game.

Before further discussion about the start of that team, other thoughts can be conjured up about the early 1940's to exemplify the significance of baseball for the Huinker family, and, more specifically, for me. Whenever there was free time on our farm, it was occupied by an activity related to our "national pastime,"- - - what an appropriate nickname for baseball , especially for our family. Family ball games, involving all five of the children occurred frequently, most often in the inside yard next to our house. And yes, there were a few broken windows. The three brothers all played town team baseball but sister Irene possibly could have been the best athlete if there had been an opportunity for her to play. Kenny especially played a major role in my development as a baseball player. We sometimes just played catch. That often involved our playing pitcher-catcher, with the catcher being the umpire. We often tried to see how hard we could throw that little sphere. Control became important because you could not win without throwing strikes. Both of us being left-handed, we even convinced our father that we needed a left-hand catcher's mitt so the ball being pitched didn't sting so much. Often we would throw each other ground balls in a game format, always competitively. It was the same way with throwing fly balls, or batting fly balls to each other, again competitively. This means that someone had to make judgments about fair or foul, out or safe. And that decision-making is one of the skills we

4

developed while playing, something that I think our children today are deprived of doing. Now all decisions are made by umpires because it is all controlled by adults. This explains an opinion that I voice quite frequently.

In the middle to late forties, the game between Kenny and me evolved into a pitcher against batter contest evening after evening most of the summer in our outer yard. The barn served as the backstop. In the early games, three years of age made a major difference ability-wise. To counter that, an agreement (decision-making in order to keep on playing) was reached that Kenny got only one out and two strikes was a strikeout, while the little brother received the standard quota of strikes and outs. Watching our own children grow up and compete athletically with each other, the older sibling usually wins regardless of the rules established. By the time it was possible for me to compete on a more level field, Kenny was already pitching for Festina and I for a local legion team we will cover later.

At the same time, Kenny, being older, had more work responsibilities. Games had to be planned for time spent on my own. One consisted of throwing a rubber ball against our wood-sided house frequently and for long periods of time. While doing this, I was broadcasting a game that was being played—Cardinals most of the time. And, believe it or not, they frequently won. Maybe even all the time. Our wood siding was a three inch horizontal board and if certain parts of that board were hit, the ball would bounce differently—further or shorter, etc. That led to outs, hits, runs, maybe even a home run. Looking back on that effort, Mom must have gone wild inside the house with that repetitive banging against the siding, pitch after pitch. She never complained, however.

Another game version, using good imagination, was to visualize a ball diamond in the yard, sometimes out in a field where there was some level ground. Then a stick from a tree would be found that had some semblance of a bat and using it as a fungo bat, we would pick up little rocks and hit them to various parts of the imaginary diamond. Again, the Cardinals, or Festina, always seemed to win. This took place during my early grade school years.

With all this ball activity, and in a depression and/or war, we never seemed to have a shortage of baseball equipment. Bats, balls, gloves (even the left-handed catcher's mitt) were found among the limited presents that were under a Christmas tree that was cut from the top of one of our many evergreen trees around the house. Again, an example of its importance. One year, the day after a brown Christmas day, we took our new bats and balls, and possibly gloves, and created a ball diamond near the house and played baseball. It was like playing golf on December 26 in northeast Iowa.

Back to that Festina baseball team in 1946. The big war was over. This team played their first game of the year at the diamond on the school playground across from our Church. During those days games were always played on Sunday afternoons. It happened that it was the same afternoon that Archbishop Beckman

5

of the Dubuque Archdiocese was in Festina, conducting a confirmation ceremony that included me, eleven years old and in fifth grade. During the ceremony, we could hear the sounds of the baseball game—the crack of the bat meeting the ball (it must have happened quite frequently because the final score was 14 to 10), the yelling that goes with any game that is attended by fans of the sport. The confirmation ceremony "wore on for over 90 minutes. " Definitely the ceremony had a priority for our parish priest, Father Rubly, and for my parents but it was questionable for me. It became very difficult to give devotional attention in church. After that difficult afternoon, the family attended all the games that year, much to my delight. The highly-demanding task of being batboy for the hometown team became my responsibility the following year. Although that team, with my brother Linus playing centerfield, wasn't very successful that first year, most of the players stuck together, and by 1948, they were a team to be reckoned with in the old Upper Iowa baseball league. In fact, they shortly moved to the Northeast Iowa League which placed them against teams like West Union, New Hampton, Cresco, Spillville and St. Lucas, considered to be a much improved brand of semi-pro baseball in the area. Some teams close to Festina that were in the previous league were Ossian, Castaila, Nordness, Burr Oak, Ft. Atkinson, Calmar, sometimes Decorah. Ossian and Ft. Atkinson provided the toughest competition in the earlier league and led to some memorable games that will long be a part of baseball folklore in the Winneshiek area. One game in particular stands out. A Festina/Ossian conflict played at Ossian involved a lack of complete ground rules prior to the game. The diamond had a farm fence from the right field foul line to center, but in left, there was about a ten foot dropoff from left field to center and no fence. My brother, Linus, playing center, actually jumped down the embankment, regained his balance and caught a long, high fly ball, climbed back up the hill and showed the ball in glove to umpires. My other brother, Kenny, playing left field had witnessed the catch. Umpires, never having experienced such a play before, ruled in Festina's favor and all bedlam broke loose in a crowd they estimated as better than 400 people. The game, for the championship of the league, ended in a tie because darkness was setting in by the 12th inning when Ossian tied the game on a three-run home run by Harold Bengfort in the bottom half of the inning. They played another entire game the following Sunday on a neutral diamond and Festina won 10-5. And I was batboy. Ironically, Linus caught a ball below the hill the following year also but this time they had a third party sitting down the left field line that could witness such actions. There is much more Festina baseball history but I will hold that for later chapters completely dedicated to Festina baseball.

So far, there were no organized baseball games for me except a few Catholic school games arranged by our priest in Festina, then Rev. Henry P. Nosbisch, and the development of a legion baseball team at Calmar that I was invited to play with. The times overlap so I will cover the legion team baseball first.

6

In the summer of 1950, a lumber yard manager in Calmar, John Hodina, started a Junior Legion baseball team. He had just been transferred to Calmar by the lumber company. He had experienced such an effort in his previous location and felt it would be good for his new area, especially because he felt there was a strong interest in the sport. It was the first opportunity to play an organized ball game. I was fourteen (close to 15) when Mr. Hodina drove into our farmyard and talked with my Dad and myself about my playing with the team. Here again is illustrated the interest my Dad had in the game of baseball. He did not need a lot of convincing and I was going to have my first big opportunity.

Regretfully, I have very little memory of the first year and even the number of games we played. Leroy Schneberger, my first cousin, also played on the team. The second year, Jerry, Leroy's younger brother, also played. So did Carl Schupanitz, a catcher who also hailed from tiny Festina. There are three brief write-ups of this first venture and all are from the summer of 1952, the third year of the Legion team. No stats, no interesting stories, but some considerable experiences. The 1952 season follows the first high school season that had just been completed and will be covered in chapter 3. Write-ups follow.

CALMAR JUNIORS 4, LANSING 3,
The Calmar Junior Legion baseball club scored three
runs in the sixth inning of their game at Lansing Sunday to edge
that team 4 to 3.
Huinker, pitching for Calmar, struck out 15 men, and
Schweinefus, on the mound for Lansing, had eight.

HUINKER STRIKES OUT 18 AS CALMAR JUNIORS
FALL
After the Calmar Junior Legion defeated Lansing and
Manly, in the third round at Charles City Saturday, July 7,
Elkader won a terrific 11 inning battle. Huinker struck out 18
men. Leroy Schneberger knocked a triple for Calmar.

During that same time, while playing baseball or softball at recess, our parish priest organized four games for the St. Mary's players that I can recall. The first one was way back when I was in seventh grade in the spring of the 1947-48 school year. We played St. Luke's of St. Lucas, a neighboring Catholic school. Get this one—my position that day was "catcher." Leroy Schneberger, mentioned above, and a year older, was the pitcher. We definitely lost and there is a specific reason why I know. We apparently were down one run and I know that I occupied third base, the tying run, in the last half of the 7th inning. Two out, a three ball and two strike count on the hitter. I readily admit that I thought I really knew the game of baseball considerably better than anybody out there, somewhat of a "hot dog" at that time. I broke for the plate because I knew with two out and a three-two count, you can break on the pitch. Well, what little show-off didn't know was that you do that only when forced to advance. Got a little lucky

7

because the batter struck out; but, otherwise I am a dead duck at home plate. That was one of the ways that the game and its strategy was learned. Another game with the same team a year later, when I was the pitcher, we again lost. That was when I was in eighth grade. These games did not get written up in the paper and that certainly was not their intent. No, I have no clue what the score was. Another rule learned, however: when a pitcher has taken his stretch position with hands together, he cannot break those hands without first stepping off the rubber. The priest from St. Lucas, Father Schuh, was umpiring and he called a balk on me, then kindly explained what I had done wrong.

The next game was played against Ossian De Sales, their high school varsity baseball team. This was in the fall of 1951. An explanation is needed right now because a major change was being implemented by the Festina Catholic parish. They were going to have their own Catholic high school, one year at a time, until they were a 1-12 school system. It started with ninth grade when I was going to be in 6th grade and, therefore, brother Kenny was going to be in ninth grade. The reasons for his decision not to go on to the new 9th grade were never completely explained to me. The general understanding obtained over time indicated that he wanted to go to Calmar High School, spoken of earlier, so that he could play baseball. From something that happened later in my own life, my parents as confirmed Catholics living in a total Catholic community, felt he should continue his Catholic education instead. Kenny did not go beyond the eighth grade, not uncommon in our community at that time. My four older siblings completed only those first eight years. Of Kenny's class, only two boys continued to ninth grade. By the time I reached the ninth grade level, the intent of having a full four-year high school was discontinued, education stopping with 10th grade. This was the situation—my high school class had 2 girls and 6 boys. The class behind mine had a few more, not sure the exact number. We had one nun, Sister Teresita, who taught Math (both Geometry and Algebra) World History, Science, Foreign Language (which was Latin) and 9th and 10th grade Language Arts. It was mostly Literature. She was one of my all-time favorite teachers but she faced an impossible task. No human being can be that expert in that many subject areas all at the same time. Enough for now. Back to baseball. Father Nosbisch scheduled a ball game against the varsity baseball team from Ossian De Sales (where I was later to coach baseball for four years). We had eleven boys in our 9th and 10th grades. When the game was over, De Sales had been shut out; had no hits; hit one ball, a ground ball to the pitcher for an out. Twenty-one out of 22 batters struck out—one batter reached first base on a missed third strike. This was in the fall season and I do not think they won many games. Another first cousin, Leroy Einck, was the catcher for that game. Two years later we were battery mates in our senior year of high school at Calmar.

The next spring, Father Nosbisch convinced the high school staff to schedule our team with the high school varsity at Calmar High School. They were a solid ball club, which I found out when I joined that team as a junior in high school. Calmar High School beat us, 4-0. Again, no writeup that I could locate

8

(or maybe I didn't want to; who knows). A parent of one of the players, a senior, whose family used to live in Festina gave Father Nosbisch a little grief; but Father's response was very simply, "If I remember correctly, I believe your son went 0 for 4." We lost the game but it was fun. The following school year (1951-52) many of the players on those two teams were teammates. Many had also played together on the Legion team.

Another aspect of those early years of growing up caused great implications for the life I have lived. And the grades 1-10 school system at Festina played a major role. A few twisted smiles may occur as you read this section, especially those familiar with our family history. As a ninth grader, girls in the Festina community began to influence my attention---especially one in particular. Yes, she was a seventh grader by the name of Anna Mae Thuente. This opportunity to connect with her possibly may not have offered itself except for the fact that I was still enrolled at the Festina Catholic center. Had it not been for the two extra years of Catholic school, this remarkable gem may have been missed.

Anna Mae, now Ann to most of us, was a spirited young teen. The more she responded to my glances and smiles, the more I was getting hooked. By the following school year, notes began to get passed back and forth. That wasn't easy; sort of like the Underground Railroad of the Civil War. A network of communication developed, with certain necessary contacts established. But it was a network that was eventually discovered by the respective teachers in our two rooms—Sister Rita (Ann's teacher) and Sister Teresita (my teacher). This led to a "D" in conduct for a 9-week report card and one that did not sit too well with my Mom. I remember to this day, when she was given the report card, her first reaction got right to the point, "If that's how you are going to behave, you might as well stay home and help with the work around here." No more "D's" in conduct, but the feelings I had for this young Fraulein kept growing.

The youthful age we both were, opportunities for us to get together were limited. You may think that recess provided an opportune time to get together. Think again. Most of the guys still played ball during that time. "Priorities." At the time no thought of a conflict of life's goals.

A bit of Festina culture provided a few opportunities to get together beyond the school day. Whenever a young couple tied the marriage knot, if one or both were from the Festina parish, the couple would sponsor a shower dance in the evening after a mostly all-day reception for invited guests. Community members not at the reception would bring a gift to the "shower dance" and dance the night away, usually at the Inwood Pavilion in another small town in our area called Spillville. Typically, old-time music- - -waltzes, polkas, etc.- - -prevailed. This cultural habit provided Anna Mae and me some evenings where we could see each other. Lest you let your mind wander, this consisted of sitting in booths

9

around the dance floor, maybe sometimes sneaking into the middle of the floor and attempting to dance.

This foundation chapter has exceeded my initial planning. But, intentionally, it provides the background for that which is to follow. Baseball permeated our entire family life. Its strength was a driving force in many key steps to follow. Then there is the slowly building courtship that played right into all these discussions. The path taken for my life really is the life that "we" have lived. Through both forces, it is amazing to think how different life would have been if Daddy had not loved the game of baseball as much as he did.

Each ensuing chapter will look at a particular phase of my baseball life. In each, the content incorporates primarily newspaper write-ups. Any pictures associated with that particular baseball era will all be included in a picture section in the center of the book. Built in are, hopefully, interesting tidbits of those games and the wonderful friends (teammates and opposing team players) that were such a significant part of all the games, and the teams played. I know that my family has heard me talk about so many of these people. It is my sincere desire to do justice in this memoir to their significant role in my successes and failures and in the great memory of those days past. That and the beautiful relationship with Ann that permeated the playing of all these ball games.

MY HOMETOWN HEROES

Baseball with the hometown Festina team, an aspect of my baseball life that proved to be something very difficult to describe. For that group of players, there exists an emotional attachment that possibly is beyond words. They were a very special force in my developing life. Ever since 1946, they and the games they played were a strong part of my life, particularly as it ties to baseball. But even beyond baseball, their attitude toward the game and to life influenced my growing up greatly. A great majority of the games and their highlights that I had the privilege to be part of occurred from 1951, prior to my days at Calmar High School, to 1956 which coincides with the first three baseball years at Loras College. During that span there were so many games played with Festina that placing some games in certain summers proved extremely challenging. Hopefully, our research places all of them correctly.

Beginning with the start of the baseball season for Festina in 1946, as mentioned in Chapter One, until the 1951 season when I became a playing member of the team, the players had remained much the same. And their won/loss record soared upward every season.

Let me go through that lineup and identify an amazing fact—nearly everyone of the team was related. Using myself as the basic relative, here goes with the starting lineup and their relationship to me:

Linus Huinker –center field; my brother;
Leo Luzum—third base; married a Schneberger relative;
Jim Schneberger—shortstop; first cousin;
Norb Einck—right field; first cousin;
Ken Huinker—left field; my brother;
Ken Schneberger—pitcher; first cousin;
Romauld Elsbernd--second base; farm neighbor;
Bob Schneberger—catcher; first cousin;
Nily Huinker—first base; first cousin;

Nily was the first to retire. When that happened, my brother Kenny usually played first base. If my brother pitched, pitcher Ken Schneberger went to second base and Romauld Elsbernd moved from second base to first base. Romauld also was a pitcher and you will see that in the six years we will be covering. The left field position, vacated by brother Kenny's move to first base, became my place in 1951, fifteen years old and planning to be a junior at Calmar High School in the fall . This move, an opportunity almost built of eager dreams, occurred after several seasons serving as batboy and/or score keeper for the Festina team.

With a few exceptions, the core of that lineup listed above was on the 1946 team. John Wenthold managed that '46 team but shortly after, another

11

farmer, Florian Nienhaus, no relation, took over the managerial reins, a job he kept until the late fifties. Besides the games themselves, one does not realize the number of hours spent on organizational league and tournament planning meetings, scheduling non-league games, postponements, phone calls, etc. that the manager takes care of. It was his quiet leadership that enabled the players to do what they loved the most—play baseball. And that they did. And very well. As the 50's rolled on, they gained the respect of other teams and fans in the area. It was not unusual to have several hundred people at the home games on Sunday afternoons, many more than the population of the "community" that made up Festina. Rivalries were built up between next door towns, Ossian, Calmar, St. Lucas and Fort Atkinson. They felt great when they could defeat their little neighbor. Soon towns further away like West Union, Sumner, New Hampton and Cresco were included in those rivalries as Festina spread its wings further and further.

The first game playing my new left field position stands out in my mind, so very typical of our long-term memory. We remember that which comes first and that which is last, but the many games in between sort of become muddled together. The game was contested at West Union, against a strong team that in 1951 became Festina's chief rival for winning the championship of the Northeast Iowa League. Lionel "Baldy" Weston, a veteran hurler, took the hill against us and shut our hitters down. I batted four times with no hits but he did not strike me out. But I try to justify my being in the lineup that Sunday afternoon by leaping up in front of the left field fence, all 5ft, 8 inches of me, to take an extra base hit away from a West Union hitter. We lost our next game, another game without a hit for me.

There is another aside that I remember from that first game. After the game, right fielder Norb Einck singled me out and offered a "good game, Art, for your first start. That meant a lot to me and maybe that comment might be the reason he became my favorite first cousin. Ann and I visited Norb and his wife, Rosaria, many times in later years. One of those visits occurred on Norb's, 80th birthday, shortly before he was called to his eternal reward. It was that day when, in our sharing, I mentioned that I was very proud to have grown up in the Festina community. Quickly, Norb's response was "You better be." And that gesture also paints a picture of the quality of people that made up that team. As of the year of this writing, all starting lineup players including my two brothers, except the three Schnebergers, have passed on to their next life.

Our third game against neighboring Calmar, we faced left hand pitcher Randy Russett, older brother to Don Russett, who later was the second baseman and teammate at Calmar High School. The batting average got off zero when I had back to back singles to left center field. That buoyed my confidence and enthusiasm. The year before that, while playing American Legion baseball, there were pitching opportunities for me. To pitch for the Festina baseball team at this

12

time was far from my mind. Ken Schneberger, Romauld Elsbernd and brother Kenny were our pitchers that 1951 season. It was exciting for me to just play.

Write-ups of games that first year are scarce but there are two of them that still sit in my memory. The first was a return engagement with rival West Union on our home diamond. A short write-up of the game follows. The final score was 4-3 with Festina scoring all of its runs in the bottom of the ninth. The first two batters for us reached base safely (don't remember how). Now it was my turn. I still hadn't struck a base hit against the veteran pitcher, "Baldy" Weston. Prior to my at-bat and immediately after the second batter had reached base safely, Leo Luzum, an experienced veteran in his own right, suggested that I try to bunt for a hit. I managed to place one down the third base line, catching the West Union team off guard and now the bases were loaded, still with no outs. Now the top of the batting order was coming up. Before the inning was finished we walked away with four runs and a victory that eventually led to a tie for first place in the league standings between West Union and Festina. "Small ball can be very valuable," is definitely a big part of the game.

> *FESTINA 4, WEST UNION 3*
> *Things looked a little dark for Festina playing on their own diamond Sunday after being held scoreless and trailing 3 to 0 as they came to bat in the last of the ninth. But then--- everything began to happen. Suddenly all the gears began to mesh and when the dust cleared at the end of the inning, the home team won by the score of 4 to 3. This put both of these contestants into a tie for second place on the league standings.*

The other game in my recollections was against Elma, another small town west of Cresco, Iowa. It was a make-up game and played under the lights at New Hampton. Our starting pitcher, Ken Schneberger, was knocked unconscious when hit by a pitched ball and taken to the local hospital. That incident provided the first pitching experience for me with town team Festina.

> *SCHNEBERGER HURT AS FESTINA WINS*
> *New Hampton, Ia. --- Festina clung to its first place Northeast Iowa baseball league spot with West Union Friday after a decisive 12-0 victory over Elma here Thursday night, and the two teams headed into Sunday's "D" day with equal 12-2 records.*
> *Thursday's makeup win over Elma, a no-hitter turned in by two Festina pitchers, may have been a costly one for the winners. Regular Festina pitcher Ken Schneberger was hit on the neck with a pitched ball in the first of the eighth and was knocked unconscious. He was removed to the New Hampton hospital after he was revived. He spent the night there, but reportedly was not seriously injured.*

13

Art Huinker fanned six men to protect the no-hitter in the final two innings.

If both teams win their scheduled games on Sunday, the two will play off Sunday night here for the Northeast Iowa league's position in the Waterloo Courier's Northeast Iowa Baseball Tournament of Champions starting next Tuesday in Waterloo. The regular league season doesn't end, however, until Sept. 9.

Winning the league title qualifies the team for the annual Waterloo Courier Northeast Iowa Baseball Tournament played at the Waterloo stadium, which at that time had a major league affiliated professional team. For the Festina team this was a big trip, very similar to the years that the team played in the Dubuqueland Tournament. We will cover that affair later in this chapter. In 1951, the winner of the Courier tournament qualified as the Iowa representative for the national American Baseball Tournament (AABC), eventually leading to the crowning of a national champion for amateur or semi-pro baseball in the United States.

Because there was a tie between West Union and Festina, a playoff game was necessary. It was played under the lights at New Hampton. Festina claimed an 8 to 2 victory, and I had probably the best hitting night of the entire season, with a single, double and triple against the veteran Weston. Festina was off to Waterloo for the third consecutive season and the New Hampton diamond became one of my favorites.

FESTINA NIPS WEST UNION IN PLAYOFF, 8-2

New Hampton, Ia, --- Festina Sunday night won the right to play in the Waterloo Courier Northeast Iowa Baseball Tournament of Champions for the third straight time by defeating West Union 8-2, in a first place playoff game here.

Festina's second victory in three games against West Union was witnessed by nearly 900 fans on the neutral diamond under the lights here.

The game was necessary to determine the Northeast Iowa league's representative in the Courier tournament because both teams were tied at the top of the standings with 13-2 records following victories in regular league games Sunday afternoon. Joe Staebel pitched West Union to a 7-2 victory over Spillville while Romauld Elsbernd was pitching Festina to a 8-1 victory over St. Lucas.

Hero of Sunday night's playoff was Art Huinker, 16-year-old outfielder, who got a triple, double and single to lead

14

Festina's 12 hit attack,while West Union was getting only four safeties off Ken Schneberger.

The first round at the Courier tournament proved to be a nail-biting 4 to 3 victory over Parkersburg. It was the first time in three tries that Festina moved into the semi-final round.

FESTINA 4, PARKERSBURG 3

Relief pitcher Ken Schneberger forced pinchhitter Maynard Petersen to ground out with two out and the bases full in the seventh inning to protect Festina's 4-3 victory over Parkersburg Tuesday night.

Parkersburg whittled the Northeast Iowa loop pacesetters' leads from 3-0 and 4-1, but went out in order in the sixth inning and failed to score after getting the first two men on base in the seventh.

The winners went out 1-2-3 in the first inning, but Ken Schneberger led off the second with a single. Ken Huinker sent him to third with a line single to right. A walk to Linus Huinker loaded the bases. A strikeout produced the first out, but Art Huinker and Neil Huinker added one-basers to drive in three runs.

Jim Basler's single preceded by an error and a walk sent home Parkersburg's first run in the third.

Ken Huinker's safety and four errors gave Festina what proved to the marginal run in the third, but they left three men stranded on base and had another potential run thrown out on a force play at home. Festina got only one hit and couldn't muster a runner beyond second base after that.

Meanwhile, Parkersburg cut the margin to 4-2 in the fourth when Ken O'Dea walked to force in a run after two other bases on balls and Jack Smiley's single had loaded the sacks. Basler singled and Whip Engelkes walked to put runners on first and second with none out in the fifth when Ken Schneberger, who defeated West Union Sunday to gain Festina's berth in the tournament, replaced Ken Huinker on the mound.

Schneberger fanned the first batter to face him, but Smiley lashed his second single scoring Basler. Engelkes was out at third when pitcher Schneberger cut off centerfielder Linus Huinker's throw and tossed to third baseman Leo Luzum. Andy Buseman grounded out to end the inning.

Don Prior was safe at first on an infield hit to open the seventh. He went to second when the shortstop's throw got away from the Festina first baseman for an error. Basler walked, but Engelkes popped out to second. Les Kampman drew a walk to load the bases. Smiley, trying for his third

15

straight hit, popped a high fly to rightfielder Norb Einck, whose
quick throw drove Prior back to third.
Pinchhitter Petersen hit a 2-2 pitch right at Festina
second baseman Romauld Elsbernd, who handled it on the
bounce and threw to first for the final out.

The next game resulted in one of those you wish you
could forget. It was a disaster. Our pitching staff, worn thin by
four games played in 10 days, could not stop the Sumner Cubs
attack, seventeen hits in all, while we finally managed our first
hit in the seventh inning. We were now scheduled for the
consolation game. In the write-up, the flat tire describes our
transportation system.

SUMNER 11 FESTINA 0
Festina's pitcher, Ken Schneberger broke up Sumner
Lefty Marv Buhr's no-hitter with a well hit double in the seventh
inning of Sumner's 11-0 semifinal round victory Friday.
Festina had only five baserunners as Buhr pitched his near
perfect game. He retired the side in order in the first, second,
third, fifth, sixth and seventh innings.
In the fourth inning, after 10 men had failed to reach
first, Festina's Jim Schneberger was safe on an error. He got
as far as second. In the fifth, Linus Huinker lived on an error
but was retired in a doubleplay.
In the seventh, Schneberger's drive to the leftfield
corner with two outs was followed by a hit batsman for the only
inning Festina had two men on base. Art Huinker was safe on
an error to lead off the eighth for the losers, but got no farther
than first.
Meanwhile, Sumner was pounding 17 hits, including a
double and a triple, off two Festina pitchers. Successive singles
by Louie Buhrows, an error and an infield out gave the Cubs a
run in the second. A walk and four hits including Bill Hughes'
double made it 5-0 in the third and brought Ken Schneberger in
to relieve starter Romauld Elsbernd on the mound for Festina.
Sumner went scoreless with only one single off
Schneberger until the seventh when it broke out for four runs on
six singles. It added the two runs that proved enough to end the
game on two more one-basers and Mel Harms' triple to the
scoreboard in the eighth.
One car load of Festina players took the field without a
warmup after arriving at the park 10 minutes after game time
because of a flat tire on their auto.

Sumner made a habit of making things miserable for Festina. I never attempted to determine wins and losses against them but we were on the short end. Not many teams could claim that advantage. The consolation battle for third place provided a huge surprise for me. Manager Nienhaus announced that I would be the starting pitcher. If you ask "were you nervous," there admittedly had to be many, many butterflies flying around in my stomach. But more than nervousness, I think the excitement of having an opportunity to pitch in the big stadium for my hometown was stronger. The game results were unbelievably better than anything I could imagine. There was a new feeling of belonging to this ball club with all its veteran players. The game write-up follows.

BUNT IN LAST FRAME SPOILS NO HIT GAME

A perfectly executed bunt by Independence manager Glen Maynard in the seventh inning ruined Art Huinker's bid for a no-hitter in his first full game as a pitcher for Festina in the seven inning consolation game. The hit also led to Independence's only run of the game and broke up Huinker's shutout.

The 16-year-old lefty, whose brothers Linus and Ken, also play on the team, has been with the Northeast Iowa loop leaders as an outfielder all season, but his only previous pitching experience with Festina was a two inning stint a week ago.

That night he hurled the final two innings and struck out the six men that faced him to collaborate with Ken Schneberger in pitching a no-hitter against Elma in a Northeast Iowa league game.

Huinker, who entered Calmar High School as a junior Monday, pitched for the Calmar Legion team this summer. It was his first season on the Festina club.

Independence had only five baserunners on four walks and an error through the sixth. Maynard led off the seventh with his bunt down the third base line. He advanced to third when Huinker overthrew first on a pickoff attempt and scored as Jim Hearn grounded out to third.

Successive hits by Leo Luzum and Jim Schneberger and a walk loaded the bases for Festina in the first. Ken Schneberger forced Luzum at home, but Jim Schneberger scored the first run of the game on a sacrifice fly to leftfield by Norb Einck.

Hits by Jim Schneberger, Ken Huinker and Einck produced another run for Festina in the third. Three more hits, including Ken Huinker's double, wound up the scoring for Festina in the fifth.

The season was not over. Festina received another invite to the Dubuqueland Baseball Tournament, always held early in September. This late in the season allowed many Midwest area players playing the professional minor leagues to play in this tournament. Festina had played in the tournament previously. In 1949, they had lost to the quality Dubuque Old Timers in the finals, a great accomplishment for the team from tiny Festina, a pimple on the map as described by the Dubuque Telegraph Herald. As a sixteen year old junior in high school, going to Dubuque to play a baseball game at the old Fourth Street ballpark spoke big-time for me.

Our first game was against a team from Lansing, Iowa who had added three good players from tiny Castaila, second baseman Dewey Reisner, first baseman Rodney Anderson and left hand pitcher Earle Koenig. Koenig was famous in the Dubuqueland tournament for his pitching duel with Tom Breitbach, top Dubuque pitcher. He and Tom battled each other in the longest game ever played in this tournament. Festina slugged out a convincing 11-2 victory and another date with the Dubuque Independents, formerly the Dubuque Old Timers. They collected an 8-3 victory over Platteville and pitcher Thornton Kipper, a future big league pitcher for the Philadelphia Phillies. The score of that game was a bit unusual because few semi-pro teams seldom had much luck scoring against him.

INDEPENDENTS ROMP

Little Festina, hailing from the northeast corner of Iowa, stamped itself as one of the teams to watch in the sixth annual Dubuqueland baseball tournament, slugging out an impressive 11-2 triumph over Lansing after the Dubuque Independents had bumped Platteville, 8-3, in Friday night's first round doubleheader.

Festina now meets the Independents in a second round game Tuesday night and those members of the Dubuque team who stuck around to see the Festina-Lansing scrap watched a bit apprehensively as the Festina nine rattled 16 solid base hits off the fences.

Festina scored a run in the second and another in the third but Lansing came back to tie up the game with single tallies in the third and fourth. In the fourth, Lansing slashed out three consecutive doubles, but could score only once. A great throw by centerfielder Linus Huinker cut down the potential second run at the plate.

Kenny Huinker, a lefthanded powerhouse, sparked Festina to a three---run rally in the sixth with a long home run over the right-field fence with a mate aboard. After picking up another tally in the seventh, the boys then put the game in deep freeze with a five-run outburst in the top of eighth.

18

>*In all, Festina gathered 16 base hits, including a home run and five doubles. Ken Huinker picked up four for five, a homer, double and two one-baggers, and batted in four runs while scoring twice. Jim Schneberger had three RBIs with two doubles and a single.*
>
>*Lansing had nine hits off winning pitcher Ken Schneberger. Anderson picked up two doubles in four attempts and Cloy Schultz punched out a double and two one-base hits in four trips.*

Of Festina's 16 hits besides my brother Kenny and Jim Schneberger, four players had two hits each- - -Leo Luzum, catcher Rudy Wenthold, Norb Einck and brother Linus. Romauld Elsbernd had one hit. That leaves the pitcher and the left fielder without any hits. The latter was yours truly.

Prior to the game with the Independents, the following editorial blurb appeared in the Telegraph Herald: "Tuesday night, the Dubuque Independents tackle little Festina, one of the crowd favorites. The Festina nine has been playing together for several years and entered the tournament with its season's lineup unchanged. Festina has three of the hardest-throwing outfielders yet seen in the meet." That was Norb Einck, my brother Linus and myself.

The game itself became an outstanding defensive struggle and a game that I remember as much as any game I ever played in. Both pitchers were outstanding, Tom Breitbach for the Independents and Ralph Kneeskern for us. (Ralph was an outstanding pitcher from Harmony, Minnesota that we played against quite often). There was no score going into the bottom of the ninth inning. Prior to that, in the second inning my brother Linus threw a runner out at the plate. Something more unusual happened in the fourth inning. Dubuque had a runner on first. Bob Hoerner, another special baseball friend and former professional baseball player, hit a ground ball to the second baseman. Playing left field, I immediately moved toward second base to back up a possible throw to the shortstop for a forceout. But, enthusiasm doesn't always lead to wise decisions, especially if the knowledge used to make the quick decision is incomplete. To back up the throw to the shortstop was correct, but how close to second base you come hadn't been totally reasoned out. I came so close that when the throw went quite wide on the third base side of second base, so wide and my being too close, the ball flew by me almost all the way to the left field corner before I was able to catch up with it. The runner, safe at second because of the wide throw, headed for third on his way to score. As quick as possible, I retrieved the ball and fired it on the fly to home place. Luckily, it was on line and was on time to catch the runner at the plate. It was bad thinking originally but with a good outcome. We get lucky occasionally.

Now it is the bottom of the ninth, with a runner on second for the Independents. Festina wasn't too high on strategic thinking for their baseball. We

19

probably should have walked the batter, John Deckert, but we didn't. Don't really know if was on anyone's mind. He grounded a single to left (contrary to what the paper's write-up stated. I charged the ball, hoping for some additional luck, but I had to catch the ball first, then throw. I failed in that regard and the game was over. A great ball game, some interesting plays, but we lost. We garnered only four hits off Tom Breitbach, two by right fielder Norb Einck who had a single and double. By the way, this write-up is copied word for word with the ninth inning error being blamed on my brother, Linus. Often, in the later years of our lives, many team members of the Dubuque Independents would get together for a Friday lunch at Breezy's Café in downtown Dubuque. They always kept urging me to come and on several occasions I did join them. Conversation would so often turn to the wonderful game of baseball and past memories.

DECKERT BLOW BEATS FESTINA

Big John Deckert, Dubuque Independents catcher, came through with a timely single with two out in the last of the ninth and a teammate on second base to break the heart of little Festina, 1 to 0, Tuesday night in what turned out to be the finest game the sixth annual Dubuqueland tournament has seen so far this season.

Festina, the underdog but crowd favorite, all but had a victory in its grasp when an error, passed ball and Deckert's line single to left broke up the game in the final inning.

The victory was a particularly tough pill to swallow for Ralph Kneeskern, the losing hurler. Kneeskern pitched a masterful five hit game, baffling 14 Dubuque batters with his strikeout pitch while walking but one man.

He was opposed by Tom Breitbach, and Tommy was also in rare form Tuesdday night. The ace of the Independents' mound corps twirled a four hitter, fanned five and did not issue a pass.

Once again it was the slingshot arms of the Festina outfielders that caught the fancy of the crowd while cutting down potential runs at the plate. The Independents threatened in the second inning when Deckert walked and moved to second on a passed ball. Tom Schlueter laced a ground single through the box into centerfield and Deckert headed for home. Linus Huinker, Festina centerfielder, scooped up the ball and tossed a strike to catcher Rudy Wenthold to nail Deckert.

In the fourth frame, Art Dalhauser got a life on an error by the second baseman. Merle Mathis fanned. Bob Hoerner then hit to second and the second baseman elected to try for the putout at second. The throw was wild and rolled far into the leftfield corner. Art Huinker dashed after the ball and from the dim-lit corner of left field rifled the ball to home to get

Dalhauser by 10 feet. The throw never touched the ground and hit the catcher shoulder high.

Long after the game, fans were speculating about the Independents' run in the ninth inning. Deckert's single to left was hard hit and Mathis was just making the turn at third when the strong-armed Linus Huinker got set to make the pick-up and throw. However, the ball got by him and Mathis scored in a walk.

Deckert, who split a finger on a foul tip in the eighth inning, had two hits in three trips. Bob Schlueter, Mathis and Tom Schlueter picked up the other bingles off Knerskern.

Norb Einck had a double and a single to lead Festina.

The following editorial appeared in the Dubuque Telegraph Herald, written by T-H staff writer Gene Mullins:

It was beginning to look like no tournament hurler was going to toss a shutout this year. . .then suddenly the fans are treated to a pair the same night. That first game looked like it could have gone on and on. Second guessers believed Festina should have loaded the bases in the fatal ninth when two were out. Festina, big favorites with the crowd, received an ovation at the end of the game. It was Festina's second appearance in the tournament. In 1949, it lost to the Old Timers, 6 to 3, in the finals.

There is little room for outsiders on the Festina club. It's strictly a family affair. . . .an outsider has little chance of breaking off any of the limbs of this family tree. There are three sets of brothers---Neil and Bob Huinker, then cousins Linus, Ken and Art Huinker and finally Jim, LeRoy, Bob and Ken Schneberger. The Huinkers and Schnebergers are all cousins. Then there is Leo Luzum. Leo wanted to play ball, too so he married into the family. All were on hand Tuesday night except LeRoy Schneberger, who had to remain behind for football practice with Calmar High School. What a hot stove league this family must have.

The season was over, almost. All the hoopla surrounding Festina's play in the Dubuqueland tournament brought the Dubuque team to Festina in October for a friendly rematch of the competitive rivalry. Again they beat us, this time by a score of 5 to 4. My brother Kenny pitched for us, Tom Breitbach again for Dubuque. There exist limited memories, but I feel the Dubuquers enjoyed the trip and did their share of celebrating on the trip home. At least I garnered two hits for a change.

21

Festina, Ia.---The Dubuque Independents notched their second win of the season over Festina here Sunday, 5 to 4.

Tom Schlueter, Midge Delaney and Bobby Budden came through with consecutive singles in the eighth inning to break up the tie game and give the Independents the victory.

Dubuque had to come from behind after Festina jumped off to an early lead. A walk, an error and a two-run double provided the host team with a 2-0 lead in the second inning.

Festina went out in front again in the bottom of the fifth on a pair of singles and a double, only to have the Dubuquers knot the score in the seventh with two doubles and a single.

Dubuque chopped the margin to one run in the fourth on an error and John Deckert's double. A walk and Bob Schleuter's two-bagger tied the count at 4-4 in the next frame.

Tommy Breitbach earned the decision for the Independents. He scattered seven hits, struck out six and walked five. Ken Huinker gave up 12 blows, fanned seven and walked four in taking the setback.

Fifty years after the 1 to 0 loss the Dubuque Independents, Tom Breitbach and I met at the wake of dear friend Bob Hoerner, Tom was with someone when I walked up to him. He introduced me to his friend this way, "This is the sixteen year old left fielder from Festina who threw the ball from the left field fence all the way home on the fly. And he got the runner." Tom remembered that so well.

NEW SCHOOL SURROUNDINGS

In the fall of 1951, my junior year began at Calmar High School. I was now a Cahawk with classmates numbering thirty-four, a 300% jump from the days at Catholic school in Festina. There were greater numbers of new girls at CHS but my eyes still focused on the ninth grader back in Festina. This was also a new experience in a public school after ten years at Festina St. Mary's.

Football filled the fall sports schedule but I did not participate. My Father had said that I could play in one sport "besides baseball." It was taken for granted that baseball was one of the choices. Basketball was my other choice. Two of my Festina classmates, Leroy Einck and Ron Schuler, chose football besides baseball. They joined senior first cousin Leroy Schneberger, also from Festina, on the football team. He was a strong football player as well as a great left hand batter for the baseball team in the spring.

For some reason that has never been understood, the junior class selected yours truly class president. Including monthly meetings held during the school day, this did not carry a big responsibility until the following spring. Being the emcee for the annual spring prom fell on my shoulders as well as directing all the planning for that event. There were many wonderful helpful hands who completed all the decorating of the gym, organizing and preparing the meal, getting music lined up for the dance and getting all the invitations and related activities completed. Never having been involved in any affair as major as the prom was a great learning experience for me, but also one that caused millions of butterflies in my stomach as the evening drew near.

Despite the scary Emcee job the prom created an emotional opportunity that far outweighed the duties of president. This event provided the opportunity for me to invite Ann on our first real big date, a night with formal dress, corsage and the works. The invitation was warmly accepted by Ann. However, it was not that simple with her parents. Her Mom and Dad had reservations about their freshman daughter going to a junior-senior prom. They finally relented.

Once the fall football season finished its final game, basketballs replaced the odd-shaped football. Practices became a great learning experience. The extent of my basketball experience consisted of brother Kenny and I playing one-on-one in a cleaned out hay mow with two wood backboards nailed to the interior of the barn roof besides recess pick-ups on a dirt court on the playground at St. Mary's. Having witnessed only one live basketball game (and that was a girls' six-on-six game) before becoming a junior at CHS, learning about "team offense and team defense" did not automatically become a clear picture for me and the result was very limited playing time that first year. We practiced after school every day before the games began. The weather was still warm enough that senior Gerry Elsbernd (also from Festina) and I would walk and/or jog home to our farms every day after practice, a distance of about three miles. At least six of the

23

basketball players also ended up on the baseball team in the spring so basketball provided an opportunity to become good friends with them before baseball started.

Gerry Elsbernd was, academically, one of the sharpest individuals you could find. Under his senior picture in the Cahawk yearbook, the following quote was very fitting, "there may be men smarter than I, but I doubt it." He later attended the United States Air Force Academy and was a pilot for the US Air Force.

The baseball season would be next. By the time that season began I had already participated in every game played by the Festina semi-pro team the previous summer. How different from the start of basketball season. Many sideline stories add interesting scenarios to the games themselves but first the games.

In this section, write-ups of all thirteen games, ending with a trip to state tournament, are reproduced for the reader to enjoy. We smashed our way to twelve consecutive wins before losing to eventual state champion Kanawha in the state semi-finals. As you will see, our first pre-tournament games led to lop-sided victories. Pay close attention to the 11-4 Decorah write-up where a certain player you know by now had a grand slam home run, the first of really not too many more. And an unwritten part of the 17-2 sectional tournament write-up over neighboring Ossian listed three home runs in the first inning. Lead-off batter Don Russett hit a triple. Then the next three batters, Russ Hillman, Leroy Schneberger and Larry Herold hit back to back to back home runs. Ironically, my memory focuses too clearly on what happened next to the fifth batter in the lineup. My mighty swing resulted in a slow roller hit back to the pitcher who easily threw me out at first base. My only defense against the resulting "ribbing" directed at me was to simply explain "the pitcher was playing way too deep for me."

Prior to spring baseball tourney play, the 1952 Cahawks won four games. Unable to find the write-up for the first win over Ossian, the write-ups for the next three games are listed below: Fort Atkinson, Decorah and Ridgeway.

CALMAR DEFEATS FORT 5-0
*The Calmar Cahawks won their second game of the
season Tuesday by shutting out Fort Atkinson. Huinker
struck out 15 men, walked five, and allowed three hits.
Smith allowed eight strike outs, nine walks and one hit.
Leroy Schneberger tripled in the first inning with two men
on, bringing in two scores. This is Calmar's second straight
win, defeating Ossian 22-3, in the season opener.*

CALMAR WINS 3RD GAME, 11-4, OVER
DECORAH
*Art Huinker, Calmar moundsman, limited the
Decorah nine to three hits. He struck out seven and gave up*

24

three walks. Huinker also hit a home run in the fourth
inning with the bases loaded to spark the victory. First
baseman Larry Herold went four for four for the Cahawks.

CAHAWKS COP 4TH WIN, 17-2, OVER RIDGEWAY
Leroy Schneberger pitched a two-hitter for Calmar.
Meanwhile, left fielder Russ Hillman and catcher Don
Hageman each had two hits. In this game, Larry Herold
scored four times in the victory.

Fort Atkinson had two very good left-hand pitchers. Notice Jene Smith, a tall, slender left hander (probably about 6 foot 3) allowed only one hit, that to Leroy Schneberger---but, true to the lie that lefties were always wild, he walked nine batters. Pro scouts followed him but in the end he settled for pitching many town team games around Northeast Iowa.

CALMAR VICTORIOUS IN SECTIONAL OPENER
Art Huinker allowed Fort Atkinson only two hits in a
tight ball game broken open by the Cahawks with a four-run
sixth inning. Calmar had only four hits, two by Leroy
Schneberger and one each by Huinker and Mickey Griffin.

We played against Fort Atkinson again, but this time lefty Clem Reicks did their pitching. Clem was born with an undeveloped right arm. He became very adept at placing a left-handed glove under the deficient right arm. Once he threw the pitch, he would slide his left hand into the glove and be ready to field his position. He didn't throw as hard as his counterpart, Jene Smith, but had a more than adequate curve ball that fooled many of us, especially left-handed batters, nos. 1, 3 and 4 in our lineup who consistently led our hitting attack. Throughout the years, Clem and I had many opportunities to exchange baseball thoughts. Later, he ended up in the same senior home at Decorah as my siblings, Shirley and Kenny.

CALMAR CLAIMS 6th STRAIGHT, 17-2, IN SEMI-FINALS
Calmar scored 7 runs in the first inning. Russ
Hillman, Leroy Schneberger and Larry Herold hit
successive home runs, three of the eleven hits for the team.
Schneberger pitched a one-hitter while having three hits
himself. Don Russett, Herold and Tom Iverson each
garnered two hits.

CALMAR WINS 7th STRAIGHT TO COP SECTIONAL
Leroy Schneberger pitched a no-hit, no-run game for
Calmar and struck out 14 men and walked four. Three

25

Calmar men had home runs. They were Russ Hillman, Mickey Griffin and Larry Herold. Herold also had a triple and single.

The district tournament was hosted by Calmar High School starting with a game against Fayette. Monona and Waukon were the other two sectional champs competing in the four-team tournament.

> ### UNBEATEN CALMAR TOPPLES FAYETTE
> *Calmar High School notched its eighth straight win of the season Wednesday by defeating Fayette 6 to 1 in the first round of district tournament action at Calmar. In the second game, Monona edged out Waukon 2 to 1 in a tight pitching duel.*
> *Calmar's win was made possible by two big innings, scoring three runs in each of the fourth and sixth frames. Art Huinker pitched tight ball for Calmar yielding only two base hits.*

Although the final score of 6 to 1 does not make it sound tough, Fayette always gave opponents a battle. Their Legion baseball coach, by the way, was a Catholic priest, Father Mullen. They beat our legion team when I was pitching the year before. Two players, Galen Mack and Terry Stevens, were very strong hitters and opposing pitchers found out quickly if the pitch wasn't located to their weaknesses. Speed alone wasn't going to get the job done. Stevens, attending Fayette High School, was the first team all-state quarterback in his senior year. Two years after we both graduated from high school, Terry and I were teammates on Sumner's town team.

> ### CALMAR ENTERS SUB-STATE PLAY
> *Calmar High School's baseball team won its district title here Friday afternoon, defeating Monona, 4-2. Huinker, Calmar pitcher, allowed only four hits and fanned eight. It was Calmar's ninth win of the season, and is the first time in the school's history that a team has entered sub-state play. Monona didn't get a man on second base until the seventh when it scored its two runs. Calmar scored two runs in the first and again in the fourth.*

I don't remember much about the game, but Monona's coach, Pete Peterson, was well-known as one of the more successful and knowledgeable baseball coaches in the state. His team from Monona won the state baseball title in 1948. First cousin, Don Huinker, was the catcher for that team. (Many people associate the name Huinker with Monona because they had seen the Huinker Chevrolet sign along Highway 52 by Monona. The business was operated by my Dad's older brother, Alfred). For the two substate games that followed, Coach

Peterson attended and would ask me how my arm felt. He said that as long as it didn't hurt in my shoulder or my elbow, it was okay to pitch, even though I had one or two days rest. Later, I coached against him while teaching at Ossian De Sales. When you played against a Pete Peterson-coached team, you had to be ready for almost anything. He was always thinking "strategies" to put pressure on the opposing team's defense. I learned much from Coach Peterson.

> *CALMAR BASEBALL ONE GAME AWAY FROM*
> *STATE*
> *The Calmar Cahawks won their 10th straight victory*
> *by defeating Clear Lake, 9-3. Art Huinker, Calmar pitcher,*
> *allowed four hits and struck out 14 men in the game on*
> *Thursday. Calmar's Larry Herold and Leroy Schneberger*
> *had home runs in the first inning, leading to three runs. They*
> *added six more in the fourth. Russ Hillman and Herold each*
> *had two hits.*

If all line scores were included for the games won thus far, a very important statistic would jump out at you. Many runs crossed the plate in the first inning. Don Russett, although only a freshman, was a very patient hitter and received many walks. Russ Hillman, batting second, and our only right hand hitter in our first four, was by far our fastest runner and did a good job of putting the ball in play. Then the two left hand sluggers, Herold and Schneberger, followed. A very tough challenge for most high school pitchers. As a pitcher, it was always nice to have early run support.

> *CAHAWKS DEFEAT MCINTYRE 7-1 FOR SUB-*
> *STATE TITLE*
> *The Calmar High School baseball team won the sub-*
> *state tournament against McIntyre 7-1, Saturday at La Porte*
> *City, and will go against Exira in the first round match at*
> *Mason City on Monday, May 26.*
> *The Calmar nine scored two runs in the first inning,*
> *two in the fourth, and three in the sixth in defeating*
> *McIntyre. Art Huinker, star pitcher for the Cahawks,*
> *blasted a homer with two on in the big sixth stanza.*
> *The state meet will feature West Waterloo and*
> *Roland as the two favorites to cop the tournament*
> *championship. Coach Silvey and his baseball boys will be*
> *out to go as far as they can. Monday night Calmar is paired*
> *against Exira from southwest Iowa.*

This game brings back memories, not for the pitching but for the three-run homer uncorked in the sixth inning. First of all, the game was scheduled for Wednesday at Calmar. Finally, after four straight days of rain and the state tournament scheduled to start on Monday, the game was played on Saturday

27

afternoon at LaPorte City, located just south of Waterloo. In the first game, West Waterloo gained the right to go to the state tournament where they played Roland, a school that possessed a big-name player, Gary Thompson, who later had an outstanding basketball career at Iowa State. West Waterloo's shortstop was Jim Berry, who coached basketball at Loras in the early 1970's. Back to our game. McIntire, located not too far from Mason City, had a pitcher (Newhouse by name) that stood 6 feet, 7 inches and was a very menacing figure on the mound. With the score 4-1 in the bottom of the sixth, our favor, he hung a curve ball and I probably hit it further than any other ball in my entire baseball life. There was no outfield fence in left field. The ball cleared a county road and landed in a house yard beyond the road. Miracles do happen.

What's more interesting is that some thirty plus years later, we were attending the wedding of our niece, Cindy Bruess, at Protivin, another one of those small northeast Iowa towns. A man looking to be in his forties came up to Ann and me, introducing himself as the left fielder from McIntire who chased that baseball down in the farmyard "through two ditches, across the road" as he described it. The town of Calmar was getting excited, having never reached the state tournament in any sport before that day. They had a welcoming for us when we returned home after the game.

The two games played by Calmar in the state tournament at Mason City can be read below. The Exira write-up appeared in the Mason City Globe Gazette.

> *CALMAR DEFEATS FAVORED EXIRA IN FIRST ROUND, 5-1*
> *Calmar was outhit by Exira but it wasn't noticeable in a 5-1 Calmar win because Art Huinker, a classy lefty, was racking up the top strikeout mark of the first day's play. He set 14 Exira batters down via whiffs and left the losers, who were making their fourth straight spring championship bid, with nine base runners stranded.*
> *The only run against Huinker was unearned and came as a result of a walk, a fielder's choice and an error in the fourth frame. He personally ended each inning with a strikeout.*
> *Calmar made the most of its five hits, bunching them in two innings for all its runs. An error, a walk and two singles and a groundout produced three runs in the first. In the fifth, a walk and an error opened the inning after Ron Albertson's single and Leroy Schneberger pounded another single for the final pair of runs.*
> *Chuck Kline pitched hitless ball except for those two frames but the Exira ace had a rough time in his cleanup hitting spot as he fanned all four trips to the plate.*

28

The following comments were part of an editorial by sports director Brad Wilson of the Mason City Globe-Gazette:

Mason City, IA—Some of the dugout chatter heard around the state finals—

Art (Lefty) Huinker, the Calmar junior who led the strikeout artists with 14 victims in the opening round, is being touted as the "beauty" among all the hurlers up here this week.

Scouts from several major league clubs who are watching the performers with a critical eye, say Huinker, 165-pounder who stands only 5 feet 8 inches, has a sly delivery. He comes down overhand, releasing the ball with a hefty wrist snap, his chest serving as a background that virtually hides the ball until it is almost upon the hitter. Whatever it is, Arthur has averaged nearly two strikeouts per inning in his 8-0 record this spring.

The Calmar left-hander has two older brothers, one of whom is Ken, who was good enough to get a look-see from the Chicago White Sox. Art, who with Leroy Schneberger commutes to Calmar from near Festina, are both cousins of Monona's Don Huinker, who caught for the 1948 champions. Monona is only a hop and a step down the highway east of Calmar.

Calmar, which becomes a full-fledged Class A school next year, also managed to include track in its spring program and developed a crack mile relay quartet. Huinker was the lead-off of the baton exchangers that included Tom Iverson, Mickey Griffin and Russ Hillman. After winning at the Comet Relays, Calmar's mile team was forced to pass up the district trials because of the senior banquet.

Ann and I often reflect on the life we have experienced and enjoyed. A common thread of discussion centers on two young kids from the "giant village of Festina" and how far we have come. Because we grew up in this rural, small-town atmosphere, did we appreciate more the opportunities that came our way? Participating in this state tournament exemplifies one of those opportunities. You dream of things like this and all of a sudden here you are. Combine that with the "dream" or "goal" of playing professional baseball. We were now one of eight teams, playing in the big city (I know, Mason City) and on a baseball diamond with a grass infield. We had never played on such a field before (not in high school anyway). Ron Albertson, our senior shortstop and a very steady fielder, never adjusted to that field and never successfully fielded a ground ball in the two games. In case you are wondering, that is the only reason why Leroy Schneberger and I played shortstop in the loss to Kanawha. And I booted one in my two innings there, too. And both Leroy and I were left-handers.

Pitching with one day's rest (McIntire on Saturday and Exira the following Monday) didn't seem to be a problem during the Exira game. But my recollection of the following morning painted a different story. By 6:00 the next morning, I, along with Festina teammate Ron Schuler, were out of our rooms at the Hanford Hotel in Mason City and walking the streets, hoping to find a drug store, or any kind of store where I could buy some analgesic balm to put on my arm. But it still was the arm muscle that hurt, so according to Coach Peterson, it should not be a problem. But it did hurt enough that I couldn't sleep. Leroy Schneberger started the second state tournament game but had control problems. After one inning plus, I went back to the mound, hurting or not. Then, another first experience happened in the bottom of the third. A pitch got away from Kanawha's pitcher and I took one on the head. Remember, this is 1953 and before batting helmets. Coach Chuck Silvey left me in the game but he said no more pitching. I often wonder what the outcome might have been if the beaning had not occurred. I also struggle to see the connection between the beaning and my arm.

CALMAR WINNING STREAK CUT IN SEMI-
FINALS
After 12 straight wins, the Calmar Cahawks baseball team was ousted by Kanawha in the semi-finals at the State high school baseball tournament at Mason City Tuesday night, 14-6. The tournament was won by Kanawha last night in the finals, 4-3 over Roland.
Calmar opened with LeRoy Schneberger on the mound and he alternated in pitching with Art Huinker for three innings with Calmar in front 4-3. Jerry Sjulle took over to start the fourth frame and finished but he took a pounding in the 11-hit Kanawha attack which included a pair of doubles and a triple. Calmar pitchers gave up 10 walks in the game and uncorked four wild pitches and coupled with three passed balls, it was an easy march for Kanawha which won its 12th game against two losses for the season.

Readers, believe me. Playing in the state tournament for all of us on the team was gratifying. The memories are still very strong, and so positive. Sure, we were disappointed when our 12-game winning streak was snapped. But, just to be there, in the state tournament. We had reached the final four.

There are some additional reflections on that junior school year. To me at least, the relationship with Anna Mae continued. The Spring Prom was a memorable night with her in her formal dress, corsage helping to impress. This high school freshman was my "belle of the ball." This prom also caused something else to happen that spring. The editorial above mentioned that Calmar started track for the first time that spring.

Well, our boys' coach for all three boys' sports Calmar offered (football, basketball and baseball) was Chuck Silvey whose real love was track. He took it upon himself (I would imagine he cleared this with our School Superintendent) to require any person that went out for baseball also had to participate in Coach's track program. To my knowledge, no one really questioned that requirement.

Every "baseball" practice after school began with the baseball players practicing for different running events. Several of us involved with competing in the quarter mile, half mile and mile plus related relays would run from the high school to a meat-processing plan out of town and back to the school, a distance that Coach Silvey had measured to be about two and a half miles. As we would near the finish line, Coach would drive his car up behind us, "pushing us" to run a little harder. Let me describe that more clearly. He would drive his car up behind us and actually cause the car bumper to "touch" us, causing us to push even harder. True story. No further comments needed. Once the running was finished, we could go to the baseball diamond and practice baseball. We were entered in two track meets, the Panther Relays in Cedar Falls and the Comet Relays in Charles City. As the editorial states, we did win the mile relay at Charles City. I do know that Coach Silvey later became one of the top track coaches in the state of Iowa at Valley High School in West Des Moines. Several times, he would look me up at the state basketball tournament when Dan Conry and I were refereeing basketball games there. It is possible that even though his baseball knowledge was limited, we were better baseball players because of the conditioning we completed.

Now, what does this have to do with the Spring Prom? Well, it just happened that the district track relays were scheduled for the same evening as the prom. You probably guessed which one won out. And I wasn't the only one that had to handle the conflict. Thus ended our "elective" track season. A question to ponder. What would we have decided if the baseball tournament was the conflict with our Spring Prom instead of track?

STILL STAR STRUCK

My first season as a player for Festina will always be cherished. The veteran players accepted me and helped make me feel comfortable. They were a group that took the game seriously but they also thoroughly enjoyed the results of their efforts. By the start of the second year, I knew that I had full membership because after-game refreshments under a shade tree next to our diamond included not just beer for the players but also cold pop as well. My brother Ken was only 19 and didn't touch the beer either. The diamond, by the way, was located on the school grounds where all of us had attended grade school.

The successful high school season which included the trip to the state high school baseball tournament had just been completed It was a spring where, in three weeks plus, I pitched ten times, nine being complete seven inning games. The left arm was weary and Festina had two regular pitchers, veteran Ken Schneberger and my brother Kenny. Schneberger was a very successful veteran right hander who took over the team's pitching chores in 1947. And even, after my success pitching for the high school team, I wanted to pitch as often as possible. But with the two Kens available for the team, I was going to be their left fielder. Pitching for the Calmar Legion team was my challenge for this summer. Because of the heavy toll on my arm in the spring, it was probably just as well.

The summer season of '52 saw Festina win the Northeast Iowa League championship for the second straight season, and the third in the last four years. This time we did not get to play in the big Waterloo Courier tournament because at the time it was played each year, many of the leagues had not completed their schedule. At the time of the selection process for the tournament we were a half game behind West Union even though just prior to the opening games Festina had walloped our major rival 13 to 0. Game specifics have long escaped my memory but reviewing records of the games show that I pitched one league game that summer. A write-up of the game follows.

ELMA AT FESTINA
Art Huinker pitched a no-hitter for Festina as it defeated Elma 8-0 Sunday. Huinker had 11 strike-outs to his credit.

The next write-up verifies the league championship for Festina.

FESTINA SEWS UP TITLE IN NORTHEAST IOWA
Calmar (Special)---Festina marched home with the 1952 championship for the Northeast Iowa baseball league Sunday afternoon by blasting New Hampton 14 to 4 at Festina, in the last league game of the season.
Ken Schneberger pitched the win for the hard hitting loop champions. Festina clinched the game with six runs in the

32

*fifth inning and gained insurance in the form of four more
markers in the eighth.*

It is interesting to look at the pitcher and catcher names on the line scores usually placed in the local papers every weekend. Maynard Hovden pitched for his home town of Ridgeway. Don Rimrodt, a 6-5 giant on the mound was pitching for neighboring Calmar; Nipper Goerend was on the mound for his hometown of St. Lucas; Galen Mack of Fayette did some pitching for West Union; Jene Smith also pitched for St. Lucas. The last two—Mack and Smith--- were high school opponents in the spring. Clint Leuenberger was a catcher for Spillville for years, while his brother Carl was a left hand pitcher for the same team.

The powerful Dubuqueland tournament had changed its dates of play. It was now being played earlier in the summer and the change made it almost impossible for Festina to participate. However, the rivalry with the Dubuque Independents was enjoyed so much by the Festina players that we traveled to the big city for a non-league game. Again, another loss but a very exciting, hotly contested game.

INDEPENDENTS GET BY STUBBORN FESTINA, 6-5
*The Dubuque Independents found the Festina team just
as tough as ever Wednesday night but managed to squeeze out a
6-5 victory at the Fourth Street diamond to extend their victory
string to six straight games.*

*It was the second time in as many years that the
Independents won a one run decision from the Northeast Iowa
league powerhouse. The two met in the Dubuqueland
tournament a year ago and the Indees won, 1 to 0.*

*This time the Dubuque club had to score in the bottom
of the ninth to win the game. Festina had scored three runs in
the top of the ninth to knot the game and it took a series of
errors for the winning run to come home.*

*Bob Hoerner led off the bottom of the ninth with a
single. He started to steal second and when the catcher's throw
went into centerfield, Hoerner sped for third. The center fielder
retrieved the ball and threw wild to third and Hoerner romped
home with the game-winning run.*

*Festina had taken the lead in the fourth inning of the
ball game with two runs to break a scoreless tie. The
Independents came back with three runs in the fifth and one in
each of the sixth and seventh innings to take a 5-2 lead.*

*Festina rallied in the ninth when Leroy Schneberger
singled with one down. He advanced on a wild pitch. Linus
Huinker drew a base on balls and Leo Luzum slapped out a
single to keep the rally going. Jim Schneberger was safe on the*

33

third baseman's error. Norb Einck went down swinging but
Ken Schneberger singled. Bob Schneberger ended the inning
with two men still on base.

  Art Huinker, Leroy Schneberger, Leo Luzum and Jim
Schneberger were the top hitters for Festina with a pair of
singles each.

  Hoerner and Tom Schleuter were the Dubuque big
guns with three hits each. Schleuter got his in three times at bat
and included a double. He drove in two runs.

  Midge Delaney went the distance for Dubuque and
struck out six. Ken Huinker started for Festina but gave way to
Elsbernd in the eighth. Huinker struck out four, walked two.
Elsbernd fanned one.

  In early October, the Dubuque team completed the home and home
exchange by travelling to Festina for another contest. This time, as hosts, Festina
defeated their Dubuque rivals 2 to 1. This was my second pitching opportunity
and the outcome was satisfying, even though there were no league or tournament
championships tied to the win. Probably because it was not tied to any of these, I
could not locate a write-up to verify the game.

  There is a little highlight that occurred two times during the 1951 and
1952 baseball seasons with Festina that illustrates a pride or an intensity in how I
felt the game of baseball needed to be played. In two different games I made
putouts at third base while playing left field. How my baseball thinking
developed for this I don't remember, but no doubt observation and experience
were the teachers.

  The situation is a very simple and often repeated one. There is a runner
on first base and nobody out, a possible sacrifice bunt situation. If the batter
squared to bunt, I would begin moving closer to the infield, thinking if he would
still adjust and swing away, he would not have the same power had he not
squared. If no bunt, step back. If the bunt is executed, keep moving in to back up
third base. Often, with the shortstop covering second for a possible force out and
the third baseman charging to possibly field the bunt and a throw to first, a good
runner sometimes keeps right on going to third because who is covering? If I
noticed our third baseman fielding the bunt, I just kept on going to cover third,
getting there in plenty of time to take a throw across the diamond from first base.
Result—a put out if the runner tried to stretch it. No matter what position one
plays in baseball, once a ball is hit (or bunted), every fielder has to be on the move
and on the alert. That is just one of the views of the game I grew up with and
coached.

  In the meantime, the romantic feelings for Ann kept getting stronger.
Now getting ready to be a senior in high school and she a sophomore at Festina,
going out for a movie or spending time at her home became more frequent. Her

Dad attended many of the Festina baseball games, especially the ones at the home diamond, and that provided many opportunities for us to be together. And the wedding dances were still a common practice for our community and another opportunity to be together. Life's two goals were not changing, just getting stronger.

Before that final game with Dubuque was played, a fantastic experience for a seventeen year old fell into my lap. Sumner, one of the semi-pro rivals for Festina that I have spoken of before, won the Waterloo Courier tournament, qualifying them for the American Amateur Baseball Congress (AABC) tournament, the first leg of which was to be played in South Dakota. The winner of this series involving teams from the western half of the United States would move on to play the eastern half champion for the national championship. This, to my knowledge, has always been played in Battle Creek, Michigan. We will often discuss this tournament structure in later chapters while covering the years when the Dyersville Whitehawks became involved in the AABC.

After Sumner's capture of the Waterloo tournament, they had the opportunity to select additional players from the other teams in that tournament. Most often, pitchers are chosen to deepen their pitching staff. In this case, they chose my brother Kenny and also Festina catcher-infielder Jim Schneberger. The South Dakota tournament is a double-elimination set-up, which often means a high number of games played in a few days time. After losing their first game to a team from Dallas, Texas, Sumner came back to win five straight, including a revenge win over the Dallas team, to claim the Western Regional championship and a trip to Battle Creek. Kenny pitched a very strong winning game in that streak of five victories.

The national championship was a best three out of five series against a team from New York City, sponsored by the Equitable Life Insurance Company. Minus one pitcher who was unable to leave work for the length of time required for this challenge, Sumner manager Ray Siegfried called on the Leo Huinker residence a second time asking if son Art could fill the roster vacancy. School was already in session and it would mean missing two to five days of school, a distraction that didn't seem to be too serious in making the decision. For myself, it was more like "when do we leave?" Suffice to say, it really overwhelmed me--a national championship stage for a kid who had pitched at this level of competition not even a half dozen times.

The trek, on mostly two-lane roads in 1952, covered seven hours plus. There was no Interstate 80 at that time. It took me further from home than I had ever been. The world had just become larger.

The baseball experience itself was not very successful; in fact, not successful at all. New York took three straight games from the Iowa champions in which we were able to score a total of three runs, one in each ball game. We led only once in the three games and committed a scary total of ten errors leading to eleven unearned runs.

DROP THREE STRAIGHT TO NEW YORK TEAM AT BATTLE CREEK

Apparently the pressure of their victorious uphill battle to gain the Western Division National Amateur title struck the Sumner Cubs in the Amateur World Series at Battle Creek, Mich., as they errored 10 times in dropping three straight games to New York City.

Cub hitting also fell off sharply from the pace they had set in the Watertown affair as they hit safely only 11 times in the three games.

Their loss to the powerful New York team still left the Cubs with a ranking of second best amateur team in the nation, and scanning the rosters of some of the teams they met at Watertown, as well as that of the New Yorkers, leaves little doubt the Cubs are tops among "purely amateur" teams in the country.

Sumner appeared tense and tired as they gifted the New Yorkers with three unearned runs in the Sunday afternoon game won by New York 4-1, then handed them six more runs of the unearned variety in their 10-1 evening loss.

Chuck Anderson, Cub righthander, worked brilliantly against the New York team, but was handed his third loss of the season when untimely errors started both of New York's two-run innings.

Buhr, Rechemmer and Art Huinker worked the evening game, but again five costly bobbles made a run-away of the affair for the Metropolitan team.

The Cubs grabbed the lead for the first time in the Tuesday game, when they scored a single run in the second inning, behind Ken Huinker's brilliant pitching. But they couldn't hold the edge, and New York tied the game in the fifth, then went on to win with a run in the sixth and two in the ninth.

It was again errors that started the New Yorkers on their way to victory, when they used errors and a walk to knot the count in the fifth inning.

The Sumner Cubs had to be content with runnerup honors in the American Baseball Congress National finals, with New York City's Equitable Life Insurance team walking off with the National Amateur honors.

Brother Kenny threw the third contest for the Cubs and pitched a strong game, allowing only three earned runs. He also had one of four Sumner hits, a double which drove in the only run of the game. The run was scored by fellow

36

Festina teammate, Jim Schneberger. My opportunity came in game two when New York had already taken control, having scored ten runs in the first five innings. My task was a "mop-up" role as they call it. Remembering that outing, even with the game out of reach, stage-fright was present. I just threw as hard as I could. There is an expression that fit me that night. It is called being a "thrower, not a pitcher." My mind was frozen emotionally. Thinking back, there was so much to learn, so much to experience, even though I did register five strikeouts in the three plus innings of work. But I also walked two and hit one batter.

Sumner's ace pitcher, Chuck Anderson, made a solid Sumner baseball team an outstanding semi-pro team. Time and time again, he shut down opposing hitters with a sharp breaking curve ball and excellent control. There is little doubt that Anderson had more victories against Festina than any other pitcher.

Some interesting sidelights of the trip. The third and final game of the Battle Creek tournament was postponed on Monday because heavy rains fell most of the day. What does a baseball team far away from home do all day when they can't play baseball? For one group of five or six players it meant a many-hour poker game in a hotel room—a room that I remember was filled with smoke, almost as though a haze fell over the table itself. Drinks were also plentiful. Finally, after several hours of sitting and observing, Sumner shortstop Mel Harms, a class act of a person, took it upon himself to offer me a visit to a huge bird sanctuary just outside of Battle Creek, even in the rain. My feeling of being out-of-place attracted his compassion, and I recall how impressed I was that he would take the time to spend several hours with a non-Sumner player.

A final story, often told, highlights the limited background that Kenny and I had lived so far. If 'homebodies' is a word, it characterized the two of us, even though baseball had provided many opportunities that took us beyond the hills of southern Winneshiek County. The final night of the three games, after the Tuesday afternoon 4 to 1 loss, the insurance company sponsors of the winning New York team, hosted a dinner banquet at a local "Italian" restaurant. This was a cultural experience new for the two of us. Heavy platters of spaghetti and meat balls were brought out and it was help yourself. Both Kenny and I had good appetites and the food tasted good. Unknown to both of us was the following main entrée still to come- - -huge T-bone steaks with all the trimmings. That recognition came too late. We had already had eaten more than our share of spaghetti and there was little room left for the delicious T-bone that was set in front of us. It was a cultural learning experience, plain and simple. By Thursday it was back in school as usual with only three school days missed. It was just one of many experiences with Sumner and seeds were planted for the future.

The second year of playing with Festina was over. Another league championship had been won but the prize of playing in the Courier Tournament was not realized. It was time to think of completing my senior year in high school and maybe another successful spring in high school baseball.

37

FINAL YEAR AT CALMAR HIGH

My last year of high school. What direction would life take after graduation? Really, except for some not-so-serious discussions between Anna Mae and me, that type of thinking didn't occupy my mind too much. My older brother Linus, already married to Lory and with family, operated his own farmstead. Kenny, now twenty, had obtained a farm bordering our home farm, ready for his occupancy. Naturally, as the youngest member of the family, I could be destined for the home place. That made sense to both of us. For that reason, vocational classes and the FFA (Future Farmers of America) were built into the instructional classes in my school schedule both years. Besides the logical view of being another farmer like the two brothers, the" dream" of playing professional baseball continued to be one of my goals, whether realistic or not. Going on to college had not entered the planning process, at least not yet. Remember the Festina culture which saw none of my brothers and sisters go beyond eighth grade.

No matter the route of even the shortest of future planning, for me it certainly included Anna Mae. This was probably myself speaking. As for Anna Mae it possibly wasn't quite as certain for the sophomore still back at Festina St. Mary's. How would the senior year of high school affect the two future-directed goals of professional baseball and marrying Anna Mae be impacted?

Both the junior and senior years of high school included participation in the school drama productions. The junior year play proved more memorable for me. Playing the role of a young high school kid named "Kip", I fell asleep on the couch (it was in the script) and while putting on the play for the elementary grades, some of the younger kids in the front rows starting talking to me, asking the sleepy head to wake up. Thank heaven my head was turned to the back of the couch so they could not see me reacting.

As mentioned earlier, vocational agriculture took up part of my academic program in both my junior and senior years. The position of president for the FFA (Future Farmers of America) demanded some of my time in that last year. In "shop" class (it now bears a much classier moniker) as a junior, my project was the building of a hay feeding manger. Dad grumbled at the lumber cost (it was built to last) but I sometimes kidded him that the labor was cheap. There is a strong awareness that he could have built it for much less cost.

Although baseball held the primary focus of athletics, it was exciting in the senior year to be a starter on the basketball team that captured seventeen victories while losing only three. It may be difficult to comprehend that I was the third tallest player in the starting lineup making me a forward on offense, or as they say today, the "small" forward. Our center, Russ Hillman, was about six foot even. Every one of the five starters also was a starter on the baseball team. I have kept a few write-ups but have not included any of them here. When the season was over, my point total averaged slightly more than ten points a game. On defense, it depended on who the main scorers were for the opponents or who the point guard was.

A sad tale for the end of the basketball season. We played Postville in the Class A competition although we played Class B competition (smaller schools) most of the year. Postville had a 6-5 center (Clyde Jarms who starred for Upper Iowa for the next four years) which put us at a disadvantage. We lost 50 to 48. However, with about four seconds remaining, yours truly intercepted a pass in our back court and, although challenged all the way, had a semi lay-up that would tie the game. That play highlighted my lack of experience because it should have called for a charge to the basket, in hopes of making the shot and/or getting fouled or being called for a charge, none of which occurred. The player I guarded that night was Jim Rima. We later roomed together as freshmen at Loras. Then he transferred to Upper Iowa where he played baseball for the Peacocks.

The 1953 baseball season proved to be less exciting than the 1952 state tournament season. Although winning our first nine games, our nemesis Fayette eliminated us in the district finals. Most of the game write-ups are included below but I don't remember too many highlights. We lost two key players from the 1952 team (both good hitters, Leroy Schneberger and Larry Herold) but three Festina players stepped in along with freshman Bill Luzum from Calmar who played third base. Bill was a younger brother of Festina town team third baseman Leo Luzum. Leroy Einck (first cousin) took over the catching duties. Ron Schuler became the starting center fielder and Jerry Schneberger (another first cousin) came from Festina and took over at shortstop. We lost our power but otherwise had as good a team as the year before.

The Fayette loss proved very discouraging because with runners on second and third with two out a short blooper was hit to short center. Ron Schuler made a great diving catch but the umpire ruled that the ball was trapped. Two runs scored and that was the difference. We all thought he caught the ball. Ron himself claimed he caught it. But, is it possible that we are a little biased? It was the end of the high school year and my first and only high school loss.

A few game write-ups are reproduced below. Most of the games were very lopsided except for the 1-0 game with Decorah. Fort Atkinson still had Clem Reicks whose presence provided a tougher challenge than the other games.

CALMAR WINS ONE-HITTER BY HUINKER
Art Huinker of Calmar High School pitched a one-hitter
as his team took a 9-1 decision from the Fort Atkinson Indians
here Monday afternoon. In addition to allowing but one hit,
Huinker struck out 15 players and hit 3 for 4 at the plate. Fort
Atkinson scored its only run in the seventh inning.

Pitchers Art Huinker of Calmar and Carleton Kittelson of Decorah fought a tooth and nail mound duel on the Luther College diamond, where the Cahawks took a 1-0 five-inning victory over the Vikings. Both Huinker and Kittelson limited their respective opposing teams to one hit in the exceptionally close game. Huinker whiffed 10 batters and Kittelson fanned six and also gave up one walk. Two hits—both singles—were registered by Huinker in the first inning and Jerry Young, Viking catcher, in the second stanza. Kittelson's lone walk and three Viking errors gave the Calmar nine the lone run.

The teams agreed to limit the game to five innings, because the Luther baseball team had to use the diamond at a certain time. But it was an opportunity to play on a grass infield. Sorry that we didn't make another Mason City trip to use that experience.

HUINKER OF CALMAR HURLS NO-HITTER

Art Huinker pitched a no-hitter for the Calmar Cahawks and struck out 15 men to shut out Fort Atkinson 9-0. Leroy Einck was the catcher. Russell Hillman had three hits for the Cahawks including a double. Ron Schuler added two singles.

CALMAR, DECORAH GATHER OPENING SECTIONAL WINS

In Calmar's win over Ridgeway, Jerry Schneberger was the winning pitcher, allowing only three hits and was credited with 14 strikeouts. Huinker, Russett, Griffin, Einck and Leonard Kuboushek each had two hits for the winners. Einck and Kuboushek included doubles in their hits.

HUINKER'S 2-HITTER ADVANCES CALMAR TO THE SECTIONAL FINALS

Art Huinker pitched a two hitter and fanned seven men to help his teammates defeat Decorah, 15-2, and give Calmar its seventh straight win. The game was called in the fifth inning because of the 10-run rule. Schneberger and Hillman each had two hits while catcher Leroy Einck slammed out three of them.

CALMAR CAPTURES SECTIONALS

The Calmar Cahawks defeated Cresco, 14-3 to win the finals of the sectional tournament played at Calmar. The Calmar club posted its eighth straight triumph in winning the championship. Gerald Sjulli was on the mound for the

Cahawks. Mickey Griffin and Bill Luzum each garnered three hits while two big triples by Russ Hillman drove in two runs each time. Leroy Einck and Ron Schuler each added two hits to the 15 game total.

HUINKER PITCHES NO-HITTER AS CALMAR WINS 13-0

With Art Huinker pitching his second no-hitter in the current baseball season, Calmar advanced to the finals of its own district tournament by blanking Waukon, 13-0. The Cahawk star hurler struck out 13 men and smashed out a two-bagger to give Calmar its 9th straight triumph so far this year. Extra base blows were also credited to Mickey Griffin, a double, and Russ Hillman two doubles. Hillman, Huinker, Einck, Luzum and Heying all had two hits to their credit.

CALMAR LOSES 3 TO 2 TO FAYETTE IN FINALS

The Calmar Cahawks winning streak of nine straight games ended here Wednesday, when Fayette took a 3 to 2 decision in the finals of the district tournament. Fayette had five hits to Calmar's four.

Looking back on the district tournament games, I wish we could do it over. The first game with Waukon ended being an easy victory in five innings. Unknown to us until shortly before the start of that game, Waukon's star pitcher, a tall right hander whose last name I believe was Schultz, was unable to pitch. He had suffered an injury that made it impossible for him to take the mound. Their back-up pitcher could not stop our hitters and consequently ended quickly. I should not have pitched and saved myself for the Fayette game. It is easy to look back and make better decisions, but thank heaven we can't do that.

Below is a write-up announcing the selection of valedictorian and salutatorian for the class of 1953 from Calmar High School. Talk about naïve people. Classmate Russ Hillman came up to me at school and offered congratulations to me on earning the high honor of valedictorian for our class of 34. With a blank look, I asked him what it meant. I had no clue. It added a new word to my vocabulary. Coming out of Festina, it just did not appear in our cultural dictionary.

HUINKER, HILLMAN WIN HONORS AT CALMAR HIGH

Two of Calmar High School's top athletes have been named valedictorian and salutatorian of the senior class. Valedictorian is Arthur Huinker, outstanding baseball pitcher for the Calmar team who has pitched two no-hitters, son of

41

Mr. and Mrs. Leo Huinker of Calmar. Salutatorian is Russell Hillman, outstanding football player who made the all-state seventh team in his senior year, son of Mr. and Mrs. Earle Hillman of Calmar.

Huinker attended St. Mary's High School at Festina for his first two years of high school. While there he was a member of the choir at St. Mary's, president and vice-president of the Knights of the Altar, secretary of the sophomore class and a member of the 4-H club at Festina.

He was a member of the FFA in Calmar during his junior and senior years and was president of the Calmar organization during his senior year. He was a delegate to Hawkeye Boy's state in his junior year. Art was president of his class during his junior year and editor of the Cahasa, the school paper in his senior year.

One more high school story. In the section of pictures you will see a team photo of a girls' softball team. And it includes that girl, Anna Mae. All the players were from Festina. Anna Mae either played third base or left field. Their coach every year was Nick Schuler. They played games throughout northeast Iowa over several summers. Anna Mae also played girls' basketball at Calmar during her junior and senior seasons. At that time it was the very popular 6 on 6 game that attracted sportswriters from across the country. Anna Mae played defense, thus not getting a chance to do any scoring.

That ended two years of education. What happens after high school? It was two good years with that class of 1953. Fifty years later, we would celebrate our fiftieth class reunion with 28 out of 34 graduates participating. Of the six missing, three had passed on to the Creator. Many memories. The school is now the South Winneshiek Community School District. The original Calmar High School building is still being utilized as well as several additions, in particular, a new gymnasium. As a reorganized school district, it usually averages between forty and fifty students a grade.

SHOULDER TO SHOULDER

Now for the third year of being a Festina regular (almost a veteran at age 17 but not when you look at the veterans in center and right field, third base, shortstop, second base, pitcher and catcher). My brother Kenny had returned from a White Sox contract and spent most Sunday afternoons pitching for Rushford, Minnesota. The senior year in high school at Calmar is now history and so is playing high school baseball. The 1953 summer evolved around the big decision to attend Loras College in the fall. That will be covered in the following chapter. Regarding summer baseball and Festina, we were going to see if we could win a third consecutive Northeast Iowa League baseball title.

After an opening non-league victory over New Albin, Festina won fifteen straight league games before losing to New Hampton, 6 to 5. Brief write-ups of some games follow. Included is another non-league game at the Winneshiek County Fair, a common custom in those days. Today most county fairs have been taken over by stock car racing, a more profitable endeavor.

> *FESTINA NIPS NEW ALBIN, 2-1*
> *Postville, Ia.---Art Huinker took the edge on a pitching duel with Carl Dresselhaus as Festina nipped New Albin, 2 to 1, here Monday.*
> *New Albin took a one-run lead in the third inning, but a home run by Leo Luzum in the seventh knotted the count for Festina.*
> *In the same inning Norb Einck singled, advanced to second on an error and scored the winning run on Jerry Schneberger's base hit.*
> *Art Huinker allowed only four hits and fanned 11 men in earning the victory. Carl Dresselhaus was nicked for five blows and was tagged with the loss.*

Why the non-league contest before the league opened? The decision-making that set this game up was something I was not involved in. But I have always felt that some of the veteran players felt that playing a non-league game first would help them be prepared for the league opener. If that was the reason, it worked. Festina reeled off 15 consecutive league wins before a loss, leading to a league championship, and entitling them to another trip to the Waterloo Courier tournament.

> *KEN HUINKER STRIKES OUT 18; FESTINA BEATS ELMA, 4-0*
> *In other contests (in the NEI League) Ken Huinker of Festina turned in the best performance of the day by pitching a three hitter against Elma. Huinker allowed three hits and had 18 strikeouts.*

43

FESTINA RALLY TRIPS NEW HAMPTON, 7-6

Festina, Ia. ---Festina scored three times in the seventh inning to nip New Hampton here Sunday afternoon, 7 to 6, for its sixth straight win in the Northeast Iowa league.

Festina trailed 5 to 4, going into the bottom of the seventh, but came to life for three runs to knock out starter Ave Johnson, and take a 7-5 league. New Hampton tallied its final marker in the eighth. Art Huinker, who took over the mound duties for Ken Schneberger in the seventh, picked up the decision for Festina.

FESTINA BLANKS IONIA 8-0, ON THREE-HITTER

Calmar, Ia.---Art Huinker blanked Ionia on three hits Sunday as Festina notched its eighth victory 4-0. At Ionia, Huinker faced only 30 men and displayed perfect control. In addition to spinning a three-hitter, he fanned 15 batsmen. Festina bagged 13 hits off loser, Dean Weydert, but five Ionia double plays cut down the scoring.

FESTINA RECORDS 13TH STRAIGHT VICTORY 8-1 OVER ST. LUCAS

Festina continues to rule the roost in the Northeast with 13 victories and no defeats by defeating St. Lucas, 8-1. Joe Huinker homered for St. Lucas in the sixth inning but the heavy blow wasn't enough to stem the powerful Festina nine which racked up five runs in the second, two in the fifth, and one in the seventh on eight hits and five St. Lucas errors. Ken Schneberger was winning pitcher for Festina.

This write-up was included primarily because Joe Huinker from St. Lucas was also my first cousin. His Dad, Arnold, was my Dad's oldest brother. Another first cousin, Dennis Huinker, was playing baseball for Calmar during this same time period. Often times, throughout our lifetime, we would meet new people, and when hearing the name, Huinker, would ask if we were related to the people who are well-known for the raising of pure bred hogs from Decorah. Dennis lived between Calmar and Decorah.

FESTINA IN FIRST LOSS, TO PLAY IONIA SUNDAY

CALMAR (Special) ---The league-leading Festina team, which suffered its first loss in the Northeast Iowa league to New Hampton, last Sunday night, will entertain the bottom-place team this Sunday, Aug. 30.

Playing under the lights Sunday, Festina absorbed its initial defeat at the hands of New Hampton in the bottom of the ninth.

44

In that frame, with one away, there was a walk and single, then a double by Knight, a double by Johnson, and a single by Chambers for the victory margin for the New Hampton Merchants.

Festina scored five runs on 12 hits and two New Hampton errors and New Hampton rallied six runs on five hits and four Festina bobbles.

Ave Johnson and Gates formed the winning battery for New Hampton. Ken Huinker and Bob Schneberger pitched and caught respectively for Festina. Huinker had 11 strike outs to his credit. He also had a home run in the seventh with one mate aboard.

The catcher for New Hampton, Dale Gates, played professional baseball in the late 1940's before returning to continue his career with the New Hampton team. The loss to New Hampton brought the Merchants within one game of Festina, sporting a 14-2 record while Festina's record dropped to 15-1. We needed a victory over cellar-dwelling Ionia to claim our third consecutive crown.

FESTINA GAINS LEAGUE TITLE

Festina scored three runs in the first inning to defeat Ionia, 3 to 0, Sunday behind the three-hit hurling of Art Huinker in the Northeast Iowa league. Huinker fanned seven men in his three-hit chore against cellar-dwelling Ionia to lead his team to the league title.

FESTINA SPANKS CUBS, 16-6, AT COUNTY FAIR

The Decorah Cubs took a 16-6 spanking by the powerful Festina baseball team in a special exhibition contest at the Winneshiek County fair on Friday afternoon, August 21.

After a scoreless ball game for two and a half innings, the Northeast Iowa league-leaders exploded with one run the third, five in the fourth, two in the fifth, five more in the sixth and three in the seventh. Decorah, a member of the Scenic loop, scored one run in the fourth, four in the fifth, and one in the eighth.

Elsbernd started for Festina, but was removed in the fifth inning after yielding five runs on five hits. He was replaced on the mound by Ken Schneberger, who spaced out one run on six safe base hits.

Randy Halverson was the losing pitcher. He allowed eight runs on 11 hits. Bob Gerleman finished for the Cubs and relinquished eight runs on eight hits.

The inning that spelled Decorah's doom was the bottom of the fourth when Festina notched five runs on four hits. Norb Einck grounded out, Elsbernd walked, and Ken

45

Schneberger hit a double to set up the initial runs in that inning. With men on second and third, Art Huinker singled to bring them home.

The next man up, Schupanitz, grounded out and G. Schneberger got a base on balls. Linus Huinker and Luzum followed up with singles and Art Huinker, Schneberger and Linus Huinker crossed the plate. Ken Huinker flied out to centerfield to end the rally.

Decorah's big inning came in the next stanza, with four runs scoring on three hits. Roger Spilde got on base via a walk, Paul Dresselhaus and Marlyn Knutson singled to score one run. The bases were loaded when Gay Halverson was given a free ticket and two runs tallied on a single by Uhlenhake. Syverson struck out for the first out and Bob Gerleman took a base on balls. A long fly ball hit to into right field by Ranny Halverson accounted for the fourth and final tally in that inning. Lomen grounded out to end the rally.

Ken Schneberger, Festina's second baseman, hit two doubles and one single in five times at bat. Randy Halverson of Decorah hit a three-bagger in the seventh to no avail.

Again, a "one game and you are out" stopped the Festina season at the Courier Tournament in Waterloo, after a 16 and 1 league championship season. Sumner used three hits to score eight runs and beat us easily, 8-3.Sometimes you are a good pitcher; the next time out you aren't. Following is a write-up of the game but first I have included a write-up which explains how the Waterloo Courier tournament operated. I thought it might be interesting to amateur baseball enthusiasts.

FESTINA TO MEET CEDAR VALLEY LEADER AT WATERLOO AUGUST 16

The Festina baseball team of the Northeast Iowa league is paired with the leader of the Cedar Valley league in the annual Waterloo Daily Courier tournament of Champions, which begins August 15.

The Waterloo Daily Courier, sponsor of the tournament of champions, will pay all expenses and teams participating split gate receipts on the basis of number of tournament games played. Team and individual trophies will be awarded the champions. A trophy will go to the runnerup and a plaque to the third place team.

Last year teams that played three tournament games received $480.30 each as 5,598 fans turned out for the four sessions. In seven years, northeast Iowa teams have received $16,704.20 in Courier tournament money. Expenses paid by the Courier last year amounted to $1,121.68.

46

FESTINA IN 8-3 LOSS TO SUMNER CUBS

Sumner spotted Festina two runs in the first inning, but came from behind for the 8-3 victory. Pitcher Chuck Anderson set the Northeast Iowa league leaders down with one hit in the last six frames in a first round game of the tournament of Champions at Waterloo, Ia., Sunday, Aug. 16.

Sumner solved two lefthanded Festina Huinker brothers' deliveries for only three hits, making one in the third for two runs, two in the fourth for five and scoring in the first without a hit.

Three left handed batters for Festina jumped on Anderson for the two runs in the first. With one out, Linus Huinker bounced a single to left. He stole second and scored on Ken Huinker's line single to right. Ken came around as LeRoy Schneberger slammed a triple off the right field fence. Norb Einck walked and stole second, but the next two batters went down on a strikeout and a roller to the pitcher respectively.

Sumner's run in the first was the result of two walks, an infield out and a wild pitch.

Mel Harms' single, an error, a sacrifice and a hit batsman filled the bases for the Cubs in the third and drove starter Ken Huinker from the mound. His 17-year-old brother, Art, came in and was tagged for a long fly to right by Bob Sawvell, producing one run. The second scored as Sumner worked the double steal.

A walk, a hit, a walk, a passed ball and another walk filled the bases and gave Sumner one run in the fourth, all starting after two outs. Then Bob Topp lined a double to right to plate three more runs, and he went to third on the throw in. Another walk and a double steal produced the fifth score of the inning.

An error and Romauld Elsbernd's triple accounted for Festina's third run in the sixth.

All we could do is accept another defeat at the hands of a very good pitcher, Chuck Anderson, and his Sumner teammates, try to look back on a successful third consecutive Northeast Iowa league championship and hope we can get another crack at the Courier tournament next year.

High school teammate and Festina first baseman Leroy Schneberger signed a professional contract with the Chicago White Sox shortly after tournament play and the season were over. Leroy reported to the Chicago White Sox team for spring training. He stated later that he was one of 16 first basemen working out for placement on the White Sox' minor league teams. "I knew I was

47

in for a tough time against that many first basemen," he said.   He later returned to his hometown and played with the Festina baseball team the following summer.

Associated with the Courier tournament a picture was taken of my two brothers and myself.   It shows the three of us with our left-handed gloves, including a left-handed catcher's mitt used by both Kenny and me during our earlier years. We played "imaginary" games while playing catch, with the catcher being the umpire determining whether the pitch was a ball or a strike. That possibly factored into the development of our "control," although that led to being questioned quite often, especially after the Sumner loss in that tournament. The picture is found in the picture section of this book.

Finally, a 1953 team picture is in the same section with the above picture of the three of us. The team picture has all team members present except shortstop and sometime catcher, Jim Schneberger. Notice that if Jim were in the picture, that would add up to five Schneberger brothers in uniform. Jerry, the youngest, entered his senior year at Calmar High School in the fall. Also missing was sometime catcher, Carl Schupanitz, a classmate of Ann's and going to be a junior at Calmar High School. By the way, he is not related to the rest of the team. His Dad ran a grocery store and post office in Festina.

Another baseball season entered the record books. Obviously we would all welcome the opportunity to be able to change some things, such as fewer walks in the Sumner game. But then it would even be a crazier world than what it already is. Accept the successes and the failures, learn from them, and now on to Loras College in the fall of 1953. What does that future hold?

FROM CAHAWK TO DUHAWK

"If you want God to bless you, we think you need to go to Loras." An unusual introduction to my college days but its significance will become clearer as we explore the college experience, with primarily the two major focuses of my life driving most steps taken during the 1953-1957 years.

But first, the impact of one teacher's extra attention to his students deserves sharing. The senior year of high school at Calmar High was rapidly drawing to a close. It was May of 1953. Part of our daily schedule included a 45 minute open noon hour. Students living near to the school could go home for lunch while most of us were served a hot lunch, a real treat for someone who had just completed ten years of cold sandwiches, etc. in a lunch pail. In fact, the cooks and I became friendly and they actually made a couple of recipes that my Mother made at home. And, of course, they were favorite recipes of mine. The time left after lunch could be spent as students wished. A small playground at the rear of the school usually was the place for wild, scrambling football games or something of the sort. Those of us who chose not to participate in such activities could walk the streets, could go up town, less than three blocks away. Oddly enough, a few of us walked to the Catholic Church for a short visit as part of the walk. This was an infrequent endeavor but one that caught the eye of the local priest living next to the church. More of that later. There was playground equipment in front of the school where lower elementary kids would gather in nice weather. And some of us, once in a while, would push the little ones in the swings, much to their enjoyment. Note that while Anna Mae was a sophomore at Festina, most of my classmate friends were all male.

It was on one of those days when the Vocational Agriculture instructor, Spencer Williams, approached and directed a very simple but significant question to me, "Art, have you ever thought about being a teacher?" My immediate response was one of surprise, maybe even shock. In none of the infrequent reflections Anna Mae and I had on what seemed like a very distant future, had we ever considered the teaching profession? In Chapter 5 I explain that the most common futuristic thinking centered on farming and/or professional baseball. When the "surprise" factor evaporated, Mr. Williams expressed his reasons for offering the career-focusing question, "Art, I think you would make a very good teacher. And I think you enjoy kids, otherwise you would not be here pushing the little ones in the swings during your free time."

The wheels in my brain started churning. The possibilities were exciting. Selfishly, it created additional opportunities for extending my dream of a professional baseball career. Mom and Daddy appeared to support the possibility of my going to college. In later years, looking back at this particular episode, it just seemed possible that my father did not really see a very interested young farmer in his youngest son. Be as it may, within three weeks my application had been completed and accepted at Iowa State Teachers College in Cedar Falls (now the University of Northern Iowa). At the same time, our Superintendent J.C Iverson, on a trip to Iowa City, asked me to go with him to meet Baseball Coach Pops Vogel. But Coach Vogel showed little interest in my baseball credentials, something that did bother me. Yet, not very much because I never really had thought about the value, baseball-wise, of playing Big Ten baseball relative to the thoughts of playing professional baseball.

Just a brief look at teacher Spencer Williams and the impact it had on my life. Not only did he redirect my entire life, his reaching out to me probably was a major influence on how I looked at my role as a teacher.

Now, a month or so later (the exact day is not in my long-term memory) the summer before college was filled with helping my father on our farm and playing baseball for hometown Festina. Daddy and I were in our barn, completing the evening chores, which consisted primarily of milking about 30 plus Guernsey cows. Both of us observed a shiny black boat of a car drive into our yard. A priest and another gentleman dressed in a dark suit complete with white shirt and tie, exited the car and walked toward the house. We were puzzled and also concerned because a priest's unannounced visit fueled thoughts of "bad news," possibly a tragedy. "Finish the milking, Art. I better check out what is going on." He did not return. The cows had been milked and turned out to pasture for the night. The visitors had departed. "What had happened," I pondered.

Upon entering our home, I noticed my parents seated at the kitchen table. My father said, "Art, we need to talk. The two people that were here were Father Ernsdorff and Vince Dowd, the athletic director and baseball coach from Loras College. They want you to come to Loras." After limited further discussion of the situation and realizing that I had an offer of a tuition-free college education, my Daddy added, "We both think if you want God to bless you, you should go to Loras College." The decision was made. Loras College, here we come. Deep inside, I felt that my Mother had hopes that my education at Loras might lead to a vocation as a priest. Also notice, the above-mentioned gentlemen never even stayed to meet with me. Times have changed. I went from being a Cahawk to being a Duhawk. Looking back on those four years as a Duhawk, I sincerely believe that God did indeed bless me in so many ways at Loras. For both Anna Mae and me, going to college would extend my drive for a baseball career, just that we would be 100 miles apart.

Back to the priest from Calmar, Father Friedman. He called my Mother and Father, once word was out that Loras College was "my" college of choice, and asked if they wanted to visit the Loras campus. The visit was set up and Father Friedman, my parents and I, spent an entire day visiting with some campus people, having a tour of the buildings, etc. After that was completed, Father drove past St. Bernard's Seminary and remarked, "After four years at Loras, Art will be enrolled here at the seminary." Whoa. For Mom, that had to be an exciting thought. For me, it did not appear to fit.

50

Four years later, many significant events of great impact took place; not the least of which was a successful baseball career and a record of 19 wins and 0 losses over all four years. Scouts began to follow more frequently, particularly Runt Marr of the St. Louis Cardinals. Secondly, I acquired a strong, faith-based education with a Bachelor's Degree and the preparation to be a teacher and coach. Third, and very, very important, teammates on the baseball team have become some of the greatest life-long friends that impact me continuously. Baseball teammates—Bob Wolfe (Lost Nation), Gene "Tiny" Potts (Dubuque) , Dick Wright (Garnavillo), Joe Ottavi (Dubuque), Bill Leonard (LaCrosse), Dick Winter (New Hampton) have stayed close throughout all the years after Loras. They, and so many of my other teammates were wonderful human beings as well as strong baseball players. There is a major reason beyond me for the perfect pitching record. Last of all, and possibly most important, that wonderful young woman from Festina, agreed to be my wife, my friend and my partner sharing her dreams, her life with me. That happened after the sophomore year at Loras and Anna Mae's graduation from high school. Now my two long-range goals are within reach.

Baseball—freshman year (spring, 1954)

Coming from the tiny town of Festina to the "big city" of Dubuque a person doesn't know what really to expect. What was college baseball going to be like? Determined to impress the coaches and be a starting pitcher, maybe my efforts were a little out of line. When asked to pitch batting practice during one of our first practices, I probably threw harder than I should have for batting practice. Frank Noonan, our assistant coach has told this story hundreds of times. Bill Howie, veteran second baseman with close to a .400 batting average his first two seasons, took a few cuts at the pitches. After the first four or five, he yelled to the coaches" Get him out of there! This is supposed to be batting practice."

When we were ready for game one against Wisconsin State College of Platteville, Coach Dowd announced that senior pitcher, Joe Elbert, would pitch. When he announced the remainder of the lineup, I was excited when he put this Festina native in left field. I had made it and even got a single the first time up and added another single later, while scoring three runs. And also pitched for one inning. The write-up for that game follows.

DUHAWKS GAIN 9-5 DECISION IN OPENER
Loras College won its 1954 baseball season opener
Friday afternoon by downing Platteville 9-5 on the Loras
Diamond. Joe Elbert started for Loras and was the winner. He
gave way to Art Huinker in the fifth and Leo Schlueter finished
for the Duhawks. The three Loras hurlers held the Teachers to
nine hits while the Duhawk sluggers were pounding out 14.
Pacing the Loras attack were second baseman Bill Howie and
catcher Bob Kaliban, each with three hits.

After three additional team wins in which I played left field, the attached write-up announced my first starting role as the Duhawk pitcher against an Upper Iowa team that had seven left hand batters. In the Upper Iowa lineup that day was Galen Mack, a real nemesis from high school days. This game I had the better of the battle. Two brief write-ups of the game itself follow, one being from the local home town papers, either the Ossian Bee or the Decorah Journal.

DUHAWKS BATTLE UIU
Coach Vince Dowd's Duhawk diamond nine will be host to the Upper Iowa Peacocks Thursday in a single tilt on the Loras College field.

In an attempt to stop Peacock hitting power, Coach Dowd plans to pitch freshman Art Huinker, the sole lefty in the Loras mound corps. The Upper Iowa squad has seven left-handed batters in its lineup.

The Peacocks have lost only one game this spring, a 4-1 thriller to the University of Minnesota. Loras had downed Platteville twice and Cornell once.

ART HUINKER FANS 17, HURLS LORAS PAST UPPER IOWA
Art Huinker, southpaw from Calmar, struck out 17 batters here Thursday as he pitched Loras to a 4-0 baseball victory over Upper Iowa University.

The freshman mound star scattered four hits in tossing his shutout, and the 17 strikeouts set a school record in the Iowa Conference tilt. It was the fifth straight victory for the unbeaten Loras squad.

I won't include here all game write-ups, but will make an effort to describe all the games for which I pitched. After the Upper Iowa victory, the team traveled to Luther College in Decorah. Both Iowa Conference games were losses by the scores of 5-4 and 7-4 for the Duhawks but the Norseman had an infielder-pitcher by the name of Eli Crogan from Soldiers Grove, Wisconsin. About seven years later we were teammates at Grove where I did some semi-pro pitching for a couple of years.

The next pitching opportunity came against the Wartburg Knights of Waverly, Iowa. Loras won both games, with the first game being my second victory. The write-up is below.

DUHAWKS COP PAIR FROM WARTBURG '9'
The Loras College baseball team copped both ends of an Iowa Conference double-header, defeating Wartburg College, 6-2 and 9-2.

52

In the first game, southpaw Art Huinker pitched a two-hitter as the Duhawks picked up 7 hits. It was Huinker's second win of the year in as many starts. Holm was the loser in the first game. Brad Winch and Tom Schneider led the hitting attack for the Duhawks. Schneider had two doubles and Winch a single and a double in the first contest.

In the second game, freshman right hander Bill Kezman went all the way for his second victory of the season. Kezman and his teammates picked up 14 hits to coast to their seventh victory in nine starts. Bill Howie and Tom Schneider each had three hits in the second tilt.

Brad Winch, with two hits, was a senior speedster from Elkader, Iowa. He split his time between baseball and track. We became good friends and the two of us plus his Clarke girl friend travelled to the Inwood Pavilion at Spillville for a dance by way of the Thuente farm to pick up that special high school junior. After graduation, Brad settled in California and our paths have crossed a couple of times since that first year at Loras.

After the Wartburg victories and another victory over Upper Iowa, the team traveled to western Iowa where the Duhawks swept two games from Westmar College.. Next, back at Loras came a big twin bill with Iowa Conference powerhouse, Buena Vista College from Storm Lake. Two wins would give us the league championship. On the mound for the first game, we pulled out a 4-1 victory. Another victory and the championship would be ours. But it wasn't meant to be and we lost 6-4. Recollections of the second game had me trying to come back in relief to pitch to a real good left hand batter. Didn't do very well. He got a base hit and Coach Dowd brought Leo Schlueter, the starting pitcher, back in. The write-up follows.

DUHAWKS, BEAVERS SPLIT

The Loras College baseball team split a double-header with Buena Vista here Saturday afternoon in the windup of their 1954 season. The Duhawks won the first, 4-1, and dropped the second, 6-4.

Art Huinker won his third decision of the season as he pitched the Duhawks to their eleventh victory in 13 starts. The lefty scattered six singles. Bill Howie, Loras second-sacker, and Art Whipple, Duhawk catcher for the first game, led the hitting for the Loras men. Each picked up a single and double in three trips.

In the second contest, Loras jumped off to a 3-1 lead which they held until the end of the fifth. The Buena Vista Beavers then rallied for a couple of runs on three consecutive doubles. Loras tied it up again in the sixth when the Duhawk first baseman, Tom Schneider, homered with no one on.

53

The Beavers collected two more runs in the top of the sixth to notch their sixth Iowa Conference sin in eight starts. Loras closed its long baseball history in the Iowa Conference with a 7-3 record.

That brought an end to the 1954 college freshman season. Eleven victories with three losses. It also ended membership in the Iowa Conference for Loras. The news article below summarizes the season statistically. College baseball was over but the summer would be filled with playing baseball for hometown Festina. Those games are addressed in the following chapter. The end of the season also meant going back to the farm, helping my father for the summer. It also meant getting back closer to my special Anna Mae.

The first year in college added 100 plus miles between us. And, even though the first semester saw me hitchhike home nearly every weekend, it still created some strain on our relationship. Even though letters were written several times a week back and forth, absence causes new stresses for a rapidly blooming relationship. During baseball season, the last three plus months of the school year challenged that relationship even more because weekends were usually tied up with games. Even though there were several suitors pursuing Ann, now a junior at Calmar High School, I felt I was winning the competition. After these challenges, by the end of the first year at Loras our feelings and our love for each other was becoming more special.

Hitchhiking was the mode of transportation for getting home from Loras College on Friday afternoons. Returning to the college on Monday mornings for 8:00 class, transportation was provided by my first cousin, Larry Schissel from Monona. Larry was also a student at Loras and usually travelled home every weekend but at an entirely different time than I did. My father would get up around 4:30 every Monday morning and take me to Monona where Larry, his sister Mary who was attending Immaculate Conception High School in Dubuque, and I would make the journey back to our schools. One icy morning we made the ditch and a farmer's fence near Rickardsville, north of Dubuque. Otherwise, the trips were made without incident.

Living on campus in Keane Hall, a student will walk back and forth past or through Christ the King Chapel several times a day. Short visitations became the norm for many of the on-campus students, including myself. It was a great opportunity to pray for special intentions. Progress toward my two life-long goals, playing professional baseball and claiming Anna Mae as my partner for life, were becoming increasingly a reality.

Inserted is a season-ending statistical summary of the season, provided by the college newspaper, the Lorian. Fourteen games for a season compared with thirty to forty games per season that teams play today.

54

LORAS '9' CLOSES SEASON; SPORTS 11-3
RECORD
The Loras College diamond nine wound up its 1954 season last weekend, winning a pair from Westmar and splitting a twin bill with Buena Vista 4-1 and 4-6. Seven of the eleven tilts completed were played in an 11-day span. The three losses came at the hands of Luther (2) and Buena Vista.

Bill Kezman finished with the best pitching record, 4-0. The frosh hurled the Loras nine to wins over Platteville, Wartburg and Westmar twice. Another frosh, Art Huinker, finished his pitching season undefeated. The lefty won three and lost none. He also broke the school strikeout record in the Upper Iowa contest. Huinker fanned 17 batters to break the record held by Vince Tiano. Tiano struck out 13 in 1951.

Five homers went into the books this season. Tom Schneider clouted a four-bagger in the Upper Iowa game and one in the Buena Vista game, Art Whipple in the Westmar tilt and Frank Sovich connected for round-trippers in both the Buena Vista and Cornell games. The team batting average for the year was .357. WOW!

As for baseball in my freshmen year, even though only starting and winning three games, confidence for a baseball career appeared possible. Even though the seventeen strikeout game against Upper Iowa received the most attention, the 4 to 1 victory over Buena Vista was probably more significant. They were a much stronger baseball team and to allow only one run against them said more than the 17-strikeout game. At least, that was my evaluation.

Following is an interview that the Loras Lorian sportswriter put together at the end of my freshmen year.

ART MAKES BIG SPLASH WITH FAST BALL
by Dave Hingtgen
In college, if you are looking for a student who graduated first in his high school class, you might expect to find him engaged in some scholarly pursuit, even on a balmy spring afternoon.

At least, you usually do not expect to find him out on a baseball field setting a new strikeout record for a varsity pitcher.

But that's where Art Huinker, valedictorian of a class of 32 at Calmar high School, Calmar, Iowa, was one warm afternoon early this May as he blazed his fast ball past 17 Upper Iowa batters to win a 4 to 0 shutout.

The northeastern Iowa freshman broke the school record of 13 strikeouts set by Vince Tiano in 1952 in his first

55

college start, too. He didn't give up his first hit until the sixth inning and allowed only four hits in nine frames.

"I was just trying to get them out," Art said when I interviewed him in his room. "My control was good. I didn't even know there was a record," he added as he polished a pair of shoes.

The little lefty's 3-0 record and dangerous bat played a prominent part in helping the Duhawks to one of their best records in recent years.

Art got his second start May 11 in the first game of a double-header against Wartburg. Again he didn't surrender his first hit until the sixth, pitching a seven-inning two-hitter, 6 to 2.

Last Saturday he protected a Loras hope for a championship by beating a strong Buena Vista team 4 to 1 in seven innings. The run was unearned as he went the distance in the first game of the crucial double header. Besides pitching three complete games, he appeared in relief in the first game of the season with Platteville and in the second game with Buena Vista Saturday.

Art's bat has been a consistent part of the Loras attack. The well-built, blond haired athlete divides his time between left and center field when not pitching. From his usual number three position in the batting order behind Ottavi, he has rapped out 14 hits for a .298 average—all singles. "Very seldom get an extra-base—too small for that," he grins.

Appearing in all but one of the college's 14 games, Art has played errorless ball. He has also got on base 24 times in 47 at bats and has averaged a run a game. He was the difference in the first game with Platteville. His hit started off a three-run rally in the second inning, and another came in the middle of a scoring spree that put Loras ahead in the third. His four runs were the margin in the 9 to 5 score.

Art, who will be 19 Saturday, got started in baseball in Calmar. St. Mary's high school in Festina, which he attended, offered only the first two years of high school and had no athlete teams.

Art first went out for baseball in his junior year at nearby Calmar high school. Behind his 8-0 hurling Calmar went to the state tournament. He struck out 14 batters in winning the first game of the tournament, then lost the next game in the semi-finals.

"The only reason we went to the state tournament was because we had two good hitters," Art says modestly. "one would come up with a key double a game. Both had professional contracts. It's funny—both were turned down because of bad knees.

56

*In his senior year Art had a 6-1 record. His control
bothered him a little, but remembers one game with the bases
loaded and nobody out when he struck out the next three
batters. "But that was because my girl friend was there," he
smiles, returning to his polishing.*

*Art estimated he averaged around 50 games a year,
playing for the Calmar Junior American Legion and Festina
teams besides the high school nine. He had a .375 average in
high school, and as an outfielder in Legion ball for three years
he continued to hit over .300 each summer.*

*With the Festina team also for three years, he batted
around .285. He threw a one-hitter in his first start for the town
team as a high school sophomore and spent his non-pitching
days in the outfield.*

*The mild-mannered, agreeable student with the poised
confidence came to Loras on a scholarship for his academic
record. Art was high up on the freshman semester honor roll
with a 3.529 average and plans to go into coaching.*

*When asked about a possible baseball career after
graduation, "I'd go on in baseball," Art says, "if I changed my
mind about coaching high school baseball or basketball.
Baseball?" he muses. " No, I don't think I'll ever stop,"
meaning that he intends to keep in touch with the game.*

*Art is thinking of going out for basketball to give him a
background for coaching. He was also introduced to basketball
in his first year at Calmar, and he averaged 10 points a game as
a senior.*

*Track and football are two more of his activities.
Although his high school efforts as a half- and quarter-miler
were pretty much limited by baseball, he learned enough to win
the 100 yard dash in the intramural track meet held last week.
In football, he was a member of the Comets, who got beat in the
semi-finals of the intramural football championship last fall.*

*Art's brother went into the service during the year, and
his dad is running the farm alone. Art will return this summer
to help his dad out- - -and try to get in the rest of this year's 50
games.*

These were nice comments afforded me by Mr. Hintgten. Hopefully,
there is some degree of truthfulness in them. One that strikes me is the "poised
confidence." Throughout my years of pitching, I quietly felt confident that I could
get the batter out, at whatever level of competition. It certainly didn't mean an out
was the end result, however. In saying that, I don't mean to come across as some
cocky player who felt he was better than everybody else. It is my hope that such a
disposition was never displayed. I also need to thank Dave Hintgten for the
interview.

57

ENGAGING SUMMER

A good start at Loras College as a freshman. Now for another summer with the home town "heroes." That word, representing my feelings, is meant in the strongest sense. For the little hometown of Festina, these players, especially the veterans, had gained considerable attention from the northeastern Iowa baseball community. When Festina began to win the first titles in the Northeast Iowa League and also represented themselves in the Dubuqueland Tournament in a very competitive and positive light, the most common question asked was "where is this town called Festina?" But by 1954, when the same question was asked, the response was different. Now the responder said "that's the little town north of West Union that has a great hometown baseball team." Personally, even admitting my biases, I don't think that recognition was as significant as the way the players handled themselves. There wasn't a "Wow, we're good" attitude. The players enjoyed their successes but they seldom bragged about them. They played together as a team. In all the years playing with them, I don't recall a dispute or argument between the players. And I don't recall any consequential disagreement with an umpire. The summer of 1954 wasn't any different.

The summer of 1954 witnessed a major step toward the long-range goals that we have discussed earlier. Having just turned nineteen, and this may raise some highbrows, I was convinced that Ann was destined to be my spouse. The proposal was made, the response was affirmative and the engagement ring placed on her finger on July 15. Later, when we shared our news with her mother, she simply responded "ahh, you!" A red dress for Ann accompanied the ring because that was my favorite color for my wife-to-be. Irony of ironies, that color was proven not to be the best color for her to wear. Oh, well, I am a little color-blind too.

Baseball also held its highlights. For the fourth consecutive year, the Festina team won the Northeast Iowa League championship. Only one league loss marred an otherwise perfect record. And that loss, although not earth-shaking, triggers some vivid recollections. We experienced a heavy rainfall the night before that had left a huge water puddle on the first base side of our home baseball field. The diamond drained poorly and consequently many of the players, including myself, worked for most of Sunday morning to get the field ready for play. We even resorted to pouring gasoline on the muddy section and lighting it in hopes of burning the ground dry. Lastly, we hand-raked about fifty percent of the infield. We obviously, in 1954, were not privy to having a grass infield. Very few around Festina did. By game time the field, although it was not ideal, was satisfactory enough to begin the game. On a very humid afternoon, the conditions resulted in a very unusual seven errors afternoon for our team and all we could do was blame the conditions for a loss. "Well, why not?" Brief write-ups of the most of the league games follow. Most of these write-ups came from the Ossian Bee weekly publications.

58

FESTINA AND ST. LUCAS TAKE EAST DIVISION LEAD

Festina and St. Lucas took first place in the two-week-old Northeast Iowa league with Festina rapping Ossian, 27-0 in seven innings, and St. Lucas edging Calmar, 5-3.

In the west division, New Hampton and Cresco are running neck and neck for the first place division, both having posted their second wins. New Hampton took Fredericksburg, 5-3, and Cresco nipped Lawler, 9-8.

In the Festina-Ossian game, Festina stroked out 26 hits in the six innings they batted. Ossian managed one hit off Art Huinker.

FESTINA DOWNS SPILLVILLE, 12-4

Festina won its third straight victory in the eastern division of the Northeast Iowa loop Sunday as they defeated Spillville, 12-4. In other games West Union downed St. Lucas, 12-7, and Calmar humbled Ossian, 21-5.

Art Huinker struck out 12 Spillville batsmen as Festina kept its league lead with a 12-4 win. Romauld Elsbernd smashed a round tripper for Festina in the third with one on.

FESTINA TIPS CALMAR 8-1 FOR FIFTH WIN

Art Huinker struck out ten as Festina registered its fifth straight win in the east division of the Northeast Iowa baseball league, defeating Calmar 8-1 Sunday.

There were three triples in the Festina-Calmar game, with Don Rimrodt and Rod Anderson each hitting one for Calmar and Jerry Schneberger for Festina. Festina had 12 hits to eight by the losers.

CALMAR DEFEATS OSSIAN, 11-2 IN NEI LEAGUE

Important game of Sunday's action was the St. Lucas-West Union contest as St. Lucas handed the West Union team its second defeat of the year, 6-2, and moved into a second place tie with the losers in the east division. Both teams have 6-2 records, trailing Festina which has a 7-1 mark to date. Winning pitcher in the St. Lucas-West Union game was Jene Smith who had 10 strikeouts. Orlinger was the loser.

The third game in the east division was between Festina and Spillville, with Festina posting its seventh win, 7-2. Art Huinker was credited with 15 strikeouts for the victors.

ART HUINKER PITCHES FESTINA TO VICTORY

Festina continued its torrid winning pace in the eastern division of the Northeast Iowa league as they blanked St. Lucas

*3 to 0. In other division games, Spillville downed Ossian 6 to 3
and West Union routed Calmar 13-3.*

*A pair of sixth inning doubles following two walks in
the sixth inning provided Festina with its runs in its 3-0 triumph
over St. Lucas. Hurler Art Huinker of the winners set St. Lucas
down on four scattered hits, striking out 14 batters in
registering the win. Jene Smith, the losing pitcher, gave up five
hits. He had 11 strikeouts.*

FESTINA GETS BY CALMAR IN EAST DIVISION, 4-2

*Festina barely got past Calmar in Sunday's east
division play of the Northeast Iowa league, taking a 4-2 victory
after trailing 2-0 in the sixth inning.*

*Festina got its four runs in the bottom of the seventh on
four singles and a double by Leo Luzum, the only extra-base hit
of the game. Calmar's two runs came in the top of the sixth on
two errors, a hit and a player hit by a pitch.*

*Art Huinker tossed the one-hitter for Festina. Rimrodt
of Calmar gave up 13 hits.*

*Highlight of the west division was Cresco's 9-2 victory
over New Hampton, which tied the two teams for the division
lead with eight wins and two losses.*

With more teams wanting to play in the NEI league in 1954, the
league split into an eastern and a western division, with an end-of-year
best two of three games playoff between the two divisions. Festina
controlled the eastern division with Cresco winning the western half over
rival New Hampton. The two-out-of-three winner would claim the right
to represent the league in the coveted Waterloo Courier Tournament.
Because Festina did not have baseball lights, the Festina home game of
the playoffs was scheduled to be played at New Hampton under the
lights.

That first game, a Festina 4 to 2 victory over the western champs stands
out as one of those "highlight reel" games. We need to step back into the middle
fifties and visit a typical farming operation first. By the middle of August each
summer, "threshing" was a harvesting activity that brought together a neighboring
group of farmers, one of whom owned a threshing machine, a huge machine
pulled from one farm to another to separate the oats seed from the bundles that
had been cut and built into shocks in all the oats fields. This was an era before
the huge self-propelled combines that glean our fields today. Each of the eight to
ten farmers had special responsibilities in this process that usually lasted about
two weeks in early to mid August. With my brother Kenny in the armed forces
over in Korea, my task centered on building loads of bundles out in the oats field
and bringing them to the threshing machine. There were several other farmers
that had the same task. At the machine, my task consisted of throwing each

60

individual bundle into the conveyor. But, each bundle had to be turned so that the head of the bundle which held the oats grain went into the machine first. This forced the hauler (me) to do lots of twisting and turning the bundle with my fork. By the end of a long day, both wrists were so sore that I wasn't sure I could pitch a baseball game. The opposite effect became the reality.

Warming up that evening, I struggled with my control. The fast ball was alive like it never was before. For the Cresco batters, it was difficult to follow the ball's movement. The result: In the nine-inning game, twenty-three outs were recorded via the strikeout route. Out of 27 outs, it leaves very little for the fielders to do. The result was a huge learning experience for me. I realized that the more flexible my left wrist, the more movement on my pitches. Many different ideas and resulting practices occupied my spare time after that to reproduce the feeding of a threshing machine with oat bundles—squeezing rubber balls, rolling a brick up tied to a rope with both hands, etc. It is amazing how much we know comes from actually experiencing it. One summer, living in Dyersville, I actually volunteered to haul a few loads of manure for the Al Goerdt farm, in hopes that the wielding of the manure fork and twisting and turning it to fill the spreader would create similar results to the oats threshing experience. Don't remember the results of that endeavor.

In the next play-off game, behind Ken Schneberger's pitching, Festina grabbed an easy 15 to 4 victory and gained a trip to Waterloo. For the first time, nine leagues sent their champions to the Courier tournament. Seven teams drew byes; Festina did not. Our opponent, also losing the draw, came from the area just south and west of Cedar Rapids, a town called Norway. It is another small town with a great baseball history. With my fastball still moving sharply, Festina won 6 to 1, this time with nineteen strikeouts. However, our '54 season came to an end in the next round, losing to Janesville, a town just northwest of Waterloo. The final score: 7 to 0. These four games receive further description below.

ART HUINKER FANS 23 AS FESTINA TIPS CRESCO
Art Huinker, ace Festina hurler, struck out 23 in leading his teammates to a 4-2 victory over Cresco in the first game of a play-off for the Northeast Iowa league title at New Hampton Tuesday night.

Huinker held Cresco scoreless until the eighth inning when the west division champs scored two runs. He allowed but four hits while Festina, the east division winners, collected seven blows off the pitching of Paul Sir and Randy Halverson.

Longest hit of the evening was a triple by Linus Huinker who started a two-run rally for Festina in the fifth stanza.

The next game in the two-out-of-three playoff will be held at Cresco Thursday, Aug. 5. Winner of the play-off will also represent the NFI league in the tournament of champions at Waterloo, starting August 9.

FESTINA WINS NEW LOOP TITLE

The powerful Festina nine copped the Northeast Iowa League championship here Thursday night as it humbled Cresco, 15 to 4. The victory was the second straight for Festina over Cresco in the best two-out-of-three playoffs.

The champs took an early lead with three runs in the first inning and rallied for six runs in the fourth to insure the triumph. Pitcher Ken Schneberger of the winners limited Cresco to five hits while his teammates tagged four opposing hurlers for 11 hits.

FESTINA TOPS NORWAY, 6-1, IN TOURNEY

The Festina baseball team, champions of the Northeast Iowa league, defeated Norway of the Iowa Vally league, 6-1, in a first round game of the tournament of champions at Waterloo Monday night, Aug. 9.

Art Huinker, ace Festina hurler, struck out 19 and allowed but four hits in leading his teammates to victory. In step with his pitching, Huinker also collected two hits in three trips to the plate.

Festina got the scoring off in the first inning with two runs. Norway tallied its single run of the game in the bottom of the second. From then on it was Festina's game all the way.

Leadoff batter Linus Huinker lined a single into right field to start the game off. The next batter, Leo Luzum, reached first on an error while Huinker moved to third. A double down the right field line by Romauld Elsbernd scored Huinker and put Luzum on third, still with none out. A second run also scored.

In the bottom of the second Huinker walked two batters with two out. This set the stage for Norway pitcher Dick Emmanuel's line drive single to score Dean Alberts from second base.

Festina added insurance runs with a single tally in the third, two in the seventh and one more in the eighth. Elsbernd had two doubles and a triple for Festina.

JANESVILLE WINS WATERLOO TILT

Tom Meinders, a Teachers High of Cedar Falls athlete last year, banged three singles and a triple and drove in two runs to spark Janesville's 7-0 triumph over Festina in the Wednesday opener of the Baseball Tournament of Champions Wednesday. His hitting provided pitcher Maurie McDonald with all the support he needed to put Janesville in the semi-finals.

Festina had lead off runners on base in all but the third and fourth innings, but never could touch McDonald in the clutches.

Singles by Stan Chapin, Dick Rath and McDonald and Meinders' triple to left center provided the Orphan League champions with three runs in the first and chased Festina starting pitcher Ken Schneberger. Romauld Elsbernd came in to get the side out on a fly to the outfield. He finished the game and yielded a run each in the third, fourth, sixth and seventh. Linus Huinker had two hits to pace Festina's hitters.

After Festina's elimination from the Waterloo Courier Northeast Iowa Tournament of Champions won by the Sumner Cubs, the Cub management asked if I would accompany them to the Northwest Regional Championship of the American Baseball Congress. The invite was accepted and we travelled to Watertown, South Dakota for the double elimination challenge. Watertown is located in extreme northeastern South Dakota.

Going into Thursday, September 16 games, Sumner remained unbeaten after two games. Ace right hand pitcher Chuck Anderson was winning pitcher in both games. Seattle, Washington also remained unbeaten.

Manager Ray Siegfried informed me that I would pitch the early game on Thursday against Seattle, in the battle of the unbeatens. We won the game 6-3 to now be the only unbeaten team in the double-elimination tournament. Anderson came on in the top of the ninth to preserve the victory. An abbreviated write-up of the game follows.

SUMNER IN ABC FINALS; DOWNS SEATTLE, THEN LOSES TO PORTLAND
WATERTOWN, S.D.---Sumner, the Iowa American Baseball Congress champion, will play either Portland, Ore., or Seattle, Wash., for the Northwest regional championship here.

The Cubs entered the final round with a 3-1 record Friday after defeating Seattle and losing to Portland in a pair of games Thursday. Those two teams, also owners of 3-1 records, were to play at 1 p.m. Friday with the winner to face Sumner in the finals and loser ousted from the double elimination meet.

The Portland team stopped Sumner 6-4 Thursday after the Iowa team had defeated Seattle 6-3 earlier.

In the loss the Beavers held on as Sumner loaded the bases on two walks and single in the seventh and did not score. In the eighth, a walk, a hit batter and Bob Topp's hit made it 6-

63

3. Chuck Anderson singled in a run in the ninth behind Stevens'
hit, an error and a fielder's choice.
    In the first game, Sumner's ace pitcher, Chuck
Anderson, came in for a ninth inning relief job as Sumner
knocked Seattle from the undefeated class Thursday afternoon.
    Sumner chased in five runs in the first inning and then
held on to win. Anderson relieved starter Art Huinker with two
men on and none out and retired the next three batters.
    Leadoff man Mack McKenna walked as Sumner's big
first inning started. Stevens singled for his sixth hit in three
games. Mel Harms' hit batted in one run. Walks to Jim
Anderson, Carl Warrington and Glen Hummel followed forcing
in two runs and Huinker singled in two more. Another scored
on the error handling Huinker's hit.

This game was a struggle for me throughout. Seattle had nine hits, all singles but one. In addition, control problems continued as seven batters received free passes. But the final score was 6-3 in our favor. We were still unbeaten, the only one left. After the next game the same day, we also joined the ranks of teams with one loss.

With three teams having 3 wins and 1 loss, Sumner enjoyed the bye while Portland and Seattle battled each other for the right to play in the championship. Seattle won a tight 2-1 victory over the Beavers and the pairing was ready for the final game.

Even though the Washington team had to come right back and play again, they topped Sumner 5-2. Down by four in the bottom of the eighth, in a pinch-hitting role, I managed to drive in our second run with a single. But that was the extent of any kind of comtribution. We, the Sumner Cubs were going back home. Seattle headed for Battle Creek .

For the first time in the summer of 1954, an invitation was received to pitch for a team other than Festina. The opportunity is very likely the result of the successful pitching at Loras College in the spring. The Dubuque Merchants, a second semi-pro team in Dubuque, was scheduled to play powerhouse Cascade in the semi-finals of the Dubuqueland Tournament, now being played earlier in the summer. Two players on the Merchants, Gene "Tiny" Potts and Rocky Schiltz eventually were teammates at Loras College. Both were very skilled and speedy players. Because of the weather as you will see by the write-ups below, Ann and I made two long trips to Dubuque, a better than two hour drive each way in those days, with a full day's work in between. The praise in the article may be a little heavy but that's what the reporter shared.

64

MERCHANTS WIN EXTRA-INNING AFFAIR

A twelfth-inning single by catcher Eddie Schiltz scored the winning run, as the Dubuque Merchants edged the Cascade Reds, 5 to 4, in one of the most exciting games in the history of the Dubuqueland Baseball tournament Wednesday night.

The victory, the first of two semi-final games in this16th annual classic, moved the Merchants into the tournament finals Thursday night against their city rival, the Dubuque Brewers, defending champs, who defeated Dyersville, 10 to 3, in the semi-final windup.

Schiltz's line single to right field, following a single by teammate Tommy Haye, climaxed a see-saw battle which saw the Merchants rally in the seventh inning for the game-tying run in order to set up the stage for the extra-inning triumph.

Meanwhile, Huinker of the Merchants, displayed a brilliant mound performance as he pitched the entire distance, looking stronger as the game progressed. Huinker fanned 12 Cascade batters and, although being tagged for 10 hits and seven bases on balls, the young lefthander looked more impressive with runners on the bases.

Cascade drew first blood in the game, mixing singles by Pat Clarke, John Sullivan and Don Harmon to score its first run in the third inning.

The Merchants sent the first of three Cascade hurlers to an early shower in their half of the third inning as they pounded starting pitcher Jim Geelan for three runs before Orrie Arntzen could come in to put out the fire.

The Reds combined four hits in the fifth inning to score three times and take their final lead of the ball game. Arntzen started the rally with a double to right with one out, and moved to third on a single by Clarke. Leftfielder Ade Kurt followed with a run-scoring single to left and Harmon kept the uprising alive with a two-base poke through the box, scoring Clarke and Kurt before the rally ended.

In the seventh, after leadoff man Gene Potts had grounded out, Tommy Haye came through with his first of two hits to pave the way for the game-tying run, as Rocky Schiltz lined the very first pitch into the right field corner for a double. Cascade immediately brought in ace hurler, Del O'Hea to put out the fire.

The Reds made several bids to score during the following innings, only to see Huinker settle down to pitch his way out of trouble with his blazing fastball. Cascade's most desperate attempt came in the bottom half of the seventh as it took advantage of two walks to put runners on first and second with two away.

65

A strategic move, involving an intentional pass to clean-up hitter Harmon to load the bases, worked for the Merchants as Huinker tossed three strikes past Kurt to cut down the rally,

Haye opened the twelfth with sharp single to center, but the scoring hopes for the Merchants faded as O'Hea forced Rocky Schiltz and Paul Smiley to pop out to second. Then Ralph Teeling gained a life when Jim Burke fumbled his grounder at shortstop, moving Haye into position for Ed Schiltz' hit.

COURAGE PAYS OFF FOR HUINKER

Art Huinker is only a freshman in college but he has more pitching heart than many a seasoned veteran.

The young lefty proved his courage to some 840 fans in the semi-final game between the Dubuque Merchants and the Cascade Reds Wednesday night.

Hurling for the Merchants, Huinker went the entire 12 innings to gain the decision over three veteran Cascade hurlers. Pitching the 12 innings and gaining the decision was only part of the story, however.

Some fans probably didn't realize Huinker had hurled three scoreless innings against the potent Cascade club Tuesday night before rain halted play.

Manager Bob Bradley consulted with Art as the game wore on, but Huinker still felt he could stay in and pitch. But unfortunately the Merchants couldn't come through with a run after tying the game at 4-4 in the seventh inning.

It came as no surprise when the youngster came off the hill after the 11th inning and informed Manager Bradley that he was getting weary. Bradley immediately made plans for Darrel Koch to go in the next frame in relief.

It was plain to see that Huinker was downhearted. Of course there was good reason to be---he had puzzled the Cascade hitters for 14 innings over a two-day stretch. He had done his best to win the game, now he was forced to leave without a chance of winning.

But Tommy Haye brightened the Merchants' outlook with a single to open the twelfth. The next two men were retired but Ralph Teeling reached first on an error.

Eddie Schiltz stepped to the plate and lined Del O'Hea's first offering into right field and speedy Tucker Haye came around to score.

Huinker's face lit up and he was no longer tired. He told Business Manager Louie Schlitz he thought he could hold them for one more inning. Schiltz conferred with Bradley and the field manager elected to give him the chance.

Huinker had to face the cream of the Cascade batting order in Johnny Sullivan, Don Harmon and Bud Kurt. The lefty tossed two bad pitches to Sullivan, then a strike and another ball. The crowd must have wondered if Huinker could hold up. The manager paced about nervously.

Sullivan connected on the fifth pitch but Paul Smiley hauled in his fly ball to center. Harmon became Huinker's 12th strikeout victim. But Kurt, hitless in four previous trips, blasted a double down the left field foul line, and again the outlook was bleak.

Huinker, who paces himself well on the mound, displayed the courage that helped him win the game. He picked up the rosin bag, looked around the outfield and set himself to face Jim Burke. The Cascade shortstop had fanned four times previously.

But Burke connected with Huinker's first pitch and slapped a looping liner to center, and once again Smiley came in fast and made the catch to retire the side and end the ball game.

Young Art Huinker dragged himself off the playing field a mighty tired young man. But it was plain to see, he was a mighty happy young man, too.

The writer of this report from the newspaper is not known to me but he (or she) probably deserves a thank you. In this game, shortstop Ralph Teeling collected a double and two singles. In later years he became a baseball umpire and officiated many of the baseball games when I was playing for Dyersville. In the above writing, the author used the expression, "pitching heart." This helped us choose the title for this publication with the second usage of that word in the Waterloo Courier by Sports Editor Russ Smith.

A good summer was now complete. Another successful year for Festina baseball. Could the second year at Loras College be as good as the first year? Time will tell, obviously, but I looked forward to it. Life was good.

And, the question was popped. A sweeter than sweet "yes" came back from Ann and we began to do some wedding planning for the following summer. Success on both goals.

A SECOND YEAR ON THE HILL

After a full summer of playing for the hometown Festina team, a more confident left-handed pitcher looked forward to a second season of Loras College baseball. Eleven returning players from the 1954 team plus a returning letter-winner Romie Gales, after two years of military service, a strong transfer from the University of Iowa, Dubuquer Rocky Schiltz, were joined by strong freshmen candidates, Dick Winter, Bill Hyland, Jim Swann (all pitchers), and a catcher from LaCrosse, Bill Leonard. Gales, a 6-0 junior, led the Loras nine to the Iowa Conference crown in the 1952 season, with the most number of hits (17), the most runs (12), three home runs and a neat .362 batting average. Native Dubuquer Rocky Schiltz, the U of I transfer, took over duties at first base, a position vacated by hard-hitting Tom Schneider who completed his three-year pre-med program and had gone on to graduate school.

A very unexpected event happened in the first semester of my sophomore year at Loras. Our intramural touch football team won the Loras Intramural Championship. One of our touchdowns that helped win it was the famous flea flicker play described in the write-up below. The write-up was taken from the college newspaper, the Lorian.

WILDCATS CHAMPS
The Wildcats bruised their way by the Dragons in the championship game of the touch-tourney, 21-6. The Dragons drew first blood in the opening plays of the game when Fred Pergande passed to Tom Tucker for a T.D. The extra point was no good.

The Wildcats came right back with a great play when Bill Kezman passed to Dick Wright. Wright lateralled to Art Huinker, who raced the distance for the first Wildcat T.D. The point after touchdown was no good and the Wildcats kicked off.
The Dragons lost the ball on downs and Kezman passed to Huinker for the touchdown. The extra point was good, Kezman to Green.
A series of passes put the Dragons on the 3-yard line but they failed to score. The Wildcats took over and immediately scored on a pass from Kezman to Dave Schultz. Dick Wiley, charging Wildcat, then caught Pergande behind the line for a safety to end the scoring.

By the time the 1955 baseball season started, a date for our wedding had been set. Some people thought we were crazy. And maybe we were, a little. But fifty years later we felt just as crazy.

68

Back to baseball and the '55 season. With all the returning letter winners and the added personnel, there was great enthusiasm for the year. We were prepared for a season-opening doubleheader against Winona St. Mary's, at that time a perennial baseball champion from the Minnesota Intercollegiate Conference. Their coach, Max Molock, was well respected among baseball coaches in the Midwest. He also had a left hand pitcher by the name of Joe Shrake who had lost only one game in his first two years in college. The game was built up as a great match-up between the two lefthanders. The day of the game, the huge bank back of Keane Hall and next to the ball diamond was crowded with students and other fans.

The season opener proved worth the pre-game hype. Freshman outfielder, Bill Leonard, ended the game in the bottom of the ninth with a monstrous home run over the bank in left field. There was no fence in left field and in order for a ball to be a homerun, it had to clear left field on the fly. Bill's shot definitely did. If his ball carried to the street below the 20 plus foot embankment, it probably bounced into the Rock Bowl, the college's football field. There were many questionable ground rules on the Keane Field diamond but we enjoyed playing there primarily because fans attending the games had an ideal place to watch. Loras won both games by the way. All write-ups and excerpts of the Loras baseball games are taken from Dubuque's Telegraph Herald.

LORAS TRIPS ST. MARY'S

Loras College's pitching staff appeared in mid-season formTuesday as the Duhawks started their 1955 campaign with a twin victory over Winona, Minn., St. Mary's College on Keane Field.

Lefty Art Huinker went the distance in the first game for a 4-to-3 extra-inning victory. Huinker allowed only five hits, striking out 14. In the nightcap, Loras right-hander Bill Hyland held St. Mary's to two hits in posting a 5-to-0 shutout. Hyland struck out 12.

Freshman Bill Leonard broke up the opener with smash over the left center field bank in the Duhawks' half of the ninth inning. The game was scheduled for seven innings.

Loras jumped off to a two-run lead in the first inning on a single by Dick Wiley, a double by Rocky Schiltz, a fielders' choice, a single by Bill Howie and an error. The Redmen drew their first blood in the fourth inning on a single and two miscues by the Loras defense. They added single runs in the fifth and sixth to take a 3 to 2 lead. Loras tied it up in the bottom of the sixth on a single by Rockty Schiltz, a sacrifice by Romie Gales and an error and a fielder's choice. Leonard's smash as the first hitter in Loras' half of the ninth was the clincher.

69

First baseman Rocky Schiltz was the big gun for the
Duhawks. He had two singles and a double in four trips and
scored two runs. Loras catcher Art Whipple picked up two
singles in three trips and drove in a pair of runs while Huinker
scored three runs in the second game.
  Huinker bested the Redmen's ace hurler Joe Shrake in
the opening tilt. The loss was only Shrake's second in three
seasons at St. Mary's and also his second in six years of high
school and college pitching.

The next game I was to pitch obviously is not a highlight, except for my
hitting. The Lewis game was played on a Sunday afternoon and it was the one
game where I was knocked out of the game. It was an afternoon where I did not
have my best stuff and it was in front of my parents as well as Ann who had
driven down for the game. Maybe the pressure of their being at the game caused
more than the usual pre-game jitters. But that does happen to pitchers, something
that fans not real close to the game of baseball don't realize. My brother, Kenny,
and I had occasional discussions trying to figure out why. We explained this
phenomenon by describing our fastball, on the bad days, as still going after we
took a second look at it. On good days, when we took the second look, it was in
the catcher's mitt. Not very scientifically sound but it was one way of explaining
why some days a pitcher has good "stuff" and other days he does not. But Loras
came back to win the game.

KEZMAN GIVES UP ONLY ONE HIT IN SEVEN INNINGS

The Loras College Duhawks spotted Lewis College a
pair of runs in the second inning and then went on to blast the
Flyers in a baseball game on Keane Field 9-2.
  The Duhawks posted their third straight victory of the
season before a large crowd of parents and high school students
on the campus for the school's "Open House" celebration.
  A four-run burst in the bottom half of the second sent
the Loras nine into the lead after the Flyers had picked up two
runs on three hits in the upper frame. Romie Gales started the
rally with a single to right. Bill Howie walked and Art Huinker
and Bill Leonard singled. A combination of stolen bases, a
Lewis miscue and a hit to left field by Sam Azzinaro rang up the
four Loras tallies.
  Huinker scored run number five for the Duhawks in the
sixth after he singled to deep left. Art Whipple singled in
Huinker and Whipple rode home on Dick Wiley's base hit. A
homer by Howie with none on in the seventh was followed in the
eighth by Azzinaro's round tripper with Whipple on board.
  Huinker started the game for Loras but was relieved on
the mound in the third by right hander Bill Kezman. Huinker ,

who moved into center field, allowed six hits and struck out four in his two and one-third innings of pitching. Kezman struck out seven, allowing only one hit. The lone blow was a short single to right.

The big gun for Loras was Wiley. The diminutive third baseman had two singles and a double in five trips. Huinker, Whipple and Azzinaro each had two hits. Azzinaro was credited with four RBI's in Sunday's contest, two of them coming on his homer. Huinker had two runs batted in and Wiley, Howie and Whipple each had one to account for the Duhawks' nine runs.

For the Flyers, Coach Gordon Gillespie let Ray Fedo handle the pitching all the way. Fedo, though giving up 11 hits, only walked one man and struck out seven Duhawks.

Notice the name of the Lewis Flyers' baseball coach. Today he is probably considered one of the most successful small college coaches in the entire country. It was ironic that our first three games of the 1955 season, all of them Loras victories, were against two extremely successful small college baseball coaches.

The next two games were played against Iowa State Teachers College of Cedar Falls. The second game of the ISTC series was our first loss. I pitched two shutout innings in relief (the eighth and ninth) but what is remembered the most is a batting experience in the eighth. With two men on and a chance to gain the lead I hit the ball over the fence at the professional Fourth Street Park in downtown Dubuque. However, it went foul by about three feet. That memory is still very vivid, sad to say. Our next game involved Knox College from Galesburg. We were the visitors. A write-up of the game is next. No special highlights recalled.

DUHAWKS WHIP KNOX

Loras College's baseball squad got back on the win trail at Galesburg Tuesday as they bumped off the Knox nine, 4-2. Lefty Art Huinker went the distance in winning his second of the season. He allowed five hits, all occurring in different innings, and struck out nine. He also led his own team in batting with two hits in three trips to the plate.

In posting their sixth win in seven starts, Loras collected eight hits to push four single runs across the plate.

For Knox, Al Stegman hurled eight innings and was relieved in the last frame by Ron Pihera. Stegman is one of Knox's top hurlers and was partially responsible for the school's winning the 1954 Midwest Conference championship.

After two innings of scoreless ball, Loras picked up a single tally. Sam Azzinaro tripled as lead-off man in the top half of the third and scored on Joe Ottavi's sacrifice. Run number

71

two came in the fifth. After Azzinaro tagged the Knox chucker for a single, he was walked across the plate.

Art Huinker was walked as the lead-off man in the sixth, reached second on Dick Wright's hit, third on Art Whipple's putout and scored on Azzinaro's fielder's choice. Loras picked up its final run in the eighth.

Dick Wright and Sam Azzinaro each picked up two hits in four trips to follow Huinker's .667 afternoon.

In the next game against Coe College of Cedar Rapids, I came on in relief for the final four innings, giving up one run to save an 8-5 victory. No specific memories but the grand slam by Romie Gales. In the write-up, it stated that Huinker was credited with the victory. Not so. Hyland received credit for the victory. Even though the definition of who received credit for a victory was not so clearly defined as it is today, because Bill Hyland had pitched five complete innings, he should be credited with the win.

> DUHAWKS TRIP COE
>
> *A grand slam homer by Romie Gales in the fifth inning meant the difference Saturday as the Loras College baseball nine notched their seventh victory in eight starts, dumping Coe College, 8-5.*
>
> *Lefty Art Huinker was credited with the win, his third straight of the year against no setbacks. Huinker relieved Bill Hyland in the sixth, giving up one run on four hits. Charlie Strassberger received the loss. He was replaced in the fifth by Jack Schmidt.*
>
> *The big blow for the Duhawks came in the six-run fifth. Gales unloaded one over the center field bank. Two walks and an error set the stage for Gales' blast, which put the Duhawks back into the lead after trailing 4-1.*
>
> *Hyland got off to a good start, giving up only one run to the Kohawks in the fourth on two hits, but three singles, two walks and two hit batters in the fifth accounted for three more Coe runs.*
>
> *Bill Leonard went to bat for Hyland in the bottom of the inning and scored on a ground ball to account for Loras' other run in their big fifth stanza.*

Next, Western Illinois (of Macomb, Illinois) came to Loras for a make-up game that had been rained out to start the season. I pitched a complete game for an 11-3 victory but the best part of that game was my bases-loaded double in the fourth inning that provided an 8-2 lead. The visitors scored only one additional run the remainder of the way.

72

DUHAWKS WHIP W. ILLINOIS, 11-3
Art Huinker pitched and batted the Loras College
Duhawks to an 11-3 victory over Western Illinois here Tuesday.
Huinker went the distance for the Duhawks, scattering
seven hits and striking out 10 for his third win of the season.
His bases loaded double in the third inning put Loras in front to
stay.
The Duhawks blasted three Western Illinois pitchers
for 14 hits to notch their eighth win in 10 starts.
A four-run spurt by the Duhawks in the third inning
proved to be the deciding margin in the game. Joe Ottavi led off
with a single and advanced to second as Dick Wiley drew a
walk. Bill Howie's sacrifice was followed by another walk to
Dick Wright to load the bases.
Huinker then stepped to the plate and smashed a
double down the left field line to score three runs. Rocky Schiltz
singled Huinker home.
The Duhawks added three more tallies in the fourth
and an identical number in the sixth. A walk and a single in the
first inning produced Loras' other score.
Joe Ottavi paced the Loras hitters with four hits in five
trips including a pair of doubles. Rocky Schiltz also had two
doubles as he collected three bingles for the afternoon.

Next, in a double-header split, we won the second game 10-7. Our
opponent was the tough Lewis team from Lockport, Illinois and their famous
coach, Gordy Gillespie. They clobbered us 9-1 in game one but in game 2 we
beat them 10-7. My role was that of closer in the second game, pitching two
scoreless innings to close out the game. My next starting job was three days later
against Wisconsin State College of Platteville, Wisconsin. We won the game
rather easily, but the score was 1-0 until the sixth. It probably was the closest I
came to pitching a no-hitter at Loras. A single and double in the seventh took care
of that.

HUINKER POSTS FOURTH VICTORY OF THE
SEASON
Loras College won its 11th victory in 14 starts
Wednesday as it defeated the Platteville State Pioneers for the
second time this season. Art Huinker posted his fourth win
against no losses this season, and his seventh in as many starts
in a Duhawk uniform.
He had a no-hitter going till the seventh inning when
Pioneers Jim Jackson and Bill Collein tagged him for hits, a

73

*double and a single. The Platteville nine picked up two more
hits in the eighth. In all, he struck out 14.*

*Loras broke the ice early in the contest as Dick Wiley
doubled and Joe Ottavi singled. The next man up, Rocky
Schiltz, hit into a double play but scored Wiley. The Duhawsk
collected run number two in the sixth when Romie Gales blasted
another round-tripper, this time with none on. It was his third
of the season. A five-run rally in the seventh iced the game
which gave the Purple and Gold contingent the same record
that they ended the '54 season with. Doubles by Schiltz and
Sam Azzinaro accounted for the only hits in the inning but three
costly Platteville errors filled in the rest for Loras*

*Eight different Duhawks got hits off the Pioneer's
pitcher, Howie Murphy. The only Lorasman to grab a pair of
hits was Azzinaro. He had a double and a single in three trips
to the plate.*

Two victories over Beloit College of Wisconsin were followed by the
final two games of the season. The first involved a road trip to Cedar Rapids to
play Coe in a return engagement. The Duhawks wore "hitting shoes" and scored
another offensive victory 10-4 over the Kohawks. The final game played on
Keane Field at Loras against LaCrosse State College also ended up in a romp, 12-
3. Both were complete game victories. Both write-ups follow.

HUINKER, LORAS TOP COE 10-4

*Lefty Art Huinker pitched the Loras College to their
13th win this season as Loras dumped Coe College at Cedar
Rapids Tuesday, 10-4.*

*Dick Wright had the only homer in the game as he
chased his Loras-mate, Romie Gales, across the plate in the
seventh inning. He also had a double to pick off two hits in his
five trips. Romie Gales had three hits and scored three runs.
Five of Loras's 13 hits were for extra bases.*

LORAS WHIPS LA CROSSE

*Loras College decisively capped its 1955 baseball
season with an easy 12-3 win over La Crosse State at home
Saturday. The win was number 14 for the Duhawks against four
earlier losses.*

*Southpaw Art Huinker went the distance for the
Duhawks, giving up seven scattered hits and striking out eight
Indians. The victory was his sixth of the season without a loss
and his ninth straight since he first donned a Loras uniform two
years ago.*

*Loras drew first blood in the contest when Bill Howie
singled and Dick Wright doubled to score one run. Sam*

74

Azzinaro followed with a single to plate Wright. La Crosse came back in the top half of the third as pitcher Ed Winarski homered as lead-off man.

The Duhawks iced the contest in the bottom half of the third as they climbed on Winarski and reliefer Bob Olson for six hits, good for a seven-run barrage.

As the inning started, Winarski faced Loras' lead-off man Dick Wiley. Wiley singled, Joe Ottavi walked, Rocky Schiltz singled, while Romie Gales tripled to send all three scampering across the plate.

Howie and Wright got together once again to clip the Indian chucker with another single and double. Azzinaro homered with Howie and Wright aboard to account for Loras' seventh score in that inning.

Next inning, Schiltz doubled and Howie tripled to send one run across, but the new La Crosse hurler held on to retire the side.

The Indians tagged Huinker for doubles and a run in the top of the fifth; a Loras error helped them push across a second. The Duhawks had one more punch left as they capitalized on Wright's walk and a double by Huinker to score two more runs in the bottom of the seventh.

The Lorian, the college paper, also provided a summary of the 1955 season along with some pictures, including a team photo. The photos will be found in the picture section of the book. Let's look back on the season and reflect. First of all, senior catcher Bob Kaliban from Lisbon, Iowa, had a unique college experience. Only at a small college could he accomplish the dual role of baseball player and lead actor in the huge musical production put on by Father Karl Schroeder every spring which included a team of dancers brought in from New York City. He missed over half of the ball games during the season. Luckily we had two other good receivers in sophomore Art Whipple and freshman Bill Leonard. By the way, Bob Kaliban has made a career of acting, and still performs to this day in New York City.

Dear friend Dick Wright (affectionately called "Garny" because he was from Garnavillo) also did some catching in his freshmen year and only after several games into the '55 season did he take over a starting position in left field. From there he proceeded to lead the team in hitting, batting .385, including a pair of home runs. Before that, he wasn't in the starting lineup unless I was pitching. I was now relegated to the bench when not pitching, used only for pinch hitting situations. Of this there was no doubt. We had a good ball club.

Then there was senior second baseman, Milham "Bill" Howie. What a sweet hitter. Not a power hitter normally, even though he did have two round trippers in the 1955 season, he constantly drilled line drives all over the field. He

75

led the team in hitting in two of his four years and in the 1955 season was nosed out by Garny by two points, .385 to .383. He was going to be a hard player to replace in '56.

Another thing happened this season that was somewhat humorous. The exact game and situation I cannot recall but Coach Dowd made a remark one day that few of us have forgotten, especially if you were a left-hand pitcher. The team was having difficulty solving the slants of an opposing left-handed pitcher when Coach, between innings, challenged the hitters with the following statement, "There is no reason you guys should not be able hit left-hand pitchers. You can see the ball so much easier than against right-handers." Many eyes came my way. And it was a statement I was kidded about many times in the next couple of years. Here I always figured it was to my advantage being a lefty.

> ### HUINKER LEADS DUHAWK STAFF
> *Southpaw Art Huinker finished his second season on the Loras College pitching staff undefeated to lead Coach Vince Dowd's 1955 staff. Huinker, a sophomore, posted six straight victories this year to add to his 3-0 mark as a freshman.*
> *Sophomore Dick Wright copped batting honors with a .385 mark. The team hit for a combined average of .296 in stacking up a 14-4 record. Loras pounded out 13 homers, with Sam Azzinaaro and Romie Gales, both juniors, cracking out three apiece.*

If one takes a closer look at the statistics for the 1955 baseball season, you will find an interesting fact. For all of you who are pitchers, how would you like to pitch for a team that averages over nine runs a game. That is what the Duhawk hitters accomplished. In eight of the eighteen games, ten or more runs were scored. We batted .296 as a team. Five starters had batting averages above .300. That made a pitcher's job easier.

Another year, another day to dwell on the introduction to Chapter 7, "If you expect God to bless you, we think you need to go to Loras." Another successful season. And another enjoyable one because I had the privilege of sharing it with fantastic teammates and two coaches who quietly managed the team in their easy-going demeanor that created a very positive atmosphere. Another summer with Mom and Dad on the farm and playing baseball for Festina, and a couple of other teams. And God was really blessing me with my upcoming marriage to sweetheart Ann, the only special person that I ever dated and I can honestly say that I have no regrets. She made my life very fulfilling.

That sophomore year was a second year of living on campus—in Keane Hall, Room 222, right next to the refrigerated water fountain. But, best of all, my roommate was Bob Wolfe from Lost Nation, a small town about 30 miles south of Dubuque. He also was a member of the baseball team as well as the basketball

76

team. What is interesting is that we had met the summer after our high school junior year when both of us were selected by our local American Legion posts to attend a state-wide camp held at Camp Dodge just northwest of Des Moines. We lived in the same dorm together and played on the same softball team. His background is very similar to mine. He was a wonderful roommate, personally and academically. The friendship that has carried on through our entire lifetime was strong enough that Ann and I asked Bob to be one of our groomsmen for our wedding that summer. He became a very successful business person but throughout all his financial successes Bob never changed. He was always that down-to-earth small town individual (also grew up on a farm), that was so easy to relate with. Ann and I have enjoyed so many wonderful times with Bob and his wife, Kathy. Both full Irish, by the way, sharing with two full German people in Ann and me. We get together frequently, sometimes just staying at each other's home for several days. God does not make them much better than the Wolfes.

MARRIED, WITH TEAMMATES

The summer of '55 is a summer that belongs in my personal history book. Our wedding date was set for August 3. We made it. Because of our youthfulness, especially Ann's, there were people who harbored doubts. For the two of us, those doubts fell on deaf ears.

Next, baseball-wise, the question is: Will Festina win its fifth consecutive league championship? The answer was a resounding "yes," winning eleven straight games before suffering a loss. On that day Festina clinched the title with a two game lead and only one game to go. Waterloo here we come, once again.

The team was still without the valuable abilities of brother Ken, serving his second year in Korea for our country. Also, we had two Schnebergers, Ken, the pitcher and Bob, the catcher, who both basically retired from baseball. Talking with Ken Schneberger's younger brother Jim, he stated that Ken was having baseball related health problems and his older brother Bob, from all his hot summer Sundays of catching, decided he had enough. Most of the catching duties were taken over by eighteen year old Carl Schupanitz who had just graduated from Calmar High School. Jim Schneberger, normally at shortstop, also toiled behind the plate for many games in '55. With the two Kens not available, second baseman Romauld Elsbernd and I did almost all of the pitching. Romauld was a neighbor to us less than a half-mile from our farm. In earlier years, as we were growing up, there were many family gatherings, with pick-up ball games happening at every one of the get-togethers. Romauld was a tall, slender right hander, normally the second baseman, who came at the opposing hitters with a side-winder motion that caused his pitches to dive downward, causing lots of ground ball outs. Quiet, with a shy, comforting smile, he continuously provided solid defense while getting many slashing hits to support the Festina offense. Following are some of the write-ups from the Northeast Iowa League games.

FESTINA, ST. LUCAS UNDEFEATED AFTER FIRST TWO WEEKS
Festina and St. Lucas posted their second straight wins in the Northeast Iowa baseball league Sunday. Festina toppled Postville, 15-2 and St. Lucas routed Spillville, 19-1. Romauld Elsbernd was the winning moundsman for Festina. Art Huinker hit a triple for the winners in the fifth.

FESTINA WINS FOURTH STRAIGHT IN NE IOWA
Romauld Elsbernd pitched Festina to its fourth victory without a defeat, an 11-3 triumph over Spillville in the Northeast Iowa League here Sunday. Elsbernd allowed nine

hits as Festina romped. Spillville bunched part of their nine hits in the seventh to score all of its runs.

FESTINA STILL UNDEFEATED
Festina posted its fifth win of the season, downing West Union, 6-1. They climaxed the victory with three runs in the eighth as Norbert Einck doubled with one on and Romauld Elsbernd tripled with one on. Art Huinker, striking out 12, was the winning pitcher.

FESTINA RUNS STRING OF NEI VICTORIES TO SEVEN
Festina registered two wins in two days to run its string of victories to seven in the NEI baseball league Sunday and Monday. The league leaders shut out West Union in a regularly scheduled game called after seven innings Sunday, and defeated Monona, 7-2 Monday in a game that had been rained out earlier in the season.

Two late home runs provided the edge for Festina over Monona, newest member in the league. The victors were trailing, 2-1, when Elsbernd homered in a three-run seventh. Jim Schneberger homered with two on in the ninth.

In Sunday's game, Art Huinker hurled a one-hitter and struck out seven for Festina. Jim Schneberger tripled in the third with two on scoring both runs.

FESTINA DRUBS CASTALIA , 20-5, FOR NINTH STRAIGHT
Festina rolled to its ninth straight victory by scoring a 20-5 victory over Castalia in NEI action, including a 10-run ninth inning. Romauld Elsbernd, Festina hurler, had four for six at the plate, including a three-run double in the fourth. Jerry Schneberger homered in the eighth with no one on for the victors.

1955 witnessed the creation of a baseball night league in northeast Iowa that played all their games on Wednesday nights. It consisted of teams who had lights on their own ball diamonds. Sumner, being one of those towns, asked if I would pitch for them on their Wednesday night games. Write-ups of some of those games follow. Sumner ended up winning the night league and chose that championship as their way into the follow-up Waterloo Courier Tournament and the state AABC tournament. Playing with Festina on Sunday afternoons, they were my team for those two tournament challenges and Sumner knew that.

Playing for the two teams made for a hectic summer if you add working with Dad on the farm during the day besides getting ready for our big August 3

79

wedding event. For all the night league games, Ann always accompanied me. Several of the trips amounted to two-hour drives each way. Game over, now try to stay awake on the way home after pitching the game and working on the farm during the day before and after. Ann's challenge amounted to "keeping me awake" or driving herself. Dad always accepted the responsibility to complete the evening chores, including milking about 35 to 40 cows.

SUMNER 17, WAVERLY 3

Sumner's Cubs scored their first Bremer-Chickasaw Night League victory of the season Wednesday night at Waverly, 17-3 with an exhibition of long-ball hitting that included four home runs and three doubles.

Southpaw hurler, Art Huinker, kept the Bear bats in check after their three-run first inning and yielded only four hits over the six-inning route.

The game opened as a marathon of base hits and runs as the first four Cub batters scored before an out was made. Mel Harm, in the leadoff spot, drew a walk and Whitford bounced a hit over the fence for a ground rule double to leave runners on second and third.

Bob Topp followed with another clothes line double that bounded out of the park over the left center field fence and then the cleanup batter, Jack Soener, powdered a line drive over the right field fence to account for two more runs.

Waverly's three runs came in the bottom of the first inning on two errors, three walks and two hits. Huinker blanked the Bears the rest of the way, striking out a total of 13, only five less than par for the six-inning course.

SUMNER TAKES JANESVILLE IN SEVEN INNINGS

Sumner's Cubs got off to a running start in the Janesville Night League game at Sumner Wednesday night, scoring three runs in the first and then coasting to an 11-1 victory, while southpaw moundsman, Arty Huinker, was fashioning a brilliant one-hitter. The game was called after Janesville had batted in the top of the seventh, with the 10-run rule in effect.

Huinker had a perfect ball game going until he walked Meinders in the fourth inning. Then in the fifth, another walk put Rath on and he scored on Carpenter's single, the only Janesville hit of the game.

Huinker recovered after losing his control momentarily in the fifth and again retired the side in order in the sixth and seventh innings. He struck out nine and walked four with three of those walks coming in the fifth.

Mel Harms and Terry Stevens each had two hits for the Cubs.

SUMNER TAKES OVER SECOND PLACE IN NIGHT LEAGUE

The Sumner Cubs moved into second place in the Bremer-Chickasaw Night League Wednesday on the strength of a 5-1 victory over the Allison Cats.

Southpaw hurler Arty Huinker was on the Cub mound and gave up only five hits in going the route against Allison. Allison's only run in the first inning came on a walk, a single, a sacrifice and an infield out.

Sumner trailed through the first two and a half innings, but moved into the lead in the third on an error, a walk, and three successive singles by Siegfried, Soener and Barnholdt.

Swisher, the Iowa State Teachers' College mound ace stayed on the Cat mound all the way, but was touched for 12 hits and five runs. He walked three and struck out eight. Huinker, an excellent control pitcher, struck out eight and walked only two.

While the baseball games were consuming two days a week, the date of Tuesday, August 3 rapidly approached. Starting with the weekend before and six days following for a short honeymoon trip, baseball took a back seat. The wonderful wedding day itself started with the marriage ceremony at Our Lady of Seven Dolors Catholic Church in Festina at 8:30 in the morning. We were officially hitched. After a full day of celebrating with the many guests from the Thuente and Huinker families as well as other friends (many of them baseball players) and neighbors, we concluded the day with a dance at the Inwood Pavilion in Spillville from 9:00 to 1:00. As mentioned earlier in Chapter One, that was the customary practice in the small communities like Festina. It was after 2:30 in the morning before we reached our motel, having to deal with a few specially-prepared suitcases that could not be found.

At the completion of the six glorious days, I was scheduled to pitch for Monroe, Wisconsin at Milwaukee County Stadium on Tuesday, August 10. Almost daily on the honeymoon, Ann and I would play baseball catch. Following that, I would throw hard against the backstop of a baseball diamond we would try to locate at least every other day. Then some jogging and/or running would follow. In fact, Ann would follow me in our car and she would drive up close behind me to make me run faster, similar to what our coach did in our junior year in high school. Yes, on our honeymoon. Apparently it wasn't enough. A horrendous game was pitched for the Monroe team and they came out on the short end of the score. Teammate Bill Hyland from Loras College took over the pitching chores about the fifth or sixth inning. The Monroe game was part of the National Baseball Congress tourney, this game being part of a single elimination

81

set-up. The playing conditions were unbelievably "ideal", especially the pitcher's mound. No excuses. There will be later opportunities of playing on Milwaukee's big league diamond with more positive results, thankfully. Disregarding the outcome of the game, our honeymoon still lives in our beginning of marriage memories. We did not get very far on our travels, maybe a hundred miles beyond Chicago, when we had intended to reach Niagara Falls. Spending all that time driving to get to that far away destination all of a sudden seemed a foolish waste of time. Enough said.

Back home after the week-long trip, married and together forever, I pitched for Festina, undefeated in the league so far, against second place Volga. The title already in our camp, Volga clobbered my pitching, 8-4. The following week, the tournament important to all baseball leagues in northeast Iowa, the Waterloo Courier Tournament of Champions, opened. Again, Festina, with its fifth consecutive NEI championship under its belt, opened against Winthrop from the Buchanan County League. Only once had we been able to reach the semi-finals of this tournament, that in 1951.

And again, the 1956 tournament efforts by Festina are wrought with problems. Especially one big problem. For the third straight time, their main pitcher doesn't have his good stuff. In just plain English, my pitching was horrible. Only five hits were garnered by Winthrop in five plus innings, but nine, yes, nine walks will ruin any game, especially in that length of time. The box score says that only two of the six runs I gave up were earned, but it was a night not to be remembered. And I felt so bad for my teammates. They looked forward to this tournament and then to pitch the way I did, it was just deplorable.

WINTHROP DROPS FESTINA, 7-3
Winthrop's first round victory over Festina was a come from behind win after Festina scored all three of its runs in a 7-3 loss in the second inning.
The two clubs got only five hits apiece, but Winthrop was the recipient of 11 bases on balls off two Festina pitchers.
The Northeast Iowa Loop champions shut off a Winthrop threat with a third to home to first bases loaded double play and then scored on three singles, a hit batsman, two walks and a sacrifice fly by pitcher Art Huinker. Leo Luzum drove in the other two runs with his bases full single. Les Lammers, a spring graduate of Winthrop High, never was in serious trouble otherwise although he had the help of two double plays.
Winthrop took the lead in the fifth on four unearned runs. Two errors and a walk loaded the bases with Dean Gritton driving in two runs on the only hit of the inning. An infield out and passed ball produced two more runs.

82

Winthrop opened the sixth with a walk and a hit and Festina starter, lefty Art Huinker, who has a perfect record for two seasons on the Loras College pitching staff, retired in favor of Romauld Elsbernd. Elsberned walked two more and gave up two infield hits- - -both as the pitcher slipped while fielding rollers in front of the plate---as Winthrop scored three more runs.

LaVerne Gritton stole home to account for one of the runs.

Leo Luzum and Norb Einck each had two hits for Festina. Einck's two hits included a double. A quick end to another Courier Tournament of Champions effort.

For the first time in Iowa, the American Amateur Baseball Congress (AABC) held a separate tournament to determine the state representative in the Northwest Regional Tournament to be held in Watertown, South Dakota. The change came about primarily by the entrance of a semi-pro league out of the Des Moines area, a league that did not fit into the structure of the Courier's Tournament of Champions in northeast Iowa. Confusion over the new rules for the AABC led to New Hampton's sports writer, Harry Gundacker, in his weekly editorial, addressing these issues, "tongue in cheek." The entire editorial, because of its length, is not included.

THE COMPLICATED ABC SETUP
The Bull Pen by H. Gundacker
Whoever is responsible for the set of rules governing the American Baseball Congress tournament representation, must have put them together on a "Lost Weekend." It would take all the lawyers in Philadelphia to interpret them---and chances are, they'd end up in an argument. A sheer masterpiece of enigmatic confusion.

The generally accepted thought all along was that the league leaders were to represent their leagues, or if not the leaders, any team the league designated. A few weeks back they pop up with a demand that each team designate the league they intended to represent. Let's take a look at a couple of examples of the confusion this premature designation has caused.

Merchant management definitely has a shot for both their league titles and as the picture brightened in both races, hopes rose that if we won them both the team could choose to represent the stronger of the two leagues---the B-C nite league. The reason for this being that a draft of 3 "battery men" (and believe me they use that term loosely) could be picked from other teams in the league. So what happens? You have to make your choice in the middle of the league race—so naturally the

83

management chose to represent the Tri-County day league---one they felt more confident of winning.

> *What it amounts to is that next week will be a very interesting baseball week. A possible six games in nine days, with the ABC berth at stake three times and the B-C nite league championship twice. It we win it all (and the odds are against it) the Merchants should be established as undisputed kings of northeast Iowa baseball. And to make that definite we could shoot the Festina ball team and drown Artie Huinker . . You've had it . . .*

Well, the latter didn't happen. It is not known if Harry Gundacker was aware of my lack of swimming ability.

The new AABC set-up actually opened its schedule of games while the Courier tournament finals were still being played. It caused many teams to really scramble for players, especially pitchers. Festina was an example. We picked up pitchers Jim Rima from Postville and Tom Weston from West Union and catcher Don Hubacher from Monona, all teams in the NEI league. Add to the need for pitching, the AABC tournament is also a double elimination arrangement.

Our first opponent in the AABC was the New Hampton Merchants, home of sportswriter Harry Gundacker and author of the above article.

> *FESTINA WINS AABC OPENER OVER NEW HAMPTON, 5-0*
> *Festina's opening round win came behind the two-hit pitching of Art Huinker as his teammates picked up two in the first and one each in the third, fourth and sixth. Huinker struck out 13 in the seven-inning game.*

Finally, after three terrible outings, Festina could count on me again. We also beat Loras College teammate, Dick Winter, in the process. He is an excellent right-hander, strong, tall, and probably throws one of the heaviest balls I have ever experienced. I don't mean the ball is heavy. It is just the way he throws it that causes that feeling when your bat connects with his pitch. Dick, in four years at Loras, lost only one ball game. We do get to see each other once in a while. He ended up in Omaha, Nebraska, but for a short while he and his wife Ellen lived in Dubuque and the four of us would play bridge together.

And, as per Gundacker's quote in his editorial, he should have gotten rid of the Festina team before the AABC tourney. New Hampton was already down one game.

In game two of the AABC, our opposition was Petersburg of the Delaware County League. Festina picked up Jim Rima, pitcher from Postville in the NEI, but Petersburg jumped on us for four runs in the first two innings.

84

Except for the sixth when we scored three times, we did not threaten the pitches of Gary Bush, a Colesburg high school grad. A grand slam by Bob Krapfl in the sixth had built the lead to 8-0 before our three-run sixth. The coming summer, when I played for Dyersville, Bob Krapfl was a teammate and a very good hitter.

Dick Wright, Loras teammate, exhibited his athleticism in this game. He put on the catcher's tools and caught the game for Petersburg. Reviewing Loras games in our freshman year, Dick was listed as a catcher/outfielder.

Festina's third-round game brought the Winthrop team that beat us in the Courier Tournament of Champions to the diamond as our opposition.

> *FESTINA TOPS WINTHROP; PETERSBURG LOSES*
> *FOR THE FIRST TIME*
> *Petersburg, defeated for the first time Friday, and one-time loser Festina play at 2 p.m. Sunday with the winner meeting Sumner at 8:15 Sunday in the final game of the Sumner sectional playoffs.*
> *Petersburg suffered its first defeat of the double elimination tourney Friday, taking a 13-2 pounding by undefeated Sumner in a game called after five innings because of the eight-run rule.*
> *Festina remained in the running for the championship by stopping a Winthrop sixth-inning rally to win 7-6.*
> *Festina shot into a 7-0 lead over Winthrop after the first four innings before Winthrop picked up a run in the fifth and five in the 6th.*
> *In the sixth, Dean Gritton and Tom Hearn singled, Harlan Halford doubled and Festina pitchers Art Huinker and Tom Weston walked four and hit one batter.*

Bases on balls again hurt us against Winthrop, just as it had in the Courier tournament loss. Again this time, Winthrop collected only five hits. But we hung on for the win.

> *FESTINA KNOCKS OUT PETERSBURG; SUMNER*
> *THEN BEATS FESTINA*
> *Festina earned its way into the championship finals by eliminating Petersburg 4-0 in the afternoon game---but Sumner ended Festina's ABC district championship hopes by winning the title 13-2 in the second game Sunday.*
> *In Festina's victory, Romauld Elsbernd was in trouble in almost every inning but managed to pull through with a six-hit shutout as Petersburg lost its second game in the double elimination tournament.*

85

Jim Redel paced Festina with three hits in five trips and each of his hits came on the first pitch. He had two singles and a triple.

Sumner, recent winner of the Waterloo Courier Tournament of Champions, ran off with its fourth victory without a loss in the tourney. Festina scored a run in the first and again in the second off Bob Boderman, but after that the lefthander couldn't be touched for a score. He struck out 10, loaded the bases on three hits in the sixth with two out but Festina failed to score.

In the game against Petersburg, Festina collected 12 hits but could only put together four single runs in the first, second, third and fifth. LeRoy Willenbring, another teammate next year on the Dyersville team, pitched into the ninth inning for Petersburg.

Sumner jumped on me for four runs in the first inning. After that, we held them scoreless until the sixth. Meantime, the score had changed and was 4-2. Then the roof fell in. Elsbernd, who had pitched nine innings in the afternoon, relieved in the 6th, Jim Rima relieved in the seventh. By the end of the seventh, Sumner had gained a seven-run lead. Jim Redel, playing shortstop for Festina in the Sumner game, was the current high school boys' basketball coach at Calmar High School.

Festina played a make-up game with Postville after the ABC tournament and won easily, 22-4. Romauld Elsbernd and I shared pitching duties. Jim Schneberger collected two home runs while Leo Luzum and Romauld Elsbernd each had one homer. Our league record ended at 13 wins and 1 loss. Volga City was second at 10 wins and four losses.

As Sumner prepared for their trip to South Dakota, they again asked if I would accompany them. Despite the poor performances of the previous weeks, maybe they had hope. But the trip was short-lived. After winning their opener over South Dakota state champion Eureka, 11-2 behind the pitching of John Chezik, the Cubs were blasted by Seattle 17-0. Sumner collected only two safeties in the seven-inning affair, cut short by the eight-run rule. Bob Boderman took the loss.

In game three, on the brink of elimination, Sumner battled back. Behind the pitching of tall right hander, Darold Swisher, despite nine walks, the Cubs were tied 2-2 going into the sixth. Omaha then exploded for six runs. Chezik replaced Swisher, issued three more free passes and in the eighth Omaha scored two additional runs and end the game again by the eight-run rule. Final score: 10-2.

For one of the first times in my life, Sumner put me into the line-up to play first base and bat lead-off. I managed to pick up two base hits from that position in the line-up but neither figured in any scoring. Terry Stevens, our Fayette nemesis from high school days, played both infield and outfield for Sumner. He was also in college at this time.

In the Omaha game, their catcher for the Sumner game was Bob Gibson. He had pitched the previous game against Portland, Oregon in a losing cause. Thank heavens.

It is not important what inning the following incident occurred but Gibby was at bat. He swung mightily at a pitch and lined a shot one bounce to Mel Harms at shortstop. He swung so hard that he fell down at the plate after hitting the shot to Harms. Mel saw that he had fallen down so he just lobbed the ball to first. In doing so, I was pulled off the base a few feet. By the time I caught the ball, unbelievably it became a race to see who was going to get to first base, Gibby or myself. He had picked himself up and, in his usual competitive spirit, came roaring down the line. We got the out but we were amazed at how fast he raced to get to the first base bag.

Sumner must have realized my lack of success on the mound and therefore did not attempt to put me in to pitch. The last three weeks of the season, baseball-wise, were not pretty. Three straight losses, all of them horrible pitching performances, brought me down to earth and wondering why my dream of professional baseball had exploded. Never had I lost three games in a row. No further comment.

In the meantime, we are back at Loras College , now a junior, and loving married life in a small apartment at 258 Bluff Street in Dubuque. Ann had started a job at Roshek's Department Store and I was preparing to start the 5:30 to 11:30 part-time shift at Dubuque Packing Company. Oh, yes, I had to go to classes too.

A MARRIED JUNIOR

Now married and sharing a small two-bedroom apartment across the street from the St. Raphael's Rectory on Bluff Street, the third year of experiencing Loras College education and Loras College baseball opened. With new responsibilities, Loras helped me find a part-time job at Dubuque Packing Company, working from five–thirty until eleven-thirty Monday through Friday evenings. The pay for 1955 and for a small-town, rural guy was excellent. Memories do fade but $5.95 an hour sounds right. On a Sunday before Christmas, my shift was called in and we received triple pay. Imagine how that was appreciated in meeting expenditures right before the Christmas celebrations that are so much a part of the life of both Ann's and my families. Also a recollection of this overtime was my Mother's reaction. She was very concerned. How could I have felt comfortable about working on a Sunday? That symbolizes the strength of our Catholic faith in my home growing up.

A family situation existed that made that Sunday's work valuable. Ann had announced that she was pregnant in late October and added responsibilities faced us. But the exciting joy that we both shared over upcoming parenthood far overshadowed that added weighty responsibility. A full time academic load also required considerable time obviously but all these factors seemed worthwhile for the life that the two of us were sharing.

The first two to three months of working at Dubuque Pack placed me at a building removed from the actual building that all Dubuque area people usually picture when they reflect on this highly successful business developed by the Wahlert family. A side product of the Dubuque packing company was fertilizer made from parts of the hog and cattle meat processing operation. Work on the bagging and stacking of the fertilizer, making it ready for shipping was a two-man operation for six hours each evening. The partner who shared that work with me is one of the finest human beings I have had the privilege to know and to play baseball against. We also refereed baseball (even some football) games together in the years ahead. Many of you know and respect him. It was Tom Breitbach. Believe it or not, we were the only two people working in this huge building. No supervision. We determined our lunch break. During that break, we brought our baseball gloves along and played catch (inside the building), worked on and discussed pitching with each other most evenings. What a joy that was. And we did keep those breaks to the suggested length of time. We appreciated the opportunity given to us. The enjoyment came to an end when colder weather

88

prohibited working in the building. The rest of the year, until baseball season started in the middle of February, the kill floor was my workplace, much less desirable but still much appreciated.

Season number three (1956) and preparation for it began in the third week of February. The players not playing basketball (at least six baseball players were on the basketball team, three of them starters) started working on their own several weeks earlier. A write-up in the Lorian announced that 75 candidates reported for the first practice. Key players lost from the previous season were infielder Bill Howie, right hand pitcher Bill Kezman who had signed a professional contract with the Philadelphia Phillies, senior catcher Bob Kaliban and sophomore catcher Art Whipple, who discontinued his education at Loras.

Even though this writing is in a small way autobiographical- - -meaning it is based on reality and that it all actually happened- - -the following story is about 50 percent true and 50 percent fiction. But for the Loras baseball team and its players who really enjoyed life together, it is humorous. One of the students who enrolled at Loras (I believe it was 1955, but possibly 1956) was Frank Quilici from the Minneapolis/St. Paul area. Does that name ring a bell? He later played second base for the Minnesota Twins, then after his active playing days, actually managed the Twins. My high school catcher for four years at Dyersville Xavier and later at Loras College, Steve Tierschel, knew him well. He was in infielder, and obviously a good one. Now for the fiction. He was one of the seventy-five candidates. But as he was working out for the team and for an infield position, he saw that the entire infield, including the first baseman, was no taller than 5 foot, 9 inches. Quilici was about 6 foot tall, and felt he was too tall for this infield and decided to withdraw from school. That is the fiction part. Reality explains the situation this way: He came to Loras thinking it was many miles south of the Twin Cities and would mean much warmer weather. But by the time he had lived through two tough winter months in Dubuque, he decided that the Twin Cities was a much better place for him and he withdrew. The latter is the true story.

The 1956 baseball season for the Duhawks was scheduled to open again with a single game against the Redmen from Winona St. Mary's, the same team we opened with the previous year. The following article appeared in the local Telegraph-Herald

> ### LORAS OPENS SEASON; ST. MARY'S NINE HERE
> *Lefty Art Huinker, Calmar, Iowa junior, has been named as starting hurler for Loras College Sunday when the Duhawks take on a powerful St. Mary's of Winona, Minn. nine on Keane Field, starting at 1:30 p.m.*
> *The season opener for the Duhawks finds Huinker shooting for his tenth straight collegiate win without a blemish on his pitching career. The blond-haired chucker registered*

89

three wins in his freshman year and blazed his way to a 6-0 mark last spring.

Waiting in relief will be another lefty, Pat Kapsch and two right-handed tossers, Dick Winter and Jim Swann. Bill Hyland, right-handed number two pitcher on the club, is currently out of duty with a sore shoulder, but is expected to return sometime next week.

The rest of the Loras lineup has five veterans and three freshmen. Vets include Dick (Rocky) Schiltz at first, Joe Ottavi at second, Dick Wiley at third, Dick Wright in left and Romie Gales in right. Frosh starting Sunday are Bob Willhite in center, Gene Potts at short, and Terry Brennan behind the plate.

Coach Vince Dowd has listed four utility players for reserves Sunday; they include Jack New, first baseman, Bob Wolfe, utility infielder, Duke Prazen, utility outfielder, and Jack Schrandt, catcher.

The Redmen have 11 returning lettermen, including four pitchers. The big loss is pitcher Joe Shrake who is ineligible for conference games. Shrake was undefeated in college until he was downed by Huinker last season.

The game was played as scheduled in somewhat typical Iowa weather for so early in the spring. It turned out to be a much easier contest than expected. Again, a write-up from the Telegraph-Herald

DUHAWKS WIN, 9-1

Loras College's lefty Art Huinker won his tenth consecutive game without a loss in college ball Sunday afternoon as the Duhawks opened their season with an easy 9-1 win over St. Mary's of Winona, Minn.

Loras' nine runs came on seven hits and three walks, while the Redmen tagged Huinker for just three hits, one in the third, and a pair in the fourth, all singles. The port-side chucker walked two and fanned three.

Dick Wright, left fielder and returning batting champion from the 1955 Loras club, paced the hitters with two safeties in three trips. One of Wright's hits was a double.

Catcher Bill Leonard, right fielder Romie Gales, center fielder Dick Schiltz, and second sacker Joe Ottavi each hit doubles, while shortstop Gene Potts had a single to account for Loras' seven hits.

The lone score for the losers came in the fourth when left fielder Dick Kuehl reached base on an error and moved around on a pair of singles.

The game, played in near-freezing temperatures, was part of Loras College's Open House celebration for high school seniors.

Following the St. Mary's victory, the Duhawks put their hitting shoes on in defeating Iowa State Teachers College 8-1 and 14-0. Those games were played at Cedar Falls. Joe Ottavi, not really known for his power, took advantage of a stiff wind blowing out and blasted two homers in game two. Returning home, Winona State became the fourth victim, a 5-2 win for the Duhawks. A brief write-up of those three games follows:

DUHAWK NINE SPILLS WINONA; CLIP ISTC TWICE

The Duhawks blasted 27 runs allowing only 3, in defeating Iowa State Teachers College twice and Winona State once. The Hilltoppers looked needle-point sharp, minus their brilliant right-handed pitcher Bill Hyland.

In their most recent encounter, April 15, Loras clipped Winona State, 5-2. Dick Winter allowed seven hits in going the distance for his first victory of the year. The tall right hander fanned eight, while giving up only three walks.

The big sticks for the Duhawks included Dick Wright, Tiny Potts and Rocky Schiltz. Dick Wright coupled a pair of singles with a double in tabulating four RBI's. Potts had three hits and Schiltz picked up a double and a single. The Duhawks scored a run in the first, two in the third and single tallies in the sixth and eighth frames.

Last Friday and Saturday, April 12 and 14, found the Duhawks at Cedar Falls, Ia., where they annihilated Iowa State Teachers 8-1 and 14-0.

A pleasant surprise for Coach Dowd was the pitching efforts of Pat Kapsch, Albert City, Ia. freshman. It was all Kapsch in the second game with the Teachers. His six-hitter introduced him as a prominent member of the polished Duhawk pitching staff.

While Kapsch, a lefty, was puzzling Tutor hitters, Loras showered four I.S.T.C. hurlers for 19 hits. Among this barrage of base-knocks were two homers by Dick Wright and Dick Wiley.

In Friday's contest, Art Huinker posted his second victory of the season, as he hurled a three-hitter. The slick southpaw struck out 12 and walked just two to gain his 11th victory without a loss.

Joe Ottavi had a perfect day at the plate, as he belted four safeties, two being home runs. Romie Gales and Sam Azzinaro also homered.

91

Next, the Duhawks had a three-game road trip over a weekend, playing at LaCrosse on Saturday morning and Minnesota on Saturday afternoon as well as Sunday afternoon. The team lodged at a dorm on the St. Mary's campus Saturday night. After the first four victories, the Duhawks were batting .336, with Dick Wright leading the way.

> *DUHAWKS SPLIT ON SATURDAY; BOW TO St. MARY'S ON SUNDAY*
>
> *Art Huinker spun a seven-hitter to give the Loras College Duhawks a 6-2 victory over Winona State at Winona on Saturday afternoon.*
>
> *In the first half of their two-state double header Saturday morning, the Duhawks took their first defeat, 4-3 from La Crosse State College in Wisconsin.*
>
> *Jack New supported Huinker's pitching with a second inning homer. The Duhawks pounded out 11 hits including two each by Joe Ottavi, Gene Potts, Rocky Schiltz and New.*
>
> *Loras left eight men on base against La Crosse, losing the game despite outhitting the host team, 11 to 7. Rocky Schiltz belted a three-run homer for all the Duhawk runs in the fourth inning. La Crosse rallied in the fifth and won on a three-run homer by Richardson. Jim Swann was on the mound for Loras, later being relieved by Dick Winter.*
>
> *In the last of the three road trip encounters, the Duhawks fell victim to the seven hit pitching of St. Mary's right hander, Szumlas. The crafty moundsman also contributed a homer and a single in four tries.*
>
> *Loras scored once in the first inning on a walk to Ottavi, and a double by leftfielder Wright. The Duhawks tallied in the fifth and seventh frames also, but in the process stranded 17 men. Tiny Potts continued his hitting pace in collecting a pair of hits in five times to the plate. Dick Wright had a double and a single in four tries.*

Even though I pitched the Saturday afternoon victory, I don't have many recollections of the game. Looking back at the box score, two Winona players became future teammates playing semi-pro baseball. Fred Hoeft played left field for Rochester, Minnesota during the 1959 summer when we won the Southern Minnesota Baseball League and Lee Paul, opposing pitcher, was a teammate when Soldiers Grove, Wisconsin went to the state baseball tournament in Milwaukee County Stadium in the early '60's.

The St. Mary's game provided me only an opportunity to pinch-hit in the ninth inning, yet there are some vivid pictures of the loss. First of all, the last two or three innings were played in snowy conditions. Needless to say, it was not very comfortable sitting through the game. Remembering the playing field, it was in

92

wide-open spaces with no outfield fence. There were several balls really blasted a great distance by Duhawk hitters that would have been home runs in most fenced-in parks; here they were just long fly ball outs. Dick Wright, particularly, blasted one that we all thought was over the outfielders, even as deep as they were playing. But no cigar.

The next three games of the schedule were rained out as was typical of many of the scheduled games that spring. The next game played was against Knox College. Once that game was played, three more games for Friday, Saturday and Sunday were rained out. The Knox contest proved to be one of those hi-lite reel games. The strikeout record of 17 from the freshmen year was raised to nineteen. Write-up follows. Team record for the year stands at 6 wins, 2 losses.

> ### ART HUINKER FANS 19
> *Art Huinker, port-sided pitcher from Calmar, Iowa, upped his own modern strikeout record at Loras College Wednesday, as he fanned 19 Knox College batters to take a 6-0 decision for the Duhawks and his 13th consecutive win without a loss in college ball.*
>
> *The 5-8, 165-pound junior walked just one man and allowed five scattered hits, four singles and a double. Only once was he in trouble. In the seventh frame, he walked one hitter and was tagged for the double, but then tightened to strike out the next trio of Knox players to face him.*
>
> *Two years ago, Huinker downed 17 batters in a single game with Upper Iowa to set the modern record which he held until facing Knox.*
>
> *The Duhawks were able to pin three Knox hurlers for just four hits but capitalized on seven errors and nine walks. Junior Bob Wolfe, third sacker, led Loras' hitting with a double and a single in four trips while first sacker Jack New and catcher Bill Leonard each connected for doubles.*
>
> *The Duhawks picked up single runs in the second and fifth innings and used two walks, Wolfe's single and Leonard's double to pile up four runs in the seventh. Loras now had a 6-2 record for the season with single games scheduled at Great Lakes on Saturday and Sunday.*

The entire schedule for the week-end following the Knox success was rained out. We started playing the Saturday tilt with Great Lakes Naval Station. It was only three days rest for me but we played into the fourth inning, leading 1-0, when the game was called. Coach Frank Noonan always enjoyed sharing a Gene "Tiny" Potts story about that game played in a foggy, heavy mist before it was called.

93

Tiny had reached first base. Whether he had singled or walked I don't recall but it is not important for Coach's story. Great Lakes had a left hand pitcher with a good pick-off move to first base. Making a good move, the pitcher came very close to picking Tiny off but the umpire ruled that he had gotten back in safely. On the very next pitch, another pick-off attempt was made and on another close play, the umpire called Tiny out. Tiny disputed the call and begged Coach Noonan to also argue for him. Coach Noonan responded by telling Tiny he could have been called out on the first pick-off and if he wasn't sharp enough to learn from the first pick-off, he deserved to be called out the second time. That exemplifies the fun we had as a team playing baseball at Loras during those years. Coach Frank Noonan utilized a cool sense of humor throughout the four years he served as Coach Dowd's assistant. Coach Noonan also carried high respect from his teaching of economics. He and his brother, Gerard (Bud) Noonan, were outstanding supporters of the sports program at Loras College.

The following Friday we traveled to Beloit, Wisconsin to play Beloit. Another victory, 5-1. We had only four hits, but 6 Beloit errors took care of the rest of the victory. Thirteen strikeouts this time but I finally got a hit myself, a double.

DUHAWKS TOPPLE BELOIT BEHIND HUINKER, 5 TO 1

Loras College managed only four hits off Bill Wagner but defeated Beloit, 5-1 here Friday afternoon.

The victory gave the Duhawks a 7-2 record for the season, and Art Huinker personally chalked up his fifth straight win of the year.

Loras' hitting did little to help in the victory. The Duhawks jumped off to a 3-0 lead in the first inning on two errors, a walk, a sacrifice fly and a single by Jack New. That was all the scoring for Loras until the ninth when another error and a walk led to the final two runs. This time no hits figured in the scoring.

However, after Beloit managed a single tally in the second inning, Huinker was complete master of the game. The smooth southpaw allowed just four singles while fanning 13 and walking three. Huinker, undefeated in the college ranks, has now posted 58 strikeouts in his five games pitched this season.

Dick Wright garnered half of the Duhawks' four hits with a pair of singles. Huinker had the only extra base hit, a double.

More bad weather and more rainouts followed before we got to play Platteville and our eighth win. This was one of those days where defeat #1 came very close. Leading 5-3 going into the ninth and another thirteen strikeouts, I was relieved in

94

the ninth after Platteville scored two runs to tie the score. Loras scored in the eleventh to win it. Terry Brennan, a reserve catcher from New Orleans, Louisiana drove in the winner. I remember very vividly that I could not get Jim Timmons out that day, primarily because I couldn't get the pitch inside against him. I think he had three extra base hits, including a questionable drive that was called a ground-rule double because it went over the short picket fence set up in right field. He hit it close to the end of the fence where the umpire had to rule on whether it was a ground-rule double or a home run. In the ninth inning of that same game Dick Wright threw a runner out at home and "Garny" always claimed that because of his great throw I did not suffer my first loss. He might have been right.

LORAS NIPS PIONEERS

A pinch single by Terry Brennan in the bottom of the eleventh inning gave the Loras College Duhawks their eighth win of the season Tuesday as they nipped Platteville State 6-5. Brennan singled home first sacker Rocky Schiltz who walked as the lead-off man.

Platteville tied the contest in the top of the ninth with a two-run rally after trailing from the third inning. The Pioneers had picked up single runs in the third, fourth and sixth innings. Loras scored three runs in the third, one in the fourth and one in the seventh.

Right fielder Romie Gales was the big gun for the Duhawks with three hits in six trips. The win was credited to right-hander Bill Hyland who relieved starter Art Huinker with two out in the ninth frame. Huinker had fanned 13 Pioneers before retiring.

Following is a brief summary of the 1956 season, a season that saw the Duhawk nine lose almost half of their schedule because of rainy weather. The write-up appeared in the Loras Lorian as well as the Telegraph Herald. The third Loras season was history. In the summer of '56 because Ann and I were staying in Dubuque, Dyersville asked me to pitch for them. That will appear in the next chapter covering some of the Dyersville baseball activity. In addition to that commitment, we were going to play enough games with hometown Festina to be eligible for end-of-the-season tourney play. It was also the summer for the birth of Terry, our first child. Sounds busy, and it was.

DUHAWKS CLOSE SEASON; BEST IN HISTORY

A veteran Duhawk nine turned in Loras College's best baseball record during the 1956 season as they won nine games and lost two. The two miscues were by identical 4-3 scores to La Crosse State and St. Mary's of Winona, Minnesota.

Lefty Art Huinker, Calmar, Ia. junior, finished his third year of college without suffering a loss. As a freshman, he won three and lost none. Six straight wins and no losses were added

95

to his record during his second year. This year he posted five more wins and no losses.

Huinker appeared in six games, pitched a total of 51 plus innings, gave up just 28 hits and 17 walks. He had ten runs scored on him while fanning a total of 72 opposing batters. The 5-8 hurler holds Loras College's modern strikeout record for a single game at 19. This spring he broke his own record, set at 17 two years ago. Red Faber, former major league player and ex-Duhawk, downed 24 in the early teens.

Dick Winter and Bill Hyland, both right-handers, went undefeated for the Duhawks along with Huinker. Winter racked up two victories over the slate, while Hyland was credited with a single win. Pat Kapsch, a port-side hurler, and Jim Swann, righthander, absorbed the only Loras defeats, one apiece, but Kapsch was able to balance his ledger with one victory.

Eight homers were hit by Loras this year. Second-sacker Joe Ottavi was the only player to hit a pair, while Rocky Schiltz, Jack New, both first basemen, Romie Gales, Dick Wright, Sam Azzinaro, outfielders, and Dick Wiley, third baseman , each collected a single fourbagger.

For the second straight year, it was Wright carrying the big bat as he led the RBI department with 13 and finished third in average with .371. New copped the batting crown with a .417 average while Bob Wolfe, utility third baseman, was second with a .384 average. Schiltz followed Wright with .368 and three others, Gene Potts, shortstop, Terry Brennan, catcher and Swann finished with a .300 plus averages.

From a won-loss perspective, it was a successful season. From the number of rainouts, allowing us to play only eleven out of the scheduled eighteen games, it was a disappointment. Once again, our offensive attack provided strong support for the pitchers. Often, victory was made easy. And you will be amazed at the number of Loras baseball players who were picked up by Dubuque County semi-pro teams looking for help in all the invitational tournaments.

A WHITEHAWK NOW

Now three very satisfying years completed at Loras. We completed our first year still in the same apartment located on the second floor at 258 Bluff Street in Dubuque. We applied for and were fortunate to land a summer job with Geisler Brothers Roofing Company located in downtown Dubuque. That meant we were going to stay in Dubuque for the summer preparing for our fourth and final year at Loras. Also number one addition to our family was expected in early July.

When the Dyersville Whitehawks' manager, Tom Jenk, contacted us to pitch for them for the summer of 1956, we were interested. They were one of the better town baseball teams around and offered a strong challenge competition-wise. But Festina still was on our minds for baseball as well. After arranging for financial coverage for mileage back and forth to Dyersville on crooked old Highway 20, we accepted the Dyersville opportunity with the understanding that we would still play sufficient games with Festina so that we would be eligible to play with them in the tournaments in northeast Iowa if our home town qualified. At that time, the semi-pro league in which Dyersville competed did not participate in the big Waterloo Courier tournament.

One of the first Sunday afternoons after the Loras College baseball season ended, Ann and I drove to Ryan, Iowa, for an opportunity to watch the Whitehawks play a ball game and get to meet some of the team members. They won handily. The Sunday afternoon cruise built some acceptance with the new teammates and the hectic summer began.

The Dyersville Whitehawk baseball year, as well as Festina baseball in 1956, brought some fantastic experiences that stay front and center in our baseball highlights. Most of those highlights related to the tournaments that each of the two teams participated in. For the Whitehawks in '56, there were four local tournaments, held in Monticello, Worthington, Cascade and Dyersville. Probably the key factor that keeps the interest in town team baseball so strong in Dubuque County and the immediate surrounding area is the opportunity for the area teams, whether having a good season or not, to participate in these local tournaments with a chance of being a champion. And fans continue to maintain continued interest in their local teams and support the tournament setup. Even though the interest has diminished drastically from the '56 season, it is sufficient to make them financially feasible. An example of the difference is the 4,000 plus fans for each of the final two nights for the Dyersville Commercial Club Tournament versus several hundred in recent years. Today, twice as many tournaments are

97

held, giving local teams even more opportunity to break through, though certain teams tend to still dominate each year. But exceptions do happen. Baseball games, like any sport, are played to determine the winner. One never knows when that upset occurs. And personal memory can vouch for that.

Dyersville's manager, Tom Jenk, is a baseball legend for the Dubuque County area. A Dyersville native, he has been associated with the game now for nearly sixty years. Besides high school ball, then college ball, all the while, being a member of the Whitehawks, he still assists his highly successful son, Tom Junior, who coaches baseball for Beckman High School. Three times state champions, the baseball program at Beckman is considered one of the best in the entire state of Iowa.

Tom himself was a very successful manager for the Dyersville town team. He always had a solid team ready when a new season rolled around, including getting strong pitching help for the team in the likes of Jim McAndrew from the Lost Nation, Iowa area, later a major league pitcher and also Eddie Watt from the Iowa City area, who also later pitched in the majors. There was always a full slate of both league games and non-league games with top teams in the area as well as participation in all the local tournaments. Besides that, he continuously hit for a high average himself year after year. The team proved very competitive continuously under his leadership.

Even though the Dyersville team played over 40 games yearly, we will just present a few write-ups of the non-tournament games. I have not bothered to put these into any sequence of the order in which they were played. The non-tournament write-ups come from the Dubuque Telegraph Herald or the Dyersville Commercial. Because these write-ups were cut out of newspapers back in the 1950's, the specific paper is uncertain.

DYERSVILLE NIPS RYAN NINE, 4-1
Ryan, Ia. --Dyersville scored three times in the ninth inning to defeat Ryan, 4-1, here Wednesday behind the seven-hit pitching of Art Huinker.

A walk and singles by Paul Krapfl, Ned Walling and Ray Olberding produced the three runs. Dyersville had scored first in the sixth.

Ryan got its lone marker on two hits in the ninth. Huinker fanned 14 in gaining the victory. Don Recker took the loss for Ryan.

WHITE HAWKS TRIUMPH, 19-5
Dyersville, Ia. –The Dyersville White Hawks went on a batting rampage Thursday night, and when the dust cleared they had beaten Independence, 19-5, swatting out 16 hits.

Leroy Willenbring had three for three, Tom Jenk had
two triples and a double and Art Huinker also had three hits.

DYERSVILLE RIPS MONTICELLO, 10-2
Monticello, Ia. –The Dyersville Whitehawks ran their
consecutive game winning streak to six with a 10-2 win over
Monticello Sunday.
Tom Jenk with a double and two singles led the assault
on losing pitcher Wally Krause. Art Huinker, Paul Krapfl and
Dick Mescher each hit safely twice for the winners while
George Neiters and Jim Russell had two apiece for Monticello.
Earl Lampe and Huinker combined to strike out 14
batters for Dyersville. Huinker fanned eight of the nine batters
he faced.

Dick Mescher, the catcher for Dyersville in 1956, was also a catcher for the Loras Duhawk baseball team. Dick grew up in Dyersville, served two years in the military, before coming back to obtain his college education. The two of us will, ten years later, become part of the newly-opened Beckman High School which we will talk about later.

Earl Lampe, the other pitcher in the Monticello game, is a left-hander also. Years and years later, Earl and I, as grandparents, met frequently at student programs put on at St. Columbkille's Catholic Elementary School in Dubuque.

WHITEHAWKS HAVE SLUG-FEST SUNDAY AT
COLESBURG
Timely hitting, good fielding, and a neat pitching job
by Art Huinker helped the Dyersville Whitehawks to their
eleventh straight win, a 14-2 romp over Colesburg, at the
Colesburg diamond Sunday. The Whitehawks season record of
11-0 represents the top mark of any semi-pro club in the state.
Dyersville held a slim 4-2 lead at the end of seven innings of
play but a three run outburst in the eighth and a seven run
deluge in the ninth provided an ample margin of victory.
Ned Walling smashed a two-run homer to right
centerfield to highlight the Whitehawks' eighth inning outburst.
Two errors, a pair of walks, and hits by the three Krapfls and
Tom Jenk accounted for their seven runs in the final frame.
Colesburg scored their only runs in the sixth on a
double by Rollie Sampson, a triple by Robin Tangeman, and a
single by Rich Sampson. Two spectacular catches by leftfielder
Don Lakeman and a fine play by Ray Olberding stopped
Colesburg's final bid for victory in the ninth.

99

The Whitehawks' lone error came in the third when catcher Dick Mescher dropped a third strike. Meanwhile Huinker set Colesburg down on five hits. He displayed pinpoint control in striking out 10 without issuing a walk. Huinker has walked only 3 men in 31 innings. He has struck out 31 over the same span to lead the Whitehawks in that department.

Brothers Rich and Rollie Sampson from Colesburg were members of a high school team in this tiny town that terrorized high school baseball teams for several years. When Ann and I and family moved to Dyersville five years later, Rollie was playing right field for the Whitehawks. There never was a ball game that Rollie played in, where he didn't work his hardest to be the best player he could be. That is the only way he knew. For that reason, teammates enjoyed having him on their team. A simple sports phrase fits Rollie. "He came to play."

His brother Rich was the pitcher in the family. He was the leader for his high school for four years. When he graduated, Colesburg had another top-notch hurler named Gary Bush. Colesburg was one of those small towns known for their baseball, similar to Festina, to Norway, and to Bancroft. All are proud of their baseball heritage. We find one major difference between these examples. Festina did not have a high school team. Actually, five starters on the Festina team from 1946 through 1956 did not even attend high school.

The write-up on the Colesburg game stated that the only error of the game was a dropped third strike by Dick Mescher. It would be my guess that the batter swung at a very wild pitch that Dick couldn't corral. Dick was too good a catcher to just drop the third strike. Also, the name, Don Lakeman, popped up for some defensive plays in that game. Don and his wife, Mary Ellen, were one of the couples that befriended Ann and I, both in the summer of '56 and again in 1961. Good friends.

WHITEHAWKS SPILL MONTICELLO HERE FRIDAY NIGHT, 7-1
Amazin' Art Huinker fashioned a four-hitter, struck out 13, didn't issue a walk, and collected 2 hits himself to lead the Dyersville Whitehawks to a 7-1 triumph over Monticello at Dyersville Park Friday.
Second-baseman Paul Krapfl and leftfielder Dick Wright teamed up with Huinker to garner six of the nine hits that the Whitehawks were able to muster off the slants of Chaplin and Lubben. All three picked up two hits in four trips.
Huinker upped his strikeout total to 64 as he notched his fourth win of the season. He has not walked a man in his last 20 innings on the mound and has given up only 3 bases on balls all season. In addition, the Loras College star is the Whitehawks' top sticker with a .460 average.

100

Outfielder Dick Wright's name should strike a familiar chord. The star athlete, out of Garnavillo High School, is in the same grade with me at Loras College and has been among the hitting leaders at Loras College.

In the meantime, the Cascade Reds gave the Whitehawks their first regular season loss by the score of 3 to 1. Sal Willenbring pitched a strong game for Dyersville and only allowed four hits, walked two and struck out seven. The Whitehawks had seven hits but could not put them together for a score.

WHITEHAWKS WHIP VOLGA CITY IN RAIN
Art Huinker hurled a one-hitter but faced only 15
batters to lead the Hawks to a 2-0 win over Volga City in a
contest halted at the end of four and one-half innings because of
rain at Dyersville Park, Tuesday evening, July 2.
Huinker didn't issue a walk and sent 10 batters down
swinging. Volga's only hit came in the fourth when lead-off
man Dick Heiden belted a double. He took third on an error by
the catcher, but was nailed at the plate on an attempted steal.
The lefthander struck out the last five hitters to face him.

About one year ago, hometown Festina played against the same team at Volga City, and they hit the ball all over the park against me. It was part of my losing streak right after Ann and I were married. Might there have been some motivation to gain revenge.

Another Loras College teammate, Dick Wiley, from Strawberry Point, Iowa, played second base for the Volga City team. He played third base most of the time for us at Loras. After graduation from Loras, he immediately moved out to the west coast and we never had an opportunity to see him again.

Now for the tournament trail, one that started poorly but ended in a roar. After an opening loss in Monticello, the Whitehawks reeled off 12 consecutive tournament victories to capture the three tournaments in Worthington, Cascade and Dyersville. Quite an accomplishment. That did not happen too often.

As we cover the remainder of the baseball season with the Dyersville Whitehawks in 1956, there is one observation that I would like to stress --- and that is the number of Loras College baseball players that appear in the lineups of teams playing in these local tournaments. In most cases, they are outside players picked up by the local teams to improve their team for the upcoming competition. That supports my belief that Loras College had a very strong team, both offensively and defensively. Very seldom were we held to just a run or two. There were not many errors made per game either.

MEMORABLE IN CASCADE

There's little doubt that Dubuque and surrounding county semi-pro teams looked forward to the wealth of tournament playing opportunities that existed in their area. Dyersville team players certainly did. For the Huinkers, it would be a first experience. For me, the experiences of the Dubqueland Invitational Tournament playing for Festina, and the pitching experience for the Dubuque Merchants in the 1954 summer provided some preparation for what was ahead. These tournaments were a challenge that I found easy to get up for.

The first tournament brought 16 teams, including the host, to Monticello. Farley provided the opposition for the Whitehawks in the opening round. We left our bats at home, having only five hits and we came out on the short end of a 3-2 score.

DYERSVILLE DROPS MONTICELLO TOURNEY OPENER TUESDAY

Jack Scherrman drove in the winning run with two gone in the bottom of the eighth, rapped out two other hits and hurled a masterful five-hitter as Farley defeated the Dyersville Whitehawks by a 3-2 score in a spine tingling extra inning contest that opened first round action in the Monticello Invitational Tournament, Tuesday, June 26.

Dyersville was in command until Farley picked up a run in the bottom of the seventh to send the contest into extra innings. Buck Hintgen started the rally by coaxing a walk after a full count. He advanced to second when Jack Scherrman tapped a bunt hit past the mound and the incoming Dyersville infielders. Wayne Drexler put both men in scoring position with a sacrifice and Larry Scherrman delivered a scratch hit to score Hintgen and send Jack Scherrman to third. Dyersville's Art Huinker summoned a last reserve of energy as he bore down and sent Farley's third hitter Jeep Schrandt and cleanup hitter Vernon Kennedy down swinging on seven pitchers.

Huinker also retired the first two to face him in the eighth striking out Joe Ottavi and getting Jerry Gaffney on a bounder to the mound, but Dick Wiley came through with a hit. The pressure mounted steadily as Hintgen ran up another 3-2 count before again coaxing a base on balls. This set the stage for Jack Scherrman who punched a hit between Dyersville shortstop Roy Krapfl and the second base bag to score Wiley, who was off and running at the crack of the bat.

Huinker had one of his rare "off nights" as he
absorbed his first loss of the season. The Loras star yielded 9
hits, and walked four while striking out 13.

Yes, it was probably one of those nights when a pitcher doesn't have his best stuff. It happens. What is important is that it is "rare" as the above write-up says. There are nights when a person doesn't have it and gets breaks and still gets by. This wasn't one of those.

Many interesting aspects of this ball game. As stated earlier, a local team always has a chance to have success in one or more of these local tournaments. Also notice the names of Dick Wiley and Joe Ottavi. Both were outside players who were brought in to improve the quality of the team and, subsequently, to help them win the game. Both are Loras College teammates. It also further exemplifies the quality and depth of that Duhawk team in the middle fifties. Ottavi did not get a hit in those last two innings but did have a double in the second inning and scored Farley's first run.

In a later chapter we cover the St. Louis Cardinals flying me to Omaha for a workout in the spring of 1957. Tied to that experience, with some extra time before the workout, was a visit with Loras fellow student, John Scherrman (or Jack as most people called him). He came back to his hometown Farley and was the winning pitcher and batting hero.

Another little sideline thought. In the spring of the previous year, when the Loras season wrapped up, and school was still in session, Farley called me at Loras and asked if I could come to play outfield with them in a game against Epworth the coming Sunday afternoon. Enjoying the game and its challenges as I did, I accepted. Jack Schrandt, a Loras substitute player at the time, accepted the responsibility for getting me to the game. No car as a student at that time. Ralph Buchman toed the rubber for Epworth that afternoon. A left-hand chucker, he later was a fellow worker with me at Western Dubuque, a time when he was high school principal at Epworth. In extra innings, a ground single to center drove in the winning run against "Buck." It was my third hit. Mr. Buchman was another one of those many wonderful people I met and got to know because of baseball. Ironically, Jack Schrandt's father grew up, where else but in my hometown of Festina. And he had also played some baseball back there in the 1930's. It was the only "game" in town, as people say.

We now had plenty of preparation for the next tournament starting two weeks later in Worthington. As it turned out, our first round opponent for that tournament was none other than our opponents at Monticello. Yes, it again was Farley. This night they did not have Jack Scherrman to lead them. Sal Willenbring pitched a brilliant two hit shutout and the Whitehawks won the opening round game 4- 0. Again, the Whitehawk bats were silent. Three total hits for the team, two by catcher Dick Mescher and one by the lead-off batter who was

103

yours truly. That drove in Mescher with the third run. The first two runs were scored on three Farley errors and a wild pitch.

The name of Wayne Drexler appears in the line-up for Farley in both games. He later became the Superintendent of Schools for Western Dubuque and my boss for 20 years. For that working relationship I am truthfully thankful. Wayne was an outstanding educator and administrator. There were many days during those twenty years when I worked as his assistant, that we had school lunch together in his office. Wayne was an avid baseball lover also, which resulted in our discussions often including baseball. He himself was a devoted follower of the Los Angeles Dodgers, formerly the Brooklyn Dodgers. In one of those discussions, talking about local baseball, he recalled getting a base hit off my pitching one game. That loss at Monticello had to be the game.

It is interesting that many players of that era have similar recollections. In retrospect, maybe that should be looked at as a compliment. Hard to believe but maybe that meant that they felt pretty good about getting a hit off a pitcher who they thought was tough to hit. That might be stretching the truth a little but so be it.

Although I have been unable to obtain any kind of write-up of the second Worthington tournament game for Dyersville, I did not pitch because I had injured my hand when I was hit by a pitched ball. I believe LeRoy "Sal" Willenbring pitched again and Dyersville won and secured a position in the semi-finals. Our opponent in the third round game was the host team, Worthington. In the other bracket Petersburg met the Cascade Reds.

DYERSVILLE AND PETERSBURG GAIN FINALS IN TOURNEY

Bernard Olinger scattered 10 hits to lead Petersburg to a 4-2 win over Cascade in the Worthington semi-finals. Joe Hoerner collected two hits to help Kerper carry the Petersburg batting load. Kurt and Ressler had two for five to pace the losers. The game went 10 innings.

The Dyersville Whitehawks advanced to the finals with a 4-1 win over Worthington. Art Huinker scattered seven hits and fanned ten to notch the win.

With one out in the first, Jenk and Wright slashed singles. Ned Walling singled scoring Jenk with the opening run. Worthington came back with a run to knot the score in the second. In their half of the inning the Whitehawks proceeded to load the bases as Paul Krapfl singled, Mescher was hit by a pitched ball and Roy Krapfl beat out an infield hit. Jenk came through with a double to score two runs. Olberding opened the third inning by hitting a home run.

104

Jenk and Bob Krapfl each had two hits for Dyersville. Dick Breitbach had three hits for Worthington and Jim Digman two for three for Worthington. Carter issued one walk and fanned one.

Dick Breitbach, with three hits for Worthington, is another Loras College teammate. In addition, Worthington's lineup included Bob Hoerner and Tom Breitbach, both strong players from the Dubuque Independents, or sometimes known as the Dubuque Old Timers. Both were part of the Dubuque team that knocked off my hometown Festina team in the Dubuqueland Tournament in that great 1-0 ball game four years earlier. When Worthington played Cascade for the consolation championship the following night, they had Leo Schlueter pitching for them. He was a senior shortstop, sometime pitcher for Loras my first year at the college. The first baseman for Cascade was Wayne Ressler, still a high school student. A very solid athlete in his own right, not only in baseball but basketball as well.

We won our first tournament title of the year the following night. But a side story to share. It is tied to baseball in that it happened during the Worthington baseball tournament. The Dyersville Commercial Club, in conjunction with their baseball tourney, also sponsored a Queen's Pageant with each of the sixteen teams participating in the tourney selecting a young girl (always the beautiful one) from the town they represented, to be their queen candidate. On an off night for playing baseball, the Commercial Club would hold a big dinner for each of the candidates, and judges from outside the communities would interview each candidate and make their selections for the runner-up and the queen herself. Representatives from area radio, TV and newspapers often were selected to do the judging. The night of the semi-finals at Dyersville, between games all queen candidates would get to ride on a convertible around the baseball field and the winners would be announced. This practice helped bring huge crowds to the two games that night.

Worthington asked their queen candidate to attend the last two or three nights of their own tourney. She would be introduced between innings and asked to stand so she could be acknowledged by the home town crowd. Not opposed to looking at a beautiful girl even if I was warming up on the pitcher's mound, I paid attention to the announcement. The candidate's name was Deanne Lighthart, a candidate that I was impressed with. Don't take this story wrong because I already wore a wedding ring and my wife and I were within days of having our first-born come into our family. But the incident has stayed with me. While doing research on all the baseball information available, the pictures of the Queen candidates appeared on the back side of one of the write-ups needed for this chapter.

She now is Deanne George, married to Tom George, and retired in Sun City, Arizona. They are good friends of Ann and me and many of you who read

105

this may remember Deanne George through all the musicals she performed for the Barn Community Theatre in Dubuque. Key among those were "Hello Dolly!" where she had the lead role and the "Nunsense" series where she played the comical little nun that caused the entire order to get into trouble.

> HAWKS TAKE TITLE
> Dyersville's Whitehawks won the championship of the Worthington baseball tournament here Tuesday night with a one-sided 11-4 triumph over Petersburg. In the preliminary game Worthington rallied late to stymie Cascade, 5-1, for the consolation title.
> Dyersville pounded four Petersburg pitchers for 12 hits and used a six-run uprising in the third inning to assure the win. Lefty Meyers and Art Huinker shared the pitching duties for the Hawks and allowed nine hits.
> In the big third inning Dyersville did its scoring on hits by Bob Krapfl, Tom Jenk, Ray Olberding, Paul Krapfl, Dick Mescher, and Meyer and one Petersburg error. Jenk led his mates with three hits in five trips.
> Willy Moorman with three-for-three and Marty Engelken and Rocky Schiltz with two hits each paced the Petersburg hitting.

Another Duhawk name appears in the Petersburg lineup. It was first baseman Rocky Schiltz, one of our top hitters for the Duhawks. And the name of Lefty Meyers brings back memories for many Dyersville and area baseball fans. Lefty, now nearing the end of his strong Dyersville baseball career, still could throw his famous "drop" ball as it was often called in those days.

Big things were about to happen. First and foremost, Ann was due to deliver our first child any day. Doctors had "predicted " the big day would occur about the fifth of July. By the time that the tournament at Worthington concluded, that date passed without activity. But Ann and I were delighted. Our health insurance, which covered delivery and hospital charges, went into effect Sunday morning, July 15.

On Saturday night, July 14, I treated Ann to a dinner date at Timmerman's Circle Supper Club in East Dubuque. We were confident by Saturday evening that the birth would not happen anymore that day and tomorrow was the magic insurance date. Ann does call me the "last of the big spenders" quite often. Think of it. The cost for the night was about $10 including tip. Neither Ann nor I had drinks at that time in our life. Now 21, I still was determined that professional baseball might be in my future and it was best for me not to consume alcohol. It is amazing what big dreams for the future will do for you. Ann felt it better if she did not have alcohol because of the baby that she was carrying. Plus, the legal age for drinking was still beyond her.

106

Guess what! Ann woke up early Sunday morning, July 15, with labor pains. It wasn't until Monday, the sixteenth of July, when our first son came into this world. Actually, it was about noon of that day. Dubuque hospital practices at that time did not allow fathers into the delivery room. But what a picture to come into the room after delivery to see Ann with our son in her arms. A memorable moment for the new, excited father. And, of course, we named our first son after a St. Louis Cardinal player of earlier years, Terry Moore. Now, we introduced Terry Huinker to the world and to his grandparents. For Ann's parents, it was their first. For my parents, let's see, probably about their twelfth. They ended up with thirty-five.

While this event kept Ann from attending the Cascade Invitational Tournament games, the four games played by the Dyersville Whitehawks at Cascade never will be forgotten. My parents encouraged me to attend Loras College if I wanted God to bless me. It strikes me that the same blessing must have carried to the games we played at the Legion Park in Cascade. Maybe it was a combination of that blessing and the birth of our first son. We will let the write-ups, mostly from the Dubuque Telegraph Herald tell most of the story.

> *CASCADE WINS; HUINKER IN NO-HITTER*
> *Baseball fans had to wait three days and nights here before the Cascade American Legion could resume its first round Friday night.*
>
> *But a large crowd found out it was well worth it as the home Cascade team won the first game over New Vienna 7 to 0 and Dyersville's Art Huinker shot into the limelight in the nightcap with a no-hit, no-run 4 to 0 conquest of Petersburg.*
>
> *Huinker, the lean lefty from Loras College, completely baffled Petersburg over the seven-inning route. He set down 14 batters on strikes and walked only three who were the only runners to get on base.*
>
> *Huinker also had a hand in Dyersville's four-run fifth which sewed up the game. Up to the fifth, Joe Hoerner had blanked the Whitehawks.*
>
> *Huinker opened the splurge with an infield hit after one out. Mescher singled to right and walks to Roy Krapfl, Lefty Meyers and Bob Krapfl brought two runners home.*
>
> *Tom Jenk hit into a force play scoring Roy Krapfl, and when the second baseman threw wildly on a double play attempt, Meyers also romped home.*
>
> *Darrell Rothrock was almost as effective as Huinker in hurling a three-hit shutout for Cascade. He struck out 12 and had near-perfect control with only one walk.*

Games such as this first game in Cascade come very rarely and it was on a very positive note that I arrived back at 258 Bluff Street to share the news and to be with the our family addition. Terry was born on Monday, and Ann brought him home from the hospital the day of the no-hitter. Maybe the newborn son created the momentum I was experiencing. Why not?

Two names are included in the above write-up. The first one is Joe Hoerner, Key West left hander and graduate of Senior High School in Dubuque, who signed a contract with the Chicago White Sox later in 1956. Eventually, he became an all-star reliever for the St. Louis Cardinals and the Philadelphia Phillies.

Darrell Rothrock, Cascade left-hander, played professional baseball for several years. Once he left the pro ranks, he settled in the Cedar Rapids area and raised havoc with opposing hitters in the tournaments held in the Dubuque County area. The above game is one example of his ability. Also a wonderful individual. Round two coming up.

HUINKER MISSES NO-HITTER; CASCADE, DYERSVILLE TRIUMPH
By John Carlton, T-H Sports Writer
Art Huinker was only one out away from pitching a second no-hitter in the Cascade American Legion baseball tournament Wednesday night in Dyersville's 2-0 victory over Worthington.

In the first game the Cascade Reds opened second-round play with Jack Nora narrowly missing a no-hitter in a 3-0 white washing of Holy Cross.

It was strictly a pitchers' night Wednesday with 34 strikeouts going into the books and not a hit for extra bases. There were only 11 hits made all evening.

Huinker, the Festina product who has not lost a game for Loras College in three years, seemed well on his way to his second masterpiece of the tourney. He stopped Petersburg without a hit in a 4-0 first-round triumph.

Only two men had reached base for Worthington through the first six innings, both on walks, and Huinker opened the seventh by getting Midge Delaney on a ground ball to short.

He walked Ralph Walkers and ran the count to 3-2 on ever-dangerous Tommy Breitbach before striking him out. Then Mert Gassman, who had fanned in two previous attempts, cracked a clean single through the middle on Huinker's first delivery.

The Whitehawk ace made LeRoy Gassman his sixteenth strikeout victim to end the game. No Worthington player got further than second. Walters made it on Gassman's hit. Breitbach reached the keystone by theft and Marv Funke advanced to second on a ground out.

108

Huinker used speed and control with a nice curve to
stop the Worthington hitters. He walked three. Jake Carter
took the loss for Worthington but allowed no earned runs and
only five hits.

Again, no explanation for the successful pitching. It is possible that the work being done with Geisler Roofing at this particular time had demanded considerable stress on my wrists that caused the pitches to have more movement than normal. Or was it still the two reasons I stated after the first game? To be truthful, I didn't worry about it. Happy to see the results.

Another night of many outside players being brought in by the different teams. Nora was a Dubuque Senior High School graduate, just as was Joe Hoerner. Nora was at this time pitching for the University of Iowa. Walters and Delaney were both members of Dubuque semi-pro teams. Holy Cross against Cascade had Leo Schlueter pitching and Tiny Potts playing second base.

Our win over Worthington was tournament victory number six in a row. The semi-finals were next.

CASCADE, DYERSVILLE BOTH SCORE 6-0 WINS;
TITLE BATTLE MONDAY
The long-standing rivalry between the Cascade Reds
and the Dyersville Whitehawks will reach its peak Monday night
when the two clubs battle it out to decide the championship of
the Cascade American Legion baseball tournament.
Both teams turned in 6-0 victories in Friday night's
semi-finals. The Reds throttled Key West on Darrell Rothrock's
two-hitter while Hawks' LeRoy Willenbring shut out Colesburg
on two hits.
Rothrock faced only 24 batters in the seven innings.
He walked none and registered nine strikeouts. It was his
second shutout of the tourney.
Willenbring was almost as effective for Dyersville.
Four runners made the base paths and only Bob Johnson, who
singled in the first and again in the second, made it as far as
second.
Willenbring sent 13 Colesburg hitters down swinging
and walked but one. He also figured in the Whitehawk scoring
off veteran Rich Sampson.
Sampson pitched no-hit ball for the first three innings
but the Hawks solved him for four runs in the fourth. Bob
Krapfl led off with a single, Dick Mescher was safe on an error
and Roy Krapfl singled in Bob.

Willenbring then singled to right to load the bases and Huinker slammed a triple to clean the sacks. The Hawks scored their other two runs in the fifth on back-to-triples by Ray Olberding and Bob Krapfl, and Mescher's sacrifice fly.

Reviewing the scores of the games covered and the number of shutouts recorded indicates pitcher domination throughout the Cascade tournament. Will it continue? A write-up of the championship game follows.

HUINKER'S NO-HITTER TOPS REDS IN CHAMPIONSHIP

Southpaw Art Huinker produced his second no-hitter of the Cascade American Legion baseball tournament Monday night as the Dyersville Whitehawks took the championship with a 5-0 triumph over Cascade.

The consolation title went to Key West, whose ageless Red Kenney throttled Colesburg on two hits for a five-inning, 11-1 victory.

Unanimously chosen Most Valuable Player of the tournament, Huinker registered his third triumph of the classic and completed one of the most spectacular tourney records in a long time.

In 23 innings he permitted but one hit, struck out 47, and walked eight.

Only two batters reached base for Cascade –both by walks. Huinker allowed no runner past first. After pitching five and two-thirds innings of perfect baseball, he issued a pass to Darrell Rothrock, and in the eighth Jake Emerson led off with a walk for Cascade. Huinker fanned 17 and whiffed every opponent at least once. Only one ball was hit out of the infield when Emerson lifted an easy fly to Dick Wright in left field in the fifth.

As the Whitehawk ace took the mound in the ninth the crowd came to life and applauded continuously as Huinker struck out Rothrock, Morrie Klocker and Ade Kurt to preserve his masterpiece.

Huinker, who has lost only one game this year, and is undefeated in three seasons with Loras, posted his first no-hitter of the meet in the first round against Petersburg.

He shoved the Whitehawks into the semi-finals by whipping Worthington, 2 to 0, as Mert Gassman ruined Huinker's bid for another no-hitter with two out in the last inning.

Meanwhile, the Whitehawks scored in the first inning as the Cascade defense fell apart. Wright tallied the first run off Peters, on a pair of Red errors.

Peters, former Notre Dame star who played for Tulsa, San Diego and Cedar Rapids in the Cleveland chain, pitched creditably for the first three innings but the Hawks got to him in the fourth.

Dick Mescher doubled and Pete Willenborg walked. Consecutive singles by Bob Krapfl and Tom Jenk brought in two runs. In the fifth an error, and singles by Huinker and Mescher finished Peters and brought in Rothrock.

We had just won our second tournament for the year with the biggest one at Dyersville coming up. The crowd reached into several thousand for the championship game, an awesome sight again for a small-town player from Festina. Both Cascade and Dyersville were stocked with veteran ball players in 1956. When I returned to Dyersville in 1961 and again played for the Whitehawks, many of those veterans were no longer playing.

Cascade saw several retire from the game even from the 1954 team that opposed the Dubuque Merchants when I pitched for them in the Dubuqueland Tournament. Bud Kurt, John Sullivan, Bob Moran and Doc Bisenius from that team were gone by 1956. By 1961, Ade Kurt, Patty Clarke and Jake Emerson had also retired.

Dyersville's 1961 team no longer had Bob and Paul Krapfl, Lefty Meyers, Don Lakeman, Ned Walling and third baseman Ray Olberding. Dick Mescher graduated from Loras College and left Dyersville to coach at Potosi, Wisconsin. Only Roy Krapfl, LeRoy Willenbring and Tom Jenk remained. Several years later, while coaching at Beckman High School Krapfl's son, Keith, was a great defensive centerfielder on the 1968 state championship team.

For many years, the number four hitter in the Dyersville lineup had remained the same. Ray Olberding was one of the most consistent left-hand batters in the Dubuque area. In addition, his slingshot arm planted him as a very capable defensive third baseman also. Two of his brothers, Spike and Del, had also played on the Whitehawk team.

There are several pictures included in the picture section from the victory over Cascade in the 1956 championship. In the box score for the game, they listed the time of the nine-inning game at 2 hours, 1 minute and attendance at 2,764. Not bad for town baseball.

About two years later, Bill O'Neill, sports writer for the Dubuque Telegraph Herald, published the following write-up related to the 1956 Cascade American Legion Baseball Tournament.

111

GREAT MOMENTS IN SPORTS . . . HUINKER
MOWED 'EM DOWN

There were numerous great moments in the college and professional baseball career of Art Huinker, present coach of Ossian De Sales High School, but the southpaw is quick to point out his greatest thrill came in the semi-pro ranks.

Few pitchers have ever run up the remarkable record Huinker turned in during the 1956 Cascade semi-pro tournament.

That was the year Dyersville won the championship of the 16-team meet ---and the year none of the four opponents could score off the Dyersville pitching staff.

Making this possible in a big way was Art Huinker. In the first-round game, the lefty blanked Petersburg, 7-0, and turned in a no-hitter. He walked three batters and fanned 14 over the seven-inning contest.

A few nights later Huinker came within one out of pulling off a double no-hitter. Dyersville won the game, 2-0, and it wasn't until Mert Gassman of Worthington singled with two out in the final inning that the losers could muster a hit.

Gassman had been a strike-out victim in his first two appearances, but his hit spoiled Huinker's bid for a second no-hitter. It was Worthington's only safety. Again Huinker had his strikeout ball working, fanning 16 and issuing just two passes.

The third game found Dyersville slipping past Colesburg, 6-0, to gain a spot in the finals. Huinker wasn't on the mound, but he did more than his share. His triple with the sacks loaded drove in more than enough to spell victory.

Now came the showdown with arch-rival Cascade. The two pre-tourney favorites had reached the final round and everywhere the talk was that war would be waged.

But Dyersville had elected to go along with Huinker, hoping he still had enough left to pull out the big one. His heavy duty in the tourney had done no harm to his ability.

He not only hurled Dyersville to the tourney championship but pitched another no-hit, no-run game against the rugged hitting Reds of Cascade. The final score was, 5-0.

Maybe the fact that his first son born that week gave him added ability---but more likely it was his tremendous desire to win.

Huinker's talent was not overlooked.

And little wonder---two no-hit games and a one-hitter---that's a lot of pitching.

Thanks must be given to Bill O'Neill and the TH for that write-up. It is hard to imagine that over that stretch of 23 innings only one batted ball found all the open spaces on a ball diamond. There are too many good ball players in the Dubuque County area to go unscathed over that stretch.

Close to 20 years after Bill wrote that write-up, I had the privilege of serving on the Loras College Athletic Hall of Fame selection committee with him. He was a fantastic source of information for that committee and the accomplishments of so many athletes that performed on the athletic fields and arenas of Loras College. He did another little write-up after Kerry Woods struck out 22 Houston Astros in his rookie season. O'Neill compared that to the 22 strikeouts at Loras College in my senior year.

THE GRANDADDY OF TOURNAMENTS

The final tournament, the one held at the Dyersville Commercial Club Park, is called the "granddaddy" of the small-town tournaments. Each year, the first two weeks in August are set aside for this 16-team challenge. Because the Cascade tourney experienced frequent rain delays early in the tournament, the opening round for Dyersville began shortly after our championship win at Cascade. The Whitehawks' opponent for the first round was Epworth.

HAWKS ESCAPE, 3-2
Spunky Epworth threw a terrific scare into the highly-touted Dyersville Whitehawks before the Hawks managed a 3-2 victory in the opening night of the Dyersville tournament. In the first game, New Vienna took out Peosta, 2 to 1, in another close game.

The Whitehawks, pre-tourney favorites, advanced to second round play after fighting off a seventh inning uprising by Epworth.

Each team picked up five hits, including an inside-the-park homer by Dick Mescher with one aboard.

Dyersville picked up runs in the first and second innings off of Ralph Buchman and topped it off with Mescher's homer.

After two were retired in the seventh, Epworth suddenly came to life when Sid Bradfield singled preceding another bingle by Bill Beyer. Jim Schultz was inserted as a pinch batter and got on through a fielder's choice. Jerry Urbain then uncorked a liner scoring both Bradfield and Beyer. Roy Willenbring nailed down his fourteenth strikeout of the game when he fanned Ralph McDermott for the final out.

A banner crowd saw Peosta taking a 1 to 0 advantage in the second frame of the opener, only to have New Vienna come back in the fifth with two counters. In that game, winning pitcher Don Kerper singled, followed by hits by Jim Oberbroeckling and Harry Trenkamp, for the final 2-1 winning margin.

Epworth's line-up had all the familiar names on their town team. It included Urbain, McDermott, Callahan, Buchman (the losing pitcher but he pitched a five-hitter, and had us off balance most of the night), Beyer and Kramer. Meanwhile, Peosta had three Burds players, a McGovern, a Schueller, a

114

McAndrew, and finally, a Dardis, also familiar Peosta names. The Dardis name has been carried on by Frank Dardis who has been an active Peosta Cubs player and manager for over thirty years, starting in the 1970's.

New Vienna, winner over Peosta, is Dyersville's opposition in the second round. By now, our three-week old son, Terry, had his great aunt Agnes as a baby-sitter, and his mother decided that the four games missed at Cascade were sufficient. I now had company again making the trip from Dubuque to the ball parks in western Dubuque County.

> *DYERSVILLE'S ART HUINKER SHUTS OUT N.*
> *VIENNA, 6-0*
> *By John Carlton, T-H Sports Writer*
> *Colesburg staved off a late-inning rally by Worthington which ended in a wild dispute Thursday night and eliminated the defending champions of the Dyersville baseball tournament, 6 to 5, behind right-hander Jerry Martin.*
> *Dyersville's talented Art Huinker handcuffed New Vienna on two hits in the opener as the Whitehawks scored a 6-0 triumph, their 29th of the season against only three losses.*
> *With the score 6-5 in favor of Colesburg, the bases loaded and two out, catcher Funke for Worthington, grounded to Rich Sampson at third but the throw was low at first and Funke was called out in a very close play. There immediately ensued a heated argument which persisted long after the game was over.*
> *Huinker, meanwhile totaled the greatest number of strikeouts so far in the tournament with 15. After the first inning Huinker made the next 10 outs strikeouts. He walked only one.*
> *Marty Bockenstedt spoiled any chance of a no-hitter by Huinker when he led off the game for New Vienna with a Texas-league single to left. The only other hit was Bockenstedt's single in the sixth.*
> *Dyersville scored first in the third off Don Kerper who let in Bob Krapfl and Dick Wright with wild pitches. Tommy Jenk's Hawks opened up again in the sixth. Huinker singled, Dick Mescher doubled and Pete Willenbring walked to load the bases. Ned Walling's sacrifice fly, an error and a two-run triple by Roy Krapfl let in four runs.*

There are no stirring memories that I can recall about the game. Somewhat foggy is my recall of the dispute but whether the ball was in the dirt and juggled by the first baseman, or whether it was strictly a bang-bang play, I can't remember. It is very likely that a few Worthington baseball fans can still remember.

115

The box score shows a single and double for me, and a single and triple for Roy Krapfl. There also was a double play for Dyersville that went from second baseman Bob Krapfl to first baseman Ned Walling to catcher Dick Mescher. New Vienna must have had a runner on third who tried to score after Krapfl threw to first but then was nailed at home.

The semi-final game again placed the Whitehawks into a last-inning situation where you have to score or watch the championship from the sidelines. With the Queen's pageant and crowning the same night, attendance reached 4,124.

DYERSVILLE, PETERSBURG VIE FOR TITLE
By John Carlton, T-H sports writer
Dyersville's red-hot Whitehawks did it the hard way Monday night but qualified to meet Petersburg for the championship of their own tournament.
The Hawks came from behind three times and finally dealt Colesburg a 7-3 defeat with five runs in the last inning in Monday's semi-finals while Petersburg eliminated Monticello in the second game, 7 to 4.
A crowd of 4,124 watched the Whitehawks chalk up their 30th victory of the season against only three setbacks in dramatic fashion. Up until the last inning Jerry Martin had held the Hawks to two runs and held a 3-2 lead.
It was veteran Bob Krapfl who smote the key blow for the winners. The Hawks shortstop was unable to start the game after spraining his ankle Sunday but came through in grand style as a pinch-hitter.
Dick Wright was safe on an error to open the inning and with one out Krapfl hobbled off the bench and nailed Martin's first pitch for a double to right field, scoring Wright with the tying run.
That was all for Martin and young Cleo Hyde replaced him. Dick Mescher hit a fielder's choice but Don Lakeman, running for Krapfl, was safe at the plate with what proved to be the winning run.
Art Huinker belted a three-run double after Roy Willenbring walked and Roy Krapfl singled to wind up the scoring in the inning.
Petersburg grabbed a four-run cushion in the first inning off Monticello's Glenn Drahn and coasted to victory in the last game. Singles by Tiny Potts, Bill Moorman, Jim Hoerner and John Witte and Joe Hoerner's double did the damage. The Cubs had scored first on Tucker Haye's double and an error.
Then Drahn settled down and retired the next 11 batters while the Cubs cut the Petersburg lead to 4-3 in the fifth.

116

But Petersburg iced it in the sixth. Moorman led off with a walk and Joe Hoerner cracked a long triple to score him. Jim Hoerner then whacked an inside-the-park homer for two more runs.

In our game, LeRoy Willenborg pitched into the sixth inning. I relieved Sal with two out, then also pitched the seventh inning. Tom Jenk, Roy Krapfl, and I each had two hits in the victory.

The Petersburg team was led by their manager, Bill Moorman, who tended to be a tough out for many years. He added Dubuquers, Rocky Schiltz and Tiny Potts, the Hoerner brothers from Key West, Jim and Joe to the Petersburg squad for the "big' tourney. In addition, he brought another pitcher, Jim Rima, from Postville. Recall that Jim and I guarded each other in the sectional basketball game our senior year where Postville defeated Calmar by two points. The following year we were roommates for a half a semester at Loras College.

Monticello's pitcher, Glenn Drahn, came from Monona, Iowa, before attending the University of Iowa where he was an outstanding football player and baseball player. He played with a famous Elkader Vets baseball team in the early fifties with the likes of Jack Dittmer, Milwaukee Braves second baseman, Lefty Cassutt and other top-notch players too numerous to mention.

There are vivid mental pictures of the huge crowds at the last two nights of the Dyersville tournament. After over 4,000 for the semi-finals and Queens' Pageant, the finals brought in 5,200. The field did not have bleachers sufficient to hold anywhere near that many. A large majority sat on the ground all the way down the left and right field foul lines. There were no fences to hold the crowd back and as the crowds grew larger, the fans edged closer and closer to the actual foul lines, often eight to ten deep all the way down to the outfield fences. It was often claimed in discussions by people afterwards, that there were as many beer cans lying around as there were fans. And those crowds were enthusiastic and raucous. Probably a combination of exciting baseball and the content of the cans.

The championship game was a pitcher's dream with limited runs and hits and the right team winning. Biased, of course.

DYERSVILLE WINS OWN MEET
By John Carlton, T-H Sports Writer
Invincible Art Huinker came through in flying colors again Tuesday night, this time hurling the Dyersville Whitehawks to a 2-0 victory over spirited Petersburg for the championship of the Dyersville baseball tournament.
In another fine game the Monticello Cubs captured a 2-1 verdict from Colesburg to take consolation honors before a capacity crowd of 5,200 fans.

117

The husky little Huinker, whose curve was not working as well as usual Tuesday night, relied on his fast one to baffle Petersburg and win a pitching duel from veteran Bob Hoerner.

Huinker, who recently pitched the Hawks to the Cascade tournament title with a no-hitter, enabled Dyersville to hang up its third tournament championship of the summer. The Whitehawks also won at Worthington.

As a fitting climax to his performance Huinker was named most valuable player of the Dyersville classic, a title also bestowed upon him at Cascade, and was chosen as left-handed pitcher for the all-tournament team.

He scored the first run of the game for the Whitehawks in the second inning when he walked and scored on an error of Paul Krapfl's fielder's choice.

Dyersville's other run came in the seventh when Dick Mescher doubled, advanced to third on Krapfl's single and scored on a sacrifice fly by Lefty Meyers.

Hoerner permitted the Whitehawks only five hits in the nine innings and only one earned run. Bill Buhr had three of the four hits off Huinker.

Joining Huinker on the all-tournament team were Jerry Martin of Colesburg as right-hand pitcher, Rocky Schiltz of Petersburg at first base, Bob Johnson of Colesburg at second, Rich Sampson of Colesburg at third, Tucker Haye of Monticello at short, Bill Moorman of Petersburg in left, Jim Whitford of Colesburg in center, Johnny Harris of Colesburg in right, and Mescher as catcher.

Robin Tangeman, Colesburg's catcher, was presented a trophy for sportsmanship.

The game itself took 2 hours 5 minutes. A time of 1 hour 40 minutes was listed for the consolation game. For a change, I only walked one batter and collected 11 strikeouts. Bob Hoerner, who normally didn't take the hill, allowed four walks and registered no strikeouts. Petersburg had four hits with three by Bill Buhr. My true friend and great competitor, Tiny Potts, garnered the fourth one.

Tournament-wise, the Whitehawks had just rung up twelve consecutive victories. Personally, I had just completed 40 plus consecutive scoreless innings. But that was going to come to a resounding ending in the next game pitched for Dyersville.

This next game requires considerable explanation. Maybe this is an effort of defending how poorly I pitched. Anyway, things were not good.

The Dyersville Whitehawks scheduled a game with the Three-I professional Waterloo White Hawks. The game took place on a Wednesday night shortly after the Dyersville Tournament. It happened to be the same week as the Waterloo Courier Northeast Iowa Tournament of Champions in which Festina was competing. I had played a sufficient number of games for the hometown team that I was eligible to play for them in this tournament, one of only two tourneys the team can play in.

Although those tournaments are covered in the following chapter, I refer to them here because they probably impacted the Whitehawks game with Waterloo's pro team.

Festina was scheduled to play their first game on the preceding Sunday night, with second round games if necessary, played on the same Wednesday night as Dyersville's game. So Festina asked that I pitch the first Sunday night game. The game went 12 scoreless innings before we finally won in the 13th. I pitched all but two outs of the game. Not a good preparation for Wednesday's big game in Dyersville. This is especially true because my dream of playing professional baseball could get a big boost with a good game against the Waterloo professionals. The opposite outcome could have a negative effect.

With two days rest, after twelve plus innings pitched on Sunday night, the tank was empty, as the write-up indicates below.

WATERLOO ROMPS 20 TO 3; DYERSVILLE
SUFFERS 4th LOSS
By John Carlton, T-H Sports Writer
Ira Hutchison's Waterloo White Hawks, labeled
"definitely a defensive club" this season, were anything but that
Wednesday night, unleashing a display of power which buried
host Dyersville, 20 to 3.
The leaders of the Three-I League humbled five
opposing pitchers to the tune of 20 hits which went for 44 total
bases, and scored in every inning but the third.
A spirited rooting section from Dubuque was treated to
an evening spotlighting many former Packers. Fritz Ackley,
Dick Grant and big Ollie Brantley, all formerly with Dubuque,
combined to hold Dyersville to six hits.
And Jim Lynn, the Packers' leading hitter in 1955, set
the pace for Waterloo with Gene Martin and Dick Patton,
among the game's leading hitters.
Art Huinker started on the mound for Dyersville but the
little lefthander, who pitched more than 12 innings Sunday,
didn't have it Wednesday night. He lasted until the fourth when
Waterloo scored four runs.

Huinker, who dropped only his second decision this year, had held the winners to just two hits and one earned run before the fourth. Then Jim McAnany tripled; Ackley, Don Bacon and Jerry Olesko each singled, and Norm Cash provided the finishing touches with a home run.

Jim Hoerner, Lefty Meyers, Earl Lampe and Dick Wright took their turns on the hill for Dyersville after that with Wright coming in from left field to finally stop the Hawks.

Dyersville made its only threat in the first inning off Ackley. Tommy Jenk's club tied it up in the first round when the manager walked, moved to third on Wright's single and scored on a single by Huinker.

In the second inning, the losers shaved Waterloo's lead to 3-2 as Roy Krapfl walked with two out and raced home on Bob Krapfl's line-drive double to the right field fence.

Ackley retired the next 10 batters in a row before bowing out in favor of Grant in the sixth. Grant gave up singles to Wright and catcher Dick Mescher in the two innings he worked.

Dyersville gained its final run at the expense of Brantley in the eighth inning. Wright was safe when his fly ball popped out of Lynn's glove in center and scored when Mescher doubled with two out.

Thank heavens that one is history. The home run by Norm Cash is vividly remembered. I know the pitch I threw. I know the count. And I can still see the ball go far over the right-center field fence. It was a no-doubter, as soon as he hit it. There were two out, one run in and the bases loaded. The count was a full three ball, two strike situation. I threw a hanging curve ball. Enough said.

The visitors had 7 hits against me in 4 innings, six against Joe Hoerner in 3 innings, and the other 7 hits were collected the last three innings. A happy camper I was not. But you have to put it behind you and go on.

The next ball game to report on is a bit unusual. Dyersville completed a great season with three tournament championships to top it off. In the next chapter, you will see that Festina continues to win their Northeast Iowa League, and had a great tournament at the Waterloo Courier Tournament of Champions. I was one of two main pitchers for Dyersville. My brother Kenny definitely was the leading pitcher for Festina.

How about a game between Festina and Dyersville? How about a game in which the Huinker brothers pitched against each other? Someone in northeast Iowa had that brainstorm and convinced the two teams to do battle. The game was scheduled for 2:15, September 9 on a Sunday afternoon. The planners felt the

120

most fan interest would be around our home town so the game was played at Calmar, the same diamond where I had played high school baseball.

KEN HUINKER OUTDUELS ART

A large crowd was treated to a fine baseball game here Sunday with brothers as mound rivals.

Art Huinker of Dyersville faced Ken Huinker of Festina on the hill, and Ken was the victor by a 4-2 score.

Dyersville had a 2-0 lead until the eighth when Festina solved Art Huinker. Linus Huinker opened the frame with a single, Jerry Schneberger walked, Leo Luzum doubled, Norb Einck singled and Romauld Elsbernd singled, accounting for the four runs.

Art Huinker's double was the only extra base hit for the losers. Art yielded 10 hits and struck out eight and Ken gave up eight hits and fanned five.

Later, people often asked if I found it difficult to pitch against a team that I had played with for so many years. Also, did you find it hard to throw against your two brothers (Linus and Ken) plus others who held so much respect in your eyes? Yes, it was a difficult game to pitch. This Festina team included the dearest of friends, the dearest of family. It was hard to make them opponents.

But, at the same time, I never pitched a ball game that I did not try to win. It has always been a "pride" thing for me. This game was no different. For me, pitchers have the advantage. The tougher the situation, the harder we can work effectively. For the hitter, coming up once every nine batters, the greater the pressure situation, the tighter muscles become that are needed to hit .

In this particular situation, the greater drive to win the game belonged on the side of my home town Festina. They were playing in front of fans from their area. Dyersville who had not played for about 17 days, actually finished playing after the big Waterloo White Hawks loss. That had been their final scheduled game. Now they were playing another game, in a way, for me or because of me. It was somewhat similar to the Dubuque Old Timers/Independents coming to play at Festina after their season had ended. That doesn't mean that Dyersville didn't try to beat Festina. Once a player walks on the field, you play to win. And the game met the expectations.

This game proved to me that Festina had good hitters, and experienced hitters on their team. It just reinforced the reason why they had just won their eighth straight Northeast Iowa League pennant and also their first ever winning of the Waterloo Courier Northeast Iowa Tournament of Champions. Similar to the Dyersville Whitehawks, they had their best season ever, and I am proud to have been part of it. Considering they had just beaten me on the diamond, you could take that final "part that I played" a couple of different ways.

121

Another memorable, hard to accept, moment took place in the eighth inning of that game that I will not forget. It is one of three such happenings in my baseball career that I can recall where I felt I made the pitch I wanted to make and where I wanted the pitch to be, resulting in the type of batted ball I expected to get, only to see the batted ball find a location where a fielder or fielders could not get to it. In each of the cases it resulted in a significant loss rather than a significant win. Each situation will be addressed in later chapters. In every case, it was no fault of my defense behind me. Only if they would have been playing out of position, they probably would have made the play.

In Festina's eighth inning rally, they had already scored one run, had runners on second and third with two out. With strong-hitting Norb Einck at the plate, ball and strike count unknown, I threw a three-quarter arm fastball low in the strike zone and breaking away from him. When he hit the ball into the ground, I thought, "Good, a ground ball to second and the third out."

Instead, the ball eluded the gallant effort by our second baseman, Norb had a base hit to right and the score went from 2-1 in our favor to 3-2 in Festina's favor.

It was solid hitting on the part of veteran right fielder, Norb Einck. He did not try to pull the ball, went with the outside pitch and produced the winning hit. Despite that, he has always been one of my most favorite first cousins.

My final concluding thought on that "battle of the brothers." Just like the years when we were much younger trying to strike each other out against the barn as a backstop on the farm, "the older brother always wins."

The entire baseball season, with the exception of one or two games, proved exciting and rewarding. The dream of a professional baseball future was still alive, not only in my mind, but in the minds of some baseball scouts.

A FINAL YEAR WITH FESTINA

The summer of 1956 provided many unique twists and turns in my baseball world compared to previous summers. It also proved to be my last year as a member of the wonderful Festina team. As mentioned in the previous chapter, the official team roster included my name. If I wanted to be eligible to play for Festina in the Waterloo Courier Northeast Iowa Tournament of Championship, it was required that I play in at least half of their league games. The Dyersville Whitehawks were the team where most of my games were played. Quite simply, living in Dubuque and working there in the summer of 1956, it made sense to play with a closer team rather than drive all the way to Festina or further.

Memory doesn't bring back all of the games played with Festina. The newspaper write-ups below do identify some of the games. Rain prevented my playing in the seventh game to make me eligible. We were ready to play when the skies opened up. The umpires confirmed to the league brass that I was ready to participate. That met the requirements in a season when Festina went 13 and 1 to capture a sixth consecutive title.

For me, there is a very interesting highlight in the coverage of the Monona doubleheader. Linus, my older brother, normally batted lead-off for the Festina team. In all those successful years, he probably batted lead-off nine out of every ten games. A left-hand batter with good speed on the basepaths, he was a slasher-type hitter who seldom struck out and had as many base hits to left field as he did to right field. Mostly a singles hitter, he sometimes managed an extra-base hit down the line or between the outfielders. But home runs? Yet, in the first game of the double-header, he hit back-to back home runs that afternoon. WOW!

I really miss my older brother. He was always so helpful, in that quiet leadership style, so much like my father parented. If we had done something out of the acceptable range, our father usually found extra tasks that had to be completed the next day. All of a sudden, the chicken coup had to be cleaned out, something none of us cared to do. For Linus, cancer shortened his life with us at the age of 57. Gone but never forgotten.

Maybe this is the place to share one of those memorable moments that happen in each and every one of our lives. Linus was in the Winneshiek County Hospital located in Decorah, Iowa. Ann and I volunteered to help his wife, Lory, by staying with him at the hospital through the night. It turned out to be the last night of his life. He died the next day in the early evening hours.

It was my opportunity to be with him in his room. For the most part, heavily sedated, he slept most of the time. I also had nodded off. All of sudden, Linus grabbed my arm, woke me and asked me a question I was not prepared for, "Art, has it made any difference that I have lived?"

123

The suddenness of his question has never left my memory. Going back to that particular moment, I am not sure of the length of the following discussion, but I would estimate at least a half-hour, possibly more. We talked about his being a good husband and father. Together, he and Lory had raised three boys and one girl. We discussed all the food that had been produced under his direction for thirty plus years. We even tried to estimate the number of people that had been fed through the farm's production. We discussed the role he played in his community, one of them being his leadership on the baseball team for an estimated 15 years and the entertainment he and the team had provided. Leadership in his church in Festina was covered. How often had he helped neighbors when they were in need of assistance. We went on and on. As awake as I was because of our discussion, weariness began to set in for my brother. We agreed to agree that, indeed, his life had made a profound difference on the people of his family and community, and maybe even further. His question still plays in my mind and has often made me ask that question of myself. "Have I made a positive difference in the lives of the people that have entered my life?" Back to 1956 Festina baseball.

FESTINA WINS OVER ST. LUCAS

Festina, Volga, West Union and Postville notched victories Sunday in the Northeast Iowa baseball league.

Festina beat St. Lucas 6-2. Art Huinker hurled six-hit ball as Festina gained its first win. Festina collected 11 hits off three St. Lucas hurlers.

VOLGA NOTCHES THIRD WIN

Volga now leads the league with three straight wins after an 8-2 triumph over West Union here Sunday. Festina and Monona who were rained out in the first week of action have 2 and 0 records.

Sunday, Festina and Monona won by identical 10-2 scores. Festina collected 13 hits in routing Castalia. The winners got three runs in each of the two opening innings. Leo Luzum whacked a two-run homer in the first for Festina. Art Huinker hurled for Festina limiting Castalia to five hits.

HUINKER SHINES; FESTINA TAKES TWO FROM MONONA

Art Huinker, who did little else but play baseball Sunday, helped Festina to a twin victory over Monona in the Northeast Iowa League as the league leaders sank their teeth deeper into first place.

Festina posted victories of 9-1 and 9-3 to go two full games ahead of second-place St. Lucas which lost to West Union, 12-10. In other games, Spillville won its first, beating Castalia, 13-7, and the Volga-at-Postville game was rained out.

124

Huinker, who helped Dyersville to its 3-2 opening-round victory in the Dyersville tournament Sunday night, started both afternoon games for Festina, striking out 15 batters and allowing two hits in the opener and throwing two scoreless innings in the second.

Meanwhile Linus Huinker furnished the power in the first game. He belted a solo home run in the fourth and bashed another with one aboard in the fifth. Don Hubacher's homer in the second was Monona's only run.

Romauld Elsberned replaced Huinker in the third inning of the second game and the two combined for an eight-hitter. Carl Schupanitz cracked a three-run homer for Festina in the first inning.

FESTINA DECLARED CHAMP AS NORTHEAST IOWA ENDS

Rain cut the Northeast Iowa baseball league to a .250 average Sunday as only one of the four games was played. It marked the end of the league season although several rainouts will be made up. Festina has been officially declared champion with its 12-1 record. It will play in the Waterloo tournament Friday. Rainouts included Festina-St. Lucas, West Union-Monona, and Postville-Castalia.

At this point in the season, Festina's record of 12-1 gave the repeating champions a two-game lead over St. Lucas with a record of 10-3. Following is the make-up game played after the Waterloo Courier tournament is over.

HUINKER PITCHES NO-HITTER IN FESTINA-ST.LUCAS GAME; STRIKES OUT 18 AS FESTINA WINS

Art Huinker strikes out 18 batters, walked one and hit one batter as he pitched a no-hitter Sunday, Sept. 2 to lead his team to a 1-0 victory over St. Lucas.

In the game with St. Lucas, Festina scored its run on a walk by Norb Einck and a triple by Romauld Elsbernd. Elsbernd's triple was one of the two hits allowed by Don Kuehner, St. Lucas hurler.

The following is a blurb that appeared in the local paper, the Ossian Bee, briefly highlighting a Festina non-conference victory over Waukon at the Big Four Fair, held in Postville every year over Labor Day weekend. It was "Huinker" day.

FESTINA OVERWHELMS WAUKON BY 20-7
Festina routed Waukon 20-7 at the Big Four Fair here
Monday. Festina got 18 hits, including home runs by Carl
Schupanitz, Ken and Art Huinker and two by Bob Huinker.

Bob Huinker is another first cousin, the same age as my brother Ken. Ken is three years my elder. In looking at records of other victories for Festina that summer, Kenny was the winning pitcher in most of them. In a game against West Union, won by Festina 5-1, he struck out 17 and allowed only one hit. Against Castalia, he pitched a shut-out, again only allowing one hit. On a given day, he could be as tough as any pitcher in northeast Iowa. Later, he would often travel to Dyersville or other tournaments in that area and pitch for a team. Sometimes it was the Dyersville Whitehawks.

The Festina club had the leadership of excellent veterans who started playing in 1946 and kept going beyond 1956. The big names were outfielders Norb Einck and brother Linus Huinker, third baseman Leo Luzum, shortstop Jim Schneberger and second baseman (sometime pitcher) Romauld Elsbernd. From these five there were always two or more who stepped up to the plate, game after game, and provided the offense that carried the team to many of its victories.

With the league championship sewed up, Festina again prepared to play in the Waterloo Courier Northeast Iowa Tournament of Champions.

126

FESTINA WINS! FESTINA WINS!

For the seventh time in eight years, Festina represented the Northeast Iowa League in the Waterloo Courier Northeast Iowa Tournament of Champions. The eighth year, 1952, Festina ended up winning their league title but at the time of the Waterloo tourney, they stood in second place behind West Union. For the sixth consecutive year, yours truly was playing at the professional Waterloo Stadium.

Only once have we managed to reach the semi-finals. That was in 1951 when we grabbed third place. Because there were nine leagues now vying for this title, there had to be an extra round to get the number down to eight teams. We defeated Norway in that extra round in 1954 but then were blistered by Sumner in the quarter-final round. We carried a paltry 3 wins, 6 losses into the current tourney.

The opening round of the 1956 tournament pitted Festina against Cedar Valley champion, Denver. The Waterloo Courier write-up labeled the thirteen-inning game that followed to be the "top pitching duel in the tournament's history." The write-up explains it well.

> *FESTINA WINS IN 13 INNINGS, 1-0*
> *In three games so far---two of which have gone overtime—a total of 30 innings have been played instead of the scheduled 23. Sunday night's opening game in which Festina's Northeast Iowa League champions nipped Denver's Cedar Valley League kings 1-0 in 13 innings, goes into the records as the top pitching duel in the tournament's history.*
> *The game, played before 900 fans, had everything but poetic justice. Little lefty Art Huinker of Festina pitched all but two outs, struck out 21 batters, allowed only six hits and drove in the winning run with a sharp single to center field, but didn't get credit for his team's victory.*
> *He was replaced on the mound by brother Ken Huinker, also a lefthander, with one out in the first half of the 13th. Ken retired the side with the bases loaded, the 14th, 15th and 16th runners left on by Denver in the three hour and 10 minute contest.*
> *On the other hand, righthander John Kurtt went the route for Denver, allowing only eight hits and one walk and struck out eight with his sharp-breaking curve ball. But Festina bunched three of its hits in the last of the 13th to win the game with one out. Kurtt had not allowed a runner to reach third base in the first twelve innings.*
> *Raymond's Corn Valley League champions reached Wednesday's 9 p.m. semifinal round game opposite Festina with*

a 7-3 victory over St. Ansgar's North Central League champs in the nightcap that wound up at 12:15 a.m. Monday.

The 1-0 Festina-Denver game finally ended in the 13th inning on successive hits by Festina's Bill Luzum, Linus Huinker and Art Huinker.

It wrapped up one of the most tense games in the 11 years of the Courier tournament, for Denver made threat after threat, only to be denied each time by the pitching of Art Huinker and then Ken Huinker.

Denver stranded 16 runners in the brilliant pitching battle between the Huinkers-- -two of three brothers on the club- - -and John Kurtt.

Art Huinker fanned 21 batters---16 of them in the first seven innings---and allowed only six hits. He walked six men. Ken Huinker got Festina out of trouble in the 13th when the potential winning Denver run was thrown out at the plate by centerfielder Linus Huinker to end the inning with a doubleplay.

Kurtt gave up just eight hits and walked only one man before bowing.

Art Huinker was relieved in the top of the 13th with Denver runners on first and third and one out. Both men had reached base as the result of fielding errors. Ken Huinker came on to pitch and walked Jerry Guenther to load the bases and bring up Kurtt. Kurtt lifted a high, short fly to centerfield. Linus Huinker made the catch and rifled a perfect peg to the plate to catch the Denver runner coming in to end the inning.

The 13th was not the only inning that Denver was on the verge of scoring. In the first frame, the losers had men on second and third with no one out. At this point, Art Huinker became master and set down the next three Denver batters on strikes. Huinker fanned two more Denver hitters in the third frame after allowing a single and a walk with one out to get out of another jam.

Denver threatened again in the sixth inning when it loaded the bases with two out. However, Huinker set Kurtt down via the strikeout route.

Kurtt didn't come close to matching Huinker in strike outs, but he was never in serious trouble until the final inning. Not a Festina runner got around to third base during the first 12 innings and only three times did a runner get as far as second base.

Festina opened its winning inning with a ground out to the third baseman. The next hitter, Bill Luzum, a cousin of the Huinkers, doubled sharply down the left field line. Linus Huinker hit a looping fly to left for a single, but the runner on second base had to wait and see if the ball would be caught, and

was forced to stop at third. Art Huinker, who had two singles
up to then, then smashed a 1-1 count pitch on the ground into
centerfield to drive the run across ending the game.

What a ball game. In a small way, another "great moment in sports." At least for my Festina teammates. John Kurtt pitched a brilliant game for Denver. But destiny appeared to be on our side that night. Just by reading the lengthy write-up, tense feelings can set in. John became head baseball coach at Wartburg in Waverly after serving as high school baseball coach at New Hartford, a small school just northwest of Waterloo. A wonderful, poised individual who always seemed in control of whatever he was doing including throwing the baseball. He is a fine example of another outstanding baseball citizen.

Bill Luzum, Festina shortstop, had just completed his junior year in high school at Calmar High School, where he played regular third base already his freshman year. We were teammates his first year when I was a senior. His older brother is Festina's third baseman, Leo Luzum, whom I have spoken of before. He is related to us, but only through marriage.

Meanwhile, Bob Huinker played left field. Another first cousin of our family. His brother Nily, was the original first baseman on the Festina team formed in the later forties.

Something to think about. The news article mentioned the tenseness of the game. It is almost as if I am asking other athletes, or just baseball players, or maybe even just baseball pitchers, what their feelings are, or what their awareness of the tension of the situation is while they are playing the game. As a pitcher, thinking back on that game, I don't feel that I was tense because there were runners on second and third with nobody out. Sure, you realize you face a tough situation. You bear down. You tell yourself that I am going to get out of this. But it is not as if you stand out there on the rubber and start worrying about your situation. You don't have a lot of time to worry. You just go after them, still thinking straight and not all tensed up. Just some inner thoughts about what was going on in my mind. For the most part, I believe that I was thinking positive even if I was in a tough situation.

The semifinal game against Raymond brought Festina back on Wednesday night with brother Kenny ready to pitch. Remember the 20-4 shellacking we took at the hands of the Waterloo Whitehawks pro team at Dyersville? That was the same night as the Festina-Raymond game at Waterloo. Kenny shut out Raymond while striking out 11 and the Festina bats scored nine runs to win the game handily. Guess what.

Festina was in the finals. Finally. And enough has been said about that "other" game in the last chapter.

What is so interesting is that Festina found itself competing in the AABC state double-elimination tournament at the same time and had reached the finals of that tournament as well. Who was pitching for the home town? We will come back to that after we complete the Courier finals.

HUINKER PITCHERS UNSCORED UPON; FESTINA TO COURIER TOURNEY TITLE; SOUTHPAW WINS 3-0 OVER URBANA; EINCK HOMERS

Lefty Art Huinker celebrated the fifth anniversary of his Waterloo Courier Northeast Iowa Baseball Tournament of Champions pitching debut Sunday night with a shutout.

It won his Festina baseball club a trophy just as had his first mound appearance on Sunday, August 25, 1951, but this time it was the big one --- the trophy emblematic of northeast Iowa amateur baseball supremacy.

The little Winneshiek County community, which had tried six times before and had won only the third place trophy in 1951, Sunday became the first team in the eleven-year history of the meet to finish a tourney unscored upon. It stopped Urbana 3-0 in the finals at Waterloo Stadium to go with a 1-0 thirteen-inning victory last Sunday over Denver and a 9-0 triumph over Raymond Wednesday.

Parkersburg, edged 8-7 by Urbana in the semifinals, defeated Raymond 13-10 in the preliminary game Sunday, to win the consolation championship this year.

Norb Einck, in right field as he was in 1951, provided the only earned run of the title game with a line drive wallop over the left field wall to lead off the sixth. It was the seventh homer in the history of the tourney and the second this year. Parkersburg's Butch Dave hit one Monday.

Festina already had a lead of 2-0 on a pair of unearned runs --- more than enough for Huinker, the 21-year old Loras College student who retired the side in order in five of the nine innings and allowed only two base runners to reach third. It was manager Florian Nienhaus and Festina's seventh try for the title since 1949. They missed winning their loop championship in 1953.

The lineup Sunday night included six playing the same positions they were playing in 1951 when Festina was the consolation champ. Jim Schneberger caught, Leo Luzum played

130

third, Romauld Elsbernd at second, Norb Einck in right field and Linus Huinker in center, as well as Art Huinker pitching.

Ken Huinker, who played left field in 1951, was at first here Sunday, where another Huinker, Neil, played in 1951. This year Jerry Schneberger played at shortstop in place of Ken Schneberger, the 1951 shortstop, and there was another Huinker, Bob in left field.

As Art Huinker powered his way past batter after batter he compiled nearly an inaccessible record of 37 strikeouts in tournament competition, adding 16 Sunday to the 21 he fanned against Denver a week ago, yet Sunday night's victory was his first in the tournament.

He was replaced by Ken last Sunday for the final two outs of the 13-inning game and Ken received credit for the victory as Art drove in the winning run with a single in the last of the 13th.

Ken, a couple years older than Art, hurled the shutout against Raymond, fanning 11 for a total of 48 in the three Festina games.

Art, who has been pitching baseball for Festina and the Calmar Legion and high school teams since he was 13, had a one-hitter in his Courier tournament debut. A bunt in the seventh inning broke up his no-hitter as his club defeated Independence 5-1 for the consolation championship.

Jack Nora, who was the starting pitcher for Urbana in all four games, went the route for the first time Sunday and struck out eight. Only the homer among Festina's six hits figured in the scoring.

Urbana got three hits for a total of nine allowed by Art Huinker in 22 plus tournament innings.

Urbana, which faces a battle to win its Iowa Valley League championship, finished second in the Courier tourney for the second time in three years and has yet to score in a championship game. Urbana lost to Sumner in the finals, 13-0, in 1954.

Festina, the Northeast Iowa League champion, can win its second tournament championship this season Thursday night when it plays the winner of a Wednesday game between Sumner and Des Moines in the finals of the American Amateur Baseball Congress tournament at Sumner.

The 891 attendance Sunday brought the tournament total to 3,157, with each team's purse amounting to about $90 a game, pending a final audit of tournament receipts. The Courier pays all tournament expenses with the entire gate receipts, minus taxes, split among the teams at the rate of 1/18th of the total for each game played.

131

Festina snuffed out a scoreless Urbana ninth inning rally Sunday to preserve its shutout victory. Trailing 3-0 going into the last of the ninth, Urbana loaded the bases with one out and then failed to score as in infield fly and a fly to right field ended the game.

Festina opened the scoring in the first inning with a single run. Linus Huinker walked, was sacrificed to second by Art Huinker and took third when Leo Luzum grounded out second to first. The run scored when the Urbana catcher missed a third strike on Jim Schneberger and Huinker scored while Harrison chased the ball.

Festina scored its second run in the fifth inning on a situation similar to the happenings in the first. Linus Huinker was safe on first on the shortstop's fielding error. He was sacrificed to second by Art Huinker for the second time and took third on a passed ball. Leo Luzum struck out but the ball got away from the Urbana catcher. Huinker scored as Luzum was thrown out at first.

The third and final run for Festina came in the next inning when leadoff batter Norb Einck, rightfielder, powered Nora's second pitch 335 feet over the left field wall for a home run.

Festina threatened more runs in the sixth when Ken Huinker walked and moved into scoring position after one out when Jerry Schneberger was also walked. However, both men were stranded on base when the next two batters went out in order. Festina had singles by Leo Luzum and Jim Schneberger in the ninth but the former was thrown out trying to score from second to end the inning.

Festina finally gave its fans a long-awaited reward for their support. They had won a championship. I don't recall a wild celebration. They had another championship to play in four days --- the AABC state championship and the privilege of playing in the Northwest Regionals in South Dakota. That may have tempered a wild celebration.

Reflect back on this team, with so many veteran players in the lineup. For the ninth time in 1956 they waded through their Northeast Iowa league schedule and claimed the title. In those nine years they had some easy wins. Often they had to battle hard for nine innings, sometimes ending up on the victorious end, other times on the losing end. Eight times they looked forward to playing in the Waterloo Courier Northeast Iowa Tournament of Champions but never came home the champion.

Twice they received an invite to the Dubuqueland Tournament, one of 16 teams to compete each year for a prestigious championship. Each year they were knocked out, once in the championship game. I competed with them in all but one of those Courier tournaments. Only one of the two Dubuque tourneys included me in the lineup. But just this summer, while with the Dyersville Whitehawks, three tournaments were won with me playing in all twelve games.

For my Festina teammates, there had been no championship to claim, no championship to reflect on with pride and a feeling of accomplishment. The wait was finally over. The team laid claim to the biggest trophy available when the dust on the diamond settled. The depth of feeling had to be immeasurable. They had to savor the moment more than could be imagined. That is why, at least for the players on the Festina baseball, it was one of the "greatest moments in sports."

It was a well-deserved victory for the Festina players as well. The players and their wives were almost like family. They did many social things together, not always the entire team but several different groupings of families. They attended weddings together and also funerals together. If the small Catholic parish sponsored an event, they usually would be in attendance. Many of their children were successful athletes, both sons and daughters, at Calmar High School. But then, why not? A community, counting the farm families surrounding Festina, of less than 200 enabled everybody to know the affairs of every family that lived in that tiny circle.

The planning meeting of all the managers prior to the start of the Courier tournament included a vote by those in attendance of my eligibility to play for Festina. Tournament rules require that a player, in order to be eligible must be on the field in uniform and ready to play in at least half of his team's regularly scheduled league games. The managers voted in the affirmative that I was ready to play in the seventh game the Sunday previous because the game was ready to start, the umpires had said "play ball" and the two teams were on the field when a heavy rain washed out the efforts.

In a separate article about the championship game, there was a short paragraph heaping praise on our rightfielder Norb Einck that deserves re-printing. This was also in the Courier.

> *One of the highlights of Festina's spectacular string of victories in both tournaments has been the hitting of Norb Einck, veteran rightfielder. He has been hitting consistently and driving in important runs which have been the difference between victory and defeat.*

Bob Howard, a close friend, golfing buddy, and a professional colleague of mine, tells about his experience with Norb Einck when Bob was growing up in, of all places, Sumner. Too young to play yet, Bob would sit on the score board beyond the right field fence and put up the scores inning by inning. Almost every inning when Festina was taking the field, Norb would jog out close to the scoreboard and share thoughts. Some of the thoughts assured Bob about how we

133

were going to beat Bob's hometown Cubs. Always friendly, always good to have around. That probably describes our right fielder.

Bob also always recalls the night he was on the scoreboard and my brother Kenny came up to bat. Kenny lined a shot to right field and Bob said "I started to duck because I thought it was going to hit the scoreboard. But the ball was hit so hard, it just kept on going and flew right over the top of the scoreboard." Bob Howard, by the way, ended up being an all-state fast pitch softball player going to many national tournaments with Dubuque championship teams, besides participating in many baseball tournaments in the Dubuque County area while playing for Farley.

There are several pictures from the three games in Waterloo in the picture section of this book. Now for the AABC tournament.

Festina played five games in the double-elimination tournament, starting before the Waterloo Courier Tournament of Champions and finishing after that tourney was completed. Pitching demands placed the most pressure on the team---5 games in the AABC and 3 games at the Waterloo tourney --- in a stretch of about 18 days. The driving distance from Dubuque to Sumner made it almost impossible for my participation but Ann and I did drive up for the finals against Sumner. Also, with the Waterloo games and one game in between for Dyersville made it almost impossible for me to do much pitching for my home town besides the Courier tournament. That was a major reason why we drove to the championship game. With four days rest I possibly could have helped in relief if necessary. But, even though we lost the game, my brother Kenny pitched well enough to win the game if we had given him defensive and/or offensive support.

Festina opened the AABC tournament by defeating Des Moines, 3-0, in extra innings. Don Kuehner, picked up from the St. Lucas conference second-place team, pitched his first of two outstanding games in the victory over Des Moines. Next, we had another good pitching outing, this time from Kenny, but we lost the game to Denver 3-1, the same team we defeated in Waterloo in the 13-inning thriller the following week.

Next, Festina eliminated Independence, 6-1, with Jerry Schneberger and Romauld Elsbernd doing the pitching. Schneberger was tossing a shutout into the fourth inning but had to leave the game when he was hit in the hand by a line drive. Elsbernd pitched the remainder of the seven-inning game and also helped his own cause with a two-run single in a four-run sixth to ice the game for Festina.

Kuehner came back to throw his second strong game in defeating host Sumner, giving them their first loss of the AABC tournament. This game provided one of the rare times when we punched out a win over the Sumner Cubs. The championship game is written up below.

134

SUMNER WINS AABC TITLE 5-0 OVER FESTINA
For the second year in a row, Sumner reigns as the
Iowa AABC Tournament champion. Sumner downed Festina
behind the four-hit pitching of Chuck Anderson 5-0 here Friday
night in the finals of the double elimination tourney. Both teams
had lost one game going into Friday's action.

The winners were able to score only one earned run off
of the pitching of Ken Huinker, but two Festina errors allowed
four other runs to cross home plate.

Sumner was leading 2-0 going into the top of the ninth
inning but then the roof fell in on Festina. An error allowed
three big runs to score wrapping the contest up for Sumner.

Festina had three singles, one each by Leo Luzum, Norb Einck and myself, plus a double by Jim Schneberger, the only extra-base hit of the game. Don Kuehner was selected as one of the two top hurlers in the AABC tournament. Sumner again prepared to make their third consecutive trip to the Northwest Regionals.

Festina still had an additional highlight game to play besides the Festina-St. Lucas league make-up game presented earlier. That awaited the pitching battle between Dyersville and Festina on September 9, pitting the Huinker brothers against each other. I call it a highlight because for Festina it was another opportunity to show the northeast corner of the state of Iowa that they were one of the premier teams of the 1950's. The game has been covered earlier in the previous chapter, again a victory for Festina, 4-2.

That officially ended the 1956 baseball season for semi-pro baseball except for the Sumner Cubs going to South Dakota. They eventually were eliminated from that competition and not able to go on to Battle Creek for the national finals.

On to the senior year at Loras College and one more year of college baseball.

It had been a very strong summer, pitching-wise. The "professional dream" was still alive. While the second dream was a reality, that of being with Ann every day, we didn't know the status of the baseball dream.

135

UNDEFEATED

The final year of a wonderful experience at the college on the hill in Dubuque had come. The academic studies continued with a load of nineteen credits in hopes of making the final semester during baseball season somewhat softer. Most of my classes were interesting and challenging, made so by some wonderful professors, mostly archdiocesan priests. Regretfully, those times have changed at Loras, with very few priests among a strong lay faculty today. Three of those priests from the fifties were still around the college, at least still in the Dubuque area when our class celebrated their fiftieth class reunion. We invited them to our house for a pre-reunion gathering of about forty members of the class. The presence of Msgr. Friedl, Msgr. Manternach and Father Vogl was the highlight of the evening. All were in the late eighties by this time but their sharing with all of us was stimulating.

The summer just completed saw full-time employment with the Geisler Roofing Company in Dubuque. Most of the work consisted of repairing or replacing flat roofs on major buildings in the Dubuque area, such as Jefferson Junior High School (where I first met Johnny Orr, at that time head basketball coach for Dubuque Senior High School), the huge Montgomery Ward building at the corner of 8th and Main, a dormitory on the Wisconsin State of Platteville campus, plus insulating of the ceiling in St. Anthony's Church in Dubuque, as well as the Catholic church at Balltown.

Parenthood was going well, with little Terry occupying much of our time. A summer of baseball playing, mostly with the Dyersville Whitehawks, some with hometown Festina, had gone very well. Now it was time to get ready for the fourth and final year of Duhawk baseball. We had lost slugger Romie Gales, outfielder Sam Azzinaro, first baseman Jack New and third baseman Dick Wiley. Wiley completed his necessary program in three years and went on to graduate school. But again, we added three new faces which provided a major boost to both the offensive and defensive skills of the Loras squad. Infielders Bruno Kowalkowski and Dick Breitbach plus outfielder Bob Willhite stepped right in. Another interesting addition to the team was catcher Dick Mescher from Dyersville. Dick was my catcher for the Dyersville Whitehawks the entire summer of 1956. He also was a colleague at Beckman High School during the two years that Ann and I were there. More on that later. Also added to the team were pitchers Don Jennings (Cedar Rapids), Frank Delaney (Dubuque) and Dick Kressin (Beloit, Wisconsin) plus utility infielder Duke Coughlin (La Crosse). I ran into Duke many years later as one of the main organizers of the Rising Stars Little League tournament held in La Crosse each year.

Our season started with a three day, six game swing through northern Missouri and western Illinois. Pitching the first game of a doubleheader at Culver-Stockton (Canton, MO) the fifteenth victory was realized on a 7-0 two-hit shutout, a game where we held a one-run lead until a six run seventh inning explosion. Notice two hits for the pitcher. We lost the second game. On the entire trip we ended up three wins and three losses, sweeping a doubleheader from Quincy College and losing two to Western Illinois University.

Allow me to stray off the topic of baseball for a paragraph. The hotel that was our residence for one night at Canton, Missouri was of unique interest. It was an old two-story building whose fire escapes consisted of heavy ropes tied to a hook in each room. Throw the rope out the window and slide down. Quite a few players took the challenge and found the "ropescape" to be a successful plan. But even better, they found it to be a "fun" escape plan. The rooms were huge, most of them with two double beds with plenty of additional space in each one. Fifty years later the building is still there but now has several retail shops on the first floor and apartments on the second floor.

HUINKER LETS DUHAWKS SPLIT

Canton, Mo.--- Art Huinker was in top form here Saturday hurling two-hit ball as the Loras Duhawks shut out Culver Stockton in their season opener. But the host team dampened the afternoon for Loras by winning the nightcap of the doubleheader, 4-3.

Huinker yielded just a pair of singles, while striking out 13. He didn't walk anybody. The brilliant lefty hasn't lost a game in his college career; and has a fifteen game winning streak going.

Loras picked up a 1-0 lead in the top of the fourth which would have been good enough.

But Vince Dowd's team sewed up the game with a six-run burst in the seventh. Dick Breitbach and Bob Willhite slammed doubles and Kowalkowski powdered a home run. All told, the Duhawks collected 11 hits off two Culver Stockton pitchers. Breitbach, Kowalkowski and Huinker each had two hits.

The second game was a different story. The home team took a 1-0 lead in the first and built it to 3-0 in the fourth. Loras tied the contest at 3-3 in the fifth with Bob Wolfe and Bill Leonard sparking the rally with triples.

The winners got a run in the bottom of the fifth which proved decisive. Bill Hyland pitched for Loras, giving up six hits.

An interesting note on the opening game write-up. The three hitters that led the sixth inning scoring explosion were all newcomers to the team. What a way to start out. The next game was a home game against tough Lewis College and Coach Gordy Gillespie. First, there was a write-up of the upcoming game in the Telegraph Herald inserted below.

137

Loras College returns home from a six-game road tour Sunday to meet Lewis College at Keane Field. Game time is 1 p.m. Coach Vince Dowd's boys have broken even in the early games, holding a 3-3 mark and will be seeking to push above the .500 mark Sunday against the Flyers.

It will be no easy matter from the looks of things, though. Lewis is stocked with 14 returning lettermen, seven of whom are seniors. The Flyers are expected to start a letterman at every position.

But Lewis Coach Gordon Gillespie may feel the loss of his top performer, catcher Jerry Pennie, who has caught every game for the Flyers in the past two seasons. Pennie, also one of Lewis' top basketball players, has suffered a head injury in recent practice, and it is doubtful if he will be able to see action Sunday.

Dowd is in good shape. His staff of six pitchers has a week's rest, and Art Huinker is scheduled to open for Loras.

Gillespie's teams were always considered a stiff challenge, so what happened that Sunday afternoon was a major surprise and also a little revenge for me because they are the team that knocked me out of the game in my sophomore game with my parents and Ann watching. Although I addressed interesting aspects of pitching, when you have it and when you feel you don't have it in an earlier chapter while pitching for Festina, this was one of those games where every pitch was alive and moving, sometimes shooting up, other times a big movement to the left, away from a right hand-batter, and sometimes down. That, more than speed, is still a most important aspect of making the pitch tough to hit. Plus throwing the ball in the low nineties as determined in pro ball later, made for a very successful day. As second baseman Joe Ottavi said after the game, "It is the only time in all my playing that I was booed by the fans when I fielded a ground ball and threw the runner out at first in the ninth inning." But Joe, I'm still glad you threw him out. This was indeed one of those good days.

HUINKER STARS IN LORAS WIN; STRIKES OUT 22
BATTERS
Art Huinker fanned 22 Lewis batters, broke his own modern strikeout record at Loras, and drove in the final run while leading the Loras College Duhawks past the Lewis College Flyers, 4-0, at Loras Sunday.

Huinker posted his16th consecutive college win against no defeats while breaking the strikeout record of 19 he set at Knox College last year. He also came within two strikeouts of the all-time record of 24 set by Red Faber, later a star for the Chicago White Sox in the '20s.

138

The Duhawks, behind Huinker's outstanding pitching, had a no-hitter going until the seventh when Sugar Kane and Frank Karpowicz of Lewis posted the only marks in the Flyers' hit column.

Loras scored three runs in the first three innings on five hits. In the first inning, Dick Breitbach singled off Karpowicz, who was handling the mound chores for the Flyers. Rocky Schiltz walked and Dick Wright smashed out a double to send Breitbach in for the first Loras run.

Huinker gave up his only walk of the ball game to Tony Janc of Lewis in the first. Joe Ottavi walked in the second inning and scored on a sacrifice fly by Bob Wolfe after catcher Bill Leonard singled.

In the third, Rocky Schiltz singled and moved to second on a passed ball. Bruno Kowalkowski belted a double which enabled Schiltz to score.

In the sixth, Gene Potts singled and stole second. Ottavi walked and Potts moved to third on a sacrifice by Leonard. Huinker drove one through the box for an RBI as Potts scurried home to score the fourth Loras run.

Tony Janc of Lewis reached first on an error in the seventh, Kane singled and Karpowicz was credited with a scratch hit when Huinker covered the infield single and was forced to switch the play from third to first where the throw was too late.

With one away and a loaded bases situation, Huinker struck out the next batter and threw the last Lewis man out at first. Both teams went hitless in the eighth and ninth innings as the Loras chucker added four more men to his strikeout list. Breitbach had two hits for the Duhawks.

Notice in the above write-ups that roomie Bob Wolfe is finally getting considerable playing time and doing very well. The next game apparently was one of those days when you don't have it. But when your teammates score twelve runs, the pitcher grinds it out and manages to be successful, with much less fanfare.

HUINKER WINS 17TH
Loras College gained its seventh baseball win of the spring, whipping Winona State, 12-4, Saturday afternoon on the Loras field.

Art Huinker, the sharp lefty star of Loras, won his 17th straight win although giving way to Bill Hyland in the eighth inning. The game lasted three hours and Loras was in command all the way. The Duhawks got single runs in each of the first four innings and four more in the sixth and seventh.

139

Winona got all of its runs in the seventh when Huinker
was touched for three singles and two doubles. He struck out
eight and gave up all nine hits. Hyland looked good in finishing
up, striking out five of six men.
Dick Breitbach socked four hits and Dick Wright, Joe
Ottavi and Huinker had two hits apiece for Vince Dowd's team.
Huinker scored three runs. Loras got a total of 14 hits off two
Winona pitchers.

In the next game, I pitched into the fourth against the Luther Norsemen at
Decorah until I was hit by a pitch on my left elbow. The score was 3-0 at the
time. It is questionable whether or not I should have been credited with the win.
Loras won 5-3, never trailing but by today's rules, starting pitchers are supposed
to go at least half the game.

LORAS DOWNS LUTHER, HUINKER SIDELINED
Decorah, IA --- Art Huinker ran his victories to 18
straight Wednesday, but the star Loras pitcher wasn't around at
the finish of a 5-3 victory over Luther. Huinker was hit by a
pitched ball in the fourth inning and was forced to leave the
game. He had six strikeouts before departing (he was struck on
the left elbow).
Loras started fast with two runs in the first inning.
Gene (Tiny) Potts reached base on an error and stole second.
He rode in on Ricky Schiltz's double and Schiltz then scored on
a single by Dick Breitbach.
In the second the Duhawks picked up another run when
Huinker and Bruno Kowalkowski each walked, advanced on Bill
Leonard's sacrifice and Huinker scored on a passed ball.
Luther got its first run off Pat Kapsch in the fourth.
Dick Halvorson singled, stole second and scored when Dave
Ramness singled. Singles by Bruno Kowalkowski and Potts
helped score its final two runs in the seventh.

A week later, with the arm showing no ill effects of
the game at Luther, the Duhawks were on the field against
Wisconsin State at Platteville. After two runs in the first, in the
fourth the Duhawk offense got rolling and piled up thirteen
more before it ended in a 15-1 rout of the Pioneers. Again,
notice two hits for the pitcher.

HUINKER GAINS VICTORY NO. 19
Art Huinker ran his victory skein to 19 as Loras
humbled Platteville, 15-1, at Platteville, Wednesday. The Loras
lefty allowed four hits and gave up one base on balls, while

140

collecting 12 strikeouts, raising his season total to 55 in four games.

Loras scored two runs on two hits in the first inning to take the lead, which they never relinquished. The Dowdmen tallied four runs in the fourth and sixth, then finished their scoring with a five-run seventh on four hits.

Platteville scored its run in the eighth when Bill Ewing reached first on a fielder's choice, and scored when the lone Loras error made Rick Malson's long fly ball good for three bases. Huinker closed out the inning with two strikeouts to leave Malson stranded.

Bob Willhite collected three hits in five trips to the plate and had five RBIs for the Duhawks. He also scored three runs. Joe Ottavi and Huinker each collected two safeties.

At this point, there were seven games left on our schedule. The following article from the Loras Lorian identifies the weather difficulties the team experienced and none of the games were completed, although we had started the final scheduled game against LaCrosse State only to have it halted with a downpour after three and one-half innings. Oddly enough, I can remember the day as being extremely hot and humid until the front came through and showed who was boss.

DUHAWK NINE ENDS SEASON; PITCHERS PACE DUHAWKS TO 13-3

Art Huinker just missed collecting his twentieth game without a loss when yesterday's contest with La Crosse was rained out, one inning short of being an official game. After three and one-half innings with Loras leading 2-0, a steady downpour commenced which closed out the Duhawk nine's season with a record of 13 wins in 16 games.

Highlight of the season was senior Art Huinker's fanning of 22 Lewis College batters to break the modern strikeout record of 19 he set at Loras last year. The Calmar, Ia., lefthander notched five wins this season, pitching a total of 35 and 2-3 innings. He gave up 16 hits while striking out 62 batters, and walking five during the entire season.

Nineteen wins without a defeat in four years of hurling were chalked up by the stocky speed-baller who posted an earned run average of 1.0 for this season and 1.5 for his career.

Dick Winter, a junior from New Hampton, Ia., pitched a total of 30 innings to collect his four wins in as many starting calls. He raised his three-year record to eight wins without a loss, allowing only 15 hits while fanning 33. The control-wise righthander gave up only eight walks during the campaign.

141

A 2-1 record was posted by junior Bill Hyland of Chicago, Ill., who bounced back from his first defeat to earn two wins and turn in over four innings of relief pitching. In 25 and 1-3 innings he gave up 17 hits and 6 walks while collecting 16 strikeouts.

Pat Kapsch, a sophomore from Albert City, Ia., hurled two wins for the Duhawks. He struck out 30 in 21 and 1-3 innings while giving 13 hits and 15 walks.

Two freshmen, Dick Kressin of Beloit, Wis., and Don Jennings of Cedar Rapids, Ia., suffered defeats in their lone appearance during the year. Each pitched one game of a doubleheader at Western Illinois at the opening of the season. Kressin gave up 3 hits, 2 walks and struck out 2 in seven innings, while Jennings allowed 5 hits, 3 walks and struck out 2.

A .364 batting average turned in by Bob Willhite was tops for the season in the hitting department. Willhite connected with 12 hits in 33 trips to the plate to cop the hitting crown. Bruno Kowalkowski, third baseman, had 13 for 36 to post a .361 average to finish second.

Dick Wright went to the plate 61 times to collect 20 hits and finish third with a .328. Huinker was the fourth hitter to go over the .300 mark, belting out eight hits in 26 trips to the plate.

The four seasons were over. What an experience with some fantastic teammates, both as very strong baseball players and also as just plain old good people. In the above write-up, notice the two players who led the team in hitting--Bob Willhite and Bruno Kowalkowski, both new players. We encountered Bob many years later when he became pastor of the parish in Aurora, Illinois where Ann's sister, Stella, taught school. Bruno was a student preparing for the priesthood with the Dominican Order. Don't know where his life has taken him.

Following are some honors received during the final semester of our senior season as they appeared in the Lorian. Pictures associated with the 1957 senior year are found in the picture section of this book.

ATHLETIC AWARDS

After the various athletic seasons are over, it comes time to pass out honors to those who have played the game well. Despite the ups and downs of the Duhawk sports slate, several outstanding individuals were singled out during the year for their accomplishments on the mound, gridiron and the hardcourt.

Senior Arthur T. Huinker, Loras' lefthanded pitching ace, was awarded the Chicago Alumni Club's annual "Scholar-

142

Athlete" trophy, during halftime of the Loras-Ambrose basketball game. Still in the process of rewriting Loras pitching records, Art has consistently displayed his ability in the classroom during his school career as well.

During the same ceremony, basketball star Dick Wright, was presented with the Delta Sigma fraternity trophy as the most valuable player of the 1956-57 season. Another honor soon followed for the senior cager when he received honorable mention on the 1957 All-American Basketball Team, selected by the Tablet, diocesan newspaper of Brooklyn, New York.

HUINKER, RUGGLE RECEIVE SENIOR AWARDS
The Rev. Lawrence J. Guter, dean of studies, has announced that Arthur T. Huinker, Calmar, Ia., and Leo A. Ruggle, Perry, Ia., will receive the annual senior awards. The men were selected by a school-wide faculty vote.

The O'Connor award was given to Huinker. This award is based on scholarship, leadership, cooperation and contribution as a student at Loras College. The presentation is made to the outstanding member of the senior class.

The Catholic Action award is based on unselfish devotion to the college and cooperation in its spiritual, physical and social activities. This year's recipient was Leo A. Ruggle.

He was chosen for his contribution to the betterment of Loras College, by the members of the religion department, under the direction of the Rt. Rev. Msgr. Ernest P. Ament.

Huinker, the son of Mr. and Mrs. Leo J. Huinker of Calmar, Ia., is Loras' outstanding scholar-athlete and was honored last Feb. 27, when he received the Chicago Club award for scholastic and athletic achievement while at Loras.

Huinker has been on the honor roll every semester and maintained a 3.5 scholastic average.

The Duhawk hurler holds the modern Loras strikeout record with 22 in one game and has never been defeated in four years of intercollegiate competition. He has a record of 19 wins.

Huinker is a member of the LI club, the IFTA, Delta Sigma and the History Club.

He is married and the father of one child, a son. He has accepted a teaching and coaching job at Ossian, Ia., Catholic high school and will pitch for an independent semi-pro team this summer.

Graduation was a terrific day. My Mom and Dad treated us to a big family picnic at Eagle Point Park before graduation, then took our entire family to

143

the Circle Restaurant in East Dubuque for a fantastic dinner. A great band of the fifties, Wayne King, was at the Melody Mill Ballroom that night and that is where most of my brothers and sisters and their spouses ended up. At 2 a.m. Ann and I tried to eat a big meal at the Red Pagoda but realized finally that we really won't that hungry.

It has been a fantastic four years at the Catholic college at the top of Loras Boulevard. How the grade point of 3.5 was maintained throughout the four years, I don't think there is a simple answer. First of all, with maybe one or two exceptions, the quality of my professors was outstanding. Even to the current day, I believe I could name almost every one of them. If there is any suggestion I can make to a student beginning his/her college career, it is simply this: ATTEND CLASSES EVERY DAY THEY ARE SCHEDULED. Our older grandchildren have heard that advice quite often. In four years, the only classes I missed were those that conflicted with a Loras baseball game. I will not claim that I was always attentive throughout but just being there helps.

Reflecting back on the four years what great advice from my parents. "If you want God to bless you, we think you should go to Loras." Oh, how true that was. After the four years of earning a degree at Loras College there was still much small-town farm boy in me. Even today Ann thinks that is still true. Otherwise, why would I enjoy taking care of a good sized flower garden at our home. She uses the quote, "You can take the boy off the farm, but you can't take the farm out of the boy."

THE ST. LOUIS CARDINALS CALL

Ever since the completion of my first year of baseball at Loras College, opportunities to play in advanced semi-professional baseball leagues became available. These leagues consisted of mostly college players, many of whom were aspiring professional baseball players. The first two summers after the spring seasons at Loras, the calls came from a league in South Dakota. The players consisted almost entirely of players from colleges, big and small. Also included were some players who had received professional contracts but had been let go. Yet they held the dream of "someday we can still be a big league ball player. " The offers for both 1954 and 1955 were declined for a variety of reasons. First of all, Festina was still a favorite place to play. It enabled me to help my Dad on the farm. There may have been another reason, the opportunity to be close to Ann in pursuit of that other dream. And wedding plans for August cemented that closeness even more, with the wedding taking place in the summer of 1955.

In looking back on those two summers, the offers possibly provided the challenges that big league scouts were looking for me to prove myself. In their evaluations, success in those leagues would solidify, or not solidify, in their minds, my ability to compete in the professional ranks.

In the summer of 1956, after a third spring baseball season at Loras, an offer came from a league called the Southern Minnesota State League, or "Southern Minny" for short. This league also consisted of many top-level college players on the uphill climb to the pros, as they hoped. But this league also included many ex-professionals whose baseball careers were in the downhill slide. This offer was not accepted when the Dyersville Whitehawk opportunity presented itself. Again, the Southern Minny would have provided greater challenges but the opportunity for full-time employment in Dubuque, while not having to move for three months and then return to Dubuque for the final year at Loras, sounded much simpler. Plus, we had our first child coming in July.

Now, as Ann and I planned for the summer of 1957, prior to beginning teaching at Ossian De Sales in the fall, a move out of Dubuque was inevitable, one way or the other. The opportunity to play again for Dyersville was there and probably a job in Dubuque, similar to the previous summer. However, this time, when an offer came again to play in the Southern Minny, we accepted. The offer came from Emil Scheid, a huge plumbing contractor from Austin, Minnesota who was attempting to find an eighth team for the league and planned to place the team in Mason City, Iowa, a new entry into the Southern Minny and the first non-Minnesota team ever allowed in the league.

The eight teams in the Southern Minny for the summer of 1957 now were Albert Lea, Austin, Winona, Faribault, Mankato, Rochester, Fairmont (all Minnesota cities) and the Mason City Braves. This league, along with seven other leagues, were considered the top class of semi-pro baseball in Minnesota. I am only familiar with the Southern Minny and the Western Minny, along with several leagues in the Twin Cities.   In reviewing the Southern Minny league history, I found that it had started already in 1912. Shortly after 1957, in the early sixties, the league was disbanded, brought about by   a drastic reduction in attendance, and therefore, a lack of sufficient funding.

In the fifties, the league was considered comparable to Class A professional leagues in ability. At that time, the minor league baseball system went from the lowest D leagues up to AAA. It was very common in the first year of play with Mason City, that crowds of three to four thousand per night were the norm. By 1960, the last year I played in the Southern Minny, we were excited if we had a crowd of three to five hundred fans.

In the schedule for the summer of 1957, three league games were to be played each week. For the new league entry, home games were held at Roosevelt Field, the same diamond that hosted the state high school baseball tournament in 1952 when the Calmar Cahawks competed for the state championship.

How did these towns finance the caliber of players they needed to be competitive? It was an interesting arrangement and one probably used by many leagues of this competitive level so that college players did not lose their college eligibility. Each player was fully employed by a business in the local community. However, if the team had any commitments that interfered with the hours of work, the players were excused from their work schedule but still received full hourly pay for the time missed. With that many games and some of the road games over 100 miles away, full eight hour work days were limited. There probably were variances in these arrangements for former professional baseball players and for a player who happened to be from that local area. And, with attendance figures in the lower thousands for every game, there was a sizable income for the home team that could be utilized as well.

My employer ran a wholesale door company where my official responsibilities consisted of sanding and shaving interior wood doors preparing for shipment to retailers. Because my hours were often shortened by the baseball responsibilities, it was a serious commitment from the employer. They did have some rewards, such as free advertising at the ballpark and free tickets for employees and their families at the games.

Our move to Mason City, after our four-year experience as a Loras Duhawk, included a stop at my brother's farm where our furniture, dishes and other items not needed in a furnished apartment were stored for the summer. We moved into an apartment on State Street, near downtown Mason City. The apartment was part of a family home, now divided into a two-apartment set-up with the owners living in the other half. The stay was short-lived. We stayed there one month and moved to another duplex, this one an upstairs apartment, because the landlady of the original house was impossible to please, impossible to live with.

After three days of organizational meetings and practices, the new Mason City Braves were ready to take the field. To start the season, the team played under the leadership of the organizer of the team, Emil Scheid. Emil was well known in the Southern Minny for his year-after-year involvement with the Austin franchise, both financially and as manager. Taking charge of the team he was responsible for starting, his role lasted for only the first ten games, before he was forced to again take charge of his hometown Austin Packers team. For the summer of 1957, and the return summer of 1958, high school coaches (and baseball players) managed the Mason City Braves. Those coaches were Ed Colbert, quite familiar to Dubuque sports fans, and Paul Bruns. Paul coached in the neighboring town of Charles City, Iowa.

The Braves team consisted of the rookie and the veteran. Veteran players were led by Roy Gilmore, Art Pennington, Frank Brown, Freddie Folkes, Junie Floyd, Don Petschow and pitchers Jim Lawler and Bill Freese. Freese, a 28-year old former professional relief pitcher, born in Wiota, Iowa, had just signed his first teaching contract at nearby Corwith, Iowa High School. He later coached high school baseball at Davenport Central High School where he had a very successful and lengthy tenure.

On the rookie side were three current college baseball players, besides myself, on the Braves' roster. Two players, catcher Chuck Lindstrom and pitcher Tom Scheuerman, played for Northwestern in the Big Ten Conference, where they helped the Wildcats win the Big Ten baseball title. Lindstrom had a .364 batting average for the college season. He was the son of former major league baseball star, Freddie Lindstrom, head baseball coach at Northwestern. The other college player was infielder Don Brummer, nineteen years old, who, as a sophomore at Creighton University in Omaha, Nebraska, had already won two letters in baseball and in basketball. Don had graduated from little Woodbine High School in southwestern Iowa.

We had another new challenge. Again, some nervous anticipation but not to the degree of what I experienced the first game I pitched for Loras College. This time the challenge was more difficult however.

In the month of June, I started seven games and relieved once. After going no wins and one loss in the first two starts, there were four consecutive victories for a four and one won-loss record by the fourth of July. For some unknown reason there are no write-ups for the first two starts. Possibly another example of omitting games I don't want to remember.

MASON CITY DEFEATS MANKATO 5-0 FOR THIRD
WIN IN ROW; HUINKER AND
FREESE APPLY WHITEWASH
By Jim Vanheel
Sharp defense still has a big place in baseball. The
Mason City Braves provided exhibit No. 1 in this department

147

Thursday night at Roosevelt Field as they blanked the Mankato Merchants 5-0. In doing so, they came up with four important double plays.

Third sacker Don Brummer and second baseman Fred Follkes each figured in three of them as the winners sparkled afield. Hal Harrison came up with one great play from shortstop on a slow bounder and the lone Merchant trying to steal was nailed on a fine throw by catcher Dick Noterman.

It takes sound pitching to go with fielding and the Braves had that, too. Lefty Art Huinker and Bill Freese combined for the goose-egg against Mankato and between them they fanned nine batters. Huinker was moving towards a shutout when he ran into trouble in the eighth on a pair of walks and a single. Freese was called in from the bullpen to retire the side and gave up no hits in relief—the second straight time he has starred in a fireman's role.

Leo Evans, tall right hander who held a previous 4-2 win over Mason City, suffered his second loss as against four victories as he was rapped for 10 hits. Still, he went into the last of the seventh inning with the Merchants trailing by only a 1-0 score.

The Braves picked up an important run in the second frame. Frank Brown, who had two doubles and a single in the game, lofted a high ball into leftfield which went for a double when second baseman Charley Frey tried to make a long run for the catch. Don Petschow singled to send Brown to third and Dick Noterman then had a sacrifice fly to centerfield to score Brown.

Evans sailed into the seventh frame with a 5-hit job but then hit trouble. Huinker got his second hit of the game but Brummer fanned for the second out. Then Fred Folkes singled and Art Pennington walked to load the sacks. The dependable Brown drove a single to centerfield for two runs and fans breathed easier.

In the eighth, Mason City got a pair of gift runs. Junie Floyd and Noterman singled and Hal Harrison put down a bunt. Evans fielded the ball and tried to get a force play at third but threw in the dirt at the side of the bag and Floyd and Noterman both scored on the error.

Each club was left with eight baserunners stranded. The win was the first for Huinker, who has pitched well in all three starts. The victory was the first for Mason City over Mankato this season.

Notice the pitcher getting two hits. Actually my hitting was better than usual in this league.

148

MASON CITY, AUSTIN PLAY TO 3-3 TIE; CALLED
FOR RAIN;
By Jim Vanheel, Sports Editor
The Mason City Braves and Austin Packers played
nine innings to a 3-3 tie Saturday night at Roosevelt Field with
the game then called because of rain. The ninth frame had been
played in a light rain and the game earlier had been held up for
a few minutes. Playing conditions were too poor to continue.
ALL RECORDS FOR THE GAME GO ON THE
BOOKS BUT THE ENTIRE GAME MUST BE REPLAYED. IT
HAS BEEN RESCHEDULED FOR NEXT WEDNESDAY
NIGHT AT ROOSEVELT FIELD.

If the game had been called a few minutes earlier, the
Braves would have had a win because they went into the top
half of the ninth frame holding a 3-1 lead. Pitcher Art Huinker
had allowed Austin only three hits to this point, all singles.
With one down, Dick Cordell got a single. Then Art Seguso
fanned. But Jim Wilkinson, last year's loop batting champ,
came through with a double to leftfield to score Cordell.

Then Huinker uncorked a wild pitch and Wilkinson
went to third. Huinker threw wild again pitching to Red
Lindgren. Catcher Chuck Lindstrom recovered the ball and
pegged to Huinker at the plate who made the tag on Wilkinson,
then dropped the ball for an error for the tying run.

Bill Knox, the Austin pitcher, allowed only six hits in
the game, four of them for extra bases. Don Petschow homered
over the right field fence in the second inning and Frank Brown
duplicated the feat in the fifth frame. In the sixth, the Braves got
their third run when Art Pennington and Huinker cracked
doubles.

Austin got its only run in the seventh prior to the ninth
frame. Cordell walked, took second on a wild pitch and went to
third on Seguso's single. Then Wilkinson hit into a double play
with Cordell scoring.

There were only two errors in the well played game
before 733 rain-soaked fans and each club left only three
baserunners stranded. Knox didn't walk a batter while Huinker
chalked up eight strikeouts. Until Seguso's single in the
seventh, Huinker had allowed only one hit. That was an infield
roller between home and third base by Phil Morris in the fourth
inning.

Not one of those games you write home about, even though Austin only
had one run going into the ninth. Three walks and two wild pitches in one game.

But pitchers, including me, have those nights. There were two hits for the home town pitcher again, however.

MASON CITY DEFEATS AUSTIN 6-5; GET WINNING RUN IN 8TH ON ERROR

By Jim Vanheel, Sports Editor

You can't count those Mason City Braves out of the first half pennant race in the Southern Minnesota League until they lose a game. They downed Austin in a much postponed , replayed game by a 6-5 score.

That made it the fifth straight win for the club and left Mason City only a game and a half behind loop leading Mankato—the difference being all in the win column. While the Braves still are in third place, they're considered the hottest team in the league.

Art Huinker, the stocky lefthander, got his second win for Mason City Wednesday despite giving up three "gopher" balls. Bill Freese came in to pitch the ninth frame and got his third straight scoreless relief job.

An oddity of the game was that Austin never got more than one hit in any inning (only seven in all) and yet the Packers got five runs and all were earned. Here's how it happened: Catcher Gene Steiger poked a solo homer over the leftfield fence in the fourth inning. Huinker walked Phil Morris and Bob Riggenbach in the fifth and Dick Cordell smacked a pitch a mile high but it still cleared the rightfield fence for a homer. Then Steiger knocked another 4-baser over the leftfield fence in the eighth.

Freese got in trouble in the ninth. After fanning pinch-hitter Red Lindgren, Riggenbach walked, Cordell singled and Art Seguso was safe on Hal Harrison's error. Wilkinson then grounded to Harrison who pegged to Fred Folkes at second base and Folkes relayed to first for a double play to end the game.

Another game with too many walks, five in total. Plus three home runs given up. That will come up again. The only consolation is the fact that we won and now we were in a battle for first place. One hit for the pitcher this time.

MASON CITY BRAVES FLATTEN AUSTIN; HUINKER FANS 11 IN THIRD WIN

By Jim Vanheel, Sports Editor

The Mason City Braves broke a 3-game losing streak by drubbing the Austin Packers 15-3 Tuesday night in a long game played at Roosevelt Field. The victory gave the Braves a

3-game sweep over the Packers in the first half of the season in the Southern Minnesota League.

Art Huinker pitched the distance for Mason City and stopped the Packers on seven hits while posting the highest strikeout total for a Mason City pitcher this season, 11. The win was his third. He was backed by errorless ball afield.

His only trouble was in the third when Austin shot ahead 3-1. A double by Bob Riggenbach,, a single by Dick Cordell, a walk to Roy Gilmore and Junie Floyd's single produced all the runs the Packers were to get in the game.

Four players for the Braves got credit for all the runs driven home. Frank Brown hit a high point by plating six markers, Fred Folkes knocked in four and Denny Rinaldi had three RBIs. Brown now has 26 RBIs, one more than Art Pennington.

Again in this game, two hits for the pitcher. In between these two victories, Manager Bruns called on me for relief in a game that the Braves lost 7-4 to Albert Lea. Two outs, two strikeouts.

The fourth victory, a game played on July 4, was a 10-4 victory over Rochester. It ended the season for us at Mason City.

Unknown to me and to Ann, long-time Cardinal baseball scout, Cliff "Runt" Marr was in the stands that night. When I came out of the locker room, he was waiting for me. "Can we go someplace to talk, Art?" Just that statement raised the heart rate a little. Because Ann and little Terry were waiting in the car for me outside the stadium, I suggested he come to our apartment. He agreed and followed us back to our new home of four days. Runt had never approached me in this manner before and the Huinkers were not too sure what to expect. The brief discussion held on our drive home with the scout following held more questions than answers.

After some introductions and usual small talk, Runt got to the point and offered me a baseball contract with the St. Louis Cardinals starting immediately. The offer included a $4,000 bonus. At that time, anything over $4,000 required a major league contract as the write-up below states. The heart rate sped higher. We do not have many specific recollections of the moment but there had to be an exchange of looks between us. Was it possible? Was my second life-long dream coming true? That did not seem possible.

First, we had to solve the conflict that would exist between this contract and the teaching contract already signed with Ossian De Sales Central High School. Do I ask to be excused from that contract? School at De Sales would begin before the conclusion of the professional baseball season. Marr acknowledged that and informed us that we would be allowed to leave the pro

151

team early to fulfill my commitment to the teaching contract. We were not ready to put our future teaching career in jeopardy by breaking that contract. We would also report to our professional team only after completion of the teaching contract. It sounded too good to be true.

Next, how soon will we be expected in Columbus, Georgia. Ann decided we could get back to Festina, meet with both of our parents to share our exciting news and say our goodbyes and be back on the road to Columbus by the seventh of July. Our furniture and other belonging were already in storage so packing was relatively simple. I remember being puzzled by my Father's reaction to the contract. He was very positive in his support of our effort, but very reserved about it. Thinking about that, I realize that my Dad never became overly excited about most things. Thinking that we used less than half of the bonus to buy a new car that fall, then thinking about purchase of a new car today, the $4,000 was a fair amount.

How long was the trip from northeast Iowa to Columbus? Ann and I had no clue. Runt Marr suggested that it would probably take three days of solid travel. There were no interstate highways to speed up the trip.

The contract was accepted and signed. We still have a copy of the contract framed and hanging on our family room wall about our desk. Manager Paul Bruns was notified of our decision the next day. The season was over at Mason City. We were going to play professional baseball. Following is a short clip of the signing that appeared in the local papers back home.

> *CARDINAL PACT FOR LORAS ACE*
> *Art Huinker, 22-year-old left hand pitcher, has signed a bonus contract with the St. Louis Cardinals, and has been assigned to Columbus, Ga., of the South Atlantic League, a class A circuit.*
> *Huinker will report next Tuesday. His bonus was under the $4,000 limit which would bind him to a major league club.*
> *Huinker, from Calmar, posted a 19-0 record during his four years at Loras College, where he was graduated this June. He has been pitching for the Mason City Braves in the Southern Minnesota League, a semipro circuit. He has a 4-1 record.*
> *He is to teach and coach this fall at De Sales High School at Ossian.*

A question that has whirled around in my mind often since that night when the Cardinals made the contract and bonus offer: Why now? Why not sooner? Why now after one month with Mason City in the Southern Minny League? Although I never questioned Scout Runt Marr, the reason may relate to a somewhat successful month in the league considered comparable to Class A

152

professional baseball. Who had established that comparison I do not know. That may be the reason why I was assigned to Columbus in the South Atlantic Coast League (called the SALLY league for short). It was a Class A league in the hierarchy of minor leagues. Catcher Chuck Lindstrom of the Mason City Braves signed a professional contract with the White Sox and was also assigned to Class A Colorado Springs. There may have been a connection.

Another interesting tidbit about that memorable July 4th night was a bit of advice offered by Marr as our deliberations were drawing to a close. Remember the night that I had given up the three home runs. One of Marr's closing statements to me was "You have to keep the ball down better, Art. That's too many home runs." I had much to learn.

As baseball discussions among professional baseball players go, both past and present, there are challenges for a baseball family which is what Ann and I now were. As mentioned earlier, we had just signed a monthly lease on an apartment and moved the first of July. The full month's rent was paid and none was coming back. We had moved to Mason City around the first of June, moved a month later to a new apartment, four days later we were moving to Columbus, Georgia. In the next month, more interesting challenges of baseball life would occur, especially for the love of my life.

The next few days remain a blur in our memory capsule as we return to Calmar, say our goodbyes to our parents and siblings, and prepare for the three-day trip to Columbus, Georgia. Because of time limitations, I doubt that we even saw all my brothers and sisters. We would be back in two months. This young Mom and Dad and not quite one-year old Terry were ready to go on an adventure. And the trip proved to be quite an adventure. Instead of the three days as planned, it took four. Our 1951 Chevrolet broke down in Kentucky on a Sunday. Not able to find anyone to repair it on a Sunday, we lost an entire day waiting for the needed repairs. We were a family in a strange town, with no means of transportation, little money, and nothing to do.

To occupy ourselves, the entire family went to a movie. The title of the movie was "Tammy." And, of course, the key music in the movie was the song, "Tammy." When our first daughter came along two years later, we named her Tammy after the movie, giving us our third child with a name that began with the letter "t."

On Monday, the car was repaired but in the meantime we had to call ahead to Business Manager Chief Bender, located in Columbus, Georgia, to see if we could get an advance on some of the bonus money to pay the repair bill. Using Western Union, Bender wired the money to us and we were back on the road, but one day late. For this young couple from the small town of Festina in rural northeast Iowa, the many new experiences kept whirling around us daily.

153

A QUIET FIRST WEEK

We arrived in Columbus about the middle of a hot, sunny afternoon and checked into a motel for another night. A phone call was made to Chief Bender, the business manager who had bailed us out of a jam covering the emergency car repairs. He suggested I come to the ball park as soon as possible after informing him of our location. He wanted me to pitch some batting practice for the Columbus Red Birds who were preparing for a home game that evening.

Ann and Terry proceeded to get settled at the motel . Don't expect us to remember the name but in 1957 a Holiday Inn might be the answer. Following the directions of Bender, the ballpark was located. Again, excitement flowed through my brain as never before, due to the expectations of my "dream" coming to reality. Chief Bender met me upon my arrival at the park, probably recognized the Iowa license plate, and proceeded to lead me to the Cardinal dressing room where he introduced me to some of the players still getting their uniforms on. A uniform with the two cardinals seated on a baseball bat was hanging there waiting for me. WOW! I had my own Cardinal uniform. After dressing, he took me out to the field where I met manager Skeeter Newsome, who instructed me to get loose and throw some batting practice. Newsome had played shortstop for the Philadelphia Athletics and Boston Red Sox, mostly in the late thirties and forties.

I tried not to make the same mistake that I made my freshman year at Loras. But later it hit me that the batters probably felt I was throwing too slow. Somewhat shaky to start, I managed to throw strikes quite consistently and that is probably all they wanted to see for the time being. The experiences expanded rapidly.

Once batting practice ended, Business Manager Bender called me over and informed me of what lay ahead. After the game that night, the team would be heading out of town for a six-game road trip to Jacksonville, Florida and Savannah, Georgia. I was to accompany the team. Whoa! Wait a minute! What about Ann and Terry. They can't stay in the motel for an entire week. I shared my concerns.   He told me to shower, then go out to the motel, pick up my wife and son and bring them to the ballpark.

"What we will do, Art," Bender said,   "Is find one of the players' wives who will let your family stay with them for the week." Long-term memory was working because I can still see where we were standing, just down the left field line beyond the infield. It was a beautiful sunny evening and we were standing in the shadows of the third base bleachers.

I had a disappointed wife when I returned to the motel and informed her of the upcoming road trip. But Ann is a gamer, much more mature than most people for her age. That is the excuse I have given for marrying her just out of high school. Clothes were gathered for the week's trip and we returned to the ball park where the game was already in progress. Throughout all this, contemplating what was all taking place, wouldn't it have been great to have cell phones about that time?

Ann and little Terry were introduced to some of the players' wives and sat with them throughout the game. Chief Bender made them aware of our situation and by the time the game was over, arrangements had been made. She would stay with the center fielder's wife until we returned from the six-day baseball trip. Notice no names appear in this entire section except for Chief Bender and Manager Newsome. That will become more understandable as we proceed through the first week of our introduction to professional baseball.

After the game's completion, the players showered and we prepared to board a bus with what was to be about a seven-hour night trip to Jacksonville, Florida. Ann and I said our goodbyes after she assured me that she and Terry would be okay and wished me good luck. Off to Jacksonville on one of those bus trips that minor league players talked about in those days. They still do.

Still not much baseball to talk about. And there will not be much for me on the week-long trip but many other memories abound for this 22-year old from tiny Festina.

Getting on the bus, I noticed a broken back on a seat towards the front, and being a rookie, that would be the place for me. I thought wrong. It was the only seat on the bus that you could almost recline to a sleeping position. Ken Toth, later a major leaguer with the Cubs for a short time, stepped on the bus and immediately let me know "Rookie, that is my seat." I retreated toward the back of the bus where a reserve catcher, Paul Davis, invited me to sit with him. We discussed professional baseball for the first part of the trip and some of his thoughts about what I should expect. Sleep finally overtook both of us, even though we were both sitting up.

Experiences the next day imprinted some lasting images on my brain's storage system. Early daylight greeted us by the time we arrived in Jacksonville. The bus pulled to a stop at the front of a less than desirable looking hotel. Immediately the reaction "Wow, is this what we are going to live in?" But, no, only the two black Americans, Toth and Davis, got off the bus. Now you realize why their names were remembered. I was in the southern United States for the first time. The bus, meanwhile, continued to a better facility where the remainder of the team stayed. This was 1957, ten years after Jackie Robinson broke the color barrier in professional baseball. But only on the baseball diamond.

That cultural situation proved to be only the beginning. That evening, when we arrived at the baseball park, a huge stadium, I observed a huge screened fence in the bleachers on a line starting at the far end of the dugout on both sides of the field. As fans started to arrive, its purpose became apparent- - -whites on the home plate side of the fence, black Americans on the outfield side. This

155

picture combined with another memory that occurred at the same time, my being on the professional diamond in a Cardinal uniform.

The remainder of the trip provided more reminders of the segregation being experienced first- hand. Signs indicating these water fountains were for whites only. And the signs outside of restaurants stating that no blacks were allowed inside. In less than two months, American History would be taught in my classroom.

As for the baseball side of the trip, there was limited action for me. The Columbus Redbirds proved to be a very light hitting team, but with strong pitching. We lost all six games on the trip, with all but one being very low-scoring games. In the second game at Jacksonville, the score found Columbus losing by several runs late in the game. Manager Newsome indicated he wanted me to start warming up to complete some mop-up duty. He brought me in to start the bottom half of the eighth.

As stated earlier, it was a huge baseball stadium, located right next to the Gator football stadium, where bowl games have been played for years. When I reached the mound, I had the feeling of being smaller than what I already was. Also, there was more space between home plate and the backstop than usual. This added to my feeling that the pitcher's mound was more like 70 feet away from home plate than the normal 60 feet, 6 inches. That feeling actually helped me keep the ball low like Scout Runt Marr suggested.

The first two batters were Lee Maye, a lefty, and Mel Roach, a right-hand batter. Both later spent several seasons with the Milwaukee Braves, but never were able to become a permanent fixture. Roach was challenging Braves' second baseman Jack Dittmer from Elkader, Iowa but never succeeded. This was the period when the Braves were a national league powerhouse with names like Aaron, Mathews, Bruton, Crandall and Adcock and pitchers like Lou Burdette and Warren Spahn.

What happened in this first opportunity? Well, I walked the lefty-hitting Lee Maye but induced Mel Roach to pop up to the second baseman. The next two batters made outs and the inning was over. Because of nerves maybe, but my best stuff wasn't exhibited. That would be my only experience of the week. The names of Maye and Roach never dimmed in my memory. Maye was with the Milwaukee Braves from 1959 to 1966, then spent five more years with Houston and the Chicago White Sox. Meanwhile Roach played in 44 games for the Braves in 1958. He played at the major league level for eight years but most of the time for short call ups, then back down again. Interesting.

On to Savannah. Not a huge stadium like the one in Jacksonville. It was a football stadium with a baseball diamond, similar to what the Los Angeles Dodgers played on initially when they made their move from Brooklyn. Savannah's left field fence was very, very short. It was a Cincinnati affiliate.

Two familiar names for all of us oldtimers were Curt Flood, later a star centerfielder for the St. Louis Cardinals, and Chico Cardenas, later with the major league Cincinnati ball club. Of course Flood is remembered most as the player who led the fight for player free agency toward the end of his career.

Also, Haven Schmidt, a Maquoketa, Iowa native, was the catcher for Savannah. I believe it was either his fourth or fifth year with that organization. His high school team lost 9-1 to eventual champion, Kanawha, in the opening round of the state tournament. That was the same night that our Calmar team beat Exira, then lost the next night to Kanawha. On that particular night where we both played, I remember meeting some of the Maquoketa players back at the hotel but I can't remember if Haven was with that group.

Haven, after retiring from professional baseball, returned to his hometown area to raise his family. His home is located right along Highway 61 between Zwingle and Maquoketa, about 15 miles south of Dubuque. Shortly after he came back from the pros, he played with a team that played against the Dyersville Whitehawks. It was my night for pitching. Once I realized he was playing, catcher Dale Digmann and I met and discussed our pitching strategy. It actually was quite simple. All pitches would be off the outside corner making it difficult to pull the ball because he hit from the left side. The Commercial Club Park, now called Jenk field, has a relatively short right field fence. It is short in comparison to left and center anyway. Finally, on Haven's fourth trip to the plate, he hit a double to the fence but he hit it to the deeper part of left field. We have encountered each other periodically over the years since we both left playing the game to younger players. He is a great individual with a wonderful outlook on life.

There were no pitching opportunities for me at Savannah. One of those nights after the game, I was able to make a phone call to Ann or she connected with me. How, we don't recall but she informed me that she had found an apartment in Phoenix City, Alabama, across the Chattahoochie River from Columbus. The town's reputation was terrible. It had been known as a wild red-light district for the paratroopers in training at Fort Benning, Georgia. At the time that Ann had located the apartment there, things had changed and it appeared to be a quiet bedroom community to Columbus. She said, "I'll tell you more when you get back. Another challenging experience for my young wife.

One last fascinating experience to wrap up the Columbus story. When the team bus returned to Columbus from the six game road trip, Business Manger Bender had left word at the stadium that I was to report to the Cardinal farm team in Albany, Georgia the next day. Albany was a Class D affiliate in the Georgia-Florida League. Columbus needed hitters, not pitchers, while Albany, in a pennant chase, had lost two pitchers who were out out with injuries. The Cardinal organization wanted me to pitch, not to sit idle on the bench.

Visualize, if you can, the scenario when I arrived at the apartment early in the morning and had to tell her the news. She had found a new apartment for her family and had lived in it for four days. After a wonderful welcome hug and kiss, it was "Ann, I have something I have to tell you. We are moving." You got the picture. Another challenge for the Huinker family, especially for Ann. But she continued to be positive and supportive of my "dream" quest. Let's move further south to Albany, Georgia, also the spring training site for the St. Louis Cardinal minor league teams at that time.

CHASING A DREAM

The same morning we were informed of the Albany transfer, the Huinker moving company picked up their belongings and headed for our new location. Before the end of the day we planted ourselves in a nice, but small, one-story, one-bedroom apartment in Albany. Other players and their wives were located in the same development. With Chief Bender's assistance (He also was the business manager for the Albany Cardinals) he contacted a few of the Albany players who directed us to the available apartment in their complex. One of the couples especially helpul was Jim Hickman and his wife. Jim became my roommate on overnight road trips and his wife and Ann got along very well. He was one year younger than I and was leading the Albany team in home runs for the season.

Jim Hickman, the only player on the Albany team to eventually reach the majors, was picked by the New York Mets, an expansion team, in the 1962 player draft. He eventually ended up with the Chicago Cubs, playing mostly first base for the northsiders for six years. His best year was 1970 when he clubbed 35 homeruns. Two other years he hit over twenty four-baggers. He retired from baseball in 1974, at the age of 38 and returned to his family's tobacco farm in Henning, Tennessee. Sounds similar to the Columbus experience for the Albany team was leaving town for a night game at Fitzgerald, Georgia. However, they were returning home after the game because it was only a two hour trip from Albany to Fitzgerald, and they informed me to stay home that first day. Much better.

The next afternoon, Ann took me to the park for a home game. This time, more formal introductions of the other players and player-manager Chase Riddle were made. Riddle immediately wanted to know the last time I had pitched, then informed me that he wanted me to start the next road game to be played at Thomasville, Georgia, a Los Angeles Dodgers' minor league team. I was told to go to the bullpen and do some throwing both this night and the next day, as well as considerable running, and running. The "big moment" was almost here- - -my first start in a Cardinal uniform, bearing the baseball bat and two Cardinal birds on the front.

Both Thomasville and Fitzgerald were about a two-hour trip from Albany, Thomasville being directly south and Fitzgerald directly east. Both compared to a Dubuque to Clinton trip or a Festina to Waterloo trip but on two-lane roads. The team always returned the same night after road trips to those two opponents. Looking at the three towns today, Thomasville's population compares with the size of Mason City, approximately 30,000. Albany itself is now about 75,000. Fitzgerald today claims a population of about 10,000.

A short write-up appeared in the Albany Herald daily paper the morning after the Huinkers arrived, introducing two new pitchers to the Cardinal staff. The write-up follows.

159

CARDS RAINED OUT; ADD TWO PITCHERS
Albany and Brunswick, unable to play the past two
nights in Brunswick because of rain, move into Cardinal Park
tonight at 8 o'clock to test the Albany weather.
Manager Chase Riddle still has Tony Stathos, a lefty,
ready to start. Stathos hasn't seen duty now since last Saturday
night.
The Redbirds also added pitching help for the torrid
battle ahead, adding two men to their mound staff.
One is limited service righthander Dick Wodka, who
comes here from Decatur, Ill., where he had a 7-5 record with
the Midwest League leaders.
The other moundsman is southpaw Art Huinker, a red-
hot prospect recently signed out of Loras College of Dubuque,
Iowa where he posted a fantastic 19-0 record. Huinker spent a
brief time with Columbus, Ga., before being sent to Albany.
Huinker arrived in town late yesterday and Wodka is
expected in a day or two. The addition of this pair greatly
strengthens the Albany mound staff which has been the club's
chief weakness in recent weeks.
Bender, elated over the acquisitions of the two,
commented: I believe we have a pitching staff that will match
any other in the league. Both Huinker and Wodka should win
for us.

The second pitcher added, Wodka, was pitching in the Midwest League before coming to Albany. That league included Dubuque at that time.

Now comes the big test—my first opportunity to start a game in professional baseball. I admit to some "butterflies" while warming up. But once on the mound, there's work to be done (fun work playing a game) and the nervous energy becomes a helping factor. The eruption of three runs scored in the top of the first by my teammates didn't hurt either. Those runs came off the ace of the Dodger pitching staff, Scott Siebert. The following article tells the rest of the story.

HUINKER BLANKS THOMASVILLE, 13-0
Rookie Southpaw Art Huinker pitched a sparkling four-
hitter in his pitching debut for Albany and Al Morris and Jim
Hickman hit a home run each as the Cardinals crushed the
Thomasville Dodgers, 13-0, in Thomasville.
Huinker had smooth sailing from the first inning on, as
the Red Birds jumped off to a 3-0 lead and kept up a savage 17-
hit assault against three pitchers.

The stocky lefty, who compiled a fantastic 19-0 record for Loras College in Iowa, fanned six men and walked just three. All the hits off him were singles.

Thomasville's ace righthander, Siebert Scott, was the initial victim of Albany's murderous barrage, eventually surrendering 13 hits and 12 runs before he was lifted in the eighth frame.

A Kiwanis' Night throng of 1,046 looked on in dismay at the Cardinals' power display. A homer for Hickman was his eighteenth. Morris, battling his teammate for top honors in this department in the league, now has 17.

Lou Brown got the ball rolling for the Red Birds when he walked to lead off the first. Morris and Manager Chase Riddle then singled to load the sacks. Hickman laced a double to score Brown and Morris, and DeGraaf's sacrifice fly got Riddle home.

In the fourth a walk to Boyer and Kabbes' triple made it 4-0 and the Cards picked up two more in the sixth when Brown walked with two gone and Morris clubbed the ball over the leftfield wall at the 350-foot mark.

Morris, Riddle and Hickman, Albany's "big three" in the power department collected three hits each and Hickman drove in five runs. Every member of the team hit safely at least once with the exception of Huinker.

That first start ended up better than what I had ever expected. Despite the emotional feelings of that first "trip to the mound," sleep was secondary as I shared the news of the shutout with Ann. I felt like the little kid who again just had his first ice cream cone.

First, notice the only Cardinal batter who did not get a hit. In fact, 0 for 5. Also notice the name of our third baseman, Bob Boyer. He was a younger brother of the famous Boyer third basemen, Clete who played third base for the Yankees, and the other, Ken, who was a great third-sacker for the St. Louis Cardinals.

Thomasville's third baseman was future big leaguer Bob Aspromonte. Bob played for the Los Angeles Dodgers for eleven years from 1960 to 1971.

That night, and the duration of our stay with the Albany Cardinals, we began to experience the heat of southern Georgia in July and August. Invariably, we received a short period of rain in the early afternoon, followed by sunny skies and extreme humidity caused by the rainfall. Almost all our games were played at night but even at that time of day, the humid conditions were oppressive. For all our games, we had a bucket of ice water with a towel soaking in it. Between innings, pitchers immediately had the towel wrapped around our necks. With a

161

special chemical added to the icy water, the cold, wet towel drew much of the perspiration out of our bodies. I can't recall the chemical's name but it is available over-the-counter at most pharmacies.

Later in the book, we will cover the Beckman Blazer baseball team winning the state tournament in the 1968 season. Both nights the heat was in the 90's and we tried to reproduce the icy bucket of water soaking a huge bath towel for use between innings. Again, we learn so much by experiencing situations that later become a valuable memory to be used again.

Professional game two was another road game. An overnite two-day trip was taken to Valdosta, Georgia, a city that today is on Interstate 75 just north of the Florida border. In the opener of a doubleheader that evening, scheduled for seven innings, the score was 0 to 0 after six innings. The Cardinal bats were silent for my second outing. The write-up below explains what happened in the top half of the inning. Manager Riddle pinch hit for me as well he should. In two times at bat, I had not touched the ball.

> ### HUINKER, COY GAIN CREDIT FOR VICTORIES
> *The Albany Cardinals swept a double-header from Valdosta in Valdosta last night, 1-0 and 9-2, stretching their string of victories to five, four of them over the Tigers.*
> *The opener was a brilliant pitching duel between Albany's rookie sensation, Art Huinker, and Valdosta's Dick Walter.*
> *Albany broke a scoreless deadlock in the top of the seventh when Walter walked Jim Hickman and Bill DeGraaf and Jim Smith collected a single to load the bases with none out.*
> *The Tiger righthander bore down at this point to fan Bob Boyer and Ron Kabbes but Manager Chase Riddle, batting for Huinker, rifled a single to center to drive in Hickman with the winning run. DeGraaf was thrown out at the plate on the play by Briner.*

A second pitching stint with still no runs allowed. And also, now zero hits in seven at-bats. This, even though I had a bat with my name on it. However, if my memory serves me correctly, the bat was considerably heavier than what I felt comfortable with. The purchaser must have felt I needed that weight to get the ball out of the infield. The opposite was true for me so the Huinker bat was never used by yours truly. Statistically, records show four strikeouts for the game with two walks. Five hits were allowed in the six innings pitched. And no home runs allowed so far.

Our family started to settle into some routine. Ball games at home were 8:00 starting time for the night games. During the short time at Albany we only played one day game, that being on a Sunday afternoon and one of the games I pitched. Ann and little Terry went to all our home games, which meant many late evenings for all three of us. Invariably bedtime was around midnight. We did not eat before the game so the family would have a light dinner after the game. That led to sleeping in the following morning unless Terry decided otherwise.

After breakfast at home, we often loaded up the family and went to the city's public swimming pool to combat the intense humid heat we experienced most afternoons. The players themselves were urged not to swim. Swimming can take considerable energy, energy needed for the game itself later in the day. Lacking adequate skills in the water anyway, it wasn't difficult to meet the request. And the baby pool doesn't require much effort.

We were expected to be at the ball park by 4:30, with an 8:00 start. A short team meeting was followed by batting and infield practice for both teams. The practice before the game for me meant shagging fly balls during batting practice and running, and running some more. Seldom did pitchers take batting practice, even on days we pitched. That did not seem right to me, but it gave me an excuse for my lack of hitting. Ann would usually take me out to the ballpark, unless we rode with other players who lived in the same apartment complex. They would then come back to the park in time for the game.

Game number three for my next pitching assignment came against the Fitzgerald Orioles and their manager Earl Weaver. Weaver, similar to our manager Chase Riddle, also played quite often. We would do battle on our home field after two road appearances.

The string of shutout innings continued with a 5-0 whitewash of the Orioles, a game that included Weaver pinch-hitting in the top of the ninth. This is the same Earl Weaver who later piloted the Baltimore Orioles to four World Series, including one world championship. He demonstrated a testy approach toward umpires on many occasions, both at Fitzgerald and in the majors.

> HUINKER BLANKS FITZGERALD 5-0; HICKMAN
> SMASHES 21st
> Young Art Huinker, who believes the only sure way to win is to shut the other fellow out, turned in his third straight whitewash job last night, stopping the Fitzgerald Orioles on eight scattered hits, 5-0.
> The Cardinal southpaw, fresh from Loras College, Iowa, where he posted a 19-0 record, made just three starts since joining the local club and now has a string of 24 scoreless innings.
> Huinker's first shutout was at the expense of Thomasville, 13-0. Next he blanked Valdosta, 1-0, although he was removed for a pinch hitter in the top of the seventh of the first game of a twin bill. The Cardinals scored their lone run in the seventh and Huinker got credit for the victory.

163

Huinker was in serious danger on several occasions last night but fine clutch pitching and a couple of fancy defensive plays by his teammates helped him keep his amazing record intact.

In the fourth inning, after being held hitless by Phil Heisler for three frames, the Redbirds tallied twice when Manager Chase Riddle walked and Jim Hickman followed with his twenty-first home run, a towering blast far over the fence in left. Paul Leslie got the only other hit off Heisler and it too was for the circuit, coming in the sixth stanza.

Heisler went out for a pinch hitter in the top of the seventh and the Birds got to reliever Joe Grusin for a marker in the last of the seventh on a walk to Boyer, a stolen base, a wild pitch and Huinker's bingle.

Fitzgerald had a fine opportunity in the second. Bird lived on an error by second baseman Sam McIntyre, the only bobble of the night, and Barth singled to right, Bird holding second. Both advanced on a wild pitch, putting runners on second and third with nobody out.

Shortsop Jim Smith came to Huinker's rescue at this point, racing into the hole between second and third to make a leaping, back-handed stab of Stroyzk's liner and doubling Barth off second. The next batter grounded out to Smith and the inning was over.

Huinker gave up two hits in the seventh but fanned pinch hitter Bishop for the final out. He then surrendered singles to Barth and Stroyzk to open the ninth, then set Kolar down on a foul pop to first, Bednar on a fly to center and Earl Weaver on a grounder to second.

One streak, the shutout innings, increased to 24. But another streak ended. My first hit finally became a reality. Probably not as significant as the scoreless innings, but to me it was wonderful.

Prior to the fourth start for the Cardinals, Manager Riddle brought me in to relieve starter Dick Wodka in the bottom of the eighth with the bases loaded and two out against Waycross. The batter was retired on an infield ground out. Now a twenty-four and one-third inning streak.

My next starting pitching assignment came against the Brunswick Phillies at home. The headline in the Albany Herald daily paper that morning has always struck my fancy. A copy appears in the picture section of the book and an abbreviated write-up with the headline is included here.

164

*HUINKER TO PITCH---CARDS MEET PHILS
TONIGHT*
*Rookie pitching sensation Art Huinker will put his 24-
inning scoreless streak on the line here tonight when the Albany
Cardinals take on the Brunswick Phillies at Card Park at 8
o'clock.*

In studying the headline, let your imagination run freely. Could it be the
St. Louis Cards meeting the Philadelphia Phillies tonight? OK, we know better
but a person does get to dream once in a while.

That night the scoreless streak came tumbling down. Reality set in.
Both streaks, the shutout string and my one-game hitting streak ended. The game
was tied at one until the sixth. Brunswick scored two in the sixth and a two-out
bases-loaded triple in the seventh by Leber, their big catcher added three more.
He hit a high, outside fastball over Hickman's head in center field. And, sadly,
this clearly sticks in my memory , primarily because another pitcher told me
earlier in the game, "don't pitch him high and away." Reverse psychology was at
work. He should have informed me to pitch him inside. Oh, well. My night was
over after the seventh inning. Newspaper coverage follows.

CARDS LOSE TO PHILS 7 TO 1
*Young Art Huinker's brilliant string of shutout innings
was halted at 25 in the initial frame last night by Brunswick as
the Phils turned back the league-leading Cardinals in the first of
a two game series at Card Park, 7-1.*
*Huinker was pinned with his first defeat of the year,
following three straight shutout victories.*
*The southpaw pitched well for five innings but began to
weaken in the sixth and was rocked for five runs in the sixth and
seventh.*
*Brunswick grabbed a lead last night by scoring in the
first inning on a walk to Graham, Price's single and
Harrington's sacrifice, on which Hickman made a poor throw to
the plate.*

What can be said? My feet were back on the ground and I wanted a
quick chance to pitch again.

In the meantime, we experienced a complete surprise sometime during
our stint in Albany. We had a visitor from the north. Our groomsman, college
roommate and Loras baseball teammate, Bob Wolfe, walked into the baseball
stands, identified Ann and Terry, and sat with them throughout the game. What a
joyous night for all three of us. I wasn't pitching that night, but that didn't matter.

Bob joined the naval air force shortly after graduation from Loras
College. After basic training, he located at the naval air base outside Pensacola,

Florida, not far from Albany. We enjoyed dining out after the game with Bob. He stayed the night, then resumed his journey to Pensacola the next morning. His visit demonstrates the kind of friend he has been throughout our life.

The winning ways returned the next game when the Cards beat Thomasville 6 to 1. This was the lone day game in which I pitched. It did not result in a shutout although the visitors had no hits until the sixth. It is important that you notice I collected my second, and last hit. It was a ground single to right field but most important, it drove in a run, just as my first hit had done. According to the game's write-up, victory number four took just 2 hours, 14 minutes. Notice also in this game that the Thomasville manager pitched in relief. Playing managers were all over the league.

> ### HUINKER TURNS BACK THOMASVILLE NINE
> *Lefty Art Huinker, beaten last week after making his Georgia-Florida League debut with three straight shutouts, resumed his sensational pitching here yesterday when he beat the Thomasville Dodgers on four hits at Card Park, 6-1.*
>
> *Huinker had a no-hitter until the sixth when Larry Buhl grounded a single over the mound. Ironically, the hit also cost him a fourth shutout, scoring Larry Burright, who had walked and moved to second on a wild pitch.*
>
> *The Cardinals staked the young southpaw to a fat lead in the third when they scored six times in routing Thomasville starter Tony Hopey.*
>
> *The Thomasville lefty, a highly touted prep star who was signed in mid-season by the Dodgers, lost his control and walked Brown, Morris and Leslie to open the third. Manager Chase Riddle then beat out a high bouncer to third for a hit that scored Brown and when third baseman Buhl heaved the ball over first, Morris and Leslie also scored and Riddle moved to third.*
>
> *DeGraaf grounded out but Hickman walked and Boyer singled to drive in Riddle. That finished Hopey, Bill Booth taking over. He was greeted by a single by Smith that scored Hickman. Huinker also singled, Boyer scoring. Manager Roger Wright took over on the mound for the Dodgers and, although hit freely, escaped without giving up another run.*

At this point in the season, Albany had built a comfortable lead in the league for the second-half championship. Nearest competitors were Waycross, Valdosta and Thomasville in that order.

We had another left-hand pitcher on the team by the name of Pete Shultis. He was a tall, slender southpaw who had one of the liveliest fast balls I had ever witnessed, probably so lively that he struggled to control his pitches. He

166

maintained a high strikeout rate, in fact, he led the league, but averaged as many walks. In one game he started, he struck out fourteen batters in seven innings. He walked "fifteen." The game took forever. It was one of the longest games, time-wise, that I had ever witnessed. The next game I pitched took one hour and fifty-nine minutes. No TV of course.

Start number six found the Cardinal team traveling to Waycross (also in Georgia), where we edged our nearest opposition by the score of 2 to 1. Looking at the entire box score of the game, it was interesting to note our first baseman had twelve putouts, indicating there were many ground ball outs. In the previous game there were ten putouts for the first baseman. And in the last game I pitched before leaving to meet my teaching contract commitment, there were eleven putouts credited to our first baseman. Strikeouts on the other hand, ranged from four to seven per game started. The strikeouts were being replaced by ground ball outs, which most professional teams prefer. On the other hand, remember Scout Runt Marr's statement when he signed us to a pro contract. Something about keeping the ball down and not allowing so many home runs. In the seven games started, the opposition did not hit a single home run. That was a far cry from the Southern Minny semi-pro league where I had allowed an average of one home run per game.

> CARDS EDGE WAYCROSS 2-1
> *Albany's Cardinals, driving hard for an early clincher in the second half Georgia-Florida League pennant race, whipped Waycross again last night, 2-1, to stretch their lead to 10 games, counting the suspended contest in Brunswick as a loss.*
>
> *Lefty Art Huinker, who will leave the Red Birds next Wednesday to take over a high school coaching job, spun a fine five-hitter in recording his fifth victory against one loss. Three of his victories have been shutouts, the other two one-run performances.*
>
> *The lone tally off the young southpaw came in the fourth when McKeon doubled, moved to third on Nester's single and scored on successive walks to Bergdoll and Morgan.*
>
> *Hugh Coy, who was scheduled to have pitched last night, will work tonight's final game in Waycross. Coy was passed over in order to give Huinker two more starts, including last night, before he departs.*

The final professional pitching challenge again was on the road, this time at Valdosta, where we had a previous 1-0 seven inning victory. This game provided less of a challenge, the Cardinals collecting 16 hits and a 9-1 victory. This game was played on August 20. The next morning the Huinker family was on the road back to northeast Iowa and our first teaching responsibility. In this game, seven Cardinal batters had two hits each, against a future pitcher for the

167

New York Yankees by the name of Rollie Sheldon. Rollie had a limited big-league career, while his pitching teammate, Fred Gladding, had a lengthy major league career as a relief pitcher for the Detroit Tigers.

> HUINKER HANDCUFFS VALDOSTA; LEFTY
> LEAVES AFTER WINNING HIS SIXTH
>> *Albany's rampaging Cardinals moved a step nearer to the 1957 second half championship by blasting Valdosta, 9-1, behind the four-hit pitching of rookie southpaw Art Huinker.*
>>
>> *Unfortunately, it was Huinker's last start of the season. He leaves today to take a coaching job.*
>>
>> *During his short term in Albany the ex-Loras College of Iowa star won six games while losing just one. He spun three shutouts and in his other three victories he gave up just one run each time.*
>>
>> *Albany staked Huinker to a 1-0 lead in the second when Leslie singled. Hickman walked and Smith singled to drive in Leslie.*

The brief summer of professional baseball was over. Six wins, one loss, and according to one of our grandsons, an earned run average of 1.23. Grandson Tony Huinker googled it. He also found that my batting average was just about as low, a paltry .125.

The news publication that all people interested in professional baseball seriously read in the 1950's went by the title of "The Sporting News." Published weekly in St. Louis, Missouri, the publication not only thoroughly covered Major League baseball activity, but it also devoted an entire section to baseball's minor leagues. Following is an excerpt of an article that appeared in that paper on August 28. The brief, but entire, article is included to give the reader a flavor of the coverage. First in the article they listed the standings as of the previous week.

> LEFTY LEAVES WITH VICTORY
>> *Southpaw Art Huinker, who came off the campus of Loras College of Dubuque, Ia., to baffle the batters in the loop, left the Albany Cardinals August 21, after hurling a four-hitter to beat Valdosta, 9 to 1, for his sixth victory against one loss. In his winning performances, Huinker pitched three shutouts and three other games in which he held the opposition to one run each. He departed early to take over a high school coaching job.*
>>
>> *Clarence Ingram, continuing his comeback after being sidelined by an injury, posted his fourteenth victory for Albany, August 15, blanking Waycross, 6 to 0. Al Morris hit his twentieth homer of the year in the game, matching teammate Jim Hickman's total and marking the first time in history that*

168

two Cardinals had reached the 20-homer mark in the same season.

An interesting section of a different Class D league included a short article on Bill Hoffland, a young pitcher from Soldiers Grove, Wisconsin, a semi-pro baseball town that in the early sixties brought me in to pitch for them.

The time that we spent in Albany and with the baseball team remains a very vivid and positive memory in the lives of the Huinker family. The climate of the team itself exhibited a warm relationship between the players themselves and with the manager. Manager Riddle quietly, but firmly, handled the on-field operations without fanfare. He managed in the Cardinal farm system from 1955 through 1962, then became a scout for the Cardinals for the next 16 years. At that time he became head baseball coach for Troy University in Alabama where he won consecutive NCAA Division Two national titles in 1986 and 1987. He died in 2011.

I deliberately asked the following question twice. You will notice there is a difference between the two. First, did I feel good about the five plus weeks that I spent in Albany? Second, did we feel good about the five plus weeks that we spent in Albany? Speaking for myself, the response is a resounding "yes." I loved it. The success was much greater than I ever anticipated. Teammates were appreciated and enjoyed. Road trips consisted of two games and the four further towns from Albany included one-night stays. Now looking at the second question, the response is the same except you need to add "teammates and their wives," The dream was alive. Could both be realized?

TOUGH CHOICES

An article appeared in the Dubuque Telegraph-Herald in early September following our professional baseball experience that is a good lead-in to our not continuing a career in the professional baseball arena. Below is that write-up.

PROMISE THREATHENS CAREER, BUT...HUINKER WON'T BREAK WORD

Ossian, Ia.—For a man who has always dreamed of a career in professional baseball, Art Huinker is starting with two strikes against him. And what' more, if he had it to do it over again, he'd do things exactly the same way.

Huinker, now 22 years old, started his professional baseball career in Class D ball this year because he insisted on some unusual conditions in his contract. And chances are, Huinker will be back in D ball again next year, too, for the same reason.

But that is fine with the little Loras College alum. He would rather keep his word then make the big leagues.

The St. Louis Cardinals were after Huinker from the time he graduated from high school. Their scouts watched him pitch 19 straight victories at Loras College and pitch semipro ball with Dyersville, Festina, Sumner, Monroe, Wis., and Spring Grove, Minn.

But Huinker refused to sign until he completed his college education. "If I didn't have a college education, I wouldn't have anything to fall back on when my baseball playing days were over," he explained.

Huinker wouldn't accept the first contract offered him by St. Louis this spring and accepted a job teaching history and coaching at Ossian De Sales Central Catholic High School.

When the Cardinals were ready to meet his money demands, Huinker insisted he be allowed to leave the team the last week in August so that he could honor his teaching contract. He also refused to sign unless the Cards would agree to let him finish the school year at Ossian and not report until June.

That's a tough contract to expect from a major league club but the Cardinals realized that Huinker would not sign if he had to break his word to the Ossian school. So the terms were written into his contract.

It was explained to the left-handed pitcher that without spring training next year, he'd have to take his chances about assignment. All Cardinal farms will have their rosters completed by the first of May.

170

But Huinker's philosophy hasn't changed. Being older than most rookies, he feels the Cardinals won't waste much time with him. If he's got it, they'll find room for him. If he hasn't, they won't take up roster space because there isn't much chance that he will still develop at 22.

His professional debut this year was nothing short of remarkable. He won six and lost one but he had three shutout games, three one-run games and was tagged for five runs once. His earned run average for Albany of the Georgia-Florida was 1.1.

Although he appeared in only seven games, he was nominated for Rookie of the Year honors.

Huinker started playing baseball when he was 14 years old. But he then wanted to be an outfielder.

When he reported for Junior Legion ball, he found there were lots of outfielders so he announced he was a pitcher. And that was an understatement. Although no accurate record has been kept, Huinker believes he has won between 18 and 20 games each year.

And yet, he still would prefer to be an outfielder. "When we would practice at Loras, the pitchers would shag fly balls in the outfield. That was really fun. I love to catch fly balls.

Huinker, however, plays wherever he's needed. And that has included shortstop, second base and the outfield when not pitching.

He is a native of Calmar and spent two years at the high school there. His first two years were at a parochial high school in Festina.

At Ossian, he teaches history and coaches baseball, boys' basketball and girls' basketball.

He played high school basketball and college baseball himself so he's well qualified in those sports. As far as girls' basketball goes, his wife, the former Anna Mae Thuente of Calmar, played two years of the sport.

So you might say, the coach's wife will coach the coach in Ossian girls' basketball.

There are several points in the article about the Cardinals and their thinking. First of all, I frequently had "my size" brought up in discussion with their scouts. They would express thoughts like "I wish you were about three, four inches taller, Art." So size was an issue for them but apparently, in the end, the idea that maybe I could be a second Bobby Schantz, was in their mind. Schantz, a left-hand pitcher mostly with the Chicago White Sox, stood about 5-6 and had a great major league career.

Also, in the article, the reporter mentioned that I was considered for "rookie of the year" honors in the Georgia-Florida league. That was news to me. Obviously, someone else received it. And well that it should have been someone else. I only played for Albany for five weeks plus. Yet, I appreciated the fact that the people responsible even considered me deserving of consideration.

The writer also mentioned that the Cardinals would offer me a Class D contract for the coming summer. Actually, when the offer came for the 1958 season, the assignment sent me to Winston-Salem, North Carolina, a Class B Cardinal affiliate. That boosted the "morale" and played a role in my decision-making in the winter of 1958. Yes, it made it more difficult.

Certainly, prior to the summer of '57, contract offers had been made by the Cardinals, but never by any other teams. Did the fact that I already was a Cardinal fan enter into these considerations? I would not think so. However, early contract talks with the St. Louis team before the summer of '57 never included a bonus offer. For that reason, we never gave the possibility much consideration. In the article above, the author mentions that I was firm in rejecting any offers until I graduated from Loras. In my reasoning, and because of their concern about size, staying at Loras held priority. Until the Cards showed a strong belief in my ability to win in the pros, that priority did not change. As mentioned in a previous chapter, it was perplexing to me that all of a sudden in Mason City, they made up their mind. Some of these thoughts may imply that I was upset with the Cardinals and their efforts, but that is far from being true.

In late spring of my senior year at Loras, baseball season completed, the Cardinals offered to fly me to Omaha, Nebraska for a try-out at their AAA minor league site. That trip consisted of pitching in the bullpen in front of their manager, Harry Walker, former Cardinal star outfielder. Then, they wanted me to pitch batting practice. The latter opportunity was rained out. Because the round trip ticket included a flight back to Cedar Rapids later that evening, I returned to Dubuque without really spending much time with any Cardinal officials.

The flight back, my first airplane ride ever, proved somewhat harrowing. We flew straight through a heavy rainstorm, complete with considerable thunder and lightning. Besides being a rough flight, it seemed as though the lightning was exploding right next to the plane. But we made it.

The flight to Omaha, in bright sunshine, gave me the opportunity to look for baseball diamonds in all the small towns around the state. I found many of them. At that time, baseball was the key sport in all the small towns. Many of them were located next to what looked like a school building. Also, early in the day after our arrival in Omaha, I had the privilege of getting together with college classmate John Scherrman from Farley as mentioned in Chapter 12. He already was in the graduate program at Creighton.

172

Now for the tough task. Why the decision not to return to professional baseball in the summer of 1958? What happened, Art? Why didn't you continue the next summer? Were you offered a contract for '58? You had a very successful start, why not keep going?

These are questions that often have been asked of me throughout the years, especially from baseball enthusiasts in the northeast Iowa area. The decision to be made certainly carried as many consequences as any decision made in my life.

First, you need to know that Ann came through like the real trooper that she is. It will be my decision. "Whatever you decide, Art, I will be with you and support you. I know this is a dream of a lifetime for you." And, even while at Loras, Doc Kammer from Loras, who loved baseball, claimed that a girl friend was something I did not need, And he was partially right. But she approvingly left it up to me.

When the contract offer came from the Cardinals in January of '58, we were excited about the possible jump to Class B baseball, ready or not. What bothered us was the pay scale. It was $400 a month and just for the months of the baseball season. Questions bounced around quickly and often. What do we do in the off months? Where will we live? I definitely will not be able to accept another teaching contract, with baseball starting by March first and ending in September. And I really truly enjoyed teaching and being with the students. The first year doing it offered many challenges but also as many, if not more, joys.

When we inquired about the pay scale for the baseball contract, and any chance of a boost in pay, we found that there were required maximums that could be paid for a minor leaguer. And $400 was it. Also, by the way, when on road trips our food allowance was $4.00 per day.

What were my chances of success? How long before I might reach the major league level? We were now expecting our second child. It turned out to be our second son that we named Tim, in March of 1958.

There were other quandaries floating around in my mind. What kind of life would it be, especially for Ann? And for our children? It wasn't only me that this decision was going to impact. How many times would I come home and say, "Ann, we are moving to another team and another league. Pack up the family." I would be the first to say, it is a heck of an opportunity for a single guy with few other ties.

One person who I wished I had discussed this more deeply with was my father. He provided all the opportunities for me to play the game we both loved. What were his feelings? Did he want me to fight for this dream of mine all the way? Today I think back on this decision and realize I did not share my concerns, or my thoughts with him very extensively. Also, today I wonder if I truly prayed

173

over the decision and asked for guidance from above. The response would probably have gone something like this, "Art, you have a free will. It's your decision. You created the situation. It's up to you."

Growing up in an environment where family life provided so much satisfaction and contentment…and love, where do I go? In the end, there were three factors that weighed in on the choice that was finally made. First of all, it was a financial one. If it would take three to five years, or even more, to reach the majors, how would we meet our financial needs? Second was the factor of uncertainty for the love of my life and the children we already had. Sure, it would be great to have a husband and father playing major league baseball but what if that did not happen. The percentages are not favorable. Hindsight tells me we would always be able to pursue the teaching/coaching career, but that feeling wasn't so clear for me at the time. And finally, experiencing that profession of teaching/coaching, even for just five months, I had very positive feelings toward the responsibilities that accompanied the profession.

The decision was made. I was a baseball holdout. To my favorite St. Louis Cardinals. In a way, I guess I still am a holdout, technically. The Cardinals gave me an opportunity to pursue one of my two favorite "dreams." And I thank them for that. To friends and baseball mates who may have wished I had continued the pursuit of a career as a left-hand pitcher in the professional circuit, I apologize. I let you down.

Just recently, Gene "Tiny" Potts shared his thoughts with me. He said, "Art, you should have kept going. You had good stuff. You had good control."

Then he added, "Especially for a left hander."

Now, the question asked of me, "Do you ever have second thoughts?" The response is "Yes, I have." But I have also been told that once you make a decision, don't look back. I have tried to remember that advice. I have sometimes kicked myself for not talking with Sister Claire of Assisi, my principal at Ossian De Sales, to see if they would have allowed me to teach until the first of March in the spring of 1958 so I could go to spring training, but truthfully, that never entered my mind at the time of the decision making.

Ann and I have had a wonderful life together. We have never had to worry about where we are going to live. We have never had to worry about a job. We have had a strong home, filled with love and security. This far overshadows any second guessing that we might do. I thank God for all the opportunities that fulfilled my life but there is none more important than the woman that probably made Doc Kammer's viewpoint a viable one. I made the decision. I have few regrets. Admittedly, the "end of a dream."

Our early departure before the season ended at Albany led to a fascinating story unknown to us until the "Field of Dreams" movie had created a famous baseball diamond out in the middle of a cornfield near Dyersville, Iowa. Part of our baseball future included teaching and coaching baseball at the Catholic high school in that small town of about 5,000.

Several Labor Day celebrations were held at the Field of Dreams diamond bringing in entertainment stars as well as baseball Hall of Fame players, including the likes of Bob Feller, Reggie Jackson and Bob Gibson, just to name a few. It became my privilege to chauffeur Gibson around once he arrived in Dyersville. We played against each other in several AABC regional baseball tournaments discussed earlier. As a result of that, we had become familiar with each other and retained a distant relationship, Bob continuing to live in his hometown of Omaha, Nebraska after his retirement from professional baseball.

The two of us were renewing old times in the Dyersville Beckman High School locker room when I realized we needed to hustle out to the Field of Dreams ball diamond some three miles northeast of Dyersville. Many of you already know that and have probably visited the place.

As Bob started to put on his uniform, he asked "Art, how many children do you have?" When informed that Ann and I had seven children, he peeled off seven baseball cards, autographed them and gave them to me. As he continued to finish dressing, I was reading one of the cards.

Suddenly I stopped. "Bob," I said, "it says here you signed a contract in August of 1957 with the Cardinals and you played for the Albany Cardinals."

Bob looked at me, "Yeah, I took the position of a pitcher who left the team early to satisfy a teaching contract he had."

Utterly flabbergasted, I looked at him and replied, "That was me."

True story. I found it hard to believe. He went on, of course, to have a memorable career, all with the parent St. Louis Cardinals. Now, he is one of the few who has made it into the Baseball Hall of Fame. I always maintain that is as close as I will come to those hallowed halls.

By the way, our children often ask where those seven cards are that Bob Gibson signed and gave to me. And my answer regretfully is "I really don't have a clue."

TRYING TO BE A TEACHER AND A COACH

It was the spring of 1957. Undergraduate student days at Loras College were nearing their completion. The fourth and final year of college baseball was winding down. Ann and I behaved like most new parents, wild about our son, Terry, as he neared his first birthday on July 16 of the coming summer. We watched for his first step as we prepared for graduation.

With the many closure issues facing us, there was another more significant issue that became our central focus, job hunting. Where would the Huinkers plant their teaching and their family roots? Thankfully, the opportunities were out there, starting with a small public school within thirty miles of Dubuque, to a much larger school system in Brainerd, Minnesota north of the Twin Cities. Although the latter was a strong school system, the extreme northerly location bothered me, especially as a baseball coach. In between those two, a new central Catholic high school had been formed in our home town area. Called De Sales Central High School and located in Ossian, Iowa, it included six parishes from Ossian, Clermont, Postville, Decorah, Calmar and our home parish of St. Mary's in Festina. After several interviews were completed with the different locations and we had deliberated over whether or not we wanted to be that close to home, the De Sales offer was accepted. And seriously, we were excited about going back home. The contract included the teaching of Social Studies and Physical Education, while coaching all sports, including boys and girls basketball along with fall and spring baseball.

Yes, this is the same De Sales baseball program that seven years earlier our nine freshmen and sophomore boys at Festina had wiped out so thoroughly. However, the school now carried the label of "central" and all six parishes were officially supporting the school with hopes that children from their community would continue their Catholic education. With this move, the ninth and tenth grade program was discontinued at Festina. The De Sales enrollment almost doubled with the centralization, including students from baseball-rich Festina. One of those students from Festina happened to be Ann's sister, Stella, who would be a junior at De Sales in the fall of 1957. Was that supposed to create special problems for me? I was either too ignorant to realize what those problems could be or too vain to admit that I would have any difficulties. Thank heaven she was a top-notch student. Something similar happened to me when teaching part-time in the education division at Loras College much later in life. Granddaughter Autumn (Terry's daughter) was in my classes. I could say the same thing. She was also a top-notch student and no difficulties. At least, in both cases, I don't know of any.

A write-up that appeared in the Dubuque Telegraph Herald and is included as part of the chapter dedicated to the professional baseball experiences attempts to unravel some of the complexities of the situation between playing professional baseball and the first teaching/coaching contract. It identifies the anxieties that I was experiencing in the spring of 1957 when the St. Louis

176

Cardinals talked several times with me about signing a contract, yet never offered anything. It was impossible for us to not seek a teaching/coaching position as long as we were uncertain of the professional baseball opportunity. The teaching contract was offered and accepted. Three months later the Cardinals offered exactly what we were waiting for.

For the next four years, from 1957 to 1961, De Sales Central Catholic provided such a satisfying teaching experience that I was ready to dedicate my life to working with "kids." I was working with an excellent group of fellow faculty, most of them Franciscan nuns from Mount St. Francis Convent in Dubuque. Chief among them was our principal, Sister Claire of Assisi Miller. What a wonderful gift it was for me to have her as my principal for ten of the eleven years when I was developing what should be my role in the classroom. Add that to the input that Ann provided during the same time, how blessed I was.

Baseball-wise, the first year was a losing season, both fall and spring. But for the next three years, the won-loss record was consistently on the positive side. Farm neighbor Andy Hemesath, a dearest friend throughout life for my Dad, discussed that trend with me. "Art, you have your opponents respecting your baseball team now. They know it will be a contested game any time they set foot on that diamond against you," is the way he put it.

The first year of baseball coaching saw four seniors lead the way. Catcher Gervase Hanken, infielders Jerry Schrandt and Dick Leibold and outfielder Bob Moellers were the veterans. Pitching-wise, juniors Allen Nienhaus and Phil Hemesath and sophomore Carl Heying led the way. Phil's Dad was the farm neighbor mentioned in the previous paragraph. Although we put a question mark by the game, Phil pitched the only no-hitter for the eleven years of coaching high school baseball.

The following year, our experienced pitchers brought our first winning season, both spring and fall. Larry Heying, Julius Martinek, Matt Vollmecke and Roger Gerleman, also seniors in 1958-59, supported the stronger pitching.

In the third year, Carl Heying was now our pitching ace. Carl went on to pitch for Loras College after his graduation from De Sales. Besides Heying, Elwyn Dotzenrod and Terry Lensing provided senior leadership for a successful 1959-1960 baseball team. Additional pitching was coming from sophomores Jim Leibold, Rick Henely and Danny Frommelt.

By the fall of 1960, what turned out to be the final year for Ann and me at De Sales, the ball club displayed fundamentally sound baseball skills that led to a record thirteen wins and one loss, that loss being in the state championship game against defending fall champion Bancroft St. John's and their well-known baseball coach Vince Meyer. Our players enjoyed playing the game of baseball.

Six straight wins placed the De Sales Falcons in the favorites' role for the sectional tourney which was to be played on the De Sales diamond. This diamond, by the way, was built one summer, using an old-time tractor with steel lugs (no rubber tires for those of you too young to remember) with a blade on the front. Many hours were spent pushing dirt from the previous diamond to its new location. The diamond was just flipped over. Home plate, formerly in the southeast corner right next to the school, was moved to the northwest corner. Believe it or not, we had a grass infield on the new diamond. The backstop was donated and built by Falcon boosters. My wedding ring slipped off my finger during all that activity and probably is buried in the dirt of the grass infield.

We had a wonderful music teacher, Sister Mary Arnold, who wasn't too happy with the diamond change. A huge sports fan who supposedly could watch the games from a window in the chapel during after-school prayer services when it was directly behind the school, no longer was afforded that opportunity. By the way, students loved her and her music program did not lack for student participants. About a year ago we attended an organ recital at the Dominican nunnery in Sinsinawa, Wisconsin where this wonderful music teacher entertained us with her great organ-playing talents. She is still as enthusiastic about life as ever.

Back to the 1960 fall baseball season. The six non-tournament wins were posted over Oelwein Sacred Heart, St. Luke's of St. Lucas, Lansing St. George, Waukon St. Pat's and Cresco Notre Dame twice. Doing the pitching were Jim Leibold, Rick Henely, Dan Frommelt and Bob Heying, all juniors. The catching was split between freshman Ron Leibold and sophomore Dave Thuente, Ann's first cousin. The first win against Oelwein Sacred Heart belongs in the record books as a rarity. It was a no-hitter but the team getting not a single hit was the winner, De Sales. The Falcons won the game 6-4 on 5 walks and 6 Sacred Heart errors. During those six games, local newspaper write-ups showed the Falcons executed five successful suicide squeezes.

Tournament Trail to the State Finals

Every baseball team, also other sports for that matter, will begin the tournament trail by dreaming of eight consecutive victories to a state championship, or possibly it is the coaches who dream that. We probably could be included after we had garnered six straight wins going into the tournament. Looking back to that trail, so much had to happen, including breaks that had to go our way, for us to keep our winning streak alive. As a matter of fact, we were losing our first game against Pete Peterson's MarMac team, 2-0, going into the bottom of the fifth inning. One of the finest baseball coaches in the area, teams competing against Pete Peterson-coached teams had to be ready for anything. Pete is the same coach who followed me after we had beaten his Monona team when I was in high school. Up to the bottom half of the fifth, MarMac controlled the tempo of the game. Gary Peterson, no relation of Coach Peterson, a good ball player and later a very successful baseball and basketball coach himself, had silenced our bats. With two outs and runners on second and third for us, a high infield pop-up was dropped allowing both runners to score. Had the ball been caught, as it normally should have been, would we have caught fire and gained that first victory 5-2? It is what it is.

All the write-ups in this chapter were taken from the Ossian Bee and written by its publisher, Dirk Amundson. The articles did an excellent job of creating a feel for the game and the excitement that accompanied it.

> ### FALCONS WIN TOURNAMENT OPENER
> *The De Sales Falcons won their seventh consecutive game of the season from Mar-Mac of McGregor, 5-2. Mar-Mac jumped off to a 2-0 lead in the first inning. From there on, however, Falcon righthander, Jim Leibold shut the door. He allowed only four hits the remainder of the game while fanning seven and walking three.*
>
> *De Sales tied the score in the fifth. Ron Leibold led off with single. After an infield out, pinch hitter Dale Nienhaus was walked. A balk advanced both runners. Garvin Nienhaus fanned and Terry Kelly popped up to the infield for what appeared to be the third out. However, the ball was dropped and both runners scored.*
>
> *In the bottom of the sixth, with two out and nobody on, the Falcons broke the game wide open. Bob Pankow walked and stole second. Ron Leibold doubled him home and scored a minute later on Rudy Tekippe's single to center. Tekippe later scored the fifth and final run of the game.*
>
> *Top defensive play of the game was made in the seventh when right fielder Tekippe threw out a runner at first base to take a hit away from him.*

The second and third wins to capture the finals of the sectional tournament saw Dan Frommelt and Jim Leibold provide strong pitching outings. The finals against Garnavillo High School also saw the Falcons wrap out fifteen hits led by Rudy Tekippe's three singles and Rick Henely's four hits including two bunt singles and a three-run homer. Our bats were coming alive.

> ### DE SALES 3, ST. LUKE'S 0
> *De Sales advanced to the finals of the tournament by winning a 3-0 victory over St. Luke's of St. Lucas. The game was closer than the final score indicates. In the top of the seventh inning St. Lucas loaded the bases with one out on a walk and two singles off left-hander Danny Frommelt. With their best hitters coming up, the situation looked very bleak. However, Jim Leibold took over the pitching chores and struck*

179

*out the first man he faced and forced the next batter to ground
out to Rick Henely to end the ball game.*

*The Falcons collected only three hits off the hurling of
Ivan Bodensteiner. The first two runs were made without a hit.
The Falcons' first hits came in the fifth inning, three straight
singles by Frommelt, Henely and Leibold, which scored the final
run of the game.*

DE SALES WINS SECTIONAL BASEBALL MEET

*The Ossian De Sales Falcons won the fall baseball
sectional championship Monday afternoon by walloping
previously undefeated Garnavillo 11-2. It was the ninth
consecutive victory of the season for the Falcons without a
defeat and sweet revenge for less than two years ago in the
finals of a sectional tournament the same Garnavillo team beat
De Sales, 3-1, at McGregor.*

*De Sales scored three quick runs in the first inning of
Monday's title game. Terry Kelly and Danny Frommelt walked.
A bunt hit by Rick Henely was followed by an infield out and
Bob Pankow's two-bagger to the left field corner. A wild pitch
scored the third run.*

*Meanwhile, the Falcon offensive machine kept moving.
They picked up three more runs in the third on five singles, two
of which were bunt hits by Henely and Jim Leibold. Frommelt
led off with a single and two bunts followed. Pankow then
singled, scoring two runs. After an infield fly, Rudy Tekippe got
his first of three straight hits to made the score 6-1.*

*De Sales really iced the game in the fourth when
Henely slapped a home run over the left field fence with Kelly
and Frommelt on base. Defense again stood out for the Falcons
as the infield handled 12 ground balls without a misplay.*

The first district round game against Cedar Rapids St. Pat's and long-
time coach Jim Kenney provided a batter's dream. The final score was 11-10.
Rick Henely again led the hitting attack with a single, double and triple good for
four runs batted in. Bob Pankow had two doubles driving in three runs. But what
I remember the most is the heads-up defensive play by Jim Leibold in the top of
the seventh. The score stood 11-9 in favor of De Sales at the time. St. Pat's led
off the inning with a double. When the next batter followed with a single to
center, Leibold cut off Frommelt's throw to the plate and flipped to Garvin
Nienhaus at second base, nailing the runner easily. That changed the complexion
of the entire inning. Instead of no outs, one run in and the tying run on first base,
there was one out and no one on. Two quick outs followed and a wild comeback
victory was sealed.

180

FALCONS OVERCOME 8-RUN DEFICIT TO BEAT
ST. PAT'S
In the first round of the district tournament at
Hazelton, the De Sales Falcons spotted St. Pat's of Cedar
Rapids eight big runs in the top half of the first inning, then
fought back to win 11-10. Outstanding relief hurling by ace
righthander, Jim Leibold proved the deciding factor for the
Falcons. Leibold took over the pitching chores in the top of the
third with De Sales down, 9-7, and shut the door in the face of
the Irish. He gave them only one harmless run in the seventh
and final inning. St. Pat's did collect six hits off his curves but
they were well scattered. In his five innings of hurling, Leibold
did not walk a batter while fanning five.

Meanwhile the Falcon hitters showed that they were
not to be denied immediately in the last half of the first inning.
They put together a triple by Rick Henely and doubles by Jim
Leibold and Bob Pankow to tally two runs.

De Sales closed the gap some more in the second
inning. Three bases on balls, mixed with three hits, tallied five
big runs. Rightfielder Rudy Tekippe opened the inning with a
long triple to center. Two walks and Terry Kelly's single
brought in three runs. Then, with two out and two men on,
Pankow boomed out his second straight double to bring across
the final runs of the inning.

Three walks and Henely's second of three hits tied the
game at 9-9. Henely proved to be a thorn in side of Irish
hurling as he drove across four runs on his single, double and
triple. He also was on the initial end of a third to second to first
double play in the third.

With the score all tied, the Falcons pushed across the
tie-breaking and winning runs in the bottom of the fifth. Lead-
off man Kelly gained life on the only error of the game by St.
Pat's, Danny Frommelt received his third straight pass, moving
Kelly to second. Then Henely picked on a 2 and 0 pitch and
drove a long double to deep left center, scoring both Kelly and
Frommelt.

De Sales Central Catholic's first district title was another comeback
victory. Trailing 2-1 in the top half of the sixth, three runs were plated, one on a
successful squeeze play, another on Dale Nienhaus's third single. The actual
winning run also scored on another successful squeeze play. On to the substate, a
first for the De Sales baseball teams.

The name Nienhaus should be recognizable from my playing days with
hometown Festina. The manager of the Festina team was Florian Nienhaus, father
of freshman Dale and junior shortstop Garvin Nienhaus. They joined senior Rudy

181

Tekippe and junior Bob Heying in representing the Festina parish on the De Sales team. Florian and his wife Helen provided an earlier athlete with an older son, Allen, who played both baseball and basketball while I was coaching. Of all the "baseball" athletes that played under my tutelage at De Sales, Allen was one of the finest baseball players I had the privilege of coaching. He was a tall, slender left hand hitter, most noted for tremendous power, who also did some pitching. During his senior year in high school, Allen was diagnosed with leukemia. Less than a year later we said goodbye to the fine youngster, a victim of the cancer.

Other Festina baseball players in earlier years were Terry Lensing, Matt Vollmecke, brothers Larry and Richie Heying, and their cousin Carl Heying. The Heyings also played basketball. Carl, baseball coach at Western Dubuque Schools and I coached against each other when I was at Xavier and Beckman High Schools in Dyersville.

DE SALES DEFEATS WINTHROP BY 6 TO 4

Good defensive ball, two squeeze bunts and strong pitching by junior Rick Henely with a mop-up job by Jim Leibold, gave the De Sales Falcons their first district baseball win Friday afternoon.

Winthrop's Jim McEnany seemed to have Falcon hitters baffled by his assortment. He allowed only a single by Dale Nienhaus in the first three innings. McEnany lost control and walked Danny Frommelt and Henely to open the fourth. Jim Leibold's sacrifice and Bob Pankow's infield smash off the shortstop's glove scored Frommelt with the Falcon's first run of the game.

The score remained 2-1 in Winthrop's favor until the sixth when walks to Henely and Pankow, mixed with two stolen bases and a throwing error, plated Henely with the tying run, and put Pankow on third base with one. Then the suicide squeeze was performed to perfection as Pankow broke from third on the pitch and freshman Ron Leibold dropped a good bunt down the first base line. Pankow scored easily with the third De Sales run of the game. Another run was added on a walk to Tekippe, his steal of second base and freshman Dale Nienhaus' third straight hit.

With the score tied, the Falcons showed their desire to win and quickly iced the game in the top of the seventh. Terry Kelly led off with a base hit, was sacrificed to second base, then moved to third on Henely's line shot to left. Henely stole second and the stage was set for the big play. Again, Kelly, the runner on third, broke with the pitch. Again the hitter, Jim Leibold, put down a good bunt to score Kelly with the winning run. When third baseman Coffman threw wildly to first attempting to get Leibold, Henely scored the last run of the game.

182

The substate games were played on the same diamond as the district games. Hazelton High School, in a small town just south of Oelwein, hosted both tournaments. Another long-time baseball and basketball coach, Bill Murphy, had the diamond ready for each of the four games. Bill is best known for his great, comedic story-telling abilities as well as a very successful coaching career.

The diamond itself had only a short backstop of about 30 feet in length behind home plate, with the entire diamond surrounded by huge trees. There was no other enclosure fencing. Down the left field line, tree branches actually hung over the left field foul line into fair territory. This played a role in the Falcons' 6-5 victory over Van Horne in the opening round of the substate. Their shortstop/pitcher, a giant of an athlete, estimated to be in the 6'5" range with a strong build, teed off on a Jim Leibold pitch and pulled it high and far down the left field line, destined for at least a double. The ball caught a high branch in fair territory, and bounded back toward left fielder Dale Nienhaus. A quick pick-up and Nienhaus made this one of the longest singles in my high school memories.

The other oddity of the game came in the top half of the seventh with the score tied and the "big man" on the mound for Van Horne. After a failed squeeze play (how many successful ones versus failed ones, I don't know) following a Bob Pankow lead-off triple, two small in stature freshmen provided the winning fireworks. A single by Ron Leibold, a stolen base, and another single by Dale Nienhaus scored the winning run. Another freshman, short but strong Jerry Linderbaum, was making it difficult for the 6-5 pitcher to get the ball over. When the big guy decided to just lob the ball to the plate in hopes of throwing strikes, little Jerry promptly hit a hard ground ball right back through the pitcher's legs for a base hit.

> FIRST ROUND SUB STATE
> The grit and determination of a ball club that just won't say "no" paid off once again for the Falcons as they came from behind to beat Van Horne, 6-5, last Wednesday at Hazelton.
> Jim Leibold survived a shaky start and blanked hard-hitting Van Horne over the last four innings. He was aided by a sharp defensive effort by Terry Kelly at second with two out and a man on third in the sixth. Leibold, in picking up his seventh win of the season, struck out five and walked only two.

The Falcons' thirteenth victory that placed them in the state championship offered many highlights, exemplified by a final score of 13-9 over Grand Mound, a small town located near Clinton, Iowa. Scoring eight runs in the first two innings tends to build a false spirit of complacency. After the next two innings, if a complacent feeling had developed, it disappeared when Grand Mound scored seven runs. In this victory, good defense (no errors versus seven for the

183

opposition and ten walks by Grand Mound pitchers) made the final difference. The Falcons were off to the big one.

SUB STATE FINALS

In a hard fought game Friday at Hazelton the De Sales Falcons piled up a quick 8-0 lead, saw it vanish, then came roaring back to defeat Grant Mound, 13-9. In the first inning with one out, a walk, back to back singles by Henely and Jim Leibold, and an error, gave De Sales two runs. In the second inning the Falcons really opened up their attack. Dale Nienhaus walked. After a strikeout, Terry Kelly walked. Then Danny Frommelt bunted safely and two runs scored when losing pitcher Bob Fey erred. Henely then walked, Jim Leibold singled to load the bases and Bob Pankow hit the first of two sacrifice flies. Ron Leibold singled and Rudy Tekippe smashed a liner to left center to clean the bases. Total result: six runs on three hits.

An error, two walks, Rudy Tekippe's second straight hit and a squeeze play by Garvin Nienhaus gave De Sales two big runs. Leibold settled down and held Grand Mound scoreless in the fifth and sixth innings. At the same time the Falcons were adding to their total. Two runs were scored in the fifth when Henely got life on an error, Jim Leibold doubled to left and both scored on sacrifice flies by Pankow and Ron Leibold. They scored their final run in the sixth on a walk, another error and Jim Leibold's fourth hit of the day.

Excitement was hitting fever pitch in the high school's home town of Ossian by this time. Following is a clip taken from the local paper, the Ossian Bee:

OSSIAN DE SALES GAINS STATE FINAL

Mayor Terrance Vikre has proclaimed Monday "championship day" at Ossian and regardless of the game's outcome one thing is certain--there is going to be a celebration in the little Northeast Iowa town.

The baseball team's success has created more of a stir than the World Series. The town's Commercial Club has been sponsoring radio broadcasts of the games. And there is talk of closing every store in the city for Monday's game.

The excitement of thirteen straight victories and of playing for the state championship quickly succumbed to a four hit, five run first inning by perennial fall state champion Bancroft St. John's. Yet Cedar Rapids St. Pat's scored eight runs in the first inning against us, so the young Falcons fought back with three runs of their own, without a base hit. However, that is where the St. Pat's

184

similarity ended. Led by future major leaguer, Dennis Menke, who went three for four, the state champs connected for twelve hits and that, combined with seven De Sales errors from a normally reliable defense, put the Falcons in a hole they were unable to climb out of. The final score was 13-3.

FALCONS TAKE SECOND IN STATE

The De Sales Falcons, pride of Ossian and northeastern Iowa, returned home Monday night to a heroes' welcome after winning second place in Iowa's fall baseball tournament.

Ossian's streets were lined with fans who had waited two hours for the Falcons to return. The South Winneshiek Commmunity high school pep band livened the homecoming with snappy tunes and about 50 cars with horns blaring, added to the happy din.

At the west edge of town the Falcons were met by the Ossian fire truck and the young Falcons and their coach, Art Huinker, were given a ride they never will forget. The fire truck with the team, two chartered buses carrying De Sales students and rooters, an open truck transporting the pep band, and a long line of cars drove slowly through the business district with horns and sirens blaring.

Supporters of the Falcons had the business district ready for the celebration. All business windows were decorated with whitewash, congratulating the Falcons on their achievements during the fall state tournaments. At each end of Main Street large banners stretched across the highway.

The long line of cars proceeded to De Sales School at the east end of town, then returned to the town hall where a short program was conducted.

STATE FINALS

The De Sales Falcons played defending state champion St. John's of Bancroft for the state title Monday afternoon and were defeated, 13-3.

The powerful state champions erupted in the first inning when they collected four straight hits off De Sales' overworked ace right-hander Jim Leibold. Five runs crossed the plate before the inning was finished.

The Falcons, without the benefit of a base hit, fought back with their usual determined vigor. They scored three runs on four walks, a hit batsman and Rudy Tekippe's sacrifice fly.

A neat double play, Rick Henely to Terry Kelly to Bob Pankow, pulled Leibold through the second inning. But too much pitching was starting to tell on the spunky little hurler and

St. Johns scored once in the third, added three more in the
fourth to force Leibold's withdrawal from the mound.
Rick Henely succeded him and allowed three hits and
four more runs over the last 2 2/3 innings. He was the victim of
shaky defensive work on the part of the Falcons, as was starter
Leibold. Seven costly errors by the otherwise alert defense gave
St. Johns eight unearned runs in the contest.
The pressure of participating in state championship
competition took its toll of the Falcons. Inexperience very
definitely played the major role for a weak defense. On the
offensive picture, the Falcons seemed to suffer the same fate.
Only two hits were collected, both singles by Bob Pankow and
Rudy Tekippe.
It was the only loss of the season for the Falcons after
13 consecutive victories.

A write-up in the Dubuque Telegraph Herald identified the pressure of playing in a state championship in this way: "Almost utterly without tournament experience---the Falcons had never before gotten through a district meet---little De Sales was strung tighter than a drumskin when the game started, and tighter yet when it was over." The same write-up addresses how the game ended up being played at Corwith. Originally to be played on Bancroft St. John's home field, the Iowa High School Athletic Association made last-minute arrangement changes when they received protests from northeast Iowa baseball fans who expressed grave unfairness of the original plan. One of the major leaders in pushing for the change was our pastor at Ossian De Sales, Msgr. Vernon Peters.

Reflecting on the successful thirteen game winning streak now some fifty years later, the young men on the fall 1960 team must carry exciting memories of their accomplishments, memories that cannot be taken away. There are several pictures in the picture section of the final game and related activities. Yes, we could have lost the first sectional game but these players "made their own breaks" many times throughout that 13-game run. Strong defensive plays at key times, timely hitting, and significant stops by our pitchers support that statement. Other reserve players on that team who did not get to see action during the tournament trail were Lee Schissel, Jim Moellers, Larry Keefe and Bob Carolan, all freshmen and sophomores.

We're going to take one more step with that team---to the 1961 spring baseball season. It was still the same school year, 1960-1961. The baseball team included the same players who were looking forward to another tournament trail beginning with the sectionals to be played on our home diamond again. Going into that challenge the Falcons again were undefeated, with a big win included over arch rival South Winneshiek, formerly our alma mater Calmar High School. Three of the four towns that were officially now South Winneshiek---Calmar, Ossian and Festina---also were part of the De Sales Central Catholic system.

Parents were able to make their choice as to which system their children attended. The rivalry was primarily a friendly one because most of the children grew up together in those three communities. At least it was for a majority of the people.

A major change was coming. Ann and I received a letter from Xavier High School in Dyersville, inviting us to look at a teaching/coaching opening at their Catholic high school. The invitation had been sent to the De Sales school address. Its return address peaked my interest immediately. Because I had received it in my mail at school, I proceeded to open it while monitoring a study hall held in the library. In that study hall happened to be our regular and much loved baby sitter Janet Barthelme. She observed my reaction to the letter and informed Ann and me later that she immediately feared that the letter involved a new teaching opportunity. By this time, the spring of 1961, Ann and I had four children—Terry, almost five, Tim three, Tammy 19 months and Peggy 5 months. They kept Ann busy and they also kept Janet (Jody as we called her) busy with her babysitting opportunities. Our children loved her and she loved them.

Why did we respond so positively to the new opportunity? In a previous chapter, we covered baseball-playing for Dyersville's semi-pro team, the Whitehawks. We had a very successful summer with that team already in 1956, between the junior and senior years at Loras College. That summer, we sensed a baseball-crazy town where coaching baseball could find considerable talent. We also had made some strong friendly ties with several couples during that summer. For those reasons, we responded to the invitation, had several interviews with the school officials at Xavier, and accepted the position. We would be leaving De Sales Catholic Central school. Probably the most difficult duty we now had was the notification of school officials that we would be leaving at the end of the school year. But possibly the most difficult task was to talk with the baseball players, all but three who would be back the coming fall, prior to the start of the sectional tournament. But the days ahead were about to become much more difficult.

Those meetings covered, the team prepared for a Monday, May 10 sectional baseball game against Lansing St. George. Although the particular inning escapes my book of memories, we were losing. We were at bat when suddenly the umpires called "time." Why? Then, as we turned our heads toward centerfield, we had our answer. Monsignor Vernon Peters, our pastor at the Ossian parish and also the official head of the central Catholic school, was walking through the playing field, eventually turning toward the umpires who had gathered down the first base line. I was dumbfounded that he chose to go to them rather than me, the person in charge of the game as its host. Somewhat puzzled, or maybe asking to myself "what the heck is going on?" I walked slowly over to the meeting with Monsignor and the umpires. When I entered the group, Monsignor grabbed me firmly by the shoulders, "Art, I have very bad news for you. Your Dad was just killed in a tractor accident." My knees buckled but he kept me from falling. "Your mother wants you out at your brother Linus's farm

187

right away. And she wants you to also stop at your sister Shirley's house and inform her of what happened." Shirley lived only two blocks from the baseball diamond.

"The baseball game! My team! I'm their coach!" Those thoughts raced through my mind, but without hesitation, I knew where I belonged. I asked the umpires and Father Gerald Condon, the St. George coach, for some time so that I could share the horrible event with Ann, who was at the game with all the kids. Then I wanted a brief meeting with the players and co-teacher, Paul Vaassen, who volunteered to help assist me in coaching. Paul stepped in as the game's coach and I informed Jim Leibold, Rick Henely and Terry Kelly at the meeting that they would share the responsibility of coaching third base and make the usual decisions that they felt most appropriate for the situation. Ann in the meantime was seeking our faithful babysitter, Jody, so that Ann could accompany me out to the farm where my mother waited. For the Leo Huinker family, baseball ground to a halt Monday afternoon, May 10,1961. Our family value system clearly told us that there was something much more important than baseball.

Thinking back to the opening chapter, trying to answer the question, "Why was baseball so important to the Leo and Matilda Huinker family?" the answer so often came back to my father. Ironically, one of his children was involved in a baseball game when he was taken from us. Maybe that is why the loss of our "Daddy" in the end was much more significant than the game that he loved.

The entire baseball team came to the funeral home in Ossian on Wednesday at a time that the school had arranged with the undertaker. There are no words to describe my "breakdown" when the players walked into the room where my father lay in his coffin. It overwhelms me even now as I try to find the words to describe the players sharing their thoughts and emotions with me. As they left to go back to school, their heads were hanging low, as was mine. Tears were abundant. Was that gathering a significant experience for them? Or was it the other around? Possibly the significant life's experience was for me.

The following morning at the funeral mass, Reverend William Kunsch (Yes, the famous biology professor at Loras College during the four years of my college education and now pastor of our home parish in Festina and biology teacher at De Sales) in his homily hit an emotional chord when he said that Leo's family always lovingly called him "Daddy." Just two months before his sudden death, Daddy made the first retreat of his life at the American Martyrs Retreat House. He was fifty-eight years old and had just semi-retired the previous fall.

Now for the baseball game and its outcome. The Falcons lost by one run with Jim Leibold being tagged out at home plate for the final out of the game. Father Gerald "Tait" Condon, the St. George Coach, wrote a most beautiful letter to Ann and me following the game in which he wrote how proud we should be of the wonderful way the players handled themselves the remainder of the game. "I

188

never saw a group of high school baseball players, emotionally stunned as they were, try so hard to win as your kids did." With those words the 1960-61 baseball season and first coaching years at De Sales Catholic Central High School drew to a close. How fortunate Ann and I were to spend our first four years in the De Sales community. Even though I often apologized to the students later at class reunions and other celebrations for being such a "green horn" rookie who lacked so much of the knowledge and ability that today I feel are essential to be a good teacher, for the Huinker family it was a positive and memorable four years.

On a side note, Paul Vaassen, the man who took charge of the team while Ann and I chose to support family, was inducted fifty years later into the Dubuque County Baseball Hall of Fame for all his years of umpiring in the Dubuque area. Umpiring was a side role that Paul started at Ossian De Sales only because it was difficult to get umpires for our games. Upon my begging he gave it a try. He became a highly respected arbiter in Dubuque County where he and his wife Mary Ann took over her home farm for their livelihood.

The summer of 1961 was scheduled to be a difficult year for Ann and our family. I already had agreed to run the summer recreation program at Ossian which included little league baseball. I also agreed to play for the Dyersville Whitehawks during the summer. Add the selling of our house in Ossian (or renting it out as we eventually were forced to do), the moving to Dyersville and finding a house to rent in our new community, to the mix. Then, the loss of my father.

With his death, Ann and I, because we were preparing to move later in the summer anyway, moved our family to the farm home where my Mom was living to help her get through the summer. It was a difficult three months for her and yet sometimes I wonder if all the hustle and bustle (and noise of four less than school-age children) made it more difficult for her. Our own lives became very complicated and hectic. It became so overwhelming at times that one day we took Mom and our family to visit my Daddy's mother. Only after driving a good four to five miles, one of our older children asked "Where is Peggy?" She was our six-month old. She was back at the farm home in her crib. It was that kind of summer. That woman that agreed to share her life with me forever became a saint if she hadn't already reached that status earlier. There were so many loose ends to bring together. Many of them remained loose.

Above: Leo & Mathilda (Einck) Huinker family about 1951
Linus, Kenneth and Arthur
Irene, Mathilda, Leo and Shirley

Above: 1951 Festine Team from left to right, back row: Linus Huinker,
Manager Florian Nienhaus, Bob Huinker, Linus Rothmeyer, Norb Einck,
Ken Huinker, Rudy Wenthold; front row: Leo Luzum, Jim Schneberger,
Ken Schneberger, Romauld Elsbernd, Nily Huinker, Ralph Kneeskern,
batboy is Allen Nienhaus

Perfect Peg Gets Festina Runner

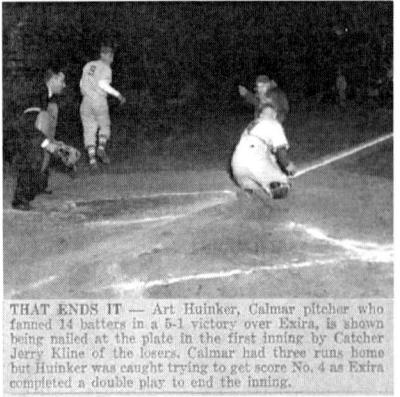

THAT ENDS IT — Art Huinker, Calmar pitcher who
fanned 14 batters in a 5-1 victory over Exira, is shown
being nailed at the plate in the first inning by Catcher
Jerry Kline of the losers. Calmar had three runs home
but Huinker was caught trying to get score No. 4 as Exira
completed a double play to end the inning.

To the left Leroy Schneberger, walking away fr
the plate, just scored ahead of Huinker.

Bucheit Produce Champs

Calmar High School baseball team, spring 1952. First athlete team to go to state. Left to right, front row: Ron Albertson, Art Huinker, Larry Herold, Russ Hillman, Leroy Schneberger, Mickey Griffen, Tom Iverson. Second row: Richard Winn, Ron Schuler, Leroy Einck, Jerry Sjulli, Denis Bengfort, Eldon Holten

Signs White Hawk Pact

To the left is a picture of Anna Mae, the girl that started stealing my heart!

County Champions

The Festina Pitcher? Lefty Huinker

Duhawk Hurlers

Three pitchers likely to see action for the Loras College Duhawks in Friday's opener with the Platteville Pioneers. Left to right are Joe Elbert, who will get the starting call, Phil Huewe and Art Muinker who will be ready for relief duty if necessary.

The 1954 Duhawk baseball squad notched an excellent 11-3 record for the season. Squad members were front row: (l-r) Frank Sovich, Joe Ottavi, Bob Wolfe, Art Huinker, Bob Kaliban, Joe Elbert, Bob Hart, Paul Marterud, Bill Howie, and Dick Wiley; (back row) Coach, Vince Dowd, Brad Winch, Sam Azzinaro, Dick Wright, Bill Kroman, Leo Schlueter, Phil Huewe, Art Whipple and Tom Schmeider.

Festina – Northeast Iowa League Champion

E. Schneberger, Russell Jr. Schneberger R. Schneberger Schupanitz A. Huinker L. Huinker Mrs. F. Nienhaus, Leo Lenius, R. Schneberger Norb Einck, Romauld Elsberud B. Huinker

Winnah!

Ralph Teeling, left, and Manager Bob Bradley, right, carry Art Huinker off the field after the young southpaw retired the last Cascade batter in the Merchants' semi-final victory Wednesday night. Huinker went the full 12 innings against three Cascade hurlers. (Telegraph-Herald Photo)

cade Caper

Pat Clarke, Cascade third baseman, dances on one foot as he reaches for a throw from the outfield that arrived too late to retire the sliding Art Huinker, Dubuque Merchant pitcher. The action took place in Wednesday night's semi-final contest, won by the Merchants, 5-4, in 12 innings. (Telegraph-Herald Photo)

Lefty Art Huinker, Calmar, Ia., sophomore, is one of the top pitching prospects on the Duhawk diamond squad. Huinker took three victories without a loss as a freshman and has three wins to date for the current season.

Missed the .400 Goal, Eh?

Bob Kaliban (right) congratulates Bill Howie (center) while looking over the latter's batting average for the season, as the third senior on the Loras nine this year, Tom Curoe, looks on. Howie is near the top again this season with a .383 average. He has been top man or runner-up in the average department since first donning a Purple and Gold uniform four years ago.

Duhawk Baseball Squad

Shown above are the members of the Loras College baseball squad which completed its 1955 baseball season Saturday. Seated, left to right: Dick Wiley, third base; Bill Howie, shortstop; Dick Schiltz, first base; Sam Azzinaro, center field; Bob Kaliban, catcher; John Saeman, pitcher; Albert Kehm, first base; Bob Wolfe, third base; Joe Ottavi, second base; Art Huinker, pitcher; and Tom Curoe, right field. Standing, left to right: Vince Dowd, coach; Romie Gales left field; Art Whipple, catcher; Dick Wright, left field; Dick Winter, pitcher; Bill Hyland, pitcher; Don Kerz, catcher; Bill Leonard, left field; Jim Swann, pitcher; Bill Kezman, pitcher; and Francis Noonan, assistant coach.

1954 FOOTBALL CHAMPS

The Wildcats won the fall intramural touch football championship. Members of the squad are, kneeling (left to right) Dick Wiley, Harold Mogenson, Art Huinker and Dwight Green. Standing are Dick Wright, Bill Kezman, Dick Schultz, Paul Lendman and Dave Schultz.

NICE FORM

Romie Gales, hard-hitting outfielder for the Duhawk nine takes his turn at bat, while Bill Leonard fills in as catcher.

Above: Anna Mae Thuente and Art Huinker married, Tuesday, August 3, 1955 at Our Lady of Seven Dolors Church, Festina, Iowa.

Dyersville's high-flying Whitehawks captured the championship of the Cascade baseball tournament Monday night as Art Huinker shut out Cascade 5 to 0. For Huinker (first row, far right), it was his second no-hitter of the tourney. First row L to r: Lefty Mayer, Ray Willenborg, Roy Kregel, Ray Oltendorp, Tom Jack. Paul Kregel and Huinker. In back are Jim Nadermann, Don Luhman, Bob Kregel, Dick Mather, Dick Wright, Pete Willenborg and Earl Lampe. Not pictured is Rod Walling. (Telegraph-Herald Photo).

* * * ▼ ▼ ▼ * * *
Huinker Scores

—Photo by The Pioneer-Advertiser

Huinker Got MVP

Art Huinker, right, received the "Most Valuable Player" trophy from Vern Weber, tournament chairman, after the final game Monday night of the Cascade American Legion tourney. Huinker threw a no-hit, no-run game against the Cascade Reds in the finals as Dyersville won, 5-0. Huinker had a no-hitter against Petersburg in Dyersville's opening tourney game and was only one out away from another perfect game against Worthington when Mert Gassman got the only hit off him in the 3 games he pitched. The diminutive lefthander's tournament record shows 23 innings pitched, 1 hit, no runs, 8 bases on balls and 47 strikeouts.

Art Huinker (left) tears down the baseline to score the only run Dyersville needed to win its championship game with Petersburg Tuesday night in the Dyersville tournament finals. Huinker, the tourney's most valuable player, hurled a 5-0 shutout. Jim Hoerner is the Petersburg catcher. (Telegraph-Herald Photo)

1956 Courier Baseball Tournament of Champions

Cheer as Denver Rally Halted

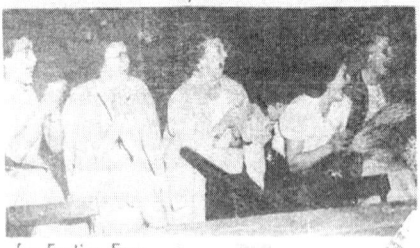

for Festina Fans

Above top: For 1956 Courier Baseball tournament of Champions; Ann's father, Hugo Thuente is standing up and cheering for the Festina team. In the same row to the left is Ann's mother, Thecla. Bottom: Third from left is Darlene Luzum, wife of third baseman Leo Luzum; second from left is Aileen Huinker, wife of Ken Huinker.

Festina Returns to Courier Tourney as Northeast Iowa Loop Champ

FRONT ROW—Romauld Eichenol, Florian Nienhaus, Ken Huinker, Bob Huinker, Norb Einck, Jerry Schneberger. BACK ROW—Art Huinker, Bob Schneberger, Linus Huinker, Leo Luzum, Carl Schupenitz, Don Russett, Jim Schneberger.

Trophy Winners in Courier Tournament of Champions

Each of the first three place teams and each member of the championship Festina team was trophies in the 1956 Waterloo Courier Baseball Tournament of Champions. Left to right are front row: Petersburg manager Donald Twlehart Bob Schneberger, Romauld Eichenol, Leo Luzum, Festina manager Florian Nienhaus, Linus Huinker, Jerry Schneberger, Art Huinker, Jim Schneberger, Carl Schupenitz, Norb Einck, Ken Huinker, Bob Huinker, Bill Luzum.

Mr. and Mrs. Art Huinker and nine month old Terry. Art had a perfect record of 18 straight wins on the mound for the Loras baseball team at the time the book went to press.

Coach Vince Dowd congratulates Art Huinker on compiling a perfect record of 19 wins, no loses, in his four years on Loras pitching staff.

Huinker To Pitch

1957

Cards Meet Phils Tonight

Headline: Could be announcement for Huinker to pitch for St. Louis Cardinals against the Philadelphia Phils.

rty years later, roomates and baseball teammates b Wolfe (on right) and myself

Members of the 1957 baseball team are front row (l-r): John Jowcrski, Bob Roth, Bob Wolf, Art Huinker, Rocky Schultz, Joe Ottavi, Gene Potts, Dick Breitbach, Don Jennings, Tom Hirtz, Duke Coughlin. Standing: Coach Vince Dowd, Pat Kapsch, Frank Delaney, Dick Mescher, Bob Willhite, Bill Hyland, Dick Winter, Terry Brennan, Dick Kressin, Dick Wright, Bill Leonard, Bruno Kowolkowski.

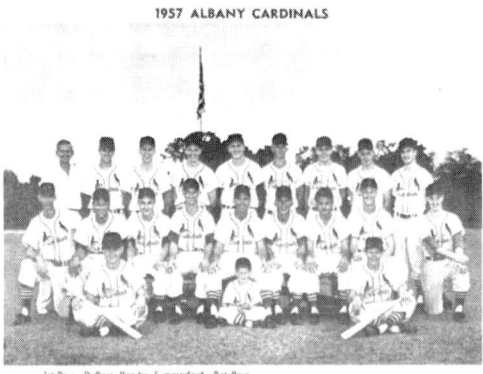

1957 ALBANY CARDINALS

1st Row—DuBose, Bender, Summerford—Bat Boys.
2nd Row—Hickman, Smith, Heinzer, Leslie, Mgr., Ingram, Eoyer, Morris, Wood
3rd Row—Bender, Gen. Mgr.; Wadka, McIntyre, Shultis, Cox, Brown, DeGroof, Kobbes, Passaro

Huinker's a Teacher Now

Art Huinker, the popular former Loras College baseball pitcher, leaves Ossian DeSales Central Catholic High School after completing his first week as a teacher. Huinker teaches history and coaches girls and boys basketball as well as ball. (Telegraph-Herald Photo)

Falcon Baseball Squad, Runner-up State Tournament, Fall 1960. (l. to rt.): James Leibold, Garvin Nienhaus, Richard Hanely, Robert Heying, Rudy Tekippe, Robert Pankow, Terry Kelly, Daniel Frommelt, Ronald Leibold. (TOP ROW): Father Paul L. Weis, Athletic Director; Lee Schissel, Dale Nienhaus, James Moellers, David Thuente, Robert Carolan, Larry Keefe, Jerome Linderbaum, and Mr. Arthur T. Huinker, Coach.

TOASTS OF THE TOWN—Ossian DeSales moved into the finals of Iowa fall high school baseball tournament by beating Grand Mound, 13-9, Hazleton Friday—and the boys hang a banner in front of the town's water tower after returning Saturday. The team will meet St. John's of Bancr Monday for the championship.

To the left:
Sporting News
write -up
August 28, 1957

Georgia-Florida League

STANDING ON THURSDAY A. M., AUGUST 22

	W.	L.	Pct.		W.	L.	Pct.
Albany	88	17	.691	Thomasville	25	28	.472
Waycross	29	27	.518	Fitzgerald	23	33	.411
Valdosta	28	27	.509	Brunswick	22	33	.400

LEFTY LEAVES WITH VICTORY

SOUTHPAW ART HUINKER, who came off the campus of Loras College at Dubuque, Ia., to baffle the batters in the loop, left the Albany Cardinals, August 21, after hurling a four-hitter to beat Valdosta, 9 to 1, for his sixth victory against one loss. In his winning performances, Huinker pitched three shutouts and three other games in which he held the opposition to one run each. He departed early to take over a high school coaching job. . . . Fitzgerald scored ten runs in the fourth inning to beat Thomasville in a slugfest, 14 to 11, August 16. Seven of the runs were scored off Siebert Scott,

Above: players on the picture are, at top, freshman Jerry Linderbaum across the bottom, junior Jim Leib freshman Ron Leibold and junior Da Frommelt.

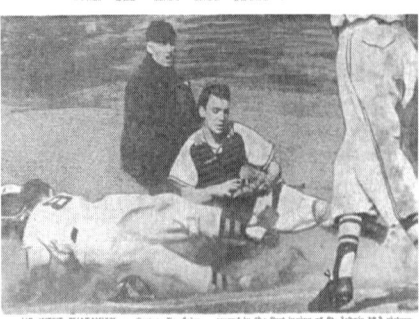

HE WENT THATAWAY — Ossian De Sales catcher Ron Leibold is just a little late with the tag as a Bancroft St. John's rooster slides across home plate with the fourth of five runs his team scored in the first inning of St. John's 12-3 victory Monday in the championship game of the Iowa fall high school baseball tournament at Corwith. (Telegraph-Herald Photos)

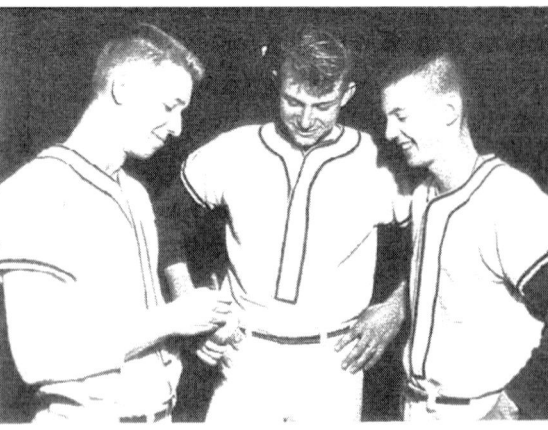

Seniors, Robert Pankow, Rudy Tekippe, and Terry Kelly, autograph the state victory ball.

ART HUINKER
—Pinpoint Control

BOB TRAVERS
Yankee Opportunist

HISTORY REPEATS—Dave Iverson accepts the semi-pro championship trophy from Oscar Torvilt, right, Sunday night after Soldiers Grove defeated Tomah 8-7 in 10 innings. Iverson managed Grove to titles in 1956 and this year.—Tribune Photo.

TOP TOURNEY STARS

Peth, Tomah, batting champion; Mike Sund, Tomah, best pitcher; Dick derson, Melrose, best pro prospect and Art Huenker, Soldiers Grove, valuable player, from left to right, received awards Sunday night follng the championship game played before 800 12th District tourney fans angor. Grove won 8-7 in 10 innings.—Tribune Photo.

Gets Deserved 'Support' After Victory

It's finally time to relax and Art Hinker, a pair of bats supporting his tired left arm, takes full advantage of his well-earned rest period Sunday at the Wisconsin State Baseball Tournament. Hinker toiled through 15 hot innings to give his Soldiers Grove entry a 4-1 win over Borgwardt Poultry in the tourney's opening game. (Story on Page 3.)

Sentinel Photo by Kevin Anhaeuser

Wisconsin State Championship Baseball Tournament 1961 Milwaukee County Stadium

To the left: Soldiers Grove Baseball Team First row: Ray Fleming, Richard Halverson, Roger Phiel, Bill Hoffland, Eli Crogan, Roger Iverson and Dennis Boardman. Second row: Duwayne Fortney, Ronnie Helgerson, Dave Iverson, Mgr. Robert Thompson, James Wiley, Mark Dilley, Gary Campbell and Art Huinker.

QUEEN AND AWARD WINNERS—Miss Wisconsin, Joan Engh of La Crosse, left, presented awards Sunday night at Bangor following the championship game to Ron Helgerson, second from left, Soldiers Grove, batting champion; Art Huinker, Soldiers Grove, best pitcher; Bob Smith, Black River Falls, best pro prospect and Mark Dilley, Soldiers Grove, most valuable player.—Tribune

Couple of Valuable Guys!

Honored following the final games of the 1961 tournament were these two ball players. At the right is Art Huinker, Dyersville's pitcher-outfielder, who was named the tournament's "Most Valuable Player". Huinker pitched the Whitehawks to the tournament crown with his victory Tuesday night. He won three games for the Hawks during the meet, and played a big role with his bat during the 1961 tourney. Huinker was Dyersville's leading hitter. At left is Jim Hosch, Cascade who was named "Outstanding Manager" of the tournament. Hosch guided the Cascade Reds to the finals of the meet but team lost in the finals in a "thriller" Tuesday night. The popular Cascade player-manager wields a big bat too. He connected for a home runs in the finals and was one of the Red's best hitters of the eight day tournament.

Another Title, Another Trophy

These victorious Whitehawks, only four of the squad of 19, show off the big trophy with 1st place honors in the Great Plains Regional Amateur Baseball Congress tournament held here last week end. The Whitehawks, repeat winners in the regional AABC, clobbered Fargo, N. D. 10-3 in the final game Monday night. Big guns in the tournament were Jim McAndrew and Art Huinker, kneeling and Dale Digmann and Tom Jenk, standing. McAndrew and Huinker were hurling stars while Digmann and team manager Tom Jenk were big hitters in the tournament.

Whitehawks Awarded Runner-Up Trophy At AABC

To the right: 1963 Whitehawk team at Battle Creek, Michigan. Left to right, back row: Jim McAndrew, Kirk Rentschler, Dick Wright, Tom Fessler, Leroy Willenbring, Tom Jenk, Larry Poock, Rollie Sampson, Ben Kern; Middle row: Dick Wold, Don Huber, Dale Digmann, Jim Wegmann, Bob Goldsmith; Front row: Art Huinker, Jim Digmann, Bob Decker, Roy Krapft, George Benn

HE FINISHING TOUCH—Tom Jenk of Dyersville, puts on the finishing touch of an eight-run inning rally that carried his club to a 9-4 triumph over Louisville, Ky. yesterday in a Stan Musial Series game in Bailey Park Stadium. Jenk hit a two-run homer after Bill Goldsmith hit a run shot. Jenk is greeted by teammates.

—Enquirer and News Pho

'Atta Boy, Jim!

Dyersville third baseman, Jim Digman, gets a big pat-on-the-back from fellow teammates as he comes off the field Monday night after slamming a hard hit ball into deep left-center driving in Art Huinker and giving the Hawks a 2-1 victory over Balltown in the semi-finals of the Dyersville Tournament. The tally ended a twelve inning game that was tied at 2-3 for five innings.

Receive Player Awards

Dale Digman, left, and Art Huinker congratulate each other after receiving player trophies Tuesday night at the close of the 18th Annual Dyersville Baseball Tournament. Digman received the sportsmanship award for a fine performance behind the plate and Art Huinker was named the tournament's most valuable player. Both are Dyersville players.

Dyersville won the tournament edging Rickardsville 4-3. Balltown blanked Guttenberg 5-0 in the consolation game.

TOM JENK
... homer starts Dyersville

Pictured below, standing in the rear are: Kip Knippel, Dan Meyer, Larry Bildstein, Tom Jenk, Jan Arthur, Chris Brown, Rollie Sampson, and Charlie Lammers. In the front are: Art Huinker, Bob Goldsmith, Dale Digmann, batboy Terry Huinker, Jim Digmann and Dan Goerdt.

Most Valuable Pitcher

Art Huinker
Dyersville

**Above: Most Valuable Pitcher
1967 Holy Cross Tournament**

1965 Tournament Champions

The Dyersville Whitehawks, 1965 champions of the Dyersville Baseball Tournament, had plenty to smile about Tuesday night after edging Rickardsville 4-3 in the final game.

In the front row from left to right are: Art Huinker, Dale Digman, Tom Jenk (manager), Bob Goldsmith, Jim Gebhart, Jim Digman, Dave Reittinger, Sal Willenbring and Jim Wegman.

In the back row from left are: Rod Tangman, Kirk Rentschler, Dan Meyer, Tom Lanham, Sid Pouquette, Ron Singsank, Steve Tierschel, Rollie Sampson, Cliff Knippel, Steve Clemen and Gary Evers.

Wins MVP many times...

Art Huinker was the most valuable player twice at the Dyersville Baseball Tournament, and at least once at the Worthington meet.

This picture was taken in 1968 and shows Art receiving the MVP award at the Worthington Tournament from Chuck Engler.

Tournament Top Rate Material

Three top ranked ball players of the Dyersville Tournament are pictured above with their trophies following the championship game Wednesday evening, August 14th.

Rollie Sampson (left) was voted the most outstanding mana-

ger of the tournament and Art Huinker (right) was given the individual sportsmanship award. Both of these awards were decided by the umpires.

Bob Goldsmith in the center was the Most Valuable Player of the Tournament. Bob hit a blaz-

ing .545 in four games, scoring a total of five runs, batting in two home runs, a triple and three singles.

All three are members of champion Dyersville Whites who defeated Epworth for the Tournament Title.

Pictured above from left to right: Jennifer, Tim, Ted (born 1973) Ann, Art, Terry, Dan (born 1968), Peggy and Tammy. This picture is one from 1980, showing our completed family.

State champions reminisce

Photos by Bill Faeger

The 1968 Beckman baseball team held a reunion last weekend to celebrate its 40th anniversary of winning the Iowa State Baseball Championship in Ames. Prior to a dance and social at Commercial Club Park Pavilion on July 19, team members posed in the same position they were in in a photo taken during the state tournament. Team members are: front, Terry Huinker (ball boy); second row from left, Coach Art Huinker, John Goerdt, Ron Kramer, Keith Krapfl, Wayne Oberbroeckling and Dave Domeyer; back row, Gene Knipper, Jim Overman, Dan Goerdt, Tom Burlage, Rick Knipper, Bob Klostermann, Lee Kruse and Lloyd Koelker. In the original photo, Jerry Bildstein, who was unable to attend the celebration, was standing between Jim Overman and Dan Goerdt. **See additional photos online at www.dyersvillecommercial.com.**

ALL IS WELL—Paton-Churdan scored in the second inning as Dick Carstens slid into home plate for a run after Dyersville Beckman catcher Rick Knipper dropped the ball when Carstens appeared to be a dead duck in the top two photos. But all ended well as Beckman scored a 5-3 victory Friday night to enter Tuesday's championship game in the Iowa High School baseball tournament. (Telegraph-Herald Photos)

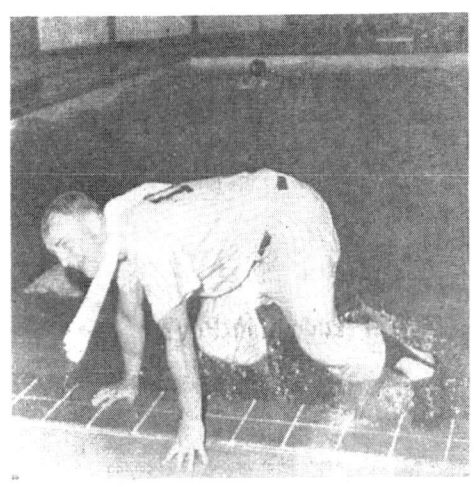

Victory Shower For Coach Huinker

Jubilant Blazers Are No. 1 Baseball Team in Iowa

Jubilant, rejoicing Beckman High School Blazers give vent on being the Number 1 High School Baseball Team in the state of Iowa after downing a 5-4 in the finals at Ames Tuesday night.

Norway, three times spring champs and once summer victors saw the Blazers take the lead away from them twice through the seven inning game and found themselves on the short end of a 5-4 final score.

For Beckman, it is the first trophy for their new trophy case at the two year old school. It is one of the very few times a school located in Dubuque county has ever won a state title in any sport.

The Blazers are pictured gathered around their new title trophy following their victory over Norway Tuesday evening, August 6th at Ames.

What if we had lost the game?

Go Get 'Em

LLOYD KOELKER
Won Both State Games

Lloyd Koelker, right, shown en route to his 1968 combined s p r i n g-summer record of 14-1. The victory was Beckman's 18th without a loss in the summer program. (Telegraph-Herald Photos)

Beckman High School
Dyersville, Iowa 52040

Friday, July 5, 1968

Dear Parents,

An opportunity has arisen for me to communicate with you and thank
you for the tremendous cooperation you have shown toward the baseball
team of the Beckman Blazers and to thank you for the fine young man you
have given me the opportunity to work with. The baseball year has been
the most enjoyable I have experienced, not so much because of the success
but because of the attitude of the young men playing.

The main reason for writing is to define our schedule for the
next few weeks and the purpose behind them. Starting Monday, July 8
and continuing through the tournament sponsored by the high school
athletic association, there will be practice at 7:00 in the evening,
unless the high school has a game. The schedule will be as follows,
rain or shine:

    Monday, July 8 -- practice - 7:00
    Tuesday, July 9 -- game: Monticello - home - 6:30
    Wednesday, July 10 -- practice - 7:00
    Thursday, July 11 -- practice - 7:00
    Friday, July 12 -- game: Manchester - home - 6:30
    Monday, July 15 -- practice - 7:00
    Tuesday, July 16 -- practice - 7:00
    Wednesday, July 17 -- tournament game - 8:00 at Dyersville
    Thursday, July 18 -- tournament game - 8:00 at Dyersville
    (one practice that week-end)
    Monday, July 22 -- tournament game - 7:30 at Elkader

        etc. etc. etc. we hope

Our objective is very easily defined. We have a good ball club, a
team that has the potential of advancing down through the tournament. In
order for your son to have the opportunity to possibly realize a highlight
of his life, we must be at the peak of our performance, both individually
and as a team. I don't want to deprive them of this opportunity. I
want them to be at the peak of their ability through practice together
as a team, to feel and know each other again that I feel comes when a
team practices together.

The last few weeks this summer we have not performed as sharply as
we have. We want to and we have to. There is something worthwhile ahead
for your young men but anything worthwhile requires work and sacrifice.
We thank you again for your constant support and hope that you will be
able to witness your son in action during the tournaments. But it all
boils down to winning the first one first.

Enclosed you will find a copy of the tourney pairings. Again thanks.

Sincerely yours,

Arthur T. Huinker

Art Huinker
Baseball Coach

Welcome Home Champs From Thousands Wednesday

e Blazers received a real
mpion style welcoming party
hey returned with the state
ner baseball title for 1968.
e Beckman bus was met in
ville, Iowa, by screaming
sirens, ringing church bells,
reds of horn blowing autos
thousands of area fans Wed-

nesday afternoon at approximately 2:15 p.m.
A caravan of hundreds of
autos escorted the Beckman bus
through Earlville, over to Petersburg, on to New Vienna, to
Worthington and back home to
Beckman High School via Dyersville's first avenue.

This photo was taken as the
caravan slowly moved out of
Earlville toward Petersburg.
The affair ended with coach Art
Huinker presenting each mem-
ber of the team with a gold
medal from the Iowa Athletic
Association marking them No. 1
for 1968 Summer Baseball in
Iowa.

Trophy For Beckman . . . No. 1

Picture above is Senior third baseman Dan
Goerdt holding the big trophy. Irvin Willenbring,
a knowlegdeable baseball fan from Petersburg,
is in the background.

Color TV To Huinkers At Ertl Dinner

The 1968 Beckman High
School championship baseball
squad and members of the cheerleaders paid final tribute to the
coach Mr. Art Huinker Tuesday
night by presenting him and his
wife with a color TV set. The
television donated by the team
and cheerleaders was given to
Huinker before a dinner at the
Ertl Round-Up Room donated to

the champs by Ertl Lanes.
In the top photo, coach Huin-
ker admires his gift with Fred
Ertl of Ertl Lanes. His ball team
from the left includes Ron Kra-
mer, Keith Klostermann, Rick
Knipper, John Goerdt, Wayne
Oberbroeckling, Jim Overman,
Lee Kruse, Jerry Bildstein,
Lloyd Koelker, Gene Knipper,
Tom Burlage, Bob Klostermann,
Keith Krapfl, Dan Goerdt and

Dave Domayer.
In the bottom photo, Mr. and
Mrs. Huinker are joined by the
cheerleaders around the television. From the rear on the left
are Sally Burger, Linda Westhoff, Carla Goerdt, Mary Ellen
English and Debbie Kramer. On
the right from the back are
Phyllis Klostermann, Pat Goerdt,
Shirley Steffen, Kathy Guden-
kauf and Joyce Kuhl.

A LOSING SEASON

The longing for a professional baseball career still occupied my mind as the first year of teaching and coaching at De Sales Central High School drew to a close. The decision, agonized over for the past few months, still stood firm. We made plans for the summer. Taking the responsibility of running the summer youth program in Ossian where we now lived would provide additional income plus an opportunity of coaching the little leaguers, solidifying the future of baseball in the community of Ossian. As it turned out, the program was allowed to include youngsters from the Festina area as well because they had no organized summer activities for their youth.

Where would baseball be played in the summer of 1958? That probably topped the list of concerns uppermost in my mind. Festina would certainly be a logical one, even though some of their veteran ball players began to withdraw from the full slate of games always played by that team.

Then one evening before the school year finished, a call came from Mason City of the Southern Minnesota League again. They were hoping to add me to their pitching roster. Even after informing them that if the offer was accepted, we would continue to live in Ossian, about 75 miles from Mason City. A job similar to the year before was not needed, but a reimbursement that would include coverage of mileage expenses plus. This meant that there would be income over and above the expenditures incurred.

With the professional career still pushing me, the Mason City opportunity sounded more desirable. The level of competition with the Southern Minny might just keep the door open. After considerable negotiating, no longer worrying about the amateur status necessary for college baseball, a commitment was made by both sides. More challenging baseball would be played game after game.

The lack of sufficient attendance at the baseball games the previous year caused four teams to withdraw from the league for the summer, bringing it down to a four-team league consisting of Fairmont, Albert Lea, Austin and Mason City. Playing a 36 game schedule meant we would play each team twelve times. Emil Scheid, who originally brought the Mason City Braves into the league the year before, withdrew that support and continued his managing of the Austin Packer team. In doing this, he took five players from the Mason City team of the year before with him. They were outfielders Brown and Gilmore, infielder Folkes, catcher Notermann and pitcher Lawler.

The Mason City Braves management was caught in a difficult position. First of all, they were financially in arrears from the previous year. In addition, they were caught short of quality player personnel with the realization they were losing so many players from the previous year's team that had not been planned on. Possible lack of experience in finding the ability of player needed and with their money problems, resulted in a challenging year, to say the least. Throughout the season, we also saw many players come and go, creating an unstable environment .

The Mason City Braves lost four games in a row before finally beating the Austin Packers 4 to 1 in a game played at Austin. We did not have a set line-up, either offensively or defensively, as the season opened. Weaknesses were not difficult to assess.

AUSTIN PACKERS DEFEAT MASON CITY BRAVES
By Jim Vanheel, Globe-Gazette Sports Editor
The Mason City Braves have had a game each with other members of the Southern Minnesota Baseball League. All have been defeats for the Braves. Before a ladies' night crowd here Sunday night, the Austin Packers beat Mason City 5-1 behind the 5-hit pitching of Dick Atkinson.

Atkinson, who started with Estherville in the Iowa State League and then worked up to class AAA in organized ball, had a shutout and had allowed only one hit through the first seven innings of play. The only blow in that span for the Braves was a ground single past second base by Paul Bruns in the fourth frame.

With a 5-0 lead, Atkinson eased up in the eighth and singles by Bill Welch, Dale Cramer and Bud Berger produced the lone run for Mason City. Atkinson walked only one batter and fanned seven in the game.

Art Huinker, the chunky lefty, pitched creditable ball for the losers. Only two of the runs scored against him were earned as the Braves made six errors, three by Berger in centerfield and two by George Dropo at third base.

The bulk of the Austin scoring was in the second frame when the Packers got four runs. With one down, Berger dropped an easy pop fly off the bat of Bob Mathias. Then Dick Notermann, who caught for Mason City last year, slammed a homer over the left field canvas at the 360-foot mark.

Carl Bellotti drew a walk, Fred Folkes hit a grounder and Dale Cramer dropped the throw on a force play at second. Then Dick Cordell, one of the league's top sluggers knocked a double to the rightfield canvas to score Bellotti and Folkes.

Huinker, who fanned six batters and walked only two, blanked the Packers from then on until the seventh inning. He walked Folkes and Cordell banged a double to leftfield for the last Austin marker.

We couldn't feel very good about our third straight loss. In reading the write-up, you will notice that two free passes were issued, each one in the midst of a scoring rally by Austin. They so often come back to haunt you before the inning is over. As a team, we had a work to do in order to be competitive in the Southern Minny.

The name Dropo might be recognizable by old-time baseball fans. George's brother, Walt, played for thirteen seasons in the majors, most of them with the Boston Red Sox and Chicago White Sox. George, our Mason City teammate, could hit the ball but struggled defensively. He played first base, third base and the outfield that summer.

Another teammate that I really enjoyed was Ken Bawek, just back from several seasons in the pro ranks as a catcher. Defensively, he was one of the smartest catchers I ever knew. He understood the ins and outs of attacking hitters and gave a pitcher confidence on what pitches to throw and when. Ken, originally from Stacyville, Iowa, a small town just northeast of Mason City, convinced me that toward the end of baseball games, the fast ball was the best pitch for me because hitters do become somewhat weary by that time. Also, he recognized, by that time, which of my fast balls had the most movement and would therefore be the one to rely on. When we lost him to injury later on in the season, it was a huge loss for the team, and especially for the pitchers.

Now for our first win.

> ### BRAVES GET THEIR FIRST WIN, 8-5 OVER FAIRMONT
> *Maybe the troubles for the Mason City Braves are finished. They've been plagued with errors and lack of hitting but that was changed Saturday night in a Southern Minnesota League game before a slim crowd at Roosevelt Field.*
>
> *Each club had a dozen hits but the Braves had a little more in the extra base department with a pair of doubles and two triples. Bud Berger and Jack Jones had the triples while Paul Bruns and George Dropo got doubles. All of the Mason City hits were stacked into the first five innings.*
>
> *Southpaw Harry Pritts was charged with the loss. He pitched the first three frames and gave up six hits and four runs. Al Thune, another southpaw, came on and was rapped for six hits and four runs in the fourth and fifth innings. After he walked the first two batters to face him in the sixth, shortstop Don Dahlke came in and finished off the game. He held the Braves hitless.*
>
> *Getting three hits apiece in the game were Dropo and Fairmont's Herb Banton.*
>
> *Lefty Art Huinker was the winner for Mason City but he was twice helped out by the hitless relief pitching of Bill Freese.*

192

Huinker, riding an 8-3 lead into the seventh inning, got
in trouble with two walks and three singles producing two
Martin runs and loading the sacks. Roger Lange popped out.
Then Bruns called in Freese from the bullpen with
Huinker going to leftfield. Freese fanned Tom Idstrom and
Huinker came back to pitch with Freese going to leftfield.
Catcher Ken Bawek snagged a foul ball off the back wall off
Tom Palmer's bat to retire the side.

Huinker, who fanned six in the game retired the
Martins in order in the eighth. He dished up a single to Milt
Nielsen to open the ninth frame. Again Freese came back to
pitch and he retired the side to preserve the margin.

Finally, I garnered two hits and a RBI to help the offensive attack.

The name, Don Dahlke, brings back memories . A graduate of Iowa
State Teachers College in Cedar Falls (now the University of Northern Iowa), Don
played professional baseball for a considerable number of years. But he gave it up
in 1958. The previous year, while playing AAA ball in the Pacific Coast League,
he had a batting average over .400 but never got called up, even to go to spring
training with his major league club. He decided to call it quits and became an
administrator in the Fairmont school system. He could hit, believe me, and we
would face his team ten more times

Inclement weather caused five postponements early in the season for the
Braves. In order to catch up with the regular schedule, we would play four to five
games a week, sometimes on back-to-back nights.

After two more losses, we picked up our second win.

MASON CITY BEATS AUSTIN 4-1 BEHIND ART
HUINKER
The Mason City Braves had a slow start last season
and then came along to be one of the top teams in the Southern
Minnesota League. They're hoping for a repeat performance
this year.

Beaten in six of their first seven loop games, the Braves
came through with a much needed win at Austin by downing the
Austin Packers 4-1 behind the fine pitching of Lefty Art Huinker.

The chunky southpaw was reached for eight hits but
scattered them well. Only one was an extra base blow. He
didn't walk a batter in the game and fanned five. He owns both
of the Braves' league victories.

He was tangling with Dick Atkinson who beat him 5-1
in an early season game. Atkinson took the loss, being bumped

193

for nine hits in the seven innings he worked. Jim Lawler pitched the last two frames and gave up one more blow.

The ten hits looked good from the Mason City side because the Braves had been blanked in their previous two starts and totaled only five hits in the two games. George Dropo, the leading hitter for Mason City, fattened his average with two singles and a double. Jack Jones had a single and double, and knocked in two runs and Ken Bawek tripled.

The most hits off Huinker came in the third. Singles by Ray Rosenbaum, Atkinson and Fred Folkes produced the marker.

After another loss, our seventh with only two wins, we make the long road trip to Fairmont for our next game.

BRAVES BEAT FAIRMONT 6-4 FOR THIRD VICTORY

The Mason City Braves got their usual good pitching here Tuesday night and in addition put on an offensive display to down Fairmont 6-4.

The triumph was the third of the season for Mason City, the second over Fairmont, and lifted the club's Southern Minnesota League mark to 3-7.

Lefty Art Huinker pitched the distance for the Braves to gain the win. Huinker has hurled all the Mason City club's loop wins this season and been beaten just once. He gave Fairmont nine hits Tuesday night, including a pair of doubles and triples, but struck out 11 batters.

Mason City banged out 10 hits off a pair of Fairmont hurlers, Harry Pritts and Loyal Bloxam. The big blows were a triple and a home run by centerfielder George Dropo. The round-tripper was a solo drive in the sixth inning over the right field fence.

The Martins opened the scoring with a run in the first inning. The Braves tied the count in the third on singles by Huinker, Ken Bawek and Jack Jones. After the Braves tallied again in the sixth on Dropo's blast, Fairmont took the lead with three runs in the bottom of the frame.

Mason City then broke the game wide open in the eighth inning with four runs. Hits by Bud Berger, Jones and Manager Paul Bruns plus a pair of Fairmont errors and reliever Bloxam's wild pitch triggered the scoring.

We again committed three errors but only one figured in any scoring. One constant in our lineup this season was our leftfielder Jack Fitzgerald. Jack was from the small town of Rockwell, just a few miles

southeast of Mason City. Ann and I stayed with the Fitzgerald family a
few nights when we had back to back games on weekends. Regretfully,
we have not had contact with them since that summer some fifty years
ago.

Another road game, this time straight north of Mason City, at Albert Lea,
Minnesota, against a team also with the nickname of Packers. We will talk often
over the next three years about the Albert Lea team. They had a core of players
who were strong hitters, but also good people who enjoyed playing the game of
baseball.

> *MASON CITY CLIPS ALBERT LEA 8-2*
> *The Mason City Braves would be in hot water this*
> *season without the services of southpaw Art Huinker.*
> *Huinker won his fourth game of the season here*
> *Sunday night as the Braves downed the Packers 8-2 before 550*
> *fans. The little southpaw's four wins account for all of Mason*
> *City's triumphs in Southern Minnesota League play this season.*
> *The win also marked the Braves' first success against*
> *Albert Lea. The Packers had won three previous tilts at*
> *Roosevelt Field.*
> *Huinker turned in an excellent performance against the*
> *hard-hitting Packers. He gave up just six hits, two of which*
> *were home runs that accounted for both Albert Lea runs, while*
> *striking out eight and walking only two. Huinker was also*
> *backed up by an errorless Mason City performance in the field.*
> *The Braves rapped out eight safeties off loser Hal*
> *Snyder, one of the top hurlers in the loop with a 5-2 record*
> *going into the game. Jack Jones, subbing for injured Ken*
> *Bawek behind the plate, paced the attack with a double and*
> *single and three runs batted in. George Dropo added a three-*
> *base blow for Mason City while Huinker helped his own cause*
> *with a pair of singles.*
> *Mason City jumped off to an early lead with two runs*
> *in the first inning and three more in the third. A walk, an Albert*
> *Lea error and Jones' double triggered the first inning outburst.*
> *Hits by Huinker, Bud Berger and Jones then sparked the 3-run*
> *second.*
> *Albert Lea tallied once in the third frame on Snyder's*
> *four-base blow and again in the fifth on Weathers' solo blast.*
> *Mason City came up with two more runs in the fourth inning on*
> *consecutive hits by Dale Cramer, Bob Gaffney, Huinker and*
> *Manager Paul Bruns.*

So much for a good game or two. Back to the other type and one of
those nights when you could have nightmares. Those nightmares never really

195

happened for me, thank heaven, but after this next game, they maybe should have. We all want to win every time out, but that creates an "impossible dream."

BRAVES ARE WHIPPED BY AUSTIN, 11-4

The umpires for Tuesday night's Southern Minnesota League baseball game at Roosevelt showed up 15 minutes late. The Mason City Braves didn't tighten up their defense nor did they start to hit until two hours later. That added up to an 11-4 victory for the Austin Packers, the fourth time Austin has defeated the Braves in five games this season.

The Braves matched Austin in extra base blows and trailed in hits by only two, 13-11. But that doesn't tell much of the story because Mason City had one of its bad nights afield with seven errors and the Braves were left with 11 baserunners stranded.

The winners had the game in the bag at the halfway point, leading 10-0 after they had their cuts at the plate in the top of the fifth.

Art Huinker was the starting Mason City hurler. He took a sound whacking in the 1 2/3 innings he pitched. Roy Gilmore got a 2-run homer off him in the first inning and Austin chased home four more runs in the second frame on five hits, a pair of errors and a sacrifice fly before Bill Freese came on to retire the side.

Freese pitched a fine game through the seventh frame. Austin got to him for four more runs but they were unearned as the Braves continued to have fielding problems.

The loss left the Mason City Braves with a record of 5 wins and 13 losses, well entrenched in the cellar, 3½ games behind third place Austin. Fairmont held the league lead with 14 wins and 8 losses and Albert Lea 1½ games behind.

The Southern Minnesota League All-Star game was scheduled to be played at the Martins' park in Fairmont on July 17. Chosen to represent Mason City were George Dropo, Ken Bawek, Manager Paul Bruns and myself. Bawek would not be able to play because he is out for the season due to injury. He is a player dearly missed, partly for his hitting, but more so for the defensive skills that he brings to his position behind the plate. By the way, the all-star game was cancelled because of rain.

MASON CITY NIPS FAIRMONT 3-2

Third-sacker Dale Cramer's Texas-league hit into leftfield tallied George Dropo from second base in the bottom of the 10th inning to give Mason City a 3-2 win over the Fairmont Martins. The victory at Roosevelt Field was Mason City's third

196

win in Southern Minnesota League play over the leading Martins.

    A crowd of 461 nervous fans witnessed an excellent hurling duel between the Martins' Loyal Bloxam and the Braves' Art Huinker, with Huinker emerging the winner in a seven-hit, 14-strikeout affair.

    Coach Paul Bruns' team unleashed a 10-hit barrage during the night but had to wait until the final three frames to score. Fairmont scored in the initial frame on Ken Staples' two-bagger and added another tally in the sixth inning on a hit, an error and a passed ball.

    After the sparse crowd had gone through the seventh-inning stretch, centerfielder George Dropo send a booming triple to left centerfield and came home on Bob Hahn's single. Hahn then evened the score via Bill Welch's single and Bloxam's wild throw to first base.

    Crafty Huinker set the Martins down in the final three innings by allowing only two singles while striking out five men to put the fire out on any Fairmont threat.

    The Braves threatened in the eighth on two back-to-back singles and again in the ninth when Bloxam gave up two walks and hit a Brave. The insurance and nerve-easing tally came in the extra inning though when Dropo reached first on an error and went to second on Welch's third hit of the evening to set up Cramer's blow.

    Huinker's brilliant mound job was backed by the bats of Welch and Dropo who went 3 for 5 and 2 for 5 respectively. To show how tight the game was, Bloxam struck out 12 men in allowing four walks while his teammates added three extra base blows, a triple and two doubles.

This victory left the Braves with 6 wins and 15 losses, now four games out of third place.

    BIG CROWD WATCHES MYRON HOFFMAN SHUT OUT THE BRAVES, 4-0.

    It was "Save the Braves" night at Roosevelt Field Thursday night. Financially, the club got a good boost with 2,162 fans on hand to see the game between Mason City and Albert Lea. But there wasn't enough stuff in the bats of the Braves to save them from a defeat as Myron Hoffman of the Packers turned in another outstanding pitching performance in firing a 2-hitter.

    But the final story was that the Braves suffered their sixth shutout of the season and the second in a row at the hands

*of Hoffman, who blanked the Braves only last Sunday in a 6-0
game.*

*The only hits off Hoffman were two doubles. George
Dropo drilled a double to the left centerfield canvas in the
fourth frame. Leon Marlow dumped a double into short right
field between three fielders in the eighth. That was all off
Hoffman as he fanned six and issued only three walks.*

*Meanwhile the southpaw pitching of Art Huinker was
no problem for the lefthanded Albert Lea hitters. The Nos. 3, 4
and 5 batters for the Packers, Charlie Weathers, Bill Ankoviak
and John Catallo, all hit from the left side. They got six of the
eight Packer hits, two apiece. Ankoviak had a pair of doubles
and drove in two runs, Weathers walked twice, doubled and
singled and scored three times. Paul Erhard also got a double
for the winners.*

*The loss was Huinker's fourth as against five victories
and he hurled creditable ball, fanning five and walking two.*

The only explanation that I have for left-hand batters getting that many
hits off me has to be too many hanging curveballs and not enough good fastballs
tight on their fists. That probably would be Ken Bawek's explanation if he had
been catching. Just some far out-thoughts of a game over fifty years ago. The
next game for me on the mound provided a different result.

*MASON CITY NIPS AUSTIN 4-3 ON HUINKER'S
PITCHING, HITTING*
By Ron Weber
*Pitcher Art Huinker carried the Mason City Braves to
a 4-3 triumph over Austin in an 11-inning thriller Thursday
night at Roosevelt Field.*

*The little southpaw went the route on the hill with a
masterful 4-hitter, then brought the Braves back from a one-run
deficit with a game-winning 2-run single in the bottom of the
11th.*

*The win was only the second for the cellar-dwelling
Braves over Austin in Southern Minnesota League play this
season. Austin had won seven previous meetings.*

*Huinker, however, winning his sixth game of the year,
had little trouble with the Packers Thursday night. After Austin
tallied two runs in the top of the third inning, the veteran hurler
retired 15 men in order until shortstop Carl Bellotti drew a walk
in the eighth.*

*Huinker chalked up an even more impressive hitless
string. After Frank Brown's three-base hit with one out in the
third, he did not allow a safety until Bob Mathias rapped a
single with two out in the top of the 10th.*

198

Despite one of the better Mason City hurling performances of the season, it took some clutch heroics to pull out the victory. After Mason City tallied twice in the bottom of the third to knot the game at 2-2, both clubs battled on even terms until the eleventh.

Austin went ahead in the top of the 11th on the only Mason City defensive lapse of the night. Joe Raso opened the 11th with a single. Then while Huinker and catcher Jim Hahn were arguing with the plate umpire over the call of a pitch to Dick Morgan, Raso swiped second and went on to third when Hahn's hurried throw to second was wild. The Packer infielder then scored when Huinker cut loose with a wild pitch.

The first two Mason City hitters in the bottom of the inning grounded out. Then Bill Welch beat out his third infield single of the evening and Austin hurler Mike Wallace followed by walking Jack Fitzgerald and Hahn to load the bases. This set the stage for Huinker's sharp single over third base that scored both Welch and Fitzgerald.

It was the team's seventh win of the season against 20 losses. My seventh win of the season on the next outing was a 4 to 3 victory that knocked Albert Lea out of a chance to tie Fairmont for the league title. With the tying run on third with two out for Albert Lea in the top of the ninth, a hard-hit ground ball to short led to the final out and our ninth victory against 25 losses.

A loss to Albert Lea at their diamond on Sunday brings us to the final game of the season at Austin. Three Mason City runs were scored in the first inning on three hits, a walk and an error. From then on, the Austin pitcher won his first game of the season by shutting us out over the next eight innings. In the meantime, I had a shutout until the sixth inning when an infield hit, a walk and two sharp singles plated one run and left the bases loaded. "Three wild pitches later," Austin had four runs and the final score of 4-3 for my fifth loss of the season instead of my eighth victory. Except for the three hits in the 6th, Austin collected only three other hits. Our final standing for the season was a dismal nine wins and 27 losses.

The summer of 1958 with Mason City certainly found many struggles on the diamond. We did not offer the level of competition game after game that is expected in the Southern Minnesota League. All of us dislike being on the losing end of a baseball game, or probably any competitive sport, but when the game is over, the loser must put it behind and look forward to the next game. At the end of the season, like this one, that becomes a bit more difficult. There will be more games in the Southern Minny.

There is another aspect of this 1958 season on the Mason City Braves baseball team that increased its difficulty. Ann and I, except for a few games,

199

immediately drove back to Ossian where we lived. There were two little ones with a babysitter that we needed to get back to. This made it hard to really get acquainted with the other players. Other than some bantering back and forth before the game and possibly a short time after the game, there was very little opportunity to get to know each other in a way other than as a baseball player. In looking at the players in the starting lineup, I remember very little about them or even what they looked like. Exceptions would be George Dropo and Ken Bawek. Of course, I will get the opportunity to play with Ken again the following year. This was a great learning experience for me that helped considerably in the years ahead. This experience helped me better understand the meaning of the concept, "team."

It is back to De Sales High School and a second year of teaching American History and coaching basketball and baseball for the boys.

A SUMMER OF SUCCESS

After the completion of the second year of teaching and coaching at De Sales Central High School in Ossian, for the first time we had more wins than losses for the Falcon baseball team. Progress was being made. Another phone call came from Emil Scheid, the baseball man from Austin, Minnesota. Continuing efforts to keep the Southern Minnesota League alive, in addition to his managing his hometown Austin Packers, he was helping sponsor a team in Rochester, Minnesota. The league would be back to eight teams, divided into an eastern division consisting of Albert Lea and Winona, plus Austin and Rochester, and a western division of Fairmont and three Iowa teams including Mason City and new teams from Estherville and Bancroft.

The Rochester Yankees (we did not wear pin stripe baseball uniforms) started slowly, splitting their first four ball games. One of those losses was a 4 to 3 defeat at the hands of Austin on May 27. That proved to be my only league loss while picking up 12 wins the remainder of the regular season. Another win was picked up in a playoff victory over Austin but also a second loss was recorded in our season-ending playoff loss to Albert Lea.

The other main pitcher for the Yankees was another left-hander by the name of John Van Cuyk. After spending three years in the major leagues with the Brooklyn Dodgers from 1947 to 1949, he jumped around the AAA leagues until he officially ended his professional pursuits in the spring of 1959. Born in Little Chute, Wisconsin, the Rochester management brought him to their roster for the entire Southern Minny season. He was 37 years old, a big hefty person who pitched very well for the team. Frequently he pitched brilliant baseball only to tire after six or seven innings. Up until that time he could consistently hit the knee high level of the strike zone. Then, suddenly, his pitches started coming a little higher and the opposing batters began to tee off. Once he could not put the pitches on the corners and down, he was in trouble. John attributed this early exit from many games to his age and lack of thorough conditioning that he was used to in the pros. That meant quite a few relief appearances for me throughout the season.

Just as I have my claim to fame, having been replaced on the roster of the Albany Cardinals by Hall of Famer Bob Gibson, John Van Cuyk had his claim to fame. He was in the Dodger bullpen when one of the most famous World Series catches was made and seen on sports pages throughout the country. Old time baseball fanatics will remember the name of Al Gionfriddo who made a circus catch for the Dodgers in front of the Dodger bullpen. Van Cuyk appeared on that picture in the background.

Our third pitcher was regular left fielder, Fred Hoeft. Fred was a hometown Rochester player who had played his college ball at Winona State University. While at Loras, we played against him two years in a row. How frequently he pitched for this Rochester Yankee team I can't specifically

201

remember. I know three times for sure. He was our power hitter and good enough that scouts were looking at him quite frequently.

The first victory of the string of twelve, was a 12-inning thriller against Austin.

YANKS WIN IN 12TH ON TRAVERS' HIT
By Gail Anderson, Post-Dispatch Sports Writer
"It felt good" was the simple and to-the-point verdict of the man whose heroics played a major role in the Rochester Yankees' 12-inning 1-0 victory over Austin Thursday night at Mayo Field.

Bob Travers, the transplanted Missourian, only minutes before had sent the 300 or so fans happily home with a ringing 350-foot double to left-center field, scoring teammate Chuck Sedor from second base and breaking up a brilliant pitching duel between Yankee Art Huinker and Austin's Jim Lawler.

"I thought it was going out of the park," Travers said. Indeed, there was some question whether or not the ball had hit the fence or eased over the barrier, but it really didn't make any difference for the drive, wherever it went, carried with it a satisfying Rochester victory.

It was, in a sense, appropriate that Travers should provide the game-winning blow, for a few innings earlier he had saved the day defensively for Manager Bob Balance's club.

The timely efforts of Travers almost overshadowed the over-all sparkling play of the two teams, particularly the pitching performances of Huinker and Lawler.

Huinker, who had lost a narrow 4-3 decision to Lawler the last time out, had the Packers eating out of his hand through most of the game and really was in serious trouble only twice. Travers' defensive gem put out the fire in the seventh, and a snappy double play pulled Huinker out of a bases-loaded predicament in the top of the 12th.

The stylish lefthander chalked up 10 strikeouts, and sent many a Packer trudging back to the dugout after biting on a tantalizing change of pace.

Lawler was nearly as tough. He yielded eight hits and struck out eight.

The stage was set for the decisive home half of the 12th. After Balance, pinch-hitting for Huinker, had popped to left, Sedor singled sharply down the center, was sacrificed to second by Bawek, and Travers stepped in.

Emil Scheid, smiling out of one side of his mouth and muttering out of the other in his dual role as administrator of both teams, summed it up. "They'll never see a better game."

Sedor and Travers each had two hits for the Yanks while first baseman Price West had three singles. There were no errors in the well-played ball game. The team record went to 3 wins, 2 losses.

As the write-up reported, Travers hailed from Missouri. He played shortstop for the professional team that was in Rochester the previous year, as part of the Three-I league. After the season finished, he stayed in town because his wife had gained a very good medical position at one of the numerous medical facilities in Rochester.

After the season ended, Rochester players parted their ways as usual. The following year Rochester again dropped out of the Southern Minny.

But, forty-six years later, "it's a small world" experience occurred. Ann and I were preparing for our 50th wedding anniversary. Yes, that marriage when I was 20 and Ann a mere seventeen, had made the magic number. You have to realize that she was a mature young woman for her age. I have stated that before. We began to put together a party to be held in the Scottsdale, Arizona area in the late winter of 2005. Part of the celebration was to be dinner and entertainment at our favorite nightclub in Surprise, AZ, a suburb of Phoenix. It was called "Jim Henry's" after the entertainer who performed there on weekends. During the week he taught English for a local high school.

Ann placed a call to the restaurant in November of 2004, well ahead of the planned February, 2005 date. A waitress answered. Ann explained that she was hoping to make a reservation for about 35 to 40 people (at that time we were not sure of a specific number, just hoping) for Friday night the last week in February. The waitress responded that she could not make reservations that far ahead but the owner was in the establishment that night and maybe he could help.

The owner picked up the phone asking for an explanation of our request. Again, Ann gave her story. In response, the owner expressed interest but replied that so often reservations of this type are made but then the people from the Midwest failed to show up. Ann quickly followed up by stating that we would be willing to make a sizable deposit to offer some guarantee for the owner. He seemed satisfied and asked for some information. Ann gave her name. There was silence on the other end and Ann figured he needed a pen to write something down.

The next words from the owner were, "Do you know Art Huinker?"

Ann responded that Art was her husband. The owner replied , " I played shortstop for Rochester, Minnesota the year your husband pitched there."

203

When she repeated to me what the owner had said, I immediately responded, "That has to be Bob Travers." The owner heard my cry in the background and reinforced my reaction.

First of all, I was amazed that his name came to me so quickly. I grabbed a second phone and we had a fantastic conversation. The end of the story is that Bob Travers treated us like royalty. We brought 38 guests to his nightclub. Each received a special menu rolled and tied with a red ribbon just for members of our group. A huge carrot cake was placed at the center of our table. There were four tables of guests for our party and he personally spoke to each table, telling a few stories on the "Huinkers" and providing appetizers for each table gratis.

Jim Henry, the entertainer played a polka honoring our 50th anniversary, and of course the couple celebrating their 50th had to dance to that particular music. Then he proceeded to pick on us and also to pick on Iowa people. It was a special night provided by a former teammate and his wife. After all our guests had left for the evening, Ann and I sat with Bob and his wife and had a private toast, again on the house. He was a fantastic ball player in 1959, one of the main reasons our club went on to win the eastern division of the Southern Minnesota League. I sent him a copy of the game just recorded above, including a picture of him that was attached.

By the way, Bob closed his nightclub in Surprise that summer. We had rumors to that effect even before he hosted our party. He also owned two eating establishments in Rochester at the time. Whether he still does, I don't know.

The next game we played was pitched by John Van Cuyk against the Mason City Braves. We held a 9-0 lead going into the seventh inning. Giving up an unearned run in the seventh, by the time I entered the game in the eighth, he had given up seven additional hits, four runs and the bases were loaded. After a strikeout ended the inning, the Yanks were in a virtual tie with Albert Lea for the eastern division lead.

We will include only a few actual write-ups of the games. The following is victory number four against the early loss, and kept us in first place by a half game.

YANKS WIN ON HOEFT HR
By Gail Anderson, Post-Bulletin Sports Writer
A sense of timing- - -picking the opportune moment- - - has kindled many a dramatic finish in sports over the years.
The Rochester Yankees' Fred Hoeft added his name to the list of crowd-pleasers whose heroics have come at that moment of decision when he rapped a 320-foot home run over Mayo Field's left field fence Tuesday night to pull the Yanks from near defeat to a 4-3 triumph over the Albert Lea Packers.

*Hoeft's sixth round-tripper of the season couldn't have
come at a better time. Not only did it save the game for pitcher
Art Huinker, but it served---coming in the eighth inning as it
did- - -as retribution for a nightmarish eighth that cost the
Yanks their only loss to Albert Lea this season.*

*Rochester had a 6-1 lead over the Packers going into
the eighth inning of that earlier game, but Bill Ankoviak's crew
put together seven hits, two walks and an error to score eight
runs and steal the win.*

*But last night it was Albert Lea that was saddled with
eighth inning woes. The Packers took a 3-0 lead into the bottom
of the eighth, and with Myron Hoffman methodically quieting
the Rochester bats, it looked like victory for the visitors.*

*Dale Timm led off with a single , but Manager Bob
Balance, pinch-hitting for Huinker, popped to short center field,
and Chuck Sedor's drive to left was caught. Bob Travers gave
the Yanks life with a single through the infield and Willard
Baker followed with another single that scored Timm.*

*That set the stage for Hoeft, the hefty hometown athlete
who has provided much of the Yankee batting power since
joining the club, but had been in the midst of a batting slump.
In fact, he had mustered just one hit in his last 17 trips to the
plate before his game-winning blast dropped over the fence last
night.*

*John Van Cuyk came in to stifle the Packers. .
.although they got two men on base via a single and an error. .
.in the top of the ninth and saved Huinker's fourth win of the
season against a single loss.*

The comeback victory kept the Yanks in first place by a ½ game over
second-place Austin. Dale Timm was not as good a catcher as Ken Bawek, but he
was a steady force behind the plate and with a bat offensively as well. He took
over the catching duties because Bawek was injury-prone and played a steady
third base while providing a strong stick in the batting line-up.

Remember the problems I had with the Albert Lea hitters last year?
Having already beaten them in the game above, and not allowing Bill Ankoviak a
hit in four tries, the advantage was on my side this year. The next game against
them, this one at Albert Lea, the results for victory number five were even better.

*HUINKER BLANKS AL, 5-0; SPINS TWO-HITTER,
HOEFT HITS HOMER*
*If there are two baseball players the Albert Lea
Packers do not like to see walk into Hayek Field, they are Art
Huinker and Fred Hoeft of the Rochester Yankees.*

205

The two have caused Manager Bill Ankoviak's Packers nothing but trouble all season, and they were at it again here Tuesday night as the Yanks maintained their one-game Southern Minnesota League Eastern Division lead with a 5-0 whitewash job on the home club.

Huinker, the little southpaw out of Loras College, hurled a masterful two-hitter, his best mound job since a 12-inning 1-0 win back on June 4, for his third victory of the year over the Packers and fifth triumph against a single setback in all games.

Only hits off Huinker were a first-inning double by Charlie Weathers and a third-inning double by Ankoviak. From that point on, Huinker retired 19 men in order in the final 6 1/3 innings. . . .that's three an inning, the minimum.

Hoeft continued his lusty slugging against the Packers with a two-run home run in the third inning. It was his fourth home run off Albert Lea pitching this season and eighth hit in 18 trips to the plate against the Packers. The four-master raised his league-leading season total to seven and gave him 18 runs batted in since joining the Yanks.

Price West and Dale Timm also had their hitting clothes on. Each got three hits, with West going three-for-three with a home run, double and single. Pete Johnson had a pair of singles, and Bob Travers was credited with the final Yankee hit.

What a difference a year makes. Ken Bawek talked at length with me about how to pitch to certain hitters, but for the most part, he kept stressing the value of depending more on my best pitch. That routinely was the fastball, either the four-seam or two-seam. Bawek would often warm me up before the game purposely to determine which of the two fast balls had the most movement. He proved so valuable to my pitching that summer at Rochester.

In the summer of 1961, first baseman Price West played for Satchell Paige's touring baseball team when I was pitching for Soldiers Grove, Wisconsin. This will occur two chapters ahead.

In our continued playing of two games a week, we played Estherville, Iowa at home and it was one of those nights where Van Cuyk pitched well into the seventh and needed two innings of relief. That wasn't soon enough as we lost that game 5-4. For the first time, I was called on to pinch-hit and picked up a single in a two-run seventh but we ended up one run short. Van Cuyk gave up 10 hits and five runs, suffering his second loss to the Estherville pitcher, Mike Sund. Two years later, I pitched in Wisconsin for the Soldiers Grove team and the opposing pitcher was Sund.

We played again at Albert Lea and once more took their measure 3-2 in eleven innings. I pitched the first eight with Van Cuyk pitching the last three and picking up the win. Price West was the hitting star for Rochester with three hits good for two runs batted in. He also had two walks. The winning hit was by none other than Fred Hoeft who had hit a come-from-behind home run in the previous game between the two teams. Second baseman Willard Baker scored the winning run after getting his second hit of the night.

YANKS HOLD 4-TILT LEAD DESPITE WEEKEND SPLIT

The Rochester Yankees retained their four-game lead in the Southern Minny League's Eastern Division despite a two-game split over the weekend. They overpowered Winona 8-4 Saturday night for their sixth straight decision over the Chiefs this season. But Sunday night at Mayo Field they suffered their second straight shutout defeat at the hands of Fairmont, 5-0. The loss snapped a five-game Rochester winning streak.

Manager Bob Balance rapped a home run and a run-scoring single to pace the Yankees to victory over their Winona "cousins" Saturday night at Gabrych Park. He collected his home run with one out in the third inning. That tied the score 1-1 after the Chiefs had opened with one tally in the first.

Pete Johnson led off a four-run Rochester rally in the fourth with a double. He scored on Bill Leach' single. Dale Timm sacrificed, Art Huinker walked and Balance singled to score Leach.

Travers was safe on an error that scored Huinker and Price West's single drove in Balance.

More Yankee extra base blows accounted for two more runs in the sixth. Travers' triple plated Huinker who had singled and Willard Baker's double drove in Travers.

Huinker notched his eighth victory against a single defeat in a route-going performance. The loser was Don Behrens who was knocked out of the box in the fourth. Manager Pete Polus finished up.

The Sunday night loss to Fairmont saw Fred Hoeft make one of his rare appearances on the mound. He pitched well enough to win many ball games but not when opposing right-hander, Loyal Bloxam pitched a beautiful two-hit shutout in the 5-0 loss. It was his second consecutive shutout against the Yankees.

Victory #9 came against "guess who." Once again, it was Albert Lea. Last year, they were my nemesis, but this year they have been the victim.

YANKS TURN TABLES WITH 'HUINKER NIGHT'

They called it Kids Night, but it should have been Art Huinker Night.

Huinker, the smallish lefthander whose pitching has been a key factor in the Rochester Yankees' Southern Minnesota League success this season, did it again Tuesday night, pitching and batting the Yanks to a 13-inning 1-0 victory over the Albert Lea Packers.

The win enabled the Yanks to maintain a four-game bulge over Austin, 9-3 winner over Winona, and dropped Albert Lea five games off the pace. It was the sixth Rochester win in seven games with Albert Lea and the third one-run triumph by the Yanks over the Packers. The two teams wind up their regular season series Thursday night at Mayo Field, with Fred Hoeft of Rochester scheduled to hurl against Hal Snyder of Albert Lea.

But last night it was Huinker's show. The stylish southpaw pitched seven-hit ball for 13 innings, and got four of the Yanks' 10 hits, the fourth a 13th-inning single that scored Bob Travers from third with the winning run. That single tally gave Huinker his fourth triumph of the season over Albert Lea and ran his over-all record to nine wins against just one defeat.

Each team had opportunity after opportunity to score during the game, but couldn't produce the timely hit when it was needed. Rochester left a total of 15 men stranded on the bases, including two in each of the third, fifth, seventh,10th and 12th innings.

The Yanks missed their best scoring opportunity in the ninth when Dale Timm and Bob Balance clubbed back-to-back doubles, yet didn't produce a run. Bill Leach was inserted to run for Timm, but only reached third on Balance's two-base rap off the scoreboard. Leach held at third as Huinker flied to right, then tried to score, but was out by 10 feet when Chuck Sedor lofted a short fly ball to center field.

Albert Lea loaded the bases in the bottom of the 11th on two walks and a single by Paul Flores but couldn't score. Then, in the 13th, Travers led off with a single, was sacrificed to second by Ken Bawek, went to third on an infield out and scored on Huinker's single to right-center field.

Huinker put the Packers down 1-2-3 in the bottom of the inning to preserve the victory, his second marathon win of the year. Earlier in the season he stopped Austin 1-0 in 12 innings.

The ability of our human brain to remember instances in our life usually involves major events in our life. John F. Kennedy's assassination has always been a key memory for me. But that 13th inning single, much less significant obviously but apparently not for me, is easily brought back into focus for me, even today. It was about a 20 foot high line drive that went directly over Albert Lea second baseman John Poliak into right center. About five years later, when Ann and I were living in Dyersville, while in the middle of doing some shopping on Main Street, I heard my name being called from a car driving down the street. It was John Poliak and his family. They were on vacation and had stopped to visit the Dyersville and Dubuque area. They also knew that we were living in Dyersville and he said later that they had not planned to look for us. Mere chance brought us together that day.

The championship for the eastern division of the Southern Minny had been clinched earlier. But there were games still to be played because the second place team in each division qualifies for the playoffs to determine which team out of the league goes on to the Minnesota State Tournament.

One of those teams battling for a second place finish was the Braves from Mason City. The crucial game, played at Mason City, was a make-up of a previously rained-out game.

> ### ROCHESTER TURNS BACK MASON CITY
> *Rochester, the East division champ of the Southern Minnesota League, defeated Mason City, 3-0, in a makeup game Tuesday night. It cost the Braves a second place tie with Fairmont in the West division and slowed down a title bid. Idle Estherville leads the West division by a few percentage points.*
> *Art Huinker, clever southpaw, picked up his 11th straight win in hurling a seven-hitter. His mates collected seven blows off Clem Ozburn and Bill Freese who relieved in the eighth inning.*

In the game, Rochester scored one run in the first and the score did not change until the Yanks put together a two-run rally in the eighth for the final margin.

The eleven straight victories are surprising considered the strength of the teams. But what puzzles me the most is the success of this season compared to the 1958 season and the 1960 season to follow. In neither of those two seasons do we come close to the success experienced with the Rochester Yanks. There is nothing in my preparation for those three seasons that differed that much from one year to another. There is little doubt that the Yanks were a superior defensive team but comparing runs scored per game that I pitched versus especially the 1960 season, the Austin Packers scored at least two runs more per game than the Rochester Yanks in this current year.

209

Frequently, we have discussed the quality of pitches thrown one day by the same pitcher and how different it is for that pitcher the next time he steps on the mound. Never have I experienced continued strong outings game after game as happened this season. This has to be rated as the best summer of pitching that I ever had. And I did not have another like it the rest of my career. The 1956 season pitching for Loras College, then both Dyersville and Festina in the summer, probably comes the closest in terms of having good control, excellent speed, and great movement of the ball coming to the batter. Successful individual games occurred during all the seasons, but none were consistent game after game. I wish I could have packaged whatever caused the success.

All baseball players and fans can accept an often-heard statement describing the game of baseball. For example: "baseball is a game of inches." One day a hard hit line drive is just out of the reach of an infielder and goes for a base hit. The next game, that same hit is a foot to the left and the third baseman makes the catch. One day every batted ball for one team is fair by inches; the next day it may be foul by inches. The closer the score, the more likely that "a game of inches" determines the outcome. The year with Rochester provided "inches" that often seemed in our favor.

The better baseball that is being played, the better the players are who are competing against each other, the greater possibility that either of the two teams can win the game. This helps understand why no one team can go through a season without being on one side of the final score or the other. In the 1959 Southern Minny season, the Yanks had many one-run victories. Many of those could have been losses, if the inches where the ball was hit would have been just slightly left or right of where it was hit.

The regular season ended with a season record of 21 wins and 9 losses. Second place Albert Lea ended with 16 wins and 14 losses and finished five games behind. There is one game, however, that I wish to cover briefly. We were playing at Austin, a game that we won and that I pitched. What inning is not important, but the bases were empty when I came up to bat. What kind of pitch, a curve ball or a fast ball, is not remembered. When it was hit, I felt it had a chance to go out of the ball park. It cleared the high left field wall with ease, my first and only home run while playing in the Southern Minny League.

Pumped as I was when I crossed the plate, I received no high fives at the plate from the next hitter but really didn't notice. When I reached the dugout, there was total silence. I sat down in the dugout and the game proceeded. All of a sudden all the players began to laugh and applaud. Led by Ken Bawek, they had given me the silent treatment. This happens every once in a while, although it had never happened to me before. Is this a sign of a baseball team that is enjoying themselves, enjoying the camaraderie that exists between players? Once realizing what they had done, I think I enjoyed it as much as the perpetrators did. One factor that built this positive relationship among the players this year possibly is tied to the same players taking the field night after night for the entire season.

Fairmont captured the Western division title and a single-game playoff with Rochester was scheduled. The Yanks again had to play on the road because Fairmont had won the series between the two teams during the regular season. In this game the Fairmont Martins were playing for their fourth league championship in the last five years. And we were playing without key player Bob Travers who had to leave the team immediately after the regular season because of other commitments.

> *YANKS WIN S-M TITLE*
> *The Rochester Yankees are the 1959 Southern Minnesota League champions.*
> *The Yanks, East division titlist, exploded for seven runs in the fourth inning to whip West division champ, Fairmont, 8-0, Tuesday night at Martin Park.*
> *It was the first S-M League title for Rochester since they turned the trick in 1956 and the second time they played the Martins in the championship game in the last five years.*
> *Lefty Art Huinker, in pitching the shutout, finished the regular season with a 12-1 record. The southpaw scattered six Fairmont hits, struck out seven and walked none.*
> *The Yanks came up with 12 blows against starter Harry Pritts and reliever Loyal Bloxam, who took over pitching duties in the fourth inning.*
> *Four of Rochester's runs were unearned in the big fourth. Two were out, two on base and two runs in when Rochester's Bob Balance hit a ground ball to Herb Banton at third. Banton scooped up the ball, but threw wild to allow another Yankee run. Before the dust cleared Rochester added four more runs.*
> *Seven of the 12 Rochester hits came in the fourth, six singles and a double by Willard Baker.*

Just to refresh your memory, the state of Minnesota holds their own end-of-season state tournaments divided into classes similar to the method used by many states in holding high school athletic tournaments. Rochester and the Southern Minnesota League participate in the top division of largest cities of the state. Their state tournament is usually held in St. Cloud, a city located about two hours north of the Twin Cities.

In the opening Southern Minny round, the Austin Packers were Rochester's opponent played on the Rochester diamond. Excerpts from the write-up in the Austin Daily Herald are found below.

211

AUSTIN ERRORS OPEN DOOR FOR ROCHESTER
VICTORY IN PLAYOFFS
By Tom Koeck, Sports Writer for Austin Daily Herald
The Austin Packers got off on the wrong foot at Mayo
Field Thursday night, losing 4-3 to the Rochester Yankees in 12
innings.

Seven Packer errors opened the door for the Yankees,
newly crowned champion of the regular season S-M League
season.

Three of the four Yankee runs were unearned because
of the errors including the tie-breaker, which came in the
bottom of the 12th with two men out.

Dick Stanton, borrowed from the Winona Chiefs
because of an injury to Ken Bawek, made it to second on Fred
Folkes' high throw to first base and after Pete Johnson hit a line
drive to pitcher Chuck Kowalski, Stanton raced to third on Dale
Timm's grounder to Jim Lawler.

Stanton scored when Bob Mathias handled Art
Huinker's grounder but pulled Lawler off first base with his
throw. The call by umpire Marvin Elman was debatable, and
touched off the last of several rhubarbs, which interrupted the
game.

Huinker, who worked the last 5 2/3 innings in relief of
Johnny Van Cuyk, grabbed the victory for an impressive 13-1
record.

The Packers collected 13 hits including a double by
Frank Brown, and nine were off Van Cuyk, who was charged
with all of the runs.

Brown's double to left-center chased Van Cuyk and
Lawler picked on Huinker for a single that tallied the tying run
in the seventh.

After that Huinker was tough. He retired the Packers
in order the next four innings and survived a close call in the
12th.

The write-up stressed several umpire calls that were objected to by both sides, one which almost ended up in a typical baseball brawl. I can't remember that as part of the game. I managed to connect with a double in three tries after I came into the game. The playoffs follow the framework of a double-elimination tournament, and the following Wednesday we lost 6-5 at Fairmont. The following night, we and our opponent, Albert Lea, both faced elimination, each having one loss.

Think with me for a minute. Wednesday, Ann and I traveled from our home at Ossian to Fairmont, Minnesota for the game we lost. The trip one way totaled about 160 miles. Back on the road the next night, we traveled to

212

Rochester, a trip of approximately 80 miles. Yes, we worked the day in between. However, understand that gas prices were less than 50 cents a gallon in 1959.

We had company on our trip to Rochester. Festina teammate and first cousin, Norb Einck and his wife Rosaria accompanied Ann and me for the playoff game. Again, the success of the summer seemingly continued but with a different outcome.

> *ALBERT LEA ELIMINATES YANKS, 3-2*
> *Albert Lea defeated Rochester, 3-2, Thursday night to continue in the thick of the fight for the Southern Minnesota League playoff title.*
> *Albert Lea collected only four hits off Yankee southpaw Art Huinker, but it was enough. They scored single runs in the fourth, fifth and sixth innings and then staved off a late Rochester rally.*
> *Hal Snyder gave up 10 hits to Rochester and stranded 13 men. He was given an assist by Myron Hoffman, who fanned Dick Stanton on three pitches with the bases loaded in the ninth.*

Norb and I thoroughly discussed the loss on the way back to Festina where Norb and Rosaria lived. This is another one of those nights where my pitches tended to be close to the location that I wanted but good hitters make adjustments too. Two singles that drove in runs were ground balls that just got past the outstretched glove of our second baseman. Both were on pitches off the outside part of the plate but hit well enough that they got through. And again, I may have been guilty of using that location too much and the hitters adjusted. A "game of inches" was certainly true in this loss.

Our Rochester Yankees were playing without two of the team's best players, Bob Travers and Ken Bawek. One can't help but wonder if that would have made a difference. Our second baseman had shifted to shortstop to fill Travers' spot. Our new second baseman was not all that familiar with his new position but I have no doubt that he tried just as hard as any other player on the team. We lost, but it was a good game.

A pre-game announcement to the team certainly did not help our situation either. The Rochester management told the players in the dressing room that there was no money left to pay players any further. I don't feel that it affected our play. At least I hope it didn't. If we were to win the playoffs, it did mean two more games for sure. Now that was behind us.

But the season wasn't over. Two weeks later, a call came for me at De Sales High School from Jerry Ackerman, catcher for the Albert Lea Packers. They had won the Southern Minny playoffs and were participating in the Minnesota State Tournament at St. Cloud, Minnesota. They needed a pitcher. Figuring a seven hour trip would require hitting the road from Ossian before

213

school was out. It meant someone else covering a class or two, cancelling our own baseball practice at the high school, and getting permission from Principal Sister Claire to leave early. Financial considerations also had been finalized.

Sister Claire, in her kindness, granted the request and we were ready to hit the road. Hold it a minute. Ann, my number one fan, was going along. We needed to get our baby sitter out of school. Ann made those arrangements, including warning Janet Barthelme, our wonderful parent assistant, that it would require an all-night sleep-over at our house with Terry and Tim. Now we are ready to hit the road. They were 3 years and 1 year old respectfully at the time.

It is now the middle of September. By the time Ann and I arrived at the baseball stadium temperatures had dropped into the mid-forties. The game started around 10:00. I can't even tell you who we played but one of the opposition players had played previously in the Southern Minny. This time of year he was playing football for St. Thomas College in St. Paul.

By the time the game was over, the clock had gone well past midnight. The final score was a lopsided 10-4 in favor of the Albert Lea Packers. The football player, a respected baseball player, had fanned four straight times. Players on the Albert Lea team felt that the emphasis on conditioning muscles other than those normally used for swinging at a baseball, had definitely made it difficult for the player's natural baseball swing. I have tried to use Google and other computer tricks to see if they eventually won the tournament or were they unsuccessful in their quest, but have not been able to find the answer.

Now for the trip home. Coming through St. Paul, we suddenly had no brakes. Thankfully, after a few miles in city driving, we found a service station open 24 hours and with three bays going for repair work. We certainly would have needed that repair job very soon anyway, but it would have been nice to have that sort of work done at a more convenient time.

We resumed our return trip home, now concerned that we may not make it back to Ossian in time to get to school and classes that morning. The remainder of the trip went peacefully. We arrived home about 7:45, giving us just enough time to get Janet back to her home a few blocks away and for me to shower and get dressed to get to school and teach.

Thankfully, we were young and could handle a night with little sleep. Ann and I took turns driving so we weren't totally without some shut-eye. We both survived the next day and now we could say with certainty that the 1959 summer baseball season was part of history.

Again, I repeat. This probably was the most successful four months of baseball for me out of all the years of organized baseball. The Yankees became a very tightly knit team and one that provided much joy and satisfaction for each and every game played. Having said that, Ann and I have crossed paths with only two of those players in later years, both very enjoyable experiences. One was Bob Travers, our shortstop, and the other was Price West, our first baseman. Both instances are described earlier. One just wonders what paths their lives have taken. And how much of a role did baseball play in the path taken.

That summer of baseball is certainly filled with "happy memories." Since that time our memories of Rochester took a more serious and sad direction for both Ann and me. Both her father and younger brother spent considerable time in Rochester hospitals before their lives ended. For myself, Rochester medical services were part of the treatment received by my mother and two brothers before they were called back by our Lord. College roommate and baseball partner, Bob Wolfe, spent considerable time at St. Mary's Hospital where we visited with him. Shortly after his return home, Bob also was called to his eternal home. By this time in our later stages of life, we have all had similar experiences.

A CHAMPIONSHIP BUT A TOUGH YEAR

Once again, in the spring of 1960, baseball enthusiast Emil Scheid from Austin, Minnesota called, this time to play for his team, the Austin Packers. The contractual agreement offered remained the same as the previous year, one that was again agreeable to Ann and me. We now had three children to be taken care of by our reliable Janet Barthelme for baby-sitting. Our first daughter was born the previous fall, October 25 to be exact. She was named Tammy Marie after the movie which we had seen on our way down to Georgia to play pro baseball. And by this time we knew a fourth was on the way for December of the current year.

At De Sales, we had just completed the best seasons in basketball and baseball since Ann and I had taken the teaching/coaching position in 1957. And, in both sports, most players were returning for the 1960-61 year.

It is time to expand upon the role and efforts of Emil Scheid to maintain a solid Southern Minny Baseball League. Starting in the summer of 1957, to my knowledge, when he organized the Mason City Braves as a new member of the league, rounding it out to eight teams, Emil was the primary leader in keeping the league operational. He fought to get support from the local town being considered for membership in the league. In doing so, he also committed his own financial support to the venture. Besides that, he was instrumental in keeping the Austin Packers solvent and a very representative member of the league. Not only did he see that the organizational structure was in place for his home town team, he managed them as well. And, watching him operate, he loved what he was doing. He could also get very worked up over umpiring decisions and they often incurred his wrath on questionable calls. To conclude, the man loved the game of baseball and gave amply of his time and financial support for his town of Austin and beyond.

This will be the first time that he managed the team that I was playing for. And he led us to the league championship. Our Packers were not as successful as the Rochester Yankees the preceding year, but our final record was 19 wins, 11 losses, finishing with a two-game lead over our next closest opposition, the Mankato Twins. The league had six teams, only one division unlike the previous season. The six teams were Albert Lea, Fairmont, and Mankato along with the Austin Packers from Minnesota and Mason City and Estherville from Iowa.

As it turned out, in studying the history of the Southern Minnesota League, 1960 was their last year as a viable top-division league. What changes occurred the following year or if they even existed, I am not sure. Attendance was way down and the paying of the players was going to be almost impossible without big-time donations. Unknown at this time, this would be our last year to commit to playing in the league because Ann and I made the decision to accept a teaching/coaching position at Xavier High School in Dyersville. This would then

216

include our committing to playing for our second home town, a team we had played for earlier in 1956.

The path to winning the Southern Minny league title in 1960 was anything but smooth. I would pitch a very strong game, then turn right around and pitch miserably. The final won-loss record was 8 wins, 7 losses, incurring three of those losses in relief roles when I failed to keep the opposing team from scoring and thus ending up on the losing end. But there was a bright side. My batting average of .380 (19 hits in 50 at bats) led all hitters on the Austin Packer team. No home runs, but 4 doubles and 2 triples. Not bad for a batter who hit .125 while in pro baseball.

Our first game of the season on May 22 (my birthday) did not start well. Never having played at Mankato, we arrived at the game late and Gary Underhill jumped in to start the game. We lost 6-2. After Underhill pitched the first four innings, I finished, giving up 6 hits and 4 runs. Not a good start. Batting-wise, I collected a double and single in three trips.

Our second game saw the Packers handle the Fairmont Martins, 9-7. Five errors by the Martin defense allowed the Packers to build an 8-2 lead going into the seventh. A short excerpt of a lengthy article in the Austin Daily Herald follows.

> *AUSTIN BLASTS 11 HITS TO DOWN FAIRMONT*
> *The Packers rewrote the script at Fairmont Sunday night. They did it behind the stout pitching of Art Huinker and reliever Gary Underhill and some lusty hitting that produced five extra base blows in an 11-hit attack on righthander, Dave Ramnes, who went the distance.*
> *Huinker gave up five hits in 6 and 1/3 innings, fanned four and walked four. Underhill allowed four hits and he whiffed three.*
> *Dick Anderson was the big hero for the Packers with four hits. His first time at the plate he slammed a home run over the right field fence with Larry Scheid aboard. It was his second circuit smash in as many games. He used his blazing speed to beat out two infield hits and he sliced one into right field his next time up.*
> *The other extra base blows included a triple by Huinker and doubles by Frank Brown, Ray Rosenbaum and Bob Folkert.*

Frank Brown normally played in the outfield, Rosenbaum covered the first base area and Bob Folkert also played outfield for this game. Anderson patrolled the center field area.

217

The next game for me was a relief job at home against Albert Lea. With a 6-1 lead and Underhill pitching good ball, the roof fell in. He allowed six hits. I allowed one which drove in the tying run. In the 10th, a suicide squeeze bunt brought in the winning run. For us, John Steffen, Rosenbaum and Underhill each had two hits.

Albert Lea had a new center fielder, Al Klinger, from West Union, Iowa, a Fayette County seat just twelve miles from our home town of Festina. Al played many games later for Guttenberg in the Dyersville area local tournaments. They also had Don Buhr playing second base. Don had played with Sumner for years. He took an educational administrative position with the Albert Lea school system. That moved him to Albert Lea and Packer baseball.

We need to present our other starting pitcher. Gary Underhill, another lefthander, grew up in a small community in southern Minnesota west of Albert Lea. He was a high school phenom and had unbelievable high school stats. He attended Upper Iowa University in Fayette, Iowa and, although successful, not to the degree that they expected from him. He pitched quite well for us at Austin as you will see in game reports to come.

What I find interesting is the pitching staff consisting of two left handers. At Rochester we had the same setup with lefty John Van Cuyk joining me on that staff. There is some bias in my feelings here but is there a reason for teams wanting left-handed pitchers. What do you think?

Our next game was a tough, extra-inning 1-0 loss to Mason City at their field. An excerpt of the game follows.

HUINKER HURLS 4-HITTER, PACKERS LOSE 1-0
By Tom Koeck, Sports Writer, Austin Daily Herald
Art Huinker wasted a brilliant four-hitter as Mason City defeated Austin 1-0 in 11 innings in a Southern Minnesota make-up game Sunday night at Roosevelt Field.
It was Huinker's second set-back against one victory and left the Packers with a 1-3 record. The run coming in the bottom of the 11th to break up a tight pitching duel between Huinker and righthander Clem Ozburn, was unearned as the result of an error.
The break came when Jerry Splinter hit a hard grounder to Bob McKay at third. McKay made the play, but the ball bounced off Rosenbaum's glove, allowing Splinter to reach second. An attempted bunt by Ozburn backfired as Splinter stayed at second when Huinker, after fielding the ball, made the play on Ozburn.
Then Paul Abraham was called out on strikes before Don Baker, lining the ball sharply into right field, scored Splinter to end the game.

218

*It was a tough game for Huinker to lose and he
certainly deserved a better fate. He found the plate effectively
with a sharp breaking curve and fast ball as he walked only one
man and finished with nine strikeouts. Bill Barnholdt gave him
most of the trouble with an infield single and a line shot to right
field.*

A good ball game and one that you like to win but that is baseball.
Looking at the Mason City line-up, Jerry Splinter was a Dubuquer who played
baseball at Loras College. And Bill Barnholdt also was an Iowa player that I
believe played at Upper Iowa. He later played games around Dyersville in local
invitational tournaments.

Outfielder Frank Brown and catcher Don Carlson each had two hits for
the Packers. Each of their hits included doubles, while the Mason City team had
four singles total.

Next, Gary Underhill gained his first victory as Austin improved their
record to 2-3. Following that game was another home game against Albert Lea.

HUINKER AND PACKERS STOP ALBERT LEA
*Austin defeated Albert Lea, 2-0, Sunday night at
Marcusen Park and this time they made it stick.*
*In the last meeting between the two teams, Austin
sported a 6-1 lead going into the top of the ninth only to have
Albert Lea tie the score and win 7-6 in 10 innings.*
*The Packers fashioned the shutout behind Art
Huinker's superb pitching and a two-run uprising in the fourth
inning.*
*Huinker, now 2-2, was never in trouble as he retired
the first seven batters before John Poliak slammed a double into
right field. But it was of no avail as Bill Ankoviak and Jerry
Ackerman went down in order to end the threat.*
*Poliak added a single in the ninth and other Albert Lea
hits, both singles, were tagged by Paul Flores and Ackerman.*
*Huinker, who walked no one, finished with four
strikeouts and allowing four hits, in pitching his first shutout.*
*The Packers pounded loser Myron Hoffman (3-2) for
six hits, three of them coming in the fourth when both runs
scored.*
*After Hoffman retired the Packers in order the first
three frames, he issued a walk to Bob Mathias to open the gate.
Mathias went to second on Dick Anderson's single to center and
both runners advanced on a wild pitch after Don Carlson,
attempting to bunt, popped out to catcher Paul Erhard.*

Then Frank Brown singled to left to score both Mathias and Anderson. Brown moved to third on Bob Folkert's single before Hoffman got out of trouble.

Frank Brown again had two hits for the Austin nine. In our next competition, a road game at Estherville, the game was more interesting than most. First of all, Gary Underhill struggled with his control and walked seven while allowing only three hits in six and 1/3 innings. It was another relief role for me and it started out good. I managed to get out of a bases-loaded, one out jam in the sixth without any runs scoring. The seventh and eighth went smoothly also. Then came the ninth.

We had a 5-1 lead going into the bottom of the ninth. After giving up four singles, our lead was one run and the tying run on first. A final strikeout of centerfielder Marv Ott and the victory was finally sealed.

On the following Sunday, we won our fourth consecutive victory at Mankato. It was a game in which we caught Mankato ace, Loyal Bloxam in one of his rare off nights.

AUSTIN GAINS 9-1 WIN OVER TWINS
By Tom Koeck, Austin Daily Herald Sports Writer
Art Huinker turned in another pitching gem Sunday night as the hustling Austin Packers chilled Mankato, 9-1, before 650 fans at brand-new Key City Park.

An unearned run, coming in the first inning, cost the little southpaw a shutout, but it did not take away from the brilliant performance.

He limited the Twins to four scattered hits, failed to walk a man and struck out 10. Bud Getta got three of the hits, all singles, and Wayne Knapp, University of Minnesota All-American first baseman, who was in the lineup for the first time, got the other.

Huinker, who got stronger as he went along, retired the last nine men in order for his third victory against two defeats.

Not only did Huinker pitch well, but he slammed a double in the third inning for the only extra base hit of the game.

The fine pitching was backed by an 11-hit attack as the Packers boosted their Southern Minnesota League record to 5-3 and stretched a winning string to four straight. It also gave Austin a 2-1 edge in the series against the Twins.

Catching the loss was ace righthander, Loyal Bloxam, who was replaced by Herb Strangland to start the ninth frame.

Although Bloxam gave up 11 blows, including two apiece by Bob Mathias, Don Carlson, Frank Brown and Larry

220

Scheid, some faulty fielding by the Twin infield added to his troubles.

Of the nine runs, only two were earned as the result of five Mankato errors. The biggest offender was third sacker Getta, who was charged with three, all coming in the seventh inning.

A three-run uprising in the third, sparked by Huinker's double and a single by John Steffen made it 4-1 and in the sixth Austin added another run off singles by Bob McKay, who had replaced Ray Rosenbaum at first base, Scheid and Mathias.

It was unusual to score that many runs, and especially, to get that many hits off Loyal Bloxam. He was a fixture year after year as one of the top pitchers in the Southern Minny. Pitching against Rochester last year, he shut us out both games he pitched against us in the regular season. Even the three walks he gave up in this game were probably a season high for him.

The Mankato trip was by far our longest. We probably left home by 3:30 in the afternoon to get to Mankato by 7:00. Three times we had to make that trek.

Our next game, after a rainout, was played at Estherville, Iowa. It was another nail-biter, with Estherville scoring the winning run in the bottom of the ninth for a 3-2 victory. We collected only five hits against a very familiar baseball name in northeast Iowa. It was Monona, Iowa native, Glenn Drahn. Just weeks prior to this game he had been appointed Athletic Director at Coe College, a small private college in Cedar Rapids. He also had two hits against me. His catcher that day was a player that the newspaper article called Bob Fitch. I wonder if it wasn't Bill Fitch, also a top Iowa player with strong ties to Coe College and who I know played for Estherville.

The Pride, team nickname for Estherville, collected 11 hits against me and, as the article stated, I got myself out of trouble several times in the contest, leaving 12 runners stranded. Offensively, I helped my cause in the third with a double and scored from third later on a sacrifice fly. John Steffen, with a home run and a single led the Packer attack.

The following Friday, playing at Austin, we were involved in another extra-inning game with the Mason City Braves. They were victorious 1-0 in eleven innings in the earlier game. This game was very much like the previous game with the Estherville Pride. We lost this one, 4-3 in 10 innings, despite my giving up 15 hits. Again, the article stated that, "to his credit, Huinker pitched himself out of tight jams and stranded 15 Brave runners this time." In the first inning, the bases were loaded with no one out. Ten pitches later and three strikeouts, the inning was over. In this game, two errors in the sixth allowed two runs to score that provided the margin of victory.

I don't specifically remember highlights of the game but the following is a paragraph from the Austin Daily Herald:

Outside of Dropo's double which failed to do any damage, Huinker did not give up anything big. The majority of blows either dropped over the infield or were just out of reach.

Again, we had just five hits. I managed to get one single off opposing pitcher, Clem Ozburn, and it did drive in a run. The big hit for us was Catcher Dick Noterman's home run in the fifth with no one aboard. All of a sudden, our record is 5-5 and we are in fourth place.

The next game I start has an unusual ending. For a change, the game was going along quite smoothly. We had a 4-0 lead going into the fourth when a line drive back to the mound caught me on the right cheek bone. Rather than continuing to pitch, Manager Scheid felt that we need to get to the hospital to have things checked out. I can't remember for sure but I believe I felt okay. If you ask if we made the putout on the liner back to me, I truly do not remember. Anyway, off to the hospital we went. Ann drove. Thank heaven, at least we did not call an ambulance. She was a little shook up but she did nicely. To end the episode, we returned to the ball park just as the game was over. No broken bones, no headache, just an imprint of the baseball on my right cheek bone. I realize there can be many conclusions that you, the reader, can make. Just keep them to yourselves, please. My only concern related to the game. We won the game by a score of 8-3. I had a chance to get a much needed win but did not qualify.

After the victory on Sunday evening, the Packers lost a one-run decision to Fairmont on Tuesday. The following Thursday, we traveled to distant Mankato and lost another one-run ball game, this time by a score of 3-2.

PACKER RALLY FAILS, LOSE TO 'KATO 3-2
Hearts and flowers may well be the theme song for Emil Scheid's Austin Packers, victim of a one-run loss to Mankato Thursday night, 3-2.
The Packers were shutout until the ninth inning when they loaded the sacks twice, but were retired when Frank Brown, who was three for four, was struck out by reliever Loyal Bloxam.
The Packers' two runs were scored by Larry Scheid who homered over the left center field fence with Bob Mathias, who opened the inning with a single, ahead of him. Then Dick Noterman singled, Art Huinker flew out, Dick Anderson singled and Don Carlson was safe on first when Bloxam threw to Dwant Mintz, covering second, trying to pick off the runner and Mintz dropped the ball.

> With the bases loaded, Noterman was forced out at
> home when Bob Folkert tapped the ball for a fielder's choice.
> Then Brown came up, and like Casey of yore, fanned.
>   Hank, the winner, worked until the ninth when Bloxam
> came in. Huinker went the distance, allowing nine hits, fanning
> five, and walking three.
>   Rosenbaum was injured in the sixth, when he collided
> with Wayne Knapp covering first base. Scheid took over second
> and Carlson was shifted to first.
>   This was Mankato's fifth straight win and they have
> won seven of their last eight games to hold the loop lead.

Our next game was a slugfest with the Estherville Pride, with our Packers winning by a score of 14-9. Gary Underhill got the win although it was one of those not-so-good pitching days for him. Another relief appearance of three innings for me giving up one run and two hits. But better than that, two hits in two trips for the relief pitcher. The following two paragraphs are taken from an Austin Daily Herald write-up.

> PACKERS WIN RUBBER WITH ESTHERVILLE, 14-9
>   McKay, in at shortstop for Larry Scheid, hit two for
> three, three runs batted in, and walking twice for a good night
> at the plate. His defensive play matched his hitting ability. Star
> hitter for the Packers was Huinker, two for two and one RBI.
>   The Packers showed fine base running, especially
> Huinker who beat the throw-in from the shortstop to score in the
> seventh and then scampered home on a passed ball that
> bounced all over the park in the eighth.

The month of August arrived with the Austin Packers in a second place tie with Albert Lea two games behind the Mankato Twins. Because we were playing make-up games and regular-scheduled games, our seldom-used third pitcher, Lou Ciola, started on the mound against Mason City. Our Packers scored seven runs in the first three innings but Mason City clawed their way back in by scoring two in the third and two more in the fourth. Ciola was lifted in the fourth and it was another call from the bullpen for me. I went until the seventh when two singles made Manager Scheid decide to bring Gary Underhill in. According to the write-up again in the Austin Daily Herald, Frank Brown, now playing center field where he was one of the best, raced to the fence and nabbed a long drive by Jerry Splinter to save the game in that seventh. I pitched four innings and allowed no runs, thanks to Brown's catch but gave up five hits during that stint. Steffens had a two-run homer for our big blow. But Mankato also won.

Next, we lost to Fairmont by a lopsided score of 17-4. Underhill again had his problems and I relieved for one batter in the fifth. Then, Manager Scheid decided that we were so far behind that he would let first baseman, Ray

Rosenbaum, finish the game. It also is a long trip to Fairmont from Ossian but we made it a little longer that night on the eve of our fifth wedding anniversary. A "well-known" bean field caused a slight detour.

The next game was even more lopsided than the Fairmont score, but this time it was in our favor. We beat Estherville, 21-8. All we can say is, "Good for the offense." But it was a victory. All of a sudden, we are pushing to take over the league lead. Mankato went into a tailspin and suffered three straight losses.

On August 9, the Packers played the Fairmont Martins and gained a 5-3 win. After that win, we were in first place all by ourselves but only a game and a half separated the top five teams. Only Estherville was really out of the race.

> PACKERS GAIN 5-3 WIN OVER MARTINS
> By Jim Koeck, Sports Writer, Austin Daily Herald
> The Austin Packers can win big or play it close to the vest. After they rapped Estherville 21-8, Sunday, the Packers edged Fairmont, 5-3 in an important Southern Minnesota League make-up game Tuesday night at Marcusen Park.
> Southpaw Art Huinker (6-7) gave up nine hits in going the distance, but it was two brilliant defensive plays by John Steffen and Bob Folkert's big bat which opened the door to victory.
> Twice Steffen threw out runners at the plate after fielding base hits by Don Saatzer and Jim McNulty, while Folkert's timely single to right field in the eighth scored Ray Rosenbaum and Bob Mathias to snap a 3-3 deadlock.
> It was an uphill fight for the Packers as twice they had to come from behind to win.
> Huinker, who blanked the Martins the first three frames, relinquished two runs off three hits in the fourth, sparked by Ed Pedersen's double, and in the seventh Pedersen singled home losing pitcher Dave Ramnes as the Martins went in front, 3-2.
> Otherwise, the Packer southpaw was tough as he fanned nine and walked only two. He capped the victory by striking out the side in the ninth.

In between several wins, we experienced another slugfest as we lost to the Mason City Braves 10-6. Gary Underhill started the game but lasted only 3 and two-thirds innings. I pitched the final five plus innings but most important were my two hits in two times at the plate. We were still in first place but by only a half-game with a record of 15-11.

Game number 28 for the season was an important come-from-behind, and I do mean come-from-behind, victory at Albert Lea. The victory left us with a one game lead in the standings with two games to go. The score stood 5-1,

Albert Lea's favor, going into the top of the ninth. Four Albert Lea errors in the inning led to seven unearned runs off Albert Lea hurler, Myron Hoffman. Two walks and five hits were included in the inning. The big hit was John Steffen's three-run homer after Austin had tied the score at five.

I worked the entire nine innings, giving up nine hits and walking five while striking out nine. Four of the five Albert Lea runs were earned. And I also had a single in the 7-run ninth. It was my seventh victory against seven losses.

Think of this season now. Our next game was a makeup game against Fairmont at the Martins' park. The date for the game was August 28. The season extended beyond three months. We started on May 22. But the makeup game at Fairmont was a big one. We won the game and the Austin Packers were undisputed champions of the Southern Minny for the 1960 season.

> ### PACKERS WIN 4-1 TO CLINCH PENNANT; HUINKER AND STEFFEN HEROES
> *The Austin Packers wrapped up the 1960 Southern Minnesota League pennant a game early, defeating Fairmont, 4-1, Tuesday night in a make-up game at Martin Park.*
>
> *By beating Fairmont, up until last night, the hottest team in the S-M League, the Packers ran their record to 18-11, out of reach for all rivals and ending what could be considered the tightest race in years.*
>
> *Six hit pitching by lefty Art Huinker and John Steffen's timely home run in the fourth inning sparked the Packers' successful pennant bid.*
>
> *Huinker, working slow and deliberate, lost a shutout when the Martins grabbed a 1-0 lead in the second inning off hits by Milt Nielsen and Herb Banton, with Nielsen scoring on Don Dahlke's grounder to Bob McKay, who made the play on Banton at second.*
>
> *Although at times in trouble, the little southpaw always seemed to come up with the right pitch at the right time. He left two stranded in the third and in the seventh a double play, engineered by McKay, shut the door after Jim McNulty opening with a double.*
>
> *In the eighth and ninth innings, Huinker, who fanned five and walked three, faced only six men.*
>
> *Steffen's big blast, which cleared the left field fence, wrecked a shutout for Harry Wise, who was left with an 8-7 record. The home run, fourth for Steffen and the 17th for the Packers in 29 games, came with Bob Folkert and Ray Rosenbaum aboard. The runs were unearned, however, because of a fielding error on second sacker Eddie Pedersen. The Packers added an insurance run in the sixth when Dick*

*Anderson led off with a single and scored on Rosenbaum's shot
into center field.*

We had won the league championship. For the second year in a row, I
became part of a league champion team in the tough Southern Minnesota league.
The previous year with Rochester everything seemed to be so simple, so easy to
win. It was just the opposite here with Austin's winning the title. Obviously, a
13-1 season on the mound versus a 8-7 record this year, gives some indication of
the difficulties. So many games this year that I pitched were battles where almost
every inning was challenging. Very few times were there three up, three down
routine innings. In the Rochester series, I felt that I had brought my good stuff to
the mound and I was in control. This year, my inner feelings were not that
positive. However, we were champions.

One good feeling related to accomplishing the league pennant for Emil
Scheid, our manager and Southern Minny enthusiast. He deserved that and we
won it for him. For the playoffs, the results were different.

We played at Albert Lea in the final game of the season. Win or lose, we
still were champions. They beat us in a one-run ball game but in the top half of
the eighth I was on first base with one out. A ground ball not hit too hard to the
shortstop told me I had to prevent a double play. In sliding high into the second
baseman, I knocked him on top of me. His knee came down upon my lower back
and it momentarily knocked the wind out of me. Finding it hard to breathe when I
again took the mound in relief, I convinced Manager Scheid that I could still pitch.
We got through the inning but still felt short of breath later. Although the
manager wasn't too happy, I told him I would be getting things checked out at our
local doctor.

Results indicated two vertebrae had been scrunched together from the
blow and that pinched situation resulted in the loss of breath. Because of the
blow, muscles along the spine were now swollen and just made the injury a little
worse. His orders were to stay away from athletic activity for a month or so. End
of season in a tough fashion.

As it turned out, as indicated in the chapter covering the Huinker family's
stay in Ossian and the teaching/coaching at De Sales Central High School, the
following 1961 year would lead to our taking a new teaching and coaching
position at Dyersville. This moved us another 100 miles away from the Southern
Minnesota League. In looking up the history of this league on a computer search,
as mentioned earlier in this chapter, the report indicated that the league folded as a
Level I semi-pro league early in the 1960's. From that it appears that the 1960
season was its final season as a salaried ball club.

What can we say about our four seasons of Southern Minnesota baseball?
First of all, we don't want to itemize the costs of our 30 plus long trips to the
games from Ossian or the baby-sitting costs incurred every year that we played. It

was tough, challenging baseball as indicated by the limited number of strikeouts that I had per game in all of the seasons. I do think back to the first year with Mason City and the frequency of home runs allowed. That changed after coming back from professional baseball played in the second half of the summer of 1957. Again, I am not a great believer in keeping each and every statistic that is available in the game of baseball. But, thinking back on all the research of the three years after the '57 experience, I don't think I gave up more than one or two home runs a season. In each of the three seasons, innings pitched reached at least 140 per season. This league and the professional experience taught me very much about pitching, more than just throwing a good fastball or satisfactory curve ball. If anything had happened, I believe the biggest was the ability to locate the pitch on the edges or just off the edges of the strike zone. Did I do that! Don't I wish! However, that is what a smart pitcher tries to do. Don't ask me for an estimate or a percentage of the time that I was successful. But I do believe that the percentage of hitting the spots successfully had increased.

It is essential that I thank Emil Scheid for the opportunity to pitch in the Southern Minnesota League. I still believe that the success that I had at that level, limited as it may be, convinced the Cardinal organization the opportunity to give professional baseball, and my dream, a chance. That causes lots of question to circulate in my mind, even today. But we make decisions and we live with them. And it does no good to look back and play the "what if" game.

Next, Ann and I appreciate so much the opportunity to meet so many wonderful players and spouses who expanded our picture of the wonderful life we were experiencing. There were too many to mention and the list includes many of the players from opposing teams as well. Today I wonder what has happened to all those people, my teammates and my opposition. That is what makes baseball the game that it is. It isn't about one's strength or one's speed against each other directly that makes the difference. It is what you do with a round ball being hit by a round bat, with time in between to think and no clock to end the game. With the Minnesota experience behind us, I looked forward to the new challenges in the game around the community of Dyersville.

Above all, it all happens with Ann at my side. There is one aspect of all the night trips to Rochester, to Austin, to Mason City, to all the other cities in the Southern Minny that we have not shared. And that is our trips home after the game was over. I don't think we were ever home before midnight. Most games started at eight o'clock in those days. By the time we showered after the games, it was eleven or later by the time we headed out of the parking lots. And, as Ann will confirm, invariably I started out driving. However, now that the stress of the game was over, I tended to relax and suddenly got very sleepy. Time to stop. Time for Ann to take over driving. That probably happened nine of ten times on our late night trips back to Ossian. And I would fall asleep. Oh, what a partner I had . . . and still have.

PLAYING FOR RIVER CITY

The summer of 1961 provided the start of a baseball relationship with a team in a small, southwestern Wisconsin river town named Soldiers Grove, an experience that followed one of the more traumatic experiences of my life earlier that spring, the accidental death of my father. The accident and related events were included in Chapter 22, covering our years with De Sales High School in Ossian.

The spring of 1961 also was the spring that Ann and I made the decision to move to Dyersville, Iowa to teach and coach. Because we would be making a move later in the summer, we packed up our family with four children, ages 6 months to 6 years, and moved out to our home farm to help Mom through her ordeal. It wasn't an easy time for any of us but it helped keep Mom occupied. The noise of the four kids all summer probably wasn't easy for Mom. She never said anything, but we wondered.

During the latter days of June, a car with Wisconsin license plates drove into the farm yard. It turned out to be Dave Iverson, the manager of the above-mentioned Soldiers Grove team. Accompanying Dave was Eli Crogran, a member of the team who played for Luther College against us while I was pitching for Loras. Eli also played for Spillville, Iowa, home of the Inwood Pavilion mentioned earlier. Spillville played in the same summer league with hometown Festina. In fact, one year in the late 50's, Festina picked up Eli to play with them in the AABC tournament.

The two men were interested in my doing some pitching for them and to pitch a game for them against Satchell Paige and his touring team. Most of my playing that summer consisted of driving back and forth to Dyersville which involved mostly playing only in their tournaments. The reimbursement received for pitching for the Wisconsin team proved very satisfactory so the trip to pitch against Satchell Paige was scheduled. The drive from our home farm to "Grove" had to be at least a 90 minute trip across the Mississippi River at Prairie du Chien , Wisconsin and then a winding trail through hilly countryside through villages like Mt. Sterling and Gays Mills, the latter known as the apple capital of southwest Wisconsin.

Soldiers Grove, known as a river town, is located on the Kickapoo River, a small river that has a reputation for frequent, disastrous flooding, so much so, that finally the entire downtown, businesses and homes, were moved to higher ground just south of the original location. It is one of the "greener" towns in the country, with most of the homes and businesses using alternative solar energy systems. The baseball diamond itself no longer exists.

When we arrived at the park, it offered an atmosphere that I had experienced many times at the local diamonds with lights around hometown Festina. The trip required more time than planned. Game time was set for 8:00

and we had barely 30 minutes before the first pitch was to be thrown. Looking around for a familiar face, the manager Dave Iverson, probably pacing nervously wondering if we were really coming, spied us among the cars parked around the ball diamond. I had worn my Dyersville uniform and Dave, although he had a Soldiers Grove suit for me, decided that the one I had on would work for this particular night.

The next thing that happened I will never forget. After again meeting Eli Crogan, and a few of the other players, a player even shorter than I and carrying a catcher's mitt, introduced himself as Dewey Fortney. He was their regular catcher. He looked me over and said, "Let's show this crowd what short guys can do."

This established a quick pitcher-catcher relationship for the game that night. And what a catcher he proved to be. Although small in stature, he handled everything expected of a receiver and then some. Extremely quick, he corralled every pitch, whether in the dirt or high above the batter's head. His arm was strong, and the quickness of his release to the bases was amazing. Later in the season, when we started playing teams that Soldiers Grove had played before, he demonstrated a great knowledge of opposing hitters' strengths and weaknesses.

The game began with Satchell's Paige's barnstormers, the visitors, batting first. The first two batters were retired, although I have no idea how. The third batter, however, slugged a line drive double to right center. As I turned to our shortstop, Mark Dilley, to get the ball and return to the mound, the runner started talking to me, "Hey, Art, don't you remember me, Price West."

I did remember well, once I took a second look and heard his voice. We were teammates at Rochester (he played first base) in 1959. We exchanged greetings and then it was back to the ball game. Today, looking back on the situation, I wish I would have called time out and gone and shook his hand. Fans, and possibly some players, would have puzzled over that action, but Price's friendship an earlier summer was memorable. The young Black American was an intelligent teammate who always looked forward to another game of baseball. We did have a brief opportunity to share some moments after the game.

Price was a good friend but now he was on the other side. After that inning, with some sharing with Dewey, every pitch to Price was upstairs and he was hitless the remainder of the game. Price did score that first inning but that proved to be the only score for the remainder of the game. The final score was 7-1.

The home half of the first inning was no less interesting. The first three batters for Grove, Ron Helgerson, Iverson and Mark Dilley, reached base against Satchell Paige. It is no use to ask how old Satchell was in 1961, but most estimates placed him in at least the fifties. Yet, with no one out, Satchel Paige decided that was enough. Three batters later, none of the next three batters put their bat on the ball, and the inning was over. After one inning, Paige's team led 1-0. "Satch" showed us that he still could pitch. He pitched one more inning, then retired for the night ready for another two innings someplace else the next night.

The game was over. Even I had a couple of hits, including a double, but the one time when Satchell was still pitching in the second inning, I did not touch the ball either. About four or five years later, the actual date not certain, we played against him while pitching for Dyersville. By that time, however, his arm was gone. He literally was playing catch with his catcher. This time, a double off the fence against him was nothing to brag about, though it made me feel quite good.

The pitching performance at Soldiers Grove apparently satisfied their needs because it was the first of several pitching opportunities in tournaments for them, both in 1961 and 1962.

"Grove" had several key players that provided the core strength up the middle making them a baseball team to be reckoned with. This is something that I believe is necessary for all successful baseball teams. In that core of key positions are catcher, pitcher, second base, shortstop and centerfield.

Leading off and playing centerfield was Ron Helgerson. Ron grew up in a tiny town of Mt. Sterling, not far from Soldiers Grove. It has been known for years for its outstanding cheese factory. Ron had good speed, a strong arm and a very quick bat that made him difficult to strike out. And he also was a "fun guy" capable of keeping up the spirits of his teammates. Ron and his wife, Gloria, have gone back and forth between Madison and Dubuque ever since the 1961 and 1962 seasons. Even today, though Ron's life was shortened by cancer, we get together with Gloria and another teammate's wife, Diane Iverson, and play bridge. Diane lost her husband Roger at a very early age. He was Manager Dave Iverson's younger brother.

At shortstop was a premier athlete whose name is well known in baseball and softball circles, Mark Dilley. In 1961, I believe Mark was about 20 years of age. In his freshman year at the University of Wisconsin, he was voted "outstanding freshman of the year" in the strong Big Ten Conference. Mark was the complete ball player, a man who also was an outstanding pitcher for the Grove team.

Manager Dave Iverson played second base and usually batted second in the lineup ahead of Mark Dilley. Another very capable player, solid on defense, who tended to put the ball in play. Dave and his wife, Phyllis, live on a farm just outside of Soldiers Grove, the same farm run by Dave's father. Dave was a baseball fanatic, on a first-name basis with Milwaukee Brewer baseball brass after his retirement. In those later years, a trip to Arizona for spring training included attendance at every one of the Brewer home games.

230

Then there was Dewey Fortney. Defensively, they did not come any better, as stated earlier. A better than average hitter, he also put the ball in play. As was true for so many of the catchers I had the privilege of playing with, I never worried about the catcher handling any pitch I threw. That statement can be taken several ways. The first way, I didn't throw many wild pitches. But if you have been paying attention to many write-ups, I recall too many wild pitches. The second way you could take that statement would be humorous in nature. It was easy for catchers to handle my pitches because there wasn't "that much on any pitch that made it difficult to catch." Readers, you can take it the way you prefer. But in all seriousness, seldom did I have a poor catcher. To have that confidence in your catcher is extremely important for any pitcher.

Then we have to introduce that other player that Grove had- - -Eli Crogran. Eli could easily be listed with the top players in southwest Wisconsin. A versatile athlete, he normally covered third base for this team. After a splendid baseball career at Luther College in Decorah, he followed his career plans and became a high school coach, primarily in basketball and baseball. In 1961, he was coaching at Fennimore High School not too far from Soldiers Grove. Later he became head basketball coach at the University of Wisconsin at Whitewater.

His baseball career took a blow early in the 1961 season. Playing third base for the Grovers, he went to his left to field a ground ball but could not get to it. Shortstop Mark Dilley fielded it behind him and snapped a throw to first, but the throw never arrived at first base. Instead, it struck Eli on the side of the head. I am not privy to the extent of the injury, if he possibly suffered a concussion, but as a result of the blow, Eli experienced double vision.

Imagine trying to hit a baseball coming toward the plate 85 to 90 miles per hour and you see two of them. The first few times Eli attempted to bat after the injury, he failed miserably. Gradually the double vision weakened but for most of the summer it was a struggle every game he played. He was far less effective batting, but he still was an important fixture in the Soldiers Grove lineup.

Other valuable members of the team in the early sixties were Ray Fleming, a reliable outfielder, Shelley Schoville who played both outfield and infield, Roger Piehl, first baseman, Richard Halvorson, first base or outfield coverage and Roger Iverson, brother of manager Dave, who played infield and was always there when his brother switched to shortstop if Mark Dilley was pitching.

Now for one more unusual oddity in my relationship with the Soldiers Grove team. The main reason they came to the Huinker farm for pitching help was the loss of their other top pitcher besides Mark Dilley, Bill Hoffland. A native of Soldiers Grove, Bill was injured in an accident involving either a car or a motorcycle, and was unable to pitch for the remainder of the 1961 season. Without his injury, Soldiers Grove probably would not have needed me.

There is an added footnote to the Bill Hoffland story. While doing research on my year in professional baseball, I perused some 1957 issues of the Sporting News for possible write-ups on my time with the Albany Cardinals. One article, dated August 18, 1957, is included in Chapter 20. Wasting time, I began to look at other minor league write-ups. Lo and behold, there was Bill Hoffland pitching for the Wytheville Cardinals in the Appalachian League while I was at Albany with the Cardinals.

Ann and I thoroughly enjoyed the years that we played with the Soldiers Grove team. It was a team that played hard on the field, but also played hard off the field. They had fun. Married couples went to all the games together and we fit right into that practice.

Later that summer, the call came from Dave Iverson. Soldiers Grove was playing in the La Crosse 12th District National Baseball Congress semi-pro baseball tournament and they needed a pitcher. They had won their first two games behind the pitching of Mark Dilley. But now they needed help in the semi-finals.

This happens in all tournaments. In a sixteen team, single elimination tournament, two games played each night, there is usually sufficient time between games for a team to use the same pitcher for the first two games. Once you reach the final four teams, a team will often play two days in a row. Additional pitching help is needed.

We agreed to a price for my services. And a very fair price for 1957. The game was scheduled to be played in Tomah, Wisconsin, approximately 100 miles from our Festina farm. My brother Kenny and his wife, Aileen, and my mother accompanied us on the trip. We were scheduled to play the first game of the doubleheader.

A brief explanation of this tournament, called the National Baseball Congress Tournament (NBC for short) which is held every summer, is offered. The winner of this district tournament proceeds to Milwaukee County Stadium, home of the then Milwaukee Braves, to compete for the state NBC championship. All state champions travel to Wichita, Kansas to play for a national title.

The entire process is very similar to the American Baseball Congress tournament in which Iowa semi-pro teams play in pursuit of the AABC national title. Which one of the tournaments the teams participate in must be a decision made by semi-pro leaders for the individual state. Why one is chosen over the other, I do not know. Later on in my baseball playing days, the state of Wisconsin had both the NBC and the AABC tournaments going on in their state.

The Soldiers Grove opponent for their semi-final game came from Onalaska, a suburb of the city of La Crosse. As in the case with Satchell Paige's touring team, Onalaska scored in the first, but it was all Soldiers Grove from there on, a lopsided 12-1 victory. An excerpt from the write-up , taken from the La Crosse Tribune, provides the information about the game.

TOMAH, GROVE MAKE FINALS; PLAY SUNDAY
FOR TITLE AT BANGOR PARK
  Tomah white-washed Bangor 3-0 and Soldiers Grove belted Onalaska 12-1 at Tomah Friday night to advance to the finals of the 12th District Semi-Pro baseball tournament.
  Tomah southpaw Mike Sund scattered five hits in pitching his second shutout of the tournament. He struck out seven.
  Art Huinker, former minor league southpaw, had too much stuff for Onalaska and racked up 14 strikeouts in subduing Onalaska.
  Huinker allowed only four hits and gave up one run to the Onalaskans in the first when Earl Johnson walked and Barry Freitag cracked a triple.
  Eli Crogan was the batting star for Soldiers Grove, collecting two singles and batting in five runs. Ron Helgerson and Mark Dilley had two hits apiece for Soldiers Grove with one of Dilley's going for a double. Freitag was the only Onalaska player with more than one hit, adding a single to his triple.

Batting ninth that evening, I had three runs scored, lead-off hitter Ron Helgerson scored four times and Dave Iverson, batting second, scored three times. The Grove team played errorless ball in the triumph.

  Mike Sund, a left-hand pitcher, pitched for Estherville, Iowa in the Southern Minny league in 1959. A good pitcher, he was a prime candidate to be picked up by a team to strengthen their chances of winning a tournament for them.

  After the game, Dave Iverson's father asked me to come with him. He walked behind the men's porta potty and handed me the payment we had agreed upon, in this case, a crisp $100 bill. I don't believe I ever possessed one before.

  This was the highest amount ever received for pitching a baseball game with the exception of the trip Ann and I made from Ossian, Iowa to St. Cloud, Minnesota (two hours north of the Twin Cities) to pitch for Albert Lea in the Minnesota State semi-pro tournament for the large city division in the summer of 1959. This was covered in Chapter 24, the summer when I played for Rochester, Minnesota. The Minnesota tournaments, at this time, were not affiliated with either the American Baseball Congress or the National Baseball Congress. They are solely for Minnesota championships and have divisions similar to what most high schools have created, based on the size of the city the team is from in this case.

The Onalaska game was played on Friday night with the championship game to be played on the following Sunday. The winner goes to Milwaukee for the state tournament. No plans were discussed about my possible return for the championship battle to be played in Bangor, Wisconsin. The next morning, however, the phone rang on the farm where we were staying with Mom. It was Dave Iverson wanting me to come back for the finals. He wanted me to play outfield and possibly be ready for some relief pitching if needed. One day's rest? "Labor negotiations" were completed and Sunday we headed for Bangor.

Meanwhile, we had a curve ball thrown at us on the way home from the Friday night game. With Kenny, Aileen and my Mom with us, we were looking for a place to get some food. It is now after ten o'clock. Driving through the town of Sparta, Wisconsin, and very slowly because we are keeping all eyes open for restaurant, I ran a red light. Then there were "red lights," this time behind us. A ticket, and $30 later, we were once again on our way. Still no food.

The city policeman who issued the ticket treated us very harshly. He kept talking about a bad accident that had just happened outside of Sparta with serious injuries, and he was emotionally upset. He placed us in the same category as the careless speeding that had caused the previous accident. It wasn't a pretty scene. At the same time, maybe his disposition was understandable.

On Saturday, Kenny needed some assistance putting in a line of field tile on his farm. In those days, all the digging and placing of individual tile were done by hand. Our next door neighbor, and valuable friend of my father, Andy Hemesath, was also helping. The conversation shifted to the ball game of the night before. When he heard the $100 figure for my reimbursement, he laughed, looked at me and said, "That's darn good, Art, for playing a baseball game." He himself loved the game.

Sunday night came and we again were playing baseball for Soldiers Gove. A win would give the team the opportunity to advance to Milwaukee County Stadium for the state tournament. This game proved anything but lopsided.

Grove jumped out to a four-run lead in the first, Tomah tied it at 5-all in the third; we went ahead by two going into the bottom of the ninth but Tomah tied in their half of the ninth at 7-all. Grove went ahead again the top of the tenth, and in the bottom of the tenth, Tomah went out 1-2-3 and it was "Milwaukee, here we come."

The game held many highlights as you will see when you read the accompanying newspaper coverage, again from the La Crosse Tribune. Playing left field lasted only two and one-third innings. Mark Dilley did not have his usual good stuff and left with one out in the third. My stuff proved sufficient, despite pitching seven plus innings on one day's rest. Interestingly, opposing relief pitcher Mike Sund had pitched a seven inning shutout on Friday for Tomah and pitched eight and two-thirds innings in this game.

> *GROVE WINS CROWN 8-7; ART HUINKER KEY PLAYER IN TRIUMPH*
>
> *By Jim Gunderson - - - La Crosse Tribune Sports Writer*

Art Huinker, Ron Helgerson and Mark Dilley were heroes for Soldiers Grove Sunday in the history-making 13th annual 12th District semi-pro baseball tournament.

Grove edged Tomah 8-7 before 800 fans in a game that was decided in the 10th inning. It marked the first time that the championship contest had gone into extra frames.

Huinker was the big difference. The former Loras College pitching sensation relieved Mark Dilley when the little Grove star got into serious trouble in the third inning. Huinker also clouted two home runs.

Grove won the title in 1956. Black River Falls, the defending champion from 1960, lost to Grove earlier in the tournament 6-5.

In the consolation game, fast-balling righthander Lee Paul fanned 17 batters as Bangor whipped Onalaska 8-3. Paul Daffinson hit a three-run pinch-hit homer for Bangor in the eighth.

Losing hurler Dick Ghelfi homered for Onalaska.

Huinker, selected the tourney's most valuable player, had to wait until the 10th inning to have the victory pocketed.

Shelly Schoville grounded out to open Grove's 10th inning bid. Helgerson doubled to right center but Dave Iverson fanned.

With two out, Dilley singled to score Helgerson with the winning run. Eli Crogran fanned for the third out.

Huinker struck out Ken Fortsythe, batting for losing southpaw Mike Sund, and Gary Grovesteen. He then got Dan Frey on a grounder back to the mound to end the game.

Grove wasted no time getting to Sheldon Rusch in the first inning, but he was the victim of some very loose infield play by his Tomah mates.

Crogan hit a two-run single scoring Helgerson and Dave Iverson and Huinker blasted a two-run homer over the right field fence.

Tomah scored two runs in the bottom half of the first as Fred Pongratz and Don Peth, both former La Crosse State College stars, hit singles. Tom Carlson walked and Jack Graf was safe on an error.

Grove added its fifth run in the second on two errors and Dave Iverson's single.

Dilley had no trouble with Tomah in the second inning, but he ran into a mess of it in the third when the Monroe County team scored three times.

After a walk to Carlson and an error, Peth stroked a towering homer over the left centerfield to tie the count at 5-5.

Huinker came in from left field to relieve Dilley, who was the most valuable baseball player at the University of Wisconsin this year. Dilley went to shortstop. Huinker struck out Rusch and Gary Grovesteen to end the threat.

Neither team scored in the next four innings as Huinker and Sund, who replaced Rusch in the second, settled down to a pitching battle.

Grove regained the lead in the eighth on Duane Fortney's homer and added another in the ninth on Huinker's second homer of the night.

Tomah tied the game at 7-7 in the bottom of the ninth. Frey singled, but was forced on second before Pongratz reached first on the fielder's choice. An error allowed Pongratz to reach second, and he later scored as Dar Date and Carlson singled.

Peth who had 11 hits in 15 trips to the plate for a .733 batting average and 12 RBIs was named the batting champion; Sund, best pitcher and Dick Gunderson, Melrose, best pro prospect.

Art Huinker pitched to La Crosse Aquinas High graduate Bill Leonard in his first college game at Loras . . . Leonard homered for a 4-3 win . . .Huinker won 19 college games without a defeat and now is coaching at Dyersville, Iowa . . . He played in the Sally League.

Don Peth got four hits in four trips for Tomah and observers agreed that Grove made a smart move when he was intentionally walked in the ninth with the potential winning run on third.

First, my two home runs. Never before and never again did this happen. The first home run with a base runner on in the first was a gift. The Bangor diamond had a scary right field fence, at least for a pitcher. It had to be no more than 250 feet down the right field four line, 275 to right center. My first "shot" was a routine fly ball to right center, but it cleared the short monster and we had a four-run lead.

The second home run of the game was legitimate. This cleared the left center field fence, a distance I estimate to be about three hundred seventy feet. The two home run night was really more memorable than most of the pitching

236

performances I experienced. That is because this is the only time something like this ever happened.

The last half of the 9th inning remains quite vivid in my recall process. We had taken a two-run lead in the top half of the ninth. But Tomah fought back to score one run and had a runner on second. Another single scored the runner from second and a mistaken throw to the plate allowed the tying run to reach second. Coming up was first baseman Don Peth who already had a four-for-four night including a home run. Manager Iverson came to the mound and without much conversation, we both concluded that we should walk him. The next batter hit a weak ground ball back to the mound for the third out.

As mentioned in the write-up, Peth was 11 for 15 in the tournament. His son, Dick, played basketball at Iowa a few years back.

Another unusual statistic on the line score of the game were the nine errors by the two teams, five by Soldiers Grove.

From a fan standpoint, this game had to be a very interesting game to watch. It was a bit nerve-wracking for a pitcher because of the short right field fence. The distance wasn't much deeper than a girls' softball diamond fence which is supposed to be 225 feet. By this time in my career, throwing many pitches on the outside part of the plate to right hand batters became a frequent pitch for me, trying to induce ground balls. At the same time it can sometimes lead to fly balls to right field. Many more pitches were directed to the inside of the plate than normal in this particular game. Please don't get the feeling that every pitch went where I wanted. Twelve Bangor batters struck out during my seven plus innings and some of them may have been due to the effort to pitch inside. Off to Milwaukee County Stadium.

237

FIFTEEN INNINGS

Luckily for the Huinkers the two tournaments played with Soldiers Grove took place between tournaments Dyersville participated in and no Dyersville games were missed. They also occurred before school started. Later years saw conflicts occur.

Our opening opponent at Milwaukee County Stadium, home of the Braves, was Milwaukee Borgwardt, out of one of the Milwaukee city leagues. And what a game it was. Whatever the planned time schedule for the four-day tournament, the schedule changed after the 4 – 1, 15-inning victory by Grove. A short write-up follows.

But first, we must take a look at the unbelievable drama in the bottom of the ninth. Grove was the visiting team and went into the bottom of the ninth tied at one. How the runners for Borgwardt gained the bases, I don't know, but suddenly Borgwardt had the bases loaded and no one out. A myriad of ways for them to score and the game is over.

We have all heard the expression, "I'd rather be lucky than good." Well, maybe that happened in this situation. With the bases full, the next batter hit a one-bouncer back to me on the mound. A quick throw to home for a force out, than catcher Fortney's quick relay to first and we had a double play. Now two were out and runners on second and third. The next batter popped out on the infield and we were out of the inning.

Six innings later, three walks issued by Borgwardt pitchers and a triple to the fence in left center and Soldiers Grove had a 4 – 1 lead. Nothing exciting that I recall happened in the bottom half of the 15th and we were moving to the second round of the 16-team tourney.

> *15-INNING BATTLE SPICES TOURNEY*
> *Milwaukee area entries grabbed two of the first three decisions, but a 15-inning marathon stole the spotlight as the Wisconsin State Baseball Tourney opened Sunday at the Stadium.*
> *Soldiers Grove clipped Borgwardt Poultry, a Langsdorf performer, 4-1, in the extra –inning thriller, with Art Huinker going the distance for the winners.*
> *Mark Dilley ended the drawn out affair when he tripled with the bases loaded - - -his lone hit in six official times at bat. His blast to left-center scored Dick Halverson, Huinker and Ron Helgerson, all on base via walks.*
> *Huinker scattered eight hits in going the route, fanning eight and walking only four.*

238

The Borgwardts tallied in the third with the help of an
error, which followed a walk, with Don Lewison's sacrifice fly
breaking the scoreless deadlock.
   Soldiers Grove knotted the count in the sixth,
Halverson's single plating Dilley, who had walked.
   John Mihalko, one of four Borgwardt hurlers, was
tagged with the loss, although he yielded only two safe blows in
seven innings.

People often ask how many pitches I threw over those 15 innings.
Estimating only, probably 170 to 180. We didn't count pitches in those days. A
picture in the Milwaukee Journal the next day accentuates the idea that my arm
had to be tired. The picture is found in the picture section of the book. It is
certainly possible that the arm was tired but I really never concerned myself with
it. As long as we were getting them out, everything was okay. I don't believe I
ever thought about coming out.

It was a thrill to play on the major league diamond. The pitcher's mound
was so smooth and I felt like I could really push off on the follow-through. The
mound seemed higher than typical town-team diamonds. That helped make me a
little taller.

There was a bigger moment that occurred for me during the game.
Collecting one of the 13 Soldiers Grove hits, I hit a line-shot that landed between
the left and center fielders and went all the way to the wall for a double. In
Milwaukee County Stadium no less. "I can see it clearly now." Forget that
remark.

Another little sidelight to the games of that first day. Benton, Wisconsin
lost in the opening round but their right fielder was Jim Timmons, my nemesis
from the Platteville Pioneers team during my Loras days. Also on the team was
Jim Nedelcoff who later became a very successful basketball coach for the
Southwestern Wildcats, located in Hazel Green, Wisconsin. How great it has
been for me, in pursuing the various write-ups of games, to encounter the many
players who have become so much a part of my later life.

The next game for Soldiers Grove became a victim of an all-day shower
in the Milwaukee area. It reminded me a little of the Battle Creek, Michigan all-
day rain back in 1952 when I was a member of the Sumner Cubs baseball team.
This time Ann was with me to help answer the question, "What does a baseball
team do all day when they can't play baseball, while far away from home?"

The answer came quickly this day. A new musical called "Music Man"
had just hit the silver screen. Although its theme was about River City, USA, it
identified itself with Mason City, Iowa where we had spent two summers playing
baseball. However, we came to find out that Soldiers Grove was often identified
as a "river city," because of the frequency of flooding by the Kickapoo River.

239

The Grove baseball players embarrassed themselves in the movie theatre that day. Every time the expression, "River City" was included in the script, a big river city yell erupted from the players. It was obvious that they were proud of the little town they represented.

Beyond the movie, many baseball stories were exchanged in rooms back at the hotel or wherever we congregated. It never ceases to amaze me, the particulars that are remembered of so many game situations played years ago. This is true for most of us. For example, my attempt to steal home in my second year playing with Festina, a failed attempt by the way. Or the pitch I threw so-and-so back when. Or how we would pitch certain hitters. Dick Wertzberger, a great Dubuquer, comes to mind, even though we met only once or twice on the diamond. Keep the pitch inside.

Talk to any baseball player. He will tell you that we also have favorite success stories to tell. Many of those long-ago accomplishments become embellished over time. Perhaps that is due to the frequency of the re-telling to the extent that we actually believe it was that way. Or is it sometimes even trying to one-up the previous story being told? Or was it the refreshments we imbibed in at the time of the story telling? The rainy day in Milwaukee was one of those days.

The next day brought sunshine and a chance to play our second round game. Our opponent was another Milwaukee team, the Milwaukee Highway Beers. The game showed great promise with a favorable 2-0 score for us, but that changed abruptly in the sixth inning for our opponents. They scored four runs and carried it to the end for a 4-2 victory, knocking Grove out of the tournament. Lee Paul, another Loras College opponent from Winona State Teachers College, pitched a strong game. The short write-up follows from the La Crosse Tribune.

> *SOLDIERS GROVE STOPPED IN STATE*
> *TOURNAMENT, 4-2*
> > *Milwaukee Highway Beer beat Soldiers Grove on the four-hit pitching of Dave Tymus, coupled with a sixth inning outburst that produced all of the Highway runs. Five hits, a sacrifice, an error and a double steal produced the tallies.*
> > *Bangor Coach Lee Paul had a no-hitter going until the sixth for Grove. Mark Dilley had a triple and single for two of Grove's four hits. Dewey Fortney and Dick Halverson each singled.*
> > *Paul fanned two and walked three while giving up eight hits.*

No hits for me to help the cause. I did throw a runner out at home trying to score from third after I caught a fly ball in left field. At least some contribution but not enough.

240

Soldiers Grove's trip to the state tournament and aspirations for a further trip to Wichita, Kansas ended with the loss. But could there be another year? In the meantime, victorious Highway Beer went on to win the tournament and advance to the national championship.

For Ann and me, the Soldiers Grove experience was another positive memory. It makes sense here to say that Grove was a team that enjoyed playing baseball. It was also a team that had a players wives' group that enjoyed the game of baseball and all the opportunities to get together that went with it. And this time it was a great and successful feeling to play on the diamond in Milwaukee County Stadium.

TO MILWAUKEE AGAIN

We have completed our first year of teaching at Xavier High School and coaching the Xavier Cardinals baseball team. Is that the reason we moved from De Sales to Xavier High School, because they are nicknamed the Cardinals? Not really, but I did like the nickname. Ann was busy trying to keep up with four little ones besides her biggest challenge of keeping up with her husband. Our oldest, Terry, completed Kindergarten successfully and becomes a first grader at Xavier Elementary in the fall.

Summer baseball in 1962 consisted primarily of playing with the now hometown Dyersville Whitehawks again. But, as in the summer of 1961, Soldiers Grove came calling. Again it was pitching help especially. The tournament was going to be the 12th District NBC tournament. Sixteen teams were participating in the single-elimination affair, which meant that for a team to win the championship, four wins were required. Financial arrangements were finalized but now we were driving from Dyersville rather than Festina, a somewhat longer trip than last year.

For this tournament, I pitched the first game and the semi finals. Mark Dilley pitched the second round game and the finals. In game 1, we defeated La Farge 10-1, the only run being unearned. In game 2, Dilley blanked Onalaska, 3-0. In game 3, the semi finals, we shut out Black River Falls 8-0, and in the championship, Soldiers Grove won the championship over Bangor, 3-0. Write-ups are provided only for the semi finals and finals.

BANGOR, GROVE REACH SEMI-PRO FINALS
By Bill Parizek, La Crosse Tribune Correspondent
Bangor squeaked past Tomah 4-3 and Soldiers Grove blanked Black River Falls 8-0 Friday night to gain the finals of the 14th annual La Crosse 12th District semi-pro tournament.
Grove's defending champions rose to victory behind the southpaw slants of Art Huinker who won his second tourney game in even more sensational fashion than the first. Against BRF, Huinker hurled a one-hitter and fanned 13 for a two game, 16-inning record of one unearned run, three hits, no walks and 27 strikeouts.
Grove got to southpaw Dan Mills, hero of the 1960 championship team when he pitched four wins, for an opening tally on two walks, a sacrifice and infield out.
Eli Crogan's single drove in the second run in the fourth and his homer accounted for two more in the sixth. Grove added three in the eighth and one in the ninth. Five of Grove's nine hits went for extra bases, including two doubles by Ron Helgerson, a triple by Ray Fleming and a double by John Solheim. Helgerson had three hits.

242

Huinker set down the first 20 batters to face him before
Tom Hayden reached first on an error with two out in the
seventh. Catcher Dewey Fortney then picked Hayden off first
with a rifle throw.

With one out in the eighth, BRF shortstop Ev Larkin
singled to ruin Huinker's no-hit bid. A doubleplay, Huinker to
Dave Iverson to Roger Piehl retired the side.

TOURNEY NOTES: A double play and a pickoff
enabled Grove hurler Art Huinker to face the minimum 27
batters although giving up one hit and having one error behind
him.

Not many highlights that can be recalled. One for five at the plate for me but it did drive across two runs.

The semi-final game was again played at Tomah, similar to last season. Friends of ours from Dyersville, Mary Ellen and Don Lakeman, travelled with us to the game. Not familiar with the roads and by-ways of southwest Wisconsin coming from Dyersville, we studied the Wisconsin map and decided the shortest route, once past Soldiers Grove, was through the town of La Farge. They were our opponents earlier in the tournament. It was not a wise choice. Players left Grove a good 10-15 minutes after we went through Grove and arrived at the game ahead of us.

With several large rivers winding through southwest Wisconsin, the terrain becomes extremely hilly. The "shortcut" we took curved so frequently that we seriously thought we made 360 degree circles around some of the major hills. Thirty miles an hour became a common speed. Teammates got a humorous charge out of our scenic drive.

The tournament finals again were held in Bangor, with the short right field fence. This time the game did not carry the emotional excitement of the 1961 championship game but the outcome was the same, another trip to Milwaukee for Soldiers Grove.

GROVE CHAMPS AGAIN, CLIPS BANGOR 3-0;
DILLEY HURLS FINAL VICTORY
By Jim Gunderson, La Crosse Tribune Sports Writer
Another magnificent pitching performance helped
Soldiers Grove earn its second straight 12th District semi-pro
tournament championship here Sunday night before close to
1,000 fans.

Righthander Mark Dilley, who won most valuable
player honors in the tourney, hurled Soldiers Grove past
Bangor 3-0. He also homered in the sixth inning with no one
on.

*Dilley had blanked Onalaska earlier 8-0 while
teammate Art Huinker hurled the other two Grove tourney
victories - - - a 10-1 decision from La Farge in which the only
run was unearned and a one-hit, 8-0 victory over Black River
Falls.*

*In four games, Grove hurlers allowed no earned runs. Huinker
was named the tournament's best hurler and Grove's Ron
Helgerson won the batting championship.*

*The championship set a precedent for Manager Dave
Iverson. It was the first time in 12th district tourney history that
a manager has won more than two crowns (Grove won in 1956,
1961 and 1962 under Iverson).*

*Iverson firmed up his team defensively by putting
center fielder Helgerson at second base, Dan Rabata at third
and Huinker in center. Rabata and Huinker are pitchers also.*

*Dilley and Huinker combined in a four-game showing
that is unmatched in tournament history - - - perhaps unmatched
by any two pitchers in Wisconsin semi-pro tourney ranks.
Dilley struck out 25 batters and walked five, giving up nine hits
in 16 innings, no runs scored for a 2-0 record. Dilley fanned 10
and walked three Sunday.*

*Huinker struck out 27 batters and walked none, gave
up three hits in 16 innings, one unearned run scored for a 2-0
record.*

*Helgerson, the tourney batting champion, hit three
singles, two doubles and a triple for a .462 average. He walked
five times and fanned once.*

We were again off for Milwaukee and a shot at the state championship
again. The losing pitcher in the championship game for Bangor, Lee Paul, was
picked up by Grove to add another strong arm to our pitching staff. As mentioned
earlier, he coached at Bangor at the time.

An interesting clip was found in the La Crosse Tribune while working
with the above write-up for the championship. The professional Northern League
was covered and in it was the name of Chase Riddle who managed the Cardinals'
Winnipeg team. Chase was my manager at Albany, Georgia, five years previous.

Also, in that 1962 season, a conflict did occur between the schedule of
the Soldiers Gove district tourney and the Dyersville Whitehawks playing an early
round game in the Worthington tourney. Dyersville won their game easily and
moved on to the next game. With Grove's win, it was once again on to
Milwaukee County Stadium again.

MVP IN MILWAUKEE, AGAIN

The state tournament scheduled for Milwaukee County Stadium experienced rain delays of the opening round. Scheduled to play at noon on Saturday, July 27, Soldiers Grove sat through a three-hour rain delay before the first scheduled game could start. As a result, Grove's first game began about 3:45.

Entering the Milwaukee County Stadium that day, the Grove team, now with time on their hands, spent time perusing a huge National Baseball Congress display in the main concourse entering the stadium. One of the displays listed previous championship teams, managers' names, most valuable player awards, etc. One of our team members became excited and rushed over to Manager Iverson, his wife, and Ann and me with something to read. It listed Art Huinker as the most valuable player of the state tournament for the previous year. Nobody, including myself, knew anything about the award. If that trophy was anything like the MVP trophy for the current tournament, it was huge.

Manager Iverson was equally mystified by the news. "We will follow up on that award," Dave said, "and find out what really did happen." Because we dropped out of the chase for the championship in the second round the previous year, none of us were around for the final night's awarding of trophies. But why hadn't they notified Dave?

It wasn't long before we had our answer. The head of the tournament both years was present. When asked about the previous year's awarding, he recalled someone coming out of the stands to accept the trophy for me. Apparently, someone has an MVP prize that they did not win. The NBC informed our manager that they would have a replica of the previous year's trophy made and have it before the current tourney was over. Would we still be around?

After the 15-inning opening round victory the previous year, then a second-round loss, we were out to better that performance this year. Playing in a slow rain throughout the game, our contest with Menasha, Wisconsin again went into extra innings. The game found me struggling to find any rhythm, any consistency of pitch location, and by the ninth inning, disaster was looming. Manager Iverson had Lee Paul warming up in the bullpen and finally brought him in. But he sent me out to left field, keeping me in the lineup.

How the following innings specifically took place, I truly can't recall. But what happened is a rarity in baseball. When a left-hand batter came to the plate, Dave would call me in to pitch. If the next batter was right-handed, Lee Paul, who went to left field when I came in, would come back in to pitch.

Finally, the umpires, knowing they were already three hours late because of the morning rain delay, and quite concerned about the time taken for the repeated pitching swaps, told our manager that every time he would make this type of change back and forth, there would be no warm-up pitches allowed. Dave accepted their request. Lee and I hustled as much as we could coming in from left field to not get the umpiring crew too upset, hoping it hadn't happened already.

The strategy worked. Grove had tied the score with two runs in the bottom half of the eighth. Then with the bases loaded in the bottom of the 11th, first baseman Roger Piehl was hit by a pitch to bring in the winning run. Both Lee Paul and I always played outfield when we didn't pitch, so Dave's managerial strategy didn't weaken the team defensively or offensively. But a walk-off hit by pitch is a painful way to win the ball game.

> ### GROVE WINS IN 11 INNINGS
> *Soldiers Grove scored a run in the bottom of the 11th inning Saturday to defeat Menasha, 6-5, in the Wisconsin semi-pro baseball tournament at Milwaukee County Stadium.*
> *The victory went to Art Huinker, who came on in relief in the 10th inning. The loser was Earl Furlow, who gave up the winning run. He came on in relief in the 11th. Mark Dilley singled for Soldiers Grove in the bottom of the 11th. He went to second on a sacrifice. Eli Crogan walked, Ray Fleming was hit by a pitched ball to fill the bases. Furlow then hit Roger Piehl to force in the winning run.*

I walked six batters in the game, not a good outing, even though I had 13 strikeouts. Lee Paul added one strikeout and walked two. The paper stated that I received credit for the win. That must imply I finished the top half of the eleventh on the mound. Ron Helgerson and I each had two hits in the lengthy contest while Iverson, Dilley and Shelley Schoville had one apiece.

The weather continued to raise havoc with the schedule of games and consequently the next Grove game was played on Monday, instead of Sunday. Soldiers Grove gained a step further than a year ago by defeating Waukesha, Wisconsin, 5-2 to advance to the final four. Mark Dilley allowed nine hits but proved tough in the clutch by giving Waukesha only two runs, both scored in the fifth inning. By that time, Grove had a four-run lead, even though collecting only six hits. Two of their six hits were garnered off my bat while Helgerson, Dilley, Crogan and John Solheim had a hit apiece.

The write-up for the Waukesha victory and the next game against Monona Grove, a suburb of Madison, were part of a bigger write-up in the La Crosse Tribune covering all the games of the state tourney. Because they covered many games of very little interest to the readers of this book, only important points are included.

The second semi-final game, originally scheduled for a routine night game, proved to be a game that started at midnight, ending at 1:45 in the morning. The opposition team, Monona Grove, was very familiar to the Grove players, having played against each other before. In a very exciting game, Grove proved the eventual winner, 5-3. The game ended after six innings, called because of a curfew rule in effect.

Lee Paul started pitching for Grove and was given a two-run lead in the bottom of the first. After Monona Grove scored a single run in the top half of the third, Grove responded with a three-run burst in the third. A pair of walks, a wild pitch and Eli Crogan's single produced two runs and Crogan scored on Dewey Fortney's single.

Monona Grove came back with two runs of their own in the top of the fourth, causing Manager Iverson to call to left field and I came in to pitch with runners on at first and third and one out. My memory does not fail me here and I can recall very specific moments, even pitches to get out of the inherited jam.

The first batter up for Monona Grove was Les Richter, star football pass receiver for the University of Wisconsin, and later its athletic director. He also played baseball at the University of Wisconsin. Before I threw a pitch, Dewey Fortney strolled slowly to the mound and shared his thoughts. "Richter has a hard time laying off high fastballs, Art, so let's go up the ladder on him." This expression means that you try to throw the first fastball at the letters and hope he will swing. Then each of the next two strikes are each a little bit higher, hoping the batter will continue to go after them. In this case, the strategy worked to perfection. Three high fastballs, all swinging strikes, and we had the second out. The next batter grounded out weakly to short and we were out of the inning.

As limited as the movement on my fastball was on Saturday, now, two days later, it had good movement and velocity. Six batters later, all outs, in the fifth and sixth and the curfew set in. Soldiers Grove was in the finals.

In the wild celebrating that followed, Roger Piehl, excitable first baseman, grabbed both my arms in the muscle area above the elbow and lifted me off the ground. Maybe sounds wonderful but truthfully, after coming back from an extended pitching outing two days previous, those muscles were so sore that I just left out a big scream and he dropped me like a lead balloon.

Celebrating is wonderful. And that we did after the semi-final victory. There was one problem. By the time the celebrating was over and we all had gone out to get a bite to eat, we finally found our beds around 4:00 in the morning. We had to play the championship just fifteen hours later.

Was it a lack of sleep? Was Milwaukee Falk that good? Those are questions a person wonders about after playing some good teams while winning our way into the championship. Admittedly, we probably were fatigued. But the emotional drive that one experiences when playing a game of this significance usually can overcome fatigue.

247

Because all the active pitchers on the team were heavily used, Manager Iverson called my brother, Kenny, to come to Milwaukee to start the championship game. Kenny is an equally good pitcher to what was on staff and I felt we had good expectations about the outcome. But it wasn't to be. We got off to a bad start in the first inning. The first batter reached base for Falk. The next batter bunted but pushed it hard to the pitcher's mound where Kenny grabbed it and turned to throw to second for a force out. His foot went out from underneath him when he hit an overly wet spot on the mound and was unable to make any throw. When the inning was over, Falk had scored two runs.

When the disaster had run its course, with Grove committing seven errors, Soldiers Grove and its dream of playing baseball in the national championship at Wichita, Kansas, was doomed. Following is an excerpt of the game as it appeared in the La Crosse Tribune the next day.

> *MILWAUKEE FALK WALLOPS SOLDIERS GROVE NINE, 15-1*
> *Milwaukee Falk was packing again today for another trip to Wichita, Kansas, and the National Semi-pro Baseball Tournament.*
> *The Milwaukee combination won its 7th Wisconsin title Monday night by going on a batting spree to smash Soldiers Grove, 15-1.*
> *Soldiers Grove was held to three hits by Carl Basco who fanned 10 and walked four in the seven inning game. Basco was named the tournament's most valuable pitcher.*
> *Soldiers Grove's hurler, Art Huinker, playing in left field Monday night, was named the tournament's most valuable player for the second straight year.*

The MVP trophies are good to look at, but they don't replace the fact that we did not get to go to Wichita. The tournament was something special in the city of Wichita. They even had a button for umpires to step on that would blow air around the plate to clean it off. Modern conveniences way back in the early 1960's.

For the next two years, Soldiers Grove tried, as a team, to reach the state tournament. In 1963, two key players were missing. Mark Dilley adjusted his career choices and was unavailable to play in the district tournament. And Dewey Fortney reported for military duty. Two key cogs of the team were missing. I found out how difficult it is to pitch when you have a catcher who is unable to handle the basic duties of a catcher, to catch the ball. Without Dewey, a high school catcher took his place, and though he tried so hard, pitch after pitch got by him. Needless to say, we did not win the game. Then, shortly after that, the tournament was moved out of Milwaukee County Stadium and brought to Madison. It didn't provide the same thrill.

248

The 1961 and 1962 experiences left wonderful memories for both Ann and me. Since that time manager Dave Iverson has gone to his eternal rest. We got together periodically with his wife, Phyllis, who comes to Dubuque to get assistance in handling the family matters she faces now with Dave gone. Ron Helgerson's wife, Gloria, goes to Arizona to be with her daughter who is a teacher in the Phoenix school system. If Ann and I are in Arizona, we will always get together. They were an enjoyable group of players and wives for us to be with.

Another chapter in our life together is over but definitely not forgotten. We saw some of the Grove players when they came to play for Rickardsville, especially in 1965, against the Whitehawks and others.

OUR SECOND HOME TEAM

The fall of 1961 would bring the Huinker family, now consisting of two boys and two girls plus Mom and Dad, to Dyersville and Xavier High School. This also meant that the summer would be spent playing baseball for the Dyersville Whitehawks, primarily during the big tournament season that took place every summer in Dubuque County. It also meant that we were going to put considerable mileage on our car, now a four-year old 1957 Chevrolet Fleetline with the big fins. The summer was spent on my home farm living with my mother after our father had been killed in the tractor accident spoken of earlier in the spring. The trip from Festina to Dyersville occurred quite often that summer until we finally made the move to Dyersville on August 15. In fact, on one of those baseball trips, Ann went house-hunting and found our home that we would rent for the next two and a half years. Located at 710 5th Avenue SE, it actually was located about four blocks from the ball park.

As was the case in 1956 when we travelled to Ryan in a regular season game just to get acquainted with our new team, this spring we decided to drive to Sherrill, Iowa for an early season encounter for the Dyersville Whitehawks with the players from Sherrill. It so happened that it was the first time in many years that Sherrill was putting a team together. We were undecided about making the trip when my brother, Linus, offered to make the drive because he and Lory had just purchased a new car.

None of us making the trip to Sherrill were very familiar with the best way to get to the town. Looking at the map, we could see that following Highway 52 all the way to Sageville, then drive back north the few short miles to the town was probably the sure way. But further investigation led us to follow a road that took us along the Mississippi River. We turned off Highway 52 at the town of Millville, followed that to a town we had never heard of before called Turkey River Town, then on to North Buena Vista, next to Balltown which finally brought us into Sherrill from the north. Today, it is part of the "Great River Road" that people take for a scenic tour of the Mississippi. Suffice to say, it turned out to be a huge mistake, one that took longer than if we had stayed on Highway 52. We arrived at the game late. It has a very familiar ring to the trip we take about a year later to get to Tomah, Wisconsin.

The game itself was an extremely lopsided affair, went on much longer than we had planned, and we were forced to leave the game early because of a Sunday evening commitment we will share later. In fact, when we left the game, Dyersville had to play the remainder of the game with only eight players. Every time my position in the batting order came up, it was an automatic out. To share only one example of the lopsidedness of the outcome, starting pitcher Roy Willenbring had seven hits in 10 at-bats. The first year was tough for Sherrill but after a few years of frequent losses, they became a team that gave area teams good battles.

Now for the later commitment. Several months earlier, my nephew, Don Kuennen, who coached basketball and baseball at Cresco Notre Dame High School, asked me if I would speak at their annual athletic banquet. It was the first Sunday evening in May, the same day as the Sherrill game. The exact time is not remembered, but by the time we returned to Ossian to shower and dress for the occasion, there was little time to waste. About that time, my Mom and Dad stopped at the house and basically, I said "hello" and "goodbye" in almost the same breath. It turned out to be the last time I would see my Dad alive. The following afternoon his life abruptly ended with the tragic tractor accident spoken of earlier. That has haunted me often throughout my life. This is again a sad example of trying to live our life faster than we should; trying to do way too many things without realizing the consequences.The baseball game was won; the evening banquet and presentation were enjoyed. But that doesn't override my memories.

Just a sideline thought of speaking at banquets such as the athletic banquet described above. Ann knows full well that I do like to eat, especially when you go to a banquet where it is basically a pot luck. So many good cooks, most of them the mothers of the athletes being honored at the banquet, bring their favorite dish, whether it be salad or vegetable or dessert to serve. It makes me want to take at least a taste from all the many wonderful-looking dishes to choose from. End result is eating too much and then I am supposed to entertain the audience with a speech after that. Not the ideal way.

About a month after the Sherrill game, the Whitehawks played at Guttenberg. It was a shorter trip than the Sherrill shortcut and was a Maquoketa Valley league game. Guttenberg was considered one of the league favorites along with Dyersville but my stuff was good that afternoon, giving up three hits and striking out 18 in an 8-1 victory. The two teams met twice again in the three tournaments that both teams were to play in. This is one of the few non-tournament games we played in that summer. But we were there for every one of the games in the three tournaments at Worthington, Cascade and Dyersville respectively.

Between these three tournaments, we were engaged in the NBC tournament with Soldiers Grove, covered in chapters 26-27.

The Worthington tournament started the second week of July, a sixteen-team, single elimination tournament spread over eight nights covering the next two weeks, barring weather cancellations. In the opening round, our opponent was, ironically, Guttenberg. Again, we defeated them by a score of 7-1, this time Guttenberg garnered four hits against my pitching.

In our second game, our opponents were the players representing Hopkinton. Four runs in the first inning, capped by a bases-loaded double by right-fielder Rollie Sampson gave the Whitehawks a big jump. Pitcher Roy

Willenbring helped his own cause with a bases-loaded triple in the second inning and the outcome was established.

In the first game that night, Balltown blasted Bernard behind the no-hit pitching of Al Eggers, a Bellevue native and star pitcher for the Loras Duhawks. He has been very deservedly inducted into the Loras College Athletic Hall of Fame. That made Balltown our opposition in the upcoming semi-final round at Worthington.

In that game, Balltown again turned to Loras College and John Willenborg, another successful pitcher for the Duhawks. John only allowed four hits but five walks and three errors behind him led to seven Whitehawks runs. My brother, Ken, was starting pitcher, later relieved by Roy Willenbring, and I came in to finish the game in the seventh. Dan Sullivan, familiar East Dubuque star player, had a home run for Balltown and Catcher Bob Meyer had two hits and two walks. Cascade won the other semi-final game and once again the two powers paired off in the Worthington championship.

HAWKS WIN AT WORTHINGTON; TRIM CASCADE IN FINALS 5-2

Steady relief work by Art Huinker snuffed out a Cascade Reds threat in the 7th inning to let the Dyersville Whitehawks cop first place honors in the Worthington Baseball Tournament Tuesday night. The Hawks scored runs in the 3rd, 4th, 5th, 7th and 8th innings to get the 5-2 win over Cascade.

Ken Huinker started on the mound for the Whitehawks and held the Reds in check until the 5th inning when Cascade's Bob Kells singled and back-to-back doubles by Jim Hosch and Wayne Ressler produced the two Cascade runs.

Ken Huinker got in trouble in the7th inning when he issued a single and two walks to fill the bases with one out. Art Huinker relieved and forced two Cascade pop-ups to end the inning.

In the third inning Leroy Willenbring led off with a double to right, got to 3rd base on a passed ball and scored the initial run for the Hawks for a fielder's choice ground out.

In the 4th inning Art Huinker singled, stole second and scored on brother Ken Huinker's single. In the 5th inning the Hawks scored again. Dale Digmann got to first on a Cascade error. A double by Bob Goldsmith scored Digmann for the 3rd Whitehawk run.

In the 7th and 8th innings the Hawks scored two more runs. In the seventh Roger Fenwick, Cascade pitcher, issued a walk to Dale Digmann, Tom Jenk singled and Art Huinker doubled to score Digmann. In the 8th an error on the Reds'

second baseman put Leroy Willenbring on first base. Dale
Digmann singled and Marv Schlichte singled to score
Willenbring.
    A capacity crowd was on hand at Worthington Tuesday
night for the tournament finale.

Roger Fenwick was a very familiar name in the baseball tournaments in the decade of the sixties. He was a right-hand pitcher who threw the ball very hard, and when you were batting, it looked like he was coming at you with all arms and legs. His motion made it very difficult for the batter to pick up the baseball. He came from the south-central Wisconsin area, possibly Beloit. Later in the sixties while pitching for the Waterloo Merchants in the American Amateur Baseball Tournament, Roger pitched against us for Beloit.

Balltown's catcher mentioned in the semi-final game was Bob Meyer, also the catcher for Loras College at this time. Growing up on a farm in the Balltown area, Bob was an excellent catcher who was a constant threat with the bat. Well-liked by teammates and opposition players, he later ended up in the Kansas City area for his career. No doubt his playing with Loras at the time led to the adding of pitchers Eggers and Willenborg, also from the college, to their pitching staff for the tournaments.

It was also neat to have my brother Kenny pitching for the Whitehawks. It felt like old home week on the farm, playing ball in our yard growing up. Kenny could hit as well as pitch. Batting left-handed, he hit one of the longest shots I had ever seen while playing legion baseball for the St. Lucas team when he was seventeen. In an open field at Charles City, Iowa, he hit the ball so far over the rightfielder's head that Kenny was practically crossing the plate when the fielder got to the baseball. The other nice part about our playing together was the fact that Kenny and his wife, Aileen, and Ann and I drove down from Festina together because we still had not moved to Dyersville.

This is 1961, five years since first having played with the Dyersville Whitehawks. Most of the players are new for me. Manager Tom Jenk, Roy Krapfl and pitcher Leroy Willenbring were on the 1956 team, but that is about it. The Digmann brothers, Dale, a catcher, and Jim at third base had taken the places of Dick Mescher behind the plate and Ray Olberding at third base. Bob Goldsmith, a left-handed hitter with power, played second base and in the outfield. We had Marv Schlichte in center and the Colesburg flash, Rollie Sampson, in right. You will find this group around for quite a few years for the Whitehawks.

All good organizations have good leaders and that was true for the Whitehawks. Tom Jenk, besides being a very strong threat at the plate, provided that on-going leadership strength that kept the team together. Long after retiring from active play, Tom assisted his son, Tom, Jr., as an assistant coach at Beckman

High School until he finally retired in 2012. Yes, the date is right, 2012. It showed the love and the knowledge that he had for the game.

Following the Worthington tournament is the Cascade Legion Tournament, played in the latter half of the month of July. First up for the Whitehawks is a game against Holy Cross.

> *DYERSVILLE, MONTI WIN CASCADE GAMES*
> *Monticello defeated Bernard, 5-1, and Dyersville whipped Holy Cross, 7-2, Wednesday night in first round games of the 15th annual Cascade baseball tournament.*
> *In the first game on the night's card, Monticello cruised home behind the three-hit pitching of Mike Hall, who struck out 15, plus some timely hitting and a couple of defensive lapses by Bernard.*
> *After Hall and Dave Hughes of Bernard had dueled through three scoreless innings, an error kicked off the fourth for Monticello. Joe Nardone followed with a triple- - -his first of three hit- - -and Gordon Westhoff, Jim Wright and Dave Westhoff added singles for three runs.*
> *Hall had a one-hit shutout working until Hughes singled in the seventh. A walk and Neil Gavin's single brought Hughes around and ruined Hall's shutout.*
> *Three walks and a single by Leroy Willenbring shot Dyersville into a 3-0 lead in the first inning of its game with Holy Cross.*
> *Two errors, a balk by losing pitcher Joe Ackerman and Tom Jenk's two-run single counted two runs in the fifth, and before the inning was over the Whitehawks added another pair on Art Huinker's double, Ackerman's second balk of the inning and a passed ball.*
> *Dick Schnier was sailing along in style for Dyersville until the sixth when four straight singles- - -by Dave Felderman, Merle Marting, Jules Kohl and Jim Fitzgerald- - scored two runs and brought Huinker on in relief.*
> *The veteran lefty struck out the side, then set Holy Cross down in the seventh to preserve the win for Schnier.*

Joe Ackerman, the Holy Cross pitcher, was also from Cassville, Wisconsin. The path to Iowa from Wisconsin was becoming a well-worn track for many good ball players across the Mississippi River. Schnier, on the other hand, was a youngster from the neighboring town of Worthington. Dick played baseball for many years in the Dubuqueland area, primarily for his home town.

Next came the quarter-final round with the Whitehawks taking on Monticello.

254

CLOSE GAMES MARK CASCADE TOURNEY
Dyersville nipped Monticello, 1-0, and Zwingle shaded Epworth, 5-4, in a pair of well-played quarter-final games at the 15th annual Cascade semi-pro baseball tournament here Tuesday night.

Art Huinker of Dyersville and Mike Hall of Monticello hooked up in a brilliant pitchers' battle in the highlight of Tuesday's card, with the Whitehawks pushing across the deciding run in the sixth inning on Marv Schlichte's double and a single by Dale Digmann.

That was half the hit production off Hall, who walked four, struck out four and got almost flawless support from his teammates.

Huinker gave up only two hits, and the veteran lefty racked up 16 strikeouts, walked only two and his mates gave him errorless backing in the field.

Haven Schmidt sparked Zwingle to its victory over Epworth, driving in a first-inning run with a single and breaking a 4-4 tie with a home run in the top of the seventh.

Dave Miller walked, raced to third on Dorrance McDermott's single and scored on a sacrifice fly to give Epworth a run in the first inning. Doubles by Howard Kettleson and Miller gave Epworth another run in the second and it tallied twice more in the fifth to knot the score. Ralph Buchman drove those two in after a single by Miller, an error and a walk loaded the bases.

Familiar names all over that write-up. Haven Schmidt of Maquoketa (although his home now is very close to Zwingle) had returned from professional baseball and was hammering most pitchers. We had encountered each other in Savannah, Georgia back in 1957. And Ralph Buchman, known more for his pitching, garnered a big two-run single for Epworth. And Dorrance McDermott still can be seen at most athletic events at Western Dubuque High School in Epworth.

DYERSVILLE, GUTTENBERG MEET FOR TOURNEY TITLE
Dyersville and Guttenberg were scheduled to meet for the championship of the 15th annual Cascade semipro baseball tournament Saturday night after winning semi-final games Friday.

Dyersville moved into the title game with a 5-1 victory over Zwingle, and Guttenberg got past Worthington, 5-3.

Dave Dewell's single and a double by Jerry Shanahan gave Zwingle a temporary 1-0 lead in the second inning against the Whitehawks, but Dyersville tied the score in the second as

255

Ken Huinker singled, moved to third on an error and scored on Rollie Sampson's sacrifice fly.

Two errors and Tom Jenk's single put Dyersville ahead, 2-1, in the fifth, and the Whitehawks sewed things up with a three-run sixth that included an error and singles by Huinker, Dale Digmann and Sampson.

Singles by Kermit Urbain and Merrill Hyde and Al Klinger's double shot Guttenberg into a 2-0 lead in the first inning of the night's second game.

After Worthington tied it in the fourth on singles by Ray Olberding, Dick Mescher and Darrell Rothrock and a double by Bob Wolfe, Guttenberg took the lead in the fifth when Klinger doubled for his third hit of the game, and scored on Kirk Rentschler's single.

A single by Gary Peterson, a walk and Hyde's double gave Guttenberg two more runs in the sixth, and Worthington closed out the scoring with a seventh-inning run on Eddie Hess's double and a single by Del Olberding.

Many familiar baseball names in this write-up of the semi-finals also. Guttenberg brought Al Klinger down from West Union. Al had played for Albert Lea, Minnesota in the Southern Minnesota State League where we had done battle quite often. Gary Peterson was Mar-Mac High School's all-around athlete the previous fall when the Falcons of Ossian De Sales edged his team on its way to the state finals. Infielder Kirk Rentschler was a strong high school player out of Maquoketa Valley High School in Delhi. And then there is Merrill Hyde, a Guttenberg native, who played college baseball at Arizona State University in Phoenix, Arizona. He played centerfield and his teammate in the outfield was Mr. October himself, Reggie Jackson. And on the mound was Rod Tangeman from Guttenberg who had a shot at professional baseball in his background. Remember, we defeated Guttenberg twice during the regular season by scores of 8-1 and 7-1. They were a different ball club now. This is an excellent example of how teams loaded up for the big Dubuque area tournaments each year. This became one of the main reasons for the strong fan appeal to attend the games. Strong baseball was entertaining the local crowds. And I suppose, in some small fashion, the mystery of what pitchers and other players were going to appear on the diamond peaked a special interest for some baseball enthusiasts.

Then we have to look at the Worthington line-up. First of all, Darrell Rothrock, strong left-hand pitcher, suffered one of his rare defeats in these tournaments. Remember, he was already challenging the hitters back in 1956 when I first pitched for Dyersville. Then Dick Mescher, the Whitehawks' catcher in 1956, who had gone over to Potosi, Wisconsin High School to coach, came back to play for his wife Jean's hometown. The Olberding brothers, Ray and Del, also got involved.

256

Last of all, my college roommate and baseball teammate, Bob Wolfe, now living in the Davenport area, suited up for Worthington. He had been playing baseball in the Marshalltown area with fellow Loras teammate, Dick Wright. Dick was coaching basketball for Marshalltown St. Mary's High School at the time.

What a collection of baseball names to reflect on. It was like a reunion of baseball figures from the tri-state area coming together to wage battle, all with many memories of past baseball games and with many new memories of great baseball games still to come.

HAWKS WIN SECOND TOURNEY OF THE SEASON OVER GUTTENBERG

The Dyersville Whitehawks won their second tournament of the season Saturday night with an 8-6 win over Guttenberg in the finals of the Cascade meet.

The Huinker brothers played a big part in the Hawks' win in the championship. Art Huinker started on the mound for the Hawks and handled Guttenberg efficiently until he tired in the 7th inning and was relieved by Ken Huinker.

Art Huinker helped his own cause in the first inning with a home run with Marv Schlichte aboard to put the Hawks into a 2-0 lead.

Guttenberg came back in the 2nd inning to score a run when Al Klinger walked and scored on a double by Kirk Rentschler.

The Hawks had a big third inning. Bob Goldsmith started things off with a home run. Tom Jenk walked, Art Huinker singled, Ken Huinker singled to center field. An error on a rundown on Guttenberg's first baseman scored Jenk and Art Huinker. The score stood 5-1.

Guttenberg scored three runs in the 4th inning when Huinker issued three walks. Rentschler singled and Tom Turner doubled scoring three runs. The score at the end of four innings was 5-4.

In the fifth inning, the Hawks scored two more runs on a walk to Jim Digmann, a single by Leroy Willenbring and two fielder's choices. Guttenberg scored one run in the 5th on a single by Bob Buelow and a double by Merrill Hyde. The score at the end of five innings was 7-5.

In the sixth the Whitehawks scored again on a single by Marv Schlichte. A stolen base and a single by Bob Goldsmith made the score 8-5. In the 7th Guttenberg's Gary Peterson walked. A wild pitch by Huinker and a single by Bob Buelow scored the final Guttenberg run.

257

Ken Huinker came on in relief in the 7th for the Hawks
and struck out 8 of the 9 Guttenberg batters to face him.

What a wild ball game. But the Whitehawks gained their second championship of the season. To add to the influx of outside players, Guttenberg's manager, Herb Borcherding, brought in Jerry Duea from the Waterloo area to pitch and he also had Bob Buelow and Tom Turner who came from Dubuque.

Just a little sidelight to the Cascade tourney. Haven Schmidt received the most valuable player award. In four games, he batted .750 (an average of three hits every four times he batted) which included two home runs and five runs batted in.

The season is coming down to its final tournament, the Dyersville Commercial Club 16-team showdown with the additional annual Queens' Pageant. Played during the first two weeks of August each year, it was getting time for Ann and I to make our big move to the host city in preparation for the start of school and the start of football practice. Veteran football coach, Paul Schramm, had to put up with a rookie football coach whose football background was very, very limited. He put up with me every fall for the next five years, several of them including practices missed because of baseball games to play with the Whitehawks and others. Before this tournament was completed, we had moved into our new home on 5th Avenue SE.

GARNAVILLO, DYERSVILLE WIN FIRST-ROUND TESTS

Garnavillo and Dyersville passed first-round tests in the annual Dyersville semipro baseball tournament here Monday night. Garnavillo ousted Winthrop, 5-1, and Dyersville sidelined Peosta, 13-1.

Jim Fiete blasted a home run after Jim Schmelzer walked in the first inning to give Garnavillo's Lou Helle all the runs he needed to win the opening game.

Art Huinker was the Dyersville standout in the second game. The southpaw hurler was touched for just five hits, struck out 15 and walked none.

Huinker also singled home a run in the first and tripled home two more in a three-run third inning to provide himself with a 4-0 cushion.

His triple came after a double by Bob Goldsmith and a single by Tom Jenk. Huinker then scored on a fielder's choice.

Goldsmith also contributed a two-run homer in the fourth and Marv Schlichte hit a solo blast in a six-run seventh inning. Huinker had five runs batted in with three singles and a triple.

258

This write-up had to be included for two reasons. Sure I pitched, but four hits. That did not happen very often. Haven Schmidt, Peosta catcher for the opening round game, was the left hand hitting catcher from pro ball that all local pitchers faced apprehensively.

There is another reason for this write-up being included. Notice the last name of the Garnavillo batter that had a two-run home, Jim Fiete. I wonder how often he was asked in his life if he was Sandy Fiete's brother. Who was Sandy Fiete you ask? Probably one of the most famous girls' basketball players in the history of the sport in Iowa. She took Garnavillo's team to the state tournament twice. Oh, and by the way, my wife Ann played against her in her two years of playing basketball at Calmar High School.

The quarter-finals found Guttenberg, Cascade, Holy Cross and the Whitehawks advancing to the semi-finals. The Hawks were scheduled to play Holy Cross in the first game with Guttenberg and Cascade battling it out in the second semi-final contest.

> ### HAWKS, CASCADE WIN BERTHS IN FINALS WITH MONDAY WIN
> *Dyersville topped Holy Cross 3-1 in a pitcher's duel and Cascade shut out Guttenberg 2-0 Monday to enter the finals of the Dyersville Baseball Tournament. The semi-finals were played before 4,700 fans that squeezed into every inch of the park to see the games and watch Miss Susan McGrew of Guttenberg crowned 1961 Baseball Queen.*
>
> *Whitehawk pitcher Art Huinker gave up only three hits and got credit for the Dyersville win. Don Kuehner gave up only two hits to take the loss but issued eight bases on balls while his teammates committed three costly errors.*
>
> *Art Huinker drove in the initial Whitehawk run in the first inning with a double with Marv Schlichte on second base. Schlichte got on base on a walk and advanced to second on an error. The Hawks got their winning run in the third inning and got an insurance run in the fifth. In the third, two walks and a single by Dale Digmann scored the second run. In the fifth the Hawks scored on a walk, stolen base and an error.*
>
> *Bob Cardelli knotted up the score in the third inning for Holy Cross with a home run over the right field fence with no one on base.*
>
> *Roger Fenwick, tall Cascade pitcher, limited Guttenberg to only three hits in winning the second game of the night, 2-0. Mark Dilley, youthful Soldiers Grove, Wisconsin pitcher, gave up five hits while taking the loss for Guttenberg.*

259

With Bob Hoerner on third base, Dan Ahearn made a
perfect squeeze bunt in the fourth inning to score Cascade's
winning run. Cascade scored another run in the sixth inning.
Bob Hoerner got two of the five hits off Guttenberg's
Mark Dilley. For Guttenberg Al Klinger connected for two hits
and Merle Hyde rapped Fenwick for one hit.

Talk about pitchers dominating. Two ball games played by four good ball clubs and only a total of 13 hits between the four teams were collected. The games were close. No runaways. Did that please the 4,700 plus fans that came out? There is a need to introduce Holy Cross pitcher, Don Kuehner. Don hails from St. Lucas, a small town just 6 miles west of hometown Festina. A 6-4 slender righthander who could successfully challenge almost any hitter. He spent most of his career coaching baseball in the large schools around Chicago.

Another interesting connection in the first game took place when left-hand hitting Bob Cardelli was given a hanging curve ball over the middle of the plate and he knew what to do with it. Over the right field fence it went. Five years earlier, Ann and I, married for one year, spent the summer living in an apartment in Dubuque, working for Geisler Roofing Company and playing baseball for the Dyersville Whitehawks plus some games for our hometown team at Festina. Ann gave birth to our first son. But that wasn't enough to fill our young lives. A baseball enthusiast named McCauley, I believe his first name was Frank but memories can play tricks with us also, was coaching the Dubuque Legion Team and he asked me if I would help him coach the team. With all the games Dyersville especially was playing, both of us were well aware of the limits it would place on my availability to help out. But help I did. One of the players I helped was Bob Cardelli, home run hitter for Holy Cross in the semi-finals at Dyersville. I don't believe I taught him how to hit a hanging curve ball from a left-hand pitcher who should know better. Better known by his nickname, Arch, I remember him well that summer five years before. We have had no contacts following that night either. I wonder where he is and what he has done. I wonder if he remembers his part-time coach from earlier Legion baseball days. Now for the championship game.

DYERSVILL WINS MEET 6-5
Nearly 4,500 rabid baseball fans got their money's
worth Tuesday night when they witnessed an extra inning
championship game and a thrilling eight-inning consolation
game.
The overflow crowd saw the Dyersville Whitehawks nip
Cascade 6-5 in the finals of the 11th annual Dyersville Baseball
Tournament and Guttenberg top Holy Cross 5-4 in eight
innings.
The tension of the crowd was at a fever pitch when the
Hawks scored the winning run in the bottom of the tenth inning.

The score was tied 5-5 when Dale Digmann singled and then Jim Digman was safe at first on an overthrow to the first baseman. Dick Schnier was intentionally walked by Cascade's pitcher John Willenborg.

With Rollie Sampson at the plate and the bases loaded with no outs, the Hawks tried the squeeze play that won the championship game. Sampson bunted, and the ball rolled toward the pitcher's mound. Willenborg attempted to grab the ball to catch Dale Digmann at the plate but fumbled it, allowing the runner to score to win the game.

The Cascade Reds drew blood in the first inning off Dyersville's pitcher Roy Willenbring. Jim Hosch connected for a solo home run to put the Reds into a 1-0 lead.

In the second inning, Cascade tallied again on a single by Jim Hoerner who advanced to second on a ground ball off the bat of Carl Heitz. A double by Dan Ahearn failed to score a run and Hoerner was out on an attempted squeeze play. However, Willenborg singled to score Heitz.

The Whitehawks tied the score in the fourth inning. Tom Jenk reached first on an error and advanced to second on the overthrow. Art Huinker, the tourney's most valuable player, then tripled to score Jenk. Ken Huinker then singled to score Art Huinker.

Cascade came roaring back in the fifth inning to re-take the lead when they scored two runs. Jim Timmons doubled down the third base line. Bob Hoerner singled advancing Timmons to third. Carl Heitz then singled to score the two runs.

The Hawks scored one in the fifth on a single by Marv Schlichte, and singles by Bob Goldsmith and Tom Jenk. Schlichte scored on Jenk's single.

In the sixth, Cascade scored again to make the score 5-3. Willenborg grounded out. Tiny Potts singled but was thrown out at second trying to steal. Then Jim Hosch tagged his second home run off Willenbring for Cascade.

Art Huinker relieved starting pitcher Roy Willenbring in the seventh inning for Dyersville.

In the seventh the Hawks knotted up the game for the second time. Marv Schlichte singled. Goldsmith grounded out, and Art Huinker was walked. Schlichte scored on an error off a pop fly by Ken Huinker. Art Huinker than scored the tying run on a wild pitch by pitcher John Willenborg.

No runs were scored in the eighth and ninth inning and it was in the bottom of the tenth inning that the Hawks made their big bid and scored the winning run.

Dyersville had six runs on 11 hits and three errors. Cascade had five runs on 11 hits but committed five errors.

261

Memories are sometimes vague and sometimes very sharp. This game had some of both. For example, the tying run scoring on a wild pitch. Even though I was the one who scored, I have little memory of it. On the other hand, the triple is very vivid. It was a sharp line drive about fifteen to twenty feet over the shortstop's head that had sufficient velocity that it got by the left fielder and center fielder. But the most vivid of all was the play that occurred on the first pitch I threw after entering the game in the seventh.

Cascade had a runner on third and there were less than two out. The score was 5-3 Cascade. But we have to go back to a meeting that Dale Digmann and I had near the mound after I had warmed up. Previously in the tournament I had attended the games on a night when the Whitehawks were not playing, but Cascade was. Their manager that year was Jim Hosch, a great athlete in his own right. On a particular situation, with a runner on third for the Reds, I happened to be watching Jim coaching at third base. He did something unusual and on the ensuing play, they successfully executed a suicide squeeze play to score a run. I remembered what he had done and realized that it had to be the signal for a suicide squeeze. I informed Dale of that and we agreed on a certain signal that I would give him on the mound for a pitchout if I saw the signal given. Sure enough, the Cascade signal was observed, I acknowledged to Dale, the pitch was made, the runner on third broke for the plate, I threw a pitchout and Dale tagged the runner out at the plate. The Whitehawks got out of a jam and the score remained 5-3. We scored two runs in the seventh to tie the game, neither team scored in the eighth and ninth innings, and our own squeeze play won the game in the bottom of the tenth. A second MVP in the granddaddy tournament. And, again, I have only a vague memory of our successful squeeze play by Rollie.

In 1956, the Whitehawks captured the championship crown at the Worthington, Cascade and Dyersville tournaments. We repeated that sweep in the 1961 season. We had several big breaks in winning all three and, similar to what I shared with the De Sales Falcons reaching the state tournament finals. Most long winning streaks find the team getting a little lucky. But I also do feel that luck we speak of is frequently related to the efforts of the team that benefits from them.

Another baseball season is behind us. The Huinkers are settling into their two-story home on Fifth Avenue Southeast in Dyersville. And our oldest, Terry, is ready to start Kindergarten. Tim, Tammy and Peggy are ready to keep their Mother busy at home. And for the father in that household, teaching at Xavier High School and helping Head Coach Paul Schramm coach football. Looking forward to it, but so much to learn. Getting a good grasp of the team concept of football did not result in my being a very helpful assistant to Paul that first year. It compared to my finding it difficult to see the picture of "team" playing basketball that first year back when I was a junior at Calmar High School. Despite that limiting factor, our first Xavier school year was interesting and fulfilling for this new Dyersville family. It continues.

REASONS WHY- - -ATHLETICISM AND INTENSITY

The Huinker family had spread their wings and moved to a big city. Well, at least Dyersville recorded a population of 3,000 or more while Ossian, our previous residence numbered in the 800's. Is it possible that when you grow up in a less populated environment, you have a different viewpoint about size than you do when you have grown up in a Chicago-sized city? Dyersville seemed fairly large to us. It even had one set of stop lights.

We rented an older home with a big front porch and a garage that you entered off the alley in the back yard. The backyard was small but still provided sufficient space for the many games that were played there by the four pre-school youngsters, especially ball games. Terry graduated from kindergarten operated by the newly-organized Western Dubuque County School System in a new building about three blocks from our home. He would attend Xavier Elementary in the fall, across the north fork of the Maquoketa River on the west side of town.

We liked the town and just as we found in Ossian, it was easy to become acquainted and make new friends. Being a coach and teacher creates many situations where your family is recognized and accepted. Playing baseball for the town team increased those situations. And, of course, we had played with the Whitehawks five years earlier and we already had met many residents of the community.

Ann always shares her experiences regarding the built-in baby sitters for our four children. As a high school teacher and having taught many of the high school students, girls in this case, often these students were ready to take care of our family when Ann attended the baseball games up at the park. "It was like my children were taken from me by some of the girls for the entire game and I would be able to sit and enjoy what was happening on the baseball diamond," she would tell me when we got home. By the way, Ann was expecting our fifth child in the fall. That seemed to make the baby-sitters more numerous.

How about games on the road, most of them being night games? Well, Ann did not miss many ball games, home or away, so regular baby sitters were necessary and frequently used. We were fortunate to have Ardell Klosterman next door with her five children, three of them high school and upper elementary daughters. They had opportunities galore to gain some spending money. And they were so good with our kids.

As for the Dyersville Whitehawks and baseball, their year was being extended. For the first time, the Maquoketa Valley League decided to join the American Amateur Baseball Congress. The Delaware County League had been members of this association for years, with teams like Petersburg always able to contend for the opportunity to play for a state championship and beyond. Now Dyersville, as a member of the Maquoketa Valley League, would have that opportunity. And what an opportunity it proved to be. That will be covered in a

263

separate chapter after wrapping up the regular league season and the local invitational tournaments.

We will include only some excerpts of the regular season games, or possibly some commentary about them. The Whitehawks went undefeated in the league games that year, winning the western five-team division of Epworth, Guttenberg, New Vienna, Garnavillo as well as the Whitehawks. The eastern division included six teams: Zwingle, Holy Cross, Bellevue, Balltown, Sherrill and Rickardsville. Holy Cross claimed the top spot in that division.

In one of the first league games of the season, Dyersville battled Bellevue, led by the Loras pitching ace, Al Eggers. It had to be one of those days for Al when he did not have his best stuff, because the Whitehawks shut out Bellevue, 9-0, collecting nine hits. And for me to get a home run, a triple and a single against Eggers proves his having an off-day. Sal Willenbring pitched the shutout, scattering eight hits, aided by two double plays.

That was an afternoon game. In the evening, the Whitehawks traveled to Independence and won their second game of the day, 6-3. This was a non-conference game. Again the Whitehawks had nine hits, with Jim Digmann, Jim Wegmann and I each collecting two hits. Bob Goldsmith pitched into the ninth inning, when Independence scored two of their three runs. I was brought in to finish up the game.

Playing shortstop for the Whitehawks that game was Xavier sophomore, Les Ernster. He was a top-notch athlete, and regretfully we lost him when the family moved to Minnesota that fall. The Dyersville team had also added two big names to our roster, Jim Wegmann in centerfield and Jim "Popeye" Hosch at second base. Both were excellent additions.

The opposing pitcher for Independence that night was Jim Reiter, a tall, strong righthander from Upper Iowa University. Jim could really pop the ball, but still struggled with control at this stage of his baseball career. He later signed a professional contract, but I have no information of his history in those ranks.

Next, the Whitehawks gained their fourth straight league victory by a very close 5-4 score. Excerpted from an article in the Dyersville Commercial are the following two paragraphs:

WHITEHAWKS IN 4TH M.V. WIN OVER BALLTOWN

Dyersville won its fourth consecutive Maquoketa Valley League by the score of 5-4 over Balltown at Dyersville on the evening of May 30th. Balltown scored two runs in the first inning on a walk to Bob Meyer, a double to Jerry Splinter and a two-run single by Leon Sigwarth. Dyersville came back with single runs in the second and third to tie up the game and the score stayed 2-2 until the seventh when the Hawks scored

*three runs. In the seventh Roy Krapfl started the rally with his
second hit of the night. Rollie Sampson followed with another
single, and two fielder's choices on ground balls by Jim
Digmann and Tom Jenk netted two runs. With two down and no
one on base, Bob Goldsmith pulled a hard fast ball over the
right fence for a solo home run. Goldsmith's home run proved
to be the winning run and gave the Whitehawks their sixth
victory against one defeat.*

Records show that Mike Schuster, another Loras College pitcher, went the distance for Balltown and I was the lucky winner on the mound for Dyersville. Jerry Splinter had three hits for the Balltown team.

A later write-up showed the Dyersville nine playing league games on Friday night and Sunday night and travelling to the Reformatory at Anamosa for a Sunday afternoon, inside-the-walls game against the Snappers. The Snappers have a definite advantage because all their games are played on their home field.

Bob Goldsmith picked up the win in relief against the Snappers. The field has no fence around the outfield. Only buildings a good 500 feet from home plate place some kind of limit on how far a ball will roll. Usually in front of those buildings, prisoners sat in the shade watching the game. Under supervision of guards, of course. One position I played that afternoon was right field, supposedly in front of the building where the prisoners with more serious offenses were seated on the ground. It may sound foolish, but I did not always have my eye on the pitcher-batter proceedings as one should. I also hurried into the dugout after we had completed the inning in the field.

The final score was 7-1 but the game was close until George Benn hit an inside-the-walls home run in the sixth inning.

In the league games, in a game played under the lights at Dyersville's Commercial Club Park, Epworth was the victim by a score of 11-0. Jim Hosch led an 11-hit attack for the Whitehawks with a home run and two singles while Tom Jenk and Dale Digmann each had two hits. It was a strong evening for me with 21 strikeouts in the nine-inning game. Epworth collected three hits. Sam Rohwedder pitched for Epworth.

In the next league game on Sunday, again played at Dyersville, the seventh league win without a loss was realized 9-3 over New Vienna. Sal Willenborg picked up the victory fanning 16 and allowing 6 hits. One of the hits was a two-run home run by Jim Recker, giving New Vienna a short-lived two-run lead. Don Kerper had two doubles for the losers. Dave Reittinger took the loss. Goldsmith and Krapfl led Dyersville hitters with two hits each. Goldsmith left the team after the game. He would be missed. No records to back up this statement, but he almost assuredly was one of our top hitters.

In a later write-up, Dyersville moved its league record to 9-0 with a surprising 20-1 victory over Zwingle, one of the leaders in the eastern division of the Maquoketa Valley League. Then, in a Sunday afternoon game at Guttenberg, the Whitehawks survived some lusty Guttenberg hitting to pull out a 11-7 victory. Following are brief accounts of those two games, again from the Dyersville Commercial.

HAWKS POST TWO M.V. VICTORIES

The Dyersville Whitehawks played two league games the past week in downing Zwingle by the surprising score of 20-1, and nosing out Guttenberg in the last inning 11-7.

In the Zwingle game, Rollie Sampson and Jim Hosch led all hitters with three hits each. Hosch had a home run, a triple and double while Sampson contributed to the cause with two singles and a double. Huinker earned the decision in pitching a four-hitter. Haven Schmidt, the ex-triple A catcher was limited to one single and struck out twice.

In the Guttenberg game, four Guttenberg men displayed their power. Gary Peterson, Merrill Hyde, Al Klinger and Jim Klinger hit home runs but the Hawks connected for seventeen hits off the Guttenberg pitching. Dyersville connected for only one home run, that being Huinker's blow in the third with one man aboard. For the Whitehawks, four players had three hits, Jim Digmann, Tom Jenk, Huinker and Jim Hosch. Willenbring and Buzz Beatty each had two hits.

The Hawks ran their league record to 13 consecutive wins without a loss on a 5-2 victory over Guttenberg and a 30-2 romp over Sherrill in a game played on the Sherrill diamond a few weeks later on a Sunday afternoon. Rod Tangeman pitched for Guttenberg scattering eight hits for the five runs. His brother Robin had two singles to lead their offensive against Art Huinker who allowed six hits in picking up the win. Rollie Sampson had a single and double to lead the Whitehawk attack.

The final 14th victory came over Holy Cross, 10-4. Trailing 3-1 going into the fourth, the Hawks put together 7 hits, including a three-run homer by Rollie Sampson and a two-run triple by Dale Digmann. I had another four-hit night with a perfect four for four, all singles. Rollie Sampson pitched the first three innings for the Hawks, Leroy Willenbring pitched the next three, and Neil Moritz pitched the three final scoreless innings. Joe Ackermann from Cassville, Wisconsin, started strong for Holy Cross, but in the fourth, Sampson's three-run homer appeared to shake him considerably in allowing four additional hits in that inning.

In a non-league game, the Whitehawks scored two runs in the bottom of the ninth to edge out Cascade 6-5. Roy Krapfl started the winning rally with a single. A wild pitch followed. Then Tom Jenk doubled Krapfl home to tie the score. An intentional walk to Huinker was followed by an infield single by Jim Hosch loading the bases. A bunt by Dale Digmann was picked up by the pitcher and thrown home for a forceout. But the catcher's throw, attempting to double up Digmannn at first base, went wild allowing Huinker to score the winning run.

Cascade's offense was led by two home runs for Jim Hoerner. His second homer in the top of the ninth had given the Reds a one-run lead. Jenk had a single and double while Huinker collected a single and a triple, and Jim Hosch had three singles to lead Dyersville hitters. All these games were played in between tournament games at the usual four sites for tournaments each summer. Addition ally, other league and non-league games were played, making the summer a very busy one, baseball-wise. The first invitational tournament for 1962 was Monticello's eight-team invitational.

DYERSVILLE TOPS LOWDEN

Hopkinton and Dyersville advanced to the semi-finals of the Monticello baseball tourney Tuesday night as Hopkinton stopped Ryan, 4-1, and Dyersville shut out Lowden, 5-0.

Ryan's only score came on Tipper McGinn's home run in the fourth inning after Hopkinton had taken a 3-0 lead earlier in the game.

Roy Willenbring hurled a three-hitter as Dyersville pounded out five hits to stop Lowden. The big blow of the game was Art Huinker's home run in the third with a man on.

Leroy Willenbring continues to pitch effectively almost every time out. I found the use of the word "pounded" a little unusual when we, as a team, had only five hits.

The next write-up, taken from the Dyersville Commercial, covered both the semi-final and final games of the Monticello tournament. It is a weekly paper and therefore, rather than separating the two games into two write-ups, they combined them into one article.

HAWKS RACE TO MONTICELLO TITLE WITH 18-4 ROMP OVER DELHI

The Dyersville Whitehawks captured the Monticello Tournament Friday evening by downing Delhi 18-4 in the final night behind the fine pitching of Willenbring and fine hitting of Jim Digmann, Art Huinker and Jim Hosch.

On Wednesday night, the Whitehawks gained a spot in the championship game by downing Epworth with Huinker going all the way for the Whitehawks.

Art Huinker, the Dyersville ace lefthander, pitched one of the finest games in the tournament by managing to give 16

267

strikeouts to account for all but five of their outs during the game. Huinker allowed only four hits to the Epworth nine and gave up only two walks.

In the championship game Friday, Dyersville walloped Delhi 18-4 after Delhi threw a short scare into the Whitehawks by leading for the first two innings.

After two outs in the third inning, things began to move as Beatty nailed a long home run over the left field fence. Jenk followed with a long double. Huinker drove in Jenk on another double and Hosch followed with a single to score Huinker. Hosch scored on an error on the third baseman and Dale Digmann scored as he and Wegmann performed a double steal. Wegmann hit Sampson in on a single to bring the total to seven runs in that one inning.

Willenbring pitched fine five hit ball. Michaels managed two hits against him to lead the hitters. Jim Digmann led the winners of the tournament with five hits in five trips up.

You will notice a new kid on the block playing baseball for the Whitehawks. He was Buzz Beatty, not really a young kid any more. Buzz, or Blair, his real name, was a Guttenberg native, and probably one of the best baseball players to come out of northeast Iowa. When he started playing high school and semi-pro baseball locally, he participated with Guttenberg in the big Dubuqueland Baseball Tournament. That tournament at one time determined the speediest player on each team by having one nominee run around the bases, starting at home plate. Each year he participated in that event, he captured the title over the fastest runners from each of the 16 teams. Later he signed a professional contract as a shortstop/second baseman. He was successfully moving up the ladder when he suffered serious injuries to both knees on double play collisions at second base. This happened as he was completing the double play defensively. Those injuries caused the end of his professional pursuit. He turned to teaching plus coaching baseball and was at West Delaware High School in Manchester in the sixties when Manager Jenk convinced him to play with the Whitehawks.

There is a need for me to share a personal story about Buzz Beatty. When asked to pick the greatest player that I played baseball with, my answer always recognized Buzz. First of all, physically, he had speed, he had an exceptional arm, and he could hit, both for frequent contact in hitting the ball and also hitting for power. What else do you need? Something happened in a game we were playing together for the Whitehawks, one in which he was at shortsop and I was on the mound.

Again not remembering exactly the score or the inning, I do recall that it was toward the end of the game and we had a very comfortable lead. The situation included a runner or two on base for the opposition and two outs. With a two-strike count on the hitter, I threw an inside fast ball and struck the batter out. As we are walking off the diamond to the dugout, Buzz came jogging past me and commented, "Boy, you really fooled me on that one, Art. I was expecting you to throw a pitch low and away and making the batter chase it."

With the game being a non-tournament game, possibly not even a league game, and for all practical purposes, a game that was basically over with, and have the shortstop behind me still thinking with the catcher and me on what pitch to throw, I thought, "That is my kind of ball player. He is going to be ready for anything that could happen in a ball game." And that is so valuable in baseball. Combine that with all his physical talents, and he was the greatest player that I played with. There are many other players that have similar qualifications but his comment at that particular time and place just impressed me so much.

Well, now we are ready to look at the next tournament. In this case, it is the Worthington Cardinals Invitational Tournament and Dyersville's opening round game was against neighboring Earlville.

> *EIGHT TEAMS SURVIVE RUGGED 1ST ROUND WORTHINGTON PLAY*
> *In the first game of the Worthington Tournament Friday night Dyersville downed Earlville in a pitchers' battle with Ken Huinker coming out on top. Huinker for Dyersville and Jim McAndrew for Earlville both pitched fine two-hit ball. The big difference in the game was that Huinker allowed only two free passes to the Earlville batters while McAndrew left seven Whitehawks get to base on walks.*
> *The Whitehawks started off strong by scoring three runs in the top of the first inning. Jim Wegmann, the lead-off batter, drew a walk. Tom Jenk laid down a sacrifice bunt, then reached first on a bad throw by the third baseman, allowing him and Wegmann to go to second and third. On the third pitch to Art Huinker, Wegmann was put out after getting caught between third and home. Art Huinker drew a walk putting two men on. Jim Hosch followed by driving out a single scoring Art Huinker and Jenk. Hosch stole second, then was driven in as Earlville made the play for Ken Huinker at first.*
> *Art Huinker scored his second run for the day after reaching first on an error. In the fifth inning, Huinker scored for the third time giving Dyersville five runs for the evening. Jim Hosch and Art Huinker had the two Dyersville hits. For Earlville, Burbridge and Smith each connected for a hit.*

Kenny struck out 10 Earlville batters to pick up the win. McAndrew meanwhile will become a Dyersville household name for the Whitehawks in the upcoming 1963 season.

In the second round game, Dyersville advanced by pounding out a 12-2 win over Hopkinton. The game was stopped after the fifth inning because of the 10-run rule. Roy Willenbring continued his fine pitching, allowing Hopkinton only five hits. Guttenberg won the other game of the night by knocking off Bernard 10-0 in six innings, also stopped by the same 10-run rule. Merrill Hyde smashed a two-run homer in the first inning for the winners. The semi-finals will now pit Guttenberg against the Whitehawks.

GUTTENBERG, BALLTOWN WIN IN SEMI-FINALS

In the opening game of the semi-finals Guttenberg scored four big runs in the fifth inning to put down Dyersville 4-2. Both teams collected eight hits for the night.

Dyersville took a lead in the second inning as Jim Hosch led off with a home run. Guttenberg came back to load the bases but could not score. No runs were scored in the third but in the fourth Guttenberg tore the game wide open as Klinger led off with a double. Rentschler followed with a single. A fielder's choice and two walks and two singles gave plenty of strength for four runs.

Dyersville came back in the last inning when Art Huinker smacked a double. He scored as his brother Ken also connected for a double. Rod Tangeman, on the mound for Guttenberg, was the winning pitcher.

Ken Huinker was the losing pitcher. He was relieved by his brother in the fourth. Art Huinker led the Hawks in batting with a single and a double.

Gary Peterson and Kirk Rentschler each had two singles for Guttenberg.

Balltown was a winner over Epworth in the other semi-final and faced Guttenberg in the championship. Now we will tackle the Cascade tournament. The competition gets tougher as the teams progress through these tournaments. Each one, in succession, offers a bigger prize for the champions. And the crowds tend to get bigger with each one.

WHITEHAWKS WIN 3-0 OVER NEW VIENNA

Art Huinker pitched a one-hitter against New Vienna Saturday to oust New Vienna from the Cascade Tournament by a score of 3-0.

The Dyersville Whitehawks moved out of first round action in the tourney as they played errorless ball for the victory. Art Huinker looked very good as he struck out 11 men during the seven inning game. The only New Vienna hit came in the second inning as Don Kerper singled but did not get off of first base as he was put out going to second and the next two

270

*men struck out. Only four men managed to reach first base for
New Vienna.*

  *Dyersville scored the first runs of the game in the third
inning as Tom Jenk drew a walk and Huinker followed with a
triple to get Jenk in. Jim Hosch hit into a fielder's choice and
New Vienna made a play on Huinker at home plate. Hosch
moved around to third as Huinker was caught in a run-down.
Hosch stole home for the second run of game. The Hawks' final
run came in the 6th inning.*

The victory placed Dyersville in the quarter finals and a game against
Monticello. It took twelve innings but Monticello came out on top, 4-3, to
eliminate the Hawks from the Cascade tournament.

  MONTICELLO, BALLTOWN WIN
  *Balltown and Monticello chalked up wins Wednesday
night and advanced into the semi-final round of the Cascade
baseball tourney. Balltown battered Zwingle, 12-2 but it took
Monticello 12 innings to subdue Dyersville, 4-3.*

  *Dyersville scored in the top of the first. Tom Jenk and
Art Huinker singled and scored on two errors and a passed ball.
Jim Wright doubled for Monticello in the second, moved to third
on an infield out and scored on an error.*

  *Blair Beatty's home run in the fifth gave Dyersville a
3-1 lead. But the winners tied it in the bottom of the seventh
when pinch-hitter Al Westhoff homered with one on and sent the
contest into extra innings.*

  *Mike Hall walked for Monticello in the 12th. He went
to second when Dave Westhoff was hit by a pitched ball and
scored on Bill Howie's single.*

An early exit for the Dyersville team and a tough loss. But that is the
level of competition faced in these tournaments and it leads to some great
baseball. The name Westhoff played a major role in Monticello baseball for many
years. There were four that played regularly including Al, Dave, Rick and Gordy.
Good ball players with lots of spirit. Those combined with brothers Jim and John
Wright, and Monti had the nucleus of a good baseball team. Add a strong pitcher
in Mike Hall and they were going to be a tough team to beat for many years.

There were no pitchers listed in the write-up and so I can't give credit to
the hurlers who must have pitched very successfully over the 12 innings.
Dyersville collected six hits and Monticello managed eight hits. Beyond that, I
have no further memories, probably because you tend to block out losses
sometimes. Now for the final local tournament coming up at Dyersville. Can the
Hawks bounce back?

The first round opponent for the host team was Garnavillo. Although not over officially after the first inning, for all practical purposes the outcome was. The Whitehawks scored eleven runs in the first and coasted to a final victory, 16-1. Roy Willenbring and Les Ernster led all hitters with three hits apiece. Our next opponent was Winthrop in the quarter-finals.

HOLY CROSS TIPS EPWORTH

Holy Cross and Dyersville advanced into the semi-final round of the Dyersville tourney after gaining quarter-final wins Thursday.

Holy Cross had to come from behind, scoring three runs in the final three innings to tip a determined Epworth squad, 3-2, and Dyersville rolled over Winthrop, 11-4. The losers added a second run in the third inning as Tom Kramer singled, stole second and scored on an error.

Shut out until the sixth inning, Holy Cross scored when Merle Marting tripled and was sacrificed home by Chuck Roling. They tied the score in the bottom of the seventh on singles by Joe Ackerman, Bob LeGrand and John Schiesl. In the extra inning Marting singled, went to second on an error and scored on two wild pitches.

A five-run second inning gave Dyersville the edge all the way. Blair Beatty's three-run homer was the big blow. Jim Hosch hit a round-tripper for the winners in the third and Les Lammers clouted a four-bagger for the losers in the first with nobody on.

The victory by Holy Cross was a big triumph for their program. They had dropped out of the top echelon of teams in the area, but with some of the present players along with an outstanding group of young players coming out of the local high school program, they had a bright future ahead for their town. One of the veterans on the Holy Cross team was Chuck Roling.

In the meantime, the semi-finals were ready to be played. It paired Holy Cross and Dyersville in the first game with Cascade and Zwingle facing off in the other contest.

DYERSVILLE, ZWINGLE POST TOURNEY WINS

Zwingle and Dyersville advanced to the finals of the Dyersville Baseball Tourney by posting semi-final wins Monday night. Dyersville stopped Holy Cross, 5-1, on Art Huinker's two-hit pitching and Zwingle scored a 2-1 win over Cascade on Bob Meyer's three-hitter. Between games Nancy Tainter of Guttenberg was named Queen of the baseball tourney. Her attendants included Kay Stevens of Dyersville, Sue Steffen of Winthrop and Erma Hirtz of Cascade.

272

Dyersville, the defending champions, scored two runs in the first inning on back-to-back doubles by Buzz Beatty and Tom Jenk. Jenk scored on an infield out. The winners added one in the second. Beatty was safe on a forceout, stole second and scored on Jenk's single.

Holy Cross scored its long run in the fourth when leadoff man Jim Fitzgerald tripled and scored on an infield out.

Jim Wegman's triple drove in one run for Dyersville in the fifth and he scored on an error.

In the second game, two errors aided Zwingle in chalking up its two runs in the fifth. Meyer was safe on an error and was doubled home by Marnell Schaefer. An infield error on Haven Schmidt's grounder allowed Schaefer to score what proved to be the winning run.

Cascade broke the scoring ice in the seventh when Cammell McDermott singled, advanced on an error and scored as Neil Gavin grounded out.

In the second game of the semi-finals, not one run scored was earned. Bob Meyer from the Cedar Rapids area and Roger Fenwick from Wisconsin both pitched outstanding games. John Schiesl pitched credibly for Holy Cross against Dyersville, allowing only seven hits but had five errors made behind him.

The championship game between Zwingle and Dyersville was played the next night. It was a fantastic pitcher's duel between Zwingle's Bob Meyer and Roy Willenbring for Dyersville.

ZWINGLE COPS MEET CROWN, 2-1

A dropped fly ball, a wild pitch and a single allowed the winning score Tuesday night as Zwingle tipped defending champion Dyersville, 2-1 for the Dyersville baseball tourney crown. In the consolation bracket, Holy Cross rolled over Cascade, 7-1, on Joe Ackerman's two-hitter.

Pitching shutout ball for Dyersville, Roy Willenbring was coasting along with a one-run lead in the eighth inning with two out and a two strike count on batter Dave Wolfe. The next pitch never got across the plate as Wolfe pounded the ball out of the park and knotted the score, 1-1. Gary Goldsmith, the next batter, was safe on the dropped fly ball. He advanced to second on a wild pitch and scored what proved to be the winning run on Terry Herkelman's single.

Dyersville broke the scoring ice in the bottom of the sixth when leadoff man Tom Jenk doubled and rode home on Jim Hosch's triple. Hosch was tagged out at the plate on an attempted squeeze bunt.

273

Two Zwingle pitchers, Terry Herkelman and Les
Webber, gave up five hits.
Holy Cross scored four of its runs in the first two
innings of the consolation game. Jim Fitzgerald led Holy Cross
hitters with three singles and a triple. Bob Meyer, Zwingle
pitcher, was awarded the most valuable player award.

The tournament was over but Dyersville was already involved in the American Amateur Baseball Congress double-elimination tournaments. This, again, was their first year for this nation-wide program (Festina and its Northeast Iowa League had been involved for over 10 years) and because of the success in this first year, the entire effort will be covered in the next chapter.

The player getting the big home run for Zwingle to tie the game was Lost Nation, Iowa native Dave Wolfe. Dave was the younger brother of Bob Wolfe, my college roommate and baseball teammate at Loras College. Both were good athletes and played lots of semi-pro baseball in eastern and central Iowa.

For the four invitational tournaments, Dyersville could show one championship and one runner-up finish. Possibly, by the Whitehawk standards, this was not acceptable. The won-lost results were 11 wins and 4 losses for the four tournaments.

Following are attendance statistics that you may find staggering. This information was gathered and reported by the Dyersville Commercial in its August 17, 1961 edition.

TOTAL OF 15,397 FANS WATCH '61 TOURNEY
HERE
A total of 15,397 baseball fans watched the sixteen
games of the 1961 Dyersville Baseball Tournament. This tops
the 1960 attendance figure by 97 admissions. Last year's total
for the entire tournament was 15,298.
The biggest single night for this year's tournament was
Monday. The semi-finals and queen's pageant Monday
attracted a total of 4,473 fans. The finals on Tuesday night
drew a crowd of 4,115 according to the figures compiled by
Gene Tauke, Commercial Club Secretary.

Not bad for semi-pro, town-team baseball. As a player, it was an appreciative sight to see so many fans at the ball park for one of your games. It also added more pressure and tension to the game being played. But with that success comes increased pressure to continue to be a winner. It also marks your team as the team to beat by every team you play against. That is the nature of the beast. Combine that aspect with a huge crowd and we are probably defining what we consider "spirited competition." Hopefully for me that idea would always be accompanied by the spirit of "good sportsmanship."

274

PLAYING WATERBALL

For the first time, Dyersville's Whitehawks had the opportunity to compete in the American Amateur Baseball Congress national tournament. Similar to Festina's efforts, Dyersville first had to win their Maquoketa Valley League championship. They took the western division title and Holy Cross won the eastern division title. To compete in the state AABC tourney, the two division champs played a best two-out-of-three series.

DYERSVILLE, HOLY CROSS SPLIT FIRST TWO GAMES IN ABC TOURNAMENT
Dyersville and Holy Cross split the first two games in the best two out of three games in the ABC Tournament held in Dyersville last week. Dyersville handed the Holy Cross nine a 5-1 setback in Friday night's encounter. Holy Cross came back to stay in the tourney by scoring four runs in the fifth inning to set up a 4-3 win.

In the first game, Art Huinker pitched a five-hitter to set the way for a 5-1 win for Dyersville. The Whitehawks threatened to score in the first, second, and fourth innings as they had men on third each inning. In the sixth inning the first run was finally tallied as Dale Digmann connected for his second single of the game. He scored as Roy Krapfl came to the plate later in the inning and smashed a double for the first run. In the eighth inning, Dale Digmann and Krapfl teamed up again to score the second Hawk run. Digmann slammed a triple with one man out and Krapfl set up his second double of the day for the runs.

In the bottom of the eighth Holy Cross came back in the game as they scored for the first time. Jim Fitzgerald scored on his single, a passed ball, and an error.

In the top of the ninth, however, Dyersville took complete control of the game as they tallied their final runs. They tallied three big ones to put the game away. Wegmann and Jenk started the rally by each receiving walks. Art Huinker singled to advance each man. An error on Jim Hosch's fly ball and a score after the ball was caught on Merrill Hyde's fly accounted for the runs.

Huinker set 10 men down on strikes as he gave up only five hits. Tom Fessler was charged with the loss as he gave up nine hits for five runs. Dale Digmann led all hitters for the game as he banged out a triple and two singles for four times at bat.

In the second game of the three game series, Holy Cross evened the count as they racked up four runs in the fourth inning to set up the 4-3 victory.

275

Dyersville scored first in the bottom of the second inning as Jim Digmann crossed the plate after he singled to lead off the inning. In the third inning, Dyersville extended their lead as they scored two more runs. Jim Wegmann led off with a single and Gary Peterson walked. They were driven home as Tom Jenk doubled. After the third inning Dyersville was held scoreless as they managed only one more hit.

Going into the fifth inning, Holy Cross was down 3-0 and were hitless to that time. Joe Ackerman opened the hitting column as he led off with a double. Feldermann scored Ackermann as he singled. Tom Fessler followed with a walk and a single by Bob Meyer scored Feldermann for the second run. Dick Dupont put the final touches on the inning as he singled, driving in Fessler and Meyer for the big four-run inning. From that inning on, Holy Cross was held hitless.

The winning pitcher was Joe Ackermann as he allowed four hits for three runs. He issued 10 bases on balls and struck out four.

For Dyersville, Ken Huinker, Roy Willenbring and Rod Tangeman combined to allow only four hits for four runs. All four hits were collected in the fifth inning. Ken Huinker was charged with the loss.

The following brief excerpt was taken from the Waterloo Courier newspaper and reports Dyersville's second victory over Holy Cross to move on to the state tournament to be held in Denver, Iowa, located just north of Waterloo.

NEW HAMPTON, DYERSVILLE QUALIFY

Dyersville nipped Holy Cross 3-0 to win their series at Dyersville as Art Huinker pitched out of a jam in a sixth inning relief appearance. Huinker came into the game at Dyersville with his team ahead 1-0 and two on with none out in the sixth. He got out of the jam and preserved the shutout while his club scored a couple of icing runs on Merrill Hyde's double and four walks in the seventh.

Thank heaven for history. It is interesting to search through old records of all kinds, in this case mostly newspapers, to bring back all this fifty year old information. Our own memories certainly cannot maintain all that has happened in our lifetime. The final Dyersville-Holy Cross game was played on Sunday evening. The state level of the AABC tourney was scheduled to begin on Wednesday.

ALLISON NIPS '61 CHAMPS; DYERSVILLE WINS IN 14
By JIM AYERS, Courier Sports Writer

DENVER- - -Defending state champion Independence and New Hampton face the win-or-else alternative as they were to play each other in the opening game of the second round of the state amateur baseball tournament here Thursday night at 7 p.m.

Both lost first round games here at Prestien Memorial Park and another loss will eliminate them from the double-elimination tournament.

New Hampton lost a 14-inning, 3 hour, 13 minute contest to Dyersville 5-2 in the first game Wednesday night and then Allison turned back the state champs 4-2 in the nightcap which ended early Thursday morning.

Allison, with Bob White on the mound, will go against Dyersville in the second game which is scheduled to begin at 9 p.m.

New Hampton's Jim Rima and Ken Huinker, the oldest of the Huinker brothers, were locked in a pitching duel in the opening contest which saw neither team score until the 11th inning.

Dyersville batted first and scored two runs after two outs. Art Huinker, Ken's brother playing right field, started what looked like the winning rally, with a single. He moved to second on an error. Huinker and Jim Hosch then stole third and second before scoring on back-to-back singles by Merrill Hyde and Dale Digmann.

Ken Huinker struck out Dave Winter and Bob Corrick in the last of the 11th before Ernie Schmitt and Duane Josephson each singled.

Tom Jenk, Dyersville playing manager, brought in Art Huinker from the outfield. Bob Soukup greeted him with a single to left field. Schmitt score when the ball was bobbled in the outfield. Josephson scored on an error on Bob Winter's ground ball to tie it again.

The three Dyersville runs in the 14th came with no outs. Dale Digmann led off with a single to right field and Jim Digmann walked. An error let Dale score and the final two runs came on a single by Jim Wegmann.

New Hampton threatened in the 13th frame. Josephson led off with a double to the 355 foot mark. After Soukup flew out, Josephson moved to third on an infield out but then Bob Winter popped out to Jenk to end the inning.

A player that seemed in our hair most of the game was future major leaguer, Duane Josephson. Duane was a catcher for the Chicago White Sox for a number of seasons. I believe, for this game, he was a high school senior that had just graduated from New Hampton High School in the spring. The double he clobbered to the fence off me in the 13th was a curve ball below the strike zone. He had no trouble bending his right knee and getting the bat head on the pitch as well as anybody. He returned to the New Hampton area after his pro career was over but ending up dying at a very young age. Athletically he also was an outstanding basketball player in high school.

We also saw Bob Soukup in the local tournaments in Dubuque County quite frequently. And we have talked about Dick Winter who had a fantastic college baseball career at Loras, one year behind me. Bob Winter who made the last out was Dick's younger brother. Both grew up on a farm outside of New Hampton.

Excerpts from the following write-up bring the state-level AABC tourney down to the final game. This article was written by Russ Smith, the Sports Editor for the Waterloo Courier. During his career at the Courier, he wrote several editorials highlighting the baseball careers of the three left-handed Huinker boys from Festina.

> *INDEPENDENCE, ALLISON, DYERSVILLE ONLY*
> *TEAMS LEFT IN STATE TOURNEY*
> *By RUSS L. SMITH, Courier State Sports Editor*
> *Jim Reiter hurled a two-hitter as Independence eliminated New Hampton 6-2 in a twice-postponed second round session last night. In the second game, Bob White won a battle of three-hitters against Roy Willenbring as Allison stopped Dyersville 2-0.*
>
> *Dyersville will meet either Allison or Independence at 7:30 tonight in what may be the final game of the double elimination tournament. If the meet doesn't end tonight, the finals will be at 8 p.m. tomorrow.*
>
> *The winner will represent Iowa in the Great Plains regional tournament at Milbank, S.D., next weekend. It will earn a $350 check from the Waterloo Daily Courier to help finance the trip to Milbank.*
>
> *Only four runners reached base for Dyersville against White- - -two on singles after two were out in the second inning and two on a walk with one out and a hit with two out in the fifth. Allison's errorless defense included a circus stop by third baseman Steve Brandt on Art Huinker's sharp grounder in the fifth.*
>
> *Meanwhile, Allison got its first batter on base in each of the final four innings and got him around in the sixth. Bob Barth, who had walked, scored all the way from first in the sixth while Ken Sutton was getting caught in a rundown between first and second after he drilled a hit-and-run single into right field.*

In the seventh, Duane Newton lined a shot past the infield to open the inning and raced all the way to third when the ball went through the outfielder. He scored on Roger Kittleson's fly to left field.

Roy Willenbring struck out 10 and walked three in a very strong losing effort. Bob White struck out eight while walking only one.

In the Independence win over New Hampton, Reiter allowed a single to centerfielder Conway and another single to losing pitcher Duane Kuehner. He struck out 11 New Hampton batters. Independence garnered 8 hits, one a Darwin Fritz home run in the fourth. Fritz played most of his games for Sumner. Another player picked up for this tournament was outfielder Larry Poock from the Tripoli area. Indy also had two of the Decker boys from Winthrop, Bob behind the plate and Jude at third base, along with their long time star player, Carl Blumenshine. Blumenshine always played shortstop, but as he got older he pulled an Ernie Banks and switched to first base.

These games were hotly contested because to the winner belong big spoils. Besides the $350 check to help with expenses, it gave the winning team the right to represent their state in what was looked upon as a great experience playing top-notch baseball against totally unfamiliar opponents.

Again, this was Dyersville's first effort in the AABC. Allison already had won the state title three times before and Independence had just won it a year ago. On the Dyersville team, none of the players except brother Kenny and myself had experienced the challenge of playing baseball games day after day, and even two in one day in these AABC tournaments. Because of the double-elimination format this was a common demand on a team. The players also experienced the highly-contested value that teams put into this championship. For most, this was the only tournament of the year for them. That plus winning meant a trip to South Dakota to continue playing baseball. Maybe even a trip to Battle Creek, Michigan for a "national championship" opportunity. Kenny and I had both been there.

There were now three teams left. Independence and Dyersville each had one loss. One more and you are out. Allison was still undefeated. I am not sure how the teams playing each other in the next game were determined. One possibility was that Allison and Independence had not played each other in the tourney. Dyersville had played both. The other possibility was the luck of a draw and Dyersville lucked out. Remember that Allison had just beaten Dyersville, 2-0 on Saturday night.

In the Independence-Allison contest, Independence jumped out to a 5-0 lead after six innings behind the strong pitching of lefthander Jim Borcherding. Scoring three runs in the top of the seventh knocked Borcherding out and brought

Allison back into the game. The game was tied 6-6 going into the bottom of the ninth before an unearned run for Independence gave Allison its first loss.

Now, with each team having one loss, Dyersville had to play one of the two other teams left. Again, how that was determined I am not sure. The procedures for this are all established so there is no argument or doubt as to who Dyersville will play. Independence was our opponent for Sunday night after their grueling win in the afternoon.

Following are excerpts from that write-up.

STATE TOURNEY FINALS MONDAY
By RUSS L. SMITH, Courier State Sports Editor
Dyersville ousted defending champion Independence, 1-0, Sunday night in the semifinal game after Independence had handed Allison its first loss in the tournament, 7-6, in the afternoon.

Jim Reiter, who threw a two-hitter just Saturday night to win for Independence, came back as a starter Sunday night and locked up in a shutout for six innings against Dyersville's cagey lefty, Art Huinker.

Reiter allowed only three hits and struck out nine- - - two of them with the bases loaded in the first inning- - -before retiring at the end of the sixth.

Then Dyersville scored the only run of the game in the seventh. With one out, Jim Digman singled off Ken Denger. He went to third on an error as Tangeman was safe at first on a sacrifice bunt attempt. Catcher Bob Decker threw Tangeman out attempting to steal second and Digmann stayed on third. Then, with two out, he came home on a passed ball.

Huinker successfully scattered four hits and left nine runners stranded as he struck out 15.

The finals were played the following night. Games had been played Friday night, Saturday afternoon and evening and Sunday afternoon and evening. Most of the Dyersville players probably worked all day Monday at their day job, then back to Denver for another game on Monday night. It does wear on the players, trying to complete such a hectic schedule.

ALLISON BOWS, 7-5, IN TITLE CONTEST
By RUSS L. SMITH, Courier State Sports Editor
Dyersville, a big Iowa baseball name, will undertake a big task this weekend as Iowa's state amateur baseball champion.

Dyersville will take a 44-7 record into the tournament. The happy Tom Jenk began making plans to depart for the

280

regional as soon as the championship game ended Monday night.

The new champions never trailed in the title game Monday night after four of their first five batters singled for a 2-0 lead in the first inning. Cleanup batter Merrill Hyde was the hitting star for Dyersville with a double and two singles. He scored one run and drove in two. Steve Brandt had a double and single to pace Allison.

The Dyersville Commercial write-up of the game listed Ken Huinker as starting pitcher, relieved by Roy Willenbring in the third and Rod Tangeman in the seventh. Although I doubt it made any difference to the pitchers involved, the Commercial listed Willenbring as the winning pitcher, while the Waterloo Courier listed Rod Tangeman as the winner. Also, Dale Digmann and Jim Hosch had two hits apiece for the Whitehawks.

Now we had to prepare for a trip to Milbank, South Dakota for the AABC Regionals. Ball players look forward to that challenge and only hope that they will be allowed to take off work.

The interesting part of the trip for the Huinkers was the pregnancy and the close delivery date for Ann and our fifth child. No, in this period of time, the sex of the newborn was unknown. For us, with the score tied- - -two boys and two girls- - -we had no preference. Because the delivery date was not far away, our family doctor, Dr. Griffin, informed Ann that it would not be wise for her to make the trip to South Dakota. That was not good news for the two of us. First of all, Ann enjoyed going to the games almost as much as I enjoyed playing them. And she shared an understanding of the game that was amazing. We would even discuss, and sometimes argue, the decisions that were made during a game I either played in or served as coach. Above all, we just thoroughly enjoyed being together on baseball trips, such as the upcoming South Dakota trip. It was a vacation of sorts for us. With our young family, there weren't too many lengthy times away from our family. The weekend baseball trip to Milbank, however, became a two-weekend trip, due to heavy rains that drenched the ball park on the final scheduled Sunday championship game(s).

IOWA CHAMPS WIN 12-1
Courier News Service
Dyersville, Iowa's champs, moved into the winners' bracket of the Amateur Regional Baseball tournament here with 12-1 trouncing of the host team and faces Fargo, N.D. in an 8 p.m. contest tonight in the double elimination meet.

Art Huinker pitched a five-hitter last night, striking out 14 and walking only four. He was backed by a 14-hit attack.

Dyersville jumped on Milbank pitcher Jim Halvorson for two runs in the second on a pair of errors and a two-run

281

double by Merrill Hyde. In the fifth Ken Huinker collected a
double, and went to third on a balk. Jim Wegmann walked,
stole second and Tom Jenk singled in both runs.
*   The Iowans ran the count to 7-1 in the seventh with*
another pair of runs. Again a two-run double by Hyde scored
the markers.
*   Dyersville completed the scoring in the eighth with five*
runs. Jim Digmann signled, Roy Kraplf walked, and Ken
Huinker singled to load the bases and Manager Jenk's single
scored a pair. Jim Hosch drove in two more with a single and
Art Huinker drove in Hosch with another base hit.

The win put us in the winner's bracket with Fargo, N.D., a major factor in double-elimination tournaments. They are our next opponent.

IOWA KINGS GAIN FINALS
(Courier News Service)
*   The Dyersville champs nipped Fargo, N.D., 4-3 in 10*
innings to become the only undefeated squad in the double
elimination tourney. The Whitehawks managed only two hits off
Curt Henre, the Fargo chucker, but were aided by 14 bases on
balls. The winning run in the last of the 10th was forced in as
Dyersville manager, Tom Jenk, drew a walk with the sacks full.
*   Jim Reiter went the distance for Dyersville Sunday,*
allowing just one earned run on seven hits and three walks. He
set 15 Fargo batters down on strikes.

I remember parts of this game quite vividly. First of all, I tried to convince Manager Jenk to start my brother Kenny in left field instead of me because I felt Kenny was hitting the ball better than I had been doing. He did that. That left me to coach first base through most of the game until Tom put me in for defensive purposes.

The next fact shows the quality of pitcher that Henre for Fargo proved to be. For most of the first six or seven innings I was able to pick up the signals of the Fargo catcher and relay that information to the hitter. Yet, we had not managed even one hit off Henre until the seventh inning.

Then, in the Fargo half of one of the latter innings after Tom had placed me in left field to play defense, his strategy paid off. A Fargo hitter laced a line drive right at me but over my head in left field. In going after it, I got turned around and at the last second managed to turn myself around and spear the ball above my left shoulder. Kenny may have gotten to the ball also but that's not what I am thinking. It was one of my better defensive plays that I remember and in a very delicate, tight situation.

After a comeback victory again by Fargo the next day to gain the tourney finals, the heavens opened and any hope of playing another game on Monday was out of the question. The only option was for both teams to come back the next weekend to play the championship, one game if Dyersville wins the first re-match, two games if Fargo wins the first rematch. All we could do is to track back to Dyersville, basically an all-day trip and prepare to be in Milbank to play for the championship the following Saturday.

The following Friday, we make the return trip to Milbank ready to play on Saturday evening. Ann stayed back in Dyersville again. But the weather was not promising. Rain had been falling most of Saturday and the hope was that the clouds would clear for a game on Sunday.

Sunday came and the rains continued. The field was filled with water puddles throughout both the infield and outfield. The dugouts (and they were deep dugouts) were water puddles. Tourney management decided that the game would be played, whether the rain ceases or continues. Well, it continued. And without any doubt, it was far and away the most miserable playing conditions that all of us ever experienced. The officials felt they could not ask both teams to come back again. Plus, the national tournament schedule was preparing to start. The end result: the game was played and the good team came away the victors in a washout.

> DYERSVILLE IN NATIONAL MEET
> (Courier News Service)
> Dyersville, Iowa state amateur baseball champions,
> won the Great Plains regional AABC crown here Sunday
> afternoon, blasting Fargo, N.D., 14-0 in a rained-on contest.
> Roy Willenborg scattered seven Fargo hits plus
> knocked in four runs with a third-inning double and sixth-inning
> single. He walked only two and struck out 11, including the side
> in the ninth.
> Other big bats in the Dyersville lineup were Buzz
> Beatty and catcher Dale Digmann. Beatty had a home run and
> a single for three runs. Digmann had three singles good for
> four RBIs. Art Huinker and Tom Jenk each had two hits also for
> the winners.

The Dyersville Whitehawks proved to be good mudders. They had twelve hits and left thirteen runners on base. Infielders actually played out of position in order to not stand in a puddle of water. I find it amazing that Roy Willenborg could pitch the entire game under extremely wet conditions and walk only three hitters while Fargo pitchers were walking 13. It is one of the few games where I scored four runs. The Whitehawks were headed for Battle Creek, Michigan, hopeful that their gear would dry out by the time we had to play again.

We should have called the game we played by a different name. A more appropriate name would have been "waterball."

We have qualified for the AABC national championship double-elimination tournament, held each year at Battle Creek, Michigan.

The tournament was scheduled to start on Friday, September 14 for the Whitehawks. However, they moved into the second round winner's group when opponent New Haven, Connecticut had to forfeit because many of their players were college football players and they had college games on the weekend and could not field their team. It was the first time in the history of the AABC that a national finals game had been forfeited. It was a break for the Iowa representative because it saved on pitching usage, and placed them in the winner's bracket.

Other teams in the tournament were defending champion Portland, OR, Houston, TX, Savannah, GA, Coldwater from Michigan, Chicago from the state of Indiana, Louisville, KY, and Dyersville. Dyersville by far represented the smallest community.

Kenny and I would be heading to Battle Creek for the second time, both having played with Sumner ten years earlier. What was Ann going to do? Her delivery date was even closer but she convinced her doctor that she could not miss this opportunity of attending the national tourney. She had not been there the first time and neither had Kenny's wife because neither of us had been married at the earlier time. So, against her doctor's wishes, she packed her suitcase and traveled with us. Several of the players assured her that they could take care of things if the baby came while we were at the tourney. That assurance didn't make me feel any better, but her going with me just in itself was satisfying, baby or not. As it turned out, Jennifer (it was a girl) was born on October 5, almost two weeks after we returned to Dyersville. She came about 6:15 in the evening, the same day as our Homecoming football game. The new Daddy/assistant football coach was able to return by the start of the varsity football game. Our opponent that night was both Ann's and my alma mater, Calmar High School, now South Winneshiek High School. Unknown to Ann's parents who drove down from Calmar to attend the football game, they heard the announcement that their daughter had given birth to a baby girl at half time of the game.

As for the tournament itself, the Whitehawks played Savannah, Georgia in the first game. Our pitching opponent was a lefthander, Woody Johnson, who just happened to be 49 years old. He set us down on four hits and we lost game one by the score of 5-1.

DYERSVILLE IN FIRST LOSS
(Courier News Service)
Dyersville now must win or be eliminated from the
American Amateur Baseball Congress national finals here
today. The Iowa champions suffered their first loss yesterday

284

*afternoon 5-1 to the four-hit pitching of 49-year-old Woody
Johnson.*

*Savannah, GA., the team that beat Dyersville, won its
first round game Friday, 2-1 over Louisville, KY.*

*Dyersville's Whitehawks were able to garner only four
hits off the offerings of lefthanded Johnson. Their only run
came in the seventh when pitcher Art Huinker walked, went to
third on a single by Blair Beatty and scored while Savannah
was trying for but not completing an inning-ending double play.*

*Savannah scored in the first on a hit batsman and two
singles off previously undefeated Art Huinker. Two more runs
came in the fourth, when with two outs a fly ball was dropped in
the outfield that let two runs score. Single runs were scored in
the seventh and eighth.*

Definitely, this was one of those days when I struggled. I felt that I had
left my teammates down. That feeling got stronger later. Thirteen hits were
garnered by the Savannah team along with three walks and a hit batsman. In
addition, they had three stolen bases. Stolen bases are usually gained off the
pitcher, not the catcher. At least, on this day, I remember doing a lousy job of
holding runners on. This dropped us into the loser's bracket.

HAWKS BOUNCE BACK IN AABC WITH 9-1 WIN

*The Dyersville Whitehawks bounced right back Sunday
in the NAABC tournament to paste a 9-1 defeat on Coldwater,
Michigan. The game saw the Whitehawks' Jim Reiter perform
masterfully when he hurled a neat one-hitter at the host
Coldwater team. Reiter's one-hitter was over the seven inning
route, since the eight-run tournament rule.*

*Reiter was hailed by the crowd of 1,500 as he neared
his no-hit goal. It was Don Nowery, a big outfield star for
Coldwater, who ruined Reiter's feat when he lofted a long home
run in the seventh inning. Reiter allowed only four runners on
base. He walked only two and struck out nine.*

*The Whitehawks, representing the smallest community
in the tournament, scored five runs with two hits in the third
inning. Jim Hosch was on second when Jim Wegmann hit a
high foul that was misjudged and missed. Wegmann then
singled Hosch home. Tom Jenk walked and Art Huinker
smashed a big double to drive in two runs. Blair Beatty walked
and was followed by back to back singles by Jim and Dale
Digmann.*

*In the fourth, Rollie Sampson singled and was sent to
second on a sacrifice by Reiter. Wegmann then singled,
Sampson moved to third and scored on an error. Tom Jenk
grounded out and Art Huinker then doubled to score Wegmann*

285

and scored himself when a throwing error was charged against Coldwater. In the top of the seventh the Whitehawks scored again on successive singles by Jenk, Art Huinker and Buzz Beatty.

The loss for Coldwater eliminated them from the double-elimination tournament. The next opponent for the Whitehawks was Louisville, KY. Both teams have already lost one game.

As for Ann, no warning signs, although she is supposedly overdue. Game 3 on Monday.

WILLENBRING HURLS HAWKS TO FINALS 7-0
In one of the best pitched games of the AABC World Series Tournament, LeRoy Willenbring gave up only four hits in Dyersville's 7-0 win over Louisville, Kentucky on Monday afternoon. Willenbring struck out eight Louisville batters and walked only one.

The second frame opened with Rollie Sampson singling, Willenbring getting a single, followed by Jim Wegmann's single that got Sampson home. Tom Jenk then singled to score Willenbring.

Tom Jenk led the Whitehawk batters with three hits. Dale Digman and Jim Hosch each collected two hits.

Now it is down to just two teams. Portland, Oregon is still the unbeaten defending champion. For the Whitehawks to win, they must defeat Portland two in a row, the challenge of coming out of the loser's bracket.

The following write-up headlines and excerpts appeared in the September 20, 1961 issue of the Dyersville Commercial.

TRIUMPHANT HAWKS HOME WITH 2nd PLACE IN AABC; LOSE TO REPEAT CHAMPS PORTLAND IN LATE INNINGS
The Dyersville Whitehawks, described as the "Darlings" of the American Amateur Baseball Congress World Series at Battle Creek, Michigan, came back home Tuesday night with second place honors in the meet.

The home folks, area and the state apparently were more than well pleased with the showing of the Whitehawks, although some of the players expressed disappointment in Monday's game with Portland, Oregon when the Whitehawks lost 11-7 in the late innings after commanding a 5-0 lead in the second inning and a 7-1 advantage in the top of the 6th frame.

Manager Tom Jenk said the boys were physically exhausted and injury ridden for the final game with Portland

286

Monday night. "We played Louisville in the afternoon. It was nearly seven o'clock before we could get to the hotel, and then we had to eat and rush right back to the park to play the big game with Portland."

One of the tough "breaks" the Whitehawks had was in the fifth inning, when Beatty hit what appeared to be a clean single with men on 2nd and 3rd base, but the"hard luck" shortstop's knee gave out running to first. In what could have been two additional runs turned out to be the third out.

It was probably the four errors that the tired Whitehawks committed in the last three innings that had a big hand in the Portland win.

"We just ran out of gas," is the words Jenk used describing the final game Monday night.

The Whitehawks scored one run in the first inning and added four big runs in the second inning. In the second, Tom Jenk cracked a long double and Art Huinker followed with a single to score the first run. In the fourth the Hawks accounted for four runs on Jim Digmann's single, a Portland error on Jim Hosch's ground ball, then a Rollie Sampson single followed by Ken Huinker's double and a single by Jim Wegmann.

The Hawks added two runs in the top of the sixth inning when Rod Tangeman singled with two outs. Tom Jenk was hit by a pitched ball. The Portland leftfielder dropped Art Huinker's long fly ball and Tangeman scored. Then Roy Krapfl, who had replaced Blair Beatty at shortstop, singled to score Jenk.

After scoring five runs in the sixth, Lloyd Lewis , Portland leftfielder, homered over the center field fence off Dyersville's Art Huinker to tie the score.

For Dyersville, Ken Huinker started and pitched one and two-thirds innings. Rod Tangeman followed and went four innings. Art Huinker finished the game and was charged with the loss.

Tom Jenk, Jim Wegmann and Jim Digmann each had two hits for the Hawks.

First, a short commentary on the unusual design of the baseball field where most of the games were played at Battle Creek. Only the first game we played was on the other field. Nearly 100% of ball fields are deepest in center field and shorter down the two foul lines. This was not true of this diamond. Down the left field foul line, the fence was 391 feet from home plate, forty feet deeper than even the Cubs' Wrigley Field where the distance is 355 feet. Right field was about 375 feet, also deeper by 20 feet than Wrigley Field. But in center field, the fence at Battle Creek was 368 feet. A common center field fence in the majors is 390 feet, and most of the time, even more.

287

The home run that spoiled Jim Reiter's no-hitter was hit to the left of center field, a location not as deep as most. It is possible that it could have been caught by center fielder Jim Wegmann if he had the room. And this was definitely true of the Portland home run that tied the final game in the seventh. Jim would have made that catch easily on a normal field. But there is no rule in baseball which says center field has to be deeper than other parts of the field. The fence went in almost a straight line from the left field foul line to the right field foul line.

It was a thrill to be playing for a national championship, to be so close. Little things happen that make such a big difference, such as the injury to Blair Beatty. But those are the happenings that make the game exciting, the happenings that cause the unexpected to occur.

For me, this tournament had a very burdensome outcome, being the losing pitcher in both games the Whitehawks lost. I don't think that not having lost all year was the reason. I really wasn't even aware of that aspect until going through the write-ups for this book. Between Roy Willenbring and myself, we were pitchers expected by the team to provide strong pitching outings. I didn't provide this for the Whitehawks at Battle Creek. It is something that a person lives with for the rest of his life. If happens often in sports. A missed shot at the buzzer, a missed putt for the championship, a missed field goal that would have won the game, a dropped baton in a relay race, these are all examples that probably remind all of us of many more examples. It doesn't destroy your outlook on life. It isn't on your mind that much. It doesn't stop you from accomplishing a satisfying life. At least, it hasn't for me. It is just there and I wish it could have been different. But that is life. What is the old saying, "If you never reach for something, you never have to worry about failing." What a miserable life it would be to live that way.

Four weeks of four tournaments for the Dyersville Whitehawks. A time period in which 13 games were played against top competition in which the team won nine games and lost four. Three of the four games we came through as champions, starting with very stiff competition from Maquoketa Valley opponent, Holy Cross. For the season the Whitehawks had a record of 46 wins and 9 losses. Lots of baseball. Lots of fun. Lots of memories. And a fifth child, Jennifer, shortly after the season was over.

The following story has to be told. My memory recall breaks down quite often so I do not recall who sponsored an informal team party held in a building at Dyersville's Commercial Club Park which in the early '60's was called the " beer garden." It held many huge city gatherings throughout the year but definitely of the informal type. This particular night, now the middle of October with a fall chill in the air, the team and other guests had congregated. The entrance to the building consisted of two huge sliding doors that had been pulled almost shut with about a two foot opening because of the cold. Across from that opening was a long service bar, possibly thirty feet away. Our famous catcher, Dale Digmann, challenged teammates to determine who could throw a baseball from the bar through the two foot opening on the opposite side of the building. Dale threw first and had no difficulty accomplishing this task. Most of the other players, including myself, followed suit but with no positive results. For most of us, we did not even come close. Dale proceeded to throw two more through the opening without fail. Try it sometime in a closed building with a low ceiling. I have often talked about the value for any pitcher to have a strong catcher. Dale is respected in this area as one of the best and he certainly gets my vote also. Add to that, he was probably one of the better clutch hitters in the game at that time as well.

Trip number two to Battle Creek, Michigan to play in the national AABC tournament has many memories. Even though, in my case, some of those memories are not very positive, it was still an enjoyable challenge to play the game you love at that level. We will be back for more. There is always a next year. For the Dyersville team, there will be two more. And, above all, I enjoyed Ann being with me for this trip, even if she was nine months(?) or more pregnant.

A HOME RUN AND A BLOOPER

We start our third year in our rental home on Fifth Avenue SE in Dyersville. Ann is now mother to five children eight years and younger with the addition of our third daughter, Jennifer, on October 5, 1962. Certainly the most dramatic of all the births of our children so far. Our Dodge Lancer wagon was registering over 90 miles an hour as we went down the long hill on Highway 20 coming into Dubuque. In the city of Dubuque, red lights caused us to slow down but if no one was coming, we proceeded through. Why did we have to drive all the way over to Xavier Hospital in the northeast quadrant of the city, you ask? It was the place where Dr. Griffin's practice did all their hospital procedures. On this particular day, Mercy appeared so much closer, especially when the baby beat the doctor to the hospital.

Yet, when the birth was over and Ann and baby were back in a hospital room, we found that Ann's roommate in the maternity room was Millie Hoerner, whose husband, Bob, was one of Dubuque's baseball greats. She had also given birth to a daughter. Bob and Millie were an amazing couple to share a room with. We also have to realize that it is the first week in October and in the sixties, the World Series was always played about that time. Besides the Hoerners and Huinkers, the chief maternity nurse was a Franciscan nun, Sister Marilla, who just happened to be a baseball fan also. So, here is Millie and Ann, the two mothers with their new offspring, getting limited attention as Sister, Bob and I discussed baseball and the World Series. Tongue in cheek, after all what is more important? I don't mean that, but the baseball talk amused the two new mothers, I think.

At the end of this baseball season and the start of a new school year, Ann and I would send our second child, Tim, off to Kindergarten while Terry moved on to second grade. That left Ann with her three daughters during the day.

The high school baseball season was winding down and the Whitehawks were preparing to kick off another busy season. We had a couple of changes. Manager Tom Jenk brought in an outstanding pitcher from the University of Iowa by the name of Jim McAndrew. From the Lost Nation area south of Maquoketa, Jim actually had pitched for Earlville against us last year in the Worthington tournament. He showed great stuff, especially an overpowering fast ball, throughout all the games he pitched. Later, Jim signed a professional contract with the New York Mets and pitched in the majors for them from 1968 to 1973. His best season was 11 wins, 8 losses in 1972. He finished his career with San Diego in 1974. He comes from the same town as my college roommate, Bob Wolfe. In fact, they are related to each other, both with lots of Irish in them. At the same time, we lost Roy Willenbring, who primarily pitched for his hometown of Petersburg. Sal, as most of us know him, had a great 1962 season with the Whitehawks. He would also be available for the Whitehawks on specific occasions and had a place on the roster for the AABC tournaments later on.

290

Another great addition for the Hawks in 1962 was college teammate, Dick Wright. Dick was now employed by his alma mater, Loras College, and he brought a strong bat to our offensive attack. And maybe best of all, he brought a very positive, fun-filled attitude to the team. Additional young talent from the Xavier High School team filled in often, particularly in Maquoketa Valley League and other non-league games.

The first game McAndrews pitched was an early June battle against Dubuque on their home field. Going into the eighth inning, he had a no-hitter going. At that point, he tired quickly and gave up three walks and two hits and four Dubuque runs. Roy Krapfl with a double and a single, and Rollie Sampson with two singles provided most of the Dyersville batting power.

The same weekend, the Whitehawks remained unbeaten after six Maquoketa Valley league games with a 6-2 victory over Holy Cross. Holy Cross managed six hits off my pitching, while eight batters fanned. Jim Wegmann and Bob Goldsmith each slapped two singles, accounting for three of the six runs gained by Dyersville.

In an earlier game against Winthrop, I garnered a home run and two doubles good for four runs driven in, while pitching the first three innings of the 7-1 victory. Bob Goldsmith and Roy Willenbring also took the mound during that game.

In another league game the same week, the Whitehawks defeated league opponent, Sherrill, by a score of 12-6. Bob Goldsmith slammed another home run for us.

In a later June game, the Whitehawks and Jim McAndrews beat Satchell Paige and his touring All Stars. The game was in control of the home towners and McAndrews yielded only five hits going into the ninth when the All Stars sent three runners across the plate and had the tying runs on base. McAndrews got the last batter to hit a lazy fly to me in left and the game was over.

As usual, Satch pitched two innings but now his pitching was almost a lobbing of the ball over the plate. I know I would not have driven a double off the fence in left if he had been pitching like all of us know he could.

Again this year the Whitehawks will play over 50 baseball games, many of them non-league games. We will not include written coverage of most of these and concentrate on a new league organized around only teams that have lights. The league was named the Quad County League, with teams from four different counties participating. The counties were Chickasaw (New Hampton), Bremer (Sumner and Fredericksburg), Buchanan (Winthrop and Independence) and Dubuque County (Dyersville). The Whitehawks won the league with a record of 6 wins and 2 losses.

On the road at New Hampton in a Quad-County league game, the Whitehawks suffered their worst defeat of the season, 9-0. We committed seven errors in the game and winning pitcher, Don Kuehner, gave us only 5 hits. Not one Whitehawk runner reached third base in the game. We often had other players filling in for us in these league games because it became impossible for some of us to play every game. Manager Jenk couldn't even make the game at New Hampton. Rod Tangeman pitched for the Whitehawks and Gary Peterson did the catching.

Later in the year, New Hampton visited Dyersville on our home diamond and we defeated them 7-3. Roy Willenbring and Jim McAndrew shared pitching duties for that game. New Hampton's great player, Duane Josephson, who had missed the first game, had three of their seven hits, including a home run. We scored two runs in the first after my lead-off double, a walk to Tom Jenk, both scoring when Dale Digmann delivered a triple. New Hampton returned the error favor of our earlier contest by committing six boots, including three in the second inning. That victory clinched the league title for the Whitehawks.

In one of those rare occurrences for me, we traveled to Sumner and came away with a 10-1 victory over the Cubs. Following are excerpts from the write-up for this earlier game.

10 RUNS ON 11 HITS IN QUAD COUNTY WIN
Dyersville and Sumner collected 11 hits apiece but Dyersville capitalized on theirs with 10 runs for a 10-1 win Wednesday night at Sumner for their fourth win in the Quad County Loop.
The Whitehawks led off in the first inning with four runs off a two-run triple by center fielder Art Huinker, a double by first baseman Dale Digmann scoring Huinker and a one run single by starting pitcher Tom Fessler.
Sumner returned with a rally of their own in the bottom half of the first bombing Fessler for five straight hits and one run. Dick Wright relieved Fessler with the bases loaded and one away and the Whitehawks' outfielder retired the next two batters.
Huinker blasted out a single in addition to his three bagger in the first, Digmann doubled and singled and left fielder George Benn contributed a double and single.

That was not your typical ball game against Sumner. They had one of the best pitchers around in Chuck Anderson but he was not present for this game. We were fortunate.

There is another interesting sidelight to that Sumner game. For some unknown reason, at the time anyway, I could not throw a baseball, even underhanded, from pitcher's mound to home plate. Playing center field in the

292

game, either the shortstop or the second baseman would run out to me in center when any kind of batted ball came my way. I would basically roll it to them, and they in turn would return it to the infield. Because of the lopsidedness of the score, that inability on my part had little impact on the game. A few days later, after various therapies had been tried by several professionals, a trip to a chiropractor, one pop, and I was back to throwing the baseball as usual.

Later the Quad County League sponsored their own league tournament. The opening round saw Dyersville down Independence, 9-6, in a game played at Independence. Following is a short excerpt of that victory.

> *WHITEHAWKS IN QUAD COUNTY OPENING*
> *VICTORY OVER INDEPENDENCE*
> *Third baseman Cliff Knippel put in a clutch single in the sixth inning with two men on and two away, to continue an eight-run scoring spree. Jim Wegmann and pinch hitter Tom Jenk each followed up with singles and catcher Dick Wright slammed a double for insurance runs.*
> *Pitcher Art Huinker and Wright were the big sticks for the visitors. Wright, batting clean-up in the initial inning, slammed a homer along with his sixth inning double. Huinker blasted a triple after Wright's round tripper and singled two times in the sixth inning.*

The next game of this tournament created a few headaches for Manager Tom Jenk. It was scheduled to be played the same night that the Whitehawks had to play Lowden in the Monticello tourney. He cobbled together a lineup for the game at Sumner but ended up losing, 6-5 to the host team. Tom Fessler allowed only five scattered hits and fanned 18 batters but still ended up on the short end of the score. Irony of ironies, the Monticello tourney game with Lowden was cancelled when the lights didn't work and the game was not played. Not fair but those things do happen.

The first of the usual local tournaments was again scheduled at Monticello, a single-elimination, eight-team tourney. First up for Dyersville was an engagement with Epworth.

> *MCANDREW HURLS 1-HITTER IN*
> *TOURNAMENT WIN*
> *The Dyersville Whitehawks made a fine opening game showing in the Monticelle Baseball Tournament Sunday night as Jim McAndrew spotted the Epworth nine only one hit to blank them 8-0 and give them their first setback of the season.*
> *Dale Digmann and Bob Goldsmith provided the Hawks slugging force with three hits and two doubles respectively.*
> *Left fielder Art Huinker provided the winning margin with a double in the first inning scoring Tom Jenk and Dick*

293

*Wright. He then followed the path to home plate on Digmann's
single. A lone tally came in the third when Digmann's double
scored Huinker. Four more runs resulted in the fourth.
Huinker's single brought in Goldsmith and Wright. Digmann
followed with another single and right fielder Rollie Sampson
doubled in both Huinker and Digmann.*

A good start for the local tournament trail. Now for a semi-final game
with Lowden, a community south of Monticello. Following are brief excerpts
from that write-up.

> *HAWKS IN 3-0 WIN OVER LOWDEN IN MONTI
> MEET*
> *The Dyersville Whitehawks advanced into semi-final
> round play in a 3-0 victory over Lowden last Thursday night.
> Hawk pitcher Art Huinker allowed only four Lowden hits in the
> seven inning contest.*
> *Dyersville runs came when Huinker singled in third
> baseman Dick Wright from first base in the second inning. Bob
> Goldsmith doubled to score Wegmann for another run. The last
> of the three runs came off a hard-hit double by left fielder Cliff
> Knippel who got a return-trip ticket from Wegmann's single.*
> *Mainstays in the Whitehawk batting lineup were Jim
> Wegmann who doubled and singled and Art Huinker who
> blasted two solos. Cliff Knippel and Dale Digmann also
> slammed doubles.*

The championship game of the Monti tournament against Petersburg was
a scoreless pitchers' battle between Jim McAndrew for the Whitehawks and
Roger Fenwick for Petersburg. Petersburg threatened in the first on an error and
two walks with one out but a ball hit back to the mound for a McAndrew to Dale
Digmann to Tom Jenk double play ended the inning.

Scoring a single run in the sixth, six in the eighth and three in the ninth
left the final score 10-0 and a Hawk championship. McAndrew and Harry
Koelker of Petersburg were named most valuable players for the tourney.

The annual Worthington tournament followed. In the opening round the
Whitehawks blanked Rickardsville, 12-0. It was a good night for me, pitching a
two-hitter and at the plate contributed three doubles and a home run. All four of
the extra-base hits were against the fence in left center with one going over.
When one hits the ball as I did that night, the memory stays with a person. And it
stayed with Rickardsville Manager Bill Sahm until the next time we played each
other in the Cascade Tournament sometime later.

Second round action saw Jim McAndrew give the Monticello opposition
only five hits in a 8-2 triumph for the Whitehawks and a trip to the semi-finals.

The following paragraph taken from the Dyersville Commercial showed that I still had my hitting shoes on.

Left fielder Art Huinker blasted a second inning homer with one aboard for the winners and followed up in the fourth with a single. Jim Wegmann, Dick Wright, Dale Digmann and Tom Jenk had two singles apiece.

Players wish they could replicate whatever they are doing to suddenly have the power to hit the ball the way I did in those two games. Maybe it was the bat itself that made the difference, and then another player used it and cracked it the next time up. Who knows?

Also interesting was the fact that Tom Jenk, with two hits in the Monti game, also had a triple and double in the previous game. Also Dale Digmann, with two against Monti, had a double and single in the first game of the tourney.

Epworth, our semi-final opponents, collected only four hits against me and the Whitehawks were in the finals of the Worthington tournament with a 6-0 victory. Three runs in the second on walks to Roy Krapfl and Jim Wegmann, singles by Dick Wright and Rollie Sampson and a double by Dale Digmann provided the lead needed for the victory.

Ralph Buchman did the Epworth pitching and did a satisfactory job but the offense was lacking behind him. Here is one of those interesting sidelights to this game that has stayed with me to this day. Ralph was a decent left-hand hitter who liked the ball out over the plate. On this particular night, the first three times up, we were able to pitch him inside and Ralph cracked a bat each of those times. Finally, the third time while running out a ground ball to the shortstop, he hollered out to the mound that I have to stop pitching him inside because bats were too expensive to crack one every time he bats. Of course, those were the wooden bat days. He did have a smile on his face as he said that to me also.

HAWKS DEFEAT PETERSBURG 10-4 IN FINALS
The Dyersville Whitehawks were named the 1963 Worthington Baseball Tournament Champions as they thumped Petersburg 10-4 in the final game Monday night. Roy Willenbring was selected as the tournaments's Most Valuable Player.
Petersburg shortstop Harry Koelker was the game's top hitter contributing four singles and two runs for four at bats. Jim Wegmann doubled and singled twice for the winners and Dale Digmann doubled and singled.
Winning pitcher Jim McAndrew allowed nine hits to the losers, struck out eight and singled twice. Roy Willenbring allowed 12 hits and struck out three.

Petersburg led off in the first inning with a run scoring single off the bat of Willie Moorman. The Whitehawks retaliated with four runs of their own in the bottom half on three singles, a fielder's choice, a wild pitch and an error.

Another Whitehawk tally came in the fourth when Jim Wegmann singled and scored on an error. Two more Dyersville runs came in the eighth when Tom Jenk blasted in Wegmann and Art Huinker with the single. In the ninth inning back to back doubles by Dale and Jim Digmann and Jim Wegmann pushed three more runs across the plate.

The huge crowd which turned out to see the finals was only part of the record showing for this year's tourney. Tournament Co-Chairman Mert Gassman termed this year's tournament a huge success and stated that tournament crowds were the largest since the start of the annual Worthington Tournament.

It was nice to see the final paragraph of the write-up on the championship game. The tournaments were drawing huge crowds. Interest was high, not only for the hosting community but from all around the Dubuqueland area.

It is also time to recognize all the hours that people from the hosting community volunteer in order to see that all aspects of running a eight-night tournament of this magnitude comes off successfully. Think for a minute about this. Ticket-takers, concession stand workers, announcers for the games, workers preparing the ball diamond, clean-up crews, to name a few. That doesn't even include the hours committed to planning all aspects of the tourney. And of course, all the people who prepare food and drink and get it ready ahead of time for serving. Players need to appreciate these aspects of having the tournament ready for their play.

While the Worthington tourney was going on, the Whitehawks played in a four-team, one day tournament on the fourth of July at Winthrop. Tom Fessler from Dubuque three-hit the Independence team for a 6-0 Dyersville victory. A brief write-up follows.

DYERSVILLE 6, INDEPENDENCE 0

Dyersville hurler, Tom Fessler, stayed on the mound the entire seven innings to hold Independence to three hits as the Whitehawks bombed Independence in the tournament's opening round.

Center fielder Jim Wegmann scored the winning run in the first stanza when he walked, stole second and was singled in by teammate Art Huinker. Another solo tally resulted in the fourth when catcher Dale Digmann doubled and was scored by Tom Jenk's single.

296

Huinker contributed a double and a single for one RBI and right fielder Rollie Sampson and Fessler peppered two singles a piece.

In the championship game, our luck ran out. Host team, Winthrop, collected eight runs and eight hits and easily pulled away for an 8-2 victory. Les Lammers pitched all the way for the champs while Rod Tangeman, Bob Goldsmith and Dick Wright shared mound duties for the Hawks. Dick Wright had a double and a single for the losers, while Bob Goldsmith and catcher Gary Peterson each had two singles for Dyersville.

Now for the big Cascade tournament, again a 16-team single elimination invitational. In the Hawks' opening round, Jim McAndrew controlled the game from the start. He hurled a one-hitter while striking out 12 and the Hawks took a 10-0 victory from Bellevue.

Tom Jenk led the offensive attack for the Whitehawks, going 3 for 3 with two doubles and a single. Third baseman Jim Digmann aided the cause with a one-run double in the third inning.

In the quarter- final game Dyersville had a real battle with Zwingle.

MCANDREW 3-HITTER PACES HAWKS OVER ZWINGLE IN TOURNEY
Dyersville ace hurler, Jim McAndrew threw a three-hitter and struck out 15 to pace the Dyersville Whitehawks into the Cascade Tournament semi-finals with 3-2 tilt over a loaded Zwingle team at Cascade Friday night.
Zwingle, represented at the quarterfinal game with variation of uniforms, held a 2-0 lead until the fifth inning when the Whitehawks came through with the necessary three runs.
Second baseman Bob Goldsmith led off in the fifth with a double followed by a walk to Art Huinker. Huinker was then put out on a fielder's choice but Dick Wright made it to first on the attempted double play and Goldsmith scurried home for the first run. An intentional walk to first baseman Tom Jenk put two men on for Rol Sampson's two-run double.

That placed us in the semi-finals against Pleasant Grove. In the other game Petersburg played Epworth. The following write-up includes both the final and semi-final results. We will include only excerpts on the two Dyersville games. First will be the semi-final Dyersville loss.

PLEASANT GROVE TIPS PETERSBURG TUESDAY IN CASCADE MEET FINAL
Dyersville held a 2-0 lead until a sixth inning two-run homer by Vernon Kennedy and a one run single put the

297

Whitehawks behind for a 3-2 upset from Pleasant Grove in the semi-finals of the Cascade Tournament Monday night.

Pitcher Art Huinker had a one-hitter going until the sixth inning eruption. Dyersville scored their two runs in the first inning when second baseman Bob Goldsmith singled, Huinker walked and Dick Wright singled to score the two runs.

In the Consolation game Epworth and Dyersville remained in a deadlock at 1-1 after the fourth inning until the eighth when Dyersville catcher Dale Digmann singled in pitcher Jim McAndrew for the winning run.

Epworth threatened to tie the game when with one out Pete Welbes singled, and made it to third on an error, but the next two batters were put out on fielding plays.

In the finals of that tournament, Pleasant Grove took the title by defeating Petersburg 3-1. Upcoming is the sixth tournament of the season for the Dyersville Whitehawks, this one on their home field at Dyersville.

As you will notice in most of these tournaments, pitching tends to dominate. There are many low-scoring, one-run ball games. Again, it is because teams feel that if they can get a well-pitched game out of someone they hire, possibly they can pull an upset and advance into the final two rounds and gain some satisfactory payouts as well as the satisfaction of winning some key games. Pleasant Grove accomplished that. The Dyersville tournament will be no different.

DYERSVILLE 4, MONTICELLO 1

Jim McAndrew won his 15th game of the season with a four-hitter as Dyersville won in the first round over Monticello 4-1. The winning runs came in the second inning as McAndrew walked and made it to second on a wild pitch. Second baseman Bob Goldsmith then singled in McAndrew and came home himself on an error.

Monticello's single tally came in the sixth off a one-run single by catcher Al Westhoff. Right fielder Rol Sampson led Dyersville hitters with two singles.

Don Recker was the losing pitcher. He was relieved in the fourth inning by Henderson.

It was not unusual for one of the Westhoffs to be involved in a key way in most of their ball games. Here it was the most seniored of the four brothers, Al, who had their only RBI.

CLOSE GAMES HIGHLIGHT TOURNEY QUARTER FINALS

Epworth dropped Winthrop 1-0 and Dyersville beat Hopkinton by the same score Friday night. Rickardsville

298

defeated Earlville 4-1 and Independence won over Balltown 4-1 in other quarter-final battles.

For Epworth, winning hurler John Willenborg led off in the third inning with a double followed by Tiny Potts' two-bagger scoring Willenborg. Each team collected four hits in the contest, Willenborg hitting two out of two.

In another one run game following Epworth's win, Dyersville pitcher Art Huinker pitched a one-hitter to blank Hopkinton.

The deadlock was broken in the sixth inning when third baseman Jim Digmann doubled and scored on a play at home following Huinker's single. Hopkinton catcher, C. Robinson, made an error on the close play.

Not one Hopkinton runner advanced past second base in what was one of the best played games of the tournament. Hopkinton made the only error.

Huinker struck out 14 Hopkinton batters.

Two 1-0 shutouts in the same night. With the score so low, it sounded like it was two soccer games with only two goals scored. And the shutouts continue.

Notice Tiny Potts coming through with the big hit for Epworth. Not unusual for him. He never stopped scrapping, no matter what game, be it baseball or basketball. A pesky, line-drive hitter to all fields and with speed to burn, he often was on the scouts' radar but never took the plunge into professional baseball.

DYERSVILLE 1, EPWORTH 0

The Dyersville Whitehawks, behind the blistering one-hit pitching of ace hurler Jim McAndrew, went 10 innings for a 1-0 win over Epworth in the semi-finals Monday night.

Dyersville's winning run came off a 10th inning single to center field by catcher Dale Digmann which sent Bob Goldsmith in from second to score on an error by the center fielder.

McAndrew gave up the single hit to pinch-hitter Tom Kramer in the 10th inning. He struck out 16 Epworth batsmen and allowed three bases on balls. Only one Epworth runner reached third base.

Losing hurler John Willenborg was combed for six hits and struck out five but was backed by almost perfect fielding.

Dale Digmann led the winners' hitting with two singles. The win was McAndrews' 16th in as many tries for the Whitehawk season.

Independence was the other winner in the semi-finals with a 3-0 advantage over Rickardsville. Roger Shelby gave up only three hits and one walk for the victory, while my brother Kenny was the loser despite giving up just four hits and two walks.

Again, the championship game is ready. Scheduled to pitch the championship game, I stayed at our home during most of the consolation game. Ann had walked up earlier to try and find a decent seat with the kids, now five strong. There were advantages living only a few blocks from the baseball park. This was probably the first time I waited that long to get to the park for a championship game in Dyersville and I could not believe the parking situation. Cars were parking almost by our house because there wasn't enough space available at the diamond. And yet, with the little league diamond and space around the swimming pool next to the diamond, you would think it would be adequate. But not for this many people.

INDEPENDENCE WINS 2-0 SHUTOUT; 3,644
WATCH BATTLEY LIMIT WHITEHAWKS TO SIX
HITS; HUINKER ALLOWS ONLY 4 HITS
Independence captured the 1963 Dyersville Baseball Championship in the second inning with two runs Tuesday night to hand runner-up Dyersville a 2-0 setback before a crowd of 3,644.

The win came when Dick Wold reached first on a fielder's choice and Roger Shelby walked. Bill Rowland came to bat after Judd Decker struck out and with two away rapped a single through right fielder Rollie Sampson scoring both runners.

Dyersville almost scored in the first inning when Jim Wegmann singled and went to third on an overthrow to second with one away. Pitcher Art Huinker flied to the center fielder and Tom Jenk struck out retiring the side.

The loss came despite Dyersville outhitting the champs 6-4. Wegmann and Huinker each contributed two hits and Sampson and Roy Krapfl had one each.

Losing pitcher Art Huinker struck out 15, giving up four hits and one base on balls. Winner Chris Battley struck out 12 and allowed one walk.

After Independence had scored its two winning runs only two runners made it as far as second base.

Independence was the tournament champion in 1959 and 1960. They won in 1959 over Worthington, 7-3, and in 1960 over Guttenberg, 9-2. They were runners-up in 1952, losing to Guttenberg, 3-2. They took third place in 1958.

Dyersville won four tournaments in its 13 years of tourney play. The Whitehawks beat Cascade, 3-0, in 1953,

300

tipped the Dubuque Merchants, 6 -1, in 1954, blanked
Petersburg, 2-0, in 1956 and edged Cascade, 6-5, in 1961.
They took runner-up honors in 1958, 1962 and this tournament.

In the battle for third place, Rickardsville defeated Epworth, 3-1. The 2-0 loss to Independence and the earlier loss at Cascade, 3-2 to Pleasant Grove, were two tough pills to swallow. But they resulted from different pitches and different results. In the Pleasant Grove loss, Vern Kennedy hit the ball hard and drove it far over the fence. The single for the Independence winning hit was not hit well at all. Time for me to be a good loser.

First of all, in looking at the scores of all the games played in the 1963 tournament, pitchers appeared to dominate. Manager Tom Jenk and I have talked about this many times in reviewing the final outcome. One statistic stands out. Not a single home run was hit in the entire tournament. That covers 16 games and not a solitary baseball left the ball park. Tom feels it was the quality of the ball that had been chosen for use in this particular tournament.

There needs to be an explanation of the description of the base hit that scored the two runs for Independence. The write-up describes it this way: "rapped a single through right fielder Rollie Sampson." The ball hit to right field was a "Texas leaguer," baseball lingo to describe a soft-hit blooper that falls in front of an outfielder for a hit. It was not hit well at all but Rollie tried to make a desperation diving catch of the ball, did not quite get to the ball, and it bounced a short way beyond him as he attempted to block it.

In an earlier chapter, I tried to describe how I felt after throwing a pitch where I wanted to throw it and Festina's Norb Einck still managed a base hit ground ball to right field. This hit by Independence player, Bill Rowland, is the same situation. The pitch again was a ball running away from a right hand hitter and he managed to hit it with the far end of the bat and got it over the infielder's head. Nobody misplayed anything. Bill did a good job getting the bat end on the ball and dropped it into short right field where no one could field it. After the game, I was upset about it, but that is baseball. It happens all the time. This happened to be a very crucial time and it was the game.

Dyersville's regular season is completed. Now, we start the AABC season. Jim McAndrew had a terrific season for us. Although he now lives in the Phoenix, Arizona area, it has been our good fortune to run into each other once in a while. Most of the time, it happens at one of Bob and Kathy Wolfe's celebrations. Bob and Jim are Irish, first cousins, both from the rural area, south and west of Maquoketa, basically near little Lost Nation.

301

A SECOND STAB AT A NATIONAL TITLE

The 1962 American Amateur Baseball Congress tournament gave the Dyersville Whitehawk baseball team an exciting run to a possible national championship only to come up short, losing to the champion Portland, Washington team in the finals. For me, the national tourney had also brought some frustration. Two losses for the Hawks, both charged to me. With the Dyersville invitational tournament behind us, we eagerly looked forward to the AABC chances.

The 1963 AABC tournaments carried a different schedule. Because Dyersville offered to host the AABC Great Plains Regional tournament normally held in South Dakota, and the offer was accepted, the Whitehawks automatically received a bid for that regional. The team did not have to play in either the local or the state tournaments. Saves a little on the wear and tear of pitchers especially but you also don't compete for about two weeks. Sometimes that is not good for keeping a sharp batting eye or the good control that pitchers work for. The home field advantage was great, however. It also meant three to five fewer trips back and forth to Denver, Iowa for the state meet. Most of those trips to Denver were made during the week, meaning many guys work all day and then play a ball game, returning home many times midnight or later. Our local games with Holy Cross, in a best two out of three, were equally as tough as the games played at the state level last year. The winner of that state meet with the right to represent Iowa in the Great Plains regional was Allison, which had won the state championship several times in past years.

Besides Allison and host Dyersville, the other teams at the Dyersville site were Renner, representing South Dakota, and Fargo representing North Dakota. The Fargo team provided the major opposition in the previous year's regional tourney at Milbank, S.D. The tournament this year started Saturday, August 31 and ran through Labor Day on September 2.

The write-up for all the games except the finals included all the games played. We will present only the Dyersville games with brief remarks on the others.

MCANDREW'S NO-HITTER IS FEATURE OF FIRST ROUND GAMES
The two finalists of the Regional AABC tournament here gave sure indication that they would advance furthest when Fargo, N.D. won over Renner, S.D., 6-2, in the opener and Dyersville followed up with an 8-0 shutout over Allison, Ia. Saturday night.
Dyersville garnered their win behind the no-hit pitching of Jim McAndrew, who allowed only one Allison runner to reach base, that being a walk. Not one hit ball made

it past the Hawks' errorless infield. McAndrew struck out 14, eight of them in the first three stanzas.

Bob Goldsmith opened up the game with a solo home run in the third inning on a low pitch off loser Bob White.

Three more tallies came in the fifth off a double by McAndrew and singles by Goldsmith, Art Huinker and Bob Decker.

In the sixth, four runs came in when Jim Digmann made first on an error, followed by McAndrew who walked. Center fielder Jim Wegmann doubled in the pair followed by a walk by Goldsmith before Huinker's two-run double.

In the loser's bracket on Sunday, Renner came from behind to eliminate Allison from the tournament by a score of 7 to 6. That brought up the winner's bracket game between Dyersville and Fargo.

FARGO 2, DYERSVILLE 1

In the most exciting and heated game of the tournament Dyersville trailed 2-0 until the ninth when the Hawks loaded the bases on two singles and a base on balls. Starter Mel Heim was relieved from the tight spot by Maynard Barta who walked Jenk forcing Bob Decker to score.

Third baseman Jim Digmann then laid a perfect bunt inches inside the third base line sending Dick Wright home for the tying run. Barta raced over, gloving the ball into foul territory. Plate umpire, Chuck Peterson ruled foul, sending Wright back to third base, causing a jabbering melee in which chief umpire Peterson's decision overruled that of third base umpire John Janz who called the ball fair.

Wright was then forced at the plate off Digmann's hit ball and Kirk Rentschler flied out to center. Larry Poock tried to score the tying run on the fly but was nailed at home on a perfect throw to catcher Mike Caraway.

Now, with three teams left, Renner drew the long straw and received a bye, forcing undefeated Fargo and once-beaten Dyersville to play each other again Sunday evening.

DYERSVILLE 14, FARGO 7

Dyersville got their sweet revenge in the Sunday night game blasting the Fargo Merchants, 14-7 after winning pitcher Art Huinker came back in for a second try. Renner rested that evening, drawing a bye.

The Hawks were never headed after scoring nine runs off six walks and four hits in the second inning.

Fargo rallied in the second with five runs on seven hits
to send Huinker to the outfield for a breather. But Huinker
came back in during the sixth inning after Dick Wold and Rod
Tangeman took turns on the mound.
   Huinker then commenced to strike out eight more
batters for a total of 14 for the game, allowing only two more
hits.
   Dyersville added insurance runs with solo tallies in the
fourth and sixth innings and with another rally of three more
runs in the seventh.
   Bob Goldmith, Rod Tangeman and Don Huber each
doubled for the winners. Manager Tom Jenk and Bob Decker
both were two for two.

Now there was a drawing between Dyersville and Fargo to determine
who would have to play Renner, S.D. on Monday afternoon. The Whitehawks
drew the bye to qualify for the championship game against either Fargo or Renner
on Monday night. Fargo came out swinging and defeated Renner, 12-2 in seven
innings on Monday afternoon.

For the third time in two days, Fargo and Dyersville would battle each
other to determine who would have the right to go to Battle Creek, Michigan for
the national championship of the AABC. You have probably observed new
names on the Dyersville squad for this tourney that did not play with them during
the season. First of all, Don Huber from Hopkinton, Ia., was selected to primarily
play shortstop for the Hawks. Don, or better known by his nickname of "Duck,"
was a veteran of many years in the semi-pro ranks and the invitational
tournaments. Also, Dick Wold, a Monona, Ia. native, was selected to give the
pitching staff an assist and also as a hitter and outfielder/first baseman. Dick, who
spent many years teaching at Maquoketa High School and coaching baseball, was
one of the better left-handed batters in northeast Iowa. Another outfielder with
outstanding speed selected was Larry Poock who we have encountered in games
previously. Also added was Independence catcher, Bob Decker, who gave good
back-up to Dale Digmann who would have to catch four games in three days
without some back-up relief.

DYERSVILLE TOPS FARGO, 10-3; NATIONAL
TOURNEY NEXT STOP
By Bill O'Neill, T-H Sports Writer
   The Dyersville Whitehawks literally "walked" their
way to the regional championship of the American Amateur
Baseball Congress tournament Monday night with a 10-3
pasting of Fargo, N.D.
   And when they weren't walking, the Hawks were riding
the strong right arm of young Jim McAndrew, who came on in

304

the first and pitched his second complete game shutout of the three-day meet.

McAndrew took over after Tom Fessler was tagged for three runs on a walk, an error, a single and a double with nobody out in the first. McAndrew promptly struck out the side to end the inning.

Fargo's Lyle Hemmingson proved to be generous in the bottom half of the inning as he walked the first four Dyersville batters before departing in favor of Doug Eiken.

The Hawks sent 12 batters to the plate before anyone even hit the ball. Fargo pitchers managed to strike out three batters in the first while walking the other six, and gave up two more walks and added another strikeout in the second before Bob Decker singled to left.

Once Dyersville gained the lead, the 6-1, 165-pound McAndrew made sure it was never in danger. He allowed just two hits, a single by Frank Brossau in the third and a triple by Jim Litch in the seventh.

The slender righthander walked four and sent 21 down on strikes. In the eighteen innings he worked in the tournament, McAndrew allowed just the two hits (he pitched a no-hitter Saturday), walked five and fanned 33. Only two putouts were in the outfield in the two games.

"I guess my fast ball was probably my best pitch, the State University of Iowa junior said after the game, "but you better ask my catcher."

The catcher, Jim Digmann, agreed. "His curve ball was working good tonight," he said, "but I would have to say his fast ball was his best pitch."

Digmann, incidentally, was the big hitter for the Whitehawks, slapping out a pair of singles and a home run to drive in three runs. He also scored three runs

The victory moves Dyersville on to Battle Creek, Michigan, as one of eight teams in the national finals. The meet will be held from Sept. 13-17.

For the second straight year, the Dyersville Whitehawks headed to Battle Creek, Michigan and a shot at the national title. This trip didn't have the tension in the Huinker family of a possible delivery of a new baby to our group of five as the previous year's trip did. We have heard the expression, "the third time is a charm." This was my third trip to the nationals so the expression had special meaning but the charm did not happen.

For this tournament, Manager Tom Jenk added another infielder to the roster. Kirk Rentschler, who had played with us before, became our fifth infielder at the second, third and shortstop positions. Jim Digmann had played all three positions during the season although he was primarily a third baseman. Bob Goldsmith was now a fixture at second base. Dick Wright had played some third base as well as outfield and Don Huber played short for us during the AABC regionals at Dyersville, over the Labor Day weekend.

With ace righthander, Jim McAndrew, scheduled to start our first game in the national tourney, we had high hopes of an opening round victory. Our record for the year, going into this tournament, was 43 wins and six losses. Once again, the Dyersville Whitehawks had played 49 baseball games from the middle of May to the end of August. The following report from Battle Creek appeared in the Dubuque Telegraph Herald the in their evening edition.

DALLAS DEFEATS DYERSVILLE IN
AMATEUR MEET
Chance-Vaught Aircraft of Dallas, Tex., sent the Dyersville Whitehawks into the losers bracket of the American Amateur Baseball Congress national tournament here Friday morning with a 7-2 victory.

As a result of the loss, the Whitehawks will face the loser of Friday's second game between Seattle, Wash., and Waterbury, Conn. The two teams will meet Saturday in the double elimination meet.

Jim McAndrew, who fired two shutouts in three nights to lead Dyersville to the regional championship earlier this month, was tagged for three runs in the very first inning Friday.

McAndrew had trouble with his control in the initial inning as he walked four batters, which, mixed with singles by Smitty Duke and Jim Laney accounted for the three tallies which proved enough to win.

McAndrew, pitching in 41-degree weather, was far off his usual form and suffered his first defeat of the season after posting 18 victories.

A two-base error by Dick Wright on Al Koonce's fly to left opened the gate for another run in the third, Koonce scoring on Laney's single to center. After McAndrew walked pitcher Glen Blackwood, he was relieved by Rod Tangemann who ended the rally.

John Tatum's single, a sacrifice and a hit by Audie Cox gave the Texans another run in the fifth, and a single by Charles McCullum, a sacrifice, an error and Blackwood's double added two unearned runs off Tom Fessler, Dyersville's third pitcher in the ninth.

The Whitehawks broke into the scoring column in the sixth when Bob Decker was safe on a two-base throwing error by Duke to lead off, and scored on Tom Jenk's single to left.

306

Jenk advanced to second when the leftfielder bobbled
his hit, and came around on Jim Digmann's shot to left.
Dyersville managed to get a runner as far as second on
only three other occasions. Hits by Bob Goldsmith and Dale
Digmann formed a threat in the first that failed; Art Huinker
tripled with two out in the fifth, and a couple of walks put
runners on first and second in the ninth, but Huinker banged
into a game-ending double play.

It was not a very comfortable morning for playing baseball. Yet, it was just as cold for the Dallas players as it was for us. Jim McAndrew had difficulty getting loose and, as I have mentioned so often throughout earlier chapters, sometimes pitchers have it and sometimes we don't. This was one of those days. We collected only six hits with third baseman Jim Digmann the only player with more than one hit.

The triple in the fifth has to be dissected. In an earlier chapter, we shared the odd dimensions of the main Battle Creek baseball field. The outfield fence formed almost a straight line from the left field corner to the right field corner, making the center field fence nearly 30 feet closer than the fence down the left field line. At 391 feet down the left field line, it makes that fence deeper than any major league left field fence. In fact, 35 feet longer than Wrigley Field which has one of the deepest fences down the left field line of all major league parks. Well, my triple bounced once and hit the fence in the left field corner. In reality, that ball would have cleared any fence in the major leagues with plenty to spare. But it was only good for a triple and because there were two out, we didn't even get a run out of it. It had to be one of the longest balls I ever hit, maybe even the longest. But what matters is that we lost the game. And that was my only hit in five opportunities.

DYERSVILLE ELIMINATES CONNECTICUT, 8-5
Dyersville, Ia., stayed alive in the American Amateur
Baseball Congress national tournament here Saturday morning
by defeating Waterbury, Conn., 8-5, to eliminate the Northeast
regional champs from the tourney.
Lefthander Art Huinker hurled a six-hitter for the
Whitehawks, Great Plains regional winners the past two
seasons, but was in hot water much of the way as he gave up
five bases on balls and saw his teammates commit three errors
behind him.
But Dyersville, which had bowed to Dallas, Tex., 7-2 in
Friday's opening game of the double elimination tournament,
came up with several clutch hits, and also benefited from walks
and Waterbury miscues.
The Whitehawks scored two runs in the first inning
when Jim Digmann walked, Bob Goldsmith beat out a bunt

single and both scored on a single by Dale Digmann after Huinker's sacrifice bunt moved them up.

A walk, Dick Nocera's bunt single, a wild pitch and an infield out gave Waterbury a run on the bottom of the first, but Dyersville got it back in the third when Don Huber singled, moved to second on a sacrifice and scored on a single by Huinker.

Two hits and a two-base throwing error by Huinker pulled Waterbury into a 3-3 tie in its half of the third, but the Whitehawks came back with two in the fourth and never trailed after. Jenk walked to start the rally, and raced to third when pitcher Don Alvino threw wildly to first on an attempted pickoff.

Jenk scored when the Waterbury left fielder dropped Dick Wold's fly ball for a two-base error, and Wold counted as Jim Wegmann and Huber followed with singles.

Two walks and an error by Goldsmith made it 5-4 in the fifth, but Goldsmith doubled a run across in the seventh, and the Whitehawks closed out their scoring in the eighth with two runs on singles by Jenk and Wegmann, a walk, an error and a fielder's choice.

Huinker, who wobbled through the first three innings, settled down after that and gave up only two hits the rest of the way, retiring 10 of 11 batters in one stretch.

Don Yurgargis walked to lead off the Waterbury ninth, and came home on Frank Fazzino's second straight double. Huinker then handled the last two outs himself to move the Whitehawks into Sunday's third round.

At least we were still alive. The Hawks outhit Waterbury with 10 hits to their six. Goldsmith, Wegmann and Huber each had two hits. The big hit probably was Dale Digmann's two run single in the first that picked the team up and helped us forget the first round loss to Dallas.

Next, the Hawks played the host team, Coldwater of Battle Creek.

DYERSVILLE OUSTED BY COLDWATER
Coldwater of Battle Creek bounced Dyersville from the American Amateur Baseball Congress national tournament here Sunday by blanking the Whitehawks, 5-0.

Southpaw Tom Schmitt had little trouble taming the Hawks as he was nicked for just five hits, walked two and struck out eight batters.

Only Art Huinker could solve his slants with any consistency. The Dyersville rightfielder had three of his team's hits, including a double---the only extra base shot off Schmitt.

Dyersville's starter Roy Willenbring managed to get past the first six men he faced, but ran into trouble in the third.

Larry Garman beat out an infield hit and moved to second on a single by Andy Howlis. Willenbring bobbled Schmitt's bunt and the bases were loaded.

When Jim Lituatis singled to left-center to score two runs, Willenbring was yanked in favor of Jim McAndrew. The second Dyersville hurler was tagged for two more hits before he retired the side after Coldwater had gained a 4-0 advantage.

McAndrew allowed at least one base runner in each of the last five innings but managed to keep out of trouble until the sixth when Garman tripled to left and came on in to score as Don Huber muffed the throw back in from Dick Wright.

Meanwhile, Schmitt retired Dyersville in order in five of the nine innings, but the Whitehawks failed to produce when they had scoring opportunities in the other innings.

Huinker singled and Dale Digmann walked with two out in the first, but Tom Jenk fouled out. Huinker led off with a double in the fourth but died on second, and two walks with one out in the fifth failed to produce a rally. The final threat came in the ninth when Huinker again led off with a hit and, with one out, Jenk gained life an error only to have the next two batters fan.

Another season had been extended into the middle of September. Dyersville's Whitehawks had again fought their way into the AABC national tournament in Battle Creek, had won 44 games and lost only eight, but suddenly it again was all over. Jim McAndrew exibited tremendous talent as our top hurler for the season. Now he was headed for the professional ranks and eventually the major leagues.

The return of Bob Goldsmith to play second base and provide strong offensive punch was a big plus for our season. Dick Wright, with his ability to play many positions in the field, including the pitcher's mound, plus his tremendous positive attitude, added an inspiring and joyous mood to our team. "It was a good year, Charlie Brown."

The Huinker family, by the fall of '63, was all settled in their new home on 10th Avenue SE. Terry had received his first communion in the spring and was now in third grade, and Tim had started first grade. God had indeed blessed Ann and me with a wonderful family and great friends. That plus a teaching/coaching position at Xavier High School in Dyersville that I really enjoyed.

DYERSVILLE WINS FIRST AND LAST

Celebrating out ninth wedding anniversary the summer of 1964, we woke up to the realization that our eight-year old son is ready to start playing little league baseball. That made Mom and Dad feel a little bit older. It had always been baseball games built around Dad and the teams he coached but now a different element existed; we watched our oldest play baseball for his age level. It was the pee-wee stage of the little league game but he was playing games. Tim had completed Kindergarten. The three girls were still keeping Ann busy in our home on 10th Avenue.

As for the Whitehawk team, many veterans from past Dyersville baseball teams played on. Tom Jenk continued to be the manager and played full time at first base. Dale Digmann, respected by other teams for his hitting, his catching and his handling of pitchers, still put on all the gear and took care of his duties in grand fashion. His brother, Jim, guarded the hot corner at third base, while Bob Goldsmith moved from second base to shortstop. Jim Wegmann and Rollie Sampson continued their patrolling of centerfield and rightfield respectively. Left field usually listed me if I wasn't pitching. Three present and former high school players at Xavier who broke into the line-up and made strong contributions were Jim Gebhart and Kip Knippel. Kip played several positions, including some pitching and had such a strong tournament at the Worthington Invitational that he was chosen MVP for the tourney. Jim Gebhart primarily filled the second base position. Another high schooler, Steve Tierschel, would provide a day off once in a while for catcher Dale Digmann.

The biggest addition to the team was right-hand pitcher, Dave Reittinger. Dave had received a professional contract and upon his return had pitched for towns around Dyersville. Now living in Dyersville, he brought probably the best curve ball of any pitcher in the surrounding area, whether right or left handed. Dave had a very successful summer and proved to be a productive hitter as well.

Because of the number of games played, both league and non-league, as well as all the tournaments, Tom Jenk always managed to find additional ball players to fill needed roles. We will pick out a few league and non-league games again before we jump into the first tournament of the season which again will be hosted by Monticello.

The Whitehawks won their fourth and fifth games of the season with a 10-3 win over Worthington and a 10-1 victory over Cascade. Both games were played at the Dyersville Park. In the Worthington game, Reittinger, Rod Tangeman and Tom Fessler did the pitching. Dale Digmann connected with a two-run homer in the second. Reittinger and Rollie Sampson each had two hits.

In the Cascade game, Tom Fessler shared pitching duties with me. We had 15 strikeouts against the Reds. Bob Goldsmith had a home run in the first inning. Jim Recker, Dale Digmann, Kip Knippel and I each had two hits.

310

Fessler, a hard-throwing right hander, and Tangeman from Guttenberg, pitched for Dyersville in past years. In a double-header win over Holy Cross to remain undefeated, another new name, Neil Moritz, took the mound and pitched an 8-0 shutout for the Hawks in the first game. Jenk slugged a triple and a double good for two runs-batted-in and Dale Digmann and Goldsmith each had two singles. Moritz was a left-hander out of Colesburg High School. Not a hard thrower but with a variety of pitches and decent control, he gained several key wins for us. Ronnie Legrand, a Leo High School player, had two doubles for the Holy Cross team. Kenny Brecht also had two singles.

In the second game, Fessler took the mound and was working on a 3-0 shutout when Holy Cross, with the aid of an error and a hit batsman, had hits by John Schiesl and Duke Lucas to tie the score.

We came back to get the winning run in the 4-3 victory when I received a walk, went to third on Dale Digmann's single and scored on a sacrifice fly by Rollie Sampson. Bob Goldsmith had another home run for the Hawks. Fessler received credit for the win and Ivan Bodensteiner was charged with the loss. Ivan hailed from St. Lucas, an old arch-rival for Festina in the Northeast Iowa League. He currently was a student at Loras College.

In two league games, the Hawks defeated Bellevue, 12-1 with the pitching handled by Reittinger and Knippel, allowing only 4 hits. Next, the team tagged a 21-0 defeat on Epworth. I pitched, allowing four hits, but do not know how many innings we played. Kip Knippel had two inside-the-park home runs. I do not remember this happening before but I had a grand slam in the game and drove in seven runs.

In a non-league game, Dave Reittinger threw a no-hitter against the only semi-pro team in Cedar Rapids, defeating them 1-0. After two walks in the second, then a steal of third, Rollie's infield out drove me in for the only run of the game.

The influence of the younger players and pitchers Reittinger and Moritz is easy to spot in the non-tournament games presented above. Guttenberg finally gave the Whitehawks their first loss in a non-tournament game by the score of 7-6.

Again, Monticello's invitational tourney started that trail. Our first round opponent was Worthington.

HUINKER HURLS 4-HITTER FOR MONTICELLO
TOURNAMENT WIN
The Dyersville Whitehawks blanked Worthington 4-0 in
the Monticello Tournament opener behind the four-hit pitching
of Art Huinker.

311

> *Victory became apparent for the Hawks in the fourth inning when they garnered three runs. Shortstop Bob Goldsmith drew a free pass and advanced on a base hit by third baseman Jim Digmann. Rollie Sampson singled in Goldsmith and Jim Gebhart followed with another run-scoring single. A third run scored on a fielder's choice.*
>
> *The final Whitehawk tally came in the sixth when catcher Dale Digmann singled and advanced to second when Jim Digmann was hit by a pitch. Gebhart then singled in Dale Digmann. Gebhart was the leading hitter for the Hawks with two singles.*

For Worthington, Darrell Rothrock did the hurling. For young Jim Gebhart to garner two hits against him showed he was ready for the competition in these tournaments. Rothrock himself had two of Worthington's four hits against us.

In the second game at Monticello, Dave Reittinger pitched the entire game, giving up only a two-run homer to Roy Willenbring. At the same time, Reittinger hit a two-run homer with Dale Digmann on base in the 2nd. In the third, Bob Goldsmith was on base when Dale Digmann hit the third two-run homer of the game. Those home runs accounted for all the scoring in a 4-2 Dyersville victory.

In that game, the pitcher for Petersburg was Carl Heying, originally from Festina and a pitcher for Ossian De Sales High School when I was coaching there. Carl was now teaching mathematics at Western Dubuque High School and served as their baseball coach. He allowed nine hits but kept them well-scattered. Carl maybe remembers how he handled his high school coach at the plate but I could not locate a full box score on the game and have no recollection of what I did against his curve ball.

Carl was not only from Festina but his home farm was about a mile from ours. In the early grades the two families took turns transporting their children back and forth to the Catholic school in Festina. Another experience playing a game against a former student and now a teacher made me feel a little bit older.

In the championship game, the Whitehawks defeated the host Monticello team, 12-3, with Neil Moritz allowing only five hits in gaining the victory. The Hawks jumped to a 5-0 lead in the first inning and were never headed. Monticello scored all its runs in the sixth inning.

With one tournament championship under our belts, we moved north to Worthington for their 16-team tourney. We won this tourney the previous year and naturally we were hoping for a repeat.

312

DYERSVILLE 15, WINTHROP 3, IN OPENING
ROUND
   Pinch-hitter Steve Tierschel poked a fifth-inning three-
run homer to end the Dyersville-Winthrop game on the 10-run
rule in the second game of first round play at the Worthington
tournament Monday night.
        Catcher Dale Digmann collected three singles for five
RBI's.
        Winthrop's three runs came off a fifth inning three-run
homer by first baseman Les Lammers.
        Winning pitcher Dave Reittinger allowed only two hits
in the route.

In the first game that night, Roger Shelby, a tough left-hander, threw a
three hitter at Monticello, in a 1-0 shutout. Vern Kennedy, a hitter who I believe
can't wait to bat against me, hit a pinch-hit home run in the fifth for the winners.
He hit a home run against us in the championship game for a 3-2 victory at
Cascade the previous year.. No, I really should say, he hit a home run against me.
And it wasn't his first.

WHITEHAWKS, EPWORTH GAIN AT
WORTHINGTON
   Dyersville and Epworth posted quarter-final victories
to advance to the semi-finals of the Worthington baseball
tournament.
        Dyersville toppled Pleasant Grove, 9-1; Epworth
defeated Bernard, 4-1.
        Dyersville jumped off to a 4-0 lead in the first inning of
its game. Two walks, a hit batsman, and singles by Art Huinker
and Dale Digmann accounted for the runs. Pleasant Grove
came back with a run in the fourth inning to cut the gap to 4-1,
but the Whitehawks put the game out of reach with three-run
fourth inning.
        Bob Goldsmith belted a two-run home run in the sixth
inning to close out the scoring. Huinker scattered five hits and
struck out nine to gain the victory.

In the second game that night, Bernard brought my brother Kenny down
to pitch against Epworth, but six errors and a 3-run fourth inning enabled Epworth
to pull out a 4-1 victory. Epworth bunched all three of their hits in that rally, led
by singles by Jim Dougherty and Ron Connolly and Jerome Urbain's triple. John
Willenborg pitched the win and high schooler Pete Welbes did the catching. Pete
played for the Wahlert High School baseball team. A great young prospect.

The semi-final game between Epworth and the Dyersville Hawks saw Epworth bring Dick Winter, a Loras College teammate to Worthington to throw against us. But Dave Reittinger threw a three-hitter, striking out seven, in leading the Hawks to a 5-1 victory. Rollie Sampson had the big hit for the Hawks, a bases loaded triple, to provide the offensive power.

IN WORTHINGTON MEET, DYERSVILLE WINS TITLE

The Dyersville Whitehawks won the 14th annual Worthington baseball tournament here Thursday night by blanking Petersburg, 2-0.

Hopkinton won third place honors by defeating Epworth by the same 2-0 score.

Southpaw Art Huinker outdueled Ken Hanley in a pitcher's battle in the championship game. Huinker allowed the losers just four hits, walked none and struck out 12 batters.

Dyersville manager Tom Jenk gave Huinker all the support he needed when he walloped a solo home run to left-centerfield in the sixth inning to break the scoreless deadlock.

The Hawks added an insurance run off Hanley in the seventh inning when Rollie Sampson doubled, moved to third on a passed ball and scored on a sacrifice fly.

Jenk added a single to his home run, and Sampson had a single in addition to his double to lead the Hawks' seven-hit attack off Hanley. The losing pitcher fanned six. Kirk Rentschler accounted for half of Petersburg's hits off Huinker with a single and double.

Cliff Knippel, who played errorless ball at several positions during the tournament for Dyersville was named the Most Valuable Player of the meet.

In the consolation game, Don Huber, who played shortstop for us in the AABC tournaments, hit a two-run homer off John Willenborg to provide the 2-0 margin of victory for Hopkinton. The Dyersville victory meant that we had successfully defended our title from the previous year at Worthington.

"You win some and you lose some." That is a phrase that is heard often in competitive sports circles. It has particular application to our next game. We had already played and beaten Monticello in their tournament and again in the Worthington tournament. Opening up in the Winthrop tourney found the two teams playing each other again. This game belonged to Monti, giving us only one run in a 6-1 final. Following is a short excerpt of how Monti did it.

314

HAWKS DROP 6-1 GAME TO MONTI, OUT OF
TOURNEY
Monticello garnered a lone tally in the first inning on a
base on balls to Jim Wright and a double by Bob Hardin.
Catcher Hoyt blasted a homer in the second inning and
teammate Long blasted a two-run round tripper the following
inning. The winners scored two more runs in the fourth when
Wright tripled in Rick Westhoff and Mike Hall.
Dyersville's lone tally came in the sixth off a double by
Bob Goldsmith who scored on a follow-up single by Art
Huinker.
The Whitehawks mustered five hits off winning pitcher
Mike Hall. Dave Reittinger was the losing pitcher.

Dave started the game and I relieved in the sixth. For this game, Mike Hall brought his A game to the mound and we didn't do much against him. Dave Hoyt did the catching for Hall that night. I believe he came out of the Cedar Rapids area but not sure of that.

This loss preceded the Cascade tournament. We have struggled at Cascade in previous years. The '64 tournament began with a game against Rickardsville and some interesting happenings are recalled.

First of all, Cascade, over the years, had difficulty with early starting games. The diamond is situated so that the batter is facing northwest. With the sun setting in the northwest in mid-summer, especially with daylight savings time, the hitter was often looking right into the sun. This particular night, Dyersville had won the toss. As I was warming up on the mound in the first inning, Dale Digmann, our catcher, struggled a little with the glare of the sun in his eyes.

Rickardsville had brought several Soldiers Grove players in to improve their chances of winning and the lead-off batter was good friend, Ron Helgerson. With everyone ready to go, I threw the first pitch. A wild scene resulted. Ron himself said he lost the ball immediately and bailed out of the box as quickly as possible. Dale could not see the ball and tried to protect himself with all the gear on, but the ball sailed past. By that time, the umpire was running away because he had no idea where the ball was either. Needless to say, the umpire declared "no pitch" and halted the start of the game. After about a half-hour delay, the sun had settled behind the big drive-in screen that the town of Cascade had purchased from the Dubuque Drive-In Theatre when it closed several year earlier. Without that, we would have waited much longer.

DYERSVILLE, MONTICELLO WIN AT CASCADE
Dyersville defeated Rickardsville, 7-1, and Monticello
blanked Key West, 7-0, in the opening run of the Cascade
baseball tournament.

Monticello's Jack Johnson hurled a five-inning one-hitter to pace Monticello's victory. The game was called after five innings because of the tournament seven-run rule.

Dyersville scored single runs in each of the first three innings before wrapping up the game with four in the fourth. Jim Wegmann's single sandwiched between two walks loaded the bases. Winning pitcher Art Huinker then stroked a three-run double and later scored on Dale Digmann's single.

Huinker had two doubles to lead the winners' eight-hit attack He gave up only four hits and fanned nine. Ron Helgerson had two of the hits off Huinker. Rickardsville's only run scored on a walk, one of Helgerson's hits and Eli Crogan's single.

The losing pitcher for Rickardsville was Mark Dilley, one of at least three players that came down from Soldiers Grove that night. Helgerson and Crogan also were Grove players.

My first double that night came in the bottom of the first. It was a high pop-up that landed in front of the center fielder. When I reached second base, Helgerson was standing there. He looked at me and said, "Where in the heck was that centerfielder playing? He must have been touching the wall out there." We laughed and then I told him that the previous year I had hit four balls off the fence or over against Rickardsville. Bill Sahm apparently remembered it and was not going to have another ball go over his head.

Bill Sahm is another familiar name to Dubuque County baseball at that time. He was the Rickardsville manager for many years. During that time he had a propensity of bringing in groups of outside players for tournaments. As an opposing team, Bill always had you guessing who would be helping him out next. He was a great guy and was fun to be around. Unpredictable, that he was. But he loved the game of baseball.

Now comes another re-match with Monticello. The first two games were ours, the third one at the Winthrop tourney, Monti claimed victory. The quarterfinal round at Cascade will be meeting number four. Situations like this add some spice to the tournaments. You have probably noticed that these local tournaments invite most of the same teams year after year.

HAWKS LOSE IN CASCADE MEET TO MONTI, 4-1
The Dyersville Whitehawks were snuffed out of the Cascade tournament in the quarter final round by Monticello 4-1. The Whitehawks only run came in the fourth inning when catcher Dale Digmann doubled and scored on an error.

Monticello scored two runs in the third inning when John Wright and Mike Hall got free passes, and scored on Gordon Westhoff's sacrifice bunt and Gerry Herr's single.

316

Another run scored for the winners in the fifth when Wright drew another free pass and scored on Herr's single. Monticello scored another run in the fifth when Dave Hoyt singled and scored on a follow-up single by Rick Westhoff.

Dave Reittinger started for the Hawks, was relieved by Rod Tangeman. Reittinger took the loss. Mike Hall was the winning pitcher for Monticello.

After four games between the two teams, the series is all tied at 2 wins, 2 losses for each. Again we have failed to win our first two games at Cascade to get into the semi-finals. We are down to our last local tournament but this one is on our home diamond and we appreciate that advantage. This loss was our fourth of the season.

The last tournament championship for us in our own tournament goes back to 1961. Last year we lost in the finals, 2-0, to Independence.

Each new tournament is like a new season, starting over from zero. That is the most interesting and valuable part of all the tournaments. If you are playing league games every Sunday and have lost over half your games, there is little, if any, chance of ending up on top. Here, the new league *starts over every two weeks.* And again, you have a renewed spirit along with the new opportunity.

HAWKS ESCAPE IN 5-4 WIN OVER WINTHROP

The Dyersville Whitehawks pulled a rabbit out of the hat in the seventh inning to edge Winthrop 5-4 in the first round of the Dyersville Baseball Tournament.

The rabbit was actually a three-run rally that brought the host team to a 5-4 advantage after trailing 4-2 in the sixth inning.

The first two runs were earned. Two runs were scored in the sixth inning when Jim Wegmann and Art Huinker drew walks and advanced on another walk to Bob Goldsmith. Catcher Dale Digmann clipped a single scoring Wegmann and Huinker.

The other three runs came in the seventh off two errors, two bases on balls and two wild pitches.

Winthrop scored its four runs in the sixth to forge ahead of Dyersville 4-2. Doug Hart singled, advanced to second when Mick Donley walked and scored on Les Lammmers' single. Jack Evers doubled in Donley and Lammers and scored on an error.

Art Huinker was the winning pitcher. Terry Fairchild and Gary Gaffney pitched for Winthrop. Cliff Knippel led the Dyersville batters with two singles.

317

A win is a win. It wasn't pretty although until the sixth it was a 0-0 pitcher's battle. In the first game of the second round, Worthington defeated Independence 3-0 on a two-hitter by Roger Fenwick. One of the two hits was a triple by my brother, Kenny. He was playing for Independence while Ray Card was doing the Indy pitching. The Whitehawks next played Holy Cross.

DYERSVILLE 4, HOLY CROSS 0
Immediately following the Worthington-Independence bout, the Dyersville Whitehawks blanked Holy Cross 3-0 in an almost identical game.
Dave Reittinger gave up only three hits in the match while the Whitehawks stormed Tom Lanham and Al Schulte for eight.
The Hawks let off in the first with a tally when Jim Wegmann walked and came in on Dale Digmann's sacrifice fly.
In the second inning Cliff Knippel singled, went to second on an overthrow, made it to third by the same means and scored on a shortstop's miscue.
Wegmann again scored in the fifth when he singled and came in on Tom Jenk's single.
Another tally came in the sixth when Knippel reached first on an error, stole second, reached third on a wild pitch and scored on Wegmann's single.
Wegmann and Digmann each had two hits. Jim Fitzgerald doubled for Holy Cross.

It is extremely valuable for teams hosting tournaments to reach the semi-finals of the tourney. This means that the host team will play four nights in the tourney, thus assuring a bigger draw for the hosting city. It is for this reason that most tournaments will have the top 8-team bracket include the host team and some of the supposedly weaker participants. This is especially significant for the four-team bracket which includes the host team. There are many discussions of the pairings determined by drawing names out of a hat. That is usually said with tongue in cheek.

The semi-finals are next with Worthington the opponent for Dyersville in the semi-final round. The other bracket found Farley playing Balltown.

MORITZ'S 1-HITTER, WINTER'S 2-HITTER PUT WHITEHAWKS, BALLTOWN IN MEET FINALS
Dyersville's pitcher, Neil Moritz shackled Worthington with a one hitter and Art Huinker homered to lead Dyersville to a 4-0 win in the semi-finals Monday night in the Dyersville Baseball Tournament.
The only hit collected off Moritz was a seventh inning single by center fielder

318

Carl Heitz. Roger Fenwick was charged with the loss, allowing four hits.

The Hawks' first run came off Huinker's 350-foot homer in the fourth stanza. A single by Tom Jenk and a fielder's choice allowing Dale Digmann to reach first set two more scores when Rollie Sampson smashed a long single to left-center.

Jim Digmann scored in the sixth when he reached first on an error, advanced to second when Sampson walked, stole third base and scored on a wild pitch.

In the second game, Dick Winter, college teammate from New Hampton, pitched a two-hitter and Balltown easily handled Farley 8-0. The game was scoreless until the fourth, but a five-run fifth broke the game open for the winners. The big inning was highlighted by a double and five singles. Winter struck out 13 Farley batters in the big win. Now it is Balltown vs. Dyersville for the championship. The Dyersville team sought their fifth Dyersville Tournament Championship.

REITTINGER HURLS 3-HITTER IN FRIGID 55 DEGREE WEATHER

Whitehawk pitcher Dave Reittinger hurled a three-hitter and collected two RBI's to lead the Dyersville Whitehawks to their fifth Dyersville Baseball Tournament crown, downing Balltown, 4-0, in the finals Tuesday night.

On the coldest night of the tournament Reittinger and Balltown chucker Darrell Rothrock were locked in a pitcher's duel until the fifth when Dyersville broke loose with two runs on three hits.

Reittinger singled home Dale Digmann after hits by Rollie Sampson and Cliff Knippel in the fourth. Center fielder Jim Wegmann then singled in Knippel who had stayed on base via a fielder's choice.

Reittinger collected his second RBI in the seventh when he singled home Sampson who was on second after a fielder's choice and an error.

Art Huinker slammed a triple setting him up for Bob Goldsmith's single in the eighth inning.

Balltown made three double plays in a valiant effort to stop the Dyersville attack. In the second inning Jim Digman grounded to the third baseman to stop runner Tom Jenk approaching from second and was put out at first base himself. Jenk hit to shortstop Doug Dunlap for a force at second and putout at first in the sixth. In the eighth Dale Digmann hit into a short to second to first double play.

319

In the championship game, two of Balltown's three hits were collected by veteran Dick Dupont. Dick played many years for the Balltown team and opposing pitchers most of the time felt he was "thee" batter most difficult to get out. Dick was another one of those opposition players who always competed to the fullest, but when the game was over, was a good friend.

Balltown's line-up also included catcher Bob Meyer, who, for once in his life, went 0 for 4 against Reittinger. They also had Frank Delaney from Dubuque playing first base that night. He also did some very successful pitching for the Balltown team. Frank was another teammate from the Loras College baseball team in the mid 1950's. And you could not have a Balltown line-up without having a Sigwarth and a Gansemer on the squad. They were on-going family names on their team for years.

For the Hawks, another regular season came to an end. Only four losses for the entire season thus far. Nowhere in all the write-ups have I found a complete won-loss record. Now on to the second season, the AABC tournaments. The Whitehawks had won the first two tournaments at Monticello and Worthington, then lost at both the Winthrop and Cascade invitationals. Then they topped off the local tournaments by winning their own Dyersville classic. This was the first home championship since 1961.

A THIRD RUN AT NATIONALS

This year with the Great Plains Regionals again scheduled for South Dakota, the Dyersville Whitehawks faced the winning of the local district Iowa AABC tournament before even thinking about a state AABC tourney usually held in the Waterloo area of the state.

Three teams, Epworth, Balltown and the Whitehawks, entered the Maquoketa Valley League play-offs to determine that league's entry. In the double-elimination, Dyersville put Balltown into the loser's bracket with a 12-3, five-inning victory, ending early with the mercy rule. High school catcher, Steve Tierschel, was my battery mate for the game. It was a unique experience for both of us. Steve mentioned to me after the game that he always hoped for the opportunity to be behind the plate for a game pitched by his baseball coach. For me, I had no anticipated fears with Steve doing the catching. He was a very strong defensive catcher, even though he had one more year of high school participation left. After he graduated, he was also good enough to become a regular catcher for the Loras College Duhawks under Coach Jim Smarjesse. In the Balltown game, Rollie Sampson, Steve Tierschel and I each had two hits, while Balltown collected three hits.

In the second game of the opening round, The Hawks put Epworth into the loser's bracket by a score of 4-0 with Roy Willenbring hurling a no-hitter for the Dyersville team. Lefty Ralph Buchman allowed only seven hits but took the loss.

The loser's bracket game between Epworth and Balltown saw Balltown squeeze out a 4-3 victory, sending Epworth to the sidelines. Frank Delaney allowed four hits in gaining the victory. For Epworth, John Willenborg gave up seven hits in a hard-luck loss. He pitched to Wahlert high school catcher, Pete Welbes who we met in the Dyersville tournament. The winning run, scored in the bottom half of the seventh, was driven in by Dick Dupont's triple. The Sigwarths were the battery for Balltown.

That victory brought a rematch between Balltown and the Hawks. Again, the Hawks scored twelve runs to down Balltown 12-2 and advance to the state AABC contest. Tom Jenk had a double and two singles while I had three singles in this game. Tom Fessler pitched six innings and Rod Tangeman the final inning in the victory.

The state AABC again was again played at Denver, Iowa. The four teams vying for the Iowa title were perennials Allison, Sumner and the Dyersville Hawks along with newcomer Traer.

The Hawks found themselves on the losing end of the first game to the newcomer Traer team, 6-2. The Hawks only connected for three hits off Traer pitcher Ed Gourley while the winners collected eleven. Dave Reittinger started for Dyersville but was relieved in the second inning after giving up four runs. He was followed by Tom Fessler and Rod Tangeman. We made five errors to aid the Traer cause, two by me in left field. I truthfully do not remember what they were but for an outfielder to make two errors in one game is unheard of. Interesting that I can't remember. What is my excuse this time. The loss placed us in the loser's bracket.

There was an interesting name in the Traer line-up that basketball people will remember. He was Bill Fleming, playing second base. Bill later became the "love me or hate me" basketball coach at Maquoketa High School starting in the seventies and continuing into the '90's. Traer was Bill's home town.

In the other opening round game, Sumner fell into the loser's bracket with a 4-1 loss to Allison. An elimination game was next between Sumner and the Hawks. Brief excerpts from the next round follow.

TRAER UNBEATEN; DYERSVILLE SURVIVES
ELIMINATION GAME
Traer jumped into the driver's seat here Friday night by humbling defending-champion Allison 8-0 in a contest limited to six innings as a result of the eight-run rule. In the first round of the tournament Traer had stunned Dyersville 6-2.
In the first game Friday night Dyersville knocked Sumner out of the competition, 8-3, behind the strong clutch pitching of veteran right hander Roy Willenbring. Only one of the three runs off Willenborg was earned. He scattered nine hits, walked just one and struck out two.

Dyersville scored five runs off Sumner starter, Delfi Kalm, in the first inning and added three more in the fourth. In the first inning three singles and two walks provided the fireworks, while in the fourth a two-run single by Dick Wright proved to be the big blow. Leading the offense for the Hawks was Jim Wegmann with two hits and two runs scored.

Roy Willenbring was stunned by a collision at third base with Sumner's Vic Belger in this game. Roy finished the game but collapsed later in the evening and ended up in the Dyersville hospital with a concussion. He threw an outstanding game in spite of the collision.

With three teams left, undefeated Traer lost a flip of the coin. Allison won and drew a bye, leaving once-beaten Dyersville to play Traer on Sunday afternoon.

DYERSVILLE TESTS ALLISON IN FINALS
By BURKE EVANS, Courier Sports Writer
Defending state champion Allison and defending regional champ Dyersville are the two finalists in the 1964 Iowa State Amateur baseball tournament.

Both defeated Traer here Sunday and earned berths in the championship game slated for 8 p.m. Monday. Ironically, it was Traer that handed both finalists their defeats in the double-elimination tourney that started last Wednesday.

Traer was never in the running Sunday. It bowed 7-1 to Dyersville and crafty southpaw Art Huinker in the afternoon contest, then dropped a 7-0 decision to Allison and hard-throwing righthander Brent Prange in the evening contest.

Actually Traer lost three contests Sunday---the two baseball games and the draw to determine whether Dyersville or Traer would play Allison in the nightcap.

Huinker stopped Traer on five hits, walked three and struck out six in the afternoon. The lone Traer run came in the first on a walk, a passed ball, an infield hit and an infield grounder by Al Albers that Dyersville shortstop Kirk Rentschler had to go to second with a forceout.

The Whitehawks scored twice in the first, added four in the fifth off relief pitcher Ed Gourley and climaxed the scoring with one in the eighth.

Jim Wegmann, Tom Jenk, Dick Wright and Dale Digmann paced the Dyersville attack. Wegmann and Wright each had three hits and Jenk and Digmann each had two.

For the Dyersville Hawks, it was back to one more victory and another AABC trip to South Dakota. Allison was standing in the way. Allison's longtime manager, Vern Harms, did a super job of having a strong contingent of players year after year, just as Tom Jenk had done for Dyersville.

DYERSVILLE IOWA AMATEUR BASEBALL KING ONCE MORE
By BURKE EVANS, Courier Sports Writer
For the third successive season Dyersville will compete in the Great Plains Regional baseball tournament. The Whitehawks won the Iowa berth in the regional tournament here Monday night by defeating Allison 10-2 in a twice-delayed, rain-soaked state amateur baseball championship contest.

By winning Monday, Dyersville earned a check for $350 from the Waterloo Daily Courier to help pay expenses during the ensuing tournament.

Despite an eight-run first for the winners Monday, it was an uphill battle most of the night. It rained off and on up

323

until game time when the rain subsided. After the Whitehawks blasted starter Frank Waterhouse and his successor Jim Rima for eight runs in the first, Allison started using as many delay tactics as possible, hoping for more rain.

Hero of the night for Dyersville was southpaw pitcher Neal Mortiz. He relieved starter Dave Reittinger with the bases loaded and one man out in the top of the first.

He struck out Larry Poock on three pitches, then got Dave Lansing on an easy fly to right. He finished the contest, allowing just five hits, walked three and struck out six. One of the two runs he permitted was unearned.

Waterhouse, the State College of Iowa ace who lost for the second time in the tournament, didn't get a man out. He left after Kirk Rentschler had doubled against the fence in left center to drive in three runs, the fifth, sixth and seventh of the inning.

Roy Willenbring was back at the game after the Friday night concussion. He appeared to be doing fine but did not play.

For the Whitehawks, Jim Wegmann continued his torrid hitting, this time getting a double and two singles. He also had two hits in the Traer game Sunday afternoon and two hits against Sumner the previous game. Admittedly, the weather conditions were less than desirable in the championship game. Would we have tried stalling tactics like Allison did if we had been in their shoes, down 8-0 after the first inning? That question does not have to be answered but I can't blame Allison for their efforts to get the game postponed at that point.

The Dyersville Hawks had another Great Plains Regional AABC Tournament to play, this time back to South Dakota. The tournament was held in Renner, South Dakota, a small community located just north of Sioux Falls. Our team actually stayed in Sioux Falls. The Renner location made our trip west considerably shorter because we were playing in the southeast corner of the state. Milbank, for example, was several hours further north and west of Sioux Falls.

The regionals consisted of only two teams, the Iowa champion Whitehawks and Salem, S.D. I do not know the actual reason, and my response is only an educated guess. Did Nebraska and North Dakota not enter the AABC this year? I don't have any other answer. The regionals consisted of a best two-out-of-three series between Dyersville and Salem.

DYERSVILLE SMACKS SALEM 9-1; HUINKER FLIPS THREE-HIT JOB
By TERRY NIELSEN, Argus-Leader Sports Writer
Dyersville, Iowa, walloped the Salem Cubs 9-1 here Sunday night behind the three-hit pitching of Art Huinker to

take a 1-0 lead in the best-of-three Great Plains Regional baseball tournament.

The Whitehawks, who were national runners-up in 1962, had a 3-1 lead after three innings, added insurance runs in the fifth and seventh, and won it in the eighth with one out.

Tom Jenk doubled home Huinker, on with an error, for the Iowans' ninth run which gave them the game. A Great Plains tournament rule gives the team leading by eight or more runs after seven innings the win.

Salem grabbed an early lead before a crowd of 1,261 in the second when Dick Sabers trotted to the halfway mark as third-baseman Jim Digmann bobbled his grounder and threw wildly to first. After a strikeout, Keith Sabers lined a run-producing single over the second sack.

The Whitehawks, known for their hitting, got to Dave Allen in the third. The lefthander, on loan from Renner, sandwiched walks to Rollie Sampson and Bob Goldsmith around a John Wright strikeout. Huinker, a .310 hitter on the year hitting in the No. 3 spot, singled up the hole driving in Sampson. Manager-first baseman Jenk and Dale Digmann plated two more runs with one-base blows. Allen eluded further trouble as Jim Digmann grounded into a twin killing.

Dyersville added a solo tally in the fifth as Goldsmith rapped a double and dashed to third when Allen's pickoff attempt went into center field. Huinker plated his second RBI with a sacrifice fly.

Wendell Maupin came on to pitch for Salem in the sixth and was touched for four runs in the seventh.

Huinker collected his second hit, a triple, and scored as Jenk hit his third safety. A Salem miscue put Jenk on third and Dale Digmann on second. Jim Digmann followed with a bouncer that got by Keith Sabers at third, scoring two more runs. Ed Gourley drove in Digmann and Dyersville led 8-1.

Huinker, hard-throwing 5-9, 160-pound southpaw, fanned 12 and walked only two.

Tom Jenk led all hitters with four hits and three runs-batted-in. Keith Sabers had two singles to lead Salem. After returning to our lodgings in Sioux Falls, we woke up to a heavy rain that did not let up, making it impossible to play the second game that day. When the rains continued to fall into Monday evening, the Salem team, realizing that any play the next day was unlikely, forfeited the second game because they were going to lose some of their players to other responsibilities. The move made the Whitehawks regional champions ready to visit Battle Creek for the national finals for the third consecutive year.

As we prepared for our trip to Michigan, Tom Jenk was busy with his managerial responsibilities. Dick Wright, who joined us for the state tourney, also missed the national tourney. Another player who was added for the regionals and who stayed for the nationals was Monticello's Jim Wright and he was joined by his brother John at the nationals. Another player added for the regionals and staying with us for the national tourney was Ed Gourley, a outfielder from Traer, who also did considerable mound work. Brent Prange, outstanding pitcher for Allison, also joined the Hawks for the trip to Battle Creek.

For the third straight year, Xavier High School administrative staff were considerate of my participation with the local Whitehawk team and gave me permission to be absent from my teaching and coaching responsibilities. And for the third year in a row, we had assistance from Ann's parents with the babysitting needed while we were absent. The team left for Battle Creek on Wednesday, Sept. 16, and played single games each of the next four days. That brought us back to Dyersville on the following Monday, Sept. 21.

For our first game in the nationals Louisville, Kentucky was our opponent.

> *DYERSVILLE WINS TOURNEY OPENER*
> *(Courier News Service)*
> *Bob Goldsmith and Manager Tom Jenk slammed home runs as Dyersville, Iowa's state champions, defeated Louisville, Ky., 7-4, in the first round of the American Amateur Baseball Congress national tournament here Thursday.*
>
> *Nashville, Michigan defeated Waterbury, Conn., 8-6, also on Thursday. Other first-round games saw Portland, Ore., defeat Knoxville, Tenn., 5-4 and Lakewood, Ohio, stop Dallas, Texas, 3-1.*
>
> *Iowan Bob Feller, a former Cleveland Indians star, tossed out the first ball before the Dyersville-Louisville game. Feller played in the first national championship tournament in 1935.*
>
> *Then Jenk hit out the first ball. His homer in the second inning gave the Whitehawks a 1-0 lead. Louisville starter Al Hayes retired the first batter in the fourth inning, but pulled a shoulder muscle and had to leave the game.*
>
> *Jim Wright and Kirk Rentschler greeted reliefer Jack Reietha with a single and double, respectively. Wright scored on Rol Sampson's infield out and Ed Gourley walked. Then Goldsmith slammed his three-run homer. Two more runs scored in the inning.*
>
> *Meanwhile, Dyersville's Art Huinker kept 10 hits well spaced except in the sixth inning when four successive singles led to three Louisville runs.*

326

Believe me, it was not a great pitched game. But we managed to keep the game under control except for the sixth. Kirk Rentschler collected three hits for the Hawks with two runs batted in. Tom Jenk had two hits, including the homer. We were in the winners' bracket.

DYERSVILLE 8, NASHVILLE 1, FOR SECOND STRAIGHT WIN

Dave Reittinger pitched an impressive game giving up only seven hits and striking out 13 batters in the Whitehawks 8-1 win over Nashville. Reittinger had a shutout until the eighth inning when the Nashville first baseman hit a home run.

Bob Goldsmith collected his second home run of the tournament for the Whitehawks in the fifth inning to account for two of the Whitehawks' five runs. The Hawks had a single run in the fourth and also single runs in the seventh and eighth.

In addition to Goldsmith's homer, Jim Digmann had a big evening at the plate picking up four hits. Art Huinker, the Hawks' center fielder had two big blows as did player-manager Tom Jenk. Rollie Sampson and pitcher Dave Reittinger each had singles in the second win.

Jim Digmann's four hits in four times at bat was a big highlight of the game and tournament. Jim was the only player in the tournament to get four hits in any one game.

Two teams had already been eliminated from the original eight that started and now only Dyersville and our next opponent, Lakewood, Ohio are undefeated after the first two rounds.

LAKEWOOD 7, DYERSVILLE 1

Two undefeated giants met in the Stan Musial World Series AABC meet Saturday and Lakewood, Ohio bested the Dyersville , Ia., entry, 7-1.

It was the third win for Lakewood and the first defeat in three starts for Dyersville. The meet is a double-elimination tournament. The Whitehawks moved into the exclusive semi-final round event with the defeat.

Brent Prange was the losing Whitehawk pitcher. He was relieved by Neil Moritz in the second inning. Rod Tangeman came in for Moritz in the sixth inning. Chuck Cooper was the winning hurler for Lakewood. He held the Whitehawks to five hits while his teammates collected 12 hits off the three Whitehawk hurlers.

The Hawks' only run came in the second frame when Dale Digmann singled, advanced to second on an infield out, and scored on Kirk Rentschler's two-out single.

327

The Whitehawk hits were produced by Bob Goldsmith, Dale Digmann, Rollie Sampson, Kirk Rentschler and Neil Moritz.

The 1964 national field was now down to four teams, three with one loss and the Lakewood, Ohio team still undefeated. Our game to be played on Sunday was our fourth game in four days. The opponent was Knoxville, Tenn., who started twenty-one year-old lefthander, Jerry Bishop, on the mound.

DYERSVILLE 7-3 LOSER IN TOURNAMENT
(Courier News Service)
Dyersville's baseball team bowed out of the Stan Musial World Series of the American Amateur Baseball Congress here Sunday 7-3 when Knoxville, Tenn., rapped six Iowa hurlers for 13 hits.

The Great Plains Regional champs got a rally going in the eighth inning to send 21-year-old lefthander Jerry Bishop to the showers when he walked the first two men to face him. Up to that time, only Bob Goldsmith had been able to get a hit---an infield single in the first inning.

When Ron Cronan took over for the Tennessee club, Dyersville got another walk and Bob Goldsmith then singled home two runs. The third tally scored when Jim Digmann sent a sacrifice fly to center field.

Knoxville, which earlier in the day had ousted Waterbury, Conn. from the meet, 5-1, jumped off with two runs in the third inning and added two more in the sixth and one in the seventh for a 5-0 lead.

After Dyersville pulled to a 5-3 score, Knoxville added two insurance runs in the last of the eighth to clinch the issue. Art Oody had three hits for the southerners.

Bob Goldsmith again led the Hawk hitters with two singles with two runs-batted-in. Roy Willenbring pitched the first 5.3 innings, allowing four runs while striking out five. Next, Ed Gourley faced one batter in the sixth before I relieved with one out. Fessler relieved at the start of the eighth and gave up two runs and had control problems before he was relieved by Neil Moritz for one batter and Rod Tangeman for the last two outs.

It was not a good hitting series for me. The two hits in the Nashville game were my only safeties in the four games. Three walks were received but that was it. In the Dyersville Commercial report of the four games, they listed nineteen players who had traveled to Battle Creek for the Whitehawks. All but two players saw action in one or more of the four games. For the Dyersville Whitehawks, this third trip to Battle Creek would prove to be its last. Personally, I was going to have one more shot with the Waterloo Merchants two years later.

328

This completed the sixteenth year of playing some sort of organized baseball. That includes the two years of playing American Legion baseball for Calmar before starting to play with my hometown Festina baseball team. This registered my fifth year of playing in a Dyersville Whitehawk uniform. Two hundred fifty ball games, more or less, had been played. There were many challenging games and they were experiences that were enjoyed.

AN OUT, NOW A HOME RUN

Another year of teaching and coaching has run its course. Talk is beginning to circulate in the Dyersville general area of a new central Catholic high school. This concept would include the four communities around Dyersville of Worthington, Earlville, Petersburg and New Vienna. At present, the Worthington community had its own St. Paul's High School. The New Vienna community was represented by St. Boniface High School which also served students from the Petersburg area. If the planned change became a reality what would that mean for the Huinker family? Would we have the opportunity to be on the faculty of a second centralized Catholic high school? When we moved to Dyersville in the fall of 1961, the Western Dubuque County Community School District had been formed to incorporate almost all of Dubuque County except for the city of Dubuque and its immediate surrounding rural area. Under the leadership of Superintendent Wayne Drexler that system was rapidly growing.

In the meantime, the Whitehawks of Dyersville were preparing for another baseball season. We would be in two leagues. The Maquoketa Valley League would continue under its normal structure. In researching old copies of the Telegraph Herald sports pages for the summer of 1965, there never appeared any standings for the second league that had been organized. Apparently the league included Bellevue, the Dubuque Truckers, Worthington, Winthrop, Monticello and Dyersville. Possibly Rickardsville and Holy Cross were part of the league but that is not a certainty. Both leagues joined the American Amateur Baseball Congress. There were many ball games to be played.

In the opening game of the season, newspapers reported a 22-10 win for Dyersville over Bellevue. The game was played at Bellevue. Listen to the list of home runs hit that day. For Bellevue, Slim Clasen, Jim Keuter, Don Even and Don Jaeger each had a homer. For Dyersville, Dale Digmann had one homer while Dave Reittinger and Dan Meyer each had two home runs. Nine home runs in all. The win must have been blowing out over the river that day. Dave Reittinger, Rod Tangeman and I all took turns on the mound.

In the write-up, Manager Tom Jenk indicated that the team would be much improved with the addition of infielders Danny Meyer and Larry Bildstein, catcher Steve Tierschel and outfielder Ron Singsank. He was also looking forward to the return of Jim Gebhart who was playing for State College of Iowa in Cedar Falls, and Cliff Knippel, also playing regularly for St. Thomas College in Minneapolis-St. Paul. These men were all current and former Xavier High School players.

We played Farley in a non-league game and have included a write-up of that game.

Dyersville clubbed three Farley pitchers for 15 hits Wednesday night enroute to a 10-5 non-league baseball victory at Dyersville.

The Whitehawsk scored two runs in each of the first two innings, but Farley bounced back with a run in the third and tied the game at 4-4 on Bob Howard's three-run homer over the fence in right in the fifth.

But Dyersville regained the lead with two in the sixth on a single by Art Huinker, one of Tom Jenk's two triples, and a single by George Benn, then added four in the eighth to seal the verdict.

Huinker had three singles and a triple in four times at bat, while Jenk added a single to his two triples as they paced the Dyersville attack.

One of those good offensive nights again. Lefty Bob Howard, originally from Sumner and mentioned above as the scoreboard keeper at Sumner when Festina played against the Sumner Cubs, later turned to fast pitch softball but he could still hit the baseball too. The catcher that night for Farley was Paul Scherrman, also a young high school player, competing at Campion High School in Prairie du Chien, Wisconsin. Paul continued playing for the Farley team into the 90's and also managed for years. Paul, along with Lenny Tekippe for Rickardsville and Frank Dardis at Peosta are fine examples of baseball men who have kept the sport alive in the Dubuqueland area for years and years.

In a Maquoketa Valley League game against New Vienna, Rod Tangeman threw the first six innings for the Whitehawks, then was relieved by Larry Bildstein. I learned something that day because he seldom pitched for me in high school. He also had two hits in the game as did Dale Digmann to lead the Dyersville attack.

In a 10-2 MV league game over Rickardsville, Danny Meyer drove in three runs while Dale Digmann led the hitters with three safeties. I pitched that one and have a very vivid memory of opposing pitcher Bill Rouse slamming a two-run home run to right center field in Dyersville. And he really hit it. Bill had pitched professionally for the Dubuque Packers, then stayed around Dubuque after dropping out of the pros. He also pitched for the Dubuque Truckers.

We played Bellevue again later in the season and this time the final score was 2-1 (the first time it was 22-10) with Rod Tangeman pitching a 7-hitter and Rollie Sampson hitting a home run to win the game.

In a 7-5 victory over Balltown, Tom Lanham, whose family had just moved to town, was our starting pitcher. Dave Reittinger came in to finish up. Jim Wegmann and I each had three hits. One of mine was a two-run homer in the eighth to provide the victory margin.

331

We played the Waterloo Merchants in a non-conference game and lost 6-5. Marv Waterhouse pitched for the Merchants, Rod Tangeman for us. Jim Wegmann had a grand slam home run to account for four of our five runs, all of which were scored in the second inning.

In the new Mississippi Valley League, I recall three games that we lost. The first was to Winthrop 6-3, Reittinger starting, with relief in the seventh by me. Next, Monticello defeated the Whitehawks in a league game, 4-3 with Tom Jenk leading our offensive attack with a double and two singles.

The Dubuque Truckers also downed the Whitehawks by a score of 8-4. Dennis Baumhover started for the Truckers and was relieved by Earl Lampe in the 6th. Reittinger started for us, relieved by Tangeman in the third and finally by Sampson in the 8th. In another game for the same league, the Whitehawks shut out Worthington, 10-0 with Rollie Sampson and I holding the visitors to three hits. And I managed three hits in three at-bats while Tom Jenk, Dale Digmann and Rod Tangeman had two hits each. One of Tangeman's hits was a home run.

Dennis Baumhover was the opposing pitcher for the Truckers. Years later Dennis and I both lived in the Peosta area and we had boys playing Little League and Babe Ruth baseball together. Their coaches were Dennis and me. Different time and different circumstances for both of us.

At the end of the season, Dyersville's Whitehawks will represent the Maquoketa Valley League in the AABC tourney again, while the Dubuque Truckers will represent the new Mississippi Valley League. This is also a good time to look at our young players and see where their future took them, answering the question of why they were not part of the future for the Whitehawks. Knippel became an attorney in the Twin Cities, Gebhart coached high school baseball in the Des Moines area, while Steve Tierschel also ended up in the Twin Cities. Larry Bildstein eventually located out of the Dyersville/Dubuque area. Dan Meyer is the one player that continued his baseball-playing days for the Whitehawks. The fixtures were not being replaced.

Now we will take a look at the four local tournaments, starting with the tourney in Holy Cross. In the opening round for Dyersville, we topped East Dubuque, 9-1. It was a four-hitter for me going all the way on the mound. Jim Wegmann led our offensive attack with three hits. Our second-round opponents in the tournament was Pleasant Grove.

*DYERSVILLE LOSES TO PLEASANT GROVE AT
HOLY CROSS*
*In Tuesday night action it was Cascade all the way in
an 11-0 rally over Worthington that was ended by the 10-run
rule. At 9:00 Dyersville went down to the strong arm pitching of
Roger Shelby as Pleasant Grove pulled out the win, 3-1. This*

matches Pleasant Grove and Cascade in the second clash of the
semi-finals Wednesday night.

Dave Reittinger and Roger Shelby were locked in a
tight pitchers' duel that lasted the entire 7 innings in a game
that was won after four. Pleasant Grove brought in all their
runs in the 4th, the first on a hit, two walks and an error on the
pitcher. The next came when Marty Kennedy singled with the
bases loaded. Jim Digmann led Dyersville at the plate with 2
out of their four hits. The Whitehawks picked up their only run
in the 7th against Shelby's tough arm with which he collected 8
strikeouts. Reittinger, the loser, had 7 strikeouts.

For us, we had to look forward to the Worthington tournament and
continue playing the league games necessary to complete the schedule. Dave
Reittinger pitched a great game for the Whitehawks but Roger Shelby continued
to have a whammy over Whitehawk hitters. I believe that Cascade eventually
captured the Holy Cross title.

WHITEHAWKS, FARLEY NOTCH TOURNEY WINS

Dyersville and Farley advanced in the Worthington
Baseball tournament here Sunday as first-round action was
completed.

Dyersville's Whitehawks blanked Bernard, 5-0, and
Farley edged Rickardsville, 4-1.

Ken Huinker allowed only a leadoff infield hit to Judd
Driscoll in the first inning as he hurled the Dyersville victory.
He chalked up 11 strikeouts.

Bob Bentley allowed just three hits in absorbing the
loss, but his teammates committed five errors. A walk, an error
and Tom Jenk's single produced a run in the first inning which
proved to be enough for the Hawks. They added another pair in
the fourth, and scored twice again in the sixth.

Larry Scherrman's double and Don Kuehner's single
broke a 1-1 deadlack and shoved Farley out in front of
Rickardsville in the sixth inning of the nightcap.

The winners added a couple of insurance markers in
the sixth. Scherrman also had two singles to support Kuehner's
four-hit pitching.

For Rickardsville, a very familiar name did the catching for them in their
loss to Farley. Dewey Fortney was the catcher for Soldiers Grove during the
years I did some pitching for them. Both Farley and Dyersville advanced to the
quarter finals at Worthington.

This time we will include the primary points of the quarter-final game against Farley from the Telegraph-Herald and then we will share some personal thoughts.

BALLTOWN, FARLEY VIE IN WORTHINGTON SEMIS

Balltown and Farley moved into Thursday night's semi-finals of the Worthington baseball tournament by scoring victories here Wednesday night, Balltown thumping Petersburg, 10-0 in five innings, and Farley rallying in the last inning to beat Dyersville, 5-4.

The Farley victory was by far the most spectacular of the tournament as the winners packaged all their runs into the climactic seventh inning after being held hitless by Dave Reittinger through the first six.

Bob Howard broke the no-hit spell with a leadoff single in the last of the seventh and moved to second as Reittinger walked Larry Svoboda. A wild pitch moved the runners to second and third, and both scored on a single by Farley pitcher Roger Fenwick.

Then Jim O'Meara lashed a home run over the center field fence, tying the score and bringing Frank Waterhouse on in relief. Jim Balik reached second base when his fly ball dropped for a two-base error, and with two out raced home from second when Gary Einwalter's grounder was booted.

The Whitehawks had taken a 3-0 lead in the second inning on a walk, two hits, two passed balls and an error, and another in the seventh on Rollie Sampson's second single, a fielder's choice, and a passed ball.

In the first game, Balltown jumped off to a 2-0 first inning lead on singles by Jack Gansemer, Dick Dupont, Bill Cummer and Dick Winter's double, and scored each of the five innings as the 10-run rule ended the game. Winter had a double and single, while Cummer and Dupont each had two singles in Balltown's 11-hit attack.

Leo Wegmann had two of the three Petersburg hits off Winter.

In our loss to Farley, the slogan tapped from famous language developer, Yogi Berra, can be applied. He was quoted one day, using these words, "The game's not over until it's over." What appeared to be certain victory with Reittinger cruising, quickly changed when left-hand hitting Bob Howard slapped a single to get things started.

Now go to Jim O'Meara's home run. The center fielder for the Whitehawks that night was "yours truly." Jim hit the ball to straight away center

334

field and I drifted back to the fence (which consisted of a five-foot high picket), jumped and caught the ball in the webbing of my glove. Yes, it was an out and not a home run. That is, it was that way until I came back down from catching the ball and my right elbow hit the top of the fence, causing the ball to drop out of my glove and over the fence. Yes, now it is the home run as mentioned in the write-up. It was not one of my happier memories. You see that happen once in a while in the major leagues but it didn't have to happen here. All I could say about that time was my favorite, "Dadburn it!"

Jim O'Meara and I were professional mates for the Western Dubuque Schools later in life. Jim served as Principal of Cascade High School for many years and was a solid educator. Then there is Bob Howard who started the rally with a lead-off single. Bob too was an administrator for Western Dubuque Schools, serving as high school assistant principal at Western Dubuque High School. Now that both he and I are retired, we are golfing buddies at Thunder Hills.

Balltown won the Worthington tournament by defeating Hopkinton, 6-2. Rothrock was the winning pitcher over Ray Card for Hopkinton.

In between the Worthington and Cascade tournaments, Winthrop sponsored a eight-team weekend tournament for the second consecutive year. With the Dyersville Commercial going to press on Wednesday afternoon, the entire tournament is reported in a single edition.

> *WHITEHAWKS TAKE CROWN IN WINTHROP;*
> *DOWN EPWORTH, CASCADE AND WINTHROP*
> *The Dyersville Whitehawks won the Second Annual Winthrop Baseball Tournament downing Epworth 1-0 behind the one-hit pitching of Art Huinker, Cascade 5-4 with Dave Reittinger limiting Cascade to five hits and in the finals beat Winthrop 9-1 behind the three-hit pitching of Rod Tangeman.*
> *In the opening round game of the Winthrop Tournament the Whitehawks scored their only run in the second inning with a single by Art Huinker, a stolen base and a single by Jim Digmann. Epworth had one hit, a Texas leaguer in the second by B.J. Featherston. Huinker pitched to only 23 men in the seven inning game. The hit in the second and a walk in the third were the only two men that got on base for Epworth. Art Huinker had 10 strikeouts in the seven inning game.*
> *Jim Digmann led the Dyersville Whitehawks in securing two of the Hawks four hits off Epworth pitcher, Ron Woods.*
> *The Dyersville Whitehawks downed the star studded Cascade team in the semi-finals with a 5-4 score. The Whitehawks started in the second inning with a home run by*

Rollie Sampson and a single by Kirk Rentschler, an error and a single by Jim Digmann. The Dyersville Whitehawks came back in the fourth inning on singles by Tom Jenk, Kirk Rentschler, Kip Knippel and Dave Reittinger to lead 5-1.

Cascade rallied in the top of the seventh on two errors, a single by Don Koppes and a home run by Larry Skowronek. Dave Reittinger limited the Cascade Reds to four hits, one each to Don Koppes and Dick Wright and two to Larry Skowronek. Reittinger struck out 10 of the Cascade batters.

DYERSVILLE ROLLS OVER WINTHROP IN FINALS

Dyersville used the home run to whip Winthrop, 9-1, and claim the championship of the Winthrop Baseball Tournament. Holy Cross edged Cascade in the consolation game, 3-1.

The Whitehawks scored twice in the opening frame on an error, a double by Art Huinker, his first of three hits, and a single by Tom Jenk.

That proved to be enough runs for Rod Tangemann who allowed only three hits and struck out 12 in going the distance for the Hawks.

But Winthrop starter Charley Lammers ran into trouble in the fifth when Huinker blasted a home run with a mate aboard to give Dyersville a 4-0 lead.

Winthrop came back to score its lone run in the bottom of the eighth, but the Dyersville power exploded again in the ninth when Rollie Sampson clouted one out of the park with the bases loaded, and the Hawks added another run to make the final score 9-1.

Winthrop used three pitchers in the ninth as the Hawks completed the game with 14 hits. Huinker also had a single to go with his double and homer to lead all hitters.

I think we were hungry for a tournament championship after being knocked out of the Holy Cross and Worthington tournaments without reaching the final four. That was an attitude that we carried into all 16-team tournaments. We felt that we had the ability to accomplish this goal but it doesn't mean we always did. That is obvious in looking at the first two where we did not get past the quarter-final round and is going to be even more true in the Cascade tournament .

MONTICELLO, WINTHROP TRIUMPH AT CASCADE

Monticello and Winthrop waltzed to easy victories here Tuesday night as the 19th annual Cascade open roster baseball tournament opened at American Legion Park.

Monticello walloped Dyersville, 12-3 and Winthrop whipped Zwingle, 11-1, both games called at the end of five innings in accordance with the seven-run rule governing the tournament.

Ray Card pitched a five-inning one-hitter, the only hit a lead-off single by Jim Wegmann in the first inning.

The winners took a 5-3 lead into the fifth, then came up with seven runs in a rally that saw four Dyersville pitchers give up six walks, the last three forcing in two runs. John Wright had a single, Card a two-run single, and Gordon Westhoff an RBI double in the big inning.

Jim Wright had a pair of doubles for Monticello, Westhoff a double and single, and Card two singles.

The second game was a romp for Winthrop with Les Lammers stroking a double and single and Doug Fairchild two singles to lead a 10-hit attack.

It was one of those really bad nights. Lasting only until the third, I had allowed four runs and six hits. When one experiences a game such as this, you wonder if you used the wrong arm to pitch, or something extreme like that. Again, we are quickly eliminated from the Cascade tourney. Our problems there continue. Now we had only the home Dyersville tournament to make amends. First opponent in the opening round was Delhi.

DYERSVILLE WHIPS DELHI, 8-0, FOR OPENING ROUND VICTORY

The Dyersville Whitehawks shut out Delhi Monday night 8 to 0 behind the spectacular pitching of Dave Reittinger. Reittinger fanned 16 at the plate as the Hawks pulled out three tallies and connected for eight big hits.

In the first inning Dyersville batted through the entire lineup as Jim Digmann walked, Art Huinker singled and Tom Jenk knocked out a double to bring in the first run of the ball game. With still no outs Dale Digmann came to the plate in the cleanup spot and drove in two more runs on a single. Kirk Rentschler came up with a fielder's choice for the first out and Rollie Sampson rapped out another single.

The next inning and one-half moved by smoothly but in the top of the third Jim Wegmann singled, stole 2nd and scored on two errors to give the Whitehawks a 4-0 lead. Jim Wegmann

connected with a three-bagger to drive in two more runs and
scored another on a passed ball.
    Jan Arthur suffered the loss for Delhi with Mickey
Jones swinging the big bat and collected two hits. Tom Jenk led
the Hawks at the plate collecting two hits.

In the Balltown 2-1 victory over Farley, Jesse Schulte bested Roger Fenwick in another tight pitcher's duel. Both Balltown runs were unearned. Larry Scherrman drove in Farley's lone tally.

Monticello topped Hopkinton 2-0 behind the strong pitching of Lloyd Brochshus as he fanned 12 and allowed only 4 hits. Losing pitcher Bob Hardin allowed only three hits in taking the loss. Both Monticello runs came in the first inning, scored by Rick and Gordy Westhoff and driven in by Jim and John Wright. A typical Monticello offensive attack.

The only game that proved not to be a pitcher's duel was the Cascade-Rickardsville showdown where Rickardsville carved out a 10-6 victory coming from a 6-3 deficit to score two runs in the fifth, two more in the sixth and their final three in the seventh. The irony of that ball game is that Cascade scored six runs in the bottom half of the fourth but had only one hit. There were three walks and three Rickardsville errors in that inning. Mark Dilley, Ron Helgerson and Eli Crogan hit home runs for Rickardsville. Look at those three names. They are all players from the Soldiers Grove team that were my teammates when we went to the National Baseball Congress state tournament in Milwaukee County Stadium in 1961 and 1962. They were good ball players.

The four victors in the quarter-final round were Rickardsville, Guttenberg, Balltown and the Whitehawks. Guttenberg handled Winthrop 5-1 behind the three-hit pitching of Bruce Hinkel, a top-notch lefty out of MarMac High School in McGregor. He pitched a no-hitter for Guttenberg in the opening round. Bob Decker's triple in the first inning drove in Winthrop's only run while Merrill Hyde connected for a round-tripper for Guttenberg in the fourth. Rick Connell collected a double and single to lead the Guttenberg attack.

In another second-round game Balltown took a wild one from New Vienna, 9-7. After building up a big 9-1 lead going into the bottom half of the seventh, New Vienna plated six runs before a strikeout closed the ball game. Home runs were hit by Dick Dupont for Balltown and Pat Sullivan and Gary Pitz for New Vienna.

In the third quarter-final game, things got back to pitchers being in control. Mark Dilley bested Ray Card, 1-0 in Rickardsville's victory over Monticello. Ron Eichorst drove in Mark Dilley in the first inning for the only run of the game. More Soldiers Grove with Dilley and Eichorst.

DYERSVILLE 8, PLEASANT GROVE 3

In the top half of the second inning Thursday night, Dyersville's Tom Jenk stepped up the plate and led off with a long homer that slammed the scoreboard and set the stage for the next six innings as Dyersville downed Pleasant Grove with an extra inning rally that collected five runs.

The Whitehawks took the lead early in the second inning picking up two runs on the homer by Jenk followed by an error, a hit batsman and an error on the catcher. Kirk Rentschler slapped out a single and went to second on an error. Rollie Sampson got a base on a wild pitch and Jim Wegmann moved the runners to second and third as he grounded out. Cliff Knippel went down swinging bringing Steve Tierschel to the plate who showed what heads-up ball can do when the catcher bobbled the third strike and Tierschel beat out the throw scoring Rentschler.

The Grovers came to bat in the bottom of seventh with the score 3-2 and one chance to pull out the big win. Jim Then led off taking a base on an error, but was forced at second when Leo Simon sacrificed a bunt. Simon stole second as Bob Goldsmith made a fine back-up play on a near over-throw. After Shelby struck out, Simon moved to third on a wild pitch and Merle Simon reached base on an error bringing in Simon.

Dave Reittinger came in to replace Art Huinker with Huinker moving to left. With the score tied 3-3, Huinker relinquished the mound with 13 strikeouts to his credit. On the next play, Merle Simon was thrown out as he attempted a steal of second.

Dyersville came to bat in the top of the eighth and sewed up the ball game scoring five runs as Jenk, Rentschler, Sampson, Wegmann and Reittinger crossed the plate with no outs. Merle Simon relieved Shelby and ended the inning.

We had made it to the final four. Now it is Balltown against the Whitehawks and Rickardsville and Guttenberg challenging each other.

RICKARDSVILLE AND DYERSVILLE SQUARE OFF FOR THE CHAMPIONSHIP

Jim Digmann's long hard fly into deep left center Monday night carried the Dyersville Whitehawks into the finals of their own tournament as it also ended a twelve-inning pitcher' duel that finally handed a 2-1 loss to Balltown's Darrell Rothrock.

The Whitehawks scored the first run of the ball game in the bottom of the sixth inning when Art Huinker led off the rally with a single to center and was sacrificed to second by Kirk

Rentschler. Hawk manager Tom Jenk came to the plate and slammed a single to left scoring Huinker.

Going into the seventh inning with one-run edge, Dyersville's Rod Tangeman walked the first two batters and was relieved by Dave Reittinger. With runners on first and second, Dick Dupont sacrificed a bunt that got a base and scored Frank Delaney on an overthrow at first for Balltown's only tally. The only shake up play of the ball game came in this inning when Dupont collided with Dyersville first baseman Tom Jenk.

With the scoreboard all tied up at one all, the pitcher's duel continued for another five innings before Digmann drove in the winning run in the 12th. Huinker again led off with a base hit, stole second, and after the next man was retired, Tom Jenk drew an intentional walk. Dale Digmann grounded out to first moving Huinker to third and Jenk to second. Digmann came to bat and connected with his first hit of the game bringing Huinker across the plate.

Darrell Rothrock went the entire distance for Balltown while Dyersville used three pitchers. Rod Tangeman started for the Hawks, was relieved by Reittinger in the seventh, who was relieved by Huinker in the 12th inning.

Huinker led Dyersville at the plate with three hits, while the winners totaled twelve. Balltown collected only two hits with Ron Sarchett and Bob Meyer taking one apiece.

In the other game, a home run with two men on in the fourth inning off the bat of Ron Helgerson gave Rickarsdville all they needed as they downed Guttenberg 5-3 to move against Dyersville in the championship game.

The game went 0-0 for the first two innings with the winners coming to bat in the third and picking up two runs on singles by Ron Helgerson and Mark Dilley followed by a triple off the bat of Dewey Fortney.

The big inning came with the fourth inning as Guttenberg scored twice on singles by Al Klinger and Dick Wold, a wild pitch and Terry Stevens' triple.

Not to be out done, Helgerson slammed one out of the park for the Rickardsville ball club with John Kosidowski and Dave Iverson on base. Kosidowski walked, Iverson sacrificed but gained a base on an error, Shelley Schoville sacrificed and Helgerson put one out of the park.

Merle Hyde slammed a homer in the sixth for the losers but it wasn't enough as they took the defeat.

Vern Geishert brought home the win for Rickardsville with 13 strikeouts. Bob Bentley and Bruce Hinkel combined for the loss.

Dewey Fortney led the victors with two singles and a triple. Dick Wold collected two hits for Guttenberg.

For the second straight game, the Whitehawks were pushed into extra innings to claim victory. The players whose names appear in these ball games for the various teams still continue to amaze me. In the Guttenberg-Rickardsville game, Terry Stevens played for Guttenberg. That is the same Terry Stevens who played and pitched for Fayette High School against my Calmar Cahawk team when we were in high school. Shortly after that, Terry played for the Sumner Cubs, tough opponent for home town Festina for so many years. Here he is playing in the Dyersville tournament twelve years after we competed at the high school level. I believe Terry was teaching and coaching at Oelwein High School at the time.

As for Rickardsville, five of their starters were players from the Soldiers Grove team that I had played for. In addition, two other players, Eichorst and Kosidowski played in the same region in Wisconsin as Soldiers Grove did. In addition, Shelly Schoville, also from Soldiers Grove, played in the Guttenberg game. Now for the championship and another barn-burner of a game.

HAWKS NIP RICKARDSVILLE FOR 6th TITLE
Approximately 3,300 fans were on hand Tuesday night as the Dyersville Whitehawks edged Rickardsville 4-3 to win their 6th tournament crown at the 15th annual Dyersville baseball tournament. In the consolation game Balltown blanked Guttenberg 5-0 to claim third place in the last baseball tournament of the season.

The spectacular relief pitching of Art Huinker for six innings as he gave up no runs and fanned nine men led the Dyersville Whitehawks to a 4-3 tournament win over Rickardsville in the final game Tuesday night.

Rickardsville came to bat in the top of the first and opened the game with two big runs that put the pressure on the defending champions. Ron Helgerson led off the rally with a single to left followed by a walk to Mark Dilley and a ground out to short off the bat of Dewey Fortney that put the runners on second and third. Ron Eichorst came to the plate and slammed a double to right that gave the challengers a two-run margin.

Dyersville made their pitch in the second inning when they retaliated with three runs. Bob Goldsmith slammed one into deep center to pull out a double as the ball went through the fence. Dale Digmann followed with a single to bring in the first tally for the Hawks and Rollie Sampson singled in the second. Sampson moved to second on a sacrifice and to third on an infield out. He came home on an error as Jim Wegmann came around to second.

341

*Mark Dilley walked, and Dewey Fortney singled in the
third inning for Rickardsville, bringing Eichorst to the plate.
He hit into a double play attempt but an error tied up the ball
game. Huinker relieved Sal Willenbring after a strikeout and a
walk that loaded the bases. With three men on, the southpaw
fanned the next batter to end the rally.*

*The game was tied until the seventh with the Hawks
scoring the winning run at the bottom of the inning. With two
outs, Wegmann slammed out a stand-up double and came home
when Kirk Rentschler put one by third.*

*Huinker fanned the next six batters he faced to keep the
one-run margin for the Hawks.*

*John Kosidowski took the loss collecting eight
strikeouts.*

*Balltown won the consolation game, 5-0, behind the
one-hit pitching of Jess Schulte. Schulte struck out ten, and
gave up only a first inning single to Kermit Urban.*

The victory over former teammates from Soldiers Grove was bittersweet.
They are a group of good players who were fun to play with. Now I had to pitch
against them. But that is the sport of competition. The final out of the game was
particularly gut-wrenching. The batter was a very close friend, Ron Helgerson.
The final pitch was a called strike three. After the call, Ron just stood there. So I
walked up to the plate to shake his hand when he looked at me and asked, "Wasn't
that pitch inside, Art?" And I had to agree with him. It was inside a good inch or
two, yet called the final strike. Are those what we call the "breaks of the game?"

More of a mystery than the question raised above is the fact that I could
go pitch five plus innings and not allow a hit to a group of real good hitters. Is it
just good pitching? How much of it can be attributed to plain old-fashioned "good
luck?" Or maybe a combination, I don't know. But we were champions for the
second year in a row. And it was still the basic group of players for the
Whitehawks—the Digmann brothers, Dale and Jim, Rollie Sampson, Jim
Wegmann, Bob Goldsmith, Roy Willenbring, Rod Tangeman, Dave Reittinger,
and especially Tom Jenk. Tom had a great tournament, batting .500 for four
games, had the most total bases and tied for the most hits with Mark Dilley. Each
had six.

Many awards are given out to individual players after the final game.
One that surprised me was the award that I received for the most stolen bases by
an individual player in the tournament. It did not give a number to let us know
how many that was. I was also fortunate to be awarded the Most Valuable Player
trophy, a trophy that I find somewhat amusing. That is an award that I think
requires much subjective judgment with several other players just as qualified
because of their contribution. I often look at our catcher, Dale Digmann, a player

who continuously provided key hits, key defensive plays, and always the same solid job of defensive catching as well as pitch-calling for his pitchers.

In the consolation battle, Guttenberg defeated Holy Cross 4-3. Guttenberg had been no-hit by John Ackerman and Holy Cross led 3-0 going into the final inning. Four consecutive hits tied it for Guttenberg and they won it in the eighth.

Again, what excitement to walk out on the diamond and experience the "buzz" of the crowd of over 4,000 fired-up fans. Oh, for the good old days. Is that a fitting statement to make here? I don't mention it to take anything away from the semi-pro tournaments played in the 21st century, but times have changed. The quality of baseball is still as good, with the exception of top-notch pitching brought in by the teams night after night in the 1950's and 1960's. In a way, that is a plus for the games today because the managers tend to stick with their own home-grown talent from the immediate area. And with the brand of high school baseball played in the Dubuque County area and immediate counties around Dubuque, there is plenty of that. Just look at the professional ranks and you will see four pitchers from those high schools pitching professionally.

On to the annual end-of-year AABC Tourney once again to be played in Denver, Iowa. Eight teams prepared to fight it out for the right to go on to the AABC Regionals over Labor Day weekend. In the opening round of the double-elimination tourney, Dave Reittinger hurled a one-hitter as the Hawks defeated Osage, Iowa by a score of 4-0. The Whitehawks scored all their runs in the first inning, getting five singles from Jim Wegmann, Art Huinker, Dale Digmann, Kirk Rentschler and Jim Digmann. The Dubuque Truckers turned back Allison, 1-0 on a six-hit shutout by Frank Delaney. His catcher was Jim Hoerner. They scored their run in the final inning on a Rick Juergens' single that plated Tom Turner who had walked and stole second base. In another area game, Petersburg lost to Fayette, 4-3 in 10 innings, to fall into the loser's bracket. In the final opening round game, the Waterloo Merchants lost a 1-0 pitchers' duel to host Denver, with Ken Folsom winning the contest over Tom Simpson for Waterloo. Folsom gave up three hits, Simpson only two.

Next, in the winners bracket, I shutout Fayette on a two-hitter, and the Hawks won 6-0. In the meantime, the Dubuque Truckers (winners of the Mississippi League League, while Dyersville had won the Maquoketa Valley League again) were also undefeated after winning their second game by knocking off host Denver. In the loser's bracket, the Waterloo Merchants defeated Allison and Osage downed Petersburg. Thus Allison and Petersburg found themselves eliminated from the tournament. The Waterloo Merchants next played and defeated Denver in the losers' bracket, thus leaving three teams to battle it out for the title, the Merchants from Waterloo, the Dubuque Truckers and the Whitehawks.

343

1965 identified a new kid on the block who proved very tough for the Whitehawks and all the semi-pro teams in the northeast quadrant of the state of Iowa. That team carried the name of Waterloo Merchants. They were able to take advantage of some good high school pitchers in Waterloo, both left-handers. One was Tom Simpson, who carried the same label that I had for years, a short, stocky lefty. The second left-hander was Rich Folkers, who had carried the Waterloo American Legion team all the way to the national finals the year before. Rich Blumeyer, now the Waterloo manager, had organized a strong support team around the two lefties and they became a team to contend with. The Dyersville Whitehawks will find that out in the remaining games of the AABC. Following is a brief write-up appearing in the Dyersville Commercial which described the progress of the remaining games.

HAWKS BLANKED 2-0 IN AABC STATE BASEBALL TOURNEY FINALS

After getting by Osage 4-0 and Fayette 6-0 in the first two games of the AABC Tournament at Denver, the competition got tougher but so did the Whitehawks. On Saturday, August 21, the winning ways of the Whitehawks turned when they met the Waterloo Merchants. The pitching of Reittinger and Tangeman could not hold the Merchants as they picked up 4 runs on 8 hits. Rich Folkers held the Hawks to only two hits, a triple and a single by Art Huinker and struck out 9 in his 7-inning performance. Final score was 4-0 with Waterloo taking the honors.

On Sunday, August 22 and Monday, August 23 the Dyersville nine knocked off the undefeated Dubuque Truckers 4-1 and 7-1. Roy Willenbring's two-hit pitching was too much for the Truckers in the first Dyersville victory. Dubuque could muster only one run in the first inning as the Hawks collected one in the fifth and seventh innings and 2 in the eighth on six hits given up by Heydinger.

Wieland hurled the Whitehawks passed the Truckers the second time allowing them one run in the second inning. Jim Wegmann and Rollie Sampson each got two singles in the Hawks 8-hit attack. Fessler was the loser as Dubuque fell out of the Tournament.

Finals Tuesday Night
The game to decide the title got underway Tuesday night with Dyersville against the Waterloo Merchants. For the first 8 innings neither team was able to push a runner across the plate. Simpson opened the top of the 9th for the Merchants with a single followed by an infield out. Then the Waterloo nine opened up. Lein received a free pass followed by a single by Ben Halupnik. Jerry Tarkett grounded out but Roger

Messingham pounded out a single to score the second run of the inning. The Whitehawks went out in order in the bottom of the 9th handing the crown to Waterloo. Simpson retired 14 hitters on strikes, allowing only three hits. Art Huinker, who pitched 2-hit ball until the ninth, was charged with the loss. Dyersville went out in order 6 of the 9 innings with no runner getting further than first base.

For the first time in four years, the Whitehawks were not going on to the AABC Regional Tournament, this year to be held in Beloit, Wisconsin. The season had come to an end for the Whitehawks. The core of our team stuck together for another year and those familiar faces continued to win most of their games, although we, by our standards, had not performed successfully in the Holy Cross, Worthington and Cascade tournaments. First of all, congratulations to the teams that defeated us in those tourneys and to the teams that won them. For us, the victory in our tournament provided the Hawks a satisfying feeling to cover the three contests we lost in the other three tournaments.

Another interesting bit of information was gathered from a write-up of a New York Mets vs. Houston Astros game next to the Telegraph-Herald' coverage of the AABC tournament in Denver. In that particular game, Jim Hickman, my roommate in professional baseball at Albany, Georgia, played center field for the Mets. For Houston, Lee Maye, the first batter I faced in my limited pro career in a game at Jacksonville, Florida, played left field and Bob Aspromonte, the Dodger farm hand and the first batter I faced pitching for Albany, played third base. At least that information was interesting for me. That was eight years after we had played against each other.

Rich Folkers, the Waterloo Merchants outstanding lefthander, had a seven-year career in the majors. From 1972 through 1974, he played with the St. Louis Cardinals. In his total major league career he won 19 games and lost 23 with an ERA of just over four.

With the baseball season over, the teachers at Xavier, getting ready for a new school year, now were quite sure that the 1965-66 school year would be the last for Xavier High School. The central Catholic high school would be completed for the opening of school in the fall of 1966. Would we be included? Time will provide Ann and I that answer. And we would now have our oldest daughter, Tammy, starting Kindergarten this fall.

And another summer had been completed relative to my summer employment. For several years I had been in charge of running the Dyersville swimming pool. Thank heaven there were always strong, well-trained life guards present because I myself could not swim. By the time my years were over with that work, at least I could swim across the Dyersville pool, but unable to keep my head above water. And I supposedly was in charge.

345

Our family is well settled in our new home. When we moved into the split-level four-bedroom house in March, 1963, it was the only house on that street. In fact for about the first three months, there was only a dirt road down to our house. There were four lots to the intersection of a hard-surface street. On one particularly rainy night, Ann went to a friend's house in another section of Dyersville to play bridge. With the road in such bad shape, I met her at the intersection in order to help her get to our home while rain continued to fall. The finishing of the street was much appreciated.

CHANGE IS COMING

The 1966 summer baseball season followed our fifth and final season of teaching and coaching for Xavier High School in Dyersville. The fall of 1966 would bring the opening of the new Beckman High School. By this tine Ann and I knew we would be staying in our present Dyersville home with a contract to teach at the new central Catholic school. My responsibilities at the new school would include the role of athletic director and baseball coach, along with the teaching of two classes of American History to junior boys, and counseling. Yes, boys and girls would be separated in most required classes.

For the Whitehawks, this summer's baseball efforts would prove to be disappointing. We failed to win the Maquoketa Valley League for the first time in the six years since moving to Dyersville. I did not research the league results prior to that time. This also meant no AABC tourney play after all the local tournaments were completed.

The same order of local tournaments was scheduled for the summer as was played in '65. The first tournament would be held in Holy Cross, followed by Worthington, Winthrop, Cascade and lastly, Dyersville.

The tournament trail started satisfactorily, winning three games and gaining the finals at Holy Cross, only to lose to the Cascade Reds. In between the Worthington and Cascade tourneys, the Whitehawks completed a four-game sweep of the Winthrop invitational to capture that title.

There the good news ends. In the three most-seniored tournaments- - - Worthington, Cascade and Dyersville- - -we were bounced from all three in the opening round. In the three games, we scored a total of two runs. First, I have to give credit to the very strong pitching that we ran into. But to score only two runs in three games is a very pathetic offensive record. This again is a great example of the domination of good pitching over good hitting, a belief I hold for all baseball levels. Another possibility may be the aging factor. The basic core of ball players were established players before Tom Jenk gathered them together in this decade of the '60's. We, the players, probably would deny that factor. In a way, that is what happened with hometown Festina. There were not enough young people to take over. That having been said, we will cover each individual tourney.

The Whitehawks and Monticello opened up the Holy Cross tournament. Following is a short write-up found in the Dyersville Commercial.

ROTHROCK'S NEAR PERFECT PERFORMANCE
HIGH-LIGHTS FIRST ROUND PLAY
Dyersville and Monticello opened the Holy Cross
Tourney one day late but with no less enthusiasm. The Hawks
pounded out the first run of the contest in the opening inning as
Art Huinker doubled to left and scored on a single by Dale
Digmann. From then on, neither team did a thing with the
sticks, until the fourth when Dale Digmann scored on a single
by Rollie Sampson. The throw in from left to get Digmann was

347

a perfect strike to the plate and would have been a close play but Monticello pitcher, Jim Rima, cut off the throw and went to second failing to get Sampson who went to second on the throw in.

Dave Reittinger held the Monticello nine with little trouble through six innings but walked two in the seventh, bringing on Art Huinker. Monticello picked up one run on an error and loaded the bases with only one out and a 2-1 score. An attempted suicide bunt failed and the runner on third was trapped for the second out. Huinker got the final out with a strikeout.

In the second game of the evening, Darrell Rothrock threw a no-hitter for Epworth against Pleasant Grove. Rothrock allowed only one base runner when Don Till reached first on an error. Rothrock allowed no hits and no walks, with the error preventing a "perfect game." The first tournament of the season and already pitchers are dominating. In that game, Tiny Potts had the big hit for Epworth, a two-run single that iced the game in the 6th.

In second-round action the Whitehawks shut out Epworth 6-0 on the fine three-hit pitching of Dave Reittinger again. Host team, Holy Cross, won their second game and would play Dyersville in the semi-finals. Other second-round winners were Balltown and Cascade.

DYERSVILLE, CASCADE GAIN BERTHS IN FINALS AT HOLY CROSS

The Dyersville Whitehawks and defending champion Cascade will battle for the first-place crown in the 2nd Annual Holy Cross Baseball Tournament. The Whitehawks advanced to the tournament finals with a first round win over Monticello, a 6-0 romp of Epworth and a 2-0 edge of home town Holy Cross. Cascade got by Petersburg, blasted Rickardsville, 11-0, and inched by Balltown in the semi-finals, 2-0.

The Whitehawks moved into the finals behind the 1-hit pitching of Mark Dilley. Dilley struck out 11 and allowed only a second inning single to Carl Farrey in gaining the win.

Dale Digmann singled in the winning runs in the 5th. Murph Lacke, humming for Holy Cross, and Dilley had a tight pitchers' duel for the first four innings but Digmann broke it open with his two-run single. Dyersville scattered seven hits through the seven innings. Dilley helped his own cause with two hits along with George Benn.

Cascade struck in the first on a walk and a single by Chuck Lannings. They added another in the 3rd on Morrie Klocker's triple and Dick Wright's sacrifice fly. Jan Arthur

348

allowed only three hits but was tagged for the loss. Balltown out-hit Cascade 4-3.

For these early Holy Cross tournaments, the games were played on the diamond located directly behind the Leo High School building. It was a very satisfactory ball park but with limited seating for the fans. The diamond itself was well cared for by the hometown Holy Cross people.

CASCADE WINS 2ND HOLY CROSS MEET IN TWO YEARS

For the second consecutive year, the team representing Cascade has won the Holy Cross Annual Baseball Tournament. This year Cascade's victim was Dyersville who fell 7-1.

Bob Bentley held the Hawks to 6 hits and one run through the nine innings. Cascade exploded for 15 big hits off two Dyersville pitchers in gaining their seven runs. They also took advantage of 3 Dyersville errors to get the win.

Dave Reittinger started for the Hawks and Art Huinker finished. Cascade got the lead right off the bat with two runs in the first. Their big inning came in the 4th when they scored 4 runs on a double and four singles. Morrie Klocker held the big stick for the winners getting two doubles.

Dyersville's lone tally came in the third on a walk, a wild pitch and a single by Dale Digmann.

Two of the six Dyersville hits finally came from my bat. But with the exception of the Epworth game, our bats were inept. The Holy Cross diamond did not have a deep outfield but pitchers kept the long ball to a minimum throughout the tournament. A few years later, the Holy Cross Athletic Association built a new diamond on the northeast side of the town and really did it right. A completely enclosed field with satisfactory outfield space as well as adequate bleachers and parking provided a beautiful facility for holding this tournament. It also provided a great diamond for the Leo High School team to play their home games. The high school also hosted high school baseball tournaments over the years until it closed in the late 1980s.

The Worthington Annual Baseball Tourney opening round games started the first week in July with the Whitehawks going head-to-head with Farley. A year ago at Worthington, the two teams met in the quarter-finals with Farley coming up with a big ninth inning rally to edge out the Whitehawks 5-4.

This year, Farley brought Don Kuehner, a native of St. Lucas, Iowa, and baseball rivals with our home town Festina ball club, to the tournament to pitch and he proceeded to allow only six hits in shutting us out, 3-0. A fourth inning home run by Dick Phillips with Andy Hollenback on base provided the winning margin. It was "one and done" for the Hawks.

Next came the lone bright spot for the Whitehawks. Expanded to a 16-team tournament at Winthrop, Dyersville opened activities with a 6-0 victory over Center Point with Dave Reittinger pitching a one-hitter and fanning 17 batters in the seven-inning game. Leading hitters for the Hawks were Roger Messingham and John Nelson, each with a double and a home run. Both players joined the Dyersville team from the Waterloo Merchants.

In the quarter-finals, the Whitehawks erupted for twelve quick runs in taking care of Ryan by a final score of 12-0. The game was stopped after five innings per tournament rules. Rich Folkers, also from the Waterloo team, pitched a perfect five innings, facing the minimum 15 batters. Rollie Sampson collected a double and a single while Dick Cathhart had a single and a home run to lead the Whitehawk attack. Steve Tierschel was the catcher for Folkers.

The next game in the semi-finals provided more of a challenge. We won the game 8-6 but only after Hopkinton fought from behind to almost overcome a five-run deficit. Dave Reittinger started for the Hawks but was chased in a big sixth-inning uprising. Rod Tangeman relieved to get out of a jam and retired Hopkinton in the seventh without any runs scoring. Dale Digmann was back catching for the Hawks. Roger Messingham was the big hitting star with a single, double and a home run. Roger was also a Waterloo Merchant player.

HAWKS DECK PETERSBURG

The Dyersville Whitehawks scored two runs in the top of the ninth inning to defeat Petersburg, 3-1, in the championship game of the Winthrop baseball tournament.

Hopkinton blanked Winthrop 5-0, to win the consolation game.

Rich Folkers, who pitched a three-hitter for Dyersville, led off the ninth inning with a double, and scored on Kirk Rentschler's two-bagger.

John Nelson singled home the insurance marker. The Hawks had spotted Petersburg a 1-0 lead in the third, but tied the game with a single marker in the fifth.

Folkers fanned 16 Petersburg batters, and was named the most valuable player of the tournament.

The Dyersville Whitehawks enjoyed the four game sweep in this tournament but the positive feeling was short-lived. First of all, two players who had played with the Whitehawks for a good four or five years, returned to their home town Petersburg in the summer of 1966. Sal Willenbring, strong right-hand pitcher, was the losing pitcher in the final game at Winthrop giving up only one run until the two-run winning rally in the ninth inning. Regular center fielder for the Whitehawks the last four seasons, Jim Wegmann, played with Petersburg that final game at Winthrop. He, like Sal Willenbring, is a native of Petersburg. His brother, Leo, had been a regular with the same team for several years. Their loss has placed a big hole in our Dyersville lineup.

Again this year, the Cascade Tournament paired the Whitehawks against Monticello in the opening round. And again, the results remained unchanged. Monticello scored five runs early and hung on for a 5-1 victory.

> *MONTICELLO EDGES DYERSVILLE*
> *Monticello upended Dyersville, 5-1 and Petersburg blanked Balltown, 4-0 in Wednesday night's action in the Cascade Baseball Tournament.*
> *Monti jumped off to a 2-0 lead over Dyersville in the second on a walk, a wild pitch, singles by Rick Westhoff and Paul Sullivan , and a fielder's choice.*
> *A triple by Jim Wright, a single by Bob Corrick, walks to Westhoff and Sullivan and one of Dyersville's three errors accounted for the other three runs in the third.*
> *Art Huinker, who took over for Dick Wold in the third inning uprising, blanked Monti the rest of the way. Dyersville's lone run came in the third on singles by George Benn and Wold, sandwiched around a walk.*
> *Benn was the only player with more than one hit, collecting a double to go with his single.*

Ray Card, a big, tall righthander by way of Upper Iowa University in Fayette, scattered five hits very effectively. At least I think that he was a student there. He was a very challenging-looking pitcher on the mound who also has a reputation of being somewhat wild, causing many hitters to hang loose in the batter's box.

While the Whitehawks battled unsuccessfully to capture the Maquoketa Valley League title, Balltown being the eventual winner, we also looked forward to the Dyersville tourney, hoping for a different result. Our opening-round opponent was pesky Pleasant Grove and their tough left-hand pitcher, Roger Shelby. Manager Tom Jenk brought in Waterloo left-hander, Rich Folkers, most recently the MVP in the Winthrop tourney.

> *PLEASANT GROVE TOPS DYERSVILLE IN*
> *OUTSTANDING PITCHERS' DUEL*
> *The second game of the opening night turned into a real pitchers' battle between Rich Folkers for the home town Hawks and Roger Shelby for Pleasant Grove. Both men hurled exceptional contests as the scoreboard was full of zeroes through the ninth inning.*

Roger Shelby, allowing only a first inning double to
John Nelson, controlled the Whitehawks the entire game.
Pleasant Grove sparked for two runs in the top of the 10th.
Lloyd Kennedy led it off in the 10th with a single. A fielder's
choice caused one out but Loras Simon kept it going with
another single. A walk and base hits by Wordlaw and
Underwood brought in two runs and brought the victory to
Pleasant Grove as the Hawks failed to score in the bottom of the
inning. Rich Folkers allowed only two hits through the first
nine innings but the Grovers exploded for four before Reittinger
came on in the 10th with one out to retire the side.

The best Dyersville chance to crossing the plate was in
the 9th when, with two men on, John Nelson hit one up against
the right field fence only to be caught by rightfielder Loras
Simon. Dale Digmann followed by getting on on an error but a
infield fly ball ended it for Dyersville leaving three men
stranded.

Loras Simon lead the Pleasant Grove gang with two
singles.

As I stated earlier, three games, including three extra innings, and we, as a team, had scored just two runs. Not many games are won that way. For those 24 innings, the team collected 12 hits. Did you notice any hits by you know who? I didn't either. This loss proved to be the final game of the year for the Whitehawks. I don't know who ended up winning all those tournaments that year. Again, no MV title and "out in the first round" for the three traditional tournaments.

The season was over for the Whitehawks, but Balltown, our AABC representative in the state tournament, asked Tom Jenk, Dale Digmann and myself to join their team at the AABC, held for the first time in the town of Dysart, located south and west of Waterloo. They also added young shortstop, Jerry Roling, from the Holy Cross team and Epworth pitcher Vern Koerperich. Vern was a left-handed pitcher also.

Eight teams were scheduled to attack the double-elimination tournament. Balltown's first opponent was Iowa defending champion, the Waterloo Merchants.

BALLTOWN IS 6-1 VICTOR IN STATE TOURNEY
Balltown scored four runs in the first inning at Dysart
Tuesday night and went on to defeat the Waterloo Merchants, 6-
1 to become one of the two unbeaten teams still remaining in the
American Baseball Congress state tournament.

352

> *Art Huinker, bothered all season by a sore arm, fired a*
> *nifty two-hitter for Balltown, and was given a 6-0 lead in the*
> *first three innings.*
> *University of Iowa pitcher Tom Staack had control*
> *trouble in the first inning, giving up four walks, to force one*
> *across, then surrendering a run-scoring single to Bill Sigwarth*
> *and a two-run double to Joe Sigwarth.*
> *Singles by Bill Sigwarth, Joe Sigwarth and Jerry*
> *Roling brought home another run In the second, and the final*
> *Balltown run scored in the third as the result of two walks and*
> *two passed balls.*
> *A walk and Jerry Tarkett's triple ruined Huinker's*
> *shutout in the fourth inning.*

Obviously I read the above write-up long before I included it here in this chapter. But reading it brought the first realization that I suffered arm problems in the summer of 1966. Seriously, I had no recollection of a sore arm but that would explain why I did very little pitching throughout the season. There was considerable relief work for me but very few games started. Combine that issue with the loss of Jim "Sal" Willenbring and no wonder Manager Jenk was forced to look beyond Dave Reittinger for additional pitching help.

Balltown also added young shortstop, Jerry Roling for the AABC tournament run. A very promising young ballplayer, Jerry was among a group of young players coming out of Leo High School about this time. Ron LeGrand, a speedy centerfielder, Dennis Roling, a catcher, Kenny Ruden, infielder-pitcher, and Hank Lucas, pitcher, were among that strong corps that made Leo High School one of the tougher small school teams in the state. Hank Lucas went on to play professional baseball for the Los Angeles Dodgers but a serious injury in an off-season car accident brought that to a halt. He and Marv Maiers from Dyersville have coached a very successful Dubuque County Legion team for many years, while Jerry Roling is considered among the elite in high school baseball coaches in the state of Iowa and beyond.

Next, the two winners, Balltown and Osage, played two nights later. This article is taken from the Waterloo Courier and was written by Assistant Sports Editor, Burke Evans.

> *OSAGE WINS; REMAINS UNDEFEATED*
> *Osage moved into the driver's seat here Thursday*
> *night in the annual Iowa State Amateur baseball tournament by*
> *nipping Balltown 3-2 behind the excellent relief pitching of*
> *veteran Vern Juenger.*
> *Balltown had two runs in and runners on first and third*
> *with nobody out in the first inning when Juenger relieved starter*
> *Jim Blood Thursday night.*

Juenger retired the side without permitting another run and hurled five-hit shutout ball the rest of the way. He walked two and struck out five, including usually hard-hitting Art Huinker three times.

It was a bad night all the way around for Huinker, who stopped Waterloo's 20-game winning streak with a two-hit, 6-1 victory Tuesday. He struck out 15 in that seven-inning stint.

Thursday, he came on in relief of starter Paul Schmitt after Denny Fossey singled to open the ninth with the score tied 2-2. Ron Foell sacrificed Fossey up a base but Huinker fanned catcher Tom Mayer. Cleanup hitter Bruce Campbell was intentionally walked but the strategy backfired when Ron Juenger lined Huinker's first pitch to right for a single to drive across the winning run.

It apparently was one of those nights for me. First, I don't remember the strikeouts but they did happen. And as far as relieving in the bottom of the ninth, it usually is a do-or-die situation. They needed one hit, they got it, and the game was over. In baseball, or in any sport, we can have those games. This was one of mine. And again, I had to accept it and we have more games coming up to prepare for.

The Waterloo Merchants worked their way back through the loser's bracket and eventually gave Osage their first loss by the score of 3-1. Balltown meanwhile played their next game and in a real tight pitchers' battle, defeated Keystone 2-1 and eliminated them from the tournament. All teams were now eliminated except for Balltown, Osage and Waterloo, all with one loss.

In the victory over Keystone, lefty Vern Koerperich pitched six innings, allowing one run and only five hits. Again, I relieved and pitched a three up, three down seventh to secure the victory.

With three teams left and all having played each other already, in a draw of some sort, Osage won the bye and the Waterloo Merchants and Balltown faced each other again, with the loser being eliminated. For the fourth time in a week, I again took the mound for Balltown.

FOLKERS OUTDUELS HUINKER
By Larry Park, Courier Sports Writer
The Waterloo Merchants advanced to the finals of the tournament as Waterloo's ace left-hander Rich Folkers outdueled Balltown lefty Art Huinker 2-1 Sunday afternoon at Dysart. Huinker previously defeated the Merchants 6-1, and he will go with them to the regionals.

Folkers gave up three hits, struck out 12 and walked one. Huinker gave up five hits, walked one and struck out eight.

354

Folkers got a slicing double to left field in the third for the game's first hit. Huinker ruined Folker's shutout with a one-out homer to left in the top of the ninth.

It was Huinker's only walk that got the stubby southpaw into a jam in the bottom of the fourth. Gary Reiners walked to lead off the inning. Steve Brandt then hit a chopper to Huinker who whirled and threw to second. Balltown's second sacker Jack Gansemer did not get to the bag in time and both runners were safe on a fielder's choice.

Bruce Lein advanced the runners with a bunt. Rieners scored the first run after Jerry Tarkett hit a sacrifice fly to right field.

Tarket also got the Merchants' other RBI when he cracked a home run over the left field fence. This blow proved to be decider because of Huinker's round-tripper in the ninth.

Folkers retired the first 13 batters he faced but Bill Sigwarth got on first on a check swing bloop single to right. He got to second as Joe Sigwarth grounded out. Folkers and shortstop Rieners tried a play to pick off Sigwarth but the ball got away from Rieners and Balltown had its only man on third except for Huinker in the ninth. Folkers struck out Jerry Roling to end the threat.

Joe Sigwarth got the other Balltown hit in the seventh on a sharp single to right. Then Roling got good wood on the ball but it went right to rightfielder Ben Halupnik. Folkers got the next two men to end the inning.

This was a very well-played baseball game on a sunny afternoon at the Dysart diamond, another ball diamond with an odd shape. It was part of a football field, either practice or otherwise. Anyway, the left field fence was extremely short, probably 280 to 300 feet down the line, then it ran a straight line out to right center, where the field was extremely deep. In the ninth inning with Waterloo up two runs, Folkers had run the count to 2 balls and 2 strikes against me. He threw a hard curveball that could have been called either way, a ball or a strike, but I got the break. On the next pitch, he threw a fast ball right down the middle, figuring no one on base, the batter either hits it or he doesn't. Well, I caught it well and it sailed between two houses beyond the short left field fence. As soon as the contact was made, there was no doubt. Folkers retired the next batter and the game was over.

Waterloo went on to nip Osage, 6-5, on Sunday evening to capture the championship. And the call came the next day asking me to go along with them to Beloit for the AABC West Central Regional Tournament. Waterloo pitcher Tom Staack walloped a three-run home run for the big blow over Osage.

Balltown had to have some degree of satisfaction for the baseball played in the state tournament. They won 2 and lost 2 but the team was in every game right to the end. Both defeats were one-run losses. They had not played in the state meet before that year. Checking the starting line-ups for the four games there were always two or three Sigwarths listed. Leon Cummer was the Balltown manager.

Waterloo, on the other hand, played six games in the time span of nine days. That is what a team faces in a double-elimination tournament if they lose in the opening round.

WEST CENTRAL REGIONALS

Playing in the West Central Regionals for the American Amateur Baseball Congress was much better for a team from eastern Iowa than driving all the way for the Great Plains Regionals. For Ann and I to reach Beloit, it is about a 2 hour plus drive. Going to South Dakota in the 60's was an all-day trip. We were picked up by Roger Messingham and his fiancée in Dyersville for the short trip by way of Wisconsin Highway 11 to Beloit.

This is the second straight year that the Waterloo Merchants had won the state championship and played the regionals in Beloit. The city of Beloit had a relatively new facility and obtained the right to host the regionals. And looking at the teams in the tournament, Beloit was very centrally located.

The Merchants opened up their quest for the nationals in Battle Creek on Saturday night but lost a 2-1 pitchers' duel to the National Electric Chiefs of Chicago. Rich Folkers pitched a strong game in the losing cause. Our next game was scheduled for Sunday night against Riverton, Illinois.

MERCHANTS STAY ALIVE IN REGIONAL WITH 7-5 VICTORY

The Waterloo Merchants still have a chance to take all the marbles in the West Central Regional baseball tournament here, with the help of a 7-5 second round game win over Riverton, Ill. , Sunday night.

The Merchants were to play the host team Beloit Blues at 12 noon Monday. Beloin is undefeated in the tourney. Beloit defeated the National Electric Chiefs 7-4 to qualify to meet the Merchants Monday.

Three teams are left in the five-team meet. Ray Buisler's of Milwaukee was eliminated 6-5 by Riverton Sunday morning, while Waterloo in turn eliminated Riverton Sunday evening.

Waterloo pitcher Art Huinker, picked up from Balltwon, got into trouble in the first inning of Sunday's game, walking six straight men after two were out, and forcing in three runs.

356

*Waterloo manager Rich Blumeyer kept Huinker in,
however, and the veteran pitcher redeemed himself by posting
no walks the rest of the game and striking out 10 while giving up
eight hits.*

*The Merchants made it 3-1 in the bottom of the first
when shortstop John Nelson got on via a throwing error, and
was knocked in by third baseman Steve Brandt's single.*

*Riverton picked up single runs in the third and fourth,
but the Merchants came back in the bottom of the fifth with a
booming triple by Huinker, and another single by Brandt.*

*The Merchants made it 5-3 in the bottom half of the
sixth on successive singles by catcher Jerry Tarkett, center
fielder John Kneeland and second baseman Roger Messingham.*

*Waterloo went ahead in the bottom of the seventh with
a four-run rally that started with successive walks to Huinker,
Brandt and Tarkett. Left fielder Rich Folkers drove in a run
with a single and right fielder Ben Halupnik drove in the tying
and go ahead runs with a two-run single. Nelson then singled to
drive in the seventh run.*

*Waterloo's win over Riverton gave the Merchants a
little revenge, since Riverton defeated Waterloo 2-1 in the
opening round of the tourney last year.*

Hitting stars were John Kneeland with four hits and one run batted in, and Steve Brandt with three hits and two runs batted in. They reported a "booming triple" by me but I have no recollection of where I hit it or to what field. But I do remember the first inning.

A veteran left-handed pitcher, normally known for having decent control, walked six straight batters after two out in the first inning. I have vivid memories of that first inning, even to the point of the discussion that catcher Jerry Tarkett and I had with Manager Blumeyer. There is no blame on the umpire for this, yet I do recall that most of the pitches, though not strikes, were all close to the location that I wanted. I often hear the expression, watching major league games, that the pitcher is not attacking the strike zone but instead nibbling at the edges, meaning that the pitcher is trying to be too fine and not having any confidence in his own pitches. I remember Tarkett affirming that with Blumeyer and the coach just challenged me to go out there and believe in myself.

No more walks the remainder of the game and thankfully our bats came alive for thirteen hits and enough runs to overcome the disastrous first inning. To say the least, if I had been manager, after six walks, that pitcher would probably have been gone.

357

MERCHANTS TO NATIONAL AFTER WINNING
REGIONAL TITLE
Courier News Service
The Waterloo Merchants amateur baseball team won
the West Central Regional tournament here Monday night with
a 9-5 victory over the host team Beloit Blues. The
championship in the double-elimination tourney means that the
Merchants now qualify for the American Amateur Baseball
Congress Stan Musial World Series at Battle Creek, Mich., Sept.
15-18.

The last Iowa team to qualify for the national
tournament was Dyersville in 1964. Dyersville finished second
in 1962.

Prior to the win in the championship Monday night, the
Merchants had defeated Beloit 9-8 in the afternoon game. The
Merchants then drew a bye and watched the next game as Beloit
beat the Chicago National Electric Chiefs, 5-3.

After drawing the bye, the Merchants were assured of
qualifying for the national tournament as both the champion
and runnerup from this tournament advance to the Stan Musial
World Series.

John Nelson was the hitting hero in the championship
game. He hit two doubles to drive in five runs. Both hits came
after Beloit had built up a 5-1 lead after three innings against
Merchants' hurler Ken Nevenhoven. Nevenhoven straightened
out after the third and shut out the Blues the rest of the way.

Second baseman Roger Messingham applied the
clincher with a three-run homer over the right field fence.
Bruce Lein, on base with a single, and Jerry Tarkett, on with a
walk, scored in front of Messingham.

Lefty Rich Folkers pitched and batted the Merchants to
a 9-8 win over Beloit earlier in the day. The loss was the first
for Beloit in the double-elimination tourney.

Folkers took over for Nevenhoven in the sixth and
pitched the final three and two-thirds innings, allowing only one
hit. Nevenhoven had relieved starter Tom Staack in the
previous inning.

Folkers stroked a single in the seventh to drive in John
Kneeland who had walked. This tied the score at 8-8.

Messingham singled to open the final frame but was
forced at second by Folkers. Nelson was safe on an error
before Art Huinker, draftee from Dyersville, knocked in the
deciding tally with a single.

That winning hit for me in the top of the ninth was against a familiar and
very tough right hander, Roger Fenwick. Between him and Darrell Rothrock,

358

there are no other pitchers who were hired by more different teams to pitch for them in the local tournaments. Over the years I have had fairly good luck against Fenwick, not an easy pitcher to bat against. I will let you in on a little secret. Though I was unwilling to share this with other hitters on the Dyersville team, or Waterloo in this tournament, I watched Roger's face and a certain twisted expression meant a curve ball, without it a fastball. There was a large degree of uncertainty about that judgment and therefore I felt very uncomfortable, not only with my own dependence on it, but with sharing it with anyone else. It worked with the game-winning hit in the Monday morning game. But I will admit to almost being hit once because I judged the expression to mean a curve ball was coming but it stayed straight and inside.

This completed the sixth Regional Tournament that I had participated in, three with Dyersville, two with Sumner, and now one with the Merchants. The Waterloo trip to Battle Creek for the national tournament would be my fifth. Three times I played with the Whitehawks and one with Sumner as a seventeen-year old.

AMERICAN AMATEUR STAN MUSIAL NATIONAL TOURNAMENT

The trip to Battle Creek for Ann and me was a very short experience. When Waterloo made the inquiry of my going to the nationals with them, there were reservations on my part. The Merchants were to play their first game on Friday night. I am not sure but I think they decided that for them to be ready to play, they would leave on Wednesday. For me, that meant taking off two days of school and unsure how many more would occur if we were successful in the Battle Creek tourney. Our brand new Beckman High School had just opened and I had a new job with some new responsibilities. If hometown Dyersville were playing at Battle Creek, the situation would have been different. But to play with a new team with no connection with my new school made me uncomfortable.

In the end, we agreed that I would take off immediately after work on Thursday afternoon and travel by bus from Dubuque to Battle Creek in time for their second game on Friday. On the return trip, Ann and I would catch a ride with a Waterloo car. Now let's cover the write-ups of the games at the AABC nationals and then talk about our bus trip.

> *MERCHANTS OUT OF MEET AFTER 5-4, 6-0*
> *LOSSES*
> *Courier News Service*
> *Waterloo's Merchants are out of the Stan Musial*
> *World Series of the American Amateur Baseball Congress being*
> *played.*
> *The Merchants, who dropped a 5-4 decision to Dallas,*
> *Tex., in the first round of the double-elimination tourney*
> *Thursday, were ousted by Evansville, Ind., 6-0 Friday morning.*

Evansville pitcher, Larry Zimmer, who hurled for the national champion Waterloo, Ind. team last year, blanked the Merchants on two hits.

Evansville, meanwhile, was collecting 11 hits and six runs off southpaw Art Huinker. Five of the runs were earned.

In addition to allowing just the two singles, by John Kneeland in the seventh and Jerry Tarkett in the ninth, Zimmer walked four and struck out nine. A southpaw, he hurled for Georgia Tech last season.

Dallas needed 11 innings to defeat Waterloo Thursday.

Lefty Rich Folkers pitched the distance for the Merchants Thursday and deserved a better fate. Only two of the five runs he permitted were earned as he gave up 10 hits, walked just two and struck out 14.

The Merchants fought back from a 3-0 deficit with two runs in the seventh and one in the ninth. Dallas went ahead 4-3 in the top of the tenth but Waterloo came back with one run and an excellent chance to win it in that frame.

John Nelson singled to open the bottom of the tenth for Waterloo and came around on a passed ball and singles by Kneeland and Steve Brandt. A pop fly out and a double play grounder ended the threat.

Dallas scored its winning run in the 11th on a squeeze by Phil Cos.

Waterloo concluded its season with a 34-5 record.

First, let's cover the bus trip to Battle Creek. Remember now, here comes a big baby-sitting responsibility. Again, I am not sure how we covered that responsibility . Did Ann's parents come to Dyersville, or did we hire a babysitter for the long weekend? As you can probably understand, we supported many good babysitter careers in raising our family.

Ann and I caught the Greyhound Bus in Dubuque Thursday evening. That transported us to Chicago with several stops on the way. At the bus depot in Chicago, we had to transfer. We were asked if we wanted to take Bus A which left in about one-half hour and was called the Express to Battle Creek or Bus B which left after a 90-minute layover. Well, we automatically said we will take Bus A. It should get to Battle Creek quicker. That, again, was not a good decision. We should have checked the arrival time of the two buses.

Bus A, the Express, made stops in almost every town of any size between Chicago and Battle Creek. Bus B made only one stop between the two locations, and actually arrived about one-half hour before Bus A. And even though the depot in Chicago was not the most comfortable of places, cleanliness aside, we could have possibly caught some shuteye during the 90 minute layover, whereas on the express bus, a person would just be getting settled and another stop would be made, arousing everyone that was trying to sleep.

We finally arrived in Battle Creek about 3:15 in the morning. After a short taxi ride, we arrived at the hotel, hoping that the Merchants had won their game the night before so that we would not have to play until Friday night. To our dismay, word left at the front desk informed us that we would be playing in the losers' bracket at 10:00 the coming morning. By the time we moved into our room and settled down, it was after 4:00. Wake-up call came at 8:00. It was not the most appropriate way to get ready for pitching a big baseball game.

Once again this author did not have his A game pitching in Battle Creek. In the five years of playing in the AABC nationals, I never pitched a game where the snap of the ball or the movement of the baseball was present. We struggled from the first pitch until the end and at this level the results are not good. We lost the game, and obviously I did not get any hits either, even though I batted second in the lineup. With two straight losses, we were eliminated from the tournament and Ann and I got back to Dyersville ahead of the planned return.

The entire experience did not sit well for me when it was over. We either should have made the commitment to go with the team, or we should simply have turned down the opportunity. First of all, I believe our decision to come in later than the other team members does not help create the team atmosphere that is so important for success. Secondly, to arrive when we did certainly did not provide the ideal conditions for performing well at the upcoming game. Both aspects did not lead to positive feelings about the situation, both for me and for the remainder of the players. Again, it is an example of trying to do more than what time allows and in the end, not doing well at anything.

But we at the Huinker household were excited about the new challenges at Beckman High School. There were many new student faces to get to know. There was a new building with many parts incomplete. Years later, students attending in the fall of 1966 still remember the messes of ongoing construction more clearly than new teaching staff and new fellow students. There also was the challenge of some new approaches to teaching and scheduling that had many of us on staff excited and also very curious. It was the start of a new high school that has had an illustrious history. And our home was located within the proximity of the new school so that I often walked back and forth to work. We were still a one-car family and would be for another four years. Looking back on that time, it doesn't seem possible that we could get by with only one, but at that time we did not know anything different. Interesting life when you reflect back on it.

361

CRUTCHES

The seventh consecutive year of playing with the Dyersville Whitehawks starts with a startling change. Tom Jenk, who had managed the Whitehawks already in 1956 when I first played with them, asked to be relieved of his managerial duties for the year. And the duties were extended to me. Besides filling that role, I continued coaching the high school baseball team into the summer. It was my request to start summer high school baseball at Beckman High School. We played in the spring season also, which included our entering both the spring and summer high school tournaments.

Conflicts were bound to happen. The non-tournament high school games that we played were already scheduled. So were the five tournaments for the Whitehawks that were played every summer. The high school season usually ended in late July unless the team's success carried the Blazers to the state tournament. Keep that possibility in mind as we proceed through this season and the next.

Under my managing, very few non-league games were played. We played the Maquoketa Valley League games and the usual five local tournaments. In looking back today, we should have played more non-league games in order to give our young players more semi-pro game experience. We relied on playing many tournament games but how many of those games we played depended on winning opening round games and even quarter final games, something we failed to do in three of the tournaments the previous year when the Whitehawks were knocked out in opening round games.

Members of the old reliable crew were back for the Whitehawks. The Digmann brothers, infielder Jim and catcher Dale, Rollie Sampson, past manager Tom Jenk and I formed that nucleus. Also back was slugging second baseman, Bob Goldsmith who greatly strengthened our team's power-hitting capabilities. And Cliff Knippel returned to play many games for the Hawks as well. Three 1966 graduates of Xavier High School, Charlie Lammers, Larry Bildstein and Danny Meyer, and long time sub, George Benn, played big roles in the Hawks' season. In addition, we had high school players Dan Goerdt, a junior, and John Goerdt, a freshman, on the Whitehawk roster. We were also able to obtain the services of Dick Wold, a strong left-hand hitter, an outfielder and pitcher, at least for the tournaments.

Besides Dick Wold and myself, we had another lefty pitcher, Jan Arthur from Colesburg, who did considerable pitching for us that summer. In a Maquoketa Valley league game against Winthrop, Jan had a shutout until they scored their lone run in the sixth. Farley's Paul Scherrman caught that game for us and collected a key 2-run single for the Hawks following singles by Bob Goldsmith and Rollie Sampson.

Rollie Sampson and I pitched a combined four-hitter against Rickardsville in another league game with Goldsmith having a triple, double and two singles good for three RBIs, while Dan Meyer and Jim Digmann each had three singles.

In another league game played at Winthrop, Jan Arthur threw a strong eight innings, allowing only two runs on four hits, in a 4-2 victory. Pat Sullivan, a Loras staff member, pitched the ninth. Rollie Sampson singled in the second and scored our first run on an error. Back to back doubles by Dale Digmann and myself brought in our second run. The game was won in the eighth when Kip Knippel gained life on an error, and singles by Sampson and this author brought in our final two runs. Sampson had two singles and I had two singles and a double.

The first tournament again was at Holy Cross, with the Hawks downing East Dubuque 11-0. The game was halted after five innings, with East Dubuque having two hits and striking out 12 times. It was a good pitching day for me and I also had two of the seven Whitehawk hits.

Our second game proved interesting because we had another battle of the Huinker brothers with Kenny pitching for Sherrill against Dyersville.

> ### WORTHINGTON, DYERSVILLE WIN
> Worthington defeated Monticello, 6-2, and Dyersville blanked Sherrill, 3-0, in the Holy Cross quarterfinals Friday night in the third annual Holy Cross baseball tournament.
> Worthington grabbed a 1-0 lead in the second inning against Monticello when Loras Wolfe singled, stole second and scored on an error, then salted things away with a five-run fourth.
> Singles by Wolfe, pitcher Ken Elam, Doug Dunlap and Tom Burlage plus three errors and a walk contributed to the big inning and gave Elam a comfortable lead.
> Singles by Rick Westhoff and Bob Hines along with an error helped Monticello break the shutout with a run in the sixth, and another in the seventh without a hit.
> In a battle of the pitching brothers, Art Huinker of Dyersville out-dueled Ken Huinker of Sherrill in the second game.
> Art gave up only one hit- - -a second inning double by his brother- - -and struck out 18 of a possible 21 in the seven-inning contest, while Ken pitched a two-hitter.
> Dyersville scored twice in the first inning on two walks, two passed balls and a single by Bob Goldsmith, and added its final run in the fourth on two errors.

Defense of one's self is an expression often used in American society. Here I must add that the other Dyersville hit besides the Goldsmith single was my

363

triple to right-center but it did not figure in any scoring. I am especially thankful that most of the time we were teammates, helping each other try to win. Also notice the name of Tom Burlage for the Worthington team. He just completed his junior year at Beckman High School providing left hand pitching services for the Beckman baseball team. In other words, one of my baseball players.

In Dyersville's semi-final game against Worthington in the Holy Cross tournament, tall, lanky Jan Arthur tossed a three hitter and Dyersville took advantage of four Worthington errors and our four hits - - - two by Larry Bildstein and two by myself, one of which drove in two runs - - - to get us into the finals against Cascade.

> ### DYERSVILLE COMES FROM BEHIND IN HOLY CROSS TOURNEY 5-4
> *Dyersville's Whitehawks had to battle back from a 4-0 first inning deficit to capture the title in the third annual Holy Cross Baseball Tournament 5-4 over Cascade Tuesday night at Holy Cross.*
>
> *Things looked bad for the Hawks in the first inning of action. Chris Brown started for the Hawks on the mound and faced five hitters, giving up 4 runs. Dyersvile made a total of 4 errors in the first inning, including a dropped fly ball and a throwing error which allowed two runs. Jim Brimeyer and Morrie Klocker got singles for Cascade in the first and with Glen Walters' walk and the four errors the Cascade team had a commanding lead after one inning.*
>
> *Dyersville couldn't get started until the fourth inning, but then kept going until they had the lead. The first tally came in the 4th when Dale Digmann got a single, Rol Sampson reached first on a fielder's choice, and stole second and scored on a single by Larry Bildstein. Dale Digmann blasted a big 2-run homer in the 5th, the first homer of the tournament, after Huinker had already scored on Jim Digmann's single and the game was knotted going into the sixth.*
>
> *The winning run came in the 7th for Dyersville. Jim Digmann took a walk and got around to third on a single and a fielder's choice, and finally scored on Tom Jenk's fly out to right field.*
>
> *Art Huinker held the losers to only four hits after coming in with no outs in the first. He got 11 on strikes and didn't allow a walk through nine innings. It was Jim Rima starting for Cascade, working 6 innings before Carl Heitz came on to finish the game. Cascade pitching allowed only 6 Dyersville hits, two of which were by Dale Digmann.*

364

There was an additional write-up in the Dyersville Commercial which identified the Most Valuable Pitcher and Most Valuable Player awards given out after the final game at Holy Cross.

TW0 MOST VALUABLES AT HOLY CROSS
Art Huinker, southpaw from Dyersville, was awarded the trophy for the Most Valuable Pitcher of the Holy Cross Tournament following the championship game Tuesday night at Holy Cross.

Huinker worked 21 innings of brilliant pitching in three different games. In the first game he held East Dubuque scoreless in five innings, allowing only two hits and striking out 12 of 15. Against Sherrill in the second round he fanned 19 out of a possible 21 outs and allowed only 1 hit getting his second win, 3-0. Then, in the final Tuesday night, he came in with none out in the first inning and went the distance again allowing no runs, giving up only 4 hits and fanning 11 for his third win.

In the three games, Art struck out a total of 42 batters in 21 innings for an average of two per inning. The opposition could muster only 7 hits off the lefthander and got a total of only 3 free trips. Huinker allowed absolutely no runs to the opposition in the three games he worked.

Cascade's player-coach, Carl Heitz was awarded the Most Valuable Player Award for his coaching and performance as a player throughout the four games Cascade played in the tourney.

A good start for the Whitehawks on the tournament trail. In the next tournament sponsored by the Worthington community, fans witnessed one of the strongest pitching duels ever played in the opening round between the Whitehawks and Hopkinton. The battle was between Lloyd Brochshus for Hopkinton and me for the Hawks. After seven innings, the score was 0-0 with Hopkinton having one hit and Dyersville having none off Brochshus. In fact, we had no base runners through the first seven innings. The only hit for either side was a single by Ron Soukup, a strong-hitting outfielder picked up from the New Hampton area, following Larry Poock reaching first on an error.

It was one of those nights when my good stuff was there, but I made the mistake of giving Soukup a curveball over the middle of the plate that should have been in the dirt and he hit it as hard as a baseball can be hit but thank heaven it was a low line drive that dropped in front of the center fielder. In the extra eighth, Dale Digmann led off the inning for us with a single followed by my bunt single. After a Tom Jenk sacrifice moved runners to second and third, Digmann raced home on a Rollie Sampson squeeze bunt. The final score ended 1-0. Seventeen Hopkinton hitters went down on strikes in the eight-inning affair.

In the second round, we eked out a tough 4-2 win over Holy Cross. Jan Arthur pitched until the fourth when Holy Cross tied the game at one, and I came on in relief. In the bottom of the fourth, we scored three runs on RBI hits by Rollie Sampson, Dan Meyer and Cliff Knippel. It was not a real well-played game as 10 errors were put in the record books by both teams, while the two teams collected only six hits. We had reached the final four of the tournament.

CASCADE, DYERSVILLE REACH WORTHINGTON FINALS
Cascade and Dyersville gained berths in the finals with Wednesday night victories over Epworth and Petersburg. Cascade ran past Epworth 3-0 behind the 3-hit pitching of Steve Bryant and Dyersville swept Petersburg 9-2.

In the semi-final game, Petersburg scored two runs early, and again I came on in early relief. Dyersville came to life offensively and tied the score 2-2, on Bob Goldsmith's two-run homer in the bottom half of the third. In the fourth, a Tom Jenk double after a walk and a hit batsman gave the Hawks a 3-2 lead. Another run was scored in the fifth and big 5-run sixth in which I managed a double with the bases loaded put the game out of reach of Petersburg.

DYERSVILLE WINS WORTHINGTON TITLE IN NINTH; HUINKER MVP
Dyersville's Whitehawks trailed through eight and a half innings but suddenly exploded for three runs in the bottom of the ninth and claimed the crown in the Worthington Baseball Tournament over Cascade.
The game was in a way a repeat of the Holy Cross final earlier this summer. At Holy Cross, Dyersville was down four and came back to win 5-4. At Worthington, the Hawks were down 4-2 going into the bottom of the 9th. Art Huinker, who was out of the game with an ankle injury he received in the semi-final game, pinch hit for pitcher Jan Arthur and doubled off the left center field fence. Kip Knippel followed with a single but was out at second as Jim Digmann hit into a fielder's choice. Bob Goldsmith hit into another fielder's choice that scored Huinker. With two out and a runner on second, Dale Digmann was intentionally walked. Rol Sampson followed with a walk to load the bases for Tom Jenk who drilled a ball to right-center scoring Goldsmith and Digmann and giving the Hawks the 5-4 win.
Bob Meyer started the game for Cascade and worked until relieved by Carl Heitz in the ninth. Cascade pitching allowed a total of 9 hits, walked 8 and struck out eight.
Three Dyersville pitchers saw action. Chris Brown started, followed by Charlie Lammers in the 2nd and Jan Arthur

366

*in the 9th with the bases loaded. He got the first hitter he faced
to hit into a double play and the second he fanned.*

*Dale Digman and Kip Knippel had two singles each for
Dyersville. Tom Jenk had a single and the game-winning
double. For Cascade, it was Jim Brimeyer with a double and a
single.*

*Dyersville player-coach, Art Huinker, was presented
the Most Valuable Player Award following the championship
game.*

*Huinker was the winning pitcher in all three of the
team's first wins. He shut out Hopkinton 1-0, allowing only 1
hit in the first round and came on against Holy Cross to pitch
the 4-2 win. Against Petersburg in the semis Art came on to
stop Petersburg scoring and get the win. In the last inning of
the Petersburg game he received an ankle injury that required
12 stitches and side-lined him for the final against Cascade.
His coaching ability showed through in the final. With the score
4-1 Cascade, in the top of the ninth and no one out, he put
Arthur, who was having trouble recently on the mound, in to
pitch. Arthur finished the inning with no runs scoring.*

*Art Huinker was equally amazing at the plate. He hit a
sizzling 4-9 for a .444 batting average in four games.*

It was another stirring comeback for the Whitehawks but an equally
discouraging loss for the Cascade Reds. For us, Chris Brown, a college student at
Divine Word College in Epworth, started but had little luck. He also started
against Petersburg in a league game at Petersburg but struggled in that game. He
had pitched against the Xavier High School team in the spring. Charlie Lammers
was brought in from Winthrop to help us out in the pitching department. He did a
very strong job that night.

*Epworth won the consolation game, beating
Petersburg, 4-1, on a two-hitter by B.J. Featherston.
Featherston also doubled home Epworth's first run and Jerry
Thalhammer made it 2-0 with a solo homer in the thirds.*

Take a look back with me to the Worthington tournament. In our first
game, we could just as easily have been victims of a perfect game pitched by
Lloyd Brochshus in that Hopkinton 1-0 extra-inning victory. If a victory has been
gained, we so often attribute the success to good playing, hitting, pitching,
whatever we choose. When we lose, it is often attributed to some tough luck. In
that first game, I believe just the opposite was true. We were lucky, plain and
simple.

The third tournament of the summer took place at Winthrop, where the
Hawks built an 8-0 lead going into the bottom of the fifth in our opening round

367

game against May City of Cedar Rapids. Bats came alive for our opponents in the fifth, as they knocked out Jan Arthur with four big runs to cut the lead in half. Brother Kenny relieved and shut the door the rest of the way and the Hawks won by a score of 9-4.

In the second round game, the Whitehawks and Hopkinton did battle again. Don Dutton did the pitching for Hopkinton and I toed the pitching rubber for the Hawks. The score was tied 1-1 going into the top of the ninth when the Dyersville team took advantage of three Hopkinton errors and singles by Dan Goerdt, Cliff Knippel, Tom Jenk and Dale Digmann, to plate four runs and put Hopkinton down by a score of 5-1.

In the other half of the bracket, the Waterloo Merchants, behind the strong pitching of Tom Simpson, knocked off Balltown by a score of 6-1 to get into the semis opposite the Whitehawks. Bob Meyer had a first inning homer for Balltown's only score. Waterloo received back-to-back homers from Roger Messingham and Ben Halupnik to help the Merchants' cause. Bill Sigwarth did the pitching for Balltown in a losing effort.

IN WINTHROP SEMIS, RYAN, WATERLOO GAIN

Ryan and Waterloo will meet in the championship game of the Winthrop baseball tournament this coming Friday following a consolation game between Epworth and Dyersville.

Ryan earned its berth in the title game Wednesday night by side-tracking Epworth 5-2, while Waterloo was forced to go eight innings before downing Dyersville, by a score of 2-1.

Denny Caldwell was the big show in the first game as he pitched a three-hitter for Ryan and also slammed a three-run home run to settle the issue in the sixth inning.

The nightcap was a pitcher's battle between Art Huinker of Dyersville and Tom Simpson of Waterloo, with an unearned run in the bottom of the seventh giving Waterloo its chance to pull the game out in the eighth inning.

Dyersville scored in the first inning when Simpson walked Tom Jenk with the bases loaded. It was one of only two walks issued by the Waterloo pitcher.

Huinker, the veteran southpaw, blanked Waterloo on just three hits over the first seven innings, but an error, two ground outs and a single by Jerry Tarkett chased the tying run home in the seventh.

Then, with one out in the eight, Simpson won his own game with a towering home run.

Jim Brimeyer had two singles and Tom Jenk a single and double to account for four of Dyersville's six hits. Simpson struck out nine. Huinker also fanned nine, allowed only five hits and did not walk a batter.

368

You win a few. You lose a few. That's life. To follow up with the 1-0 victory in the Worthington tournament where we had not a single base runner until the game went into extra innings, we still came out victorious. It could have been lost very easily. Our semi-final game in the Winthrop tourney was one that we lost. There is one place on a baseball diamond that probably more pop fly, bloop hits happen than any other. If you took the baseball and dropped it just out of the reach of the first baseman, right fielder and second baseman, it would be the exact spot where this high pop fly hit the ground. It was not hit well but despite all the extreme efforts by our three fielders, it could not be caught. Waterloo tied the game on that pop fly. Had it been caught, the Whitehawks could have claimed victory. It was one of the hardest losses I ever experienced in my pitching career. Yes, you do win some you maybe should not, and you lose some that you should not. Maybe I had one coming.

But there are more dark clouds on the horizon. The Cascade tournament was next and our success there had not been very bright in this invitational. It did not get any brighter as Epworth, behind the strong pitching of a new face in the local tournaments, Jerry Ott, stopped Whitehawk hitters with a 1-0 shutout. This again was an opening round loss at Cascade, a factor that had become commonplace in this tourney for us. Dick Wold pitched a masterful game for the Hawks but we do not win many ball games when we get shut out. Upcoming is the Dyersville finale.

DYERSVILLE, HOLY CROSS NOTCH WINS
Holy Cross nipped Earlville, 5-4, and Dyersville clobbered Farley, 13-2, in five innings as the annual Dyersville baseball tournament got underway.

Holy Cross pushed across the winning run in the top of the seventh inning in the opening game. Jerry Roling and John Schiesl each cracked out a pair of hits for the winners, while losing pitcher Gene Parkin hit a two-run homer for Earlville.

Dyersville made short work of the nightcap, scoring six runs in the second and seven in the third to end the game after five innings because of the 10-run rule.

Bob Goldsmith clubbed a two-run home run for Dyersville to highlight the big second inning. Tom Simpson, Dick Wold, Jim Digmann and Rollie Sampson had two hits apiece for the winners.

Simpson, who allowed just three hits in pitching the victory, drove in four runs with his pair of hits. The only runs he gave up came on Paul Scherrman's two-run double in the second.

Notice all the veterans with big offensive games for the Whitehawks. They came off a very good pitcher, Roger Fenwick, who did not give up many runs but it must have been one of those nights for him.

369

In the second round, Dick Wold gave up only one run while allowing seven hits, in a 4-1 victory over Holy Cross. The score was 0-0 going into the sixth when Holy Cross picked up their run in the top half of the inning to go ahead by one, but the Whitehawks, behind a walk to Dale Digmann, a single by Wold, and Rollie Sampson's triple brought in the winning runs to push the Whitehawks into the semi-finals.

By now you may have noticed that Art Huinker is not pitching. In fact, I am not even playing. The same was true at Cascade. In the consolation victory of the Winthrop tournament, my left knee gave out while scoring from second on a base hit, suffering a torn cartilage. The entire Dyersville sequence of games at Cascade and now at Dyersville I spent on crutches coaching third base. And trying to line up pitchers for the Whitehawks.

WHITEHAWKS VS. HOPINTON IN TITLE GAME AT
DYERSVILLE
Dyersville's host Whitehawks rallied for four runs in the fifth inning to defeat Balltown, 5-2, and Hopkinton bounced back twice to edge Monticello, 6-5, in Monday night's semi-final games at the annual Dyersville baseball tournament.

Balltown jumped out to a two-run lead in the top half of the first inning against Dyersville on singles by Joe Sigwarth, Bob Meyer and Jack Wiland plus an error.

Cliff Knippel singled to lead off the Dyersville first, went to second on a wild pitch, took third on an infield out, and scored as Bob Goldsmith was grounding out.

That's the way things stood until the Whitehawks erupted in the fifth. Rollie Sampson started it with a single and moved up on Dan Meyer's sacrifice. Knippel was safe on the shortstop's throwing error, Sampson stopping at third, after which Knippel stole second. Sampson scored the tying run and Knippel took third while pitcher Tom Simpson was grounding out. Goldsmith singled to right scoring Knippel with the lead run, and the last two scored on a single by Dale Digmann and Dick Wold's two-run triple.

Simpson scattered three more hits over the last six innings for a total ration of a half dozen, walked two and struck out 10 to gain the decision over the veteran Darrell Rothrock.

Hopkinton snapped a 5-5 tie with a sixth inning run when Duck Huber walked, took second on an infield out and scored on Gary Black's single to lead the Delaware County league team into the finals.

In back-to-back games, the Whitehawks faced two top-notch veteran pitchers who had so frequently been brought in by the various teams throughout the years I was playing for Dyersville. Against Farley it was Roger Fenwick on the mound. This game it was Darrell Rothrock for Balltown.

In the Hopkinton win over Monticello, the victors brought in a new pitching face, Arnie Leistad, who was Wartburg College's pitching ace that year. They also had added several other strong college players such as Dan Rourke, Gary Black and Don Dutton. They also went north to get veteran ball players, Larry Poock and Ron Herdliska. And they had Gary Peterson doing their catching. Poock, who had played for the Whitehawks in one of their Battle Creek trips, had an inside-the-park home run in the semi-final game and Don Dutton unloaded a two-run homer over the right field fence. Another Hopkinton player that night was Kirk Rentschler who also had played with the Whitehawks one year in the national tourney at Battle Creek.

On the Monticello side, they had a young newcomer who played strong baseball for their team for many years, Bobby Hines. He led their offensive attack in the losing cause. On to the finals.

> *FOR DYERSVILLE TITLE, HOPKINTON WINS, 4-2*
> *Lloyd Brochshus fired a four-hitter and Hopkinton snapped a 2-2 tie with a run in the seventh inning here Wednesday night to hand the host team a 4-2 setback in the championship game of the Dyersville baseball tournament.*
> *Monticello defeated Balltown, 3-1, in the consolation game.*
> *Brochshus, voted the tournament's most valuable player as he won two games and relieved in a third, was staked to a 2-0 lead in the first inning.*
> *Dan Rourke opened with a single for Hopkinton, stole second and rode home on a single by Ron Herdliska. Herdliska then scored when a throwing error on Don Dutton's ground ball went wide of first base and into right field.*
> *Brochshus protected that lead until the fourth inning when Dale Digmann and Dick Wold cracked back-to-back singles. Digmann scored when Wold's single got away from Hopkinton's right fielder, and Tom Jenk singled to score Wold.*
> *Gary Black's double and walks to Herdliska and Larry Poock loaded the bases for Hopkinton in the seventh, after which Black scored the lead run on Dutton's sacrifice fly. The new champions added an insurance run in the eighth when Kirk Rentschler singled, stole second, went to third on a throwing error, and scored when a grounder was booted for an error.*
> *In addition to Brochshus' MVP award, Hopkinton manager, Don Huber was awarded both the outstanding manager and sportsmanship trophies, and Wold for the*

*Whitehawks was the tournament's leading hitter with .636
average on seven hits in 11 times at bat.*

Hopkinton brought their contingent of college and veteran players to the championship and played very well. Don "Duck" Huber was a very worthy winner of his two awards. Before we forget, Elaine Brueckner, former Xavier student and one who was forced to put up with me as were all juniors in a required American History class, was selected Queen of the 1967 Queen's Pageant.

Once again, the Whitehawks were the champions of the Maquoketa Valley League, although they had a tight battle with Balltown before clinching it late in the schedule of games for the year. The Hawks picked up pitcher Jack Wiland from the Balltown team to take with them to the state AABC tourney which was held in Dysart, Iowa again.

Following is the write-up that appeared in the Dyersville Commercial for the first three games.

> ### DYERSVILLE STANDING TWO AND ONE IN STATE AMATEUR MEET
> *After losing the first game in the Iowa State Amateur baseball tournament at Dysart, the Dyersville Whitehawks have scored two victories and are still in the running for the title in the double elimination tourney.*
>
> *Dyersville took its first loss when playing the Iowa City Hawkeyes on Thursday night. In a nip n' tuck contest Dyersville came out behind, 6-3.*
>
> *Jan Arthur started for the Hawks, was relieved by Willenbring in the 5th who allowed two runs on two hits before Huinker came in to finish the game. Dyersville pitching fanned eight and walked 4.*
>
> *Jim Koering went all the way for Iowa City allowing only two hits and one walk while getting four on strikes.*
>
> *Dyersville's only tallies came in the 3rd as Jim Digmann singled, Arthur reached first on a fielder's choice, Brimeyer walked and Jenk homered. Iowa City came back with one in the 4th and five big runs in the 5th.*
>
> *In game 2, young Dan Goerdt hit a homer in the 5th with no one on that put the Hawks in front of Tripoli 2-0 and proved to be the winning run in a 2-1 decision.*
>
> *Dyersville got their first run in the second on a single and two errors. Goerdt's round tripper in the fifth made it 2-0. Tripoli was able to get one in the sixth on a single, a fielder's choice, a stolen base and a sacrifice fly.*

Jack Wiland, Balltown hurler, worked all seven innings for the Hawks, getting the win. He fanned a total of 7 and walked only 1. Bob Everding took the loss.

Dyersville outhit Tripoli 4-3 and did not commit an error to three by the losers.

Tuesday night the Hawks battled Tom Simpson and Waterloo Merchants for ten innings before breaking loose and winning, 4-1.

The defending champs of the tourney got behind in the 4th when singles by Jim Digmann, Tom Jenk and Dale Digmann made the score 1-0, but soon tied it up in the 6th on a homer by John Nelson.

It stayed 1-1 until the 10th when Huinker doubled and scored on a double by Tom Jenk. Dale Digmann followed with a 2-run homer.

Sal Willenbring worked the first seven innings for Dyersville when Art Huinker came on to get the win. Simpson for Waterloo defeated the Hawks in extra innings in the semi-final round of the Winthrop tourney and played with Dyersville in the city's tournament. He was charged with the loss.

It was this game that became the focus of the editorial, again by Courier Sports Editor Russ Smith, titled "Small Man, Big Heart," which eventually became the title selected for this book. The entire editorial appears right after the title page in the front of the book. Forgive the blotches that appear on the copy. My sister, Shirley, had cut it out of the Courier and in the exchange from her house in Ossian to our house, some moisture must have left its mark. His editorial relates back to my knee injury in the consolation game at Winthrop and my spending most of the remainder of the season on crutches. Doctor's orders were quite specific. Do not play. But the situation required a pitching change and I put myself in. Foolish, but it worked out.Waterloo was eliminated from the tourney with two losses. Dyersville, 2-1, met Allison for the championship, a game which we lost ending our 1967 semi-pro season.

Winner of two tournaments and the Maquoketa Valley League, plus runners-up in the Dyersville tourney gave us some success for the season, although we still cannot figure out our performance in the Cascade tourney year after year. For the second straight year, injuries caused setbacks in my own ability to play the game of baseball. Sure, age is obviously increasing but still at 32 years of age, that factor should not be affecting my play. At least, I don't think so.

Preparation for our second year as a counselor and teacher, along with the coaching and athletic director responsibilities, had me feeling professionally excited. More changes are in the works under the leadership of Principal Brother Michael Palmer and Assistant Principal Sister Claire of Assisi. There was a vibrancy on our staff at this point that made you glad to be an educator. I really don't know if I needed rejuvenating, but I do know that I truly felt positive about being in education. And as athletic director I had the distinct privilege of working with fellow coaches Dick Mescher (basketball), Bob Timmerman (football and wrestling), and Brother Leo (track).

Family-wise, Ann had already informed me that our sixth child was on the way, due the following March. So much for the rhythmn method. By this time, Terry was starting sixth grade, Tim to fourth grade, Tammy to second and Peggy to first grade, all at Xavier Elementary in Dyersville. Jennifer missed going to Kindergarten by two months, so she could keep Mom busy at home for the school year. Pre-school just was not a common educational factor yet at that time. But we had a happy home and so very much to be thankful for. That was probably highlighted by the popular children's song of the day, "Beans in your ears." Only in our case, it was popcorn seed in our five children's ears one night with a baby sitter, which required some attention from a doctor in getting them removed. No long-term hearing damage, but just another of many typical big family memories.

PLAYING AGAINST MY OWN PLAYERS

This proved to be my last year as an active player of the wonderful game of baseball. Many factors began to impact our life and our decisions. First came our sixth child, a son baptized Daniel. He arrived on March 2 and balanced the sexes, three and three, in our family. Ann and I promised each other that the score was now tied and we were not going to play overtime. So much for promises. Ted, number seven, came five years later. Ann and I were extremely proud of our family, starting with the oldest, Terry, who was ready for seventh grade in the next school year. Tim was close behind getting ready for fifth grade, Tammy for third grade, and Peggy for second grade. Jenny was preparing to start Kindgergarten the coming fall. Notice that we started with our three oldest children christened with names that began with the letter "T." Not true for the fourth. Ann wanted Tessie (short for Theresa) and I pushed for Trudy. We compromised and left the "t" letter and called her Peggy. Don't try to understand the change. We also found it hard to explain.

We completed our second school year at newly-established Beckman High School, including the spring baseball season. This will be covered in the following chapter. All of us involved at the school felt that the first two years were highly successful for all involved, probably most of all for the more than 500 students.

Now we throw another curve ball into the mix of many evening discussions. Do we need to make a change in our directions for the future? With a family of six, is there a need to seek opportunities that would provide higher income possibilities? All thoughts included staying in the field of education. As we came closer to making that decision, Loras College, my alma mater, entered the picture. Most investigations at the college level centered on administratve positions of various types, most of them in the field of student life. This was also true at Loras. That implied a possible advanced doctoral degree in educational administration. Needing definite help financially to pursue a doctorate, we found a federal program at the University of Illinois in Champaign-Urbana, Illinois in the chosen field which provided a monthly stipend, the value of which was determined by marital status and the number of dependents. That stipend would be good for one year (twelve months). It provided a somewhat larger yearly wage than was included in my contract at Beckman High School. That made our decision easier, although we still were in the "should we or shouldn't we" dilemma.

I told Ann that I would sit down with our principal at Beckman High School, Brother Michael Palmer and seek his input. His response revealed a depth of wisdom that I will never forget.

"Art," he said, "this must be your decision. You and Ann need to claim responsibility for whatever direction your life takes. For me to tell you what to do

375

only gives you an out if you question that decision down the road. I wish you the best, whichever way you go."

I realize that those are not his exact words, but it was his major point. Take responsibility for this decision, whichever direction it takes us. Then don't look back. Make it work. Far too often, we decide something, then continue to waver on its worth. I can do that very easily. The decision was made. We were leaving Beckman and heading for an agreement with Loras College by way of the doctoral program at the University of Illinois, complete with the federal assistance for which we had applied. With a family of six, we were leaving the security of our involvement at Beckman High School.

Besides the big decision to change the direction of the lives of the Huinker family forever, another situation began to unfold that would also impact our lives. The Beckman High School baseball team, coming off a very successful spring season, kept impressing me with their many advanced skills plus their great desire to play the game of baseball. This will be covered in a separate chapter following this one, but suffice to say that eight players in the starting lineup would also competed for their home town baseball team in the summer of 1968, five with Petersburg, two with Dyersville and one with Worthington. And they were players with ability to handle that task.

The summer baseball season for the Dyersville Whitehawks saw them with another new manager. After taking on those responsibilities in 1967, I felt that, with our decision to leave Dyersville in the fall of 1968, it would be better if I gave those reins to someone else. Veteran outfielder Rollie Sampson stepped in and led the Hawks to one of their most successful seasons ever. The final record for the summer was 31 wins and only one loss. A nucleus of veterans again led the charge for the Dyersville team. Besides Rollie and myself, Tom Jenk, Dale and Jim Digmann, Dave Reittinger and Bob Goldsmith filled the local team's lineup throughout the summer. Dick Wold found himself on the Dyersville roster quite frequently again as did newcomer Dick Miller. Miller filled the centerfield slot for almost all of the games as well as the leadoff role.

Again, we will pay little attention to Dyersville's involvement in the Maquoketa Valley League. In one early league game, Holy Cross battled hard but fell short when the Hawks broke a 4-4 ninth inning tie with a two-run rally in the top of the ninth, primarily on the strength of a Dick Miller double with two men aboard and a Rollie Sampson sacrifice fly. Ron Legrand blasted a bases-loaded triple to provide the power for Holy Cross. In a second game with the same team later in the season Dave Reittinger shut out the Holy Cross team with Dan Meyer's third inning homer the big blow for the Whitehawks.

The Winthrop tournament opened the 1968 tourney season and Dyersville started out with a 10-0 victory over Epworth. Dave Reittinger threw a two-hitter while striking out nine. The winners picked up four runs in the second on a Steve Tierschel double, singles by Dan Goerdt and Dick Wold, plus two

Epworth errors. In the fifth, Dan Goerdt with a single and Dick Miller's double, plus a walk and an error put the game out of reach. Vern Koerperich was on the hill for Epworth.

PETERSBURG, DYERSVILLE POST WINS AT WINTHROP

> *Petersburg and Dyersville rode strong pitching into the semi-finals of the Winthrop baseball tournament by notching wins Wednesday night.*
>
> *Harold Olson of Hopkinton and Lloyd Koelker of Petersburg were locked in a scoreless pitching duel until the bottom of the eighth when Petersburg pushed across the one run of the game.*
>
> *Jim Overman opened the inning with his second single of the night, and moved to second on a sacrifice bunt. A moment later, Leo Wegmann slapped a double that sent Overman home with the winning run. Each pitcher allowed five hits in going the distance. Olson chalked up six strikeouts while Koelker fanned nine in earning the decision.*
>
> *Veteran southpaw Art Huinker spaced six hits and struck out 11 batters as Dyersville downed Keystone in the nightcap. The Whitehawks gave Huinker all the runs he needed in the first inning off losing pitcher Don Haugen.*
>
> *Dick Miller singled and rode home on Bob Goldsmith's home run for a 2-0 lead. Singles by Dale Digmann, Huinker and Dan Meyer, an error and a passed ball accounted for another pair in the fourth inning.*

In a variation of the Dyersville lineup, Tom Jenk moved to left field, Dale Digmann to first base, and the catching duties were handled by Steve Tierschel. Also, note that Lloyd Koelker, the Petersburg pitcher, was the pitching ace for the Beckman Blazers' high school team.

In the semi-finals, Dave Reittinger out-dueled Sal Willenbring for an exciting 3-2 victory, when the Hawks scored the tying and winning runs on four straight hits by Tom Jenk, Dick Wold, Dale Digmann and Jim Digmann. After a first inning run for Dyersville, Jim Overman's triple with a mate aboard had tied the game. Then Bob Klosterman's single preceded a double by Leo Wegmann to give Petersburg a 2-1 lead in the top of the seventh before the four straight singles in the bottom of the half gave us a tough win.

HAWKS DOWN RYAN IN FINALS AT WINTHROP

> *Dyersville grabbed an early 7-1 lead at Winthrop Friday night, then fought off determined Ryan to score a 7-6 victory in the championship game of the annual Winthrop*

baseball tournament. The host team grabbed third place with a 4-3 consolation game win over Petersburg at Householder Memorial Park.

Paul Scherrman's grand slam homer, capping a five-run third inning, proved to be the winning blow for the Whitehawks, who needed a nifty relief job from veteran lefty Art Huinker to preserve the victory.

Dyersville carried a 2-1 lead into the third inning and loaded the bases on two walks and a hit batsman before Tom Jenk delivered the first run with a sacrifice fly. Steve Tierschel singled to re-load the bases, and then Scherrman unloaded them with his grand slam.

Ryan had taken a first inning lead as Dyersville starting pitcher Dick Wold gave up a single by J.F. Gaffney and three walks, before being replaced by Rollie Sampson.

Dick Miller's double in the bottom of the first, followed by Bob Goldsmith's two-run homer put the Whitehawks in front to stay.

Back-to-back home runs by Ron Burke and Ron Sarchett, Burke's with a man on base, gave Ryan three runs in the fourth, and it pulled within a run in the sixth, scoring twice on an error and singles by C.J. Robinson, Dough Winders and Vic Vifian before Huinker came on to put out the fire.

The crafty little lefthander than hurled 3 plus innings of scoreless relief, striking out the last five batters he faced, to lock up the title.

It is a little discouraging for me that I remember so little of some of these games in the 1968 season. Trying to reflect on that, I wonder if I was so heavily involved in the coaching duties where the Blazer team continued into the summer season, winning game after game. There were several times that conflicts occurred between the two schedules, causing me to miss a considerable number of Whitehawk games.

In the consolation game at Winthrop, additional notes in the write-up showed that the Beckman players had a hand in the Petersburg attack again. A Bob Klostermann single followed by Jim Overman's home run accounted for two of the three Petersburg runs. Winthrop scored three runs after two out in the top of the seventh to capture the victory. The Holy Cross tournament followed.

DYERSVILLE, PETERSBURG BOTH ADVANCE
Dyersville defeated Cascade, 5-2, and Petersburg edged Earlville, 2-1, to wind up first round play Wednesday night in the fourth annual Holy Cross baseball tournament.

378

Singles by Nick Wagner, Paul Kurt, Lee Simon and Mike Gehl gave Cascade a quick 2-0 lead in the second inning against Dyersville, but Rollie Sampson and Art Huinker combined to pitch no-hit ball the rest of the way.

Singles by Dick Miller and John Goerdt and Bob Goldsmith's double gave the Whitehawks a run in the fifth inning, and they took the lead in the sixth on Miller's triple, following walks to Huinker and Dan Goerdt. Jim Digmann's bases loaded two-run single provided the last two runs for the Whitehawks, who are seeking their second straight tournament title.

Petersburg loaded the bases on two errors and Bob Klosterman's single in the third inning against Earlville, and two runs scored on a single by Dale Goedken.

That proved cushion enough for LeRoy Willenbring, who allowed only two hits and struck out 14. The only run off him came in the fourth inning on Owen Rentschler's double, an error and a passed ball.

In Earlville's loss, Gene Parkin pitched a strong five-hitter in a losing cause. Another Petersburg-Dyersville matchup followed these games and I have a strong, clear memory of that one.

DYERSVILLE RUINS NO-HIT EFFORT, 4-3

Dyersville, hitless for the first six innings Saturday night, exploded for four runs in the seventh to nip Petersburg, 4-3, in the final second round game of the fourth annual Holy Cross Athletic Club baseball tournament.

Lloyd Koelker hurled a perfect game through five innings, and the only baserunner through six frames survived on an error in the sixth.

But Petersburg's second error and a double by Art Huinker started Koelker's downfall in the top of the seventh. Bob Goldsmith struck out, but Tom Jenk doubled two runs across, after which Roy Willenbring replaced Koelker on the mound for Petersburg.

He got Dan Goerdt to ground out, but Dave Reittinger singled to score Jenk with the tying run, took second on the throw to the place and scored the winning run on Jim Digmann's single.

Jim Wegmann doubled with one out in the last of the seventh for Petersburg, but Huinker replaced Dave Reittinger on the mound for Dyersville and struck out the last two batters.

It was a night to remember. But it also brought many emotions to the surface. The game itself was a classic. A no-hitter for the opposing pitcher going into the seventh inning of a seven-inning game. Then, coming up with four hits in that final inning to take a one-run lead. But that was only the surface part of the emotional aspect of the situation.

To begin with, how many high school baseball coaches get the opportunity to play a significant ball game against their current high school players, much less pitch against two of those players in a crucial, win or lose the game, situation? First, Lloyd Koelker, our high school pitching ace, had a no-hitter going against us for six innings. He pitched a great ball game against a strong semi-pro team. Who gets the first hit off him but his coach. Then, after we captured the lead, I come in to relieve our starting pitcher with one out in the seventh and the tying run on second and who do I face but two of my high school team members. Yes, the write-up states that I struck them out. It has often crossed my mind, wondering how the two players batting against me were handling it. Knowing their love of the game, I have no doubt that they had that competitive spirit making them want to get a base hit for their team. An interesting situation, to say the least. What a group of young players.

In the semi-final game, Dave Reittinger came back and threw a three-hitter to shut out Bellevue, 4-0. A Dick Miller single and an error gave us our first run in the first inning. Singles by Jenk, Sampson and Dan Meyer brought our second run across the place. The final two runs crossed the plate in the fifth, led by Dale Digmann and John Goerdt singles. One more victory and we would have our second championship.

DYERSVILLE CAPTURES TITLE AT HOLY CROSS
Dyersville grabbed its second straight baseball tournament championship Thursday night as it drubbed Winthrop, 8-1, in the title game of the annual Holy Cross tournament.

Epworth took third place with a 3-1 decision over Bellevue.

The Whitehawks, who also won the recent Winthrop tournament, wasted little time Thursday night, jumping off to a 3-0 lead in the first inning on two walks, Art Huinker's two-run triple and an error.

Gaylord McGrath's double and two Dyersville errors gave Winthrop an unearned run off Huinker in the fourth, but the Whitehawks got that back in the bottom of the frame., added three more in the seventh on Dan Goerdt's double, a walk and Dale Digmann's homer, and picked up another unearned run in the eighth.

Dale Digmann had a homer and two singles, Huinker a triple and Tom Jenk a double and single to carry Dyersville's eight-hit attack. Roger Decker had two of Winthrop's five hits.

380

*Epworth picked up single runs in the first, fourth and
sixth innings of the consolation game. Singles by Bill Sahm and
Gary Brown wrapped around a walk scored the first run, the
second one came on four straight walks, and the third on a
walk, stolen base and error.*

*Bellevue got its only run on singles by Rick Frank and
Don Even plus an error.*

Two for two for the young tournament season, but many very dramatic
highly-contested ball games. Even though it is my last season of play, if plans
don't change, so much is going on that there wasn't much time to even think about
it.

The Worthington tournament enters the picture next. In our opening
round game, Peosta failed to dent the scoring column while the Whitehawks
stepped on home plate nine times in the first inning. Dale Digmann had a double
and a single in the first inning, driving in four runs. After the first inning, the
Whitehawks collected only one hit. In the meantime, Dave Reittinger allowed
two singles for the five inning contest, one each for Dave Weydert and Bill
Spiegel.

In the second round game at Worthington, six runs in the seventh inning
changed a tight, one-run game into a 9-1 victory over Winthrop. Six hits by six
different players, Goldsmith with a double and singles by Dick Wold, Dale
Digmann, Jim Digmann, Tom Jenk and Dick Miller, erased any doubts about the
outcome of the game. It was another two-hit pitching performance, this time by
the short, stocky left-hander, namely me.

For the third straight tournament, our next opponent in the semi-finals
was Petersburg.

*IN WORTHINGTON FINALS, HAWKS VS.
HOPKINTON*

*Dyersville and Hopkinton scored one-run victories
Wednesday night and will play tonight at 9:30 for the
championship of the annual Worthington baseball tournament.*

*The Whitehawks, going for their third straight 1968
summer tournament championship- - -they won at Winthrop and
Holy Cross - - -lost two early leads before coming back for a 5-
4 win over Petersburg, while Hopkinton blanked Epworth, 1-0,
in the other semi-final game.*

*Dyersville jumped off to a 2-0 lead in the first inning
against Petersburg on a hit batsman and Bob Goldsmith's home
run, but Petersburg tied the score in the third on a walk, an
error and singles by Bob Klosterman and pitcher Lloyd Koelker.*

381

Art Huinker's double and an RBI single by Goldsmith pushed the Whitehawks back in front, 3-2, in the bottom of the third, but Petersburg went ahead 4-3, in the fourth on a single by Rick Knipper, a triple by John Deutmeyer and Klosterman's sacrifice fly.

Goldmith walked, advanced to third on a sacrifice and an error and scored the tying run on Dick Wold's single in the sixth, and Dyersville won it in the seventh on a hit by winning pitcher, Dave Reittinger, an error and Huinker's second double.

Owen Rentschler walked in the fifth inning, was sacrificed to second and scored the only run of the first game on Bob Hardin's single.

Harold Olson pitched three-hit ball for the winners, striking out nine.

Why would we think this game would be any different than the other two against the Petersburg team? Five of their players were starters on the Beckman high school team. In this game, Rick Knipper did the catching for Petersburg, with Koelker again doing the pitching. I had feelings similar to the last game. I now had three hits against Lloyd, all of them doubles. But, something else happened in this game. It occurred in the fifth inning, although I am not certain of that. I received a walk, and was thinking about a possible steal of second. I could take credit for the "embarrassing" thing that happened to me next, but it is only fair to say that Lloyd deserves all the credit. I broke for second a little too soon and he picked me off first base, the only time that happened to me in the almost twenty years of playing the wonderful game of baseball. The pick-off also increased my respect for the quality of players that were on this Beckman team that I coached. Most of that credit belongs to the players' parents and coaches who were in charge of their development in little league baseball and beyond. By the way, that embarrassing moment softened quite quickly and now is a laughable moment in the stories we share when coach and players get together.

Also, in the Petersburg contest, Dwight Long started on the hill for the Hawks, with Dave Reittinger taking over in the fourth and picking up the win.

Hopkinton, winners over the Whitehawks in the finals of the Dyersville tournament in 1967, took our measure again in the Worthington finals. Another close ball game but the Hawks came up one run short.

SHERM'S 2-RUN HOMER GIVES HOPKINTON TITLE
Harold Sherm's two-run homer in the sixth inning proved the decisive blow Thursday night as Hopkinton defeated Dyersville, 3-2, to win the annual Worthington baseball tournament and break the Whitehawks' 1968 stronghold on eastern Iowa tournaments.

382

The Whitehawks, who had previously won tourneys at Winthrop and Holy Cross, rallied from a 3-1 deficit as Bob Goldsmith hit a leadoff homer in the ninth and had the tying run on second base when Arnie Liestad came on in relief to strike out the last two batters.

Dick Miller doubled and scored on two wild pitches to give Dyersville a 1-0 lead in the first inning, but Hopkinton tied it in the third on an error and Ray Nygard scored from second on a hit by Jerry Voss. Voss also singled in the sixth ahead of Sherm's home run.

Bob Klosterman and Lee Kruse each had two hits- - - one apiece in a four-run fourth inning- - -as Petersburg beat Epworth, 7-3, in the consolation game

Bob Meyer pitched a strong game for the Whitehawks allowing only five hits. Three Dyersville errors did not help the cause. For Winthrop, Delhi native, Bob Hardin, allowed only four hits in the six plus innings of pitching before being relieved by Arnie Liestad, Wartburg College's ace.

In the consolation game, a familiar name in baseball circles but not too often as the pitcher, Larry Conrad, went the distance for Epworth in the losing cause for the consolation title.

Next on the tournament trail, the Whitehawks invaded Cascade for their 16-team challenge, hoping to change the jinx that we had lived under for several years. At the same time, the Beckman High School team is competing in the summer tournament. Our first round opponent was a solid Holy Cross team. Another decision had been made prior to the start of the high school tournament schedule. Pitching batting practice for the Blazer high school team became a priority for me, and pitching for the Whitehawks hopefully would still be strong.

CASCADE TOPS TOURNEY FOES
Cascade mauled Sherrill, 10-3, and Dyersville edged Holy Cross, 3-1, Friday night to end first round play in the annual Cascade baseball tourney.

Cascade made only five hits in Friday night's game, one of them a three-run, inside-the-park homer by Lee Simon in a four-run fourth inning. But Sherrill chipped in with six errors to help the host team's cause.

Jim Oberfoell slammed a two-run homer in the first inning for Sherrill, which got only one more hit off Bob Greene.

John Goerdt raced around the bases on a four-base error by the Holy Cross righthander, Pat Lacke, to get Dyersville off to a 1-0 lead in the first inning of the second game, and the Whitehawks used speed on the base paths to get two more in the second.

Pitcher Dave Reittinger singled and stole second, after
which Dan Meyer walked. Reittinger then stole third and
scored as he and Meyer worked a double steal. Meyer promptly
stole third and scored on Rollie Sampson's sacrifice fly.
That was all Reittinger needed as he stopped Holy
Cross on three hits. He lost his shutout in the sixth inning when
Jerry Roling walked, took second on an error and scored on a
single by Ron LeGrand.

The second round game brought perennial Dyersville foe, Farley to the
diamond against the Whitehawks. Bob Meyer took the mound for Dyersville,
Jerry Gehrke for Farley. When the dust cleared, each pitcher allowed only four
hits. Meyer fanned 11 Farley hitters. A walk to Bob Goldsmith, Dick Wold's
double and an error allowed the Whitehawks to score the only run of the game.
Dale Digmann and Dick Wold each had two hits for the winners. In the second
game of the night, Cascade, behind Bob White's one-hit pitching, won their game
by the same 1-0 score over Epworth. Bill Sahm's double was the only hit.

In the semi-finals, the Whitehawks, hoping to shake the jinx, were
tied, 1-1, against Monticello going into the 7th inning. When the inning was over,
Dyersville had connected with four singles and a double by Rollie Sampson to
claim the victory by a margin of 6-1. The singles were by Dale Digmann, Ron
Sarchett, Lloyd Brochshus and Dick Miller. Reittinger and Brochshus combined
to hold Monti to four hits.

This was the second straight game the Beckman Blazers played in the
high school tournament the same time that the Whitehawks were playing. That
took me out of those games as well as two key reserves, Dan and John Goerdt.

DYERSVILLE TOPS HOSTS TO WIN CASCADE
TITLE
Dyersville won its third eastern Iowa baseball
tournament of the season Friday night with a 3-1 victory over
the host team in the annual Cascade tourney. Monticello won
the consolation game over Epworth by the same score.
The title contest was an error-filled horror which saw
the Whitehawks commit six errors and Cascade seven, while the
two teams combined for just seven hits.
Dyersville picked up the game's first run in the second
inning when Dale Digmann walked, took second on a deep fly
ball and scored on Ron Sarchett's single.
Pitcher Art Huinker singled in the fifth and three
Cascade errors followed to produce the Whitehawks' last two
runs.
Huinker had a shutout until the seventh but was
replaced by Bob Meyer after Paul Kurt's single and a double by

384

Lee Simon- - -voted the tournament's most valuable player- - -
accounted for Cascade's only run.
    Monticello got only one hit off Dave Benter in the
consolation game, but it drove in a pair of runs in the seventh
inning to snap a 1-1 tie.
    Gordon Westhoff and Paul Sullivan walked to start the
seventh, moved up on a throwing error, and scored as Al
Westhoff spoiled Benter's no-hit bid with a single.
    An error and singles by Ken Tekippe and Bill Sahm
gave Epworth a first inning run, but it got only one more hit off
Rick Berlin.

The jinx was broken, if there was one. The write-up doesn't tell the
entire story. It definitely was a night where my stuff was anything but good.
Only control allowed me to get by as long as I did. When Manager Sampson
came to the mound after the two hits in the seventh, I was very honest and shared
my lack of having "good stuff" by that time. Meyer breezed through the last two
plus innings to save the championship victory. Again, this memory of that
evening, especially the lack of good stuff, is quite vivid. But it was a significant
victory for us after the several years of disappointment at the Cascade diamond.

We were down to the last tournament of the year. There would be no
AABC tournament in the 1968 season. I don't know the reason for withdrawal
from the AABC Did the Maquoketa Valley League members vote not to get into
this tournament? Again, if they did, I am not privy of the reason. Without the
AABC challenge to follow the Dyersville tournament, this would be my last
active baseball playing. But because of everything that was going on in the
Huinker family's life the first few weeks of August, 1968, is it possible that there
wasn't time to dwell on something that had been so important in my life up to this
time? Not only important but something that I enjoyed so much. To walk unto a
baseball diamond and prepare to play a ball game was challenging but something I
looked forward to, right up to the very end.

We obviously change physically over time and something I began to
experience while attempting to bat was a slowing of my reflexes. Getting out of
the way of an inside pitch didn't seem to happen as easily for me. In a small way,
some of these reactions aided my decision that this would be my last playing days.
But then, there was one much bigger reason that I will disclose later during the
Dyersville tournament.

In the opening round of the Dyersville tourney, the Whitehawks took
care of Earlville by a score of 8-0 in five innings with Bob Meyer pitching a no-
hitter. Bob Goldsmith had a single and another 2-run homer to add to many he
already had during the season. Tom Jenk added 2 singles.

In the second round, we beat Worthington in a five-inning 7-0 game. I
managed to strike out 12 and allowed no hits in the five innings. High school

junior-to-be John Goerdt had two singles to lead the Whitehawk attack, one of the hits being part of a 5-run fifth inning for the Dyersville team. This victory put the Whitehawks into the semi-finals against Balltown who also no-hit their Holy Cross opponents behind the left-hand pitching of Jim Hinkel.

For the annual Queen's Pageant, Dyersville's Carol Thier became the second straight Dyersville candidate to receive the crown. She was crowned by last year's Queen, Elaine Brueckner.

DYERSVILLE, EPWORTH IN MEET FINALS

Dale Digmann's two-run homer in the last half of the seventh inning gave Dyersville a 9-8 victory Tuesday night over Balltown, sending the Whitehawks into tonight's championship game of the 18th annual Dyersville baseball tournament.

The Whitehawks will play Epworth, 2-1 winners of Winthrop in Tuesday's second semi-final, following the consolation game between Balltown and Winthrop.

Digmann's winning blow off reliever Paul Schmitt followed a walk to Dan Goerdt and a fielder's choice, and offset a two-run homer by Schmitt in the top half of the inning.

It was a game of long balls, and it took little time for the first one as Merrill Macklenberg of Balltown clouted a four-bagger off Dave Reittinger to lead off the first inning.

Three walks and singles by Mike Tschopp, Jack Gansemer and Dick Dupont produced four more Balltown runs in the second to swell the lead to 5-0, but Bob Goldsmith's grand slam homer in the third got those back for Dyersville.

Catcher Bruce Kimm's homer made it 6-4 in favor of Balltown in the top of the fifth, but the Whitehawks scored once in the bottom of the inning and took a 7-6 lead with two runs in the sixth on two walks and singles by Dick Wold and Ron Sarchett.

In the other semi-final game, Dave Benter opened the eighth inning with a single, moved around to third on a sacrifice and a wild pitch and scored on Bill Sahm's single as Epworth nipped Winthrop despite 14 strikeouts by the loser's Terry Fairchild.

A walk, a wild pitch and Bob Decker's single gave Winthrop a 1-0 lead in the first inning, but Larry Conrad doubled and scored on an error as Epworth tied it in the second.

It was a night of relief pitching for me as I replaced the starter early in the ball game, but gave up two home runs, the second one to Paul Schmitt in the top of the seventh, before Dale Digmann rescued the Hawks with his homer with a man on to win for us in the bottom half of the seventh. If a person checks thoroughly the box scores over the last five to six years, I think we would be

386

amazed how often Dale's name is behind a big hit that wins the game or gets the Whitehawks back into the game. Besides that, he was a tremendous catcher, both mentally and physically. Goldsmith also collected another big home run to add to his total for the year.

For an odd reason, however, the home run by Bruce Kimm in the fifth is of great interest for me. When Beckman High School played Norway in the state finals about two weeks earlier, the high school pitchers held him to a one for four night, and the hit was a single. Now I face him for the first time and he promptly puts one over the left field fence at the Dyersville Park, and I might add, a no-doubter as soon as he hit it. The players and I have kidded back-and-forth for years, but I maintain that if the high school pitchers could stop him, and he hits one out against my pitching, that it was time for me to retire. That is either a solid reason, or a very weak excuse, whichever you want to pick.

In the 1968 championship game, the Whitehawks collected 10 hits in a 11-2 romp over Epworth. Roger Shelby, a great Dyersville nemesis, did not have one of his better nights and the Hawks made it look easy with five runs in the 6th on three consecutive singles by Dick Miller, John Goerdt and Bob Goldsmith, a double by Dick Wold and another single by Tom Jenk. Although the Hawks got only a two-run double by Dan Meyer in the ninth, they sandwiched it around four walks and an error to score five more runs. Lloyd Brochshus pitched a five-hitter, none until the eighth, when Epworth put together singles by Jim Hein, Larry Conrad, Roger Shelby and Bill Spiegel to score two runs.

In the consolation game, Balltown defeated Winthrop , 3-1, led by a two-run triple by Dick Dupont behind a walk to Jack Gansemer and a single by Bruce Kimm. Jim Hinkel pitched the win for Balltown.

The Dyersville Whitehawks, winner of four of the five tournaments in the summer of 1968, added a victory at the Monticello Fair and another victory over the touring Indianapolis Clowns to end their season at 31 wins and only one loss. Ann and I with the six little Huinkers were already moved to Champaign, Illinois and did not participate in those games. There were numerous comebacks in those 31 wins and many other tight pitchers' battles that went our way throughout the summer. Perhaps it was a satisfactory way to conclude my active playing days, but I would be remiss if I did not add that the active playing, the walking out on the ball diamond to get ready for another game, was missed. Another year over. This time, a final year over.

Yes, the actual playing of a baseball game was over for me. Some interesting tidbits occurred that should be shared. Looking back on those eighteen years of playing professional and semi-pro baseball, the first game I started as a pitcher at that level of competition was the 1951 consolation game in the Waterloo Courier Tournament of Champions with home town Festina. It was a one-hit victory over Independence. The final game I starter as a pitcher was the no-hitter against Worthington in the second round of the Dyersville tournament just covered. Those are two good <u>book-ends</u> to those eighteen years of throwing the baseball against some wonderful players on opposing teams as well as the great teammates on those Festina and Dyersville teams.

Now we have to take a look at the Beckman Blazers' 1968 baseball season. And what a year it proved to be.

BLAZERS ARE CHAMPIONS

It was the fall of 1966. A brand new Catholic high school opened its doors for almost 600, 9th through 12th grade students representing five Catholic parishes from Dyersville, Earlville, New Vienna, Petersburg and Worthington. Three existing, smaller Catholic high schools were discontinued- - -St. Boniface High School in New Vienna, SS. Peter and Paul's High School of Worthington and Xavier High School in Dyersville.

Prior to the opening of the new central high school, I taught five years, from 1961 through 1966 at Xavier High School, the school replaced by the new Beckman High School, also located in Dyersville. The Xavier school was served by the same Franciscan nuns from Dubuque who also served at our prior school, De Sales Central Catholic High School at Ossian. And starting with the 1962-63 school year, I again had the privilege of working under the guidance of Sister Claire of Assisi as principal. With the opening of the Beckman system, she moved there as assistant principal. And she continued dedicating her life to that school in various roles for almost forty years. As an educational leader and as a person, Sister Claire was tops on my charts.

At Xavier High School, my responsibilities also included head coach for baseball and assistant coach to Paul Schramm for football and boys basketball. There were no girls' organized sports at that time. This was also true at De Sales High School where a very successful girls' basketball program went by the wayside after the 1957-58 school year, my first year of coaching girls' basketball. Word had it that some leaders at that time believed that the physical demands of basketball took a toll of the child-bearing system of a young girl and could lead to future complications. We do develop some interesting positions on life! What about girls playing football? No, that would be going too far. Or would it? How about boys playing football?

Family life at the Huinker house certainly changed during those five years I taught at Xavier High School. We added our fifth offspring, Jennifer, in October, 1962, making our roster three girls and two boys. All but Jennifer were in school by now, Peggy being in Kindergarten and the older three attending Xavier Elementary. A new house had been built on 10th Avenue SE in Dyersville with four bedrooms. But we were still a one-car family, although it was now a station wagon by necessity. Trips up to the homeland around Festina and Calmar, about a two-hour trip, usually included a return trip to Dyersville late enough in the evening that we could have all five kids sleeping crossways in the back of the station wagon with the two back seats laid down. Sometimes we would experience a minor altercation because one or another of the five would roll over unto a sibling sleeping next to the mover. For the most part though, Ann and I could have a relatively quiet drive home and time to get our upcoming days organized.

389

As for baseball coaching, the first spring leading the Xavier Cardinals (Yes, our team mascot was the Cardinals, possibly another reason for accepting the Dyersville position) was a losing effort. We were fundamentally very weak. Early games were lost because of errors in the field, numerous past balls and wild pitches, and many running mistakes on the basepaths.

That began to change for the better. We had a veteran catcher, John Bartels, but he had suffered a serious neck injury the summer before and I really feared that he might take a foul ball on the mask once too often and suffer permanent injury. John took over outfield duties and a freshman from Earlville, Steve Tierschel, took over the catching duties and for the next four years, never relinquished them. Steve continued his baseball playing for Loras College in Dubuque where he lettered four years as their catcher. He also did some catching for the Dyersville Whitehawks covered in the previous chapters and was my battery mate several times. We had other players who stepped forward and provided a positive thrust for some successful years in the early and middle sixties.

Cliff "Kip" Knippel played infield and did some pitching for the Cardinals. He was a leading hitter and outstanding base stealer for the three years I had the privilege of coaching him. He later also added strong playing time for the Whitehawks. After graduation Kip attended college in the Twin Cities , then eventually on to law school which brought an end to his baseball playing days for the Whitehawks. Don Kramer, another Earlville student, became our most reliable pitcher for several years. Others in those early years that gave the Cardinal team a big boost were Jim Gebhart, Ron Singsank, Charlie Weisbrich, Terry Deggendorf, and Ron Digmann, just to mention a few.

In later Xavier years, Larry Bildstein, Dan Meyer, Dan Wieneke, Charlie Lammers, Steve Clemens, Herb Pins, Gary Schuster and Bill Wilhelm became our leaders. Wilhelm and Meyer did most of our pitching and did a very good job, bringing continuous successful years for the Cardinal baseball team. Bill Wilhelm had a strong hold on the Cascade Aquin team, never losing to them in five starts. Meyer played shortstop for the Whitehawks for a number of years and Bildstein, Clemens and Lammers later were on the Whitehawk active roster.

Dan Meyer was nicknamed "Blackie" because of his dark complexion. That created a unique experience for the Cardinal players one spring when we traveled to Cedar Rapids to take on the Regis Royals. The umpire behind the plate that day was a young black man. After a few innings, it was noticed by some of the players that he was paying very close attention to our use of the term, "Blackie," when we were yelling support for player Dan Meyer. The questionable situation was diffused after I held a cordial meeting with the umpire. We also tried to refrain from using Dan's nickname the remainder of the game. Thankfully, he was understanding of what was happening .

Starting with the spring of 1962 when I first coached the Xavier Cardinal baseball team and up until the 1966 season, we had never beaten the Wahlert Golden Eagles. Under the tutelage of Ed Colbert, who also was one of my managers for the Mason City Braves in the Southern Minnesota semi-pro league in the late fifties, the Eagles took our measure every time, quite a few of them in the sectional or district tournaments. There were some tight ball games, but we never got over the hump with a key hit or an outstanding pitching performance. In one of the losses, future major leaguer, Bill Burbach, shut us down.

In the spring of 1966, the Cardinals and Golden Eagles were locked up in another tight ball game which found the score tied 3-3 going into the bottom of the seventh inning. The game was being played at the park in Dyersville. Again, Dan Meyer was the key player involved. I don't recall the number of outs, but there were no runners on base when Dan unloaded on a pitch and hit it in the direction of the deepest part of the ball park, which at that time had a 425 foot sign attached to the fence. Our first reactions were "any place but there." However, he hit it so hard that it hit the top of the fence at the 425 foot sign and went over. At the time Dyersville baseball enthusiasts could remember only two people who had accomplished that feat, both Dyersville Whitehawk players, Bud Ross and Ed Watt. One of the Wahlert baseball players who remembers that game was Jim Noonan, son of our assistant coach at Loras College. Later, when he taught for Western Dubuque Schools. Jim and I would reminisce about Dan's powerful drive against the Eagles. The following spring, Wahlert again knocked us out of the tournament by a score of 2-1. A good game again but no victory cigar. But the loss provided indicators of a very strong ball club and most of that team's starters were sophomores and juniors with strong frosh players pushing for starting positions.

In one of those early years at Xavier, I experienced one of the weirdest situations ever in all my baseball coaching years. We were involved in a tight game with one of our neighboring schools. We were the visitors and held a one-run lead in the last of the seventh. The home team had the bases loaded, two out and two strikes on the hitter, when the coach called for a suicide squeeze with the runner on third breaking from third on the pitch. The batter bunted the ball, our pitcher picked it up and threw it to first base for an easy final out and the game was over. A very unusual situation for the squeeze play.

Our strong club returning for the 1968 season played both a spring baseball schedule and a following summer season with state tournament competition each session. The Iowa High School Athletic Association was in the midst of emphasizing a summer season more than a spring season, consequently many schools played both. There was still no separation of schools into different classes determined by the size of the student population. This was to be the last season where there would be no differentiation between large and small schools.

In the spring competition, we again lost to the Wahlert Golden Eagles but not in tournament play. The team had won all but one of its other games and captured the sectional tournament. In the districts, also held at the Dyersville Commercial Club Park, we found ourselves facing Davenport West, whose roster included pitcher Terry Williams, one who frequently attracted pro baseball scouts whenever he was scheduled to pitch.

We fortunately, or maybe unfortunately as it turned out, had several days to prepare for the district opener. It enabled our ace pitcher, Lloyd Koelker, to have sufficient rest before the showdown, but that also enabled their ace to get his rest.

Our team had the usual practice routines, such as batting practice and the defensive infield and outfield practice. In addition to that, because the players possessed an advanced state of baseball fundamentals, we did considerable work on the individual needs of the players.

There were two players that I specifically recall. Second baseman and sometime centerfielder, John Goerdt, only a sophomore and a very good right hand hitter, rarely pulled the ball to left field. He did hit the ball extremely well to right and right centerfield. So, one of those days, we worked with him to open his left hip, allowing him to get the barrel of the bat through more quickly on an inside pitch and pull it to left field. All of this while he continued to handle the outside pitch to right and center field as well as always.

Our catcher and lead-off batter, Rick Knipper, had good speed, as did John Goerdt, and often was a threat to steal once he had safely reached base. In Rick's case, his ability to hook slide to the outside of the base to avoid a tag on a close play was picture-perfect, but he had difficulty using a hook to the inside of the base when needed. Because most slides needed on close plays require the outside hook, the inside hook slide is not as important, but still needed. So, two days before the start of the district tournament, Rick went to the outfield grass, took his spiked shoes off, and under the tutelage of a teammate who could make the inside slide, observed him after we had discussed the fundamentals of the slide. I went to another sector of the diamond to work with other players.

A little while later, Rick and his player-coach reported to me that progress was being made. One of Rick's teammates good-naturedly razzed him a little and Rick decided that he wanted to demonstrate the success he was having. They returned to the outfield grass but this time Rick left his baseball spikes on, and on one of his slides, most of us heard the cracking sound around the entire diamond. His spikes caught in the grass and Rick and I were headed to Mercy Hospital in Dubuque, fearful of the worst.

It was a long trip back to Rick's home in Petersburg. First and foremost, I worked hard at trying to keep his disposition positive before, during and after the cast was placed on his broken leg. But how do you do that when one is having

392

great difficulty trying to salvage their own negative feelings? I couldn't imagine the impact this would have on the team just two days away from the challenge of Davenport West in the district tournament. The major question very simply was, "Who is going to catch?"

A phone call had been made to Ann informing her of what had happened and that I would be late getting home. Go ahead with dinner and I will get home as soon as I can. The exact time that I returned home is not recalled but I do remember Ann meeting me at the garage door into the house. We embraced and I began to cry. I can't tell you the main reason for the tears. Were they for me because I had just lost a key player from the team, or were they for the player himself who now could not play in the big game? They were probably for both reasons. The loss of a good catcher is key for any ball club, especially one of Rick's caliber. But life does go on, as we all know. We had been thrown a sharp-breaking curve ball but we had to face reality and make some needed adjustments. The advantage for having some time between the sectional and district tournaments to give pitcher Lloyd Koelker extended rest turned to a disadvantage with the loss of our catcher.

Arriving at school early the next day, second baseman John Goerdt walked into my guidance office and offered to replace Rick Knipper behind the plate, informing me that he had caught many times for little league and Babe Ruth baseball teams. He was willing to give it a try. That gave us a second option. The first was back-up catcher Dave Domeyer, also from Petersburg. Dave had caught very little at the high school level but had similar experiences at the lower levels as Goerdt had. We would hold practice that afternoon and make the decision after that for the next day's game. Dave did the catching.

Whatever the decision, we came out on the losing end of that district tournament game. We collected only a couple of hits off future pro player, Terry Williams, and the only run we scored was a John Goerdt home run over, where else, the right center field fence. In the meantime, with the wind blowing in very strong from left field to home plate, a pop fly to left field fell in front of left fielder Gene Knipper and just out of the reach of shortstop Bob Klosterman for a two-run single to give Davenport a 2-1 lead going into the later innings when they scored two more runs to ice the game. Whether the right coaching decision was made or not, Williams won the duel over Lloyd Koelker in a challenging high school ball game. Our spring season ended.   Our record at the end of the spring season, including the tournament games, was 14 wins and three losses.

A very interesting game was played that spring when the Manchester Hawks, under the tutelage of my favorite player, Blair "Buzz" Beatty, hosted the Blazers at Manchester. Buzz struggled with finding a good starting pitcher that spring and when he realized that one of his players was a very strong "softball" pitcher, he started him against us. As it turned out, the youngster found it difficult to pitch softball-style from the baseball distance of 60 feet, 6 inches, instead of the standard softball distance of 45 or 46 feet. I am not sure what that distance is. Control was an initial problem and he walked our first batter, Rick Knipper. Two pitches later, Rick was on third. Following the softball routine, he had no ability to hold runners on and Rick immediately took advantage. The game ended up in a 13-2 romp for the Blazers.

After the loss to Davenport West, the Blazers immediately began their summer schedule even before school was out with another win against the Western Dubuque Bobcats, coached by my former De Sales student, Carl Heying It was a wild, high-scoring game but we finally came out on top. By the time tournaments started in July with the opening of summer sectionals, the Blazers, according to newspaper write-ups, had won 20 consecutive ball games. Interestingly, many of those games were played with less than a full contingent players normally in the starting line-up. First of all, Lloyd Koelker pitched a considerable number of games for his hometown Petersburg. And he pitched ve well, I might add. Just re-read the previous chapter and see how tough he was against the Dyersville Whitehawks. As mentioned earlier in the previous chapter eight of the starters on the Blazer team played often with their home town semi pro teams.

There is one game in particular that summer that I remember quite clearly. At least I think I remember it clearly. We were scheduled to play Dubuque Senior at Fourth Street Park (or Petrakis Park named for the famous Dubuque Packer business manager, John Petrakis). When we left Dyersville, we had nine players, just enough to start the game. The only problem was that one of the players had a cast on his leg. It was Rick Knipper. What followed probably should not be shared. It was not something that should have happened. Our catcher for that ball game was, cast on his leg, Rick Knipper. He caught the entire game, had a couple of hits, and the Blazers won by a wide margin. Rick was a week or two away from having his cast taken off, but that still probably does not justify putting him behind the plate. Picture the catcher, with a cast up to his knee, crouching down and doing a strong job of catching. I truly do not remember any passed balls in the entire game. Mea maxima culpa.

A twist of fate struck us again in the summer schedule. Again, I do not recall the inning, but the Blazers had built a good lead against Anamosa and were extending it, when starting leftfielder, Gene Knipper, our Earlville native, raced for third base and slid in safely. The throw bounced beyond Anamosa's third baseman and I began yelling at Gene to head for home. But this was Gene's reply, "I can't, coach. I think my leg is broken." Discouragingly, he was right. This time I had no other coach or adult with me to take over the team. After consulting with the team players and the opposing coach, the players finished the game, while Coach again took one of his players to the local hospital at Anamosa. Ironic, isn't it that both of them were named Knipper. The difficult part was that Gene was out for the remainder of the season and missed all the tournament games. Jerry Bildstein filled in very well for him but for Gene it was possibly the toughest three weeks of his life. He wanted to play so badly and yet had to sit on the sidelines. As I think back on the games that followed, I saw Gene Knipper take a senior leadership role along with Dan Goerdt and Lloyd Koelker and become a vocal supporter of everything that happened after that.

Tournament time for the summer session approached. The common policy for the summer was a bit unusual. It was my feeling that I had enough players that we would always have a sufficient number of players, and because I owed a debt of gratitude to the local towns who had provided the foundational training for these young kids, I allowed them to play for their home town team if they had a game scheduled the same night as the high school Blazer team. That policy did not change except during the high school tournament season when they became solely Beckman Blazer teammates. I realized that I had a good baseball team. I realized I had a group of young men who loved to play the game of baseball. I realized I had a good pitching staff, led by ace Lloyd Koelker and ably supported by senior lefty, Tom Burlage, and sophomore righthander, Ron Kramer. We would find out later how valuable all three were. There was such a strong confidence building in me regarding the quality of that team that a letter was sent to the parents, thanking them for the baseball sons they have given me and suggesting the potential of this group. For the first time I established a required practice schedule between games to prepare for what I felt was a tournament trail of great potential. A copy of that letter is found in the picture section of the book.

Tournament game 1: Beckman 7, Dubuque Senior 1

The sectional tournament for the Blazers took place at the local Dyersville ball park. Our first opponent, Dubuque Senior, led by Hall of Fame coach Dick Core and a team we had beaten easily earlier in the summer, now were ready to throw their ace lefthander at us by the last name of Oleson. After losing the flip and batting first, the score read 1-0 in favor of the Blazers. It stayed that way going to the top of the sixth.

The floodgates opened up in the sixth when 12 Blazers went to the plate, scoring six runs on four hits and three Senior errors plus a hit batsman. The four hits, all singles, were collected by Bob Klostermann, Jim Overman, Dan Goerdt and Jerry Bildstein. Bildstein and Dan Goerdt each had two hits as the Blazers moved to the semi-final round of the sectional against Manchester.

Tournament game 2: Beckman 8, Manchester 1

The sectional semi-finals brought the Blazers an 8-1 victory led by a three-run blast by first baseman Jim Overman. The home run was part of a big six-run first inning when the first three batters in the Beckman line-up, Rick Knipper, John Goerdt and Bob Klostermann had singles before Overman's big home run. But the rally wasn't finished. Dan Goerdt collected Beckman's fifth consecutive hit. An error, a fielder's choice and a double steal got two more runs.

Tom Burlage went all the way on the mound for the Blazers allowing just six hits, three of them to Tom Gorkow who collected two singles and a triple for the Manhawks coached by good friend and outstanding player, Buzz Beatty. The sectional finals were at Elkader against the host team coached by a very familiar person, Merrill Hyde, the Guttenberg star athlete who had played his college baseball at Arizona State. Merrill also participated with the Dyersville Whitehawks in their drive for the national AABC championship.

Tournament game 3: Beckman 1, Elkader 0

The competition was building. With sophomore Ron Kramer on the hill, the Blazers narrowly eked out a 1-0 victory over Elkader. Beckman scored early on a single by John Goerdt, two errors and a successful squeeze play for the only score of the game. Ron pitched a beautiful game but needed relief help from Lloyd Koelker in the seventh. Elkader placed runners on second and third with one out in the seventh. That brought Lloyd Koelker to the mound and he promptly put out the fire with two strikeouts to protect the 1-0 win. Kramer allowed only four hits in picking up the victory. This game was the first of three consecutive games where we battled strong left-hand pitching by the opposition. The Elkader lefty for Coach Hyde was Lee Palas, who later pitched for a team competing in the Dyersville Invitational tourney.

On our trip home that night Ron Kramer obtained his nickname that has jokingly followed him the remainder of his life. It had been a relatively warm day and Ron pushed his window down on the bus and stuck out his right arm to keep cool. Noticing this, one of his teammates feared that this would prove hazardous to his pitching arm and promptly told him to protect that "golden arm" and bring it inside the window. He carried the new name, "Golden Arm," the remainder of the tournament trail and even has it today.

Tournament game 4: Beckman 1, Decorah 0

Tournament game number four found us back at Elkader in the opening round of the district tournament. The opponents were the Decorah Vikings, led by left-hand pitcher, Bill Varner. We knew we had our hands full with Varner who was leading an undefeated Viking team. His reputation had spread beyond extreme northeast Iowa.

Again, nothing much is happening offensively as Lloyd Koelker and Varner hooked up in a beautiful pitcher's duel. Decorah provided the first real threat when Jim Sersland walked early in the game, stole second, and proceeded to third on an error. Then, in an attempted suicide squeeze play, the runner broke from third too soon, Lloyd pitched out and Rick Knipper easily tagged Sersland out at home plate.

The Blazers threatened early also on a walk and Rick Knipper's double, but the suicide squeeze failed for us when we missed the attempted bunt.

With the scoreless game continuing, Danny Goerdt walked to lead off the inning, was sacrificed to second but was still there with two out. That is when the unexpected occurred. Thus far in the game, the major weakness I had seen in the Decorah line-up was the catching position. In my mind, I started thinking that we had to put pressure on their defense, with both pitchers going so well. Each ended up allowing only four hits in the game and Lloyd only walked one. All right, let's take a gamble. Danny Goerdt had average speed but was not our fastest runner. He picked up the steal signal and on the next pitch, broke for third on the delivery by Varner to the plate. The catcher's throw went way wide of third base into left field, and Dan got up and easily crossed the plate with the only run of the game. It ended again on a score of 1-0, the Blazers on the winning side. Again we played against an outstanding coach at Decorah, still coaching to this day, by the name of Len Olenzcak. He has made Decorah one of the most successful baseball schools in the state.

Remember my sharing how Coach Pete Peterson, successful baseball coach for Monona first and then MarMac High School, helped me understand the importance of keeping pressure on the other team's defense. And one important factor tied to that pressure is the use of the "unexpected" or surprise. In all competitive team sports this should be stressed in practice, through trick pick-off plays, or steals when least expected, etc. Goerdt's steal of third certainly fell into that category.

In one of the later innings of that game, Lee Kruse, our rightfielder, made a play look easy but I don't believe it was. Decorah had a runner on second when the batter connected on a low line drive to right field. Lee was not playing a very deep right field, another one of my baseball coaching philosophies, and going full speed to the infield, grabbed the line drive above his knees for the final out of the inning. Well played by Lee and a possible game-saver. For our fourth victory on the tourney trail and for the fourth game in a row, our pitching has allowed either no runs or one run.

Tournament game 5: Beckman 6, Cedar Rapids Washington 3 (eight innings)

The next challenge for the Trail Blazers came from a team that the players today feel was their toughest opponent throughout the entire eight tournament games they played. Coached by well-respected baseball figure, Pinky Primrose, the Cedar Rapids Washington Warriors proved another worthy opponent. The following is an excerpt from the Dyersville Commercial article on the game and provides insights into the challenges that the Blazers and pitcher Lloyd Koelker faced in the finals of the district tournament.

BECKMAN WINS DISTRICT TITLE
Righthander Lloyd Koelker won his third game of the
summer high school baseball tournament as Beckman High

397

School captured the district championship Monday evening, downing Cedar Rapids Washington, 6-3, in an extra inning contest played at LaPorte City.

Beckman fell behind in the very first inning against Washington when they scored on a single by Skogman. Tim Mohr connected for a home run in the fifth putting the Blazers down by two going into the 6th.

John Goerdt opened the inning with a home run. Bob Klostermann walked and, with two outs, scored to tie the game on a single by Lloyd Koelker. Jerry Bildstein reached first base on an error and then Lee Kruse batted in the leading run with a single.

Washington forced the game into extra innings in the bottom of the sixth when Mike Hurn connected for a solo homer making it 3-3.

Beckman then took over the game in the top of the eighth. With one out, Koelker walked and advanced on a single by Jerry Bildstein. After Lee Kruse grounded out, Keith Krapfl walked, Rick Knipper singled, John Goerdt walked and Bob Klostermann gave his team their third tally of the inning with a single.

John Goerdt led Beckman's offensive attack with a home run and a single. Lloyd Koelker recorded his third tournament victory and his 13th of the season against only one loss. Lloyd allowed Washington eight hits but walked only one, fanning three. Tom Hurn was charged with the loss as he was tagged for eight hits, while fanning four and allowing eight free trips.

Not mentioned in the write-up is probably the defensive play of the entire tournament trail. Cedar Rapids Washington had already scored one run and had the bases loaded in the first inning. With two out, and the three runners on the move as the ball was hit, sophomore Keith Krapfl raced back toward the center field fence and made an over-the-head, back-handed catch of a line drive that, if not caught, would have probably added three more runs to Washington's first-inning lead. Keith's catch turned the tempo of the game back in favor of the Trail Blazers and the eventual come-from-behind win was led by another sophomore, John Goerdt, who started the Blazer offensive engines with his home run in the sixth to, where else but right center. Rick Knipper's single with the bases loaded in the eighth with two out broke the deadlock and closed the gates for the Cedar Rapids team.

Game number 6: Beckman 5, Davenport Assumption 4

After the third straight high-tension victory, the Blazers were one win away. One more victory and it would be state tournament time. Standing in our road was another Davenport school, this time Davenport Assumption. Assumption had beaten opponents from the southeast quarter of the state, with their last win against Iowa City High School. Their loss in the spring tournament was to a familiar foe for the Blazers. Davenport West, victors over Beckman in the spring district tourney finals, knocked off Assumption in the spring tournament the game prior to playing Beckman. The pitcher that beat them was the same Terry Williams who had beaten Beckman. Williams now had signed a professional contract with the Boston Red Sox. The sub-state game was scheduled to be played under the lights at Solon, Iowa, just north of Iowa City. The date was Thursday, August 1, with the Blazer squad hoping the game would lead to the state tournament the following Monday.

This game had to be one of the most exciting and emotionally draining games that I have ever been involved in. We had the lead but left the Knights back in to forge a tie in the top of the seventh. Beckman went ahead only to have an umpiring decision changed which turned the winning run into an out and required us to go back out and play an additional batter before we could say, "State tournament, here we come."

The write-up for the game is taken from the Telegraph-Herald's report.

BASES-LOADED WALK SENDS BECKMAN INTO STATE FINALS
By Bill O'Neill, T-H Sports Writer
Pinchhitter Tom Burlage worked Gary Laake for a base on balls with the bases loaded in the seventh inning here Thursday night to force in the run that gave Dyersville Beckman a 5-4 victory over Davenport Assumption in a sub-state baseball game.

The win puts Beckman in the state tournament to be held next week at Ames. Other teams advancing included Norway, a 6-3 winner over West Des Moines Valley, Paton-Churdan which downed Fremont-Mills, 1-0, and Sious City Heelan, a 5-4 winner over Goldfield.

Beckman will meet Paton-Churdan in the 6 p.m. opener Monday while Norway will take on Heelan at 8.

Coach Art Huinker said Friday morning that there will be chartered buses going to Ames Monday. Anyone desiring to make reservations for the trip is asked to call Beckman High School.

399

The Trail Blazers spotted Assumption a 1-0 lead in the third inning on an error, a sacrifice bunt and Tim Pantner's run-scoring single.

But Beckman put together three of its eight base hits in the bottom half of the inning to take a 3-1 lead.

Rick Knipper opened the inning with a single up the middle, and moved to second as John Goerdt grounded out. Bob Klostermann beat out an infield hit before Jim Overman singled to center to score Knipper with the tying run.

Dan Goerdt walked to load the bases, and Klosterman came in with the go-ahead run as Lloyd Koelker bounced out. Jerry Bildstein reached on an error which plated Overman with the third run of the inning.

Beckman padded the margin to 4-1 in the fifth when Overman opened the inning with a single and eventually scored on Lee Kruse's two-out single.

Koelker saw his lead trimmed to 4-3 when the Knights scored a couple of unearned runs in the sixth.

Bob Leese survived on an error with one out, and Koelker got Phil Delvecchio to fly to left for the second out. But Tim Donohue and Steve Kelsey came up with back-to-back singles, and an error on Kelsey's hit enabled the two runs to score.

The Knights tied the game in the top of the seventh when Mike Hutcheson opened the frame with a single and moved to second when pinch hitter Dave Prodors walked on a 3-2 count.

Tim Pantner singled to right, and Hutcheson came in with the tying run. After Mike Ewen popped out, Leese was given an intentional pass, and Koelker got out of the inning making DelVecchio his seventh strikeout victim.

Beckman, which committed five errors, was helped with one of Assumption's two boots in the bottom of the inning to push across the winning tally.

Overman walked and stole second before Dan Goerdt reached on an error. Koelker forced Overman at third and Bildstein beat out a hit to deep short to load the sacks.

Kruse then bounced to the first baseman who fired to the plate where umpire Don Farnsworth first ruled Goerdt safe, but then changed the ruling and called him out.

This brought Burlage in to hit for Keith Krapfl, and he worked Laake for the walk that sent Dyersville into the state meet with an 18-0 record.

What a gut-wrenching ball game. There are several additional aspects of this game that probably could not be included in the write-up but played a significant role in the outcome. First of all, when we arrived at the diamond before the game, we had time to study the field. It appeared to be a very nice-looking field but one that had not been properly taken care of at that particular time. It included a grass infield but, because of infield dragging methods, there was at least a one-inch drop from the ground under the grass to the ground part of the infield. During infield practice before the game, the first few ground balls I hit were taking crazy bounces and I worried that our infielders would become fearful of any and all ground balls hit. For the remainder of the infield practice, all ground balls hit were bounced into the ground so that the fielders were able to gather in easy fielding balls and have a good practice session. Yes, we had five errors but only two of them were infield ground balls that were almost impossible to field. Did my hitting strategy during the practice help or hurt? I seriously do not know, but at least I had infielders who were ready to play ball.

Go back to the top of the seventh with Assumption batting. They had already tied the score and had runners on second and third with one out. The write-up states that Mike Ewen popped out. Yes, he did. But the pop fly was between the left fielder and the shortstop, and the shortstop, Bob Klostermann, who ran full speed with his back to the plate, grabbed the ball out of the air, then had the presence of mind to immediately put on the brakes, turn and fire the ball to home plate. The runner had started off third base but immediately stopped when the Coach saw how quickly Klostermann had recovered and fired the ball home. A game-saver it was, but it was just one heck of a defensive catch and throw by a high school shortstop. That definitely was the play of the game.

The reversal of the call at home plate which extended the game was maybe a correct call and maybe it wasn't. The play was close and with the umpire's thinking that the tag was too late, called him safe. But when it was brought to his attention by Knights' coach, Don Miller, that the bases had been loaded and it was a force out rather than a tag, he reversed the decision. After he gave me a full explanation stating that it was a force play which he had failed to realize, there did not seem to be much that I could protest. We had already completed a full celebration, all the players surrounding Danny Goerdt still on the ground at the plate. Bur suddenly, it's not over. That was an emotional roller-coaster for all of us.

Now, there are two out, bases loaded and Keith Krapfl scheduled to bat. Keith was a sophomore and I decided to go with senior Tom Burlage. Tom was a very low-key kind of guy who I felt might handle the pressure better. Once the count went to 3 balls and 2 strikes, Tom managed to foul off two or three good pitches, before Assumption hurler Laake threw one above Tom's head and the seventh inning plus the game was finally over. Believe this or not, but that seventh inning took over one hour to play. Just that inning. It indeed was a gut-wrenching experience .

Lloyd Koelker pitched the entire game, giving up seven hits and striking out seven. He allowed only one earned run and that possibly could also have been called unearned. Knipper, Klostermann and Overman each had two hits. Finally, we could say, "We are in the state tournament."

Something else happened that night of the Assumption game. I graduated from Loras College having completed their master's program for high school guidance counselors. I really did receive my master's but wasn't there to participate. There was something much more important than picking up that degree. That could be done by just stopping at Loras College and receiving that which I would have received at the graduation. That something else that was so much more important was a group of young baseball players who were striving for a possible state baseball championship. Being with those players and seeing them pull out one close exciting victory after another was so rewarding, words can't describe it. To help them realize the challenge they had placed in front of them was one of the most compelling charges I had ever been given. It made me think of the two goals in my life. The first, of course, was to marry the woman I had fallen so deeply in love with and who now shared her love with me every day of her life. The second goal, to play professional baseball with the dream of being a major league player wasn't happening, but it just seemed as though this new challenge of a state championship being fought for by such wonderful young people was taking the place of that major league goal. Just maybe, this current pursuit was taking its place.

Let me share a little sideline story of this team with you. When Ann and I finalized our decision to leave Beckman High School and pursue a doctor's degree at the University of Illinois, I took advantage of downtime between a high school doubleheader for the Blazers to inform them of our decision. Things were quiet for a while, but then players began to inquire more deeply of those plans and other ramifications that would go with our shocking decision.

We were playing another high school game later that week when something new began occurring with this team that I was so thrilled to be coaching. At this game, the first time our players went out to take their positions in the field, they literally ran at almost full speed. When the inning was over, they again ran hard back to the dugout. This action continued the remainder of the season, every game, and every inning of those games. One of my coaching goals always was directed at hustling throughout every game and every play. I have shared that with you before. I am not sure which player suggested the new form of "hustle," but if you were one of the lucky ones to watch this team run hard out to their positions, and back in at the end of each inning, you may have felt some of the emotion and the pride that I felt for them. And it was working.

If only there wasn't so much going for the Huinker family at this time. I really wish that Ann and I would have had more time to step back and enjoy the excitement that went with each victory these young Blazers claimed. Still playing with the Whitehawks, trying to get things together for the selling of our house, completing the master's program, and wrapping everything up at Beckman High School challenged the love that Ann and I shared. At the same time, thank heaven we had our love to fall back on as we scurried from one thing to another, with and without our six children, including new baby Danny, now five months old.

The Blazers still had practice on Saturday. I don't think we practiced on the day after the game but I don't remember a Sunday practice. One thing I do know. Whenever we practiced, I pitched batting practice, tired arm or not. All of a sudden I also had an "assistant coach" of sorts. He wasn't officially an assistant but Dave Knepper of Worthington, a good player on the previous year's team, was getting so enthused and involved that he asked if he could help out. He also warmed up pitchers before each game at the state tournament.He assisted in all our practices, helping make them more complete for every player.

Dick Mescher needs to be recognized at this time also. He was taking over the athletic director duties for the coming school year and he stepped in and made all the arrangements for the state tournament trip, taking a big load off my shoulders.

We had our beloved Beckman High School bus ready to take us to Ames. Brother Richard (now Joe Wysocki) was our chauffeur and also our mechanic who kept the bus running. We left for Ames on Monday morning and took some batting practice before the game on a separate field. The diamond itself where the games were to be played was in excellent shape. Outfield fences, particularly right field, were a little short but still satisfactory for high school play. And for wooden bats of course.

The state tournament is here. And so were the Beckman Trail Blazers. Lloyd Koelker, our ace with three days rest, would start on the mound against Paton-Churdan representing the southwest region of the state of Iowa.

> *BECKMAN GAINS FINALS IN PREP BASEBALL MEET*
> *By Hal Lagerstrom, T-H Sports Editor*
> *Beckman of Dyersville meets Norway tonight at 8 in Brookside Park for the 1968 Iowa High School Athletic Assn. Summer Baseball Championship.*
> *The undefeated Trail Blazers, playing in their first state tournament, parlayed clutch hitting and some poor baserunning into a 5-3 victory in Monday night's tournament opener.*
> *Norway blanked Sioux City Heelan, 2-0, in the second game.*
> *Beckman coach Art Huinker, bringing his second team to the state finals (he coached Ossian De Sales to the state meet in 1960) used both right hander Lloyd Koelker and Lefty Tom Burlage on the mound and both responded to the challenge as*

403

Koelker worked the first two innings and was nicked for a run after which Huinker switched to Burlage.

"Rick (catcher Rick Knipper) said Koelker didn't have too much and I took his advice," said Huinker - - -pretty fair tribute to the judgment of his junior receiver.

Burlage mowed down the first six batters he faced, then ran into trouble in the fifth as Paton-Churdan tied it up. At this point, Huinker switched back to Koelker, who had gone to second base in the third, and his ace right hander responded by retiring the last seven batters to post his 15th win in 16 decisions.

"Lloyd is a cool weather pitcher - - - he doesn't like the heat too much," said Huinker, referring to the 90-degree temperatures. "But he said the end was in sight when he went back in to pitch and really fired at the end."

Actually, Koelker and Burlage retired Paton-Churdan in order in five of the seven innings. The Rockets rallied to tie the score each time they had the luxury of base runners, but each time ran themselves out of a potentially bigger inning.

Beckman scored in the top of the first when Bob Klostermann singled with two out, stole second, took third on an overthrow by catcher Terry Fox and scored as the ball rolled through the centerfielder's legs.

But the Rockets came back in the second to put runners on second and third with none out as Dick Carstens singled and Don Hahnsen hit the first of his two doubles. One out later, Carstens broke for the plate, Knipper made a neat back-hand grab of a near wild pitch from Koelker and put the tag on Carstens - - - only to drop the ball. On the next pitch Hahnsen broke down the line faking a steal, but Knipper immediately made up for his error by picking Hahnsen off third on a sharp throw to Dan Goerdt.

Singles by Keith Krapfl, Knipper and John Goerdt produced another run for Beckman in the third, and Jerry Bildstein's center field home run over the 330-foot sign made it 3-1 in the fourth.

But Hahnsen's second double, a walk to pitcher Denny Bertelli and a sacrifice put runners on second and third with one out. Hahnsen scored as Koelker threw badly to first on Dean Fox's grounder up the middle, but Bertelli tried to score, too, and was cut down on Jim Overman's throw to Knipper. Then Jim Drayer doubled to score Fox with the tying run, and Koelker was called back to the mound.

Walks to Overman and Bildstein set the stage for Lee Kruse's game winning hit in the sixth.

Actually, Paton-Churdan unwittingly gave the Blazers one of the runs when Fox- - -who earlier had thrown two balls away on steals- - -let Bildstein take second to prevent a double steal. Then Kruse hit an outside curve ball down the right field line and it bounded over the fence for a ground rule double scoring both runners.

That, as it turned out, was the ball game, and Beckman takes a 20-0 record into tonight's state championship battle.

Now we were down to one game to win for the championship of the state of Iowa of all schools of all sizes. A comment heard quite often among the players referred to the crowd of people who came down to the game from the Dubuque and Delaware County areas. They were amazed and pleased at that support. Sophomore John Goerdt led all hitters with three safeties while Rick Knipper had two safeties in the opening round win.

Were we ready to go after Norway, defending state champions from the fall campaign and also defenders of the championship in the spring season? Well, we had to be. And I think that is the way these young, eager ball players looked at the upcoming championship game. It would be our eighth tournament game since we first defeated Dubuque Senior in the opening round of the sectional at Dyersville.

Weather forecasters were predicting another hot evening for the final game on Tuesday. We were planning on sophomore Ron Kramer as our starting pitcher. Lloyd and Tom were available for relief but hopefully we would not need them, at least early in the game. While I was pitching for the St. Louis Cardinal organization in Albany, Georgia where the weather was even hotter and more humid night after night, we had a five-gallon bucket filled with ice and water that had a chemical in it designed to soak a towel that would be placed around our neck between innings. It just drained the sweat out of you and made you feel so much fresher. We have discussed the process in the chapter when we were playing in Albany, Georgia. Hours were spent on Tuesday before the Norway game during the day, getting the same setup ready for the Tuesday night game. Finally, we located a pharmacist in Marshalltown where we were staying. He said he knew what we were looking for, and sold us the correct over-the-counter chemical. And so we were set for another hot evening

The nerves were beginning to find my stomach. The butterflies made it almost impossible to eat the late afternoon meal and that is unusual for me. I had to admit that if I were the person to help keep the players relaxed, it wasn't going to be very successful. They probably did better than their coach.

In this case, we will let the Telegraph-Herald tell the story. We had to choose between the local Dyersville Commercial and the Dubuque paper but we would have been typing forever with the huge, but wonderful, write-up in the local paper.

STATE BASEBALL TITLE HUINKER'S FAREWELL
GIFT FROM BECKMAN
By Hal Lagerstrom, T-H Sports Editor

Art Huinker ended his high school coaching career here Tuesday night and his Beckman baseball team made the final game a memorable one by defeating Norway, 5-4, to win the 1968 Iowa high school summer championship.

It was the culmination of a brilliant season for Huinker and his Trail Blazers, who blazed their way through 21 undefeated games during the summer and a 40-3 overall record for the combined spring-summer schedule.

But, despite making some inspired pitching moves during the tournament series, Huinker chose to heap all the credit for Beckman's first state championship in any sport to the team.

"They're the ones who did it," Huinker said. "They worked hard all season and never quit. They really deserve this."

The team was scheduled to be welcomed home with a parade this afternoon, beginning in Earlville and passing through several other communities, all of which have boys on the championship team.

But the route to that parade was a difficult one for the Blazers against a veteran Norway team which has won three straight spring titles and two fall championships.

Norway got to sophomore Ron Kramer - - - Huinker's choice as the starting pitcher since both Lloyd Koelker and Tom Burlage had pitched Monday night - - - for a run in the second inning when Regis Butz was hit by a pitched ball, stole second and scored as first baseman Jim Overman booted Mark Miller's grounder.

Don Stumpff was also hit by a pitch, putting runners on first and second with one out, after which Beckman got a break with some heads-up play. Steve Butz looped a drive over third baseman Dan Goerdt's head into short left, but the runners had to hold up for fear Goerdt would catch the ball.

He didn't, but grabbed it on the first bounce, whirled and threw to Kramer who was alertly covering third base, turning an apparent hit into a force out and killing the rally.

The Blazers got that run back in their half of the inning when Jerry Bildstein and Lee Kruse walked with one out, Bildstein scoring when pitcher Butz picked up Kramer's tap to the right of the mound and threw wildly to first.

John Goerdt and Bob Klostermann walked with none out in the third. Goerdt took third on Overman's deep fly to

406

right and scored on Dan Goerdt's bunt single. After Koelker walked, Bildstein grounded to first baseman Miller whose throw to the plate got Klostermann trying to score.

But Dan Goerdt raced for third on the play and scored when Norway catcher Bruce Kimm threw the ball into left field.

Regis Butz walked, stole second and scored on Roger Boddicker's single as Norway got one run back in the fourth, and the Tigers got some help from Beckman's usually reliable defense to score twice in the fifth.

Max Elliott's second double started the inning against Koelker, who came on in relief of Kramer in the fourth inning. Terry Brecht struck out, but Regis Butz walked. Miller then wrapped a double play ball to second baseman John Goerdt, but Klostermann dropped the throw to second and the bases were loaded.

Koelker walked Boddicker to force in the tying run, and the lead run scored when catcher Rick Knipper threw badly trying for a pickoff at third. Koelker then struck out the last two batters and didn't face another serious threat.

Overman's line single to center with one out started the Blazers' winning rally in the fifth. Dan Goerdt grounded out, Overman taking second, but Koelker came through with a sharp single to left, scoring Overman with the run that made it 4-4.

Koelker took second on the throw to the plate, went to third as Bildstein beat out an infield hit and scored what proved to be the winning run when third baseman Steve Butz booted Kruse's ground ball for an error.

Koelker posted his second win in the two-game state finals while Terry Brecht, who won Monday night, was the loser in relief.

There were several key moments in this big championship game. First of all, in the bottom half of the first inning, Rick Knipper, as our lead-off man, doubled off the left field fence. Even though he did not come around to score, I think his hard-hit ball gave the rest of the team the confidence they needed to say, "We can beat these guys, champs or no champs."

Obviously, the alert play of Dan Goerdt, grabbing the pop fly over his head on the first bounce and, realizing what the situation was, quickly throwing to third base for a force out was significant. The other half of the play was Ron Kramer's being on the third base bag, ready for the throw. Both players exhibited great baseball presence of mind and "hustle" to get the force out. Oddly enough, the third base umpire was also fooled and first called the batter safe because he did not realize it was a force out, and Ron did not bother to tag the runner.

In looking over the box score of the game, Norway pitchers had only two strikeouts for the game. That puts a lot of pressure on a high school defense, and with the speed of many of the Blazers, I believe it caused some of the defensive lapses of a veteran baseball club familiar with championship play. We made some errors also, but I attribute them to players really keyed up and maybe not as relaxed as they normally were. Need to recognize the big single by Koelker to tie the game. Lloyd was a good hitting pitcher. I like that for some reason.

And it is worth repeating. Norway catcher and future big league catcher for four years, Bruce Kimm went one for four against Kramer and Koelker. The following week, he hit a home run against me in the Dyersville tournament. The Blazers were good. And they continued their "hustle" by running to the diamond to begin the inning and running just as hard to the dugout to end the inning. This included our pitchers. A wonderful picture in my mind, even today.

Yes, we now were state champions. We celebrated in the middle of the diamond like any team will after winning the big one, whether it be the major league world series or a state championship. I don't think I settled down until the players threw me into the pool when we returned to the motel in Marshalltown. Then they themselves had to dive in also because I am not a very good swimmer.

The high school baseball coaching career of eleven years ended in the most wonderful fashion possible. If this team intended our success as a farewell gift for their coach, they provided the most memorable gift possible, one that still sits as a vivid highlight never to be forgotten, and always to be appreciated. What a wonderful group of young people that were given to me to coach. Twice now they have gathered together, after 25 years and after 40 years, to celebrate and to renew their fond feelings for each other.

The 25-year reunion in 1993 included a baseball game between our '68 champs and the 1986 champs under the coaching of Tom Jenk, Jr. It was one of those situations where we had everything to gain and nothing to lose. Every '68 player was at the reunion and ready to play ball except Jerry Bildstein who had a family conflict that made it impossible for him to participate. And the '68 champs won. We took extended batting practice the day before the game and the batting practice pitcher was yours truly, now fifty-eight years old. Interestingly, the arm felt good. I threw for over a thirty minutes. But the next day, it was like I had a catch in my left shoulder. As I found out later, my pitching arm, abused many times in my career, reached a bone-on-bone situation. What I wonder now connects with the decision to end my career in the summer of 1968 when we left for Champaign, Illinois. Was the shoulder that close to a bone-on-bone situation already at that time instead of occurring at the batting practice for the Blazers in 1993? Finally, about 15 years later, a brand new ball and socket replaced the worn-out pitching shoulder. It was all worthwhile for the game I loved so much.

Ann and I were still chasing around getting everything completed before we had to transport our troops to Champaign, Illinois. In the next two weeks, we

408

had three victory celebrations. The parents of the players gave us one of the parties. One was celebrated with the players and the cheerleaders at the Ertl Lanes where Ann and I were presented with a colored TV set, our first one with color. For this, I thank Fred Ertl, head of the Ertl Toy Company.

Then the Lions Club of Dyersville threw a huge banquet and celebration at Beckman High School in recognition of the team's championship season. There was one very special moment that evening when our second player with a cast on his leg during the baseball season, Gene Knipper, received a baseball autographed by all the players and myself. We all felt bad for Gene because I think we all realized how much he loved to play baseball, especially with this group of guys, and now was unable to participate in this greatest of moments. But it doesn't surprise me one bit that this team would reach out to Gene and let him know how important he was to them. That was a glorious moment.

Next, the parents of the players threw a reception for Ann and I. A beautiful chime clock was presented to Ann and me at that party. Much of the evening was spent answering questions that the parents had. They wanted to know all the inside happenings of the race to the championships.

What a way to bring closure to a baseball career. The Whitehawks had won the Dyersville tournament for the fifth time in the nine years I played with them. One loss all year. And the Beckman Trail Blazers won the high school state championship. Did these successes cause any second thoughts about leaving this all behind? Yes, it did. Yet, we had made our decision and we were looking forward to an unknown world ahead of us.

My mother and some family members were able to attend the Lions Club Banquet. She had a hard time understanding how we could leave all this. "The community is so accepting of you and Ann. How could you make this change?" she offered. Less than four months later, God called her back to be with her baseball husband. I wonder if she felt any different about our leaving when she got to her eternal reward. Wouldn't it be wonderful if we knew.

Eleven years of teaching and coaching were complete. It was eleven years during which Ann and I both were deeply engrossed in the activities revolving around the schools we worked at. They were wonderful experiences. We had tremendous faculty sharing with us at both schools. The students will never be forgotten. We have many opportunities even today to still share with them. Maybe, in a small way, that is what teaching is all about. You see them succeeding in their world and you think, "I hope that we made a positive difference in their lives."

At one of our farewell gatherings, Master of Ceremonies Father Frank Benda left us with this closing remark, "Each year you and your lovely wife, Ann, have contributed more and more of your time and energy to direct and encourage the youthful enthusiasm of our students. It would be the understatement of the year to say 'we'll miss you!' But on the other hand, it is when the rocket is freed from its pad that it really shows what it can do. Good-bye and farewell to a kindly counselor, to an inspiring teacher, to a spirited coach, and to a wonderful couple." God continues to bless us.

THE CURTAIN COMES DOWN

As I reflect back on the first thirty-three years of my life, the period of time covered in this book, there are regrets, there are disappointments, but they are definitely outweighed, primarily by the special love shared with Ann. That love is sometimes challenged by the every day events that we all experience. The death of our daughter, Tammy, was a major challenge. But our love bridged that sorrow and we probably strengthened our feelings for the marriage we share.

The sport of baseball provides memories that go beyond my realm of possibilities. I do admit that with all the games I actively competed in, or coached in, the victories far outweigh the losses. Yet, for me what tops all of those memories are the players themselves that I played with and/or coached and those that were in the opposite dugout for all those contests. And to all those people, teammates and opposing players, I humbly say "thank you". Thank you for what, you might wonder. Well, first of all, thanks for playing the wonderful game of baseball with me. Secondly, and probably more important, thank you for the wonderful sportsmanship and teamwork exhibited throughout all the years of playing the game we all loved. To my teammates, it was always great fun to wear the same uniform that you did and to share our abilities and friendship as we pushed ourselves to gain a victory. Sometimes we won, sometimes we did not win, just as all who play the game. You, and in many cases your families, are a very valuable part of the life that Ann and I cherish.

So also with players who took the field from the opposite side of the foul lines. No way can we recollect the number of times when the opportunity arose for both Ann and I, and also our children, to recall memories of those days when we took the field from the opposing dugouts. Seriously, the bridge between teams allows us to interact with each other, to have respect for each other, and that is the foundation of friendship. I thank all of you for those opportunities, even as many of those pictures are getting dimmer with age.

Then there are the many young baseball players I had the privilege of coaching who gave of their time, their energy and their enthusiasm to make themselves better ball players, and who also played the game in the right way, as good sports when they played to the best of their God-given abilities. It came down to players I coached and all young men and women who I taught in the classroom that helped me make that difficult choice of either continuing the pursuit of my dream of professional baseball or giving it up. Because I found myself enjoying the role of teaching and coaching so much, along with the tremendous love I have for Ann, it helped make the choice so much easier. Players, "arms crossed" was only a squeeze play away.

What about the regrets and/or disappointments. Obviously, there are some regrets regarding that decision. But to this day, I am comfortable with the choice that was made. The same goes for the decision to temporarily give up teaching and coaching and taking off for Champaign, Illinois to obtain the

411

doctorate. And if there were regrets, the decision can't be changed, so one cannot belabor the point and worry about it. We move on.

People may not be aware of the doctor's degree I obtained. That is the way we wanted it. You may ask why? I guess that is just us. I explain it this way. I fear that some people, especially friends and family, would put me on a level different from them. That is not the way life should be. Where you are, I want to be. Then we can communicate and be friends. The title of "doctor" has been used in only one place. You may have guessed it. In the checkbooks that Ann and I use.

A major regret relates to the playing of the game of baseball itself. In playing high school baseball as well as college baseball, I never had the privilege of having a coach who could help me better understand the basics of pitching. Not that they were not good coaches. I much appreciate every one of you that guided the teams I played for. That just was not your area of expertise. Many books about pitching were read and no doubt that was helpful. My school of learning for the most part, however, consisted of sharing with other pitchers and those wonderful people who played catch with me when we were 60 feet, six inches apart on the ball diamond, especially Dale Digmann and Ken Bawek. My brother, Kenny, and I talked about pitching a lot, but he had the same limited background that I did. If there were baseball camps available and conducted by players with advanced knowledge of becoming a better pitcher, we had no awareness of them.

For me, speaking from experience and what I did learn, pitching has three important elements: the speed with which one throws the ball, location of the pitch so that you do not put the ball over the middle of the plate, and last of all but maybe the most important, movement of the ball so that it might be in a slightly different location than the hitter thought it would be when he first gained sight of it. In this latter point of movement, I am really referring to something other than a curve ball, or slider, etc. When a pitcher just throws the ball, does it have a tendency to move, up or down, left or right? After these three comes the surprise factor, or out-witting of the batter. This was always a fun part of pitching for me. I often out-smarted myself.

Allow me to return to my parents' feeling that if I expected "God to bless me, I need to attend Loras College. " Sometimes there is reflective thinking inside me which causes me to go beyond my attendance at Loras. I feel very blessed for my entire life. I think back on all the games pitched and batters retired in key situations. Why did they not hit that ball that didn't go to the location I intended. Or maybe, after being hitless in three at-bats, and all of a sudden I managed a key hit late in the game. That happened frequently enough that I wondered about my parents' statement. Was I blessed? I obviously do not have an answer to that question. But I know I was blessed to have the parents I had and brothers and sisters I had.

412

For me, the game of baseball was to be played with an enthusiasm and a determination to be the best player I could be. My hope is that I always played it that way, but as a good sport, win or lose. Life has been good for Ann and me, surrounded by so many wonderful people we love and cherish. Many of those friendships are due to baseball. And those friendships have made a great difference in my life, in Ann's life, and in the life of our family.

Thinking back to my brother's middle of the night question about his life, I close with this very simple reflective thought: "Has it made a positive difference that I have been part of the lives of those around me?" Someone knows. I can only hope.

"Kids, I present you with your scrapbook."

ACKNOWLEDGMENTS

This book would not be possible without the cooperation and approval from the fourteen daily and weekly newspapers listed below who have granted me permission to utilize articles, pictures and even editorials from their publications for inclusion in this publication. Whenever possible, references are incorporated with the article or editorial. Again, thank you to all the following:

Albany Herald
Austin Daily Herald
Battle Creek Enquirer News
Decorah Journal
Dubuque Telegraph Herald
Dyersville Commercial
La Crosse Tribune
Loras College Lorian
Mason City Globe Gazette
Milwaukee Journal Sentinel
New Hampton Tribune
Ossian Bee
Rochester Post Bulletin
Sioux Falls Argus Leader
Sumner Gazette
Waterloo Courier

414